Population and Social Change

Population
and Social Change

Edited by

D. V. Glass and Roger Revelle

 EDWARD ARNOLD, LONDON
CRANE, RUSSAK NEW YORK

© THE AMERICAN ACADEMY OF ARTS AND SCIENCES 1972

First published 1972
by Edward Arnold (Publishers) Ltd.

Published in the United States by:
Crane, Russak & Company, Inc
52 Vanderbilt Avenue, New York, N.Y. 10017

Library of Congress Catalog Card Number: 72–80107
ISBN: 0 8448 0009 0

Printed in Great Britain

Contents

Acknowledgments

The book is the tangible outcome of two international conferences on historical population studies sponsored jointly by the Harvard Centre for Population Studies and the American Academy of Arts and Sciences. The first of these was held at the House of the Academy in October, 1966; the second at the Villa Serbelloni in Bellagio, Italy, in July 1967. We are indebted to the Rockefeller Foundation for making the villa, an ideal site for international meetings, available to us.

Conference participants who did not contribute to this volume include: Professors Bernard Bailyn, Carl Bridenbaugh, Professor Ansley Coale, Alexander Gerschenkron, John Habakkuk, John Hajnal, Harvey Leibenstein, Ralph B. Potter, Jr., Henry Rosovsky, and Gustaf Utterström; also Dr. Olive Banks and Dr. Goran Ohlin. We are grateful to all of them for provocative and instructive discussion.

The Ford Foundation assisted the Harvard Centre for Population Studies with funds for these meetings. A grant from the Ford Foundation to the American Academy of Arts and Sciences to encourage interdisciplinary studies has also been drawn upon. We are pleased that the first use of funds from this grant should have supported a project of this kind.

D. V. Glass

General introduction

The generous reception given to the Spring 1968 issue of *Dædalus*—
the first to concern itself with historical aspects of population growth
—has provided an opportunity to produce an expanded version. The
original issue, largely the result of two conferences, did not aim to
be comprehensive, but rather sought to draw attention to some of the
growing points in historical demography, a field of study that has
seen very substantial developments since the 1950s, with approaches
different from, and far more searching than, the work of earlier
periods. This expanded version includes eight additional contributions which give some indication of the wide range of new work and
suggest possibilities for future research. The previous contributions
are reprinted in their original form, save for some further biblio-
graphic references to more recent work.

Most of the new contributions relate to Western societies. This is
inevitable at present. More work has been done on such societies
and their historical data tend to be better than those for Africa,
Asia, or Latin America. In addition, there is a strong and understandable interest in the demography of the pre-industrial and early
industrializing stages of developed societies, both because we still
know far too little about them and also because we still hope that a
fuller understanding of the processes of change may throw some light
upon prospects in developing societies. But there are two contributions on Asian societies—on Japan and on India—and by no means
all the articles on Western societies deal with questions of the demographic transition. And this is as it should be, for there are many
other questions of intrinsic interest which need investigation. Moreover, a focus exclusively on changes in birth and death rates during
the transition may well prevent us from taking account of circumstances without which the timing of the transition cannot be understood.

This latter point is illustrated by Paul Demeny's contribution to the
original *Dædalus* issue, in which he drew attention to several pockets
of low fertility in Austria-Hungary—among Hungarian Calvinists
in the Transdanubian region, among German Roman Catholics
in the Banat, and among Greek Orthodox Rumanians in Krassó

Szörény. More recent work by Dr. R. Andorka has shown that in one village in Baranya county in Hungary fertility was low from at least the end of the eighteenth century, when the parish register was initiated, and the study is now being extended to the central village of the area, which has parish registers going back to the middle of the eighteenth century.[1] Such findings are in line with the argument of Gösta Carlsson that the secular decline in fertility in the West reflected a process of diffusion rather than of innovation.[2] Pre-industrial Western societies were not entirely devoid of pockets of control. In some cases control was practised by particular social groups, such as the *Ducs et Pairs* in late seventeenth-century France. Or control might have been used by larger sections of the society in response to particular economic circumstances, such as a series of harvest failures. A response of this kind in eighteenth-century Sweden was implied by the report of the Swedish *Tabelkommission* in 1761, discussing the effects of a fall in wheat prices in 1750: 'At once girls and boys were ready for the bridal bed, and for married couples love began to burn more vigorously.'[3] And if E. A. Wrigley's work on Colyton is confirmed by other parish studies—T. H. Hollingsworth's earlier demographic analysis of the British peerage also showed a fall in fertility among the cohorts born in the late seventeenth and early eighteenth centuries and a rise among later cohorts—this would provide significant evidence for the country which has customarily been taken as the model for classical transition theory.[4]

John Hajnal's examination of the history of marriage in Europe revealed the emergence, from the late sixteenth century onwards, of a pattern of late marriage and substantial proportions of never-married men and women in countries in the West and South.[5] This new and 'artificial' marriage pattern was important in restraining the rate of population growth, but Hajnal did not cite—or attempt to discover—evidence that the new pattern was consciously adopted as a means of restricting marital fertility. And this applies equally to most studies relating marriage patterns to systems of

[1] R. Andorka, 'Birth Control in the Ormánság since the End of the Eighteenth Century', *Demografia*, 1–2 (1970), 85 (English summary).

[2] G. Carlsson, 'The Decline of Fertility: Innovation or Adjustment Process', *Population Studies* (November 1966), pp. 149–74.

[3] H. Gille, 'The Demographic History of the Northern European Countries in the Eighteenth Century', *Population Studies* (June 1949), p. 49. The report also stated that it would be in periods of crop failure and high prices that 'existing bridal beds will be less fruitful'.

[4] T. H. Hollingsworth, *The Demography of the British Peerage*, Supplement to *Population Studies* (November 1964), Tables 28 and 32, pp. 40 and 42.

[5] J. Hajnal, 'European Marriage Patterns in Perspective', in D. V. Glass and D. E. C. Eversley (eds.), *Population in History* (London, 1965).

inheritance. P. J. Greven, for example, has examined in detail the
transfer of land to sons in colonial Andover. But the reason for the
delays in that community was evidently the father's reluctance to
give up ownership and, in any case, the son often had the use of the
land long before his father's death[6] Marriage was to a considerable
degree controlled by parents, as it was even later in other societies,
but scarcely with population motives in mind.[7] Michael Drake's
study of pre-industrial Norway, however, suggests that marriage
patterns were sometimes a reflection of a conscious desire to limit
marital fertility. He quotes the statement made to Eilert Sundt by
a young man whose wife was much older and who explained: 'I
thought when I took such an old woman, the crowd of young ones
would not be so great, for it is difficult for one in limited circumstances to feed so many.' One statement scarcely justifies a generalization. But Drake shows that in 1801 in Western Hedmark, with
a large proportion of cottars in the population, the wife was older
than her husband in 47·5 per cent of existing first marriages, and that
in 9 per cent of the existing first marriages the wife was ten or more
years older. In another area in Norway, Vigran, the farmers imported
agricultural workers but refused to give them crofts so that they had
to leave when they wished to marry. Of these farmers Sundt reported
that he had often heard them say 'how desirable it would be if one
could put a stop to the formation of the working class and the
increase of pauperism'. Action by individual farmers thus had the
same aim as the official attempts made in many German states, in
Austria, and in Switzerland, during the Malthusian period, to
prevent the poor from marrying.[8]

By contrast, P. C. Matthiessen's data on Denmark seem to display
the classical pattern of transition. The high point of total fertility
was reached by the generation of women born in 1850/54, with an
average of 4·4 live births per woman, assuming no mortality.

[6] P. J. Greven, Jr., *Four Generations*, Ithaca, 1970, esp. Ch. 6.
[7] Attempts by parents to control marriage are not infrequent in present-day Western
agricultural communities, especially to prevent marriage across social class boundaries. In
any case, at least in a country like Britain, the universe of possible mates is firmly bounded
by social class (and to some extent by religious) barriers, so that romantic love tends to
operate within a relatively limited social space, that space to a considerable extent being
defined by the socio-economic status of the parents.
[8] Gille, 'Demographic History of the Northern European Countries', p. 38, quotes
somewhat similar evidence from the Swedish *Tabelkommission* and from the Danish writer
E. Pontoppidan. G. Duplessis-Le Quélinel, *Les mariages en France* (Paris, 1954), suggests
that the practice was also found among the lower peasantry in France in the eighteenth
century. On the Malthusian attempts to prevent the poor from marrying, see D. V.
Glass, 'Malthus and the Limitation of Population Growth', in D. V. Glass (ed.), *Introduction to Malthus* (London, 1953), pp. 38–47; and J. Knodel, 'Law, Marriage and
Illegitimacy in Nineteenth-Century Germany', *Population Studies* (March 1967), pp.
279–94.

Thereafter fertility declined, the fall beginning among the older groups of women and gradually working down through the younger groups. This is also the type of transition found in Sweden and Britain and makes it clear that a major part of the long-term fall in family size was not achieved by 'family planning', but rather by terminating childbearing when the 'target' number of births had been reached. And as the 'target' fell from generation to generation, the age of termination also fell. The term 'family planning' has not infrequently been applied to birth control practice, as if it had the same meaning as 'family limitation'. But that is by no means necessarily so. Even today in Britain where family limitation by contraceptive practice has permeated the society, 47 per cent of the couples married in 1961/65 who had used birth control by the time of interview and had had at least one pregnancy by 1967/68, had not begun to use birth control before the first pregnancy.[9] This does not suggest anything like universal 'family planning'.

Matthiessen's findings are not, however, in conflict with Carlsson's argument. In a more detailed analysis, published elsewhere,[10] Matthiessen has shown that the decline in fertility among the older women is visible among the cohorts born from 1815 onwards. Further, for all cohorts born after 1815, marital fertility above the age of thirty was substantially higher in the rural districts than in Copenhagen or—though to a smaller extent—in the provincial towns. These differences suggest some form of control within marriage well before the time when the national decline in the birth rate became evident.

The third essay dealing with the fertility history of a Western society is that on Quebec by Henripin and Péron. Here the analysis covers an exceptionally long period—from the beginning of the eighteenth century until 1961—and an unusual population. It is a population which was originally exhorted by Colbert to be fruitful and multiply,[11] and which has been strongly responsive to control

---

[9] The information relates to British-born women (with British-born husbands), age at first marriage under thirty-five years and with first marriage unbroken at the time of the survey (or, in the case of earlier marriage cohorts, unbroken until the women were forty-five years of age). Of the women first married in 1961/65, 91·4 per cent had already used birth control by the time of the survey and an additional 3·8 per cent, who had not used it, thought they would do so in future. (Since the survey was carried out in 1967/68, the duration of marriage was very short for the most recent marriages. Taking only those women who were first married in 1961/62, 95 per cent had already used birth control by the time of the survey.) See D. V. Glass, 'The components of natural increase in England and Wales', Supplement to *Population Studies* (May 1970), Tables 3 and 5, pp. 17 and 20.

[10] P. C. Matthiessen, *Some Aspects of the Demographic Transition in Denmark* (Copenhagen, 1970).

[11] Special incentives were given to the colonists to marry early and penalties—prohibition on engaging in the fur-trade—for those who did not marry within fifteen days after

by the Roman Catholic church, at least until very recently. Crude birth rates were around 55 per thousand until the middle of the nineteenth century, and the slight fall thereafter seems probably to have been the result of changes in marriage patterns. Even in the 1920s, the crude birth rate was around 39 per thousand. Marital fertility was exceptionally high. Rural farm women aged sixty-five and over in 1961 had had an average of 8·3 births per ever-married woman, and even for urban women the comparable average was 5·9. It may well be that the mean for all women in the middle of the nineteenth century was above 8 births.

In referring to the context in which this high fertility was achieved and maintained, Henripin and Péron stress both obedience to the church and the nationalist feelings expressed in the slogan 'revanche des berceaux'. The situation is perhaps analogous to that in the Netherlands, where, as F. Van Heek put it, politico-religious competition resulted in a 'front' mentality.[12] But in the Netherlands this mentality influenced Calvinist as well as Roman Catholic reproductive behaviour.

Nevertheless the situation has been changing sharply in recent years. High fertility was in part explained by low economic and educational achievement. Aspirations have changed and high fertility is not compatible with the new aims. In 1961, ever-married women aged forty to forty-four had had only 4·3 births as compared with an average of 6·4 for women aged sixty-five and over. In an address to the Population Association of America, Ronald Freedman stressed the importance of comprehensive demographic studies of developing societies not only for practical purposes but also as a means of observing in detail—in a way impossible for the historical changes in industrial societies—the process of transition. The close observation of such changes in Quebec would be no less rewarding and probably far more practicable.

The remaining contributions on Western societies deal with rather different questions from those discussed above. Ian Sutherland's paper picks up a question raised by John Graunt, namely whether the Great Plague of 1665 in London was 'greater' than that of 1625.

the arrival of the boatloads of women sent out from France. See J. Henripin, *La population canadienne au début du XVIIIᵉ Siècle* (Paris, 1954), pp. 7–8. See also *Edits, ordonnances royaux, declarations . . . concernant le Canada* (Quebec, 1854); *Collection de manuscrits . . . relatifs á la Nouvelle-France* (Quebec, 1883–85), Vol. 1; and P. E. Renard, *Les origines économiques du Canada* (Mamers, 1928). A recent study has shown the high nuptiality and fertility of the population of one of the areas in France which contributed heavily to the colonization of Quebec. See H. Charbonneau, *Tourouvre-au-Perche aux XVIIᵉ et XVIIIᵉ Siècles* (Paris, 1970), especially Ch. 6.

---

[12] F. Van Heek, 'Roman-Catholicism and Fertility in the Netherlands', *Population Studies* (November 1956), pp. 125–38.

That question cannot now be answered with precision, since to do so would require reliable data on population as well as reliable statistics of deaths from plague and from other causes. But Sutherland attempts to reduce the range of indeterminacy by estimates constructed on a variety of bases and in so doing produces a continued and systematic account of the role of plague in what was, by the late seventeenth century, the largest urban centre in Europe. Since Sutherland completed his work, other studies of plague have been undertaken and they, too, will help to show what this cause of death meant to pre-industrial Europe. I. F. D. Shrewsbury's volume[13] presents the most detailed history of plague in Britain to appear so far, though it offers less of a connected story for London than does Sutherland's survey. And a publication by Hollingsworth[14] is based upon his discovery—or, rather, rediscovery—that for many years in the seventeenth century deaths were given by age and sex for the London parish of St. Botolph's Bishopsgate. This material may prove to be of special importance, since the demographic impact of plague clearly depended not only upon its general spread and case-fatality rate, but also upon its relative age and sex incidence. The human significance of the plague is well illustrated in the writing of Richard Smyth, a friend of John Graunt.[15] Smyth kept a record of the deaths of his acquaintances, and his lists show that whereas forty-five died in 1664 and forty in 1666, the deaths among his acquaintances amounted to 155 in 1665. The demographic significance is far more difficult to assess. Yet it is important to our understanding of whether and why the level of mortality fell in England after 1665 and before any major industrialization. K. Helleiner argued that the disappearance of plague was an important ingredient in the first, pre-industrial vital revolution.[16] T. McKeown is much more doubtful that 'prolonged changes in mortality (from all causes) and population growth can be attributed to the behaviour of a single disease'.[17] Nevertheless, Hollingsworth's data on the British peerage suggest that it was with the generation born after the effective disappearance

[13] I. F. D. Shrewsbury, *A History of the Bubonic Plague in the British Isles* (Cambridge, 1970).

[14] M. and T. H. Hollingsworth, 'Plague Mortality Rates by Age and Sex in the Parish of St. Botolph's Without, Bishopsgate, London 1603', *Population Studies*, March 1971. See also T. R. Forbes, *Chronicle from Aldgate*, New Haven, 1971, for deaths by age in the parish of St. Botolph's, Aldgate.

[15] H. Ellis (ed.), *The Obituary of Richard Smyth* (London, 1849). Smyth describes his list as 'a catalogue of all such persons deceased whome I knew in their life time . . .'.

[16] K. Helleiner, 'The Population of Europe from the Black Death to the Eve of the Vital Revolution', *The Cambridge Economic History of Europe*, Vol. 4 (Cambridge, 1967), pp. 84–5.

[17] T. McKeown, 'Medical Issues in Historical Democraphy', in E. Clarke, ed., *Modern Methods in the History of Medicine* (London, 1971).

of bubonic plague that expectation of life at birth began to rise consistently.[18] Perhaps the information which will be furnished by the aggregative analysis of the Cambridge Group's sample of parish registers will throw some light on the effect in England as a whole.[19]

The re-issue of the Walter Willcox and Imre Ferenczi volumes on international migration[20] draws attention to the gaps in our knowledge which still remain forty years after those volumes were first published. In spite of many detailed national and local studies, there are still major unknowns in the picture of nineteenth-century flows from Europe. The great discrepancy between gross passenger movements as recorded by 'migration statistics', and net outward migration, as calculated from census and vital statistics, has not been fully explained. And the examination of the economic factor in overseas migration has suffered from the inadequacy of the information on the occupations of migrants in their countries of origin. So far as emigration from the British Isles to the United States is concerned, one major difficulty has been to distinguish between emigrants from Ireland, from Scotland, and from England and Wales, regions with widely different rates of industrialization and different employment opportunities.

Charlotte Erickson's paper approaches some of these latter questions by drawing upon a source which has not hitherto been widely used—namely, the microfilms of ships lists in the National Archives in Washington. She has analysed the lists of ships arriving in New York from Britain in two periods—1846–54, with 850 adult males from England and Scotland; and 1885–8, with about 8,700 adult males. Given the information recorded, she has been able to examine the occupations in the country of origin and the last place of residence of the individuals concerned. That the data have serious defects is made clear. Nevertheless the analysis supports conclusions considerably different from those often reached by earlier writers. In particular, the migrants from England and Scotland in the 1880s—for which period the data are much more extensive—were not men driven from the countryside by agricultural depression. They came very largely from the towns and from regions of relatively high industrial wages. But among them were disproportionately large numbers of building workers, miners,

[18] T. H. Hollingsworth, *The Demography of the British Peerage*, Tables 42 and 43, pp. 56–7.

[19] Sutherland's basic data for London (the City, the Liberties and the out-parishes) for 1603 to 1665 suggest that at least 21 per cent of all deaths during that period were from plague. (Allowance has also to be made for considerable under-reporting of plague deaths, as was argued by John Graunt.) Proportionate mortality from plague in London in the period 1603–65 was thus much greater than proportionate mortality from smallpox during the eighteenth century.

[20] W. F. Willcox, ed., *International Migrations* (2 vols., New York, 1969, reprint).

clerks, and general labourers (not agricultural). As Dr. Erickson remarks, they were 'some of the least qualified members of the urban labour force, . . . the disadvantaged for whom the continued high rate of population increase and entries to the labour force narrowed the range of opportunities, particularly in a decade when building activity was low'.

Since the 1950s, studies of small communities have added considerably to our knowledge of the interrelationship between demographic and other factors. French historical demographers have made very significant contributions based largely upon family reconstitution from parish register materials. More recently, American historians have drawn upon a wide variety of local materials in examining communities in colonial America—as witness the publications of P. J. Greven, Kenneth Lockridge, and John Demos.[21] No less important have been the studies of groups insulated by religion or distance, of which the Hutterites are a noteworthy example. In the present volume, the essay by the late H. E. Lewis and his colleagues summarises the work carried out on a small group insulated by distance, the islanders of Tristan de Cunha. Many years ago, Dr. R. R. Kuczynski examined the records of that group, though his study was not published. But the systematic investigation of the islanders and of their demographic-genetic history began with the volcanic eruption of 1961, when the entire population (some 279 persons) was transferred to England. The removal provided a stimulus and a set of possibilities—a stimulus to examine the excellent records going back 150 years and the possibilities of on-the-spot medical, anthropometric, and genetic research. The result has been a series of investigations—many still in process—of great genetic and demographic interest, offering analogies in respect of historical isolates and throwing into high relief some of the problems involved in assisting small underdeveloped societies. From the point of view of demography itself, the history of the population will reward study. With a social system somewhat similar to that of the Hutterites— equality of status, common ownership of property, and freedom from governmental control—fertility has fallen dramatically. For women born before 1830, the mean number of children per fertile woman was nearly 10; for the generation born in 1900–9 it was 4·4. At the same time, the present population is descended from

[21] P. J. Greven, *Four Generations*; K. Lockridge, 'The Population of Dedham, Massachusetts, 1636–1736', *Economic History Review* (August 1966), pp. 318–44; J. Demos, *A Little Commonwealth: Family Life in Plymouth Colony* (New York, 1970). See also R. V. Wells, 'Family Size and Fertility Control in Eighteenth-Century America: a Study of Quaker Families', *Population Studies*, March 1971; Susan L. Norton, 'Population Growth in Colonial America: a Study of Ipswich, Massachusetts', *loc. cit.*, November 1971; and M. A. Vinovskis, 'Mortality Rates and Trends in Massachusetts before 1860', forthcoming.

fifteen ancestors, though inbreeding is high only in respect of half the founding ancestors. A whole range of questions immediately springs to mind, and Dr. Lewis and his colleagues have given a fascinating account of the ways in which some of these questions are being examined.

If we know too little about demographic processes in the pre-industrial phases of Western societies, we have even less knowledge of population developments in Asia. A recent study has shown how, in one country, the island of Java, ethnocentric assumptions have led to estimates of nineteenth-century population growth which, in the author's judgment, are in substantial error.[22] For a few countries, it is not lack of 'data' which is responsible for our ignorance, but lack of assurance about the changing meaning and coverage of the data. This is especially so of China, much of the earlier work on which was carried out by Western historians unfamiliar with the country or its language.[23] But for most countries, far too little effort has been made to discover what data exist and how they may best be used. India is one such country. Official censuses have provided a reasonable basis for estimating population growth since 1871, but relatively little attention was given to earlier materials, though a publication by the Registrar General of India has reprinted the results of a series of local enumerations. Population estimates for earlier periods were thus often based upon highly indirect inferences, or at best upon estimates of cultivated area, the labour needed for cultivation, and the ratio of dependants to agricultural workers.

With the aim of providing a more secure basis for estimates, Dr. Ajit Das Gupta and several colleagues have re-examined the various earlier estimates and have attempted to produce revised estimates of nineteenth-century population growth by working on the materials for main regions of India—Madras, Bengal and Bombay Presidencies, and the Northwest Province. These regions contain about 70 per cent of the population of India, and data of varying quality are available for them as far back as the 1840s, and in the case of Madras, from the beginning of the nineteenth century. On this basis, new estimates of total population (excluding Pakistan) have been reached—154 million in 1800, 189 million in 1850, and 237 million in 1900.[24] But this is just the beginning of the new work.

[22] B. Peper, 'Population Growth in Nineteenth Century Java', *Population Studies* (March 1970), pp. 71–84.
[23] But see Nanming Liu, *Contribution à l'Etude de la Population Chinoise* (Geneva, 1935); and Ho Ping-ti, *Studies on the Population of China, 1368–1958* (Cambridge, Mass., 1959).
[24] See also S. S. Gupta, M. Ghose, A. K. Dutta, and A. Das Gupta, 'Estimates of Nineteenth Century Population of India', *Bulletin of the Socio-Economic Research Institute, Calcutta* (January 1969), pp. 16–22.

Given the rich and unused materials relating to the seventeenth and eighteenth centuries, to which Das Gupta refers—including the village revenue and poll tax records—it is to be hoped that Indian demographers and historians will find time to use such materials in reconstructing the population history of their country.

The last of the new contributions, by Dr. Susan Hanley and Professor Kozo Yamamura, draws upon a wide range of recent local and other studies as a basis for a fresh assessment of the nature of population growth in pre-industrial Japan. Once again—as has also been shown by local studies in Europe and the United States—there is evidence of substantial variation between areas and over time in the rate of population growth and in the pressure of population on levels of living. But taking the country as a whole from 1600 to 1868, the authors conclude that the demographic situation had strong similarities to that of Western Europe prior to the Industrial Revolution. Population increase was slow, held back both by famines and by restrictive practices often associated with famine conditions, though there is evidence that the age at marriage of women was higher than in India, and that the remarriage rates of widows and divorcees were low. The population of Tokugawa Japan was not involved in the 'Malthusian trap.' On the contrary, there was considerable social and economic progress, and the economy was able to generate a surplus which, subsequently, was drawn upon to foster industrialization. Mortality was high but the very fact that, as in Europe, the available medical techniques could not have brought it down rapidly, meant that the early stages of industrialization after the Meiji Restoration did not run into rates of natural increase comparable to those in many areas of the developing world today. The basic contention, then, is that not only is Japan demographically different from most other Asian countries today but that its population history—or, rather, the relation between population increase and economic development—was different in the seventeenth and eighteenth centuries. There are clearly many questions still to be answered and assumptions to be examined in the light of a wider range of local, historical studies. But the essay offers an admirable framework within which to search for more definitive answers.

In bringing this introduction to a close, it should again be emphasized that the aim of including new contributions was not to produce a representative or comprehensive survey of current work on the history of population. The intention was simply to show some of the new work being done in a field which has expanded very greatly during the past ten years. Even so, important sections of that new work are not represented in this collection. In particular, there is nothing on the history of household size and structure, a subject on which a series of extremely interesting papers was presented at a conference in September 1969.[25] And apart from the essay by Dr. Lewis and his colleagues, the collection gives no indication of the work on historical aspects of demography and human genetics which is being undertaken in France, Italy, and Sweden. Historians in the United States are re-examining colonial society: a few references to their work are given in this introduction. In Britain the enumeration transcripts of the Censuses of 1841 to 1861 are providing fresh information on the social correlates and consequences of industrialization.[26] Tax returns for the eighteenth century are making possible at least a rough quantification of the supply of skilled manpower in England and of the internal migration associated with the apprenticeship system.[27] These are but a few indications that the prospect for historical demography during the next ten years is a most exciting one.

[25] The Conference was organized by the Cambridge Group for the History of Population and Social Structure. The proceedings will be published subsequently.

[26] See, for example, M. Anderson, *Family Structure in Nineteenth Century Lancashire* (Cambridge, 1971); and W. A. Armstrong, 'Some further Comparisons between Mr. Laslett's 100 Pre-industrial Communities and York in 1851', forthcoming (the reference is to P. Laslett, 'Size and Structure of the Household in England over Three Centuries', *Population Studies*, July 1969. For some comments on this latter study, see L. K. Berkner, 'The Stem Family and the Development Cycle of the Peasant Household: an Eighteenth Century Austrian Example', forthcoming in the *American Historical Review*.)

[27] In a current study I have used these returns for England and Wales as a whole for 1712 and for three counties for substantially longer periods.

Roger Revelle

Introduction[1]

Almost everybody, including some demographers, believes that his great-grandparents had all the children they were capable of having —after they were married, of course. Today, as we all know, most couples in Europe and the United States have about the number of children they want. In the bad old days, a good many of the children died; today, nearly all of them grow up.

Demographers have erected a theory to fit these beliefs and facts: the theory of the demographic transition. In the past, according to this theory, human populations maintained themselves or slowly expanded under conditions of high mortality balanced against high, essentially uncontrolled fertility. During the Industrial Revolution, fertility remained high and uncontrolled, for a while, and the average length of life increased. As a result populations grew rapidly in the Western world, at rates higher than ever before experienced. During the nineteenth and early-twentieth centuries, birth rates began to come down, first in France and the United States and then in the other industrialized countries, due to the deliberate control of births by individual couples. This decline in fertility eventually slowed down population growth (though, on the average, populations in these countries are still growing at rates that were unprecedented on an international scale before the nineteenth century).

To date, the demographic transition from high to low fertility and mortality seems to be chiefly a European, American, and Japanese phenomenon. Only part of it—the decline in mortality— has occurred in the poor countries of Asia, Latin America, and Africa, where most of the world's people live. Because their death rates have drastically fallen, while their birth rates have hardly changed at all, the populations of these countries, which grew relatively slowly until a few decades ago, are now expanding more rapidly than the populations of most of the presently developed countries ever did; and no man knows what tragic consequences lie ahead.

[1] This introduction was written for the Spring 1968 issue of *Daedalus*. It discusses only those essays which were first published in that issue. The new contributions included in this volume are reviewed by Professor Glass in the preceding 'General Introduction'.

Except for their low mortalities, the less developed countries are much more like Japan and the countries of Europe two hundred years ago than those countries today. Under these circumstances, it seems urgent to examine the historical conditions and processes that existed before the demographic transition and during the early stages of the decline of fertility—in the hope of learning something that may be applicable to the enormous problem of reducing birth rates in the poor countries. The essays in this volume illustrate work in progress towards that end.

This is not to say that the authors undertook their research with any such practical objective in mind. They were impelled, instead, by historical curiosity, the opportunity to develop and use new research methods, and the desire to understand the conditions of life for ordinary men and women in past times—men and women who left few records beyond the austere annals of their marriages, births, and deaths.

Perhaps the most striking outcome of these studies is evidence that many married couples in some, but not all, of the rural societies of pre-industrial Europe, long before the start of the demographic transition, deliberately limited the number of their children; this was in addition to such 'social' methods of fertility control as prolonged lactation and postponement of marriage. (The latter, though highly effective and the only method endorsed by the worthy and innocent Reverend Malthus, was probably not thought of by many of the couples who practised it as a device for keeping down the ultimate number of children they would have.)

There were marked differences in levels of marital fertility and, hence, presumably in the degree of fertility control within marriage among the regions of Europe and at different times in the same region. Indeed, the wide range of marital fertility in space and time is one of the principal proofs that some deliberate fertility control existed before the demographic transition. It is hard to avoid Paul Demeny's conclusion that the decline in fertility during the transition resulted not from a qualitative change in reproductive behaviour—a 'social mutation'—but from quantitative changes in the frequency, dissemination, and techniques of old practices in response to new conditions of life.

A second conclusion comes from these studies. Despite the ability and willingness of many couples to limit the size of their families, pre-industrial populations seem often to have grown to larger sizes than they should have attained for a comfortable balance with available resources. Though most people were probably well above the level of bare subsistence, poverty and misery became widespread. Under these 'quasi-Malthusian' circumstances, the numbers of people ceased to increase, or even declined, probably through a combination of increased infant and child mortality, emigration, social customs limiting fertility, and conscious fertility control. Evidently, our ancestors had to be placed under considerable stress before they would forgo the individual benefits of excessive reproduction.

In one respect, Western Europe was *sui generis* when compared to other parts of the world. Everywhere west of a straight line running from Trieste to St. Petersburg, the age of marriage of women was high until recent times, and many women and men never married. This 'European marriage pattern', whose importance was first pointed out by John Hajnal, had several significant social consequences—including, for example, the existence of large households containing servants and unmarried relatives, as well as a married couple and their children. From the demographic point of view, however, its most important consequence was a marked lowering of fertility. As a fertility-control device, the European marriage pattern had the advantage of being quickly responsive to changes in economic conditions. When a man could not find a way to support a family, or farm lands were not available, marriages were postponed. Under conditions of prosperity or reduced population pressure—for example, after an epidemic which had killed many of the older people—the number of marriages increased.

In various parts of Europe, significant long-term changes in age at marriage can be shown. In 1626 in Amsterdam, according to Bernard H. Slicher van Bath, 52 per cent of brides were under twenty-five years of age; this proportion was only 32 per cent a century and a half later. By 1850, the average age of women at first marriage in the Netherlands and Belgium was between twenty-eight and twenty-nine years, and about the same for Switzerland. From 15 to 20 per cent of women were still single at age fifty. As Etienne van de Walle shows in his article in this volume, the average age at which women married declined at about the same time as the extent of fertility control within marriage increased, though it is not clear whether or how the two events were causally related. But the fact that brides were about as old as their husbands strongly suggests that limitation of the number of children was one of the motives for late marriages.

In most of the world, women have always married at a much younger age than they have in Western Europe, and nearly all women marry. From the standpoint of understanding possible fertility changes in the less-developed countries, as Paul Demeny points out, a study of the demographic history of Eastern Europe, where young marriages are nearly universal, is perhaps more relevant than a similar study of the West. Moreover, the Eastern European countries remained largely rural until very recent times, and, particularly in Hungary, there was great ethnic, religious, and cultural diversity. This diversity was reflected in wide differences in fertility among provinces and even between nearby villages. The modern decline in fertility began rather late in Hungary, although its average birth rate is now among the lowest in the world, probably below the level needed to maintain the population. In many Hungarian villages, however, the number of living children was already extremely small in the middle of the nineteenth century. Apparently in an attempt to maintain and increase the size of farms, numerous families succeeded in having only one child. The means used for fertility control are not entirely known, but they undoubtedly included the age-old practices of abortion, infanticide, *coitus interruptus*, and abstinence, as well as various 'folk' contraceptives.

Because of its lack of industrialisation, rural character, and strongly religious society, Spain is also of special interest in considering the problems of the less-developed countries. Making use of all the rather scanty data he could find, Massimo Livi-Bacci has been able to compute life expectancies and fertility rates for Spain from 1768 to 1910. Although as late as 1900 life expectancy was less than thirty-five years in Spain (much lower than that in either India or Pakistan today), a steady decline in marital fertility began towards the end of the eighteenth century and continued through the nineteenth, while the proportion of married females of reproductive age increased throughout the nineteenth century. Spanish fertility was among the lowest in Europe in 1860. There seems little doubt that there was appreciable and increasing deliberate fertility control among married couples. Livi-Bacci suggests that growing social mobility was a significant factor in this pattern of change.

Until the last century, human lives in Europe were cut off not only by a high level of average mortality, but also by intermittent catastrophes—widespread famines and deadly epidemics of plague, smallpox, typhus, yellow fever, and, later, cholera. The most dreadful of these was the plague, which first appeared in Europe in the fourteenth century and recurred at intervals until the eighteenth. Jean-Noël Biraben describes the last important plague epidemic in Western Europe. This began in Marseilles in 1720, following the arrival of a plague-infested ship from Syria, and ravaged Provence and Languedoc for more than two years, killing over a hundred thousand persons. Nearly half of the inhabitants of Marseilles, Toulon, and Arles died. The proportions killed were even higher in some smaller towns, but a large number of settlements escaped with relatively few deaths. The epidemic spread along highways and attacked all cities of ten thousand or more inhabitants in the affected region of southern France, as well as many small towns. It was particularly virulent during the summer; it ended suddenly in October of 1722.

Fairly reliable information on catastrophic mortalities from epidemics and 'subsistence crises' (a demographic euphemism for famine) is relatively easy to obtain, for example, from parish registers, which record the month-by-month numbers of burials. For times prior to the advent of modern censuses and vital records, however, it is much harder to estimate the average levels of mortality or age-specific mortality rates—especially infant and child mortalities. Using the powerful tool of family reconstruction from parish registers developed by Louis Henry and his collaborators, E. A. Wrigley has been able to compute the changing levels of infant mortality and life expectancy in the Devonshire village of Colyton over three centuries. Of every thousand children born in Colyton during the reign of Elizabeth I, between 120 and 140 died before the age of one. The numbers of infant deaths increased somewhat during the seventeenth century. There were between 160 and 200 such deaths per thousand live births during the first half of the eighteenth century (compared with about 20 in England today and 160 in India), but by the beginning of the nineteenth, this proportion fell back to the Tudor levels. Corresponding to the high levels of infant and child mortality, the expectation of life at birth before 1600 was between forty-one and forty-six years; from 1625 to 1699, it was between thirty-five and thirty-nine years; and in the middle of the eighteenth century, between thirty-eight and forty-five years. Today, life expectancies are about seventy years in England and about fifty years in India.

As Wrigley points out, there is considerable evidence from burial and baptismal records in other parishes that the increased mortality found in Colyton in the seventeenth century occurred throughout England. The causes are obscure; they may have been related not to a lowering of living standards, but to the presence of new infectious diseases brought from other continents during the worldwide expansion of European travel and conquest. It seems apparent from the relative constancy of numbers of births and the steady rise in number of marriages found by Wrigley for Colyton throughout the eighteenth century that there was a considerable degree of deliberate control of fertility within marriage, at least during the latter half of the century.

In the early part of the eighteenth century, deaths exceeded births in Colyton, whereas in London in 1696–98, D. V. Glass finds that baptisms and burials were about equal. At least temporarily, the city may have ceased to be, as it had been for thousands of years, 'a consumer of men'. Glass's study gives us a glimpse of pre-industrial

urban ecology: The middle classes lived in the centre, the poor on
the outskirts of the city—just the reverse of the situation in United
States cities today. Nearly two thirds of the inhabitants were unmarried, and 55 per cent were under twenty-five years of age, reflecting
both the prevalent Western European marriage pattern of the time
and the high fertility of the people (compared with 44 per cent never
married and 37 per cent under twenty-five in England today).
Mobility was also high, and the city was apparently growing rapidly,
with perhaps as many as 13 per cent of the inhabitants leaving
within a year and as many as 27 per cent coming in.

Except for the differences between country and city, not enough
research has been done to indicate the degree of demographic homogeneity or heterogeneity in pre-industrial England. Through the
work of Pierre Goubert and his students and colleagues, however, it
is clear that there were marked demographic differences among the
different regions of France. Using the methods of family reconstitution from parish registers employed by Henry and Wrigley, Goubert
shows that the levels of infant mortality and the fertility of married
women were high throughout the eighteenth century in Brittany, a
province distinguished by its 'curious economy', Catholic fervour,
and general backwardness. A woman marrying at age twenty would,
on the average, have ten or eleven children, half of whom would die
before they were ten years old. Rapid population growth was prevented by late marriage. The average age of marriage for women
was always more than twenty-five years, and 10 to 15 per cent of the
women in Brittany never married. According to Goubert, there was
not the slightest trace of birth control within marriage in Brittany,
nor were there many illegitimate children, in contrast to England.
'Virtue is French' in the eighteenth century. Birth rates and child
mortalities were markedly lower in the southwest of France and in
Normandy than in Brittany. The intervals between births were
thirty months or more in the southwest, instead of twenty months, as
in Brittany. This lower fertility was counterbalanced by the survival
of about two thirds of the children past their tenth year. A sporadic
and intermittent birth control was practised, perhaps by the use of
coitus interruptus, throughout the eighteenth century, at least in the
southwest. Systematic birth control certainly developed towards the
end of the century in Normandy and the region of Paris.

Views of pre-industrial populations in presently developed countries are given by Bernard H. Slicher van Bath for a period from 1500
to 1795 in the Netherlands and by Susan B. Hanley for Tokugawa
Japan (1679–1834). In both countries, the total population about
doubled during the early part of the period, and there was a rapid
growth of cities. Tokyo was probably, as it is today, the largest city

on earth in the eighteenth and early-nineteenth centuries, having more than a million inhabitants. Both Japan and the Netherlands apparently suffered from heavy population pressures during the latter half of the period studied, and the living standards of the poor deteriorated. In Japan, about five persons apparently had to be fed from each cultivated acre (compared with 1·7 persons per acre in India today), and agricultural productivity may have been strained near the limit, even to meet human physiological requirements. In both countries, there were marked regional differences in population growth. These were apparently determined by the extent of economic development and land reclamation. In Japan, for example, there was a marked increase in commerce, textile manufacturing, large-scale commercial agriculture, fisheries, and arable land in the regions of greatest population growth.

Some of the difficulties and pitfalls of historical demography are described by J. A. Banks and T. H. Hollingsworth. Banks warns that we must beware of 'the ecological fallacy'—the assumption that associations based on data about sets of persons are valid estimates of the associations that would have been obtained had the data been about individuals. For example, differences in fertility among regions, some of which are more urbanized than others, need not necessarily be interpreted as differences between urban and rural fertility. They may be the result of other phenomena for which urbanism is, at most, an intermediate variable. Hollingsworth observes that error, bias, uncertainty, mistakes, and outright lies can all contaminate historical demographic data. The most difficult problem results, however, from failures to record relevant events. In parish registers, for example, many infant births and deaths may have gone unnoted by even the most conscientious clergymen. He points out that a historical demographer should not let himself be inhibited by thinking about data in black and white terms. Few numbers are so good that they can be accepted without question or so bad that they are useless.

The historical determinants of human fertility are discussed by David M. Heer, using a conceptual scheme first proposed by Joseph J. Spengler. The decision of a married couple to have or not to have a child depends on the value they place on an additional child compared to the value of other goals; the cost of an additional child, both in monetary terms and in time and effort, relative to the costs of other goals; and the resources of income, time, and energy available to the couple. Per-capita resources of income and leisure time greatly increased in Europe and the United States over the last hundred and fifty years, while fertility markedly declined. Hence, if Heer's scheme is correct, changes in values and costs must have more than counterbalanced the effects of increased income, with the net result that fertility was depressed. Heer describes in some detail how this may have happened.

In a similar vein, John T. Noonan, Jr., examines the origin, dissemination, acceptance, and effects of the cluster of ideas that underlies Western Christian sexual morality and family responsibility. He believes that these ideas were at least one of the causative factors in the typical pattern of late marriages and widespread celibacy which contributed to the suppression of fertility throughout Western Europe until relatively recent times.

Joseph J. Spengler has written the only essay in this volume which focuses on the socio-economic consequences of demographic factors. In his view, the suppression of fertility that resulted from the Western European marriage pattern and the consequent low rates of population growth before the nineteenth century allowed the accumulation of savings for investment and cushioned the impact of human numbers on land and other resources. At the same time, it augmented per-capita productivity by its effect on the age distribution of the population—with relatively low fertility the proportion of the people in the productive age group of fifteen to fifty-nine is comparatively high.

'Historical demography is in its heroic age', says Wrigley. Exciting and puzzling discoveries are continually being made, and the marginal returns to research effort can be expected to increase for some time. Each new analysis helps to narrow the uncertainties of previous studies, but raises new problems of its own.

The causes of this excitement are clear. As Louis Henry points out, modern historical demography is essentially a new science. It received its greatest impetus after World War II, when longitudinal studies of the ties between successive generations began to take the place of cross-sectional studies, and powerful new techniques were developed for analysing a variety of historical population data. More fundamentally, demographers realised that human populations are inscribed in time and can be understood best when they have been traced back into the past as far as usable observations permit.

To be sure, such retrospective analyses alone may not be enough for understanding. One must also use what Banks calls the 'hypothetical deductive method' of sociology—the formulation and testing of hypotheses about a social phenomenon against a body of known facts, including especially the social environment in which the phenomenon occurred. Banks illustrates his point by stating three hypotheses about the European marriage pattern in the sixteenth to nineteenth centuries, in terms of the future time perspectives of persons who postponed marriage and the possible shift over the centuries in their attitudes from Christian asceticism to a more worldly, prudential view. He is convinced that the most trustworthy sociological results will be obtained when the historical or documentary approach and the sociologist's method of surveys of living persons can be used to confirm and reinforce each other.

Henry concludes that historical demography, as it has evolved during the last twenty years, is not simply a marginal part of demography. It is demography itself, just as demography, being a study of human populations in time, is history itself. David Landes might not disagree, but he points out that his fellow historians will be convinced only when they can see that demographic studies foster a greater understanding of underlying historical processes. The new science of historical demography has devoted almost all its efforts to the determinants of population change and very few to an examination of its consequences. We do not understand the effects of population growth or stagnation on the course of economic and social development; the consequences of greater longevity on the allocation of resources and the distribution of political power; or the effects of differential fertility and mortality on the pathology of cities. These questions cannot be answered solely by the present techniques of demographic research. Extra-demographic variables must be introduced, some of which cannot be quantified. This will require a joint effort, combining the intellectual resources of historical demography with those not only of other historians, but of sociologists, economists, and specialists in resource analysis.

David Landes

The treatment of population in history textbooks

In principle, the historian is supposed to learn and know whatever is necessary for him to understand and explain his subject. In fact, the wider the range of his concerns, the more he falls short of this ideal. No one is supposed to know so much as the writer of the general textbook, intended to cover all aspects of the history of a country, or Europe, or the West, or the world over a given period; yet all professional historians, to say nothing of students, know enough not to expect anything like omniscience from these panacean compendia. Indeed, a cynic might argue that a good teacher wants a text with just enough shortcomings to enable him to shine.

The weaknesses of general history were less apparent when history itself was narrowly confined in its interests; when the story was limited to the doings of 'important' people—kings, courtiers, politicians, generals. As the range of interests within the discipline has widened to include the mass of common folk as well as the select few and to compromise the full array of human phenomena—economic, intellectual, social, psychological, as well as political, diplomatic, and military (to embrace the realm of everyday, banal existence as well as that of the unique, eventful exercise of power)—the gap between ideal and performance has increased. This is particularly true of those aspects of the subject that have become the province of highly-trained specialists using esoteric techniques. Economic history is the most obvious example. The history of population is another.

The study of population is not so old as history (that is, history as a defined field of knowledge), but it does go back a long way, to Graunt and Petty in seventeenth-century England, to the Abbé Expilly in France a century later, to Süssmilch in the Prussia of Frederick the Great. These fathers of modern demography began with the concern to establish the facts of population change, but they and their successors rapidly moved on to the analysis and explanation of change. By the late-eighteenth century, demography had assumed the shape that has prevailed to this day—that of a discipline combining increasingly sophisticated techniques of quantification with a core of theory that aims to relate the diverse statistical data.

The development of historical demography as a defined subfield of demography and, at the same time, of history (one of an increasing number of such dual specialties) is much more recent.[1] Some of the first manifestations of interest in the subject come in late-nineteenth-century France, where demographers and historians, as well as politicians and statesmen, were exercised about the low and declining birth rate, which had obvious implications for France's status as a European power. The problem was that not only was French population almost standing still, but the number of Germans was growing rapidly, so that demography threatened to put the seal on the defeat of 1870. As a result, there was a spate of studies on the character and causes of France's demographic stagnation, most of them pessimistic and some of them frankly alarmist. In 1897, Jacques Bertillon, one of the foremost 'natalists' of his day, gave an anguished warning to his compatriots: 'In fourteen years Germany will have twice as many conscripts as we. Then that people that hates us will devour us! The Germans say it, write it, and will do it!'[2] It was in this context that Levasseur wrote his sober three-volume history *La population française* (1889–92). It remains a useful reference work to this day.

At the same time, German historians were also beginning to turn their attention to population, though less to the German population of their own day, which was obviously developing satisfactorily, or of the immediate past than to that of other countries or of far earlier times. Ignaz Jastrow did a study of the population of German cities at the end of the Middle Ages and in the early modern period (1886); Karl Bücher published his classic monograph on the population of late medieval Frankfurt (1886); Julius Beloch brought out a series of monographs on the population of the Greco-Roman world (1886, 1899, 1903), of Italy from the sixteenth to the eighteenth century (1888), and of Europe in the Middle Ages and Renaissance (1900); and Karl Lamprecht devoted a substantial chapter of his economic history of medieval Germany to demographic issues (1885).[3]

[1] On the history and literature of historical demography, there is a brief survey in David Glass, Introduction to D. V. Glass and D. E. C. Eversley (eds.), *Population in History* (London, 1965), pp. 1–19. Several of the other essays in that volume are also relevant. The most useful handbook guide to demography as a field, offering information on primary sources, techniques, bibliography, and research centres (including their addresses and sources of support), is C. Legeard, *Guide de recherches documentaires en démographie* (Paris, 1966).

[2] Jacques Bertillon, 'Le problème de la dépopulation', *Revue politique et parlementaire*, Vol. 12 (1897), pp. 538–9, cited in Koenrad W. Swart, *The Sense of Decadence in Nineteenth-Century France* (International Archives of the History of Ideas, No. 7; The Hague, 1964), p. 173. In addition to Swart, see the discussion in Joseph J. Spengler, *France Faces Depopulation* (Durham, 1938). Claude Digeon, *La crise allemande de la pensée française (1870–1914)* (Paris, 1959), pp. 328–9, alludes to the problem, but only very briefly.

[3] The most important German contribution to the more recent history of population was a series of monographs edited by F. J. Neumann, *Beiträge zur Geschichte der Bevölkerung*

In this area the British, who were the pioneers of demography as a contemporary science and were always among the leaders in population theory, were laggards. Not until G. Talbot Griffith brought out in 1926 his *Population Problems of the Age of Malthus* did the British historian find a theme that aroused his curiosity and intellectual passion; and from that day to this, the subject of population growth during the period of the Industrial Revolution has remained the central problem of British demographic history.[4] Contemporaneous with Griffith or following after, there have come Margaret Buer, T. H. Marshall, Barbara Hammond, Dorothy George, Thomas McKeown and R. G. Brown, J. D. Chambers, David Glass, T. H. Hollingsworth, K. H. Connell, H. J. Habakkuk, J. T. Krause, W. A. Cole, P. E. Razzell, and others—all of them adding fuel to the controversy.[5] Any such list is necessarily incomplete not only because space limitations prevent a complete enumeration, but because new names are added all the time.

This preoccupation with population change during the course of

in *Deutschland seit dem Beginn des Jahrhunderts* (7 vols.; Tübingen, 1883–1903). The scope of the series was widely construed to include studies of handicraft industry and social welfare.

---

[4] Griffith was preceded by E. C. K. Gonner, a student of agrarian history who published an article on the same subject. 'The Population of England in the Eighteenth Century', in the *Journal of the Royal Statistical Society*, Vol. 76 (1913), pp. 261–303; and by John Brownlee, a statistician, who wrote among other things an essay on 'The History of the Birth and Death Rates in England and Wales Taken as a Whole, from 1570 to the Present Time', *Public Health*, Vol. 29 (1916), pp. 211–22, 228–38. These quantitative studies, although laying the empirical foundation for Griffith and his successors, did not stimulate the kind of debate that arose the moment one moved from narration or description to explanation.

[5] Margaret C. Buer, *Health, Wealth and Population in the Early Days of the Industrial Revolution* (London, 1927); T. H. Marshall, 'The Population Problem During the Industrial Revolution: A Note on the Present State of the Controversy', *Economic History* (A Supplement to the *Economic Journal*), Vol. 1 (1929); B. Hammond, 'Urban Death-Rates in the Early Nineteenth Century,' *Economic History*, Vol. 1 (1928), pp. 419–28; T. McKeown and R. G. Brown, 'Medical Evidence Related to English Population Changes in the Eighteenth Century', *Population Studies*, Vol. 9 (1955), pp. 119–41; J. D. Chambers, 'Enclosure and Labour Supply in the Industrial Revolution', *Economic History Review*, 2nd Ser., Vol. 5 (1952–3), pp. 319–43; Chambers, *The Vale of Trent, 1760–1800 (Economic History Review*, Supplement No. 3; London, 1957); Chambers, 'Population Change in a Provincial Town: Nottingham 1700–1800', in L. S. Pressnell (ed.), *Studies in the Industrial Revolution* (London, 1960); T. H. Hollingsworth, *The Demography of the British Peerage*, special number of *Population Studies*, Vol. 18 (1964); K. H. Connell, *The Population of Ireland 1750–1845* (Oxford, 1950); H. J. Habakkuk, 'English Population in the Eighteenth Century', *Economic History Review*, 2nd Ser., Vol. 6 (1953–54), pp. 117–33; J. T. Krause, 'Changes in English Fertility and Mortality, 1781–1850', *Economic History Review*, Vol. II (1958–9), pp. 52–70; Phyllis Deane and W. A. Cole, *British Economic Growth 1688–1959* (Cambridge, 1962; rev. ed., 1967): P. E. Razell, 'Population Change in Eighteenth-Century England: A Reinterpretation', *Economic History Review*, 2nd Ser., Vol. 18 (1965–6), pp. 312–32. Several of the above pieces are reprinted, sometimes with revisions, in Glass and Eversley, *Population in History*. On the quantitative sources for British population history, see Glass, 'Population and Population Movements in England and Wales, 1700 to 1850', *Population in History*, pp. 221–46; for a general bibliography of studies in British population history, see, E. A. Wrigley (ed.). *An Introduction to English Historical Demography* (London, 1966) pp. 241–63.

BP

industrialization is, in part, dictated by the nature of the evidence: With discrete exceptions, continuous, wide-ranging demographic statistics begin in the late-seventeenth and eighteenth centuries. Intellectual considerations, however, have been paramount, specifically the conviction that the so-called demographic transition from a Malthusian equilibrium of high death rate/high birth rate to a new equilibrium of low death rate/low birth rate is one of the central phenomena of modern history—indeed, that it is a core aspect of the process of modernisation itself. Hence, interest in Britain and elsewhere has broadened to encompass the other stages of the process—in particular, the adjustment of fertility to lower mortality.[6] This concern has received new impetus from the general anxiety about the population explosion of pre-industrial areas in the twentieth century. Can history, asks the demographer, shed some light on the determinants of population growth—their nature, relationship to one another, susceptibility of management, and the like?

We have, then, a growing body of work in demographic history of an increasingly sophisticated character. The range of inquiry and analysis has widened, and new statistical and research techniques have been introduced by specialists who have come to the field from the demographic, rather than the historical side.[7] Few historical specialties have grown and changed so rapidly, and this change is in turn testimony to the recognized importance of the subject. It is all the more interesting, therefore, to consider the place of this new area of inquiry in the larger field of history *tout court*. Specifically, what place has it held in the general textbooks? And through these, what information about the history of population has been transmitted to the younger generation? An effort, however cursory, to answer these questions will tell us something about historians as scholars and about the quality of instruction in the discipline. It will also suggest some thoughts about the relevance of the concerns of the demographic historian (or historical demographer) to those of general history.

[6] See especially the work of J. A. Banks, *Prosperity and Parenthood: A Study of Family Planning Among the Victorian Middle Class* (London, 1954); also J. A. and Olive Banks, *Feminism and Family Planning in Victorian England* (Liverpool, 1964).

[7] The most important innovation has been the method of reconstitution of families, which makes possible a far more effective exploitation of pre-census sources. The technique was pioneered by Louis Henry and his associates in the Institut National d'Etudes Démographiques in Paris, beginning in the 1940s, and has since spread to other countries, in particular to England. For the technique, see Louis Henry and Michel Fleury, *Nouveau manuel de dépouillement et d'exploitation de l'état civil ancien* (Paris, 1965); Louis Henry, *Manuel de démographie historique* (Paris, 1967); and Wrigley, (ed.), *Introduction to English Historical Demography*. In the same volume, David Eversley offers an analysis and defence of the continued utility of the older aggregative methods: 'Exploitation of Anglican Parish Registers by Aggregative Analysis', pp. 44–95.

For the purpose of this inquiry, I have confined my searches largely to books in English on European or Western history, with special attention to the textbooks in use in American colleges and universities. Nowhere else, in the Western world at least, does the standard, required textbook hold so important a place in higher education, and nowhere else are the rewards to the author of a successful text greater; hence the readiness of even the best scholarly talent to devote itself to this kind of work. The textbook is, thus, a reasonably accurate reflection of current historical scholarship. (I say 'reasonably accurate' because these manuals have obvious built-in constraints that necessarily distort the author's message. They have to be simple, and history is usually complex. They should be as free as possible of jargon and technical matter, and it is hard to treat demography without some recourse to numbers and abstruse theoretical concepts. Finally, in order to make money, they ought to be lively; but population is not the most exciting subject for the average student in a required course in 'Western Civ'.)

The earliest textbooks and general histories—those of the pre-World War I period—devote little, if any, attention to population. This is not surprising, in view of the general neglect and ignorance of the subject and the narrow view of history that was prevalent. Still, one might have expected more from a collaborative effort like the *Cambridge Modern History*, which brought together experts from many countries and a wide range of specialties. Yet Volume 6 on the eighteenth century, published in 1909, seems to have nothing on population, even in the chapter on Ireland; and it contains no chapter whatever on the economic and social history of the period, where demography might have found a place. By contrast, Volume 11, *The Growth of Nationalities* (1909), does have a chapter, by J. H. Clapham, the future professor of economic history at Cambridge, on 'Great Britain and Free Trade (1824–52)'. Clapham makes a brief reference to the continued growth of population (to which the interested reader might have asked, continued from what?), and he treats the famine in Ireland as a precipitating factor in the repeal of the Corn Laws. Yet the chapter comments on the sharp drop in Irish population due to the famine and emigration without mentioning the rapid increase in numbers that preceded the catastrophe; and although it speaks of emigration from the United Kingdom in these years as checking 'the gloomy fears of the Malthusians' (p. 20) and easing the labour market, it sheds no light on the source of these fears or this pressure. The last volume in the set, Vol. 12, is *The Latest Age* (1910). Again there is a chapter, by Sidney Webb, dealing with economic and social history. Webb's concern, however, is primarily with social movements, conditions of work, and welfare programmes. The only reference to population, almost *en passant*, comes in a brief discussion of urbanization.

If the leading European historians, writing for a constituency that included their fellow scholars, could pass over the subject of population so lightly, one should not expect more of textbooks addressed to a more innocent clientele. Carlton J. H. Hayes brought out his *Political and Social History of Modern Europe* in 1916; the book was destined, in various avatars, to be the most successful American text of the interwar years. It disposed of population and the Industrial Revolution in three sentences (Section 2, p. 76):

> The development of commerce and industry has been attended by remarkable increases of population—for clothes could be made and food produced more easily than ever before in the world's history. In the first half of the nineteenth century, the population of England was doubled. During the nineteenth century the population of Europe, roughly speaking, grew from 175 million to 396 million.

This was more space than Hayes was prepared to devote to the subject some thirty-five years later. In a textbook entitled *Modern Europe to 1870* (1953), which he described as 'an essentially new work' in which national politics and policy would receive 'chief attention, but not to the neglect of those social, economic, and ideological factors which shape or at least condition political thought and action', he found no room for population at all.

Hayes was a political historian of the traditional variety. What, however, is one to make of the representatives of the so-called New History, who were going to revolutionize the discipline by widening its scope to include those more enduring elements and determinants of change—social, economic, cultural—that the conventional political narrative had neglected? One of the two leaders of the movement was James Harvey Robinson, who wrote an *Introduction to the History of Western Europe* (first edition, 1902; new brief edition, 1931). In the 1931 edition he took care of the population explosion in a sentence: 'Moreover, the population of Europe nearly doubled during the nineteenth century, owing to the quick and ready facilities for distributing food'—offering no statistics, no reflections on the significance of the change. He did, however, follow this with a paragraph on the rise of cities. Robinson also joined with Charles Beard in writing *The Development of Modern Europe: An Introduction to the Study of Current History* (first edition, 1907; revised edition, 1929); here the subject of population was simply never mentioned.

One could cite numerous other examples of this neglect or swift disposal of the subject in the textbooks of the interwar years—the work of such distinguished scholars as J. Salwyn Schapiro, Edward P. Cheyney, H. A. L. Fisher, Robert Ergang, Franklin Palm.[8] Nevertheless, sins of omission may be less serious than sins of commission. The Thompson-Palm-Van Nostrand text, in an unguarded Malthusian moment, declares that Great Britain, 'by her unrestrained expansion of population and facilities for production in certain lines, threw her economy out of gear to such an extent that she was threatened with a shortage of food, clothes, and other necessities of life' (p. 818). The Ferguson and Bruun volume, which tries to give more attention to the subject than most, speaks of the surge of population in the eighteenth century and then offers a graph showing a smooth parabolic increase from 1630 on.[9] The Boak-Hyma-Slosson text devotes a page to the population explosion of the nineteenth century, which it attributes to a rise in the birth rate in Russia, a fall in the death rate in Western and Central Europe.[10]

The palm in this domain, however, must go to Ferdinand Schevill, whose *History of Europe from the Reformation to the Present Day* appeared in 1925. An introductory chapter declares that the book will be representative of the New History—that is, it will be a history of civilisation. Although there is no mention of population in the Index, the book does, in fact, devote more space to the subject than any other text of these years that has come to my attention. In a chapter on 'The Industrial and Social Revolution of the Nineteenth Century', the author treats the rapid increase in numbers as a consequence of the Industrial Revolution:

Wherever the Industrial Revolution has taken root it has greatly increased population for the simple reason that the production of more goods has enabled more people to live. Statistics would seem to show that the increase is only partially due to an improved birth rate (or lowered death rate) and that it most often presents itself to view as migration from the rural districts to the urban centres in possession of the machines. In the case of England, which serves as the industrial type, the total population doubled

[8] J. Salwyn Schapiro, *Modern and Contemporary European History* (New York 1918); E. P. Cheyney, *A Short History of England* (rev. ed.; Boston, 1927); H. A. L. Fisher, *A History of Europe* (3 vols.; Cambridge, Mass., 1935–36); Robert Ergang, *Europe Since Waterloo* (Boston, 1939); J. W. Thompson, F. C. Palm, and John J. Van Nostrand, *European Civilization: A Political, Social and Cultural History* (London, 1939).

[9] Wallace K. Ferguson and Geoffrey Bruun, *A Survey of European Civilization* (2 vols.; New York, 1939).

[10] Arthur Boak, Albert Hyma, and Preston Slosson, *The Growth of European Civilization* (New York, 1939).

in the first half of the nineteenth century and has continued to increase since at a scarcely slackened rate (p. 516).

The discussion continues by noting the increase in food supply thanks to imports from abroad. Schevill then moves on to Germany and offers the following analysis: 'The German agricultural population has at best remained stationary, proving that the considerable German increase in population belongs to the towns and is of industrial origin'. Finally, he generalizes the remarkable fertility of German cities to Europe as a whole. 'Conceding that Europe's amazing growth of population is overwhelmingly industrial and urban, we are obliged, in considering the problem of the maintenance of this human increase, to take account not only of the new foreign markets but also of the improved productivity of the soil.'

Of course, if one turns from general histories to specialized textbooks, specifically to those in economic history, the picture is more reassuring. The attention accorded population varies, from the passing references of Lilian Knowles to the more extended discussions of A. P. Usher and Herbert Heaton.[11] Usher's treatment is especially impressive, given its precocity. He wrote before Griffith opened up the whole debate. In the absence of a convenient body of monographic literature, Usher went to the British census of 1841 for Rickman's estimates of population in the eighteenth century, and he hit on the interesting device of contrasting the actual course of population growth (insofar as he could establish it) with the course predicted by Gregory King at the end of the seventeenth century. King expected the population of England and Wales to reach 7·35 million by 1900; by that date the number had reached 32·5 million.[12] Usher has little to offer, however, on the causes of this unanticipated surge, except to suggest that industrialization brought with it a greater international division of labour, and that specialization made possible a larger food supply.[13] 'The dismal forebodings of the

[11] Lilian C. A. Knowles, *Economic Development in the Nineteenth Century: France, Germany, Russia, and the United States* (London, 1932); A. P. Usher, *An Introduction to the Industrial History of England* (Boston, 1920); Herbert Heaton, *Economic History of Europe* (New York, 1936).

[12] *The Industrial History of England*, pp. 269–71. Usher gives his source as the Census of 1821, but this is presumably a typographical error.

[13] It is interesting to compare the textbook of 1920 with W. Bowden, M. Karpovich, and A. P. Usher, *An Economic History of Europe Since 1750* (New York, 1937). The latter gives considerable attention to population, especially in its economic aspects: distribution in space, relation of density to economic activity, comparative rates of growth—the whole supported by tables and semilog graphs. It does little with the components of these changes, saying nothing about birth rates or death rates, for example, and makes no real effort to account for them, leaving the reader to infer that increased resources permitted larger numbers. By increased resources, moreover, is meant coal more than food; economic activity (by implication, the demand for labour) more than means of nourishment. The

Malthusians', he wrote, 'seem very remote to us, and it is equally difficult for us to appreciate Liebig's feeling that the application of scientific theory to agriculture would be of inestimable humanitarian worth by reason of freeing the world from the prospect of indefinitely increasing pressure upon food-supply' (p. 269). Usher's confidence seems as remote to us as the dismal forebodings of the Malthusians.

Heaton, writing in 1936, had the advantage of more than a decade of further demographic research and debate. His treatment, moreover, is the more interesting because it is relatively up to date and reflects the strengths and weaknesses of contemporary work. Thus he states that the population of England and Wales grew substantially (by 23 per cent) from 1700 to 1760, whereas we today are inclined to see it growing at about half that rate; he explains the rise and the fall in the death rate as being due to better sanitation and medical care, whereas we have been inclined to discount this factor, since the work of McKeown and Brown.[14] Heaton sees the increase in the supply of food as a response to, rather than a cause of, population growth.

Heaton devotes more space to population change in the nineteenth and early-twentieth centuries, relying on Marshall for Britain and on R. R. Kuczynski for Europe as a whole.[15] The discussion focuses on the final phase of the demographic transition: the general fall in the death rate from 1870 on and the concomitant drop in fertility, due to later marriage and the spread of birth control. Writing in the middle of a world depression, when birth rates had fallen to their lowest point in recorded history, Heaton offered a gloomy prognosis: 'This development must produce stationary and then declining populations in those countries which for four centuries have been the energetic and dominant economic and political regions of Europe' (p. 744). And citing Beveridge: 'Such a development, visible already over other parts of the world where the white race has gone, would indeed "be a turning point in history" ' (p. 744). Heaton went on to discuss the economic and social consequences of this change, noting a fall in the demand for food and raw materials, a shift in expenditure towards

result is a strangely simplistic model of growth. Thus the low rate of increase in France was 'mainly attributable to losses in extensive areas which were not more than offset by the gains in the industrial and commercial regions' (p. 18). No explanation is given for the diminished rate of increase from the late-nineteenth century on, but the sharp drop in the twenties is imputed to 'direct losses of life in the war, to the unfavourable age distribution of the postwar period, and to unfavourable economic circumstances'.

[14] The recent article of Razzell on the effects of inoculation against small-pox may have re-opened the issue. I say, 'may have', because there are those who feel that Razzell's evidence tends to exaggerate the extent of the practice, in that it consists in part of self-advertising by practitioners of the new art. Still, the persistence of controversy says something about the limitations of our knowledge.

[15] Robert R. Kuczynski, *The Balance of Births and Deaths* (2 vols.; New York, 1928, 1931).

consumers' durables, luxuries, and services, and an increased concern for the old as against the young. He then concluded with further tentative predictions: 'Stability and security will seem more important economically and politically than will opportunities for enterprise and advancement. But those countries which still possess youth and energy, and which want outlets for their teeming populations, may not be willing to let the older ones enjoy either stability or security (p. 745). The whole makes interesting reading and leads one to reflect on hazards of contemporary history.

After World War II, numerous changes were made in the history curriculum of American colleges and universities. Sometimes world history (or 'world civilisation') replaced European history as part of an effort to live up to the new ideal of One World, or the differentiated history course was dropped in favour of general courses in social science or social studies—sacrificed in the name of disciplinary ecumenism. Whatever the title given to the introductory survey course, the textbook usually had to say something about population, the more so as it was rapidly becoming clear that the non-Western peoples of the world were experiencing the kind of population explosion that the West had known in the eighteenth and nineteenth centuries, but under far less favourable economic conditions. Historians differed on the seriousness of the problem posed by this increase in numbers, but all agreed that population was a central issue for the world citizen of the mid-twentieth century.

In addition, the growing concern with population had its impact on scholarly research. The war had necessarily entailed an interruption of training and writing in this field; work did not stop, but it slowed down. With the return of peace, however, demography picked up again stronger than before, and this revival found expression in new research centres and publications: the Institut National d'Etudes Démographiques in Paris, with its quarterly *Population* (1946 on) and its monograph series; and the British *Population Studies*, which made its appearance in 1947. By providing opportunities for communication and publication, these further encouraged research in the subject, so that demography rapidly became one of the most creative and productive branches of social science. This advance was bound to make itself felt—first in adjacent fields like economic history, eventually in general history.

During the immediate postwar years, most schools made do with the textbooks of the interwar period, some of them hastily revised to meet the needs of a new generation of students. Such revisions, however, generally entailed no change in the treatment (or nontreatment) of population history. They usually consisted in the addition of chapters on the events of preceding years—the war, the peace, postwar reconversion and reconstitution. (These additions have the virtue of bringing a textbook right up to the minute, and both teachers and students like this; they also have the advantage for the publisher of making previous editions obsolete, which cuts down the use of secondhand copies.) It was not until the fifties, therefore, that one saw the first fruits of the new concern with population.

One of the most innovative of the new texts, and one of the most successful, was the Brinton, Christopher, and Wolff *History of Civilization* (1955), which went into six printings in the space of two years and has continued to flourish to this day. As a textbook, its great strength lies in the treatment of ideas and cultural achievements; and some might argue that this is what we mean by civilization. The book does not ignore the economic and social aspects of history, but it deals with population in passing. There is a paragraph, for example, on the European population explosion citing figures for British and Russia (tables are carefully avoided; they turn some readers off). This is followed by a brief discussion of urbanization and its social consequences: 'The most important social change flowing from the industrial revolution was not the increase in the population but the alteration in its structure and balance' (pp. 202 f.). The subject returns later, on a theoretical level in a review of Malthus, which provides the occasion for a reference to the Irish famine and depopulation. One finds in a chapter on India: 'It is clear that if the Indian masses are to attain the standards of human welfare that Westernization seems to make people want, India will have to solve—and not by starvation or war—her problem of population. Her citizens will have to interfere with "nature" and institute birth control, something abhorrent to the basic ways of Hinduism' (p. 629).

The Brinton-Christopher-Wolff text covers a lot of ground, and one can well understand why even an important topic like population can receive only brief attention. What happens when one narrows the scope of the story?

One of the standard theory courses in American colleges is the one labelled Europe since 1500, or Modern Europe. In this field, the leading text over the last decade has been Robert Palmer's (later Palmer and Colton) *A History of the Modern World*,[16] which has now seen three editions. In the latest edition, this textbook does better by demography than any other in the field. There is a full discussion of 'Basic Demography: The Increase of the Europeans', which is broken down into sections on the rapid growth during the eighteenth and nineteenth centuries, the stabilization of the European popula-

---

[16] The first edition appeared in 1951. The second and third editions (1956 and 1965) are co-authored by Palmer and Joel Colton.

tion, the growth of cities, and the transoceanic migration. The authors are not afraid to use tables or charts (this is exceptional) or to talk of birth and death rates per thousand (numbers, particularly ratios and similar compound numbers, frighten history students). Moreover, they are ready to go at length into the consequences as well as causes of the demographic transition.

How do they account for the great increase in numbers during these centuries? They start with a disclaimer: 'The causes of sudden rise in world population after 1650 are not known' (p. 559). They then become more affirmative: 'All students agree in attributing the increase to falling death rates rather than to increasing birth rates. Populations grew because more people lived longer, not because more were born.' The authors offer five reasons for why people lived longer: the rise of 'organized sovereign states', which brought an end to civil war and 'chronic violence'; the elimination of certain endemic diseases—the subsiding of plague in the seventeenth century, the 'conquest of smallpox' in the eighteenth; the increase in agricultural output, 'beginning notably in England about 1750'; better transportation, which put an end to local famines; and the rise of machine industry, which enabled Europeans to trade manufactures for food (pp. 560 f.). Most demographic historians, of course, would not accept the assertion that smallpox was conquered in the eighteenth century, and agrarian specialists would object to the notion that a significant increase in food output did not begin until the mid-eighteenth century.[17]

Palmer and Colton allude to the consequences of this surge of population for European power: 'The ascendancy in modern times of European civilization, or roughly of the white races, has been due in some measure to a merely quantitative advantage' (p. 561). But they see its effects primarily in urbanization and migration. The former was of crucial importance, at least as much for psychological and cultural reasons as for social and political: 'The great city set the tone of modern society' (p. 563). The migration, they note, involved some sixty million people (perhaps a fifth of whom later returned) and 'towers above all other historical migrations in magnitude, and possibly also in significance, for it was the means by which earlier colonial offshoots of Europe were transformed into new Europes alongside the old' (p. 565). Interestingly enough, in the actual analysis of this movement, Palmer and Colton give almost no place to demographic considerations. They note the contribution of cheap steam transport, the pull of land and jobs in the New World, and the push of famine or political persecution. Above all, they stress the

---

[17] On the latter question, see especially the new book by Eric Kerridge, *The Agricultural Revolution* (London, 1967).

permissive liberalism of the eighteenth and nineteenth centuries when governments generally suffered their subjects to pick up and leave, taking their wealth with them. They do nothing with the correlations between rates of population growth and rates and sources of emigration.

The most original feature of the Palmer-Colton treatment of demography (it has no parallel in any of the other textbooks I have examined) is the discussion of the causes and implications of the shift from large to small families beginning in the last decades of the nineteenth century. On the side of causes, the authors stress the 'codes of modern society': to begin with, literal codes like the Code Napoléon, which required a roughly equal division of inheritances and hence encouraged those who wanted to preserve their patrimony to limit the number of their children; and then figurative codes, the values of modern society—the preference for leisure and recreation, ambition for the social advancement of children, the effort to lighten the burdens of the wife and mother. The authors note, however, that small families threaten the continuity of society; that 'those societies in which individual welfare is most highly prized, by the very means they take to promote it, become smaller than the societies which value mass and collective strength'. They add that 'what people consider to be welfare easily passes into self-indulgence, and that some of the most civilized persons have few children, or none at all, for the most grossly selfish reasons' (p. 563). (For a textbook, this kind of moralizing is most unusual.) To be sure, the drop in the birth rate was reversed after World War II, but the 'permanent effect' of this reversal 'is not yet clear' (p. 561).

Another postwar textbook in this field is Paul H. Beik and Lawrence Lafore, *Modern Europe: A History Since 1500* (1955). Neither of the authors is primarily a specialist in economic and social history. Beik has concerned himself with the ideas and institutions of pre-Revolutionary France. Lafore has published on European diplomacy on the eve of World War I; he also writes novels. But the authors are concerned to link social change to other aspects of historical change. In a section on 'Society and Politics', population makes its appearance as one of an array of forces changing the European world: 'Although the countryside looked much as it had for centuries, there were accumulating during this era the people, money, roads, ships, towns, and machines which were to make Europe astonishingly different in the nineteenth century' (p. 193).

The text continues rather timidly: 'For one thing, population was growing—no one knows quite why. [Again the precautionary disclaimer.] Statistics are lacking, but good guesses can be made.' In fact, the authors proceed to offer data on population increase in

Britain, France, Prussia, Spain, and Russia—though the accuracy of these data leaves something to be desired. They do venture an explanation for at least some of this increase: 'Europe's increase was part of the great population growth which has come in the world since the eighteenth century. It is a historical fact explainable in some regions by the better order and improved agriculture which kept a greater percentage of the newly born alive, in other areas less easily explainable but none the less real' (p. 194).

This is the most extended discussion of population in Beik and Lafore. The subject returns at intervals—in a chapter on 'Revolutionary Economic and Social Changes' of the nineteenth century, in a section on 'Changing Social and Economic Problems' of the period before World War I, in chapters devoted to Great Britain, France, and Russia. In the course of these brief allusions, the authors remark on the growth of cities (pp. 411 and 569), the scope of emigration from Europe overseas (p. 568), the changing distribution of occupations, the political implications of the discrepancy between German and French demographic patterns (p. 621), and the impetus given by Russian population growth to the land hunger of the peasantry, 'which played so important a part in the twentieth-century revolutions' (p. 682). In sum, the book offers a dispersed, unsystematic, but not indifferent treatment.

If we narrow our focus even further, we come to a text like David Thomson's *Europe Since Waterloo* (second edition, 1965). Thomson is primarily a political historian, but his short study of *Democracy in France: The Third and Fourth Republics* (third edition, 1958) gives considerable space to economic and social institutions. Thomson is clearly at home in these areas. In the textbook, he has a chapter on 'The Forces of Change', which begins with a section on the growth of population: 'The speed of this growth was a completely new phenomenon. . . . No social and political order could have remained unaffected by so immense an increase of humanity; and the events of the nineteenth century remain unintelligible unless this greatest revolution of all is kept constantly in mind' (pp. 92 f.). Thomson notes that this increase 'changed the course of world history by making it possible for the smallest of the continents to colonize a good part of the rest of the world.'

Why this population explosion? Thomson stresses the fall in death rates: 'Populations grew not so much because more people were born as because more survived, and more stayed alive longer' (p. 93). And why lower death rates? For four reasons that are very close to those of Palmer and Colton: 'improvements in public order and security' effected by stronger monarchies, which ended civil and religious wars, repressed violence, and 'did much to relieve famine, plague, and destitution'; advances in medical science in the eighteenth century, which freed Western Europe from 'the worst endemic diseases and plagues that had taken a constant and heavy toll of all populations down to the seventeenth century'; improvements in transportation, which 'made it possible to end localized famine and shortages'; and increases in food output. Unlike Palmer and Colton, however, Thomson dates the agricultural revolution from 1800 onward and treats it more as a response to population pressure than as a cause of growth.

Yet Thomson does less with the consequences of population growth than with its causes. Aside from this discussion of the agricultural revolution and an allusion to the implications of an expanding population for Russian territorial expansion, he contents himself with an omnibus model linking population and general change:

> If nineteenth-century Europe appears in history as unusually restless, explosive, and prone to revolution, this remarkable demographic fact is at least one explanation. Against this tide no social and political order could stand intact. No mere 'restoration' of old institutions and traditions could suffice to meet the needs of the new masses of humanity which so abruptly made their appearance on the old soil of Europe. Only constant inventiveness, reorganization, and experiment in new forms of social life could sustain civilization. In the sphere of economic production and distribution, this inventiveness and reorganization took the form of what is traditionally called the 'industrial revolution'; in the sphere of social life and organization, it took the form of urbanism and, eventually, suburbanism(p. 94).

Thomson has more to say about population in a later chapter on 'The Balance of Power in Europe, 1850–70'. Here he provides further statistics on population growth, which he then transposes into ambiguous rates of increase: German population grew 'at the rate of 8 per cent'; that of France, 'by roughly 7·5 per cent' (p. 228). The reference is apparently to decennial rates, but this is not indicated in the text. Neither is the reader provided with a table, again perhaps for fear of rendering the text illegible to anti-quantitative undergraduates.

Thomson then alludes briefly to urbanization, noting simply that as a result of the move to the cities, 'the whole texture and fabric of social life was changing . . ., creating novel or more acute problems of urban housing, sanitation, public order, and organization' (p. 228). He returns to the topic in a chapter on 'The Pattern of

Parliamentary Democracy' in the prewar period. Again the discussion begins with a selection of statistics, with particular emphasis on differential rates of growth of various countries; this time rates are specified as per year, but there is still no table, much less a chart. Then the discussion moves on to the implications of urbanization, its political consequences in particular: 'Its significance for internal politics was that every European government now had to administer and serve the interests of larger and denser agglomerations of people than ever before in the history of mankind' (p. 226). Thomson enumerates some of the tasks this entailed: 'how to ensure adequate provision for public health and sanitation, public order, and police; how to protect industrial workers against bad conditions of working and living' (p. 228).

The subject of population comes up again at a number of points in the narrative: in regard to the implications of the divergent rates of increase of Germany and France for the international balance of power (p. 521); to the demographic consequences of World War I ('The French calculated that between August, 1914, and February, 1917, one Frenchman was killed every minute' (p. 537)); to the end of the great wave of European overseas migration ('The age of wide open spaces and boundless opportunities, of limitless expansion and dynamic productivity, had come to an end' (p. 656)); to the renewal of fertility in post-World War II Europe (p. 803); and to the drop in mortality rates during these years and the effect of continued population growth on the demand for food and raw materials. This dispersal of the material has its disadvantages; one misses, for example, a systematic discussion of the concluding phases of Europe's demographic transition. On the other hand, dispersal in the hands of someone like Thomson is an integrative device. He weaves population into the larger story and, by so doing, conveys more perhaps than if he encapsulated the subject and set it apart as a kind of esoteric special topic.

One could continue with other texts, with varying results. In general, the more narrow the focus on modern European history, the more sensitive the author is to the significance of population change. At the same time, the closer the author's specialization is to economic and social history, the more easily he handles demographic phenomena and the more space he is prepared to give to them. In a text, for example, like that of Blum, Cameron, and Barnes (two of whom are economic historians), population is treated in at least four distinct sections, as well as *passim;* and the authors do not shy away from the use of tables.[18] Whether demographers would be entirely

[18] Jerome Blum, Rondo Cameron, and Thomas Barnes, *A History of the European World* (Boston, 1966).

satisfied with the author's explanation of population growth, which takes the form of a timeless enumeration of determinants of varying specificity, is another matter.[19]

It is clear, then, that on balance the treatment of population in college texts has improved considerably over the last generation; but to some extent this improvement is implicit in the point of departure. The textbooks of the interwar period were almost invariably so inadequate in this regard that even a modicum of discussion looks good. When one compares the textbook treatment of population with the latest work in historical demography, it is clear that the authors of these manuals are inclined to rely on other general works or some of the older monographs—even on other textbooks; that they have little familiarity with the concerns and findings of the latest research; that they are usually awkward and often inaccurate in their citation and manipulation of numbers; and that they find it hard to state an explicit model, right or wrong, positive or conjectural, of the process of population change.

There will always be some gap between the treatment given in the textbooks and the work done on the frontier of the discipline. This is true of any topic. In the case of demography, however, the discrepancy is aggravated by the technical character of the research, which becomes more esoteric with time, and by the disinclination of teachers and students allergic to numbers.[20]

Obviously any effort to diminish this lag calls for work by both demographers and historians. The former have to find the time to write general studies of population that are comprehensible and relevant to the general historian; the latter have to learn to understand and deal with numbers and must be ready to insist that their students do the same.

Such a prescription is easy enough; its implementation is another matter. The operative word here is *relevant*. The readiness of historians to invest their own time in demographic studies and to offer instruction in this area to students will depend on the significance of

[19] 'The growth in population was due principally to industrialization and its concomitants, such as agrarian reform and the increase in agricultural productivity. The improvements in transportation and communication and in medical science and sanitation contributed to the growth of population even in areas that did not experience industrialization directly, sometimes with dire consequences' (pp. 562 f.).

[20] See, for example, on the techniques coming into use in demography proper, *Emerging Techniques in Population Research* (Millbank Memorial Fund, 1963). As for historical demography, the materials in the present volume are themselves evidence of the rapidity with which methods and terminology are changing in an esoteric direction. This tendency, needless to say, is not to be criticized in itself; all developing sciences take this path. Nevertheless, esoteric technique does constitute a barrier to communication with other disciplines, especially a discipline like history, which retains a strong humanistic, non-quantitative component.

these studies for an understanding of the general process of historical change. In this regard, the statements of a number of textbooks make it clear that some historians at least are already converted to the cause. These are, however, the exceptions, and even they are hard put to convey to the reader the significance of population change. The difficulty may be due in part to their own shortcomings, but I submit that it owes more to the limitations of demographic history, which has devoted almost all its efforts to the study of the determinants of population change and little to an examination of its consequences. For the general historian, it is the consequences that really count. He would like to say something about the causes of the increase of the eighteenth and nineteenth centuries—if only because historians like to say *why* as well as *what*. He will become convinced that all this is worth saying, however, only when it illuminates the larger story.

In this regard, as we have seen, there are a number of obvious implications of population change that historians have almost converted into clichés: the effect of differential rates of growth on the balance of power (France *vs.* Germany, Protestants *vs.* Catholics in Holland, Europe *vs.* the nonwhite world); the pressure of numbers on the food supply, and hence agriculture; the relation of Europe's population explosion to the great wave of overseas migration. These leave vast areas of social and economic demography unexplored. To cite a few: the effect of growth or stagnation of population on demand for goods, on the supply of labour, on the rate of economic growth; or the consequences of greater longevity for age distribution and the allocation of resources. For that matter, what are the general implications of the age distribution for the character of a society? What does it mean to be a young people or an old people? What does it mean to have an unbalanced sex ratio—as a result of war, for example? What are the psychological effects of very late marriage, or extensive celibacy, as in Ireland? (The novelists write about this, but historians have little to say.) What about differential mortality between rich and poor, urban and rural, between one occupation and another? One of the important works of postwar social history is Louis Chevalier's *Classes laborieuses et classes dangereuses*, which uses the differences in death and disease rates from one *arrondissement* of Paris to another to illuminate the social structure of the city, working these statistical data into a psychological analysis of the isolation of the lower classes.[21] For all Chevalier's originality, he is not the first to do this kind of thing; one can go as far back as Kay (later Kay-Shuttleworth), writing in 1832 in Manchester and offering the reader

[21] Louis Chevalier, *Classes laborieuses et classes dangereuses à Paris pendant la première moitié du XIXe siècle* (Paris, 1958).

what amounts to a statistical map of urban pathology;[22] the approach recurs repeatedly in later British reports.

One could add considerably to this series of questions, but to no purpose. The point is that if textbooks leave much to be desired in this area, it is at least in part because the specialists have done so little with these aspects of the subject. In a conference like the American Academy one on Historical Population Studies, we have skirted these questions repeatedly—gone to the very edge and then stopped and confessed our ignorance. If we have done this, it seems to me, it is not for want of desire or curiosity. Answers to such questions are hard to come by, specifically because they do not lend themselves easily to the techniques of analysis that have been so successful in purely demographic research. To study the impact of population change on other aspects of historical change requires one to introduce extra-demographic variables, some of them recalcitrant to quantification.

Under the circumstances, what is needed is some kind of joint effort, combining the resources of demographic history with those of other branches of the historical profession and of allied disciplines. There is already a small body of work along these lines. Chevalier's study is one example; it is no coincidence that Chevalier had had close connections with the Institut d'Etudes Démographiques in Paris. The best French regional studies—Goubert's monograph on Beauvais and the Beauvaisis, Le Roy Ladurie's recent work on the peasants of Languedoc—build much of their analysis around a demographic core.[23] This historiographical tradition perhaps accounts for the place accorded population in some of the newer French general histories.[24] In Britain, the Cambridge Group for the History of Population and Social Structure, founded in 1964, have played the role of pioneers, and Peter Laslett's *World We Have Lost* (1965) and E. A. Wrigley's recent article on London's influence in the century before the Industrial Revolution are only the first fruits of what promises to be a bountiful harvest. In central Europe, one thinks of the important and original volumes of Rudolf Braun on the industrialization of the Zürich highlands from the seventeenth century on.[26]

[22] James P. Kay, *The Moral and Physical Condition of the Working Classes Employed in the Cotton Manufacture of Manchester* (London, 1832).

[23] Emmanuel Le Roy Ladurie, *Les paysans de Languedoc* (2 vols., Paris, 1966).

[24] See, for example, Jacques Godechot, 'Le siècle des lumières', in R. Grousset and Emile G. Léonard (eds.), *Encyclopédie de la Pléiade: Histoire universelle*, Vol. 3: *De la réforme à nos jours* (Paris, 1958), pp. 288 *et seq.*

[25] E. A. Wrigley, 'A Simple Model of London's Importance in Changing English Society and Economy 1650–1750', *Past and Present*, No. 37 (1967), pp. 44–70.

[26] Rudolf Braun, *Industrialisierung und Volksleben: Die Veränderungen der Lebensformen in einem ländlichen Industriegebiet vor 1800 (Züricher Oberland)* (Erlenbach-Zürich and Stuttgart, 1960).

This new approach, moreover, is infectious. Demography and demographic history have a strong comparative bent, and both emulation and collaboration work to promote the new techniques and directions of research. If the impact on general history has thus far been limited, it promises to increase rapidly. In 1965, Louis Henry, who presents himself emphatically as a pure demographer concerned with demographic variables, wrote that the progress in demographic research during the last two decades 'could scarcely have been foreseen' fifteen or twenty years before.[27] Who is to say how far we will move towards integrating demographic history in general history in the next two?

[27] In the Preface to Wrigley (ed.), *Introduction to English Historical Demography*, p. vii.

Louis Henry

Historical demography

When I agreed to write the essay for this volume, I planned to devote
it to current studies at the Institut National d'Etudes Démographiques and to provide a summary of other French work in the field.
Being a demographer and not a historian, I thought I would also be
able to place historical demography within the field of demography
as a whole: to discuss those problems which are unique to it and those
it shares with the entire discipline. The article thus consists of two
parts, which although not closely interrelated are not altogether
independent of each other. My purpose is to analyse the place of
historical demography within the wider discipline of demography
itself and to consider French studies in the field, with emphasis on
those of L'Institut National d'Etudes Démographiques (I.N.E.D.).

THE FIELD OF HISTORICAL DEMOGRAPHY

When I first became interested in historical demography about
fifteen years ago, the object of study was the analysis of populations
which existed before the advent of demographic statistics. In France,
for example, this meant that historical demography was concerned
with population studies before 1801, the date usually held to inaug-
urate the statistical era. The Census of 1801 was considered more
reliable than those which had preceded it during the Revolution;
1801 was also the first year of an uninterrupted series of figures
recording the movement of population.

The definition of the boundaries of historical demography remains
true, but only approximately. The pre-statistical period forms far
from a uniform whole, and it is necessary to distinguish a number of
separate elements within it. The first statistics resemble, moreover, a
harvest so summarily gathered that more grain remains to be
garnered than has yet been stored. Those statistics were often
collected with other purposes in mind. Vital records furnish a
typical example.

In France, registration of baptisms, marriages, and burials was
initiated in the diocese of Nantes as early as the beginning of the

fifteenth century. The practice then spread to neighbouring dioceses, and several series of registers exist from the second half of the fifteenth century. By the end of the fifteenth century and the beginning of the sixteenth, a concern with keeping records is found in several widely separated dioceses—Normandy, Paris, Franche-Comté, Provence. In 1539, a royal edict obliged the entire kingdom to register all baptisms and the deaths of those persons holding ecclesiastical benefices. The registration of marriages became obligatory in 1579. (This edict served mainly to reinforce that of the Council of Trent, passed in 1563, whereby curés were enjoined to register all baptisms and marriages.) Finally, the registration of deaths was required by Pope Paul V in 1614.

In 1667, a royal ordinance standardized the registration of baptisms, marriages, and burials; its measures were revised, modified, and reinforced in 1736. An edict of 1787 gave non-Catholics the right (which had been suppressed in 1685) to be registered separately. The corresponding registers were, in principle, to be maintained by the judges, but were, in fact, recorded by denominational leaders. In September, 1792, registration was transferred from the curés to the mayors. The law was not substantially altered in other respects, and continuity was maintained. The old parish records were transferred to the mayor's office, and today many town halls, especially in the villages, do not distinguish between the pre-Revolutionary parochial registers deposited there and the true register of vital statistics that succeeded them.

In regard to vital statistics, the pre-statistical era in France is divided into three parts: an early period, for which few, if any, statistics exist; an intermediate period for which registration is incomplete and imperfect; and a recent period at the beginning of which registration approaches modern standards and at the end has attained them—most often in the years following the law of 1736.

Other documents besides those recording vital statistics also exist: tax rolls, listings of inhabitants, and so forth. Complete listings of inhabitants are rare, but in the eighteenth century lists for the *taille* are abundant and frequently form a continuous series. Their existence, however, does not modify the division of periods established above in respect to vital statistics; furthermore, this division can be applied to all European countries (correcting for differences in dates necessitated by an earlier or later start in registration and the time when this registration became more exact).

For demography, the earliest period is a kind of prehistory, beginning with the origins of humanity and extending to the dawn of modern times. Research in it is not impossible, but its methods are very different from those of classical demography and often belong to archaeology. The risks, as in archaeology, arise from superficial generalization from unrepresentative remains. When, however, a study of a population is joined with a knowledge of its way of life, plausible figures can be established and its distribution within a territory indicated.

The intermediate period appears to offer more possibilities. It is, however, perhaps less studied than the early period, if one excepts some monographs devoted to documents of exceptional quality. No specific methodology exists for the intermediate period, and nothing presently indicates that one will be found.

The situation is completely different for the recent period. An exact methodology exists and when carefully adhered to, it endows those interested in historical demography with a precise tool from which promising results have already been obtained. The lines between historical and classical demography have, therefore, been considerably modified; historical demography is now more and more concerned with the beginning of the statistical era, still so little known. In France, for example, historical demography tends to stretch back as far into the nineteenth century as the rules governing access to documents permit. Because vital statistics fall into the public domain only after a hundred years, 1866 constitutes the present frontier of historical demography.

HISTORICAL DEMOGRAPHY AND CLASSICAL DEMOGRAPHY

The history of demography, since the start of the science in 1662, has been marked by two preoccupations. The first demographers concentrated on the study of mortality to such an extent that the first century of demography—from John Graunt to Per Wargentin—consists of the progressive discovery of correct procedures for the measurement of current mortality. In the nineteenth century, official statistical services were created to record the size and movement of population. The information and knowledge thereby acquired had both an administrative and scientific utility.

These two facts are not independent of each other. A study of mortality is hardly possible without a census which records the number of people and their classification by age. When, at a very late date, demographers turned their attention to the study of other demographic phenomena—birth and marriage—they modelled this study on the earlier analyses of mortality, without questioning too deeply whether it was necessary to proceed in this way. As a result, in demography everything was studied by a judicious combination of the data extracted from two sources: the census and vital statistics. When vital statistics failed to provide certain information, they were supplemented by the census, so that the latter became the keystone in the arch of the demographic edifice.

Because a census could be taken only by a statistical service, this service had a monopoly on statistical observation—that is to say, a monopoly on demography itself. Until the last war, all that was not classical demography was marginal and without real importance. The lines of thought that classical demography followed often led to impasses because its methods were too rigorously focused on the present—on events of the moment. At the time, however, no one was concerned that it should be otherwise.

After 1945, the situation was modified by several changes whose repercussions will be felt for a long time. In the United States and Britain, the analysis of demographic phenomena by periods (transversal analysis) was thought to be ill-suited to phenomena other than mortality. Demographers in Britain and the United States, thus, substituted an analysis based on the experience of each generation or cohort throughout its lifetime (longitudinal analysis) for transversal analysis. Today longitudinal analysis has largely conquered demographic studies; even mortality, which has so far escaped, begins to be menaced.

Reflection on the procedures of statistical observation has made the need of the double source of data—the census and vital statistics—somewhat less imperative. It was seen that, for the past, almost everything required could be found from vital statistics alone, provided they were accurate. It became apparent, even for studies of the present, that it was not possible to answer all the needs of demography by combining the data of the census and the vital statistics.

A new means of statistical observation—sample surveys—came into wide use. Although often conceived simply as a complementary procedure, the sample survey offers new possibilities and puts demographic observation within the reach of more organizations (for example, universities and research institutes). The *de facto* monopoly of the statistical services can no longer be justified.

Requirements for information and opinions in the field of economics and demography have increased so sharply within government that the statistical services have become more and more occupied by current events. Providing data has clearly become, at the expense of scientific analysis, the predominant focus of statistical services. The disequilibrium between collection and analysis has led to an almost total disinterest in the past, even when it belongs to the statistical era.

Since the war, permanent or temporary organizations for research have been created or launched. These organizations do not pose demographic problems in the same terms as the statistical services. Scientific concerns predominate; the preoccupation with events of the moment is diminished.

Such changes have great importance for historical demography. Longitudinal analysis is naturally inclined towards a historical perspective. The importance it has acquired tends to make all demography a history of successive generations. Historical demography, which quite naturally uses longitudinal analysis, therefore became an integral part of demography as a whole, just as the history of the eighteenth century is an integral part of history as a whole.

To fail to observe demographic phenomena in the manner of the statistical services is no longer considered erroneous; moreover, historical demography is now completely independent of the statistical service and is free to pursue its observations in terms of its needs, taking into account all relevant documents. No other branch of demography now benefits from an equal autonomy.

The diminished participation of the statistical service in the development of demography as a science minimizes the importance of purely contemporary events. As a result of this evolution, the frontier between historical demography and current demography has been reduced, if not eradicated.

Demographic phenomena are inscribed in time. Such phenomena cannot be explained nor understood unless they have been traced through the concatenations of many decades or centuries, as far back as available observations and documents permit us to go. To study demography only from current events is equivalent to the study of astronomy without benefit of earlier observation or to the construction of a theory of evolution with attention to none but presently living species. Can one imagine a meteorology which did away with the information of the last century under the pretext that it was no longer current?

We do not know whether laws analogous to those which regulate natural phenomena exist for demography, but what we do know shows that any future cannot proceed from a given present. If there are no permanent and rigid statistics in demography, there are certainly relations among phenomena. By studying these, we can hope to improve our knowledge and our ability to forecast. Only the observation of as long a chronological series as is possible will furnish all the relations observable up to the present. In demography, therefore, the important factor is not to possess the most recent information about the population of a certain country or city, but to be able to dispose of homogenous retrospective statistics extending as far into the past as possible. If this is accepted, it is hardly a paradox to say the historical demography is all demography —or, to put it another way, that from the scientific point of view demography has as its object the study of all observable populations, past and present. Given the actual state of affairs, however, I prefer the first formula, for it focuses more clearly on the primary importance of time.

The paradox to which I subscribe is not inspired by a particular love of the past. I am not a historian, and I came to historical demography because I needed information on natural fertility (fertility unlimited by birth control). Because historical demography furnished this information, it was possible to advance the study of biological factors in fertility and to construct a model that could serve as a guide to biologists in certain studies of the physiology of reproduction. As a demographer, I also know that modern statistics do not furnish so much diverse information as can be collected from the study of rural families of the eighteenth century. This lack could easily be corrected by a few sample surveys—that is, if one gives, finally, more weight to studies in depth than to peripheral current happenings.

HISTORICAL DEMOGRAPHY IN FRANCE

Historical demography in France was launched less than fifteen years ago. As always, it is difficult to say after the fact exactly what role each person and each organization played. Interest in social history existed before this date, and certain scholars recognized that demographic phenomena should be taken into historical account. This was true of C. E. Labrousee, L. Chevalier, J. Meuvret, M. Reinhard, and of the Ecole Pratique des Hautes Etudes. Echoes of the idea may be found in *Population*, the journal of the Institut National d'Etudes Démographiques, although the Institut was not generally concerned with historical research. The real impulse came later, from Pierre Goubert in his study of social history, *Beauvais et le Beauvaisis de 1600 à 1730*, in which demography played an important part. An article written in the *Annales* inspired me to write an article for *Population* in 1953. This, in turn, attracted the attention of archivists, that of M. Fleury, in particular. Several years later, he and I edited *Manuel de dépouillement et d'exploitation de l'état civil ancien*. M. Fleury's role was not limited to collaboration in this work. He pointed out to me the value of the Genovese genealogies as a source of demographic research on a governing class from the middle of the sixteenth century until the present.

At about the same time I made the acquaintance of E. Gautier. He had already reconstituted the families which had issued from marriages celebrated between 1674 and 1742 in Crulai, a Norman village where his family originated. Several years later, we published a monograph that furnished a methodology not only for similar monographs, but for more extended studies.

This monograph was followed by several others, due for the most part to historians P. Girard and M. Terrisse, students of M. Reinhard. P. Girard studied Sotteville-lés-Rouen, and M. Terrisse worked on Ingouville. J. Ganiage, after having made a study of Europeans in Tunis in the nineteenth century, presented a monograph on a group of three villages in the Ile-de-France. This study indicates that fertility declined in these villages at the time of the Revolution, if not somewhat earlier. P. Chaunu, a professor at the Faculty of Letters at Caen, started his students and collaborators to work on monographs and then on more extended studies; the first finished was by P. Gouhier and discusses a Norman port, Port-en-Bessin.

In the South of France, J. Godechot, Dean of the Faculty of Letters at Toulouse, also set his students to work on monographs. For its part, I.N.E.D. published a monograph on two villages of the Lot by one of its former collaborators, historian P. Valmary. P. Goubert directed an extended study in the sixth section of the Ecole Pratique des Hautes Etudes.

I will cease this enumeration, which, although incomplete, may be tedious. It does, however, demonstrate that historical demography in France began with abundant monographs on individual villages. Although these do not constitute a strict sample of the rural population of the past, they are similar enough to provide the broad outlines of what might have been the demographic characteristics of French peasants in the eighteenth century. These are late marriage (an average of age twenty-five for women and twenty-seven to twenty-eight for men); a low proportion of older unmarried people; high marital fertility (four or five children per marriage, but six or seven children for the marriages of completed fertility); low total sterility; average interval between births on the order of 2 to 2.5 years while the woman is fairly young; low illegitimate birth rate; and frequency of premarital conception variable among regions. Infant mortality was high (20 per cent to 25 per cent), due, in large part, to diseases of the newborn (8 to 10 per cent). The mortality rate for children of one to four years, and even for children of five to nine years, was also high. Only about 60 per cent of those born survived to age fifteen. There was a life expectancy of about thirty years. Results on the subject of migration are few, although certain monographs suggest a continuous and not negligible stream of departures, either for other regions or, more probably, for the cities.

Because of the difficulties of observation, no studies presently exist for classes outside the rural population, except the 'Dukes and Peers'. The study of this part of the nobility indicates the early appearance of some form of birth control. Already obvious in the eighteenth century, birth control had probably existed as early as the end of the seventeenth century. In rural areas, a reduction in fertility occurs much later; it was evidently practised by the time of the Revolution. Authors of the period say that birth control appeared earlier, but this remains to be proven statistically.

The preparation of monographs continues, and these will be of interest for some time if they do nothing more than confirm the expected results. Meanwhile, research on a much larger scale has appeared. Cities, regions, France as a whole are the subjects of new studies.

Chronologically, the study of France as a whole was undertaken first and covers the period 1670 to 1829. Vital statistics are taken from the registers of a random sample of towns and villages. From these data, the births, marriages, and deaths of the country are estimated. As the age of death is almost always known at least approximately, it is possible to reconstitute the population by sex and age. The demographer starts with the classification of the population taken from a census year in the nineteenth century, and goes back in time so long as the registration of deaths exists. This procedure had already been used by J. Bourgeois-Pichat for the beginning of the nineteenth century; it will be necessary to continue it after the results already obtained are verified. Once the population by sex and by age is known, one can determine the mortality levels for every five or ten years.

Since the population of France as a whole was basically closed, the quality of the registration, that of deaths in particular, can be checked by comparing the total number of deaths of one generation to its initial size. If registration has been exact, the two numbers should be equal. If there is under-registration of deaths—which is often the case before 1740—the initial size is above the total registration of deaths. If the difference is not great, it can be attributed to the under-registration (also frequent before 1740) of infant deaths.

The work in question was undertaken in 1959 by I.N.E.D. and covers about thirty towns and three hundred and seventy five rural communities. The data have been collected, and collation is now in process for the period 1740 to 1829 only. For the purposes of this study, France has been divided into ten regions; as yet, only one region is finished—the extreme west of the country, Brittany-Anjou. Progress is slow because it is impossible to apply gross measures in a study of this kind; with this reservation, the collation is proceeding normally.

In forty of the three hundred and seventy five villages, a nominative extraction (that is, identification of people by name) has been made in order to permit a study of fertility based on the reconstitution of families. The forty villages represent all parts of France and constitute a random sample of the forty thousand rural parishes. The reconstitution of families is well advanced, and it will soon be possible to begin the collation for the northern part of France.

To many, the reconstitution of families seems a particularly arduous task. This impression arises, in particular, from a lack of funds and, therefore, of personnel. In reality, however, the reconstitution of families does not demand much more time than the nominative extraction. The combination of the two operations represents about ten thousand hours of work for the forty villages, approximately a year's work for five full-time persons. This is little effort if the purpose is to assemble the basic givens of a country for one hundred and sixty years. Especially is this so if one compares this effort with that demanded by the collection of facts now being made for the modern period.

The first regional study was launched by J. Dupâquier, who was then in charge of research at the Centre National de la Recherche Scientifique and is now Assistant at the Sorbonne. This study deals with the French Vexin, a region near Paris which includes about ninety parishes. A nominative extraction is being made only for those individuals whose last name begins with the letter B and for women having or having had a husband whose last name begins with B. This study should allow us to recognize those families who move from village to village and to see if their demographic characteristics, and their fertility in particular, differ from those of the families who stay in one place. Until now the monographs on villages have concentrated on families with no mobility.

An analogous study, but one with an integral extraction of facts, is going to be undertaken for a small and fairly closed region of Normandy under the auspices of P. Chaunu. Chaunu also plans a complete analysis, with reconstitution of families, of Rouen. This will be the first large-scale attempt to study in depth the urban demography of the past. A smaller study, on Caen, has been done by J. C. Perrot.

These two studies are part of a large programme of research undertaken in 1968 with the support of the Centre National de la Recherche Scientifique. The programme is as follows:

1. A systematic study of the people of France from the eighteenth century to the present, with the establishment of a national file (administrative, demographic, and economic history) of parishes and communes.

2. An effort to use the registers of the sixteenth century for regions which possess the greatest number of such registers.

3. An extension, as far as 1870, of the nominative extraction and the reconstruction of families in the forty villages of the I.N.E.D. sample.

4. A study of the causes of death before the time of Pasteur, from various documents heretofore not consulted.

The studies previously mentioned have been based on vital statistics; to conclude this survey of demography, I should like to mention studies based primarily on lists. J. Dupâquier has recently shown what can be extracted from tax rolls in regions where an adequate series of them exists. Within the framework of a village monograph, Y. Blayo has undertaken the systematic comparison of nominative lists of the census between 1836 and 1861 in order to discover who left and who arrived. This work is not too different from what can be accomplished with two seventeenth-century nominative lists of an English village.

Certain studies have been undertaken that encompass demography, economics, and social life. That of E. Le Roy Ladurie on the Languedoc peasants from the fifteenth to the eighteenth century merits special mention because it highlights man's relationship to the earth in an agricultural economy when all cultivatable space is occupied and productivity does not change.

The vitality of historical demography in France is also signalized by the creation in 1962 of the Société de Démographie historique, which has an international field of interest. This society publishes yearly a collection of studies and chronicles; three have already appeared.

At the risk of making this article a plea for historical demography, I stress in conclusion only these points. Contrary to what a superficial view might suggest, historical demography is not simply a marginal part of demography. It is demography itself, just as demography, being a study of human populations in time, is history itself.

Historical demography now has the enormous advantage of not being dependent on any organization for its observations. In spite of the evident difficulty caused by this independence, the advantages are fundamental to many of the recent successes of historical demography.

In certain countries, historical demography is today one of the most vital branches of demography; paradoxically, it is also one of the most modern. Historical demography has, in fact, been most marked by the postwar developments in the methodology of dealing with demographic phenomena. Historical demography's independence in regard to the statistical services has enabled it to adapt more successfully to modern conceptions.

Finally, at a time when one often speaks of the collaboration among scientific disciplines, frequently without making much effort to bring it about, it is a pleasure to point out that the collaboration between historians and demographers is fairly well guaranteed, in spite of considerable differences in their formation and preoccupation. It is a good augury.

ADDENDA

It is worth adding to the above text, written in 1967, some notes on subsequent developments.

The researches mentioned are being continued and, in general, are taking more time than was expected. The Institut National d'Études Démographiques has completed the study of the fertility of a quarter of the nominative sample of forty communes—the South-West quarter, the most difficult because of defects in the registers. It was expected that a very early limitation of births would be found; in fact, the decline is moderate, at least until 1830.

Many monographs have been completed; among the most thorough, that on Tourouvre (Perche), shows a lower fertility among the poorest villagers than among the less poor; that on Meulan, a small town 50 kms. down river from Paris, displays a limitation of births from the middle of the eighteenth century.

The study of urban communities has been extended; Bayeux, Lyon and Reims should be added to Rouen and Caen, already mentioned in the text.

An attempt has been made to utilize statistics which have hitherto been more or less neglected—enumerations of hearths or inhabitants.

An important study of the plague has just been completed. Naturally, it covers a much longer period than the other studies referred to. A study of mortality in Anjou in the seventeenth and eighteenth centuries should also be mentioned.

As always, progress throws up unanticipated difficulties. The multiplication of monographs has not yielded as much in the way of results as had been expected; in reality it is difficult to co-ordinate the monographs and to impose a choice of localities for study. Some people believe that the 'great day' of monographs is over; the difficulties encountered in the work on South-West France makes me believe that co-ordinated monographs would be preferable to an overall study, especially because of the substantial differences in the quality of registration in different localities.

The mechanization of family reconstitution is now on the agenda. But progress is slow, for while it is easy for a human being to identify a name which has been written in various ways, it is not so for a computer.

The present article was translated from the French by Patricia Cumming.

J. A. Banks

Historical sociology and the study of population

I

Modern sociology is scientific in intention, if not always in execution. As John Madge phrased it recently in his account of the subject over the past fifty years: 'The discipline of sociology is at last growing up and is within reach of attaining the status of a science,'[1] The point of his argument is that since the turn of the century sociologists have slowly and painfully developed techniques and concepts for tackling the special problems of their subject, and that they have at last begun to emancipate themselves from the stultifying effects of the debate about whether the social sciences can or cannot be logically assimilated into the natural sciences. Indeed, the writers treated in Madge's study ignored the controversy altogether. They set out instead to tackle a limited set of problems with whatever tools they could fashion for the purpose— content analysis, participant observation, interviewing, experiment —and from the mistakes they made in the process, they obtained a clearer grasp of what the sociological adventure is all about. Of course, at no time did they abandon what has been said to be the chief objective of a science—namely, 'to explain the phenomena in the world of experience, to answer the question 'why?' rather than only the question 'what?'"[2] In this sense, they may be said always to have had in mind the eventual establishment of scientific laws, true propositions about uniformities, universals independent of space and time.

In the present context, it is instructive to notice that not one of the twelve themes reviewed by Madge was at all historical in the way in which the writings of Comte, Spencer, Veblen, Sumner, and Hobhouse were historical—that is, in applying some kind of evolutionary or developmental conceptual framework to the history of

[1] John Madge, *The Origins of Scientific Sociology* (London, 1963), p. 1.
[2] C. G. Hempel and P. Oppenheim, 'The Logic of Explanation', *Philosophy of Science*, Vol. 15 (1948), reprinted in H. Feigl and M. Brodbek (eds.), *Readings in the Philosophy of Science* (New York, 1953), p. 310.

mankind and using evidence in the form of a variety of events from the past to illustrate it. Historical sociology of this bent, although still extant as the case of Pitirim Sorokin exemplifies, has in very recent times been superseded by a newer conception of historical sociology, more consonant in its methods and objectives with that sociology which applies scientific procedures to the study of current data. Such historical sociology uses what has been called the hypothetical deductive method[3] for the formulation and testing of hypotheses, and only differs from other scientific sociology in that its data are documents and artifacts, taken as indications of past events, rather than as observations of and answers to questions put to people at the present time. In principle, there is no logical distinction between these two procedures, since the testing of universal explanatory generalizations can be carried out through the systematic examination of documents, artifacts, observations, and questionnaire responses indiscriminately. The decision whether to use one or more kinds of data is merely a matter of convenience, although in some circumstances there may be differences in the levels of objectivity and precision which they offer.

Nowadays a clear distinction may be drawn between historical sociology and sociology of the older sort as well as the history pursued by professional historians. What separates them, indeed, is a differentiation of aim. Although both science and history make use of the particular as well as of the general, the former regards particular instances as merely the means by which one can arrive at general laws, whereas the latter does not regard the establishment of such laws as part of its province. As Ernest Nagel has explained:

> It is unlikely that anyone would find something radically wrong with a treatise on theoretical thermodynamics which did not contain a single proper name or a single reference to any particular date. But it is even more unlikely that anyone using the word 'history' in its customary meaning would classify a book as a *history* if it mentioned no particular individuals, times, and places but stated only generalizations about human behaviour. The distinction between history and theoretical science is thus fairly analogous to the difference between geology and physics, or between medical diagnosis and physiology. A geologist seeks to ascertain, for example, the sequential order of geological formations, and he is able to do so in part by applying various physical laws to his materials of study; but it is not the geologist's task *qua* geologist

---

[3] K. R. Popper, *The Poverty of Historicism* (London, 1961), Section 29.

to establish the laws of mechanics or of radioactive disintegration which he employs in his investigations.[4]

Historians may employ generalizations of a sociological or psychological order to account for particular occurrences, and in doing so they may make it plain that such generalizations are of limited validity, but they do not set out deliberately to test hypotheses in this fashion.

An example from the field of population studies will serve to illustrate the point. In his discussion of the economic and population histories of eighteenth-century Britain, H. J. Habakkuk has pointed out the unsatisfactory nature of the baptism and burial register records which the earlier historians, Brownlee and Griffith, had used to estimate the total population and the birth and death rates through the century. 'One result of the paucity of statistics', Habakkuk asserts, 'is that we cannot test explanatory hypotheses and weed out from among the many that are plausible those that fit the facts.' At first sight this looks like a hypothetical deductive statement, but then Habakkuk continues: 'Worse still, it is often not clear what precisely it is that has to be explained. How rapidly, for example, did population grow during these expansion periods?'[5] In the present context, the question is of considerable interest. What it asserts is the perfectly valid principle of historical logic that no useful purpose is served by putting forward plausible hypotheses to explain the 'facts' when we do not know what the facts are. This is the very obverse of the procedure of the hypothetical deductive method in science—namely, that the search for the facts is a consequence of the formulation of hypotheses. In such a case, of course, the point of emphasis would not be the unsatisfactory state of eighteenth-century British records, but the need to look for records of some other time or place for more reliable data with which to verify or falsify the hypotheses. Habakkuk emphasizes, by contrast, the pioneer work of Chambers and Eversley in analysing parish registers, and of Hollingsworth in examining genealogical trees. 'Another decade or so of work on these lines', he thinks, will make it possible for us 'to generalize with confidence about the nature of population change in this period'.[6] It is primarily the facts and only secondarily their explanation which interest the historian. The scientifically-minded historical sociologist, on the other hand, sees significance in the reverse order of priorities.

[4] Ernest Nagel, *The Structure of Science* (New York, 1961), p. 550.
[5] H. J. Habakkuk, 'The Economic History of Modern Britain', *Journal of Economic History* (1958), reprinted in D. V. Glass and D. E. C. Eversley (eds.), *Population in History* (London, 1965), p. 149.   [6] *Ibid.*, p. 150.

CP

There is, it should be understood, no ultimate evaluation implied in this contrast. Interest in general laws is no more or no less worthy a human trait than curiosity about and concern for specific facts. Indeed, the approaches of the historical sociologist and the historian may fruitfully supplement each other, often to the benefit of both. The former may indicate to the latter—largely by referring to tests which have been made with data from times and places other than those on which the historian happens to be concentrating— ways in which valid restrictions on the number of apparently plausible generalizations may be introduced; while the latter may be able to place the data in an economic, political, and social context drawn from systematic knowledge, a context which the former cannot possibly formulate in his concern for only those facts which seem directly relevant to the hypotheses he has in mind. The importance of this contextual knowledge can hardly be over estimated. As Karl Popper has emphasized, the scientific method of testing hypotheses depends not only on the results of controlled experiments or on the accuracy of observations, but also on whatever assumptions are involved in the process of deducing the one from the other. What he calls the 'prognosis', the conclusion of the deduction which it is necessary to check against the facts, is derived from a combination of the hypothesis to be tested and 'some other statements which for this purpose are not considered as problematic —for example, some initial conditions',[7] In the treatment of social fact, the quality of the assumption about contextual background can make or mar the relevance of data as a test of generalizations, because such assumptions usually provide Popper's 'initial conditions', leading to the deduction of a prognosis. Indeed, the demonstration that evolutionist sociologists and social anthropologists had distorted evidence by treating it out of context gave the functionalist school much of its initial advantage as an alternative approach to the study of societies.[8] Contemporary historical sociologists, anxious to avoid the errors of their predecessors, try to work on a much narrower canvas, such as the relationship between economic institutions and the quality of family life in the Lancashire cotton industry from 1770 to 1840.[9] They still rely to a considerable extent, however, on secondary sources, the best work they can find by professional historians on the same time and place.

That the benefit may also work in the reverse direction may perhaps be most clearly illustrated by reference to what William Rob-

---

[7] Popper, *The Poverty of Historicism*, p. 132, See also Popper's *The Logic of Scientific Discovery* (London, 1959), Para. 12 and Ch. 3, *passim*.

[8] Alexander Goldenweiser, *Anthropology* (London, 1937), Ch. 31.

[9] Neil J. Smelser, *Social Change in the Industrial Revolution* (London, 1959).

inson called 'the ecological fallacy', the assumption that associations computed from the means or other measures and derived from data about sets of persons are valid estimates of the associations that would have been obtained had the data been about individuals.[10] In an examination of Emile Durkheim's classic treatise on suicide, first published in 1897 and regarded by Madge as the pioneer work in the development of scientific sociology,[11] it has been pointed out that he regularly slipped into this fallacy.[12] For example, from a table on rates of suicide from 1878 to 1887 in French *départements*, classified according to the average number of persons of independent means living in those *départements*, Durkheim drew the correct conclusion that 'the more people there are who have independent means, the more numerous are suicides'.[13] But in employing this material, he intended to provide evidence for what he called 'anomic suicide'— that is, suicide resulting from the fact that an *individual's* life has come to lack regulation.[14] The full rationale behind this argument— that wealth deceives its possessors into believing that their success is inevitable and unlimited, and hence predisposes them to suicide whenever crises threaten—need not concern us here. What is important is Durkheim's bland assumption that it was the wealthier members of *départements* whose suicides inflated the figures in his table or, alternatively, that the proportion of persons of independent means in a *département* at that time was a clear indication of the proportion of people in the *département* experiencing *anomie* and threatened with crisis. Neither of these assumptions was necessarily false, but the evidence presented cannot be applied to the hypothesis tested— that *anomie* is a cause of suicide—without the intervention of initial conditions, knowledge of which is highly problematical. Consequently, if a historian were seeking hypotheses to explain the kinds of data presented in Durkheim's table, he would be well advised not to formulate those which relied on assertions about the circumstances of individuals unless he had access to other information not apparently available to Durkheim.

The relevance of this example to the study of population should be evident because giving birth to a baby is as much an example of individual behaviour as suicide is. At the present time, the Office of Population Research at Princeton is engaged in the formidable

[10] W. S. Robinson, 'Ecological Correlations and the Behavior of Individuals', *American Sociological Review*, Vol. 15 (1950).

[11] Madge, *The Origins of Scientific Sociology*, Ch. 2.

[12] H. C. Selvin 'Durkheim's *Suicide*: Further Thoughts on a Methodological Classic', *Emile Durkheim*, ed. R. A. Nisbet (Englewood Cliffs, 1965), pp. 125–9.

[13] Emile Durkheim, *Suicide , A Study in Sociology*, trans. J. A. Spaulding and George Simpson (London, 1952), p. 245.

[14] *Ibid.*, p, 258.

project of recording fertility in Europe using about seven hundred subnational units—provinces, *départements*, counties—rather than relying on the traditional practice of analysis by countries. The enterprise has been undertaken, in part, as a test of the hypothesis that there is an association between the process of modernization and the decline of fertility. There is also a subsidiary purpose to be achieved in the drawing of graphs 'to display the spread of low fertility from certain focal points',[15] A historical sociologist would want the hypotheses underlying such work to be spelled out in much greater detail. The evidence cannot be interpreted as the behaviour of individuals in any other sense than as residents in an area which, presumably, exerts some *collective pressure* that predisposes them to control, or not to control, their desire to procreate. Nevertheless, what kinds of hypotheses about the degree of urbanization, the occupational distribution of employment, the religious involvement of the inhabitants, or their political commitment can be formulated that will make good sociological sense when related to so nebulous a concept as residence?

This question should not be understood as implying that because fertility is a matter of individual decision or, rather, of the joint decision of two persons, data about couples are the only valid data which can be used to test hypotheses in this field. Sociologists interviewing a large number of families find themselves perforce obliged to group their data; often they have no alternative but to deal with summaries of aggregates provided by other people. Still, awareness of the ecological fallacy is a timely reminder always to bear in mind the implications of the methods of aggregation that have been employed. The Princeton study will have figures about the fertility of residents in regions. It will also have other kinds of data about these regions. For example, some regions will no doubt be more urban than others, as measured by the proportion of town-dwellers. Assertions about urban-rural differences in fertility, however, can only be tested by reference to urban-rural aggregates *per se*. Strictly speaking, any differences in fertility between more urban and less urban regions should be interpreted in terms of some *ecological* notion about the influence of urbanism on the region as a whole. This might further require a detailed study of some contemporary regions *ab initio*, rather than more elaborate analysis of existing demographic data; it is reasonably safe to conclude that what is true of urbanism will also be true of the division of labour, religious affiliation, political observances within regions, and other gross measures of social fact.

[15] A. J. Coale, *Proceedings of the International Conference on Historical Population Studies*, October 21–3, 1966, Vol. 1 (Boston), p. 6.

What contribution has the historical sociologist to make to the solution of such problems? In the ordinary course of events, he would not be concerned with this question, since it implies that he starts with fact rather than theory. He might, however, be required to face it were information about regions the only kinds of data available for the particular time and place he was studying. In such a circumstance, he would normally fall back on general sociological approaches to the study of, say, urbanism, although it is likely that in his final treatment of the subject he would not explicitly specify these approaches in detail. For example, he is almost certain to be aware of a strand current in urban sociology from at least the time of Durkheim which has regarded the higher physical densities of urban areas as having important consequences for social relationships. Durkheim, indeed, distinguished between physical density (*densité materielle*) and dynamic or moral density (*densité dynamique ou morale*), and argued that each was intimately connected with the other. In a series of deductions from the assumption that individuals have 'a need' for as intimate a social contact with their fellows as they can find, he demonstrated that a denser population increases the opportunity of greater intimacy and also makes possible a diversification of interests and functions in social life. Such diversification, he concluded, occurs in the form of economic, political, and social specialization.[16] Empirical justification for Durkheim's point of view is, to be sure, difficult to obtain except in a broad sense, although more recent work on densities, markets, innovation, communication, and diversity and deviance among urban populations[17] suggests that, as an assumption about initial conditions, the degree of social contact, the nature of communications in a region, and possibly the normative patterns associated with these phenomena (*densité morale?*) might be taken as ecological factors responsible for variations in the attitudes about the size of family deemed satisfactory for a civilized existence, and hence for differences in fertility.

Save where this assumption might raise difficulties in other parts of his analysis, the historical sociologist could be content with the broad notion that regional data would be satisfactory for his purpose, at least until this assumption could be shown to be false for the period he was treating. He might, however, weigh this assumption against the conclusion, gleaned from a review 'of the fluctuations, divergencies, and wide inter-area and inter-city differences in urban fertility,' that urbanization *per se* is not an important determinant

[16] Emile Durkheim, *De la division du travail social* (Paris, 1911), pp. 238–9. See also L. F. Schnore, 'Social Morphology and Human Ecology', *American Journal of Sociology*, Vol. 63 (1957–58), pp. 620–34.

[17] W. F. Ogburn and O. D. Duncan, 'City Size as a Sociological Variable', *Contributions to Urban Sociology*, eds. E. W. Burgess and D. J. Bogue (Chicago, 1964), pp. 129–47.

of fertility.[18] Thus, he might decide that it would be unwise to interpolate from city to region. To this day, sociologists do not really have much certain knowledge of what Louis Wirth called 'urbanism as a way of life';[19] indeed, some of the effects which thirty years ago seemed to be rather obvious features of changes from rural to urban are now thought to be rather more general aspects of change in *both* rural *and* urban.[20] At best, urbanism may be regarded as an intermediate rather than a determining variable in fertility decline. The sociologist must, therefore, consider the region in terms of assumptions other than those which have been used to account for differences between town and country.

Much the same kind of consideration applies to other possible characteristics of regions for which data may be available. Some evidence exists, for example, to support the view that fertility varies with what has been called 'the future time perspective' [21] of individuals and that this perspective varies from occupation to occupation, possibly because of the nature of the relationship between an individual's work (thought of as a life chance) and the time factor. Certainly the hypothesis fits the case of nineteenth-century England rather well.[22] A classification of regions by the relative distribution of different occupations, therefore, might be regarded as equivalent to classification by variations in the future time perspectives of the residents. Unfortunately, this implies rather more knowledge about the nature of occupations than we possess. It also confronts the problem that a future time perspective is likely to be an ingredient of religious beliefs—as Beshers, following Weber, suggests. Here the sociologist is aware that at least the Protestant-Catholic dichotomy, or the Protestant-Catholic-Jew trichotomy, is unsatisfactory in many ways. Gerhard Lenski, for instance, has found no distinction among white Protestants in their attitudes to birth control, but marked distinctions among white Catholics when they were further subdivided into activists, regulars, irregulars, and marginals in their degree of involvement in church activities, as measured by their response to questions about regularity of church attendance and activity in church-related organizations.[23]

---

[18] S. H. Hashmi, 'Factors in Urban Fertility Differences in the United States', *Contributions to Urban Sociology*, p. 45.

[19] Louis Wirth, 'Urbanism as a Way of Life', *American Journal of Sociology*, Vol. 44 (1938), reprinted in P. K. Hatt and A. J. Reiss (eds.), *Reader in Urban Sociology* (Glencoe, 1951), and in E. W. Marrick and A. J. Reiss (eds.), *Community Life and Social Policy: Selected Papers by Louis Wirth* (Chicago, 1956).

[20] P. H. Mann, *An Approach to Urban Sociology* (London, 1965), pp. 98 *et seq.*

[21] J. M. Beshers, *Population Processes in Social Systems* (New York, 1967), p. 85.

[22] *Ibid.*, pp. 44–7. Beshers takes his point of departure from my *Prosperity and Parenthood* (London, 1954), *passim.*

[23] Gerhard Lenski, *The Religious Factor: A Sociological Study of Religion's Impact on Politics, Economics, and Family Life* (New York, 1961), Table 33, p. 194.

The mere classification of a region as Protestant or Catholic, or as predominantly Protestant or Catholic, is a guide neither to the intensity of religious commitment there nor to the nature of the prevailing attitudes about time. Without this information, it is difficult for the sociologist to develop the kinds of unproblematical statements which can serve as initial conditions and a satisfactory bridge between hypotheses and data. The overworked *ceteris paribus* is no substitute for knowledge here.

II

All this may read as a counsel of despair rather than as a contribution to the study of population. Indeed, the immensity of the task of evaluating historical evidence in sociological terms has no doubt been one of the reasons why sociologists of this century have turned more and more to conducting surveys *ab initio* in order to test hypotheses. The task of working through other people's findings, with little knowledge of what they mean, has seemed far less profitable than it apparently appeared to previous generations of sociologists, possibly because more sophisticated techniques have promised better and more easily attained results from original work. To the sociologist, registration data on births and their subsequent conversion into fertility ratios leave much to be desired in this respect, primarily because there is little recorded information about the situations in which these births took place. Census and similar records do not enable one to distinguish between birth differentials due to variations in the natural fecundity of couples, their opportunity to copulate, and the effective use of birth control, or any mixture of these. Yet information of this kind is required if the study of fertility decline is to be related to biological and social variables. As a factor in the total birth rate, natural fecundity is probably too insignificant to influence differentials, since involuntary childlessness probably accounts for little more than 8·5 to 9·5 per cent.[24] On the other hand, there is some evidence that social mobility through marriage occurs for women who possess initial 'advantages in growth, health, and education'. Moreover, these women are 'more efficient at child-bearing than women less well endowed'—that is, prematurity rates and obstetric rates are lower for such women.[25] If these biological (?) facts also influence fecundity rates, social selection may

[24] E. Lewis-Faning, *Family Limitation and Its Influence on Human Fertility During the Past Fifty Years*. Papers of the Royal Commission on Population, Vol. 1 (London, 1949), p. 92.
[25] R. Illesley, 'Social Class Selection on Class Differences in Relation to Stillbirths and Infant Deaths', *British Medical Journal* (24 Dec., 1955), Table 1 and Figure 4, p. 1522.

act to produce variations in the fertility rates of different social classes. In the theory of demographic transition, of course, the variations referred to run in the opposite direction from that which this hypothesis suggests, but they may nevertheless have operated to keep the differences among the classes *lower* than they might otherwise have been. Moreover, recent examination of the 'trend' towards earlier physical maturation[26] suggests that the fertility of affluent Western-type societies might be explained partly in terms of changes in fecundity rates, especially when it is remembered that restrictions on opportunity to copulate have become relaxed in these societies. A failure to practice effective birth control is more likely to lead to pregnancy for a fecund than for a sub-fecund couple, and the variations in fecundity in this latter respect might affect as much as one third of the population.[27]

Clearly, the sociologists' main contribution to the knowledge of the factors underlying fertility will be in their examination of the social influences on the opportunity to copulate and on the effective use of birth control. Within marriage, the former of these has largely been ignored, possibly because evidence from the 1930s has since been confirmed—namely, that coital frequencies vary with the age of wife and not with class or religious differences among populations,[28] In societies or in sections of societies where family relationships are unstable, however, the absence of one party for relatively long periods of time might affect the fertility of *married* couples. For example, tables in the 1911 Family Census show that officers in the Navy, Marines, or the Army with wives married at ages twenty to twenty-four had smaller completed families than those of any other upper-middle-class groups except barristers (that is, for marriages contracted between 1851 and 1880).[29] Unfortunately, instability of relationships may not necessarily reduce total exposure to risk. As Judith Blake has put it in her discussion of the Jamaican conjugal union: 'On the one hand, it may reduce the rate of reproduction by decreasing the total amount of exposure to pregnancy. On the other hand, it may increase the motivation to re-

[26] J. M. Tanner, 'The Trend Towards Earlier Physical Maturation', *Biological Aspects of Social Problems*, eds. J. E. Meade and A. S. Parkes (Edinburgh, 1965).

[27] R. Freedman, P. K. Whelpton, and A. A. Campbell (*Family Planning, Sterility and Population Growth* [New York, 1959]) reckoned that 66 per cent of the 2,713 couples they interviewed were fecund, 10 per cent were definitely sterile, 7 per cent were probably sterile, 12 per cent were semifecund, and 5 per cent were indeterminate (pp. 261 and 460).

[28] R. G. Potter, P. C. Sagi, and C. F. Westoff, 'Knowledge of the Ovulatory Cycle and Coital Frequency as Factors Affecting Conception and Contraception', *The Milbank Memorial Fund Quarterly*, Vol. 9 (1962), pp. 48–9. The reference is to L. M. Terman *Psychological Factors in Marital Happiness* (New York, 1938), pp. 271–5.

[29] *Census of England and Wales, 1911*, Vol. 13, 'Fertility and Marriage', Part 2 (London, 1923), Table 35, pp. 98–143.

produce because, with each new union, there is often a desire to have children born of that particular union.'[30] It cannot be argued, therefore, that particular social situations which segregate the spouses more than is customary for their age group generally will *necessarily* result in smaller families among this minority. Nevertheless, the general point still stands that only survey research is likely to provide information on attitudes towards childbearing and their influence on coital frequency. Records from the past on the latter in particular are scanty, to put it mildly.

The historical sociologist can make a contribution to the study of the major influences on opportunity to copulate as regulated by nuptiality, especially in respect to fluctuations over time. Two kinds of statistics are available here: the proportions of men and women in a society who never marry, and the average age at marriage of those who do. Not much, it must be confessed, is known directly about the first of these, other than that marked variations exist.[31] By implication, the same social forces which produce later marriages result in a larger proportion of the never married, although at first sight there appears to be a clear distinction between what Malthus called 'moral' restraint ('abstinence from marriage, either for a time or permanently, from prudential considerations'[32]) and celibacy, accepted for ascetic and religious reasons. If it is argued that the characteristically 'European' pattern of marriage is not a simple product of urban industrialism but is *sui generis*,[33] and that sexual asceticism has always been a high ideal for European Christians (however much at times celibacy itself has been found to be impractical even for the clergy),[34] prudential and ascetic restraint might be seen as part of a single *Weltanschauung* derived from the Christian ethic. Within the same general body of doctrine, the future time perspective of prudential restraint, which is this-worldly, might in this sense be linked to another future time perspective, one which sacrifices the pleasures of this world for the beatitudes of the next. The purely historical part of the exercise then becomes that of showing, along lines which have already been made famous by Max Weber, how, if at all, the former developed out of the latter.

[30] Judith Blake, 'Family Instability and Reproductive Behaviour in Jamaica', *Current Research in Human Fertility* (New York, 1955), p. 26.

[31] K. Davis and J. Blake, 'Social Structure and Fertility: An Analytic Framework', *Economic Development and Cultural Change*, Vol. 4 (1956), pp. 218–19.

[32] T. R. Malthus, 'A Summary View of the Principle of Population' (1830), reprinted in D. V. Glass (ed.), *Introduction to Malthus* (London, 1953), p. 153.

[33] J. Hajnal, 'European Marriage Patterns in Perspective', *Population in History*, pp. 102–6.

[34] H. C. Lea, *History of Sacerdotal Celibacy in the Christian Church* (3rd edition; London, 1907), *passim*.

To be genuinely sociological, this would require the research to be conducted against the framework of a number of hypotheses, open to modification as the work proceeds. Such hypotheses might be:

1. that postponement of marriage, both absolutely and temporarily, results from its evaluation in terms of a future time perspective—that, for example, those people who refrain from marriage at any point in time demonstrate that they have done so as a result of a time perspective which also influences other decisions they make;

2. that within the body of Christian doctrine current at this point in time the future time perspective on worldly matters is positively associated with conceptions of a favourable destiny after death—that, for example, those people who hold a future time perspective express themselves on it in terms of Christian eschatology;

3. that, over time, discussions of Christian doctrine show a shift in emphasis from asceticism to prudence as realizable worldly means to other worldly ends—that is, that more of those Christians who wrote about these matters in an earlier period stressed the former, whereas more of those who wrote later stressed the latter.

The assumption here is that those writings which have come down to us are, so to speak, representative of the views of the doctrinaires of their time. It should also be noted, moreover, that in practice the historical sociologist will not be able to take a statistically random sample of those who postponed marriage. On the contrary, he is more likely to take examples of people whose biographies and so forth demonstrate that they possessed or did not possess the necessary future time perspective and to see whether they did or did not postpone marriage in terms of it.[35] Nor will the historical sociologist always know what Christian doctrine explicitly meant to these people, although he might make some kind of inference from religious adherence, provided that there was evidence of the strength of an individual's religious convictions and of the eschatological doctrines of the body of believers of which he or she was a member. The sociologist using historical data must be what Kitson Clark has called a 'critical' historian, but at the same time he must never cease to be a sociologist.

Against this may be set the view that survey research on couples at the present time is the more rewarding method of tackling such questions as the relationship between the nature and strength of a religious conviction and 'abstinence' from marriage, total or temporary. Unfortunately, historical sociology must make regular

---

[35] See, for example, Banks, *Prosperity and Parenthood*, Ch. 3.

use of indirect evidence—'that is, evidence left by men and women who were intent on their own business and had no intention of leaving behind the information which is being used'; men and women who, when they were writing it down, 'were unaware of the ghostly figure of the historian standing beside them and therefore did not modify their words to impress him, or lie to deceive him.'[36] Many sociologists would regard such indirect evidence with some suspicion, especially if it included impressions and assertions about people other than the author. Indeed, sociologists often mistrust historical data because they have found that 'many popular impressions about social relations in our own time are incorrect.' They have, in consequence, 'become sceptical of the possibility of ascertaining the facts about historical populations whose members can no longer be interviewed or observed.'[37] Such sceptics fail to see, perhaps, that historical data of one sort, such as a Victorian factory inspector's views on the effect of factory employment on early marriages in cotton areas, may be checked against census and other data of the same period to arrive at an impression of the degree of bias shown by any commentator.[38] Moreover, in spite of statistical and other devices to overcome the impact of interviewer variability and the influences characteristic of any situation of human interaction,[39] there is still no effective answer to the charge that direct evidence obtained from social surveys, especially on such emotional topics as family planning or religious dogma, is likely to be coloured by attempts to impress or to deceive the interviewer. Indeed, the kind of care which a historian takes to check his sources by internal and external criteria is often lacking in survey research which omits to check its results against what has been recorded elsewhere in documents.

Thus, there seem to be disadvantages in both methods of testing hypotheses. The weaknesses of the social survey in recording changes in attitudes and, more particularly, changes in situation over time, suggest that documentary and historical sociology are essential for the study of certain types of problem. A person's memories of what his past attitudes were on getting married or having a child are notoriously subject to modifications over time, and his present aspirations about future behaviour are not necessarily the best guide to what he will actually do. Thus, a comparison between

[36] G. K. Clark, *The Critical Historian* (London, 1967), p. 57.
[37] W. J. Goode, ' "Comment" on Lawrence Stone, "Marriage Among the English Nobility in the 16th and 17th Centuries" ', *Comparative Studies in Society and History*, Vol. 3 (1960–61), p. 207.
[38] See Margaret Hewitt, *Wives and Mothers in Victorian Industry* (London, 1958), Ch. 4, *passim*.
[39] For a detailed examination of the problems, see Herbert Hyman, *Interviewing in Social Research* (Chicago, 1954).

what engaged couples said was their preferred family size and the number of children they had about twenty years later has led to the conclusion that 'the direct approach of asking people at marriage how many children they want leaves 90 per cent of the variation fertility unexplained'[40]—a percentage which increases to 98 when non-planners alone are considered, but still leaves 80 per cent unexplained when family planners are considered separately.[41] The events and circumstances influencing a couple's decision to marry or to have a first, or another, child are so manifold that only a successive series of interviews to ascertain changes not only in views, but also in economic circumstances and other aspects of their situation could possibly provide the kind of detail in depth which would be superior to *post hoc* documentary analysis, and even then only if those conducting the research had had sufficient foresight, or luck, to hit upon exactly the correct questions to ask.

This is not meant to imply that the documentary or historical approach to the study of marriage and fertility is, on balance, superior to conducting surveys. Both methods are required, although it may well be that different sociologists will have to conduct them because the kinds of demand they make call for different temperaments or personalities. The study of family planning, using effective birth control, is surely a case in point. Contraception, has, of course, been employed throughout human history. What is particularly striking about the present era are three factors related to 'the decision to conceive' that were absent during earlier periods: the rationalization of techniques—that is, their employment in terms of a logical or even scientific cause-effect sequence rather than in terms of magic or folk beliefs; the widespread dissemination of contraceptive information; and the psychological availability, or willingness, to use contraception—a willingness supported by moral aesthetic, and related attitudes.[42] Clearly, only a survey could supply data on whether or not a couple uses birth-control techniques and why. It might also provide information on how the couple has come to learn about birth-control techniques and whether they regard them as effective—information which may be correlated with the degree of effective family planning achieved. On the other side of the picture, however, the *sine qua non* would seem to be how the information is disseminated throughout a community and how religious, political, and moral teachings on population are propagated—

[40] C. W. Westoff, E. G. Mishler, and E. L. Kelly, 'Preferences in Size of Family and Eventual Fertility Twenty Years After', *American Journal of Sociology*, Vol. 62 (1957), p. 494.

[41] Percentages calculated from Table 1, *ibid.*, p. 494.

[42] P. G. Marden, '*The Fruits of Philosophy and Fertility*: An Exercise in Historical Demography'. Paper presented at the 1967 Annual Meetings of the Population Association of America, Cincinnati, Ohio, 28–9 April, 1967, cyclostyled, pp. 21–24.

surveys like the Cornell University International Population Programme's content analysis of newspaper clippings related to population from countries of America other than the U.S.A. and Canada.[43]

Such analysis, it might be objected, still utilizes contemporary material. A more precise study of the demographic transition in the countries of its origin would, however, require the application of these techniques, as well as the traditionally historiographical ones, to documents which have survived for a hundred years or more, especially since it is reasonably clear that the process of dissemination throughout South America, Africa, and Asia is only the second stage in a democratization process,[44] which began in Western Europe and the U.S.A. At the same time, the techniques used in the content analysis of contemporary newspapers might well be used with profit by historical sociologists who have been concerned with the spread of family limitation in the nineteenth century. A coding system, similar to the one used at Cornell, would also seem to be necessary if the 12,500 newspapers and periodicals issued in England between 1824 and 1900 and offering some 25 to 50 million articles[45] are to be examined systematically for the changing patterns of attitudes toward marriage and the family at a crucial stage in the history of population trends. The continuous interchange between methods of work, documentary and survey, applied to the testing of the same hypotheses, but against the background of different initial conditions is the most fruitful approach to the study of population. The regular reassessment of the results of this work, focused upon a relatively small number of explanatory propositions along the lines at present being pursued by James Beshers, would seem to be the most promising and exciting at this time.

One final point is perhaps worth making. As Beshers himself has indicated, part of the justification for the sociological approach to the study of population is that it will help in the formation of more effective policy at a time of population explosion. Many historians do not need to be told this for their discipline, because they already believe that a knowledge of history is an invaluable

[43] I am indebted to J. Mayone Stycos, director of the programme, for details of this survey and for a copy of the coding instructions for the more detailed study which started in January 1967.

[44] The term is due to Norman Himes. See his *Medical History of Contraception* (Baltimore, 1936), Parts 5 and 6.

[45] Michael Wolff, 'Charting the Golden Stream: Thoughts on a Directory of Victorian Periodicals'. Talk given to the Conference on Editing Problems in the Nineteenth Century, University of Toronto, 5 November, 1966, cyclo-styled, p. 11. This article appears in the collection, *Editing Nineteenth Century Texts*, edited by J. M. Robson (Toronto), 1968.

basis for tackling at least some aspects of contemporary social issues. Sociologists, however, need to be convinced that the use of historical data can be illuminating for this purpose. From an examination of the part played by the English feminist movement in fertility decline in the nineteenth century, my wife and I concluded that the important factor was the attitude of the Victorian male towards family planning and that the decision to use, or not to use, birth control was generally not within the power of wives to make. We thereupon suggested that for societies *at the present time*, in which major decisions are a male responsibility, it is a waste of effort to direct birth-control propaganda at married women.[46] At about the same time, the very same point was being made independently by J. M. Stycos, from his knowledge of surveys conducted in non-Western societies.[47] Thus, historical and contemporary research may be seen to supplement each other in arriving at a policy decision—namely, that to be effective propaganda must be directed at husbands rather than wives, wherever their dominance demands it. From our point of view, this is a good example of the fundamental unity of the sociological approach, irrespective of the techniques of research used. When both historical and contemporary data confirm the same proposition, confidence in its essential accuracy is enhanced.

[46] J. A. and Olive Banks, *Feminism and Family Planning in Victorian England* (Liverpool, 1964), pp. 130 *et seq.*

[47] J. M. Stycos, 'The Outlook for World Population', *Science* (11 December, 1964), pp. 1438–9.

T. H. Hollingsworth

The importance of the quality of the data in historical demography

The population of Africa, south of the Sahara, in the seventeenth century B.C. may be regarded as an obscure enough field for statistical research, and yet we can state the birth rate and the death rate that must have prevailed to some apparent degree of accuracy: namely, to within a factor of two. Taking 28 per 1,000 per year as our estimate for each of these vital rates, the correct values would only have to lie between 14 per 1,000 and 56 per 1,000. Hardly any populations have ever been found with vital rates outside these limits, and even then they are only just outside them, so the assertion seems justified, although scarcely worth making. Methods of estimating the total size of this same African population are also necessarily vague. Some broad considerations about the level of culture, or assumed culture, may result in a figure of, say, five million people. The degree of uncertainty, however, is much greater than it is in estimating the birth and death rates. To apply to this area the highest and lowest densities of population ever found elsewhere would be absurd, and the resulting range would be very great indeed. On no reasonable assumptions, however, can the range of reasonable likelihood for such an obscure population as that of Africa south of the Sahara for the seventeenth century B.C. be made as short as a factor of two either way. A factor of five (that is, between one million and twenty-five million) would not be too small. Even for the seventeenth century A.D., we can scarcely do much better for this particular part of the world. Dire famines and droughts may have restricted population to a handful; long-forgotten cultures may, on the other hand, have thrived in their way, but left no artifacts because they happened to use impermanent materials. We do not know what the population was, and probably we shall never know it except within very broad limits.

An important conclusion can be drawn from these considerations —namely, that different kinds of statistics require different orders of accuracy. Ascertaining a birth rate (or its more refined equivalent) to within a factor of two is a pointless exercise; ascertaining the population of an area or of a city to within a factor of two is more worthwhile. Correspondingly, an uncertainty of 20 per cent in a birth rate owing to shortcomings in the data is more serious than an uncertainty of 50 per cent in a total population size from the same causes. All demographic statistics are based on somewhat imperfect data, and it is important to bear in mind the different values that these statistics have. Ordinarily, the more refined the index of demographic behaviour, the higher the quality we demand of the data. In this essay, we shall consider some examples of historical demography in terms of the quality of the data and suggest what can be done and what cannot.

CATEGORIES OF ERROR

The meaning of terms needs to be clarified first. Error, bias, uncertainty, and mistake are all used to describe similar phenomena. It is useful to be clear in what ways they may be said to differ.

The fundamental point is that our philosophy of statistics must be somewhat more sophisticated than the simple idea that a figure means what it says. There are four respects in which a figure may not be simply what it seems to be: first, random error, caused by sampling; second, the intrinsic bias of the observer who reported the figure; third, what might be called factual errors; and fourth, mistakes. The first is the metaphysical basis of standard statistical practice, and given this basis, modern statistical techniques follow by fairly simple mathematics. By logical steps, we can produce significance tests, confidence intervals, frequency distributions, and the rest of the statistician's panoply. In expositions of these techniques, the mathematics is usually emphasized at the expense of the philosophy, although there is sometimes a difficult introductory section devoted to philosophy which it is easy to leave unread, since it generally seems to have little connection with the rest.

The first respect in which a figure is not quite what it appears to be is not, however, the only kind of error that a statistician can surmount. A limited amount of observer bias also presents no more than a routine difficulty. The meaning of observer bias may be explained by an example. If an observation were made to the effect that there were thirteen baptisms in a certain parish in a certain year, we should know that exactly thirteen in one particular year has no great significance because random error causes some annual variation in the number. The thirteen baptisms might, however, have been a figure provided for us by an assistant, and liable to some observer error that was specific to him. He might have zealously copied all the baptisms out of the register, for example, ignoring references to some of them as having been performed by the parish priest, but actually occurring outside the parish. The observer in question would thus have achieved an upward bias in his figures. It is not difficult to imagine other such faulty manners of observation that could possibly occur, all of which would cause irremovable errors if the registers were no longer extant. In normal statistical practice (in doing a sample survey, for instance) such observer bias is discovered only after all the data have been collected and can rarely be traced to its ultimate cause; one only knows that A gets figures that run 3 per cent too high for consistency with the other observers whereas B is 2 per cent too low. Adjustments are then made, empirically, to the data during the process of analysis. This type of error, however, is rare in demographic work.

The third category, factual errors, is worth attention, because data containing factual errors can be grossly misleading; it is often possible to avoid some of the error by one special argument or another. By factual errors we mean misinterpretations of the data. In extreme logic, factual errors cannot, of course, occur; one could always talk of 'recorded baptisms,' for example, and never of 'baptisms'. The jump of inference between the two is essential to the inquiry, however, and not to make it would leave us with barren mathematics only. Yet there is reason to believe that the jump may not be the skip over an imaginary line we hope it is, but a leap over an immense chasm of doubt. Almost always, the trouble is not any consistent bias of the particular observer, but is caused by factors beyond his control. Generally (in fairly detailed statistics) there is a certain amount of omitted data, caused by the limitations of the observer's interests, time, and energy. It is possible, but not likely, that a vain inflation of records may have occurred; but a record-keeper is more likely to be lazy than vain. A chronicler who had no real records at all to work from, on the other hand, would no doubt have used his imagination and would be more likely to have exaggerated his numbers than to have diminished them.

Finally, by mistakes we mean errors in copying, in arithmetic, or in logic, and also any deliberately promulgated lies that the student makes the mistake of swallowing. The category is familiar to historians already, and little more need be said about it here.

HISTORY AND DEMOGRAPHY

Because contemporary demography is based upon statistics collected from the existing population, the data can be improved by a second enumeration or a sample check. Historical demography, on the other hand, deals with unique sources which can never be improved. Really reliable population figures will never be available for most people and periods, and the historian who hopes to base his argument upon a firm foundation must hope in vain. Other historical evidence will have to suggest, in part at least, what the true population levels and trends were, with the consequent risk of a circular argument. This means that more care must be given than heretofore to the degree of strength of a set of population data, and an assessment must be made of what deductions they will bear.

Professional historians seem to have acquired an unfortunate prejudice, when dealing with numbers, that small numbers are 'safer' in some sense than large ones. At the time of Montesquieu's *Lettres Persanes*[1] (1721), exaggeration was still common; since Hume's essay *Of the Populousness of Ancient Nations*[2] (1752), historians' estimates of population in the more distant past have often been minimum estimates only. When working chiefly from such reports as the numbers killed in a battle or living in a city, historians are fully justified; and in the matter of total numbers, since all the figures for the period would be deflated to much the same degree, it cannot be especially serious. When birth rates are estimated in this way, however, we can easily suppose that births were being limited, and when infant mortality is investigated, we may get absurd rates. Birth rates below the high levels found today in many parts of the world are, *a priori*, unlikely; infant mortality rates under 150 per thousand are scarcely credible. It would be most useful to attempt not only to determine the lowest conceivable rates, but also to determine the highest conceivable vital rates that could have obtained, assuming conditions favourable to such high levels. This would lead to the extent of undercounting that would be required to produce the observations, or rather to eliminate all the nonobservations. One would then have to consider whether such undercounting might possibly have occurred.

The origin of this attitude would seem to be the conviction with which Hume demolished Montesquieu's earlier view. Two samples of Montesquieu's prose will give some indication of the state of historical demography in Europe at the time:[3] '*La Grèce est si déserte, qu'elle ne contient pas la centième partie de ses anciens habitans. L'Espagne, autrefois si remplie, ne fait voir aujourd'hui que des campagnes*

---

[1] Charles Louis de Secondat, Baron de la Brede et de Montesquieu, *Lettres Persanes* (Amsterdam, 1721, and many later editions). Letters cxii to cxxii discuss population and related matters.

[2] D. Hume, *Political Discourses* (Edinburgh, 1752), pp. 155–261.

[3] Montesquieu, *Lettres Persanes*, Letter cxii.

inhabitées; et la France n'est rien, en comparaison de cette ancienne Gaule dont parlé César.' ('Greece is so deserted that it does not contain one hundredth of its ancient inhabitants. Spain, once so full, today only displays uninhabited country; and France is nothing in comparison to the old Gaul of which Ceasar spoke.') He concludes: *'Après un calcul aussi exact qu'il peut l'être dans ces sortes de choses, j'ai trouvé qu'il y a, à peine, sur la terre la dixième partie des hommes qui y étaient dans les anciens temps.'* ('After a calculation as exact as can be made in this sort of thing, I have found that there are scarcely one tenth as many people on earth as there were in ancient times.') The emphasis of the *Lettres Persanes* was, in fact, not on history, but on the contemporary world. It was a work of satire, and the *'calcul aussi exact qu'il peut l'être'* was based on no more solid evidence than sweeping generalizations, like those for Greece, Spain and France quoted above. No one reads *Gulliver's Travels* for geographical information, nor supposes that all the lands it describes really existed, merely because Swift employs some verisimilitude in his satire (such as having Gulliver visit Japan among many fictitious places).

It was easy, therefore, for Hume to refute Montesquieu convincingly enough to impress the world of learning. He produced evidence that some of the ancient figures for population must be wrong since they are contradictory, and that many others are highly unlikely. Two points he made in his essay are, however, more relevant to the present growth of work in historical demography. He says:

> The facts, deliver'd by antient authors, are either so uncertain or so imperfect as to afford us nothing decisive in this matter. How indeed cou'd it be otherwise? The very facts, which we must oppose to them, in computing the greatness of modern states, are far from being either certain or compleat. . . . 'Tis to be remark'd, that all kinds of numbers are uncertain in antient manuscripts, and have been subject to much greater corruptions than any other part of the text; and that for an obvious reason. Any alteration, in other places, commonly affects the sense or grammar, and is more readily perceiv'd by the reader and transcriber.[4]

A proper result of Hume's work would thus have been to spread doubt about the possibility of being very informative about historical populations. It was one thing to argue that Montesquieu's 90 per cent reduction in world population over seventeen centuries was wrong, but another to say what the true change had been. Hume thought that world population in his own time was probably higher

---

[4] Hume, *Political Discourses, Of the Populousness of Antient Nations.*

than at any time in the past; he clearly knew that this was only probable, not provably certain.

CRITICS OF HISTORICAL DEMOGRAPHIC DATA

In most statistical work, the data are implicitly assumed to be without factual errors or mistakes. Statisticians are no different from historians in their preference for observations that mean what they say. Some theory has been developed that suggests when outlying values should be disregarded, but even this did not receive much consideration until the computer became a practical tool for data processing. An elaborate theory deals with random errors, but factual errors receive slight attention. Even the theory of random errors is comparatively new; seventy years ago, astronomy and surveying alone used a theory of errors, essentially based on Gauss's method of least squares. The economist and the historian, where they used numerical data at all, were bound to work only with large numbers so as to avoid risk of random error, and they had to assume that their data were either good and therefore usable or bad and therefore useless. The effect was to inhibit the study of historical demography. John Rickman, who was responsible for the first four British censuses, asked for information on the baptisms, marriages, and burials by parish over the preceding century, and eventually back to 1570. But he clearly realized that the quality of the returns was very poor, and he analysed them only in a rough way, never publishing the original figures at all.[5]

According to E. Biot, the first student of historical populations who paid serious attention to the reliability of the data was not David Hume nor John Graunt, but Ma Tuan-Lin, who lived in the thirteenth century.[6] The section of Ma's *Wen hsien t'ung-k'ao* (Literary Encyclopaedia) entitled *Hu k'ou men* (Doors and Mouths) deals with population statistics for China from earliest times to Ma's own day, ending in the year 1223. Biot, and S. Wells Williams[7] also, had a great respect for this Chinese scholar, who was fully

[5] J. Rickman, *Observations of the Results of The Population Act, 41 Geo. III* (London, 1802). See also 1841 Census, *Enumeration Abstract Preface*. D. V. Glass discusses these figures in 'Population and Population Movements in England and Wales, 1700 to 1850', *Population in History*, eds. Glass and D. E. C. Eversley (London, 1965), pp. 221–26.

[6] E. Biot, 'Sur la population de la Chine et ses variations, depuis l'an 2400 avant J. C. jusqu'au XIIIe siècle de nôtre ère', *Journal Asiatique*, Series 3, Vol. 1 (1836), pp. 369–94, 448–74; Vol. 2 (1836), pp. 74–8.

[7] S. Wells Williams, *The Middle Kingdom: A Survey of the Geography, Government, Literature, Social Life, Arts, and History of the Chinese Empire and Its Inhabitants* (2 vols.; London, 1883). Chapter 5, 'Population and Statistics', Vol. 1, pp. 258–88.

alive to the errors that readily enter population statistics, especially when they are not derived from a census conducted expressly for the purpose of ascertaining the population, but are by-products of some other inquiry carried out for taxation or military purposes. Questions of completeness of coverage particularly concerned Ma.

A brilliant essay by Goran Ohlin has recently criticized three particular pieces of demographic research, considering whether it is really possible to derive any significant results from them.[8] The three topics he considers are somewhat diverse, which makes Ohlin's essay especially rewarding since it gives a variety of insight into the problems confronting the historical demographer. They are mentioned briefly here to give some indication of the diverse skills that historical demography may require and the small result that may be all that can be achieved from a laborious study.

First, Ohlin draws attention to the size of the samples from which J. C. Russell calculated, twenty years ago, his Life Tables for Medieval England. At some child ages, Russell had only single figure numbers at risk, making any calculation of Black Death mortality, for example, liable to wide error—independent of any errors in the actual data or of possible non-representativeness of the sample population.

Second, Ohlin appraises Karl Lamprecht's work, eighty years ago, on the number of villages in the Mosel Valley between the years 800 and 1237. The main argument here is that we cannot know the average size of these villages, which may well have changed greatly over as long a period as 437 years. Apart from correcting a misunderstanding of Lamprecht's figures, Ohlin points out that counting a list of place names is not quite the same as counting all the villages in an area, so that even if we knew the average size of a village, we should still be uncertain of the true population of the area.

Third, the difficulty of converting records of death taxes that were paid into death rates or even into relative death rates is explored in Ohlin's essay. His data were the heriots (a heriot was a tax payable upon a tenant's death) paid between 1246 and 1348 by tenants on five manors belonging to the Bishop of Winchester, and he shows that the sharp increase in the number of heriots paid after 1289 might indeed mean higher mortality, but it could alternatively mean that properties had become subdivided so that there were more tenants and, therefore, more deaths.

Among the many other serious studies of the reliability of mis-

[8] Goran Ohlin, 'No Safety in Numbers: Some Pitfalls in Historical Statistics', *Industrialization in Two Systems: Essays in Honor of Alexander Gerschenkron*, ed. Henry Rosovsky (New York, 1966), pp. 68–90.

cellaneous data relevant to historical research, only Louis Henry's articles on funerary inscriptions[9] can be noticed here. They should be known to anyone who is interested in the possibility of calculating mortality rates in the past from a series of ages at death as recorded. He showed, for instance, that whereas more than 40 per cent of all deaths in France between about 1812 and 1834 were before age fifteen, for a particular cemetery at Lyons less than 10 per cent of deaths with an inscription were before age fifteen. Henry thus demonstrated that only a general indication of adult mortality in the past can be gleaned from funerary inscriptions, owing to the selectivity exercised in deciding who will be given a memorial. Skeletons, the main source of demographic data for prehistoric times, must also have their limitations.

PARISH REGISTERS

The Anglican parish registers, on which demographers largely rely for data on vital rates in England before civil registration began in 1836, have been studied by J. T. Krause.[10] He estimated that 10 per cent of births and 5 per cent of deaths were omitted around 1700, and that after 1780 a deterioration set in resulting in near collapse of the system between 1795 and 1820. Among the causes of this decline in coverage, Krause cited the growth of nonconformity, the costs of burials, and the diverse ways in which the clergy obeyed the original order of 1538 that had established the parish registers. It is also noteworthy that London and the other cities about which we have most information have lower levels of completeness than Krause's guesses of 90 per cent for births and 95 per cent for deaths. In this connection, D. V. Glass[11] has recently shown that parish registers in London at the end of the seventeenth century could well have undercounted births by a very serious amount, at least 20 out of 83 known births in two parishes having been missed in the registers. Although it is possibly reasonable to expect the cities to be worse than the rest of the country because of more dissent and a more transient population,

[9] Louis Henry, 'La mortalité d'après les inscriptions funéraires', *Population*, Vol. 12, No. 1 (1957), pp. 149–52; and 'L'âge au décès d'après les inscriptions funéraires', *Population*, Vol. 14, No. 2 (1959), pp. 327–9.

[10] J. T. Krause, 'Changes in English Fertility and Mortality, 1781–1850,' *Economic History Review*, 2nd Series, Vol. 11, No. 1 (1958), pp. 52–70; and 'The Changing Adequacy of English Registration, 1690–1837', *Population in History*, eds. Glass and Eversley (London, 1965), pp. 379–93.

[11] D. V. Glass, Introduction to *London Inhabitants Within the Walls, 1695* (London, 1966), p. xxix.

the better communications and higher standard of living of the cities might be expected to work for a better keeping of parish registers. The poor coverage that is known to apply to London can hardly encourage one to expect good coverage elsewhere.

Parish registers, in fact, are the chief source of data for recent research in historical demography. For the clergyman, however, keeping a parish register may have been like keeping his diary. He remembered to write the event down at once perhaps 80 per cent of the time; sometimes he forgot and never wrote it up afterwards. There was no proper check on him, and his level of enthusiasm must have been high to collect as much information as he normally did. Keeping a register *in vacuo*, so to speak, can have been no labour of love for many of the clergy. Moreover, it is easy to assume that most children were baptized, but how do we know whether it was 90 or 99 per cent? Every village in England is traditionally supposed to have had one squire, one idiot, and one atheist, for example, and these people might have been regarded as being respectively above, beneath, and beyond the church. We certainly know of areas of downright dissent, but what of areas of grudging assent? The conscientious parent who had all his children baptized may well have been the rule, but will not have been the universal rule. For telling us roughly how large a parish was, the registers are thus adequate; questions arise only when we want to study the birth rates and death rates.

A thorough method of exploiting parish registers was first put forward by M. Fleury and Louis Henry in 1956 and has been very widely used since.[12] It cannot be improved upon, but we must consider how likely it is that the data are good enough for it to be properly applicable. If they are not good enough, nothing can be done except to omit parts of the analysis.[13] General comparisons of the level of fertility and age at marriage are less likely to be spoiled by poor data than are the more intricate calculations, such as birth-interval analysis or mortality during the first year of life. The small number of families living in a parish means that sampling errors, too, must be avoided by taking rather large time-periods—during which, the practice of keeping the parish register could have changed.

Some studies using the Fleury-Henry method of ransacking parish

[12] M. Fleury and Louis Henry, *Des registres paroissiaux à l'histoire de la population: manuel de dépouillement et d'exploitation de l'état civil ancien* (Paris, 1956): and *Nouveau manuel de dépouillement et d'exploitation de l'état civil ancien* (Paris, 1965).

[13] See also Louis Henry, *Manuel de démographie historique* (Geneva-Paris, 1967), pp. 3–26, in which he considers how to assess the quality of the observations. His methods here may be more applicable to French than to English registers.

registers and family reconstitution have arrived at suspiciously low rates of infant mortality, if we bear in mind that (allowing for probable under-enumeration) 200 or 250 per 1,000 infants apparently died in their first year of life among the high aristocracy until the eighteenth century. Thus E. A. Wrigley,[14] in what is otherwise an excellent study, found 1,480 baptisms[15] at Colyton between 1600 and 1649, but only found 138 buried in their first year of life. At such a place and time we might expect about 300 infant deaths for 1,480 births, so that unless Colyton were exceptionally healthy, it would mean that extra infants should be added who were neither baptized nor buried, owing to early death. It would be necesssary to raise the Colyton baptisms by about 200 (more than 13 per cent) to get the expected rate of infant mortality, and it would mean that only some 40 per cent of the infant deaths were actually recorded. Wrigley's breakdown of infant mortality into seven groups by age suggested to him that at most 6 per cent of the baptisms might have been under-registered, and he compared them with figures for the parish of St. Michael le Belfrey in York during the years 1571-86.

An alternative comparison with Crulai[16] is interesting. In that French parish, we have data for two periods, from 1688 to 1719 and 1720 and beyond—that is, until about 1750. The under-registration of mortality was estimated at between 3 per cent and 12 per cent for the later period and was assumed to hold for the earlier period also. These are minimum estimates, moreover, in the sense that they suppose that registration of burials was virtually complete at Crulai. Baptisms were also assumed correct, so that, in fact, the correction is for migration only. For the earlier period, the infant mortality rate (uncorrected) was 236 per 1,000 (196 out of 829 born) and for the later period 172 per 1,000 (135 out of 786 born). Under-registration of deaths would raise these rates to 243-264 and 177-192, respectively, not too inconsistent with the figures for the British aristocracy, bearing in mind that the second period is well into the eighteenth century.

Wrigley, however, has a crude infant mortality rate for Colyton of only 93 per 1,000 (138 deaths out of 1,480 births). If under-registrations of baptisms were at his maximum of 6 per cent, then 95 infants would have been missed completely, and the Colyton infant mortality rate for 1600-1649 would become 148 per 1,000

[14] E. A. Wrigley, 'Family Limitation in Pre-Industrial England', *Economic History Review*, 2nd Series, Vol. 19, No. 1 (1966), pp. 82–109.

[15] Private communication.

[16] E. Gautier and Louis Henry, *La population de Crulai, paroisse normande* (Paris, 1958), pp. 159–71, 268.

(233 out of 1,575). This figure is still well below Crulai's level a century later, itself low rather than high in relation to the British aristocracy.

Let us consider the division of deaths in the first year of life into those aged under three months and those older than that. It is convenient to take a fairly late point of division, so that difficulties over the considerable delay in baptizing newborn children that occurred in England but not in France have little importance. Mortality is much lower at the age of three months than earlier, and it will not matter greatly what the precise ages were within a week or two. On general grounds, we must expect the ratio of deaths under three months to deaths over three months to vary with the general level of infant mortality: the higher the infant mortality, the smaller the proportion of deaths in the first three months. We may verify this for Crulai. For the period 1688–1719, the ratio of deaths under three months to deaths between three and twelve months was 158 to 38 (4·158 to 1), and for the period 1720 and beyond, which had a lower infant mortality rate, the same ratio of deaths was 118 to 17 (6·935 to 1). At Colyton, the uncorrected deaths numbered 90 before the age of three months and 49 between three months and twelve. Adding 95 infant deaths, all very likely under three months, is not enough; the new ratio, 185 to 48, is still only 3·854 to 1, although the infant mortality remains less than either of the Crulai rates. The best fit of the Colyton figures to the Crulai ratios (linearly interpolating) would be to add a further 96 missed baptisms to Colyton, all assumed to correspond to deaths under the age of three months. We should then find an infant mortality rate of 197 per 1,000 (329 infant deaths out of 1,671 births) and a ratio of infant deaths under three months to infant deaths over three months of 281 to 48, or 5·854 to 1. Any under-enumeration at Crulai owing to migration would affect this calculation, and so the true infant mortality at Colyton is unlikely to have been below 200 per 1,000, as anticipated. Fortunately, Wrigley's conclusions about fertility changes are modified, but not contraverted, by such a high rate of omission.

GENEALOGICAL RESEARCH

Ideally we need a way of appraising data that does not lead us into supposing that all the observations we find are all the observations that an ideal observer could possibly have found. This, of course, will require more care than if we had no such worries, since we must accord at least some passing thought to the reliability of each observation. No observation can be discarded, and few or none elevated to the special position of being thought indisputable. If, for example, a man said his age was forty in response to an inquiry, then that is what the datum is, even if his true age was forty-six, and he later said it was. From this it follows that a comprehensive set of data must include both estimates of his age, or at least pay some attention to both of them. Although forty-six would be correct, only an ideal observer would know that it was correct, and we should be forced to pay some attention to the figure of forty. The analysis would have to include a criterion for deciding what to do about the two figures. Four possibilities exist: accept forty (because it came to us first), accept forty-six (because we believe it is the better of the two figures), accept both, or discard the data as intractable. The third is the most difficult to handle, but the most rewarding in the end. It means that not only will our results be liable to sampling error and our hypotheses confirmed or contradicted at a certain level of probability, but also that an extra error term will be incorporated into the analysis that will indicate how far any conclusions at all can be drawn.

The collection of data under these conditions is, of course, more arduous than when data are gathered in the ordinary way. It is, however, a regrettable fact of a statistician's experience that bias creeps in readily whenever a sample is not truly random, but has selected itself in some way. For this reason, some method of using the vital events of every member of a population is much to be desired, and in two studies on the British aristocracy[17] such a device has been elaborated. This method would be applicable to any study based on genealogies, although it does not suit parish register work.

Very widely varying degrees of information exist about the dates of historical events. For m any events we know the exact day, and from some Chinese genealogies, where astrological interest has preserved the information, the exact hour of a birth is known.[18] In genealogical studies at least, there is then a second group for which the dates are a little uncertain—we may know only the date of burial rather than the day of death, or we have two dates between which a birth or death occurred; marriage licences granted on a certain day may point to a marriage soon afterwards, and so on.

[17] T. H. Hollingsworth, 'A Demographic Study of the British Ducal Families', *Population Studies*, Vol. 11, No. 1 (1957), pp. 4–26, reprinted with revisions in *Population in History*, pp. 354–78; also, Hollingsworth, *The Demography of the British Peerage*, Supplement to *Population Studies*, Vol. 17, No. 2.

[18] Yuan I-Chin, 'Life Tables for a Southern Chinese Family from 1365 to 1849', *Human Biology*, Vol. 3, No. 2 (1931), pp. 157–79.

There is next a third group—those people whose age is known to the nearest year at some point, but whose date of birth seems now to be lost. For example: a man's age may be mentioned in the proof of a will; he may have stated his age in a dated letter to a friend; or his portrait may give his age at the time it was painted. There is a fourth group, which needs care owing to contradictory evidence which sometimes occurs, comprising cases where more accuracy can be achieved by making a birthdate fit in with those of the siblings, whose relative order of birth is almost always known, at least within each sex. There remains, however, a considerable fifth group of people who are poorly documented, for whom no direct indication of age exists. Yet general considerations often show, within five or ten years, limits within which they must have been born. For example, the date a man joined the army or when he entered an Inn of Court as a student may be known. Similarly, dates of death are often known to within twenty years or less from documents that mention a person as being alive or dead.

The principle used in the larger and later study on the British aristocracy to classify the raw information according to its degree of accuracy was that of the binary logarithmic scale.[19] A range of one year either way was taken as the centre, and other classifications went from one thirty-second of a year up to thirty-two years either way. There were thus eleven classes, the shortest of which was all time-ranges up to three weeks; a twelfth class consisted of a large group of dates assumed to be accurate to the day. It was then possible to include as much of the universe as seemed sensible for the different parts of the study, and to study the bad data each time to see whether or not they suggested a bias. Neither would have been possible if all data below a certain level of reliability had simply been discarded. In actual fact, a certain amount of absurdity came into the estimates of age at death because all those with the same type of uncertainty had been placed at the same age. Adult married females with no further information about them, for instance, were always made to die at age fifty-three—a figure arbitrarily derived from Indian life-tables and the usual age at marriage as found in the first study.[20] It would have been possible, and better, to distribute these cases stochastically over the range of ages suitable to them; but should further study of the raw material bring to light some of the vital dates for these people, there is at least the comfort that no bias would be expected when correcting the tentative dates.

[19] Hollingsworth, *The Demography of the British Peerage*, pp. 73–6.
[20] Hollingsworth, 'A Demographic Study of the British Ducal Families'.

If it be allowed that the general quality of information about dates of birth must be connected with complete omission of an individual, it becomes possible to derive estimates of the rate of omission. The method assumes that there was a constant sex ratio at birth, but that boys and girls were not equally likely to be left out. Almost all the omitted people probably died young, particularly in the first month or so of life. This method—the only way of deducing the omission rate that has so far been suggested, unless two independent enumerations happen to have been made of the same population—seems much better than just assuming that the results 'look good'. The levels of omission found ran from about 16 per cent of the true births for those born around 1600 to about 10 per cent around 1700, about 2 per cent around 1800, and less than 1 per cent around 1900.[21]

The child death rates were profoundly affected by these omissions, a point overlooked in a recent study in which the ratio of the corrected figures for the cohort of both sexes born between 1575 and 1599 was treated as though it had been directly observed.[22] There is no reason to claim more for such an early cohort than that female mortality was probably lower than male mortality (which was not true in the next century) and to estimate roughly how much lower it was. Calculating the female advantage for different ages is meaningless, in view of the irremovable errors in the data.

It is depressing to think that a large proportion, perhaps a sixth, of the people who ought to have been under scrutiny were phantoms, leaving no trace of their birth or death and not so much as a name to remember them by. Yet it is not incredible, and one must not pretend that complete records are common. In China, extensive population records have been kept for centuries, even for millennia. Chronic errors crept in, however, so that most of these records are probably badly wrong, with an occasional jump when they were belatedly improved.[23] It is less likely that gross lying occurred at the time of the jump than that some long-established errors were removed and the earlier figures had been far from the truth. A valuable corrective to undue belief in the completeness of historical vital statistics lies also in the study of more recent demographic data. Errors of the grossest sort occur in many registration systems today. In India, for example, the registered births suggest

[21] Hollingsworth, *The Demography of the British Peerage*, pp. 86–8.

[22] U. M. Cowgill, 'Life and Death in the Sixteenth Century in the City of York', *Population Studies*, Vol. 21, No. 1 (July 1967), pp. 53–62. Other aspects of this paper are discussed by Louis Henry in *Population Studies*. March 1968.

[23] Ho Ping-Ti, *Studies on the Population of China* (Cambridge, 1959). But compare J. D. Durand, 'The Population Statistics of China, A.D. 2–1953', *Population Studies*, Vol. 13, No. 3 (1960), pp. 209–56.

that the national birthrate is about 25 per 1,000; examination of the census and sample inquiries, however, leads to a figure of about 45 per 1,000. Even in Victorian England, some 6 per cent of births went unregistered before 1860.[24]

THE FUTURE

There has been some demand for a more detailed analysis of the social patterns of the British aristocracy following the description of their demographic levels and trends.[25] It is only prudent, when considering what could be done, to bear the limitations of the data in mind. There is no doubt that eldest sons of peers led different lives socially than their younger brothers and that the latter often did not marry or else married late. Some study of these social differences would be interesting and would not be affected by the omission rate. The heir, on the one hand, was under pressure to continue the line and produce a large family; on the other, he usually married so young that estrangement from his wife after a few years of marriage was not rare. On balance, the eldest sons probably had the higher level of fertility, adjusting for age at marriage, but a proper study has still to be made.

The most remarkable thing to a demographer that studies of the aristocracy have shown, however, is that fertility among the children of British peers fell steadily between about 1620 and 1740. At the beginning, the fertility of this group was so high that the population was tending to grow at a rate equivalent to about 2 per cent per annum; by the end, it had fallen so far (helped by later marriage and higher mortality rates under age fifty) that a net decline of population of about $\frac{1}{2}$ per cent per annum is indicated by the generation replacement rate. The subsequent changes are more familiar and easier to explain: the rise in fertility until 1830 and its steady fall since, flattening out in the twentieth century; the steady fall in mortality; the high age at marriage until the end of the nineteenth century, and its subsequent collapse. But the fall in fertility between the reigns of Charles I and George I—the main factor in the halving of the rate of replacement per generation— is beyond adequate historical explanation at present, although the French nobility behaved in much the same way during this period.[26] (They did not, however, share in the rise in fertility

[24] Glass, 'A Note on the Under-Registration of Births in Britain in the Nineteenth Century', *Population Studies*, Vol. 5 (1951), pp. 70–88.

[25] Hollingsworth, *The Demography of the British Peerage*, pp. 4–5.

[26] Henry and C. Lévy, 'Ducs et pairs sous l'Ancien Régime', *Population*, Vol. 15, No. 5 (1960), pp. 807–30.

after 1740.) It will not do to bring in external causes, such as plague, and economic factors surely had little effect on a population whose mean income must have been many times greater than the national average. Social pressure is the probable explanation, but what kind of pressure? There was a major political revolution in the 1640s which affected the social standing of the aristocrats, but it seems very odd that their fertility should have declined for a whole century afterwards as a result. The Restoration, after all, was in 1660, not 1740. Alternatively, if the 'general tenor of aristocratic life' is invoked as being anti-fertility for some reason, why did the British aristocracy reverse its fertility trend about 1740 and the French aristocracy continue theirs?

Further research would do well to concentrate on the period 1620–1740 and consider which groups of families led the downward trend. Distinctions by national group (English, Scottish, or Irish), Whig or Tory, Catholic or Protestant, high- or low-ranking peers, old or new families, and (to some extent) rich or poor are obtainable in principle and might be relevant to the investigation.

Extensions at both ends of the time-scale would also be practicable. At the later end, peers dying after 1938 were excluded, which was convenient for technical reasons. Since peers' children were the main universe studied, the numbers of those studied shrinks for all generations born after 1875. At the earlier end, although the records are poor, some attempt might be made to gather data back to 1283, when the House of Lords was constituted in something like its present form, for the number of people involved is relatively small. Here detailed consideration of the accuracy of all estimates of dates would become very important, since few dates beyond all question are available and otherwise the work cannot be done.

Historical demography is a difficult subject. The collection of data is laborious, requiring checking and a watch for hints of underenumeration. The analysis is often subtle, since errors in the data need to be assessed. The conclusions may seem too trivial to be worth so much effort. Yet the historical demographer's aim is to produce the best conclusions that can be drawn from the extant material. Scholarship that tries to do more must be vain.

This article was originally written in 1967, and the author has since published his views on the sources and methods of historical demography at some length as a book, *Historical Demography*, London and Ithaca, New York, 1969. Further work on this subject was contributed to a conference on historical demography at Florence in October 1971, which will be published in the *Annales de Démographie Historique* for 1972.

Joseph J. Spengler

Demographic factors and early modern economic development

> How slender an initial difference may come to
> be decisive of the outcome in case circumstances
> give this initial difference a cumulative effect.
>
> —Thorsten Veblen

Sometime before the seventeenth century, perhaps as early as the fifteenth, a unique marriage pattern began to develop in Western Europe. It apparently did not exist in the fourteenth century, but had become effective by the seventeenth, if not earlier. John Hajnal has described the genesis of this pattern, which seems to have been a product of both the rational elements in Western European culture and the prevailing institutional arrangements associated with that culture.

This pattern consisted of much later marriage than one found in Eastern Europe or outside Europe. It significantly intensified the birth-limiting influence of ecclesiastical and other forms of celibacy. It contributed greatly to the relatively low level of European birth rates which, 'so far as we can tell, were rarely over 38 before the spread of birth control'. Thus, it impeded the rate of population growth. This slowing down augmented, in turn, per-capita productivity as well as capital formation and cushioned the impact of numbers upon land and resources. It made average income higher than it otherwise would have been and thereby facilitated the emergence and successful launching of the Industrial Revolution, which finally freed Western man, especially the common man, from the trammels of static, catastrophe-prone, and poverty-ridden pain economies.[1]

[1] On the marriage pattern, see John Hajnal, 'European Marriage Patterns in Perspective', *Population in History*, eds. D. V. Glass and D. E. C. Eversley (Chicago, 1965), pp. 101–40; see also *Population in History*, pp. 46–51, 99, 298–9, 377, 448–85. On the fertility-controlling effectiveness of deferment of marriage, see J. W. Leasure, 'Malthus, Marriage and Multiplication', *Milbank Memorial Fund Quarterly*, Vol. 41, Part 2 (October 1963), pp. 419–35. For the impact of the Industrial Revolution on the standard of living, see discussion by E. J. Hobshawm and R. M. Hartwell, in *Economic History Review*, Vol. 16 (1963), pp. 120–46.

POPULATION AND INCOME GROWTH

The course of both population and income growth corresponded rather closely to that of a Malthusian model in Europe until around the sixteenth century, and in most of Asia and Africa almost to the present. Europe's population did not begin to grow continuously and without marked interruptions until the fifteenth century, but thereafter it proceeded at a slowly increasing rate. Europe's population, M. K. Bennett suggests, increased by about three quarters between the years 1000 and 1300, only to decline by perhaps three eighths during the next century, and then to return to the 1300 level by the early-sixteenth century. Thereafter it grew—about one quarter of 1 per cent per year in the sixteenth and seventeenth centuries and somewhat more rapidly in the eighteenth century, especially in the latter part. The long-term annual growth rate averaged about one half of 1 per cent in the eighteenth century and about three quarters of 1 per cent in the nineteenth: This increase in the growth rate seems to have been attributable mainly, if not entirely, to a decline in mortality. Before the nineteenth century, this decline is traceable chiefly to a marked diminution in the incidence of famine and pestilence and the catastrophic mortality associated therewith, especially in such periods as 1349–1470s, aptly described by Sylvia Thrupp as 'the golden age of bacteria'.

The movement of the per-capita output of goods and services in Europe was long dominated by the course of its population growth, itself often under the empire of unfavourable events and therefore very low over the long run according to modern standards. The countries of Europe were predominantly agricultural, with three quarters or more of the population being rural. The mode of agricultural production was relatively traditional and unchanging. Supply was quite inelastic, and its increase depended principally upon the extension of cultivation. English and other data suggest that productivity was low and progressed slowly even when population pressure encouraged the abandonment of the three-field system. In Western Europe, as Phyllis Deane and W. A. Cole write: 'The significant variable in the long pre-industrial secular swings in productivity seems to have been the rate of population growth. When population rose, product per head fell: when population fell, product per head rose.' The Malthusian tendency for numbers to keep abreast of agricultural output seems to have been characteristic also of Asia. Despite a generally higher birth rate, the population of Asia supposedly increased only about five sixths between 1650 and 1800, no more than that of Europe and Russia. Mortality regulated population growth in Asia much more than it did in Europe. As K. W. Taylor concluded: 'Long periods of [population] stability are best explained by the Malthusian hypothesis and the relatively short periods of rapid growth can be explained in terms of major technological or environmental changes.' Even distribution of population, A. P. Usher found, was closely associated with the availability of food. This correlation remained constant until the Industrial Revolution converted mineral resources into a major determinant of population location. Density varied, of course, reflecting in part the fact that full maturity of settlement was not achieved in Northwestern Europe until around 1600—sixteen centuries later than in the Mediterranean world, but three centuries earlier than in India and China. In Northern and Western Europe, density varied greatly even before the Industrial Revolution, ranging from 137 inhabitants per square mile in Belgium and parts of Italy through 90 in England and 110 in France to about 5 in Norway.[2]

So long as the numbers of people tended to press closely upon the food supply, average income and output could not increase greatly over the long run. The elasticity in the supply of produce was too low. Average output increased with the extension of settlement, the formation of capital, and the stimulus of the temporary economic upsurges manifest after 1100 and again after the late 1400s, but not much of this gain could be retained. Indeed, if it had been, average income in 1500 might have exceeded subsistence by 300 to 400 per cent, rather than the actual, much lower, margin. If average output in the Roman Empire around A.D. 200 has approximated 1·25 times a hypothetical subsistence level and thereafter had grown about one tenth of 1 per cent per year, by 1500 the level of output should have been about 3·5 times as high as it was thirteen centuries earlier, but it was not.

As English data suggest, in and long after the Middle Ages, population pressure tended to develop in the wake of a continuing growth in numbers. It became manifest, for example in the late-

---

[2] This paragraph and the one preceding are based on essays by K. F. Helleiner and the editors in *Population in History*; W. A. Cole and Phyllis Deane, 'The Growth of National Incomes', *Cambridge Economic History of Europe*, eds. H. J. Habakkuk and M. M. Postan (Cambridge, 1966), Vol. 6, Chap. 1; D. V. Glass, 'World Population, 1800–1950', *Cambridge Economic History*, Chap. 2; M. K. Bennett, *The World's Food* (New York, 1954), Chap. 1; Phyllis Deane and W. A. Cole, *British Economic Growth 1688–1959* (Cambridge, 1962), pp. 38, 65, 78–82; Phyllis Deane, *The First Industrial Revolution* (Cambridge, 1965), pp. 11–13; essays by K. W. Taylor, J. C. Russell, and A. P. Usher in *Demographic Analysis*, eds. J. J. Spengler and O. D. Duncan (Glencoe, 1965); W. Bowden, M. Karpovich, and A. P. Usher, *An Economic History of Europe Since 1750* (New York, 1937), pp. 3, 6–7; chapters by L. Genicot and R. Kobner, *Cambridge Economic History of Europe*, ed. M. M. Postan (2nd ed.; Cambridge, 1966), Vol. 1; Roger J. Mols, S.J., *Introduction à la démographie historique des villes d'Europe du XIVᵉ au XVIIIᵉ siècle* (Louvain, 1955), Vol. 2, pp. 425–34, on mortality, and Vol. 3, pp. 284–7, on natality.

DP

thirteenth and early-fourteenth centuries—after several centuries of growth, much of which was subsequently wiped out by the Black Death. Population pressure was again felt in the sixteenth and seventeenth centuries and resulted in complaints of unemployment as well as calls for the development of colonial outlets to absorb the excess numbers.[3]

Even so, as Deane and Cole state, England and Wales had apparently achieved by the late-seventeenth century a higher level of material welfare than any other country with the exception of Holland, whose average income, according to Gregory King, was slightly above the English average and at least one fourth above the French average. Deane and Cole add, however, that the seventeenth-century English average did not greatly exceed that of the 'rest of the world' or that of fifteenth-century England. They also observe that 'change, outside the cataclysms produced by famines and epidemics, was generally small, slow, and easily reversed' in the seventeenth-century world in which King lived.[4]

Three observations may now be made. Although our information in respect to Europe's rate of population growth before 1800 is incomplete, this rate appears to have been low, averaging perhaps one quarter of 1 per cent per year between 1500 and 1700 and about five twelfths of 1 per cent per year between 1700 and 1750. In France population increased somewhat between 1500 and 1600, though not steadily; in the seventeenth-century, Pierre Goubert believes, it oscillated around an equilibrium of about nineteen million, standing nearer the minimum than the maximum in 1700 It grew about one third of 1 per cent per year in the eighteenth century, about 0·22 percent per year in 1700–55, and about one half of 1 per cent in 1755–1801. In England and Wales, population grew about one third of 1 per cent per year between 1500 and 1700 and between 1700 and 1780. Even if English incomes and

---

[3] Manifestations of population pressure, especially in England, have been discussed frequently in the *Economic History Review*. See articles by M. M. Postan and E. E. Rich, in Vol. 2 (1950), pp. 221–46, 247–65; D. C. Coleman, Vol. 8 (1956), pp. 288–94; W. C. Robinson, with comments by M. M. Postan, Vol. 9 (1959), pp. 63–83; J. Z. Titow, Vol. 14 (1961), pp. 218–23; J. M. W. Bean, Vol. 15 (1963), pp. 423–37; G. S. L. Tucker, Vol. 16 (1964), pp. 205–18; Sylvia L. Thrupp, Vol. 18 (1965), pp. 101–19; D. Herlihy, *ibid.*, pp. 225–44; P. E. Razzell, *ibid.*, pp. 312–32; E. A. Wrigley, Vol. 19 (1966), pp. 82–109. See also Genicot, *loc. cit.*; J. C. Russell, *British Medieval Population* (Albuquerque, 1948), pp. 156–9, 232, 312-14; *Population in History*, pp. 434–85 and 507–22 *passim*; J. W. Thompson, *An Economic and Social History of the Middle Ages (300–1300)* (New York, 1928), pp. 391–2 L. D. Stamp, *Man and Land* (London, 1955), pp. 92–4; also, essay by Charles Parain, *Cambridge Economic History of Europe*, Vol. 1, and essays by R. S. Lopez and M. M. Postan, *Cambridge Economic History*, Vol. 2; K. F. Helleiner's essay, *Cambridge Economic History*, Vol. 4.

[4] Deane and Cole, *British Economic Growth 1688–1959*, pp. 38–9; E. H. Phelps Brown, *The Growth of British Industrial Relations* (London, 1959), p. 2.

wages were not much greater in the late-seventeenth century than in the late-fifteenth, the slowness with which the population grew at least permitted the standards attained in the late-fifteenth century to be retained and perhaps even improved. Given the low rate of natural increase, overall real output per head could increase something like 0·3 per cent annually in England and Wales between 1700 and the 1770s, even though the aggregate real output grew slowly throughout the eighteenth century.

Despite the slowness with which average output advanced, it rose above the levels encountered in much of today's underdeveloped world. Phyllis Deane estimates that the average income in England and Wales in 1750 (at least one third above the 1700 level, but about two fifths below the 1800 level) would have been equivalent to £70 in the 1950s—a figure nearly treble that of India and two thirds that of Mexico in the 1950s. According to Simon Kuznets, 'per worker income in the agricultural sector in today's most populous' underdeveloped countries (China, India, Pakistan, Burma, South Korea, and most of Africa) is only 'one fourth or one third of per worker income in the currently developed countries in the preindustrialization phase' when six tenths or more of their labour force remained in agriculture. Accordingly, *total* income per worker in these countries was two to three times as high as it is in today's underdeveloped countries. 'By comparison with many present-day pre-industrial economies in Africa and Asia', Cole and Deane conclude, 'the English economy of the late seventeenth and early eighteenth centuries had reached a relatively advanced stage of economic organization. So too, no doubt, had certain other countries.'[5]

THEORIES OF POPULATION AND INCOME GROWTH

A low rate of population growth may encourage the rate of growth of average income in three ways. These observations are especially true of predominantly agricultural economies that are equipped with an essentially traditional agricultural technique, are not yet subject to economies of scale, and are just beginning to assume a a more commercial-industrial form.

[5] In this and the preceding paragraph, I draw on S. Kuznets, *Economic Growth and Structure* (New York, 1965), pp. 176–93; Deane, *The First Industrial Revolution*, pp. 5–13; Cole and Deane, 'The Growth of National Incomes', pp. 3–10; Deane and Cole, *British Economic Growth, 1688–1959*, pp. 38, 65, 78–80; essays by Glass, G. Utterström, P. Goubert, L. Henry, and J. Meuvret in *Population in History*; J. C. Toutain, *Le produit de l'agriculture de 1700 à 1958* (Paris, 1961), Chap. 7, and *La population de la France de 1700 à 1959* (Paris, 1963), pp. 24–9. See also W. W. Rostow, *The Economics of Take-Off Into Sustained Growth* (London, 1963).

If a population is growing slowly, the bulk of the savings which it generates can be devoted to increasing capital per head, thereby easing indirectlyt he pressure of population upon land and facilitating the growth of nonagricultural enterprises. Capital formation proceeded at a very slow pace in the seventeenth and early-eighteenth centuries. In England around 1700 the annual rate of saving fell within a range of something like 3 to 6 per cent of the national income. The French rate was probably lower, and the Dutch rate may have been higher. With such low saving rates, capital per head could increase significantly only if the rate of population growth were negligible and savings were not employed wastefully, as often happened in ancient and medieval times. Were population growth negligible and were only 4 per cent saved and invested annually to yield a 10 per cent rate of return, average income would rise about 0·4 of 1 per cent per year, enough to increase per-capita income by approximately one half in about ninety-five years. Were population growing as much as 1 per cent per year, this growth would absorb virtually all the savings, should they amount to only 4 or 5 per cent of the national income. Not even in Europe, however, was the former option always exercised. According to E. F. Heckscher, population growth in eighteenth-century Sweden absorbed the disposable resources available.[6]

Slowing down population growth decreases the impact numbers and agriculturalists have upon cultivatable land. Accordingly, the ratio of the agricultural labour force to cultivatable land was only 10 to 50 per cent as high in pre-industrial European countries as it is in today's underdeveloped countries. Even so, in and before David Ricardo's day, there was strong evidence of a classical diminishing of returns in England and possibly elsewhere. Nevertheless, because numbers had grown slowly, and limits to production had not been reached, time remained during which yields per acre could be increased or manufactures could be developed and exchanged for imports. This time was utilized, moreover, and yields were increased somewhat, certainly in greater measure than they have been today in those underdeveloped countries whose agricultural productivity has increased little over the centuries.[7]

Potential productivity per capita in a population depends mark-

[6] Deane and Cole, *British Economic Growth, 1688–1959*, pp. 260–4; Cole and Deane, 'The Growth of National Incomes', p. 5; E. F. Heckscher's essay in *Economic History Review*, Vol. 2 (1950), pp. 266–77.

[7] On the course of yields, see C. Clark, *Conditions of Economic Progress* (2nd ed.; London, 1951), pp. 224–7; Deane and Cole, *British Economic Growth, 1688–1959*, pp. 64–7; M. M. Postan, in *Economic History Review*, Vol. 12 (1959), pp. 80–1; also M. J. R. Healy and E. L. Jones, 'Wheat Yields in England, 1815–59', *Journal of Royal Statistical Society*, Series A, Vol. 125 (1962), Part 4, pp. 574–9; C. Clark and M. R. Haswell, *The Economics of Subsistence Agriculture* (London, 1964), *passim*.

edly upon the size of the fraction of the population that is of working age. Let this group be represented by those fifteen to fifty-nine or fifteen to sixty-four years of age. This fraction varies appreciably. In 1965, for example, the fraction aged fifteen to sixty-four approximated 54 per cent in Africa, Latin America, and Southeast Asia, much less than the 64 per cent found in Europe. Therefore, under *ceteris paribus* conditions, potential productivity was about 1·185 (64/54) times as high in Europe as in Africa, Latin America, and Southeast Asia. Northern and Western Europe enjoyed superiority in this respect as early as 1850, when the fraction aged fifteen to sixty-four years ranged between 60 and 66 per cent. Of course, the increase in potential productivity made possible would be actualized only if there were not offsetting increases in unemployment.

Before we attempt to estimate the magnitude of this fraction in the seventeenth and eighteenth centuries, we may examine a hypothetical stable population to observe how an age structure is generated by past mortality and fertility patterns. The relative number of persons of working age in a stable population rises as fertility (measured by the Gross Reproduction Rate [GRR]) and life expectancy at birth decrease; the relative number falls as fertility and life expectancy rise. If, for example, we hold expectation of life at birth constant at fifty years, the proportion aged fifteen to fifty-nine rises from 45·8 per cent with GRR at 4·0 to around 60 per cent with GRR at 1·25 to 1·50. If we hold GRR constant at 2·0 the proportion falls from 64 per cent with an expectation of life at birth of twenty years to 54·7 per cent with a life expectancy of over seventy years (70·2). Thus, declining mortality cancels out a portion of the improvement in age structure asssociated with a decline in the GRR. For example, combining a life expectancy of thirty years with a GRR of 3 results in a fraction of 0·545 aged fifteen to fifty-nine; a life expectancy of 70·2 with a GRR of 1·5, in a fraction of 0·577 aged fifteen to fifty-nine.

Information on the age composition of the pre-industrial countries of Northern and Western Europe may be found from two sources. The first source, hypothetical stable populations, furnishes only inferential information. In the body of Table 1, I give the percentages aged fifteen to sixty-four in stable populations resulting from combinations of GRR (see column 1) with expectations of life at birth (see line 2 in head of table). This fraction descends from 64 per cent when a GRR of 2·25 is combined with a life expectancy of twenty-five to fifty-five when a GRR of 3·0 is combined with a life expectancy of forty. The numbers in parentheses are rough indicators of the rates of natural increase per 1,000 inhabitants associated with designated combinations of GRR and life expectancy. We see at once how the proportion aged fifteen to sixty-four declines as GRR and life expectancy at birth increase.[8]

Table 1   Proportions aged 15–64 years: rates of growth

	Expectation of life at birth			
GRR	25	30	35	40
2·25	64(—3)	62(3)	61(7)	60(11)
2·5	62(1)	61(7)	59(11)	58(15)
3·0	59(7)	57(13)	56(18)	55(22)

The problem confronting us is that of selecting those combinations in the table which most closely approximate fertility and mortality conditions in pre-industrial Western Europe. The rate of population growth must be low. Life expectancy probably did not exceed thirty-five years in whole populations before 1800. Let us suppose the most representative combinations to be those associated with a GRR of 2·25 to 2·5 and a life expectancy of thirty to thirty-five years. We would then expect the proportion aged fifteen to sixty-four to approach 59 to 62 per cent or, more likely, 61 to 62 per cent, since the rate of population growth was decidedly below 1 per cent per year. This proportion is at least 10 to 15 per cent greater than levels encountered in many of today's under-developed countries.

Extant data relating to fertility and mortality in pre-industrial Europe presumably support the suppositions made in the preceding paragraph. First, the birth rate was much lower in pre-industrial Europe than it is in present-day and pre-1900 Asia and Africa. During the 1700s the rate was around thirty-five, somewhat lower in England and Wales, France, and Scandinavia (exclusive of Finland, which had a rate sometimes just over forty). Between 1776 and 1800, when the Swedish birth rate averaged somewhat below thirty-five, the GRR averaged about 2·1. We find birth rates of roughly thirty-five to thirty-seven associated with a GRR of 2·25 and of roughly thirty-eight to forty-one associated with a GRR of 2·5. Although the birth rates reported for eighteenth-century Europe may be somewhat off the mark, they do suggest that the GRR was close to 2·25 or 2·5.

So far, information on mortality and life expectancy before 1800 is limited. Around 1800, expectation of life at birth may have been

[8] Tables 1 and 2 are based on Western-type stable populations, described in A. J. Coale and Paul Demeny, *Regional Model Life Tables and Stable Populations* (Princeton, 1966). See also on age composition and population prospects, United Nations, *The Ageing of Populations and Its Economic and Social Implications*, Population Studies, No. 26 (New York, 1956) and *World Population Prospects*, Population Studies, No. 41 (New York, 1966).

as high as thirty-five to forty years in some Western European countries; if so it was higher than it was during the sixteenth and seventeenth centuries. Life expectancy at birth rose in Sweden between the period 1755–76 and the period 1816–40, increasing from 33·2 to 39·5 years for males and from 35·7 to 43·5 years for females. Female life expectancy at birth, usually somewhat higher than male life expectancy, was 44·7 years in Denmark in 1835–44; 42·18 in England and Wales in 1841; 40·83 in France in 1817–31; 37·91 in Iceland in 1850–60; and 35·12 in the Netherlands in 1816–25. K. F. Helleiner suggests that life expectancy rose during the eighteenth century because 'the periodic erosion of growth by epidemic or harvest failure became less marked', especially after 1750. An alternative might be that other changes gave rise to a decline in mortality during this century. Mortality, however, appears to have been greater in the earlier parts of the eighteenth century and in the seventeenth century. Gregory King's data suggest a life expectancy of only thirty-two in England during 1690s, a figure which Peter Laslett finds fitting 'in fairly well with what is known for the seventeenth century both in England and France'. Studies of localized populations in the first half of the eighteenth century in France yield an estimate of about thirty-three years for expectation of life at birth. According to S. Peller, life expectancy at birth among Europe's ruling families averaged only about thirty-one years in 1600–99, three years less than in the preceding century and six years less than in the eighteenth. Generation life tables of the British peerage suggest that expectation of life at birth was thirty-three years among males born between 1680 and 1729, but almost forty-five years (44·8) among those born between 1730 and 1779 If violent deaths are not included, male life expectancy at birth for those born between 1330 and 1679 remained in the range of thirty or thirty-one years. One may infer from these diverse data that life expectancy at birth probably did not exceed thirty-five years in any country before the late-eighteenth century.

Our second source of information is the statistics available for the age composition of pre-industrial Europe as well as Japan, a country whose people controlled their numbers. Persons aged fifteen to sixty-four constituted 60·5 and 62 per cent, respectively, of Sweden's population in 1750 and 1800; 62·2 and 61·4 per cent of France's population in 1775 and 1801; and 58·4 and 60·8 per cent of Japan's population in the eighth century and 1888. The proportion of the Danish population aged fifteen to sixty-four in 1787 was similar to that in Sweden in 1750. Iceland's population in 1703 included a larger proportion aged fifteen to sixty-four. Data on the age composition of eighteenth-century Europe suggest, when contrasted with those in Table 2 discussed below, that this age composition was more favourable to economic production than that now found in much of the underdeveloped world with its high fertility and relatively low mortality. Although the conditions that made for high mortality and, hence, for a relatively low proportion of persons under fifteen years of age must have debilitated the population in some degree, they could hardly have offset the advantages derived from a low rate of population growth.[9]

Thus, the age composition of populations in Western European countries was favourable to average productivity. It is difficult, of course, to assess the change in age composition that took place after the adoption of the unique Western European pattern of marriage. This may have increased the favourableness of the age composition by at least three units, or about 5 per cent. If per-capita productivity rose correspondingly, the rate of saving could have increased by a larger fraction. In any case, until late in the eighteenth century, the slow rate of population growth permitted savings to be devoted almost entirely to improving productive capital per head. This slowness also held down the rate of increase in population pressure, perhaps sufficiently to permit improvement in yields to offset small increases in population.

YESTERDAY'S EUROPE VERSUS TODAY'S AFRICA AND ASIA

Today the economic distance separating various parts of the underdeveloped world from various parts of the developed world is many times what it was two to three centuries ago. At one time, this distance might have been easily bridged. Had, as late as 1800, the index of performance in the most advanced lands been four times that in the least advanced, and had this index continued to improve at a rate of 1·5 per cent per year in the more advanced countries, the laggard countries might have caught up by the early-twentieth century. This did not happen. The index rose most rapidly in the advanced countries. Today real private consumption per head is between six and thirty-one times as high in Northern and Western

[9] Data on natality and mortality in this and the two preceding paragraphs are based upon United Nations, *Population Bulletin*, Nos. 6 and 7; Glass, 'World Population, 1800–1950', *Population in History*, pp. 14, 52–7, 79–86, 98, 134, 215, 241, 274, 282, 304–7, 358–9, 446, 467, 469, 474–506, 506, 538, 555, 562–87; articles by H. Gille and H. Hyriennius, in *Population Studies*, Vol. 3 (1949), pp. 3–65, Vol. 4 (1951), pp. 421–31; R. R. Kuczynski, *The Balance of Births and Deaths*, Vol. 1 (Washington, 1928), pp. 6–7, 39, 94; L. I. Dublin, A. J. Lotka, and M. Spiegelman, *Length of Life* (2nd ed.; New York, 1949), pp. 41–3, 348–51; Peter Laslett, *The World We Have Lost* (London, 1965), pp. 93–4; Irene Taeuber, *The Population of Japan* (Princeton, 1958), pp. 10, 46.

Europe as it is in various underdeveloped countries; it is even higher in the United States. The increase in spread is the result of what was done in the European sphere and not done in the underdeveloped world. In the latter category must be included failure to curtail fertility.

Agricultural population density increased faster in Asia than in Europe. By 1948, it was nearly double that in Africa and Europe, exclusive of the Soviet Union (147 per square kilometre of available land in Asia as contrasted with 83 and 86 in Africa and Europe).[10] Over three fifths of the labour force of Africa and Asia remained in agriculture, although output per agriculturalist and per acre remained low, often too low, to supply minimum nutritional requirements.

Population grew faster during the nineteenth century in Europe than it did in the underdeveloped countries, with their high levels of mortality. This relationship was eventually altered. Mortality declined in European countries, but so did the birth rates. Today the rate of population growth is much higher in the underdeveloped world than elsewhere and is a number of times what it was in pre-1800 Western Europe. Most Gross Reproduction Rates in Africa, mainland Asia, and Latin America fall within a range of 2·5 to 3·5; expectation of life at birth falls below forty years in Africa, between forty and fifty years in Asia, and between fifty and fifty-five in Latin America. The rate of natural increase per decade between 1970 and 2000 is expected to range from around 20 per cent in Asia to around 30 per cent in South America and, perhaps, Africa. These prospective rates, roughly double what they were in the period 1920–40, reflect declines in crude mortality uncompensated by declines in natality. These high rates of population growth will absorb much of the capital that is formed in the underdeveloped world and hence will greatly retard growth of output per head.

The age composition of the present-day underdeveloped countries is much less favourable to productivity than that encountered in the developed world or in European countries during their pre-industrial stage. As of 1965, the fraction formed by the population fifteen to sixty-four years was as follows: East Asia (exclusive of Japan), 52·5 per cent; South Asia, 54·7 per cent; Africa, 54·2 per cent, ranging from 51·7 per cent in West Africa to 56·1 per cent in Eastern Africa; Central America, 50·8 per cent; Tropical South America, 53·4 per cent; Caribbean America, 56 per cent. The Philippines is exemplary, for the current fraction, 53 per cent, is much below the 57·2 per cent reported for 1903, but is consistent with

[10] United Nations, *The Determinants and Consequences of Population Trends*, Population Studies, No. 17 (New York, 1953), p. 269.

an estimated birth rate in the upper-forties and a death rate in the low-twenties.

These percentages are compatible with current estimates of gross reproduction (2·5 to 3·0 in Africa and 2·5 to 3·5 in Asia and Latin America) and life expectancy at birth (around or below forty years in Africa; forty to fifty in Asia; fifty to fifty-five in Latin America). In Table 2, GRR and life expectancies are combined to yield stable populations and the percentages of the population aged fifteen to sixty-four. (In parentheses, we give the approximate rates of natural increase associated with these combinations.) The data suggest that in Africa the fraction aged fifteen to sixty-four will range between 55 and 58 per cent; in Asia, between 50 and 58 per cent; and in Latin America, between 49 and 56 per cent.

Table 2   Proportions aged 15–64 years: rates of growth

	Expectation of life at birth		
GRR	40	50	55
2·5	58(15)	56(22)	56(23)
3·0	55(22)	53(28)	52(31)
3·5	52(27)	50(34)	49(37)

The relatively low rates of fertility and natural increase—in part the result of the unique fertility-regulating pattern of marriage that developed in Europe during the fifteenth or sixteenth centuries—must have contributed greatly to the growth of average income in the seventeenth and eighteenth centuries. The sustained increase in average income did not, of course, give rise to the Industrial Revolution, for this revolution, unlike the minor ones of the twelfth, fifteenth and seventeenth centuries, was a *revolutionary* transformation of the British and Western European economies. It was the product of many cooperating factors (capital accumulation, inventions, innovations, favourable factor endowments, *laissez faire*, market expansion, earlier experience, and so forth). Among its causes was the relatively low level of fertility existing in Western Europe. Because fertility was low, the relative number of persons of productive age and, hence, the potential productivity per head were high. Natural increase also was low, so that the pressure of population upon agricultural land did not build up rapidly and nearly all savings could be devoted to improving the stock of capital instead of supporting population growth. Average income could rise, albeit slowly and somewhat intermittently, and pave the way for the coming of the Industrial Revolution.

David M. Heer

Economic development and the fertility transition

Population theorists have developed contrasting views concerning the effect that economic development, or increase in per-capita income, has on fertility. One school contends that economic development inhibits fertility. This view, perhaps predominant in recent years, is expressed most succinctly in the theory of demographic transition set forth by Warren S. Thompson, C. P. Blacker, Kingsley Davis, Frank Notestein, and others.[1] According to this theory, a nation's demographic process depends on its stage of industrialization and, by implication, its level of economic development. Warren Thompson and Kingsley Davis, for example, divide the nations of the world into three classes. Class I nations are highly industrialized, have low fertility and mortality, and show little or no population growth; Class II nations are beginning the process of industrialization, have declining although still high fertility, rapidly declining mortality, but, in net balance, a high rate of population growth; Class III nations are not yet industrialized, have both high fertility and high mortality, and, at most, only moderate population growth. The theory of demographic transition, popularized around the time of World War II, is congruent with the generally inverse association between fertility level and degree of industrialization among nations today. Indeed fertility levels of industrialized nations are lower than they were before the nations became industrialized.

A second school of thought, however, argues that economic development promotes fertility. Perhaps the foremost representative of this viewpoint was the English economist T. R. Malthus. He believed that an increase in the demand for labour increased the proportion of persons marrying and reduced the average age at marriage, and that this change in marriage pattern led in turn to

---

[1] See Warren S. Thompson, *Population and Peace in the Pacific* (Chicago, 1946), pp. 22–35; C. P. Blacker, 'Stages in Population Growth', *Eugenics Review*, Vol. 39, No. 3 (October 1947), pp. 88–102; Kingsley Davis, *Human Society* (New York, 1949), pp. 603–8; Frank W. Notestein, 'The Economics of Population and Food Supplies', *Proceedings of the Eighth International Conference of Agricultural Economists* (London, 1953), pp. 15–31.

an increase in fertility.[2] Because Malthus lived during the middle of the Industrial Revolution in England, his views were presumably coloured by what he conceived to be recent trends in fertility in his own country. Later critics of Malthus, considering his views on the relation between fertility and economic development to be erroneous, generally attributed the large acceleration in population growth which accompanied the Industrial Revolution exclusively to lowered mortality. Several historical demographers have, however, recently produced evidence indicating that fertility may well have increased during England's period of industrial development in the early-nineteenth century,[3] and that similar increases may have occurred in parts of the Netherlands.[4]

Support for the school of thought linking fertility increase to economic development has also been supplied by studies indicating a relationship between birth and marriage rates and business cycles.[5] Virginia Galbraith and Dorothy Thomas have demonstrated that business cycles in the United States between 1919 and 1927 affected both marriages and births. With an appropriate time lag, marriages and births of each parity increased when business conditions improved and declined when business fell off.[6] Dudley Kirk analysed the situation in Germany during the 1920s and arrived at similar conclusions.[7] Researchers working with such data from other countries have in all cases shown a positive correlation between birth and marriage rates and the height of the business cycle.[8]

Evidence that economic development promotes fertility also comes from other types of studies. From his analysis of both the influence of general business conditions on fertility and the effects of the relative demand for labour on young persons of reproductive age, Richard Easterlin hypothesizes that the high wage and salary levels of persons twenty to twenty-nine years old was one of the

---

[2] Thomas R. Malthus, *An Essay on Population* (New York, 1914), Vol. 1, pp. 167, 277–8; Vol. 2, pp. 27–8, 132, 140, 230–1.

[3] J. T. Krause, 'Some Implications of Recent Work in Historical Demography', *Comparative Studies in Society and History*, Vol. 1, No. 2 (January 1954), pp. 164–88; H. J. Habakkuk, 'English Population in the 18th Century', *Economic History Review*, Vol. 6, No. 2 (December 1953), pp. 117–33.

[4] William Petersen, 'The Demographic Transition in the Netherlands', *American Sociological Review*, Vol. 25, No. 3 (June 1960), pp. 334–47.

[5] In citing studies whose conclusions can be interpreted as lending support to the Malthusian theory of a direct relation between economic development and fertility, I do not wish to imply that the authors of the studies necessarily themselves subscribe in whole or in part to Malthus's views in this regard.

[6] Virginia Galbraith and Dorothy S. Thomas, 'Birth Rates and the Interwar Business Cycles', *Journal of the American Statistical Association*, Vol. 36 (December 1941), pp. 465–76.

[7] Dudley Kirk, 'The Relation of Employment Levels to Births in Germany', *Milbank Memorial Fund Quarterly*, Vol. 28 (April 1942), pp. 126–38.

[8] For further bibliography on this topic, see Ronald Freedman, 'The Sociology of Human Fertility', *Current Sociology*, Vol. 10/11, No. 2 (1961–62), p. 108.

prime factors sustaining the American baby boom of the 1950s. The number of persons in this age group was exceptionally low because of the small number of babies born during the Depression. The supply of new entrants to the labour force was, therefore, abnormally reduced during the 1950s, a period when demand for labour was high. Moreover, the group entering the labour force in the 1950s was exceptionally well educated in comparison with older age groups and thus has a competitive advantage in employment during a period in which educational qualifications became increasingly important.[9]

A recent study by W. Stys further supports the conclusion that a high economic level increases fertility. Stys has shown that for Polish peasant women born during the latter half of the nineteenth century, average completed family size varied with size of farm. Among landless peasants, the average number of births per mother was 3·9; on farms of more than seven hectares, the average number was 9·1. The difference in fertility by size of farm results mostly from variations in the mother's age at marriage. There was, nevertheless, some tendency for births per year of marriage to be slightly higher among women living on the larger farms.[10]

The results of surveys conducted by Gordon De Jong imply that respondents of each social class would increase their fertility as their economic circumstances improved and would reduce it were their economic circumstances to decline. De Jong asked respondents in the Southern Appalachian region of the United States what they considered to be the ideal number of children for the average young couple today, for a 'well-off' young couple, and for a 'not well-off' couple. The respondents in the study believed that the ideal number of children for the 'not well-off' couple would be 1·5; for the average couple, 2·79; and for the 'well-off' couple, 4·02. Similar results were obtained separately for respondents of each social class.[11]

Deborah Freedman has been concerned with the extent to which the husband's 'relative income' affects fertility of individual married couples in the United States.[12] (By 'relative income' she means the degree to which the husband's actual income exceeded or was exceeded by that of men in his socio-economic reference group—that is, men of similar age, occupation, income, and region of residence.) Her analysis was made with data from a national

[9] Richard Easterlin, *The American Baby Boom in Historical Perspective* (New York, 1962).

[10] W. Stys, 'The Influence of Economic Conditions on the Fertility of Peasant Women', *Population Studies*, Vol. 11, No. 2 (November 1957), pp. 136–48.

[11] Gordon De Jong, 'Religious Fundamentalism, Socio-economic Status, and Fertility Attitudes in the Southern Appalachians', *Demography*, Vol. 2 (1965), pp. 540–8.

[12] Deborah S. Freedman, 'The Relation of Economic Status to Fertility', *American Economic Review*, Vol. 53, No. 3 (June 1963), pp. 414–26.

probability sample of fecund, white, non-farm wives eighteen to thirty-nine years old married at least five years. After controls for thirteen other relevant variables, she found that the number of children born to the wife was positively related to the magnitude of the husband's relative income. After ten years of marriage wives whose husband's relative income was low had 0·42 less children than would have been expected on the basis of the other variables; conversely, wives whose husband's relative income was high had 0·21 more children than would have been expected.

The two contrasting views concerning the effect of economic development on fertility obviously demand reconciliation. I have elsewhere hypothesized that economic development directly increases fertility, although various other factors usually accompanying the process of economic development serve to reduce fertility.[13] The indirect effects of economic development tending to reduce fertility are often, albeit not invariably, stronger than the direct effect tending to raise it. Thus, economic development frequently results in fertility decline.[14] Making use of data for forty-one nations during the 1950s, I found that the average level of national fertility was inversely associated with per-capita net national product when no other variables were held constant. The relation between the two variables was slightly positive, however, after instituting controls for other relevant variables—the level of infant mortality, per-capita newspaper circulation, population density, and the recent percentage increase in per-capita energy consumption. Controlling for these other variables, I found that per capita newspaper circulation and population density were inversely related to fertility, and that infant mortality and recent increase in per

[13] See David M. Heer, 'Economic Development and Fertility', *Demography*, Vol. 3, No. 2 (1966), pp. 423–44, where I set forth a theory which attempts to harmonise these contrasting views and offer empirical evidence of a new theory's validity.

[14] Actually there are four possible versions of this hypothesis. In the first version, we refer to one national population over time and examine the effect of aggregate economic development and the aggregate factors accompanying it on aggregate trends in fertility. In the second, we look at the effect of the aggregate level of economic development and its accompanying factors on the aggregate level of fertility in a set of national populations at a particular time. In a third version, we look at the effect of economic development and its accompanying factors on an individual basis—individual change in income and style of life associated with that income—on individual fertility for a group of persons over time. In the fourth version, we examine the effect of the individual level of economic development and its accompanying factors on individual fertility for a group of persons at a given moment in time. Ansley Coale has correctly pointed out that a demonstration of the truth of one of these versions does not necessarily constitute proof of any other version. The results contained in my article 'Economic Development and Fertility' are pertinent only to the second version, whereas my main interest in this essay is the first version of the hypothesis. Some of the other studies I have cited are pertinent to the third and fourth versions.

capita energy consumption were directly related. After control for other variables, infant mortality showed a stronger relation to fertility than any of the other four variables. Increase in educational attainment, for which per-capita newspaper circulation is a good index, and decline in infant and early childhood mortality are, of course, two of the most pervasive phenomena accompanying economic development.

An understanding of the biological factors which constrain fertility is necessary to any analysis of fertility change. Nevertheless, fertility cannot be fully explained unless voluntary decisions concerning future children are also considered. Biological factors clearly place an upper bound on the fertility of each individual. Below the limit of biologically maximum fertility (probably around twelve births for the average woman)[15], each individual is more or less free to choose how many babies to have. Excess fertility can always be avoided even though the price for doing so may be great. To consider two extreme examples, couples can refrain from sexual intercourse to avoid a further pregnancy, and the pregnant woman can decide to abort the fetus even at the risk of her own life.

Joseph Spengler has devised an excellent conceptual scheme for analysing the factors affecting the decision to have children.[16] He considers the decision to have an additional child to be a function of three variables: the preference system, the price system, and income. Provided these terms are given a broader definition than they usually receive in economic literature, the three concepts provide a complete classification of all factors that affect such a decision. The preference system simply describes the value a married couple places on an additional child relative to the value of goals they might otherwise achieve. The price system delineates the cost of an additional child relative to the cost of attaining other goals that might be achieved were the decision to have another child not made. Costs must be broadly defined to include not only monetary costs, but expenditures of time and effort. Income, too, must be broadly defined so that it encompasses monetary income as well as the total amount of time and energy available to a couple in their pursuit of possible goals. (Because the term *resources* fits the definition more closely than the term *income*, I shall henceforth refer to the former rather than the latter.) Given these definitions, the probability of deciding in favour of another child will vary di-

[15] See J. W. Eaton and A. J. Mayer, 'The Social Biology of Very High Fertility Among the Hutterites', *Human Biology*, Vol. 25 (1953), pp. 206–63.

[16] Joseph J. Spengler, 'Values and Fertility Analysis', *Demography*, Vol. 3, No. 1 (1966), pp. 109–30.

rectly with the relative value anticipated from that child, inversely with the predicted relative cost, and directly with the amount of resources foreseen as available for all goals.[17]

Spengler's scheme should prove to be useful in analysing the long-term changes in fertility in the now developed countries during the last century or so and in demonstrating further the thesis that economic development directly enhances fertility, but has indirect effects that lead to fertility decline. Any explanation of the variables accounting for the long-term fertility change in the developed nations should, however, be postponed until the magnitude of this change has been described. The accompanying graph shows,

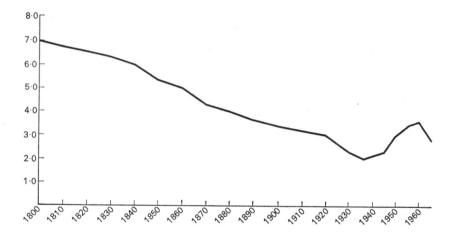

Figure 1   Total fertility rate for the white population of the United States, 1800–1965

Sources: Ansley J. Coale and Melvin Zelnik, *New Estimates of Fertility and Population in the United States* (Princeton, 1963), p. 36; U.S. National Center for Health Statistics, *Monthly Vital Statistics Report,* Vol. 15, No. 11 Supplement (February 1967).

for example, the change in the total fertility rate for white women in the United States between 1800 and 1965. The total fertility rate for a given year is a summary measure of fertility, which can best be described as the total number of children a woman would have were she to live through the entire reproductive period and bear children at the average rate for that time. As one can see from this graph, the decline in the total fertility rate from 1800 to 1965 has been very pronounced. The regularity of the decline, however, is distinctly marred by the dramatic fertility rise during the 1940s and 1950s. Since 1957, the trend of fertility decline has been re-

[17] I shall ignore the possibility that children are an 'inferior good' so that as income rises children are substituted for more desirable objects which give the same sort of satisfaction only in higher degree. I do not consider this to be a realistic assumption.

newed, and from 1964 to 1965 the United States experienced the sharpest annual percentage fertility decline in its entire history (almost 8 per cent).

It should not be supposed that the temporal pattern of fertility decline has been identical in all of the developed nations. The magnitude of the decline was greater in the United States than in Europe. Furthermore, fertility reduction began much earlier in France and the United States than in Great Britain, where decline dates only from 1876,[18] even though England industrialized much earlier. Moreover, the baby boom following World War II was much more pronounced in the United States than it was in Europe.

The developed nations have a long history of increasing per-capita monetary income. According to Simon Kuznets, the average decennial rate of growth in per-capita national product in the United States between 1839 and 1960–62 was more than 17 per cent, a rate sufficient to increase per-capita product 4·9 times per century.[19] The developed nations also have a long history of decreasing hours devoted to gainful employment and increasing amounts of leisure time. Had there been no change in either the price or preference system, one might have expected that the long-term trend in fertility would have been upward. Since fertility has tended over the long run to go down rather than up, changes in the preference and price system must have discouraged rather than encouraged fertility to an extent that they counterbalanced the elevating effects of increased money and leisure time.

On the other hand, the developed nations which did not suffer severely from World War II (United States, Canada, Australia, and New Zealand) underwent a substantial rise in fertility during the 1940s and 1950s. As I have noted earlier, Easterlin has provided extensive documentation that this period of rising fertility was also one of rapid rise in monetary income for young adults in the United States.[20] During the period of the baby boom in the United States, the amount of time, money, and effort available for child-rearing activities was markedly expanded by the increased willingness and ability of grandparents to help their married children in child-care responsibilities. The grandparents of the postwar baby crop had had relatively few children themselves and, therefore, probably welcomed the chance to share in the work of raising their grandchildren. Moreover, even though the number of children per parent was quite high during the 1950s, the number per grandparent was

[18] A. M. Carr-Saunders, *World Population: Past Growth and Present Trends* (London, 1964), p. 92.
[19] Simon Kuznets, *Postwar Economic Growth: Four Lectures* (Cambridge, 1964), p. 64.
[20] Easterlin, *The American Baby Boom in Historical Perspective.*

not large since the number in the parental generation was so small. Thus, grandparents could make a large contribution to the rearing of each grandchild in a way that will not, for example, be possible for the grandparents of the 1970s. We may therefore presume that during the period of the baby boom the elevating effects of rising resources more than counterbalanced any depressing effects of changes in the preference or price system.

In the last hundred years or so, several changes in the preference system of the developed nations have undoubtedly tended to reduce family size. One of the most important of these is the decline in mortality, which has of course been pronounced. In the United States for example, the mean expectation of life at birth increased from 47·3 years in 1900 to 70·2 years in 1964.[21] The secular (long-term) decline in mortality has had greater relative effect in infancy and childhood than adulthood. If fertility had not declined, the reduction in mortality would have tended to increase somewhat the number of living children per living parent. The United Nations estimates that for a population with high fertility (a Gross Reproduction Rate of 2·5) and very high mortality (life expectation at birth of twenty years). the ratio of population under fifteen years to that aged fifteen to fifty-nine years is 0·56. When the expectation of life at birth is increased to seventy years with no change in fertility, the ratio is increased to 0·83.[22] Thus one would expect the value of an additional birth to wane as the level of mortality declines.

There is also a possible connection between the level of mortality and the amount of emotional energy that parents invest in each of their children. It may be supposed that the pain of bereavement at a child's death is directly proportional to the amount of emotional energy that the parents have invested in the child. Where mortality levels are high, one might expect parents, in the interest of self-protection, to develop relatively little emotional involvement in any one child. A reduction in mortality encourages parents to place more libido in the existing children and thus should reduce their desire to have an additional child, since they have limited amounts of emotional energy.[23]

Lowering the mortality level should also reduce the desire for additional children because parents can be more certain of having a specified minimum number of children survive to maturity. When

[21] U.S. Public Health Service, *Vital Statistics of the United States, 1964*, Vol. 2, Section 5, Life Tables, p. 12.

[22] United Nations, Department of Economic and Social Affairs, *The Aging of Populations and Its Economic and Social Implications* (New York, 1956), pp. 26–7.

[23] This idea was first advanced in an oral communication by Dr. Laila Sh. El Hamamsy, Director of the Social Research Center, American University, Cairo, Egypt.

mortality is high, one cannot be sure that any of one's existing children will survive to maturity. When mortality is as low as it is in the developed nations, parents can be highly certain that their child will survive from birth to maturity. Thus, a decline in mortality reduces the value of an additional child as insurance against the possibility that one or more of the existing children may die. The effect of mortality reduction in this respect can be quantitatively measured. If one assumes that each couple is capable of bearing twelve children, that a perfect means of birth control is available and utilized, and that all couples want to be 95 per cent certain of having at least one son who will survive to the father's sixty-fifth birthday, the Gross Reproduction Rate will fall from 5·2 when the expectation of life at birth is twenty years to 0·95 when the expectation of life rises to seventy-four years.[24]

A second long-term change in the preference system relates to the value which parents can derive from the productive labour of their children. In the agrarian society of the United States in the eighteenth century, when the supply of land was practically unlimited, children could be productive assets to their parents at a very early age. As the amount of land per capita declined, as it did in the United States during the nineteenth century, the value to the farmer of the labour of an additional child probably declined correspondingly. In all of the developed nations, industrialization substantially reduced the value of child labour. Although such labour was quite common in many of the early factories, the situation of the child in the factory was much less satisfactory than it was when he worked under the direction of his father on the family farm. As a result, strong moral sentiment developed against child labour, and legislation restricting it emerged in all of the developed nations. In each nation, the development of this legislation was very gradual, and the early regulations were much less restrictive than later laws. The first legislation in England, passed in 1817, merely banned children under nine years of age from working in cotton mills. In the United States, the first mildly restrictive legislation appeared in a few northern states about the middle of the nineteenth century.[25] Only in 1938 did the United States Federal Government enact child-labour regulations; these prohibited the employment of children under sixteen in manufacturing or mining and banned the employment of children under fourteen from all industry, except agriculture, which engaged in interstate commerce.[26]

[24] David M. Heer and Dean O. Smith, 'Mortality Level and Desired Family Size', *Indian Demographic Bulletin*, Vol. 1, No. 1 (1968).
[25] United States Children's Bureau. *Child Labour: Facts and Figures*, Publication No. 197. (Washington, D.C., 1930), pp. 2–5.
[26] Florence Taylor, *Child Labour Fact Book: 1900–1950* (New York, 1950).

The utility of child labour was further reduced by compulsory education laws which, as they increased in severity, also lowered the productive value to the parents of an additional child. Prussia, under the leadership of Frederick the Great, became in 1763 the first nation to legislate compulsory attendance at school for all persons five to fourteen years of age. The first law establishing compulsory school attendance in England was enacted in 1876. In the United States, Massachusetts became in 1852 the first state to demand school attendance; similar legislation did not become universal until 1918, when attendance was finally made compulsory in Mississippi.[27]

The development of formal institutions to support the elderly has also brought about substantial changes in the value of an additional child. In the pre-industrial period and in the early stages of the Industrial Revolution, the elderly could expect to receive financial support only from their own kin—mainly from their sons. Gradually business corporations and governments developed social-security schemes for the aged and for widows. In the United Kingdom, legislation establishing old-age pensions for needy persons was first enacted in 1908, and in 1925 a contributory system covering all workers was established. In the United States, the first federal legislation concerning old-age, survivors', or disability pensions dates from 1935, although many private corporations provided pensions and insurance systems much earlier.[28] With the full development of social security, it became unnecessary for parents to bear children in sufficient number to assure that one or more sons would support them in their old age. Thus, the value to parents of additional children has been further diminished.

The preference system has also been altered by the decline in social rewards for bearing a large number of children. When mortality was high, a high rate of fertility was a positive necessity if the population was not to decline. Governmental and religious authorities who did not wish to see the nation's population reduced encouraged a high level of fertility. As mortality declined, however, a high level of fertility was no longer necessary to maintain the existing population level. As a result, many governments and religious bodies have shifted from a position favouring large families to one of neutrality or even opposition. A historic landmark was reached when the Church of England admitted at its Lambeth Conference of 1930 that mechanical or chemical means of contra-

[27] H. G. Good, *A History of Western Education* (New York, 1960), pp. 318, 356, 450; 'Education in the United States', *Collier's Encyclopedia* (1959), Vol. 7, pp. 79–93.
[28] 'Social Security', *Encyclopedia Britannica* (1967), Vol. 20, pp. 762–9.

ception were not necessarily immoral.[29] Since that time, the Protestant churches have, for the most part, ceased to extol the virtue of large families, and in the present decade the Roman Catholic Church has been faced with a great internal struggle, as yet unresolved, concerning this question. Although no European government has become alarmed about problems of excess fertility—all, in fact, encourage large families through their programmes of family allowances—the United States has for the first time, under the Johnson Administration, provided federal funds for the establishment of family-planning clinics, thus indicating that it no longer wishes to encourage large families, at least among the poor.

A fifth possible change in the preference system may be the result of a tendency for economic development to shift the criteria for social status from ascribed characteristics (such as birth into a particular family) to achievement. Where status is ascribed at birth, one need spend little effort in advertising one's status to others; where status is achieved, its level tends to be transitory, and individuals may develop an intense need for conspicuous consumption to demonstrate their rank. If the preference for conspicuous consumption increases, the preference for children, who do little to publicize one's status, should decline. J. A. Banks has provided extensive documentation to show that during the latter years of the Victorian Era, the British middle class felt an increasing need to engage in conspicuous consumption, and that English fertility first began its decline during this period.

The tremendous development of new and improved methods of birth control over the last century has not only reduced the relative preference for children, but has also increased their price relative to that of other goals. When available methods of birth control are crude and undeveloped, or knowledge of better methods is lacking the decision not to have an additional child involves substantial inconvenience, interference with sexual pleasure, or even some hazard to health and life incurred by resort to a primitive means of abortion. Some of the major landmarks in the development of contraceptive technology during the last century were the manufacture of rubber condoms in the late-nineteenth century, the invention of a diaphragm by Mesinga in 1880, and in the 1930s the appearance of the latex condom, which was cheaper and better than its rubber predecessor.[30] Increasing use of the highly effective

[29] Richard M. Fagley, *The Population Explosion and Christian Responsibility* (New York, 1960), pp. 194–5.
[30] For extensive accounts of the history of contraception, see Norman E. Himes, *Medical History of Contraception* (New York, 1963), and Elizabeth Draper, *Birth Control in the Modern World* (London, 1965).

oral contraceptives in the United States and other nations during the 1960s reduced the penalties in deciding against another child and may have been one of the major reasons for sharp fertility decline. Although the 'pill' was placed on the United States market only in 1960, by 1965 it was the most popular contraceptive, the method used most recently by 24 per cent of white wives eighteen to thirty-nine years of age.[31] Abortion has also been one of the principal means of birth control, and improvements in its technology have probably affected the preference for children. Little has been written about this, however, and it is difficult to ascertain the history of abortion techniques in those nations where the purposeful disruption of pregnancy is for the most part illegal.

Economic development has produced other changes in the price system affecting desired family size. Urbanization has been one of the most important concomitants of economic development. In the United States, the proportion of the population classified as urban increased from 5 to 70 per cent between 1790 and 1960.[32] In general, urbanization results in a rise in the relative price of living space. Since rearing of children demands considerable living space, the relative cost of children no doubt rises with each increase in the relative price of living space. Although the relative cost of living space has in general been increasing over the last hundred years, the rise has, perhaps, not been invariant. One may speculate that the increasingly widespread use of the automobile in the United States during the 1940s and 1950s, together with governmental policies which subsidized home-ownership, made possible the acquisition of suburban houses at a relative cost probably substantially lower than prevailed during previous decades. Part of the American baby boom of the 1940s and 1950s may be explained by this short-term change in the relative cost of living space.

The tendency for the labour cost of child care to rise relative to the labour cost of producing material goods no doubt is a factor affecting desired family size. While economic development makes possible a much larger production of factory goods per man-hour of labour, the number of man-hours necessary to supervise and socialise a child has certainly not declined and most probably has risen. When a married couple are deciding whether to have another child, they can assume that an additional child will burden the wife with the responsibilities of child care for about three years. Moreover, with another child to supervise, she will have to work harder during the period when the older children are still under her care.

[31] Charles F. Westoff and Norman B. Ryder, 'United States: Methods of Fertility Control, 1955, 1960, & 1965', *Studies in Family Planning*, No. 17 (February 1967).
[32] U.S. Bureau of the Census. *United States Census of Population, 1960*, Vol. 1, Part 1, p. 4.

This increased effort must be set against the possible remuneration from a job. Since the amount of material goods which can be bought with each hour of labour outside the home has steadily increased with each advance in national economic level, there has been a substantial long-term increase in the price of child-care services relative to the price of material goods.

A final long-term change in the price system affecting the decision to have children concerns the quality of education which parents demand for their children and which is socially imposed. A society more and more oriented to a complex technology requires that children be given an increasingly lengthy education. Parents recognize that their own child will be at a substantial disadvantage unless his education meets society's new norm. Even where the direct cost of education is met by the state, longer education increases the cost to the parent in terms of more years of child dependency. Hence the secular rise in the standard of education has no doubt helped to depress family size.

The factors connected with industrial development which I have listed have, in my opinion, tended to depress fertility to such an extent that the actual trend has usually been downward despite the elevating effect increased resources have had on fertility. It is not yet possible to evaluate the importance of the role each of these factors has played in the temporal changes in fertility in the developed nations during the past century or more. Although their relative importance may never be well established, further historical research may be of great value. I would recommend, in particular, detailed study correlating fertility change with such matters as the development of social-security systems, the decline in the prevalence of child labour, increases in the proportion of children attending school, changes in the relative cost of living space, and augmentation of the relative labour cost of child care.

Analysis of the past can be of some help in predicting the future course of fertility in both the more developed nations and in those currently less developed. For the economically advanced nations, certain of the factors which have operated in the past will in the future operate with much diminished force. It is, for example, impossible for infant and childhood mortality to drop much further. Again, provision for old-age security is now almost completely divorced from the extended kin-group, and little further shift from kin-group responsibility can be expected. Moreover, child labour has been practically eliminated, and additional change in this will be of no further importance to fertility. Thus, for the economically developed nations, at least three factors important in the past reduction of fertility will have little impact on the course of future fertility.

This might tempt one to predict that if per-capita income continues to rise in these nations, fertility will also rise. We should, however, be able to count on the continuation of certain trends which in the past have been inimical to high fertility. Most of these trends affect the price system. Since the ideal means of birth control has not yet been invented, we can anticipate some decline in fertility with each successive step toward this ideal. We can also predict that the mother's opportunity cost for spending time in child-rearing activities will continue to climb since the price of material goods will most probably continue to fall relative to that of providing child-care services. The demand for a higher level of education will in all likelihood also continue. Unless the cost of such education is completely socialized, this demand should constitute additional pressure for fertility decline. Barring unforeseen developments in transportation technology, increasing population density should make inevitable a further increase in the relative cost of living space, an important component of the total cost of rearing children. Finally, we can, I think, be fairly confident that public opinion will take an increasingly negative stance towards large family size. A withdrawal of social rewards for a large number of children might have a substantial effect on fertility preference. I believe that the public will be more and more aware of the taxes necessary to support population growth, of the ways in which a larger population aggravates urban congestion and crowds detract from the enjoyment of places of prime historic and scenic interest. If, however, the level of international tension is exacerbated, a contrary pressure in favour of larger families might ensue since each nation might fear that its power relative to other nations would diminish were its relative population size to fall.

The long-run fertility trend in the now industrialized nations will, I think, not be upward. Nevertheless, it is certainly plausible to assume that fertility may rise in several of these nations for certain short-run periods. For the less developed nations, it seems very probable that further progress in economic level should bring substantial fertility decline. In these nations, economic development should have all of the indirect effects that it had previously in Europe and North America. In many of these nations, there will also be governmental programmes encouraging small families. Furthermore, the technology of birth control is now more advanced than it was when fertility first began to decline in the West; thus, the mere introduction of the new birth-control methods may bring moderate fertility reduction into populations only weakly motivated to reduce family size. The real question for the less developed nations is whether they will be able to attain a further measure of economic development. It is, of course, not impossible that in at least some of these nations population growth will outstrip the increase in the means of subsistence. If lower living standards ensue, the level of mortality may be greatly affected. Given a rise in infant and childhood mortality, it may then be impossible to obtain fertility decline.

John T. Noonan, Jr.

Intellectual and demographic history

I

The number of human births and deaths and the number of living human beings can be recorded, calculated, or estimated for various places and periods. To the historian, the tabulations made constitute data. They are pieces of evidence which he must question for their own built-in assumptions and then fit with the evidence offered by other disciplines from geography to theology in order to carry out his job of describing human action. This historical task necessarily will involve postulating motives, purposes, valuations, and rationality in the men whose actions are described. If the historian is writing about human action in relation to population, his job is to weigh the evidence and to estimate the elements of human response that are reflected in a particular birth rate or a particular growth. The rates of births and deaths are precious material for him, but the answers to his questions come only from an interrogation of all the evidence available.

Among the evidence, fragile, intangible, and nonquantifiable, are human ideas themselves. That ideas affect behaviour is, I suppose, the assumption of everyone who writes history. At the very least, economic historians endow human beings with an economic rationality that leads men to match their behaviour to their financial prospects. In the writing of demographic history, hypotheses as to the casuality of economic calculations predominate, possibly because of the academic antecedents of demography and demographers. If a close correlation is found between the births and some economic factor—the price of grain, the size of a lot, the index of industrial production—it is often thought that the reason for a change in births has been satisfactorily accounted for. It is often assumed that some kind of economic rationality determines human habits of breeding. Such economic rationality is itself a type of idea or system of ideas.

Demographers who think of their work with contemporary data

as a science have difficulty understanding what a historian is interested in.   They are used to proceeding on the principle of parsimony—Ockham's old principle that entities are not to be multiplied in causal explanations. In applying this principle they are apt to look first to a demographic factor—if the number of births goes down and the number of marriages is found also to have decreased, the latter phenomenon may be taken as the cause of the former. If the demographic factor is not found, they turn most readily to an economic explanation, sometimes with the unexpressed conviction that, at bottom, economic reasons underlie human actions. They seek to demonstrate their causal hypotheses quantitatively. They are accustomed to measurement and are content only if measurable relationships can be worked out.

When these assumptions, useful for prediction and control purposes in a laboratory, are transferred to history, there is danger of grave distortion. Historians do not believe in multiplying causes needlessly, but they are aware that in most persons and in most societies a multiplicity of interacting, reinforcing, counterchecking forces are at play. Parsimony is a poor principle if it suppresses part of the play.

Quantitative measurement, desirable if attainable, is not the only tool for understanding the acts of human beings. Ideas other than demographic observation or economic estimations are operative in the behaviour of men. That such non-economic ideas affect births and deaths as well as other human activities does not, *a priori*, seem unlikely. The extent and force of these ideas and their effect on population may be expected to vary with the ideas and with the people holding them. Competing ideas exist in the same society and in the same men, and to take ideas into account is not to measure phenomena, but to grasp a complex structure of interactions. In a complicated system such as Christianity, some ideas may promote population growth directly, others retard it directly, and others affect it indirectly. The particular groups accepting the ideas will emphasize different ideas. The ideas themselves will not constitute a constant, but will develop, reflecting the experience of those affected. One can scarcely speak of measurement. What is sought is insight. One does not seek a standard and a kind of proof irrelevant to the questions asked. To agree to omit the influence of non-economic ideas in any history of human population because the calculation of their effect is not statistical must be regarded as an arbitrary cutting off in evidence, an inadequate depiction of human action.

Apart from the interaction of ideas with population history, demography itself depends on a number of theoretical assumptions.

Any effort to view demography as a pure science of measurement necessarily neglects to take critically into account the notions of intellectual history which honeycomb demographic enterprises. What constitutes a village or a nation or the human race itself is a matter of theory. Unless one believes that a social, religious, political, or geographical grouping has theoretical significance, it is difficult to see why the figures of a given community are tabulated. The selection of what group will be studied is not a matter of tabulation, and yet this decision to choose, to isolate, to describe a particular slice of population is decisive for demography. Even in the fundamental task of tabulation, then, there is no pure demography of numbers; the data are always determined by particular purposes; a set of social, moral, political, and scientific interests frames the determinations made.

If this dependence of demography on theory exists in the examination of the births and deaths of human beings, it becomes accentuated when other categories are introduced as relevant. The simplest additional category is marriage. What is a marriage is determined by a legal, religious, or social standard, and the demographer may either take the standard used in the records given him or uniformly apply a social standard such as 'a union lasting for a certain duration'. In either case, he has to impose on the rough flow of human interactions a pattern which he deems significant for his purpose. By supposing that what he accepts as marriage has some relation to births, he necessarily ventures into the realm of causality, theory, and intellectual history.

II

The ideas most relevant to population in Western society are of a mythic-moral character. By ideas I mean beliefs, concepts, and valuations; by mythic I mean ideas, non-demonstrable but not necessarily untrue, of the nature of the cosmos in relation to the destiny of man; and by moral I mean prescriptions for human conduct in terms of a good. Of these mythic-moral ideas the most obviously relevant are those which assign a value to population. There is, for example, the belief advanced in the Babylonian Talmud that there are a certain number of souls waiting to be born, and that until they are born, the Messiah will not come.[1] There is the belief that procreation is necessary in order to perpetuate the race until the Messiah does come.[2] There are the thoughts current since St. Augustine's time, that the population of heaven has been depleted

[1] *Niddah* 13B, *The Babylonian Talmud*, ed. Isidore Epstein (London, 1935–52).
[2] See Eusebius, *The Gospel Demonstration* 1.9, *Patrologia graeca* (hereafter *PG*) 22:77–81.

by the fall of the angels and that this depopulation must be met by human efforts at procreation, 'lest heaven be cheated of its number of citizens.'[3] There is the belief of a minority of the Fathers that the Kingdom of God expands by procreation.[4] There is the belief, in countries divided by the Reformation, that the triumph of a faith depends on the birth rate of its followers.[5] In all of these views, population itself is a positive value.

Other mythic-moral views assign a negative value to population. There is the belief, current among Gnostic and orthodox Christians of the second century, that 'the world is full': The optimum and maximum number of the redeemed exist; the Messiah has come there is no need to continue the procreation of the race.[6] There is the even more severe view of the Manichees that the most sinful of deeds is the procreative act: It perpetuates in new human beings the imprisonment of the light particles, once parts of the Princes of Light, who should be liberated from the flesh to journey to the Father of Lights.[7]

A mythic-moral view need not be expressed in religious imagery. The ancient Greek view of procreation as an answer to death—the view that man lives in his descendants—had no such explicit imagery;[8] this belief is doubtless held by many nonreligious persons today. Modern valuations of population sometimes depend on the belief that procreation either does or does not serve 'the nation', taken as an ultimate reality: Nazi Germany and postwar Japan are obvious alternative examples. Some contemporary American thought reflects the belief, common to almost all utopian literature, that a static population is best suited to human needs because it is so amenable to rational planning; in this thought, an ideal society on earth performs the function of setting population standards that Augustine once attributed to the population of heaven.

Relevant ideas need not contain direct statements on the value of population or the ends of procreation. Of almost equal immediacy to population size are ideas on marriage and sexual behaviour, on celibacy, chastity, virginity, and widowhood. The special ideas of patristic Christianity, for example, form a cluster here. Celibacy as such is not valued, but marriage is not presented as the optimum

[3] St. Augustine, *De civitate Dei* 22.1, *Corpus scriptorum ecclesiasticorum latinorum* (hereafter *CSEL*) 40:583. Again in Duns Scotus, *In libros sententiarum*, Paris Report, 4.28.

[4] St. Ambrose, *Expositio in evangelium Lucae*, 1.30, *CSEL*, 32⁴:29.

[5] For a twentieth-century expression of this belief, see John A. Ryan. 'The Moral Aspects of Periodical Continence', *Ecclesiastical Review*, Vol. 89 (1933), p. 34.

[6] See St. Jerome, *Contra Helvidium* 21, *Patrologia latina* (hereafter *PL*), 23:215.

[7] See St. Augustine, *Contra epistolam quam vocant fundamenti* 5, 13, 15, *CSEL* 25¹:197, 209, 212.

[8] See St. John Chrysostom, *On Those Words of the Apostle 'On Account of Fornication'* 3, *PG* 51:213

state; chaste celibacy is preferred.[9] Widowhood is assigned a high value.[10] Marriage is presented as the sole framework in which sexual intercourse may occur.[11] Within marriage, value is given to sexual continence, even to perpetual continence.[12] All of these valuations, if put into practice, affect the likelihood of opportunities for procreative acts. They may be contrasted in their probable effects with the Old Testament ethic where marriage is the norm, virginity is to be kept only as a condition of a girl prior to marriage, there is no word for bachelor, and widowhood is diminished by the levirate law.[13]

The ideal content of marriage is also of substantial relevance. Consider the Christian goals of offspring, fidelity, and indissolubility in marriage. That monogamy alone is permissible, that slave concubinage to produce an heir may not be practised, that divorce cannot be had for sterility are formal tenets of the Latin Christian Fathers.[14] These beliefs seem to reduce the occasions for procreation and, thus, affect the growth of population. On the other hand, the classic Christian authors of the West insist that the purpose of marriage is procreation, and they hold legitimate only the seeking of marital intercourse for procreative purposes. They condemn contraception and abortion.[15] In these ways, Christian rules favour the growth of population.

In addition to ideas on sexual conduct, ideas on education may affect population. All people rear their children, giving them both physical nourishment and some social training. That the rearing of children should include both intellectual and moral formation is not necessarily a given idea; the idea of such education is the acceptance of an option valuing the quality of offspring. The Christian theologians of the second century adopted the *paideia* of the Greeks and developed these Greek educational ideas in a new context.[16] As a result, Christians affected by this tradition were taught to value not the quantity of their children, but their quality; value was assigned not to offspring as such, but to offspring as the objects of a religious

---

[9] First Epistle to the Corinthians 7:7.

[10] E.g., St. Ambrose, *De virginibus*, 1.23, 38, 52, *PL*, 16:195, 199, 203.

[11] Matthew 5:27–8; Romans 1:24–7; First Epistle to the Corinthians 6:16; First Epistle to the Thessalonians 4:4.

[12] E.g., Canon 33 of the Council of Elvira in 306 forbids priests to have intercourse with their wives: *Sacrorum conciliorum nova et amplissima collectio*, ed. G. D. Mansi (hereafter Mansi), 2.11.

[13] See Lucien Legrand, *The Biblical Doctrine of Virginity*, p. 29.

[14] See St. Augustine, *De bono coniugali* 7, 29, *CSEL* 41:196, 227.

[15] On procreative purpose, see Clement of Alexandria, *Paedagogus* 2.10.95.3, *Die griechischen christlichen Schriftsteller der ersten drei Jahrundert* (hereafter *GCS*) 12:214. On abortion, see the *Didache*, 5.2.

[16] See Werner Jaeger, *Early Christianity and Greek Paideia* (1961), pp. 37–67.

education.[17] The patristic teaching was reaffirmed in the changed culture of the Middle Ages. To seek children on a natural level, Thomas Aquinas taught, was formally sinful; only children who were to be formed spiritually constituted a good in marriage.[18] By defining the purpose of marriage as comprising both the procreation and the education of offspring, such classic Christian formulas produced an inherent tension. Pursuit of one goal always held the possibility of endangering the other. It was always a question of how the balance was to be preserved. The answers to this question related to the growth of population.

Another set of valuations relevant to population has centred on the rules determining freedom to marry. These rules define who can choose the spouses, what classes are eligible for marriage, when girls and boys can marry, and how marriages are made. Roman legislation presented marriage as an important social act for upper-class families, open to imitation by the lower classes, and denied to slaves.[19] The model of Christian marriage presented by the Epistle to the Ephesians was that of a free and loving union open to any Christian.[20] This model was in sharp conflict with the social norms in the early Christian centuries.

Gratian's teaching that a girl could not be compelled to marry against her will marked a distinct development in European history.[21] Very gradually, in a society where arranged matches were still the model furnished by the upper classes, the principle of freedom was applied by church courts.[22] A milestone was reached when the Council of Trent affirmed explicitly that the consent of parents was not necessary for the validity of a marriage; such marriages could still be illicit, but the great sanction of invalidity was definitively removed.[23] Yet in many European societies (such as rural Ireland following the famine of 1845), the parents' control of marriage could still be decisive.[24]

Canon law challenged the legal restrictions on slave marriages during the twelfth century.[25] Until the end of the nineteenth century,

---

[17] Clement of Alexandria, *Stromata* 3:15, *GCS* 15:241; St. Augustine, *De bono coniugali* 8.8, *CSEL* 41:198.

[18] St. Thomas Aquinas, *In libros sententiarum Petri Lombardi* 4.31.2.2, reply to objection.

[19] *Codex Justiniani* 5.5.3, 9.11.1.

[20] Epistle to the Ephesians 5:25–33.

[21] Gratian, *Decretum*, Part 2, C.32, Q.2, c.1, in *Corpus juris canonici*, ed. Friedberg (1879–81).

[22] See, e.g., *Decretales* 4.1.15, 21, 29, *Corpus juris canonici*.

[23] Council of Trent, Session 24, 11 November, 1563, 'Canones super reformatione circa matrimonium', c.1, 'Tametsi', *Concilium Tridentinum* (ed. Societas Goerresiana, 1955), Vol. 9, p. 968.

[24] K. H. Connell, 'Peasant Marriage in Ireland: Its Structure and Development Since the Famine', *Economic History Review*, 2nd Series, Vol. 14 (1961–62), p. 513.

[25] Gratian, *Decretum*, Part 2, C.29, Q.2, c.1.

however, the practical social restrictions on slaves and then on servants inhibited freedom to marry. Economic class lines remained strong into the present century, and racial lines still dominate contemporary patterns. Yet in theory, and substantially in fact, the transition from the Roman model of marriage as a family affair for upper-class men and women to marriage as a personal choice open to everyone has been generally made in the United States and Western Europe.[26]

The Council of Trent channelled marriage toward greater control by the Church. Before Trent, marriages could be illicitly but validly contracted by the parties themselves. After Trent, only consent exchanged before the parish priest of one of the parties constituted a valid marriage.[27] This sixteenth-century increase in social-ecclesiastical control may have coincided with the beginning of an increase in the age at marriage. (Age fourteen for boys and twelve for girls had been established by Roman law and accepted by canon law.) The actual rise in the legal age itself, however, followed the development of a practice of late marriage. Here nineteenth century European governments set the pattern and were followed by the Catholic Church only in 1917.[28] Nineteenth-century secular legislators and twentieth-century church legislation also swept away many of the restrictions, established by the old canon law, against marriage within certain degrees of relationship and against marriages of mixed religion. There was, paradoxically, increasing freedom to choose and increasing restriction on the age when choice might be made and on the method of expressing consent.

The demographic impact of these changing rules was doubtless mixed. A system of arranged marriages is theoretically more efficient in making sure that everyone gets married than is a system of personal choice. If, however, an important objective of the arranged marriages is to control the devolution of property, the system may function to promote only the marriages of heirs, as it did among landed groups in Europe. A rise in the age of marriage necessarily means that fewer people are physically present to marry, and that the period of marital fecundity will necessarily be reduced. Yet families marrying later may be more stable and seek to have larger numbers of children. Increase in the valuation put on the inter-personal goals of marriage decreases the value of the procreative good. Persons marrying freely may, however, have a greater interest

[26] As is suggested by studies, such as Alain Girard's, the actual range of choice, at least as those now married recalled the range they had, may still be small. The family will play a role by implicitly approving the decision made. See Girard, *Le choix du conjoint* (1964), pp. 128, 156.

[27] *Loc. cit.*, footnote 23.

[28] *Codex canonici juris*, canon 1067.

EP

in having children and nurturing them to maturity. The rules adopted do not, taken alone, afford a basis for estimating the net impact on population. All that is evident is the likely relevance to demographic history of the changing norms.

Of all moral concepts I suppose that the most basic is the concept of person—an individual who is entitled to be treated as I am, who has a self-determined end, who cannot be regarded as a thing. 'Person' as an explicit concept has had a long and slow development. Many of the major moral controversies of the past can be analysed in terms of who has been recognized as a person. Are aliens persons? Are prisoners, are slaves, are Negroes, are women, are infants, are embryos? Different answers to these questions have affected population history. Non-persons have often either been exterminated or restricted in their opportunities to procreate. Prisoners, for example have almost never been treated as persons; in ancient times, this response to them resulted in their total elimination from the population.[29] In all societies, prisoners have been restricted or prohibited from expressing their procreative desires. Infants and embryos were viewed as non-persons in the Roman world and, as such, were subject to destruction on a wide scale.[30] That women were less than persons was reflected in the long acceptance of prostitution with the concomitant of contraception practised by the prostitutes. The willingness to have an economy where many servants were not expected to marry has existed in many societies nurturing the class belief that only people of a given status are persons. The enactment of miscegenation laws and the consequent restriction of procreative marital opportunities have been based, in part, on a belief that given races are less than fully human.

Who will count as a person is not assured nor given. Attribution of personhood may be affected by racial, religious, political, biological, economic, psychological, or social ideas. The literary lesson of *1984*—that persons may in their own lives become unpersons— is brought to contemporary life by the Chinese Communists' treatment of members of the counter-revolutionary classes. The perception of persons is a function of ideas about humanity; on this perception have hinged the generative opportunities and the existence of substantial numbers of the population.

To determine that ideas have been held on population, procreation, chastity, sterility, education, freedom to marry, and persons— all of which evidently bear in a theoretical way on demographic questions—is not to determine that these ideas have been followed or, if followed, that they have been influential. There are at least

[29] E.g., Joshua, 11:3.
[30] See Tertullian, *Ad nationes*, 1.15, *CSEL* 20:85; Seneca, *De ira*, 1.15.

three further questions to be asked: How have the ideas been diffused? How have they been accepted? To what extent have they modified one another or been affected by other factors?

In answering the first question, it is evident that there is inter-action between the actual behaviour of any group and the ideas pro-posed to it as models by its leaders, teachers, or legislators. There may also be interaction between the pattern of those ideas so firmly established as to be unselfconsciously held as folkways and that of the ideas proposed as new and better models by moral philosophers, prophets, or critics. In the history of Western thought on sexual con duct, two examples may suffice. Jesus teaches an equality between man and woman in the right to fidelity of a spouse (Matthew 19.9), when he applies 'adultery' to a man's sexual conduct with an hitherto unmarried woman; a similar equality of sexual rights in marriage is enunciated by Paul in the First Epistle to the Corinthians (1 Cor. 7:3-5). This idea of sexual equality was counter to current behaviour in the Mediterranean world. One striking example of the resistance of the popular culture to this idea is furnished by the Roman divorce legislation in 331 under Christian auspices by Constantine. The legislation makes adultery by a wife ground for divorce, but explicitly provides that a husband's being a 'womanizer' (*mulier-cularius*) is no ground.[31] The ideal of equality is thus repulsed even at the level of formal law. It is only in the twelfth century that canon law sets out the idea as at least a legal norm for the church courts,[32] and this legal proclamation is, of course, merely the beginning of the influence of the idea on behaviour.

A second example is the view that there is a natural position in sexual intercourse. There is nothing in Scripture on this subject, and the Greeks and Romans do not seem to have had any strong notions about it. Beginning with the penitentials of the seventh century, however, a belief appeared that there is only one lawful position, that of the man above the woman.[33] The belief must arise from some Anglo-Saxon folkway, for no other source is apparent. The rule was then accepted by the later scholastic theologians and persisted as a norm till well into the fifteenth century.[34] The case is an instance of a model being taken from the belief or practice of one group of unsophisticated people and then generalized as an ideal.

These examples show that it would be an error to postulate a straight lineal relation of ideas proposed by moral teachers to the

[31] *Codex Theodosianus*, ed. T. Mommsen (Berlin, 1885), 3.16.1.

[32] Gratian, *Decretum*, Part 2, C.32, Q.4, c.1–10.

[33] St. Bede, *Penitential*, 3.38; Egbert, *Penitential* 7.16, *Die Bussordnungen der abendlandischen Kirche*, ed. F. W. H. Wasserschleben (Halle, 1851).

[34] E.g., St. Bernardine, *De religione christiana*, 17.1.1 in *Opera omnia* (Quarrachi, 1950), Vol. 1.

behaviour of those taught. Yet in the area of sexual conduct, the ignorance of individuals has been very great as to what is 'normal' or 'right'. The channels of communication have often been controlled, and high social importance has usually been attached to the basic norms of the society. In such a context, the confident setting out by leaders of certain patterns as correct has influenced behaviour, however much instinct or folkway has modified their ideas. Most behaviour has been learned, however unselfconsciously the learning has been carried on. Relatively small groups have concerned themselves with this conduct; they have conveyed knowledge, exemplified ideals, enacted laws, and, thus, have affected larger groups. Their impact has necessarily been in the long-run, with a time lag of short duration. In general, however, a large degree of rationality has not entered into the decisions of individuals when answering such questions as: Shall I get married? How many children shall I have? Shall I determine whom my child marries? These questions have been answered by individuals within existing structures governing sexuality, the conditions of education, and the concept of person. Through these structures, which reflect ideas modified by behaviour, instinct, and earlier structure, ideas have influenced behaviour. The ideas, whose dissemination is to be traced, come from both the earlier structures and the moral leaders and critics.

For the West, ideas on population from both sources have been conveyed by liturgical acts, especially the marriage service and the sacrament of penance; by didactic forms, particularly parental homily, preaching, catechism, and elementary schooling; by imaginative literature; by law, both canon and secular, acting as much as standard-setter as sanction-applier; and by personal example. By examining these multiple sources, the broad lines of diffusion of ideas may be surveyed and some estimates made as to how the ideas have been disseminated.

The second question, the extent of acceptance, is more difficult to answer. It would evidently be a mistake to measure the force of an idea by its probability to us; its power depends on its hold on the person receiving it. A bare cataloguing of relevant mythic-moral ideas such as I have attempted in this essay is apt to seem unreal; the ideas appear as illusory, unlikely, bizarre. Their persuasive power has to be measured in the situations to which they were responsive, in the cultures in which they were embedded.

Within the historical situation of the cultures, there have been different levels of acceptance. The Gospel parable of the seed and the various soils is aptly applied to the audience of any idea. There is always a range of attitudes—from impassioned conviction to sullen compliance to open defiance. A variety of investigative means is necessary to arrive at estimates of the hearers' adherence to any given concept or valuation.

In the area of religious ideas, the crudest of tools has been the label 'Catholic' or 'Protestant'. The labels appear to be of some use for seventeenth- and eighteenth-century Europe, but, applied to contemporary societies, they are survivals of post-Reformation controversy. They have been of great interest to religious polemicists intent on attributing all the character of a country to its creed. They have been maintained in currency by ecclesiastical leaders anxious to claim as adherents 99 per cent of a country and are perpetuated by newspapers and magazines which find it paradoxical that a country can be 99 per cent Catholic and vote 30 per cent Communist.

More meaningful efforts have been made to measure religious beliefs not by the nominal classification of an ecclesiastical census, but by liturgical practice. For Catholics, the most common criterion has been attendance at Mass; sometimes the more substantial index of frequency of confession or communion has been used. These tests are helpful in a negative way. If a person never attends Mass, it is unlikely that other specifically Catholic concepts are familiar to him. These criteria are, however, inadequate to determine if specifically Catholic concepts relating to population and procreation have been transmitted to the group investigated. Ideas are not magically imparted by a liturgical action; there must be teaching, literal or symbolic, linking the liturgical acts to particular valuations. Consequently, to measure dissemination of an idea, the means used to transmit it must be ascertained and the frequency of exposure to these means determined. Only after such determination has been made, can it be said that the label 'Catholic' includes for the group investigated the clusters of concepts and valuations that formal doctrine embraces.[35]

This second question, the determination of acceptance, imperceptibly melts into the third and most difficult question, the extent to which the idea has been affected by other factors. A thousand personal circumstances bear on the way an individual receives an idea. Yet it is supposed, with some foundation where ideas of a religious character are concerned, that individuals may be grouped by social class, occupation, ethnic origin, political boundaries, historical experience, age, and geographic location. Such groupings will be relevant not only in determining the dissemination of ideas, but in estimating the probable hold of the ideas on those hearing them.

[35] For example, a recent study of abortion in Chile makes an effort to correlate Mass-going, confession-going, reception of the Eucharist, and the practice of abortion, but it makes no examination of the dissemination of the church's teaching on abortion. See Mariano Requem, 'Social and Economic Correlation of Induced Abortion in Santiago, Chile', *Demography* Vol. 2. (1965), p. 41.

Definition in terms of these seven major variables yields groups whose responsiveness to particular kinds of mythic-moral ideas may be gauged.[36]

Yet ideas are never received singly, and they are never received unchangingly. When they appear as part of a system, a complex of related concepts is imparted: The concepts balance, constrain, or modify one another. In this dynamic tension, development may be expected. It cannot be determined *a priori* which ideas will be dominant or which ideas will develop. Specific ideas on population and sexuality are only a part of a larger mass of ideas. A theology's concept of sin, for example, may be as relevant as its concepts of marriage. The popular culture's approach to leisure may have as much effect on demography as its view of women. The organization—ecclesiastical, political, educational—conveying the ideas may have enormous impact on both the shape of the ideas and the weight attached to them. Study of ideas does not exclude attention to the organizational, cultural, and broader theological or philosophical framework, but depends on a consideration of the interrelations among them.

To take the Christian example, who could say in advance that the model of the one-child family presented by the Holy Family would be more or less important than the Christian Fathers' Stoic doctrine on the procreative purpose of the sexual faculties? Who could suppose that of the three classic goods of marriage—offspring, fidelity, indissolubility—fidelity would be given less weight in Latin Catholic countries than procreation? Who could determine that education or procreation would be preferred in case of conflict? To say that one value or the other should have prevailed is to theologize. In writing history, one can only point to the existence of balancing ideas in a system and then investigate which ones became dominant in the local experience of the particular group examined.

If a group is defined by its multiple non-ideological characteristics, if the dissemination of ideas to that group is determined, and if the dominant ideas are observed with allowance both for the counteracting force of other ideas in the system and for their own development, it seems possible to relate the effect of the ideas received to the population history of the group. Such a relation will only be a matter of reasonable hypothesis. To use these reasonable hypotheses, to take them into account as factors in population

[36] See Gabriel Le Bras, *Etudes de sociologie religeuse*, Vol. 2 (1956), pp. 547–653. Substantially the same point is made by Louis Chevalier, 'Towards a History of Population', *Population in History*, eds. D. V. Glass and D. E. C. Eversley, p. 75, reprinted from *Population* (1946).

history, seems to me preferable to writing a history that, by ignoring all but the economic factors, tacitly supposes that economic rationality alone is real.

III

Three examples may serve to illustrate how demographic history might be enriched by more attention to intellectual history. First, consider the increase of abortion in Hungary in the 1950s. Therapeutic abortion boards were established in Hungary in 1952. On 3 June 1956, the principle of abortion on demand was legally established. Describing these two legal events, Christopher Tietze asks: 'What has been the effect of the legalization of abortion in Hungary?'[37] He then provides the following figures:

Table 1   Abortions per 1,000 of population

Legal abortions		Other abortions
1949	0·2	3·4
1952	0·2	4·4
1955	3·6	4·4
1956	8·3	4·2
1957	12·5	4·0

The only factors correlated by Tietze with this striking increase in abortion are the changes in the law. These legal changes are surely relevant, but laws are signs of ideas as well as causes in themselves. The spread of Communism among Hungarian workers, the suppression of the religious orders and most religious instruction, the increasing desperation of elements of the population in the mid-fifties, the ideas that burst into action in the October, 1956, revolution, the ideas that were generated by the failure of the revolution—all these intellectual events are also relevant. The two legal events afford a misleading account of the changes in the behaviour pattern unless they are placed in the context of this political and intellectual ferment.

Secondly, consider a larger example: the demographic history of Ireland before the famine. In *The Population of Ireland, 1750–1845*, K. H. Connell estimates the Irish population at something over four million in 1781, postulates its doubling (despite substantial emigration) by the time of the great famine, and hypothesizes that the population increase was due to substantially earlier marriages.[38]

[37] Christopher Tietze, 'The Demographic Significance of Legal Abortion in Eastern Europe', *Demography*, Vol. 1 (1964), p. 123.
[38] K. H. Connell, *The Population of Ireland, 1750-1845*, p. 51.

He then gives reasons for earlier marriages in largely economic terms. The cultivation of the bog, the swing from pasture to arable land, the increase of agricultural exports, the general dependence of the natives on the potato, and the subdivision of holdings made early settlements of estates possible and therefore promoted marriage for men at age twenty or twenty-one;[39] the early marriages resulted in the population increase. He adds that 'children were wanted because of their unusual value to their parents' as cultivators of the land.[40] The population increase was higher in counties like Connaught than in counties like Leinster: Connell makes the supposition that a near-subsistence economy in Connaught encouraged the improvidence of early marriage more than the greater prosperity of Leinster.[41] His general hypothesis is that greater prosperity stimulated marriages and births, but that when a certain level of prosperity was reached, other economic calculations led to some postponement of marriage and a consequent slight decline in the birth rate.

That many people married as early as age twenty in pre-famine Ireland is doubted by Michael Drake. The Malthusian beliefs of literate observers, he suggests, often lead them to see early marriages as the cause of poverty, but their casual observations are not decisive. Nor can travellers' exclamations at low ages in exceptional cases be taken as evidence of a trend.[42] The Census of 1841 shows that the median age of bridegrooms in the 1830s must have been twenty-five, and there is no substantial evidence showing that it was earlier in the two generations before 1830.[43] Drake suggests instead that the population increase was due to the spread of a potato diet between 1740 and 1780, which resulted in a lowering of mortality and a substantial increase in fecundity.[44]

This controversy between Connell and Drake has been properly conducted in terms of the meaning of the census and observer evidence. When causes for change or stability are to be postulated, however, there also seem to be political and intellectual events relevant to a history which gives reasons as well as numbers. The period described by Connell is the beginning of the resurgence of the Irish nation after a century of colonial domination. Its beginning

[39] K. H. Connell, *The Population of Ireland, 1750–1845*, p. 89. Connell speaks of 'early' marriage as around age twenty or twenty-one for men in 'Marriage in Ireland After the Famine: The Diffusion of the Match', *Journal of the Statistical and Social Inquiry Society of Ireland*, Vol. 19 (1955–56), pp. 82–3.
[40] K. H. Connell, *The Population of Ireland, 1750–1845*, p. 246.
[41] K. H. Connell, *The Population of Ireland, 1750–1845*, p. 249.
[42] Michael Drake, 'Marriage and Population Growth in Ireland, 1740–1845', *Economic History Review*, 2nd Series, Vol. 16 (1963–64), pp. 303–5.
[43] Michael Drake, *op. cit.*, pp. 303, 311.
[44] Michael Drake, *op. cit.*, pp. 311–12.

is marked legally by such enactments as 'the Bogland Act' of 1771 permitting some land-leasing by Catholics; the recognition of legal rights thus begun culminates in the Catholic Emancipation Act of 1829. The laws are both the effects of changing political ideas and the causes of new changes. The abortive revolt of 1798 is both a sign of desperation and a cause for despair of successful violence. Connell relates the effects of the Grattan parliament and the Napoleonic wars solely to the increased economic activity. He describes Catholic emancipation only in terms of its effect in making possible a Catholic middle class. He refrains from any suppositions about the effect the political changes had on thought affecting marriages and births. That the ideas which necessitated political change had repercussions on attitudes toward population does not, however, seem improbable. To consider only the economic effect of such major political and ideological changes in a country stirring with the consciousness of its oppression seems to shut out evidence of potential significance to the history of the birth rate.

The relation of religious ideas to the population increase also seems worthy of consideration. In the mid-eighteenth century, the outlawed bishops lived the lives of itinerants staying in 'places of refuge';[45] the parishes were irregularly supplied; the religious orders were criminal; Catholic education consisted in the uncertain efforts of the 'hedge schools'.[46] Clerical candidates (some 480 in all)[47] were educated abroad without reference to the language or history of their country and could not have provided more than seventy new priests a year.[48] Priests had little secular influence on their flocks.[49] A change was already under way by 1782 when the Catholic Relief Act was enacted, permitting Catholic churches to be built within towns, Catholic bishops and members of religious orders to live in Ireland, and Catholics to teach school if licensed by a Church of Ireland minister. Seventy years later, by 1850, the bishops were a powerful body firmly based on domestic soil; the national seminary,

[45] See, e.g., the letters of eighteenth-century bishops of Meath in A. Cogan, *The Diocese of Meath*, Vol. 3 (1867), p. 166.

[46] For contemporary comment on the efforts at educational reform in the nineteenth century through the suppression of the hedge schools by Catholic bishops, see the letter of James Doyle, Bishop of Kildare to the Earl of Derby, Chief Secretary for Ireland, 13 January, 1831, in W. J. Fitzpatrick, *The Life, Times and Correspondence of the Rt. Rev. Dr. Doyle*, Vol. 2, p. 232.

[47] See Letter of the Secretary of the Trustees of St. Patrick's College, Maynooth to the Under-Secretary in the Civil Department of the Chief Secretary's Office, Dublin Castle, in John Healey, *Maynooth College; Its Centenary History* (1896), p. 616.

[48] The calculation is a rough one. It supposes a distribution over five years of study, and a certain number of ordained priests remaining abroad in chaplaincies.

[49] The observation of Edmund Burke, a man perhaps interested in discounting Catholic clerical influences in Ireland, but a generally fair and intelligent observer. See Edmund Burke, *Correspondence*, Vol. 3, p. 34.

St. Patrick's College at Maynooth, had supplied 1,272 of the 2,291 Irish clergy; the parishes were well-staffed, the religious orders thriving; Catholic churches were openly and legally attended; an effort at Catholic elementary education had begun.[50] The Maynooth priest had become the dominant figure in the villages and small towns. He was now, a friendly writer declares, 'the teacher, the guide, and the counsellor of his people, their leader in social and political movements, the centre of their energies, the focus of their power, the exponent of their ways, the moderator of their excesses.'[51] Did such powerful local leaders have no effect on attitudes towards marriage and towards birth?

The formal ideas of the Irish clergy on sexual morality underwent no change in this period. In the eighteenth century, 75 per cent of them had been educated in France and another 15 per cent in the Low Countries.[52] Rigorism in morals dominated the seminaries of these countries. When Maynooth was founded, the same traditions were continued. The first professor of moral theology was a Frenchman, Louis De la Hogue (1798–1801), followed by an Irish graduate of Paris, Edward Ferris (1801–09), followed by another Frenchman, Francis Anglade (1810–28). These men devoutly maintained Augustinian sexual teachings as the law of God.[53] The textbooks in use, Antoine and Bailly, were among the most severe of moral treatises. The theory expounded by these books and by these professors condemned any premarital sexual activity, restricted sexual initiatives in marriage to the procreative act, and viewed the whole sexual area of human life as peculiarly prone to concupiscence and actual sin.

Some of the ideas thus conveyed favoured marriage and procreation. The restriction of lawful sexual activity to marriage encouraged marriage if it was economically feasible. The view that marriage was meant for procreation encouraged copulation for population in marriage.[54] Contraception and abortion were shunned. Values counter to early marriage and procreation were, however, also being transmitted. The attitude on sexual activity before marriage discouraged courtship and the occasions for the social meetings of boys and girls. Sexual incontinence was sternly rebuked.[55] A sterile

[50] Healey, *Maynooth College*, p. 466.

[51] Healey, *Maynooth College*, p. 238.

[52] See footnote 47.

[53] On rigorism at Maynooth, see Healey, *Maynooth College*, pp. 283–4.

[54] As James Joyce sees the message conveyed: 'Copulation without population! No, say I!' (*Ulysses* [1961 ed.], p. 423).

[55] See, for example, the record of episcopal visitations between 1780 and 1801 of Bishop Plunkett of Meath, in A. Cogan, *The Diocese of Meath*, Vol. 3, pp. 300–40. Typically Bishop Plunkett notes in Dunshauglin on 16 August, 1801, 'scandalous incontinence inveighed against and threatened with the divine vengeance'.

wife was a disaster, but the expedient of some peasant societies of establishing a woman's fertility in premarital intercourse was not adopted.[56] The narrow limits placed on sexual activity in marriage, the insistence on the indissolubility of a marriage once made, and the high premium put on chaste celibacy all worked against any acceptance of early marriage as an eminently desirable state. Copulation control was itself a form of population control in diminishing the number of chances in which conception could occur. The valuation the clergy placed on the education of children, reflected in the strenuous efforts to establish Catholic schools, embodied an approach to childbearing that stressed quality as well as quantity of offspring.[57] In all these ideas discouraging early marriage and early procreation, Ireland is but a more pronounced case of the Western European marriage pattern, which I shall set out as my third example.

Can one conclude from the existence of ideas working both for and against early marriage that they cancelled one another out? Such an approach would seem unduly mechanical, insufficiently sensitive to the dominant trends of the period. Connell, however, only remarks that the people were reputed to be continent, that they believed in marriage, and that they did not practice contraception. Otherwise he attempts no correlation of moral ideas and demographic history. His later account of peasant marriage after the famine focuses on the economic motives for marriage; and in the one place where he mentions moral attitudes, clerical discouragement of courting is seen as a reinforcement of the economic desire to postpone marriage.[58] His view of the peasant would suggest that the economic aspects of life so effectively controlled decisions on marriage that the moral framework was irrelevant. Alternatively, he may have assumed that, as the moral ideas were unchanged throughout the period studied, they might safely be ignored as a factor causing change.

There was, indeed, in the period 1750–1845, no change in the formal ideas imparted to the Irish clergy and presumably no change in the ideas of sexual morality actually conveyed by them to the people. There was, however, a change in the role, training, numbers, and importance of the priests, a change noticeable some time

[56] Connell 'Peasant Marriage in Ireland: Its Structure and Development Since the Famine', p. 517. Connell's observations made here on post-famine Ireland seem equally true of pre-famine Ireland.

[57] In the same visitation record of Dunshauglin, referred to in footnote 55, Bishop Plunkett also denounced 'neglect of the Christian education of children'. On the bishops' effort for Catholic schools, see Fitzgerald, *The Life, Times and Correspondence of the Rt. Rev. Dr. Doyle*, Vol. 2, p. 232.

[58] Connell, 'Peasant Marriage in Ireland', p. 572.

before 1782 and marked after the foundation of Maynooth in 1798. This change in the status of the conveyors of teaching on sexual behaviour is a factor that cannot be treated as non-existent.

In this short compass, the impact of the ideas conveyed by the clergy can only be raised as a possibility. Parish by parish information would be necessary to trace the effect definitively. Nevertheless, it seems relevant to population history to inquire if this clerical influence helped to establish a pattern of increasingly later marriages well before the famine. The lower birth rate of Leinster, for example, might be associated not only with economic prosperity, but with more extensive efforts on the part of clerics to educate the people. An account of Irish population changes that does not consider the net effect of ideas favouring and discouraging marital procreation seems to have the burden of showing the irrelevance of the ideological elements in an era when this complex of ideas was being conveyed with increasing vigour, by an increasingly strong ministry, to people responsive to ecclesiastical leadership.

My third example is the relation of marriage in Western Europe to the Christian ethic. Hajnal pointed to the existence of a marriage pattern in Western Europe distinct from that in Eastern Europe, Asia, or Africa.[59] The picture drawn by him is now being confirmed by the detailed studies of Ansley Coale and his associates.[60] The pattern is that of a society distinguished by two features: Marriages for both men and women occur at a relatively late average age; many persons do not marry. In these two aspects, Western Europe is distinguished from societies where almost everyone gets married and almost everyone gets married by age nineteen or twenty. This distinctive pattern begins to develop slowly in Europe, probably by at least the seventeenth century; it is strongest in nineteenth-century Europe, where Coale's work, based on census reports, is able to show fluctuations on a province by province basis. It is common to both 'Catholic' and 'Protestant' countries, but not to Eastern Orthodox countries. It obtains more or less regardless of an area's degree of industrialization. It is specific enough to Western Europe and general enough within Western Europe to ask for an explanation that will fit Western Europe as a unit. A hypothesis, then, is needed that is not related to sectarian religious differences, nor to exclusively economic factors, nor to specifically national characteristics.

[59] J. Hajnal, 'European Marriage Patterns in Perspective', *Population in History*, p. 106.
[60] See the essay in this volume by Ansley Coale, 'The Decline of Fertility in Europe from the French Revolution to World War II'. The essay was also published with the title 'Fertility and Family: A World View', as part of the Sesquicentennial Celebration of the University of Michigan.

Such a hypothesis is one relating the pattern to the cluster of ideas constituting Western Christian sexual morality.

These ideas are sixfold: the confinement of sexual intercourse to marriage, the treatment of marriage as monogamous, the emphasis on the ideal marriage as permanent, the justification of marital intercourse by procreative purpose, the condemnation of contraception and abortion, the insistence on the education of children. These central Christian ideas were present, with slightly different emphases, in both Catholic and Protestant cultures.[61] They combined to encourage both sexual restraint and postponement of the serious step of entering marriage and raising a family. They operated against the background of a religion whose founder was presented as celibate. They produced a very different approach to marriage than that of, say, the Talmudic teaching to marry young in order to avoid impure desires or the secular injunction to marry young to ensure heirs to one's property. They did not, of course, operate alone; they were reinforced by other ideological, political, economic, and physical influences; nevertheless, they were the common denominator upon which other influences produced variations without altering the basic pattern.

Negative confirmation of this hypothesis is found in the changes which had already begun to occur at the end of the nineteenth century. By then, for example, in the most anti-clerical portions of France, the marriage age had fallen significantly as had the fertility per marriage.[62] In these areas the relevant ideas on desirable morality had been rejected or partially rejected by the populace. The Western European pattern changed more generally in the next sixty years. This development corresponded both to a rejection of Christian ideas by much of Western mankind and to changes, such as the acceptance of contraception by the Protestant churches, in the formal Christian ideas themselves.

Why did the pattern occur in post-Reformation rather than in medieval Europe? The timing reflects the time lag between the acceptance of ideas by the moral teachers of Europe and their diffusion by law, literature, liturgy, preaching, and example. Only in post-Reformation Europe did the education of a parish clergy in

[61] 'Catholic' and 'Protestant' are used here to denote cultures which have self-consciously different ecclesiastical organisations. The difference in other respects needs close analysis. E.g., in 'Protestant' England divorce with right to remarry was not made generally available before the nineteenth century. In some sociological writing there is over-emphasis on Weber's concepts of 'the Protestant ethic', despite his own later severe qualifications of the idea and his own later approach to the special characteristics of European capitalism in more general terms of a spirit of rationality. See Max Weber, *Wirtschaftethik der Weltreligionen in Gesemmelte Aufsatze zur Religions Soziologie* (1920), pp. 536–46.

[62] Ansley Coale, 'The Decline of Fertility in Europe'.

both Catholic and Protestant countries assure the dissemination of the formal ideas.[63] To take two other instances of this kind of time lag, it has been argued that the witchcraft hysteria of the late-fifteenth and early-sixteenth centuries reflected the effect of the preceding several centuries of theological work in elaborating a theory of witchcraft and providing detailed information on the behaviour of witches.[64] The virulent outbreak of anti-Semitism in twentieth-century Germany has been related to the conditioning of attitudes by centuries of Christian theologizing in which the Jews played the roles of scapegoats or villains.[65] In both these cases, the theological notions involved were relatively peripheral to the main body of doctrine—indeed, were contradictory to more central Christian ideas. Yet it is plausibly contended that witchcraft theory and anti-Semitic theology, detached from the central Christian concepts, powerfully affected popular behaviour centuries after the ideas were put forward by the theological elite. If peripheral elements of Christian theology could work so strikingly for ill in these popular manifestations, it is not unreasonable to suppose that more central ideas operated with profound, if delayed, effect on European behaviour to influence sexual conduct along the main lines to which the Christian moralists had so seriously committed themselves.

Why was there such a marked difference between Western and Eastern Europe? One factor to explain this difference might be found in the greater vitality of the parish ministry in the West and the greater interest of the Western clergy in affecting moral conduct. The institutions of preaching in the Protestant countries and of confession in the Catholic countries were not matched in the East. A tendency to restrict asceticism to the monasteries and a relatively more tranquil acceptance of human failings in the secular Christian also marked the Orthodox of the East. In addition, two doctrines were treated differently in the East: Divorce was accepted, and the procreative purpose of intercourse was not stressed. In sum, both the complex of ideas on sex and marriage and their communication were significantly different in the hands of the Orthodox. The differences, when combined with many non-ideological factors, help to explain the different pattern.

The general hypothesis of any relationship between the formal Christian ideas and the Western European pattern and my answers to specific difficulties with this hypothesis are put forward only tentatively. I hope that they are plausible enough at first sight to

[63] On the very slow development in the seventeenth century of a seminary-educated clergy, see Paul Broutin, *La Réforme pastorale en France au 17e siècle* (1955), pp. 11, 89, 296.

[64] Hugh Trevor-Roper, 'Witchcraft and Witches' *Encounter*, Vol. 28 (May 1967), pp. 3–25.

[65] Georges Friedmann, *The End of the Jewish People?* (English translation, 1967), p. 268.

provoke refutation or confirmation. They may serve, at least, to suggest the relevance of intellectual history to a specific demographic pattern.

It has been the discovery of the historians of legal institutions that such history cannot be written without more attention to general cultural and political factors than they were at first prepared to give. Demographic history would seem likely to undergo a similar expansion of its concerns. What it has to deal with is evidence of human behaviour. That behaviour points to thoughts. To account for that evidence, to integrate it, to understand it require a history not only of births and deaths, but of ideas, if the history is to be a history of men.

Etienne van de Walle

Marriage and marital fertility

The relationship of marriage to general fertility is at the heart of the preoccupations of nineteenth-century demographers in Western Europe. During his stay in Switzerland, T. R. Malthus met a peasant who 'appeared to understand the principle of population almost as well as any man I ever met. . . . [The] habit of early marriages might really, he said, be called *le vice du pays*; and he was so strongly impressed with the necessary and unavoidable wretchedness that must result from it that he thought a law ought to be made restricting men from entering into the marriage state before they were forty years of age, and then allowing it only with *des vieilles filles*, who might bear them two or three children instead of six or eight.' Malthus relates, however, that he 'found upon inquiry that the [man] had himself married very young.'[1]

MARRIAGE AND THE BIRTH RATE

Although no law so extreme was ever passed, there were many restrictions to marriage at that time in Swiss cantons, German states, and elsewhere. Some of these laws had been passed long before Malthus, when there was a general belief in the importance of population growth. Although it was acknowledged that a large population was necessary for the welfare of the state, marriage laws were instituted to protect local finances against the prolificacy of irresponsible paupers who might otherwise have a claim on relief or charity. During the first half of the nineteenth century, under the influence of Malthusian ideas, marriage restrictions were reactivated.[2] They were intended to relieve the pressure of population by compelling the poor to 'moral restraint'. In Switzerland, restrictions of marriage on economic grounds were abrogated only with the passage of the federal constitution of 1874 and the civil status law of 1876. Until then, various regulations had been effective in barring a large proportion of the population from marriage.

---

[1] T. R. Malthus, *An Essay on Population*, Vol. 1 (London, 1927), p. 212.
[2] On the German marriage laws, see J. Knodel, 'Law, Marriage and Illegitimacy in Nineteenth-Century Germany', *Population Studies* (March 1967), pp. 279 ff.

For instance, in the canton of Lucerne, where the restrictions on marriage were particularly pervasive,[3] the proportion of women single at age fifty reached 39 per cent in the Census of 1870. After age fifty, the chances to marry are slight and, in any case, fertility is not affected. A population in which almost 40 per cent of the women of childbearing age are unmarried will find its birth rate seriously lowered, numerous illegitimate births notwithstanding.

Legal restrictions on marriage, whether introduced before or after Malthus, created a general atmosphere of restraint, which had to be borne by a large proportion of the population. The older generation was obviously worried by the early marriage of the young. Malthus's hostess in a Jura inn complained 'that boys and girls were marrying who ought still to be at school'.[4] The conflict between the generations may have been the source of the belief, in the absence of adequate statistics, that the age of marriage was, in fact, going down.

In an earlier era of populationists, J.-L. Muret, the minister of Vevey in the canton of Vaud, worried about a decrease in the number of people; he inferred this from a study of parish registers and attributed it mostly to out-migration. In 1764, he tabulated data from the marriage registers of his parish which showed the age of marriage among women to be twenty six years and two months.[5] He wrote at the time:

> A means which would seem very efficient, and be the more appropriate since it would enhance population more directly, would be to bar from all employments the non-married men; to tax inheritance accruing to a single man aged twenty five years and over; and to favour in various ways those having the most numerous families.[6]

Half a century later, Dean Bridel, the minister of Montreux in the same canton, spoke favourably of the region's low birth rate. He computed the age at first marriage of women in his parish at twenty six years and nine months, a figure very close to that indicated by Muret's data, and he commended late marriage as the cause of the low birth rate. He wrote:

> The obvious, overriding and, to my eyes, sufficient cause to explain it is a pronounced, general and already ancient tendency towards

---

[3] W. Bickel, *Bevölkerungsgeschichte und Bevölkerungspolitik der Schweiz* (Zurich, 1947), p. 155.

[4] Malthus, *An Essay on Population*, p. 211.

[5] J.-L. Muret, *Mémoire sur l'état de la population dans le pays de Vaud*, in *Mémoires de la Société Economique de Berne*, Vol. 1 (1766), p. 57. Muret notes that women in the countryside marry much earlier.

[6] J.-L., Muret, *op. cit.*, p. 107.

postponing as much as possible the age of marriage. . . . Where women rarely become mothers before twenty eight, twenty nine or thirty years, they have acquired the maturity needed to give their infants more intelligent and conservative care than very young mothers. In fact they also have a lesser number of children, since, at least in my parish, they consider it a duty to nurse them for a long time; this leaves less margin for pregnancies, and results in the latter following on one another at intervals of three years.[7]

Whether writers deplored too early marriage or the excessive postponement of marriage—whether they rejoiced because women married early, thereby checking depopulation, or married late, thereby indicating forethought and restraint—they all agreed that the 'incidence' of marriage was the main factor affecting fertility. By the incidence of marriage, we mean the combined result of the age at marriage and the proportion who never married. In many European countries, the two combined to limit to 35 to 40 per cent the proportion of women of fecund age that were married. This pattern of marriage, which probably had no equivalent elsewhere in the world and has now disappeared everywhere except Ireland, markedly lowered the birth rate in Western Europe.

The possibility of fertility control within marriage was hardly ever mentioned, even in France, before the second half of the nineteenth century. Such writers as Cauderlier attempted to refute evidence which might have suggested the contrary. As late as 1900, Cauderlier denied the importance of 'artificial causes of fertility limitation'.

I think these causes have always existed, and I don't see very well why they would suddenly have become more powerful, to the point where they would have caused the recorded decline in the French birth rate. . . . In brief, the fertility of women is a constant in time; in other words women are as fertile today as fifty years ago. The increase and the decrease of marriages are sufficient to account for the greatest demographic phenomenon of the last half-century.[8]

There is ample evidence in nineteenth-century Europe to indicate a close association between fluctuations in the number of births and fluctuations in the number of marriages. Economic conditions— depression and prosperity, drought and good harvests—affected the number of births by influencing the number of marriages. Many authors of the time attempted to relate nuptiality and fertility

[7] F. d'Ivernois, 'Montreux, enquête sur les causes patentes et occultes de la faible pro- portion des naissances', *Bibliothèque Universelle de Genève* (May 1837), pp. 11–13.

[8] Cauderlier, *Les lois de la population et leur application à la Belgique* (1900), p. 190.

to the price of staples, particularly grain. The relationship of marital fertility (as opposed to the birth rate, the number of births over the total number of persons in the population, be they married or not) to the incidence of marriage deserves to be examined further.

STRATEGIES OF FAMILY FORMATION

Control of marital fertility by contraception, as we know it today in Western countries, is without doubt a fairly recent development. It probably did not appear on a large scale much before the Revolution in France, and 1870 or later in most European countries. Moreover, in most of the world today and even in Europe in the past, uncontrolled fertility has most likely been accompanied by a pattern of early and universal marriage, at least among women.

According to J. Matras's scheme, there are four conceivable 'strategies of family formation', combining either early or late marriage with either uncontrolled or controlled fertility.[9]

	Uncontrolled fertility	*Controlled fertility*
Early Marriage	Strategy A	Strategy B
Late Marriage	Strategy C	Strategy D

Strategy A is still the rule in most of the world, as it was in Europe during Antiquity and the Middle Ages. Strategy C was advocated by Malthus and adopted, on the whole, in Western Europe in the nineteenth century. J. Hajnal argues convincingly that there had been a shift at an earlier date from Strategy A to strategy C; from a pattern of early and general marriage to what he calls the European (meaning Western European) pattern, characterized by high age at marriage and a large proportion of people who never marry when fertility is uncontrolled.[10] One might speculate that the adoption of Strategy C was a preliminary step in the development of fertility control within marriage. Eastern Europe, however, underwent a fertility decline without abandoning the custom of early and almost universal marriage.

The transition from Strategy A to C occurred at an unknown date, and there are not many statistics to document it. We are concerned here only with the transition from Strategy C to Strategy B. In several countries, statistical records (censuses and vital registration) are available for the period during which this shift took

[9] J. Matras, 'The Social Strategy of Family Formation: Some Variations in Time and Space', *Demography*, Vol. 2 (1965), p. 351.

[10] J. Hajnal, 'European Marriage Patterns in Perspective', *Population in History*, eds. D. V. Glass and D. E. C. Eversley (Chicago, 1965), pp. 101 ff.

place. We shall examine the evidence for four countries in which
the transition has apparently occurred—namely, France, Switzerland, Belgium, and the Netherlands.

The two paths from C to B on Matras's diagram (the first is by
way of A, the second by way of D) correspond to two theories on
the relationship between changes in fertility and those in marital
habits. The first theory follows the lead given by economic historians.
H. J. Habakkuk and W. L. Langer, for example, contend that
population growth in eighteenth-century England may have
been due not to mortality decline, but to a decline in the age at
marriage and to the resulting increase in the number of births.[11]
Since this theory relates to a time when vital registration and censuses provide no usable information on the topic, we cannot test it
here. We can only say that the proportion of single women in the
beginning of the nineteenth century was extremely high in those
areas of Europe which we are considering (with the exception of
large parts of France) and that it is unlikely that it could ever have
been much greater.

The Dutch historian E. W. Hofstee, however, has involved a
similar argument to explain the recorded increase in the birth
rate of the Netherlands between 1850 and 1875, a period covered
by reliable national statistics. Hofstee attributes the rise to an increase in the frequency of marriages as the population departed
from what he calls the 'classical agrarian-artisanal pattern of reproduction'.[12] According to this view, marriage had previously
depended on the possession of a house and the means of livelihood.
Among rural populations, the eldest son would often be the only
one who could afford to marry, and then only when his father had
died or was too old to take care of the farm. Younger brothers and
unmarried sisters would live on the farm as dependents with ancil-
lary status. During the 'proletarian transition period', the old institutions started breaking down as a result of industrialization and
urbanization. The ties become looser between employers and servants—or unlanded members of the family, the two often being
synonymous. People married earlier and in larger proportions; they
went to towns where they were able to earn a living in ways other
than agriculture. The number of holdings ceased, therefore, to
limit the number of households to the extent that it had during the

[11] See W. L. Langer, 'Europe's Initial Population Explosion', *American Historical Review*
(October 1963), where it is argued that the spread of the Irish potato in Europe made it
possible to feed a family on less land, and therefore to marry earlier, and H. J. Habakkuk,
'The Economic History of Modern Britain', *Population in History*, pp. 147 ff.

[12] E. W. Hofstee, 'Regionale vercheidenheid in de ontwikkeling van het aantal geboor-
ten in Nederland in de 2e helft van de 19e eeuw', *Koninklijke Nederlandse Akademie van
Wetenschappen, Akademiedagen*, Vol. 7 (1954).

earlier agrarian period. The birth rate grew, and many of the old values based on tradition were abandoned. A dynamic pattern of culture fostered the acceptance of fertility control, and the birth rate began a sustained decline.

Hofstee's theory is of interest here because it describes a sequence of events where changes in marital customs antedate a decline in marital fertility. (The proportions married increased during the nineteenth century in all parts of the area we are considering.) To the extent that the theory attempts to make this shift a decisive feature in a general succession of historical changes, it is vulnerable to many objections. Was there ever an agrarian = artisanal pattern of reproduction in Europe? If so, when did it start to disappear? The European pattern of marriage appeared relatively late, if Hajnal's interpretation of the historical evidence is correct. The Dutch population in the Middle Ages, for example, probably married early and universally. On the other hand, when did 'proletarization', as Hofstee calls it, occur? There must have been previous changes in the proportion married. Such changes in nuptiality happened to coincide with the beginnings of national population statistics in the Netherlands, but it is questionable whether the recorded changes can be attributed to fundamental and irreversible social trends occurring decisively in a relatively well-defined period.

The second theory put forth to explain the transition from Strategy C to Strategy B entails passage through an intermediary stage (Strategy D) in which fertility is controlled and marriage is late. This hypothesis holds that recent declines in age at marriage were made possible by the substitution of contraception for late marriage as the means of curbing population growth. Joseph Spengler, for instance, has employed this hypothesis in the case of France:

> Evidently men have tended to marry in relatively greater numbers as they have acquired the practice of family limitation. Or, stated in other words, in France the population has always (since 1860 at least) sought to limit natural increase, either by deferring and/or avoiding marriage, or by limiting fertility within the married state.[13]

It has sometimes been argued that the European pattern of marriage disappeared because late marriage had lost its function, which was to keep the family small.[14]

[13] J. J. Spengler, *France Faces Depopulation* (Durham, 1938), p. 73.
[14] K. David, 'Statistical Perspective on Marriage and Divorce', *Demographic Analysis*, eds. J. J. Spengler and O. D. Duncan (Glencoe, 1956), pp. 243 ff.

THE COURSE OF NUPTIALITY AND MARITAL FERTILITY

We can gain some insight into the validity of the theories described by comparing the trend of the age at first marriage and of the proportion never married among women in France, Belgium, Switzerland, and the Netherlands during the period covered by national statistics with the trend of marital fertility. (See Figure 1.) It is sufficient to say that the age at first marriage is estimated from the proportion of single women at each age in the censuses, comparing one census to the next; that the proportion of women never married around age fifty is a good measure of the proportion who never marry; that our index of marital fertility is free of the influence of age differentials in the populations considered, and that it indicates marital fertility as a proportion of the highest fertility ever reliably recorded in a human population (which would be equal to 1).[15]

The decline of marital fertility in Switzerland, Belgium, and the Netherlands after 1850 is almost surely the result of large-scale adoption of family limitation; the decline began much earlier in France. The statistical record encompasses the transition from high to low marital fertility (including some of the pre-decline plateau) in Belgium and the Netherlands, but not in France and Switzerland.

In all instances, the mean age at first marriage shows a marked tendency to decline. By computing from censuses ten years apart, extreme fluctuations are evened out. There is a suggestion of a rise in Holland and Belgium at mid-century caused by the economic crisis of 1846–48. A potato blight struck at this time and represented a major catastrophe not only in Ireland, but also on the Continent. All four countries show an increase in age at marriage during the 1880s. This led some writers of the time, Cauderlier among them, to speculate that fertility decline was caused by delayed marriages. In retrospect, the change in age at marriage clearly appears to have been only a fluctuation in a secular trend which resulted most probably from economic causes. The trend is interrupted by an occasional economic crisis and by World War I. Fertility, however, continued to decline despite the ups and downs in age at

[15] The computation of the mean age at first marriage has been described in E. van de Walle, 'La nuptialité en Belgique de 1846 à 1930 et sa relation avec le déclin de la fécondité', *Population et Famille*, Vols. 6–7 (1966), pp. 42–5. The index of martial fertility, I_g, is explained in Ansley J. Coale, 'Factors Associated with the Development of Low Fertility; An Historic Summary', *United Nations World Population Conference*, 1965, Vol. 2 (New York, 1967), pp. 205–9.

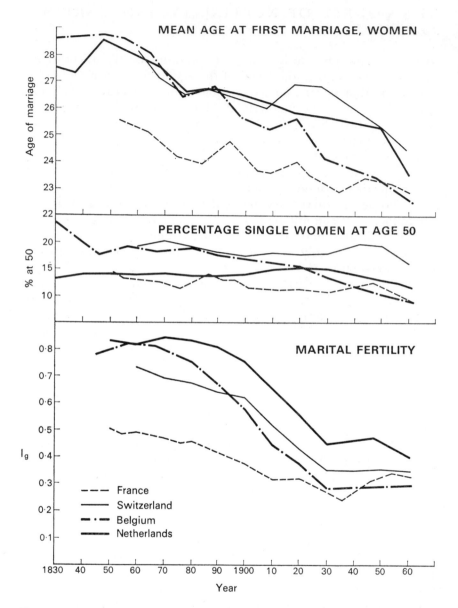

Figure 1 Comparison of the trend of age at first marriage with the proportion of women never married and the course of marital fertility

marriage. Cauderlier believed that marital fertility was a constant and failed to realize that it had started to come down.

Age at first marriage declined almost steadily in the four countries for more than a century. France was only exceptional in that its population married at a much younger age than did those of the other countries considered here. Age at marriage might possibly have come down before the first French census for which we possess an age and marital status distribution, that of 1851. Knowledgeable students of French population history, however, argue against this proposition. Louis Henry has compared the proportions single given by Moheau in 1778 for certain regions of France at the end of the *Ancien Régime* with those given for the whole country in the 1851 Census; if anything, the proportions single were higher in 1851.[16] The study of parish registers indicates an age at first marriage of about twenty-five.[17] Of course, the effect of the Revolution and the Napoleonic wars on nuptiality cannot be estimated. The proportion married might have become smaller after this period of hardship than it had been during the *Ancien Régime*. War losses, by diminishing the supply of marriageable males, tend to decrease the proportion of married women.

Finally, the percentage of women never married appears to have remained stable during the period under review. Belgium alone shows a continuous and slow decline. Fluctuations from census to census are minor, and the last census indicates an all-time recorded low everywhere. Although the decline in age at first marriage is notable in practically every administrative sub-division (*département*, canton, or province) of the countries discussed here, there is no systematic trend in the percentage remaining single at age fifty. Averages for each country even out a number of opposing changes, with a general tendency towards more regional homogeneity.

Maps 1 and 2 are meant to provide some insight into the regional differences in age at marriage and in the prevalence of permanent celibacy around 1870, a time close to the beginning of the fertility decline in three of the countries. France, where age at marriage was earlier and more women married, was well ahead in the transition to low fertility by 1866. The country had its share of areas with a late age at marriage—Brittany, the Rhine *départements*, and so on—but it also had many regions with what was, for Europe,

[16] L. Henry, 'La nuptialité à la fin de l'Ancien Régime', *Population* (July–September 1953), pp. 542 ff.

[17] L. Henry, 'The Population of France in the Eighteenth Century', *Population in History*, pp. 454–6. See also J. Bourgeois-Pichat, 'The General Development of the Population of France Since the Eighteenth Century', *Population in History*, p. 484.

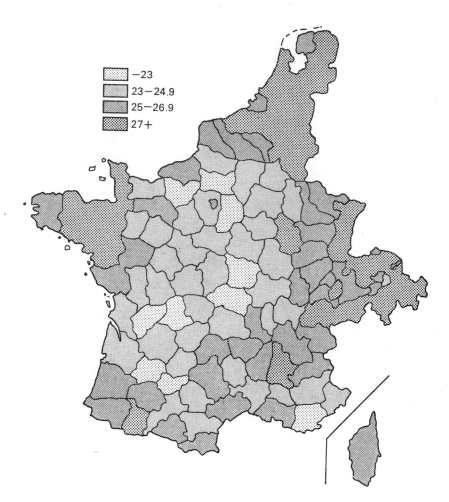

Map 1 Mean age of women at first marriage, France, Switzerland, Belgium, and the Netherlands, about 1870

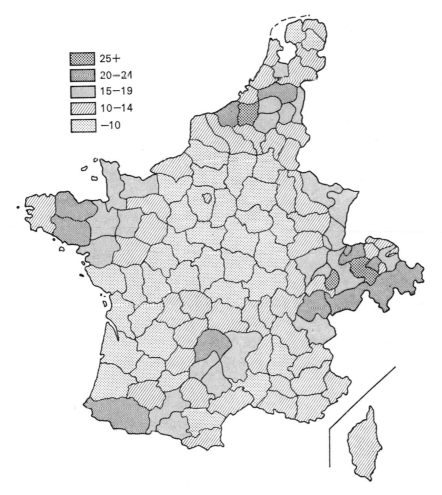

Map 2 Proportion single women at age 50 in France, Switzerland, Belgium, and the Netherlands, about 1870

Legend:
- 25+
- 20—24
- 15—19
- 10—14
- —10

an exceptionally low age at first marriage: an average of less than twenty-four years for women.

That the proportion married was higher and marital fertility started to decline earlier in France leads back to the relationship between the two factors. In the French *départements*, there is an undeniable association between low marital fertility—presumably caused by an earlier and wider use of practices of family limitation —and an early age at first marriage and low proportion of old maids. The proportion married was greater in 1866 in those areas where birth control had been accepted earliest and most widely. Similar conclusions could be reached by considering Belgium and the Netherlands, and would apply also to dates other than 1866. (Switzerland is a special case because of cantonal legislation restricting marriage.)

Table 1 lists the levels of marital fertility in the ten French *départements* with the highest age at first marriage in juxtaposition to those *départements* with the lowest. The proportion of women never married is also correlated with marital fertility by areas: the higher the proportion of old maids, the higher the fertility of those who married.

Table 1   Marital fertility (I_g) in *départements* with highest and lowest age at first marriage, France, 1866

Département	Highest age at marriage Age at first marriage in years	I_g	Département	Lowest age at marriage Age at first marriage in years	I_g
Morbihan	27·9	0·737	Var	20·8	0·440
Côtes-du-Nord	27·9	0·802	Nièvre	21·5	0·451
Haut-Rhin	27·9	0·770	Haute-Vienne	21·6	0·493
Drôme	27·8	0·481	Lot-et-Garonne	21·9	0·277
Haute-Savoie	27·7	0·689	Seine-et-Marne	22·0	0·385
Loire-Inférieure	27·5	0·601	Oise	22·1	0·350
Bas-Rhin	27·3	0·774	Tarn-et-Garonne	22·4	0·329
Hautes-Pyrénées	27·2	0·513	Charente	22·7	0·329
Ille-et-Vilaine	27·0	0·679	Allier	22·8	0·468
Manche	27·0	0·521	Eure	22·8	0·307
Average	27·5	0·657	Average	22·1	0·383

It is tempting to accept the thesis that society imposed restrictions on marriage to limit the number of children per completed family and check rapid population growth. According to this interpretation, the advent of contraception released society from the need to impose such restrictions. A pattern of late marriage and diffusing contraception is thought to have served as a transition from the time when late marriage and uncontrolled fertility had been the rule to the present pattern of relatively early and general marriage with controlled fertility. If this interpretation is correct, the path followed from Strategy C to B ran through Strategy D.

A strong argument against this hypothesis is explicit in the evidence summarized in Figure 2. The data suggest that in both Belgium and the Netherlands age at marriage started to drop earlier than marital fertility. This also appears to be true for those areas of France and Switzerland where the decline in marital fertility began late anough to be documented by official statistics. Table 2 lists the age at first marriage in 1870 and 1900 for all areas which had not undergone a clear decline in marital fertility by 1900. In every instance, there is an important decline in the age at first marriage, which is obviously not the result of the adoption of fertility control.

Even if the facts were not clear, there would be *a priori* reasons to doubt the validity of an explanation that attributes a conscious desire to marry earlier to the diffusion of contraceptive practices. Although the origins of the European pattern of marriage are

Table 2   Marital fertility (I_g) and age at first marriage in areas not having experienced a decline in marital fertility by 1900. Switzerland, Belgium, and the Netherlands, about 1870 and 1900

Country and canton or province	I_g 1870	1900	Age at first marriage in years 1870	1900
Switzerland				
Freiburg	0·816	0·861	27·6	25·6
Ticino	0·674	0·682	27·2	25·7
Valais	0·770	0·789	27·1	25·6
Belgium				
Limburg	0·866	0·881	28·7	27·0
Netherlands				
Nd. Brabant	0·931	0·954	29·1	27·6
Overijssel	0·786	0·755	27·1	26·2
Drenthe	0·750	0·757	27·1	25·5
Limburg	0·897	0·968	28·3	27·7

obscure, we have no reason to assume that it was consciously intended to reduce the number of births since high fertility was universally valued as the primary aspect of a woman's role at this time. Etienne de Sénancour, the first writer known to tolerate contraception outside marriage, has the following definition of love: 'To love is to make a choice of the person with whom, according to certain affinities, one hopes to have happily constituted children, morally endowed with precious faculties.'[18] He claims elsewhere

[18] Etienne de Sénancour, *De l'amour, selon les lois premières et selon les convenances des sociétés modernes*, Vol. 1 (Paris, 1834), p. 175.

that no woman would have any reason to divorce a man 'as long as he renders her continuously fertile'.[19] If the purpose and function of late marriage and widespread celibacy were to limit the birth rate, it is difficult to see why writers before Malthus so universally approved of high fertility. Malthus's use of the expression 'preventive check' to population growth to characterize the moral restraint of those marrying late or rejecting marriage may have misled us into believing that there ever was an intent to prevent. That the rate of growth was actually slowed down is not, of course, in question. The existence of restrictions to early and general marriage and the use of contraception are essentially different in intent; the one is no substitute for the other. As a rule, contraception is accepted or practised efficiently by couples at a rather late stage in married life, after the desired family size has been reached. Late marriage would, in many respects, be a method of avoiding or postponing a first birth only. It is unrealistic, perhaps, to suppose that engaged youths adjust the date of their marriage so that no excessive parity will be reached later in their lives.

Marital fertility apparently started to decline in many cases after the incidence of marriage has increased. Although the two events appear to be related (as was shown by Table 1), is this relationship necessarily one of cause and effect? We must be wary of the *post hoc, ergo propter hoc* fallacy. It is more likely that age at marriage and marital fertility started to come down because of the same economic or social causes. But what were these causes? We know that age at marriage fluctuated in the short run under the influence of economic circumstances, crises, and so on. The trend toward lower marital fertility, however, is generally linear from the pre-decline plateau until World War II; wars and crises hardly interrupt it.

The European pattern of marriage is contrary to human inclination. In Malthus's words, 'the dictate of nature and virtue seems to be an early attachment to one woman'.[20] As in other cultures, the normal tendency must have been to marry as early as possible. The origin of the European pattern must be left to speculation. Because it was oppressive, however, it is not difficult to explain a tendency to relinquish it. Economic constraints of various sorts discouraged early marriage. The general improvement in economic conditions during the nineteenth and twentieth centuries in Belgium, the Netherlands, Switzerland, and France made possible a lowering of the age at marriage. Under conditions of uncontrolled fertility, a decline in age at marriage would have had unfavourable economic

---

[19] Etienne de Sénancour, *op. cit.*, p. 71.   [20] Malthus, *An Essay on Population*, p. 7.

consequences—as Malthus's reasoning made clear. Thus, the continuation of the decline for a long period necessitated a change in
the attitude toward fertility control. Had the latter not come about,
the natural tendency toward earlier marriage would have been
frustrated. In this view, the decline in age of marriage was not
provoked by a decline in marital fertility; the latter was a permissive
agent without which the nuptiality trends would not have persisted
in the long run.

Paul Demeny

Early fertility decline in Austria-Hungary: a lesson in demographic transition

'In traditional societies, fertility and mortality are high. In modern societies, fertility and mortality are low. In between, there is demographic transition.' These propositions connecting basic demographic phenomena with the degree of modernity are neither subtle nor precise. Few students of population would be satisfied with this definition of demographic transition. Yet, with all their ambiguities, these three sentences unquestionably describe the central preoccupation of modern demography. Modern demography is, above all, about demographic transition. This is to be understood in two distinct, but interrelated senses. First, there is description in the spirit of the narrow, literal definition of demography—a description of quantitative aspects of human populations. Thus, contemporary demographers often ask: What is the level of fertility in traditional societies? When does fertility decline start? Where does fertility decline start? What is the speed of decline? What is the level of fertility in modern societies? On a more ambitious level, there is the task of explanation. The answers to each question about demographic facts are rephrased into questions. Why did fertility start to decline where it did? Why was the decline faster here than it was elsewhere? And so on. It is hoped that the answers to these latter questions will eventually jell into a *theory* of demographic transition: a set of generalizations which are capable of explaining the onset, the course, and the final outcome of past demographic transitions, and which will also give us a key to the prediction of transitions yet to come.

Why transition, as description or as theory, should occupy the centre of the stage in modern demography is not difficult to understand. It would suffice in the present context merely to refer to the sheer historical interest in the topic. The demographic transformations that have occurred in the now modernized countries of the world did manifestly result in historically unprecedented patterns

FP

of reproduction, length of life, age distribution, and population growth that deeply altered the lives and involved the participation of virtually every individual member of the societies which were affected. One might assume that students of history would be eager to chart and understand a process of such dimensions and to trace its presumably multifarious economic, social, and psychological consequences. But historians, with all their propensity to clarify every obscure nook and corner of the past, have neglected the study of demographic processes to an extraordinary degree. The paucity of data required for such a study and the technical difficulties of interpreting the usually rather obvious deficiencies of existent numerical information go a long way to explain (but not absolve) the historians' neglect. It is to be hoped that historians and workers in other related disciplines will eventually acquire sufficient familiarity with demographic analysis and that the present unsatisfactory state of affairs will consequently change. In the meantime, demographers, a relatively new breed among social scientists, must try to fill the gap left by the more established disciplines concerning our knowledge of past population transitions and to erect a theory on the basis of such knowledge.

The task is evidently a worthwhile one, even if judged only on its intrinsic intellectual merit. Beyond that, conditions in the present-day world seem to make the task urgent indeed. The non-autochthonous character of the process of modernization presently revolutionizing the economically backward two thirds of the world has produced a nearly general and precipitous decline of mortality. This decline, in combination with especially high levels of fertility as established in the pre-modern era, has resulted in what nowadays is referred to, awkwardly but not without some justification, as the population explosion. The outcome of the explosion, quite obviously, depends on the future behaviour of fertility. Apart from a few instances, relating to small or isolated populations, fertility in the less-developed countries has shown as yet no sign of an incipient decline. It can be demonstrated, however, that sustained maintenance of high fertility could jeopardize the process of economic and social modernization and, with it, the already achieved lower levels of mortality. Thus, more than ever, a theory of demographic transition is needed not only to explain the past and predict the future, but to guide in formulating rational and effective policies through which a decline of fertility could be induced artificially.

It would, of course, be naïve to assume that a theory specific enough to serve as a guide for policy could result from historical investigations alone. Differences between conditions in the Third World today and those in the countries which have undergone demographic modernization in the past are too deep-going and numerous for that. Nevertheless, history could provide some highly useful insights into the hierarchy of forces presently at work in shaping the levels of fertility. It might even suggest some rules for action if only by disproving certain assumptions that otherwise would lead to erroneous or at least unproductive policies. At any rate, it is difficult to say how useful history is for the present or for the future until one tries to understand the past. There can be no doubt that we have not yet tried hard enough.

The present essay examines the circumstances and certain salient features of the decline of fertility in the area commonly known with reference to pre-World War I Europe as Austria-Hungary, insofar as such an analysis appears to be of direct relevance to problems prominent in contemporary theorizing on demographic transition. The main limitations implicit in so circumscribing the scope of our discussion should perhaps be stated explicitly. First, no comprehensive nor balanced description of the Austro-Hungarian demographic transition will be offered. The focus will be on problems, rather than on the particular area. Second, the range of the problems discussed will be limited both by the points of emphasis in contemporary interest and by the nature of the area selected as the demographic laboratory—in this instance Austria-Hungary. Finally, our attention will be further restricted to the *beginnings* of the fertility decline, the perennial *pièce de résistance* of any theory of demographic transition.

A number of characteristics make the now long-defunct Hapsburg Empire of special interest as a demographic test tube for students of fertility transition. Two of these characteristics should be stressed here. The first is the population's exceptional diversity. The Hapsburg lands lacked many things, but were rich in ethnic, religious, cultural, and economic heterogeneity. Living side by side, peacefully or otherwise, in what was rightly called a multinational empire were Germans, Hungarians, Czechs, Slovenes, Italians, and Croats; Poles, Ukranians, Slovaks, Serbs, and Rumanians. The list of major religious denominations is almost as long as the list of the various ethnic groups. Contrasts among regions in terms of levels of literacy, degrees of urbanization, occupational structure, and other characteristics were always marked and remained so until the country was broken up into its constituent parts.

The potential usefulness of such heterogeneity in aiding demographic research should be obvious. Moreover, this potential can be realized because large masses of statistics of good quality and of easy comparability are available—an asset, unlike diversity, which was largely lost after 1918. This is not meant to imply that the whole region was under a unified statistical administration during the Hapsburg era. After the 1867 Compromise, separate organizations were set up for the Austrian and Hungarian parts of the dual monarchy. Diversity within each part was, however, almost as great as within the Empire itself. Furthermore, the two systems supplied data collected and tabulated on the basis of closely similar methods and principles.

Naturally, praise for the quality and quantity of data that exist for Austria-Hungary is to be understood in a relative sense only. In many respects, and particularly for the least developed regions of the country, the statistics are truly unique; elsewhere in Europe data of similar standards became available only at a substantially more advanced level of economic and social development. Nonetheless, even the best data are seldom of the sort the researcher would wish to have, as is always the case with historical statistics. Moreover, as one pushes backward in time, difficulties with the data increase rapidly, from the standpoint both of quality and of quantity. This imposes a final limitation on the discussion that follows. The problems of interpreting the inadequate data that originate from Austria-Hungary prior to 1880 and have a bearing on our topic are in some cases still unsolved. The use of these data would necessitate the discussion of intricate issues of data adjustment and interpretation that would go far beyond the necessarily narrow confines of this paper. Accordingly, data will be used here only when statistical tests have conclusively shown them to be substantially exempt from biases due to omission or misreporting.

A DIGRESSION ON DEMOGRAPHIC INDICES

In our analysis, we seek to describe and compare levels and changes in fertility. For this purpose, we need an index that measures overall fertility—that is, the reproductive performance of women of childbearing age. It is obvious, however, that in populations where procreation takes place primarily within marriage, we should consider separately the two immediate factors that determine overall fertility performance—namely the fertility of the *married* women, on the one hand, and the *proportion married* among all women of childbearing age, on the other. Thus, our discussion will run mainly in terms of three indices: the index of overall fertility, denoted as I_f; the index of marital fertility, denoted as I_g; and the index of the proportion married, denoted as I_m.

The specific method of calculating these indices is somewhat laborious and will not be described here.[1] Fortunately, the essential meaning of the indices is sufficiently described by their names, and only a few comments need to be added here to facilitate their interpretation. The value of each index may range from a low of 0 to a high of 1. Thus, for example, I_g assumes a value of 1 if marital fertility is at its theoretical maximum where married women bear children at the highest rate ever recorded among populations known to have 'natural' fertility (practising no birth control). This amounts to taking as a standard the marital fertility that characterized women in the 1920s among the Hutterites (a small North American population) and expressing marital fertility in terms of that standard. Accordingly, a value of I_g of 0·8, for example, indicates that the number of children born in a given year is 20 per cent less than would be the case had married women experienced a fertility at each age as high as in the standard (Hutterite) schedule. (It is assumed in these calculations that illegitimate fertility is zero.) In an analogous fashion, an overall fertility index (I_f) of 0·3 indicates that the number of children in a given year falls below the theoretical maximum by 70 per cent. That maximum would be attained if all women, regardless of marital status, would bear children at the rate indicated by the standard schedule. It should be noted, finally, that there is a simple arithmetic relation between the three measures, the index of overall fertility being a product of the indices of marital fertility and of the proportion married. In other words $I_f = I_g \times I_m$.

The relationship just noted permits us to represent all three indices in a simple two-dimensional diagram (see Figure 1). Once the reader has familiarized himself with this diagram, it conveys information in a highly illuminating and concise manner about the level of the indices at a given moment as well as about changes over time. By the same token, the graph facilitates comparisons among indices of various regions and among patterns of change.

The levels of marital fertility (I_g) are measured along the vertical axis of Figure 1. Distances along the horizontal axis indicate the value of the index of proportions married (I_m). Since overall fertility equals $I_g \times I_m$, lines along which the value of I_f is constant are also easily represented on the diagram. Four such 'isoquants' of I_f are drawn on Figure 1; with reference to these, the approximate level of overall fertility is easily determined at a glance.

[1] For a technical discussion, see Ansley J. Coale, 'Factors Associated with the Development of Low Fertility: An Historic Summary', *Proceedings of the World Population Conference, 1965*, Vol. 2 (United Nations, New York, 1967), pp. 205–9. It should be noted, however, that in this paper the index of overall fertility is calculated by taking into account only legitimate births.

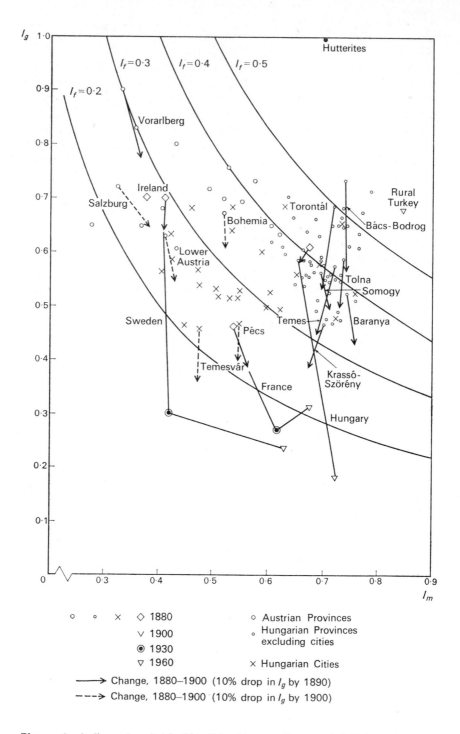

Figure 1 Indices of marital fertility (I_g) and proportions married (I_m)

FERTILITY AROUND 1880 AND AFTER: AN OVERVIEW

Statistics providing a cross-classification of marital status with age and sex are not available for Austria-Hungary until the Census of 1880. Thus, calculation of the indices (and, for that matter, even calculation of simpler measures that permit the crucial factoring of fertility into marital fertility and proportions married) is feasible only for the years around 1880 at the earliest. The results of such a calculation are given in Figure 1. Specifically, the figure shows the position, around 1880, of the seventeen Austrian provinces (*Länder*) as well as the position of the more than sixty Hungarian provinces (excluding Croatia-Slavonia). For Hungary, it is possible also to separate the cities (defined by administrative criteria) and the non-urban (rural) areas. Accordingly, the values for the cities of Hungary are indicated separately, and the figures for the provinces (*vármegye*) do not include the urban segments, if any.

If one then calculates the indices for another date—for example, for the years around the 1890 census—one can plot another set of points on the map. By connecting with an arrow the earlier point with the later one for each province, one has a visual image of the change in fertility (and nuptiality) during the decade. This procedure can be repeated—moving on to 1900, to 1910, and so on. For each population, the series of dated points interconnected by arrows describes the path that I_m, I_g, and I_f travelled over time. Since our interest is focused only on the early decline of fertility, we need not overburden the diagram by representing the change for every province and for a long span of time. We limit our attention to the leaders and to the last two decades of the nineteenth century. Accordingly, we have used 1880 as a base and have selected all provinces where marital fertility, as measured by I_g, had declined by at least 10 per cent by 1890. There are eight such provinces: one in Austria and seven in Hungary. Four of the Hungarian cities also showed a similar decline. So that we would not rely on developments in a single decade only in detecting early fertility decline, we have also selected from among the remaining provinces all those in which a 10 per cent decline occurred by the turn of the century, again in relation to the 1880 level. Three Austrian provinces, but none of the Hungarian ones, have satisfied this requirement. Some seven more of the Hungarian cities, however, did witness a substantial decline by 1900. The changes in the indices between 1880 and 1900 in the Austrian and Hungarian provinces selected by the criteria

just described are represented in Figure 1 by arrows: the head of
the arrow indicating the position in 1900. A solid line is drawn if
a marked decline has occurred by 1890; a broken line indicates
that at least a 10 per cent drop relative to 1880 was registered by
1900. None of the provinces for which only the 1880 position is
indicated in the diagram showed a similar decline by the turn of the
century. As to the cities, the 1880–1900 change is shown only
for the two that had the lowest I_g values by 1900 in absolute terms.

In order to put into perspective the 1880 levels and the declines
in the subsequent twenty years shown for the Austro-Hungarian
provinces, Figure 1 also gives the location of the indices for some
other populations that may be considered extreme in some sense.
The Hutterites exemplify populations with the highest level of
marital fertility. Late-nineteenth century Ireland is known for its
extreme restriction of marriage. In contemporary rural Turkey,
marriage is early and nearly universal, and fertility of marriages is
presumed to be very high. The Hungary of the early 1960s is described by an I_g value that is probably the lowest ever experienced
in any sizable national unit. Finally, also for purposes of comparison,
Figure 1 shows three notable patterns of demographic transition:
those for Sweden, France, and Hungary (estimated for the present
national frontiers). The transitions are traced from 1880 on, first
for the same period as given for the Austro-Hungarian provinces
(1880–1900) and then in a deliberately schematic manner up to
around 1960.

PRE-DECLINE LEVELS OF MARITAL FERTILITY

We can now proceed quickly with an examination of the demographic facts summarized in Figure 1. The first question that may
be asked concerns the level of pre-decline fertility. Let us assume
for the moment that the pre-decline situation in Austria-Hungary is
the one described by the indices for around 1880. A glance at
Figure 1 shows that differences in the overall level of fertility were
large, ranging from a value of below 0·2 to well over 0·5—that
legitimate births in the Austro-Hungarian provinces amounted
roughly to some 20 to 50 per cent of the potential maximum. Such
marked differences were a result partly of the differences in I_m and
partly of the differences in I_g. Let us consider the latter factor first.

Any reasonable description of fertility transition contains the
idea that marital fertility is 'high' before transition, but 'low' after
transition. Ordinarily, low marital fertility is the consequence of

deliberate control of what demographers call 'natural' fertility.
Couples presumably exercise such control so as to insure that the
number of children born to them conforms to their preferences
concerning size of family. Since preferences may differ considerably
from population to population, a great deal of variability of 'low'
marital fertility may result even if contraception is universally and
effectively practised. On the other hand, the notion of 'high'
marital fertility implies the absence of deliberate interference with
natural fertility; hence, one would expect a substantial degree of
uniformity within populations having pre-decline marital fertilities.
In the Austria-Hungary of the late-nineteenth century, not only is
such uniformity missing, but the quantitative differences among the
I_g values for the various provinces were extraordinarily large. To
be specific, values ranged from a high of over 0·9 to a low of about
0·46.

Such differences in pre-decline marital fertilities constitute an
unsolved demographic puzzle of the first order. One must add
quickly that no solution of the puzzle is offered here. We shall
limit ourselves simply to stating two alternative lines along which
an explanation of the facts may be attempted. The first of these
would maintain the assumption that no birth control was exercised
by individual couples for the express purpose of limiting family
size. The burden of explaining differences in I_g would then fall on
differences among populations with respect to exposure of women
to intercourse, to the capacity to conceive (fecundity), and to the
probability that a pregnancy is terminated by a live birth.[2] These
variables are, in turn, affected by such factors as racial-biological
characteristics, standards of general health and nutrition, length of
lactation, and a variety of social customs and regulations.

It is, of course, beyond dispute that significant differences in the
level of natural fertility may and do exist. For example, one would
certainly shy away from asserting that birth control was practised
in the province of Vorarlberg because its marital fertility was some
10 per cent below the Hutterite level, even though such an interpretation may well be correct. On the other hand, differences of the
sort shown in Figure 1 can hardly be attributed to differences in
natural fertility alone. Ideally to support this assertion, more detailed
data on at least the actual fertility performance would be necessary
—such as, for example, individual fertility histories, parity distributions, or age-specific fertility rates. Lacking data of this sort, one
may study differences of marital fertility among provinces and, in

[2] Compare Kingsley Davis and Judith Blake, 'Social Structure and Fertility: An Analytic Framework', *Economic Development and Cultural Change*, Vol. 4, No. 4 (April 1956),
pp. 211–35.

some instances where this is feasible, among smaller subdivisions of individual provinces that are closely similar with respect to the characteristics that presumably affect natural fertility (health, nutrition, social customs, and so forth). Our investigations for Austria-Hungary have shown that I_g levels among such populations are still apt to differ greatly, thus weakening, even if not conclusively destroying, the plausibility of the argument that natural fertility differences alone are responsible for the disparities in I_g. When an argument seeks to explain as much as is sought to be explained in this instance, however, the burden of proof is on those who have offered the argument in the first place.

This brings us to the alternative hypothesis that could explain the differences in marital fertility shown in Figure 1 in a much simpler fashion—namely, by assuming that such differences constitute *prima facie* evidence of some form or forms of deliberate birth control within marriage. According to this view, such control must have been exercised by at least an appreciable fraction of the married population in most, if not all, of the Austro-Hungarian provinces around 1880, and presumably for a long time before that date. Unfortunately, as so often happens in historical demography, this conclusion is based essentially on deductive reasoning and cannot be regarded as definitely proved, even though some impressionistic and literary evidence indicates that primitive techniques of induced abortion were indeed known and practised in certain parts of Hungary, and that various folk methods of contraception, including crude intrauterine devices, had considerable currency.

Should the reader find the postulate of pre-decline birth control an easy one to accept, let him be reminded that it is in sharp conflict with much of received theorizing on demographic transition.[3] If we admit that birth control of one form or another had been practised *before* the secular decline started, a central feature of transition theory is erroneous—the vision of the onset of fertility decline as an instance of social mutation, as a clear-cut qualitative change in behaviour. Thus, the decline of fertility would have to be viewed as the result of a merely quantitative change in the frequency of age-old practices that presumably came about as a natural response to changing environmental pressures. The implications of such a reinterpretation of demographic history are far-reaching, notably with respect to formulation of population policy in present-day high-fertility countries. Although their discussion is beyond

[3] See, however, Gösta Carlsson, 'The Decline of Fertility: Innovation or Adjustment Process', *Population Studies*, Vol. 20, No. 2 (November 1966), pp. 149–74. For a survey of the literature, excluding the most recent work, see Ronald Freedman, 'The Sociology of Human Fertility', *Current Sociology*, Vol. 10/11, No. 2 (1961–62), pp. 35–121.

the confines of this paper, a possible objection to the above argument may be considered briefly.

The preceding discussion assumed that the 1880 indices do, in fact, represent the pre-decline situation in Austria-Hungary. Is this a reasonable assumption? On the face of it, it certainly is, since we know that, apart from the notable exception of France, the downturn of fertility occurred in Western Europe only after 1875. If anything, one would expect that this event came later in Austria-Hungary. Nevertheless, the choice of 1880 as a date of reference was not dictated by such considerations. It was simply imposed on us by the limitations of the available data. Could it be, after all, that the decline in Austria-Hungary started well before 1880 and that the large differences in I_g found around this date simply reflect the result of developments prior to 1880 which brought down marital fertility from more or less identical levels, but at differential rates of change?

There is plenty of statistical evidence that bars the assumption of an appreciable pre-1880 decline as far as Austria is concerned. For Hungary, the pre-1880 record is much less clear, partly because of the deficiencies of the underlying census and vital statistics and partly because correction for such deficiencies is exceedingly difficult since certain genuine demographic disturbances affected the population during that period, notably those associated with the devastating cholera epidemic of the early 1870s. Nevertheless, there *is* evidence of a relatively small but noticeable fertility decline in a few provinces; indeed, in some segments of certain provincial populations, the downturn can be traced to the 1850s. Not surprisingly, the provinces that experienced a decline by 1880 are among those marked in Figure 1 as showing a continuing drop. Since these provinces also had low I_gs in 1880, some of the extreme marital fertility differences found for that date are, in effect, artifacts of previous downward changes in marital fertility. Nevertheless, one can find no apparent explanation in earlier declines for the mass of provincial differentials registered around 1880. The dynamics of I_gs *after* 1880 appear to support this contention. As was pointed out earlier, the large majority of the Hungarian provinces exhibited no substantial decline of marital fertility by 1900. Decline was appreciable and widespread after the turn of the century, but even by 1910 a good number of provinces (located mostly in Transylvania) had witnessed no decline in marital fertility relative to the level in 1880 (at any rate, none detectable by a cross-sectional index, such as I_g). Notably, the provinces that showed an almost perfectly horizontal plateau of I_g between 1880 and 1910 are the very provinces which had low, although not the lowest, marital fertility in 1880. To assume a pre-1880 decline from high fertility to such levels—to I_gs ranging from 0·5 to 0·6— and then a stabilization for at least some thirty years at that level would be not only far-fetched, but would raise more problems than it would help to solve. Moreover, analysis of the age distributions in these provinces indicates that the 1880–1910 plateau represents a fertility level that prevailed during the indefinite period *prior* to 1880 as well. Thus, the existence of large pre-decline differentials of marital fertility stands unshaken and with it the remarkable, though still tentative, conclusion that points to extensive inter- ference with reproduction within marriage in populations hereto- fore considered, explicitly or implicitly, as having 'natural' marital fertilities.

PATTERNS OF NUPTIALITY AND FERTILITY DECLINE

The contrasts we have found among provincial I_g values in Austria-Hungary around 1880 are fully matched and even exceeded by differences in the index of the proportions married relating to the same date. As Figure 1 shows, a few of the Austrian provinces exhibit I_m values of 0·35 or lower, the extreme being an almost in- credible 0·28 registered for Carinthia. At the other end of the scale, the rural populations in almost all of the Hungarian provinces have I_m values of over 0·65; the majority of provinces have I_ms exceeding 0·7; some provinces have I_ms exceeding 0·75.

Such differences are, of course, much less surprising than dif- ferences in pre-decline marital fertility. It has always been recog- nized that control of fertility through the classic Malthusian method —restriction of marriage—is practised in all societies, but at greatly differing degrees. Historically, Western Europe constituted a case *sui generis,* having adopted a nuptiality pattern characterized by high average age at marriage as well as by high proportions re- maining single throughout the childbearing period. As was recently pointed out by John Hajnal,[4] Austria-Hungary straddled the bound- ary delineating the area displaying this Western European pattern. Naturally, the division is not so sharp as summary comparisons would suggest, as is indicated by the distribution of points in Figure 1 with respect to the I_m scale. Even if the largely intermediate- type city figures are ignored, the provincial data still show some gradation between extremes. This point would be even stronger

[4] John Hajnal, 'European Marriage Patterns in Historical Perspective', *Population in History*, eds. D. V. Glass and D. E. C. Eversley (London, 1965), pp. 101–43.

were some large Austrian provinces, notably Galicia, broken up into more homogeneous geographical units. Nevertheless, the contrasts are clear. In Hungary, around 1880, average age at first marriage was typically twenty-one or twenty-two years for women, and the proportions remaining single seldom exceeded 5 per cent. On the other hand, the average age at first marriage for women was above twenty-seven years in all of the predominantly German-speaking provinces (in one instance, going as high as 28·3 years), and the proportions remaining single typically exceeded 20 or even 30 per cent (the extreme case being Carinthia's figure of 45 per cent).

For the present purposes, our interest in these striking differences is limited to their relations to the level and decline of marital fertility. Figure 1 shows that there is a somewhat blurred, yet unmistakable, negative relation between I_m and I_g, particularly if the cities are not considered. In other words, with respect to overall fertility, proportions married and marital fertility pull in opposite directions. Accordingly, it may be suggested that, to a certain extent, restriction of marriage and restriction of births within marriage are employed as alternative tools in achieving the goal of restricting overall fertility. While this seems to be a reasonable generalization, it is important to emphasize that the various provinces seem to differ merely with respect to the specific mixture in which they employed the tools of control—that is to say, at any given level of I_m, marital fertility shows a large enough variation to make the discussion in the preceding section applicable. Even in the provinces with low I_m values, there is clear indication of successful limitation of births within marriage. It would seem, therefore, that once modernization upsets the pre-decline equilibrium of fertility, the decline should start from essentially similar conditions with respect to tested knowledge of birth-control methods, regardless of the exact initial levels of I_m and I_g.

Nevertheless, upon further reflection, it would be reasonable to expect that the quantitative mix of the pre-decline controls on overall fertility should have an important bearing at least on the speed of decline in marital fertility. Consider, for instance, a situation where identical levels of overall fertility are maintained, but through different combinations of I_g and I_m. This obviously means that the population with the higher proportions married must be characterized by a higher average level of practice (and perhaps of knowledge and acceptance) of birth control or by a higher proportion of families practising control. In such a population, a newly generated pressure favouring low fertility would presumably result in an earlier and faster decline than would the same pressure in a population with the same overall fertility, but with a higher I_g and a lower I_m. Our inability to find provinces satisfying the necessary *ceteris paribus* clause, of course, prevents us from testing such a proposition. Nevertheless, the deduction appears to be roughly consistent with the early substantial decline that occurred in those provinces of the country in which the pre-decline fertility plateau was the result of high I_ms and of low I_gs. The single exception to this is Vorarlberg: the province with the highest single I_g value. Paradoxically, that decline may be explained by the anomaly of a disproportionately high overall fertility as compared to provinces with identical proportions married. The process was apparently one of adjustment and convergence to the norms prevailing in the immediate geographical neighbourhood.

It should be admitted, however, that *within* the group of provinces described by early and quasi-universal marriage (that is by high I_ms) the level of overall fertility appears to have no obvious relation to the onset and speed of early decline. Still, the pre-decline levels of overall fertility for these provinces, whether taken as a group or individually, were clearly higher than in the provinces with heavy restrictions on marriage. Thus, in the former group, not only did contraception have to be more widespread, but absolute demographic pressure was also probably more pronounced. This observation should further lessen our surprise that the early declines were registered mostly among provinces with high I_ms and low I_gs.

Thus far, we have tacitly assumed that the process of fertility transition involves merely changes in I_g, while I_m remains on the level established in the pre-decline equilibrium situation, at least during the early transition. It is, indeed, tempting to postulate two broad historical patterns of fertility transition that are consistent with such an assumption of early stability in I_m (as illustrated in Figure 1 by Sweden, on the one hand, and Hungary [post-World War I territory], on the other). The first is a two-phase transition of a characteristically Western European type. In this pattern, I_g drops steadily during the initial phase without any appreciable change in I_m, whose absolute level is low. Once overall fertility is drastically reduced by highly effective control of fertility within marriage, the natural tendency to marry, and to marry early, is released and I_m increases; nuptiality ultimately loses its distinctive Western European pattern. The second type of transition starts from the condition of early and quasi-universal marriage. The fertility transition is dominated by, and largely limited to, a decline in marital fertility. The pattern of nuptiality is preserved throughout the process in its essentials, and the post-decline equilibrium of nuptiality is the same as the one established in pre-modern times, perhaps with some tendency toward even higher proportions married.

An examination of the detailed record of the Austro-Hungarian transition suggests that these models should not be taken too literally. As far as the early stage is concerned, Figure 1 tends to indicate that some element of convergence in marriage patterns was present during the last decades of the nineteenth century. In provinces where I_m was initially low, it had a tendency to increase and vice versa. This finding would at first seem to be highly significant since it would suggest that nuptiality has played different roles in the transition—reinforcing the transition toward low fertility where it was high to begin with, and militating against fertility reduction where it was low initially.

A closer analysis of the data, however, discourages such interpretations. In particular, changes in age at marriage and proportions married showed only minor variations during the early phase of the transition in the provinces with a high I_m; moreover, these were short-run variations quickly reversed and not systematically related to the drop in I_g. For the low-I_m (Austrian) provinces, the record is somewhat more ambiguous. Without question there was a noticeable drop, particularly in the German-speaking provinces after 1880, in the age at marriage and an even more pronounced increase in the proportions eventually marrying. These changes are well illustrated by the data for women in Table 1.

Table 1

Province	Index of proportion married		Mean age at first marriage		Proportion single around age 50	
	1880	1910	1880	1910	1880	1910
Lower Austria	0·412	0·440	27·8	26·8	0·155	0·168
Upper Austria	0·407	0·436	27·8	27·2	0·223	0·166
Salzburg	0·323	0·400	27·2	26·4	0·389	0·232
Styria	0·366	0·416	27·3	27·1	0·300	0·208
Carinthia	0·276	0·372	27·9	26·0	0·447	0·319
Tyrol	0·350	0·413	28·0	26·4	0·291	0·238
Vorarlberg	0·330	0·385	28·3	26·9	0·317	0·248

This, of course, is far from a static situation. Since the changes were well under way before marital fertility started to drop (indeed, the trends were already operative before 1880), it may be assumed that an autonomous increase in the proportions married was an important factor in upsetting the pre-decline equilibrium. Such an increase must have led to higher overall fertility, thus creating new demographic pressures and requiring countermeasures which, given the new and higher propensity to marry, were necessarily controls *within* marriage. Indeed, it is possible that a change in marriage patterns may be credited with a catalytic role in bringing about a decline of marital fertility in the Austrian part of the Hapsburg Empire. The quantitative significance of these changes must, however, be kept constantly in mind. In comparison with the impact of changes in marital fertility, it was decidedly minor. Once marital fertility started to drop, its impact went quickly beyond any reasonable compensation for earlier marriage. As the limited sample in Figure 1 indicates, the effect of I_ms increase was far overshadowed by the effect of I_gs drop, even by the end of the initial period of fertility decline. All in all, even the German-speaking Austrian provinces can be said to have followed fairly closely the pattern exemplified by Sweden. The significant step toward earlier and general marriage had to wait until control of births within marriage brought overall fertility well below the level needed for the sheer reproduction of the population from one generation to another.

FACTORS IN EARLY FERTILITY DECLINE

Apart from the demographic characteristics of the pre-decline situation narrowly defined in terms of indices of fertility and nuptiality, what factors help to explain why fertility declined early in some areas of Austria-Hungary and not in others?[5]

First of all, an outline of the geographical pattern of early decline is in order. The only Austrian land achieving a substantial drop in marital fertility by 1890 was Vorarlberg, at the westernmost end of the Empire. As was suggested above, an early decline in this small Alpine province, wedged between Tyrol and Switzerland, is not particularly surprising in view of the exceptionally high level of the pre-decline I_g that was bound to become anachronistic as the population's contacts with the outside world multiplied. In this sense, the province was a follower, rather than a leader. The real centres from which modern fertility transition spread in Austria were the provinces reducing I_g appreciably only in the last decade of the century—in particular, Lower Austria and Bohemia. In the present context, Lower Austria should read simply 'Vienna', the capital city which is also the centre of the province. In the rural

[5] In view of the complexity of the socio-economic causes underlying the fertility transition, an answer to this question calls for the marshalling of large masses of information and for a detailed analysis, tasks that cannot be attempted in the present essay. As a conclusion to this paper, only a few descriptive comments will be offered which point to some of the factors involved.

areas of Lower Austria, fertility did not change until after 1900. Early decline was more general in Bohemia (the Western third of present-day Czechoslovakia), which was the most advanced region of the Empire economically. Thus, in the Austrian lands, fertility decline does seem to fit the conventional picture of demographic transition as a process associated with urbanization, industrialization, and their various correlates.

The same cannot be said, however, about the seven Hungarian provinces that constitute the important example of early fertility decline in the Hapsburg Monarchy. Remarkably, the seven provinces that met the test of early decline form an unbroken string, stretching along the north bank of the rivers Drava and Danube in what was then southern Hungary. The westernmost member of this group is the province of Somogy, south of Lake Balaton. Some three hundred miles to the east is the other end of the string with the province of Krassó-Szörény,[6] located south of the river Mures and north of the section of the Danube ending at the Iron Gate. The whole area, now divided among Hungary, Yugoslavia, and Rumania, contained somewhat over three million people around the turn of the century, a population that was and has remained predominantly agricultural. The lack of appreciable urban-industrial development in the area suggests that the single most important factor regularly invoked in explanations of transition is inapplicable here. In fact, it can be positively shown that the decline of fertility originated and developed in and among the peasantry. The few urban centres of the area were distinguished neither by especially low I_gs nor by especially fast declines of fertility. This is to be understood in relation to the surrounding rural areas. Fertility in Pécs or in Temesvár—the centres of provinces Baranya and Temes respectively—was below that in Vienna or Budapest. Krassó Szörény, in some respects the most backward among the seven, had by 1880 a level of marital fertility as low as that reached in Vienna twenty years later.

If the provinces are compared with other areas in Hungary with respect to such characteristics as infant mortality rates, proportions literate, or rates of in- and out-migration—elements believed to affect the timing of the onset of fertility decline—once again they show no distinguishing characteristics that could account for the story told by Figure 1. Nor is the story explainable in terms of some peculiarity of the area with respect to standards of health, nutrition, housing, climate, or topography.

---

[6] Unless common English terms can be substituted, administrative divisions are referred to here with the names that appear in the official statistical publications of the period.

Following the classic approaches, we thus seem to reach an impasse. Negative lessons are, of course, not entirely worthless; it can at least be said that late-nineteenth-century Hungary supplies a remarkable proof for a possible adoption of increasing degrees of voluntary control of marital fertility in the absence of any fundamental modernization of the underlying socio-economic structure. In a more positive vein, three points should finally be made. First, it can be shown that the process by which family limitation spread within the seven-province area was to a significant degree one of geographic diffusion. This is by no means a trivial proposition; there are few documented instances of such a process. Only too often geographical differences observed cross-sectionally at a given time are interpreted as evidence of diffusion when, in fact, the differences may be of a quite stable nature that persists unaffected even in a period of change. To some extent, this was the case in the area in question, but there is also clear evidence of transmission in the form of time lags determined by geographic location. The process of transmission need not be interpreted as a transmission of contraceptive knowledge. Our discussion of provincial differences in pre-decline levels of I_g suggests that it is unreasonable to assume the lack of such knowledge in practically all provinces of Austria-Hungary. If we carry the analysis to a sub-provincial level (examining, for example, differences among the several thousand villages located in the seven provinces), an analogous picture emerges. The variance of fertility is so large that with the possible exception of a relatively small number of villages the assumption of a state of natural fertility is highly questionable. If so, the diffusion observable within the provinces leading the fertility decline was presumably one of ideas, aspirations, and attitudes, rather than techniques. Conscious manipulation of exposure to outside contacts, thus, may affect the speed of fertility decline. At the same time, the presence of persistent earlier differentials within the area shows that such exposure is insufficient in itself to induce a change in behaviour not otherwise desired.

Second, although the ultimate chemistry of the agent that makes people *prefer* smaller families remains elusive, the description of the groups that moved in this direction is instructive. By isolating villages that are homogeneous with respect to certain statistical criteria and by observing trends and levels of fertility within such villages, we can isolate at least three 'leading' groups. In the Transdanubian region, the nucleus of change is found among the Protestant (Calvinist) Hungarian population. In the Banat region, the leaders were Roman Catholic and German. Further to the east, in Krassó Szörény, early fertility decline is a characteristic of the Greek

Orthodox Rumanian population. In the first instance, the relevant factor can be shown to be religion. There is a sharp contrast between Hungarians depending whether they are Protestant or Catholic, although the spread of birth control among Catholics in Transdanubia (in Baranya, Tolna, and Somogy) can be traced at least to the early 1890s, perhaps three decades after the Calvinist example. In the Banat and Krassó Szörény, the emphasis is on nationality: The Hungarians and Serbs of the region (Roman Catholics and Greek Orthodox respectively) were late in reducing marital fertility. The demographic behaviour of the leading groups was extraordinary in many respects. By the first decade of the twentieth century, reproductive performance in a large number of villages was well under replacement levels, and birth rates sank below twenty or even fifteen per thousand, consistently remaining below the level of crude death rates. The evidence indicates that an increasing proportion of the families sought to raise only a single child.

To assert that such behaviour is somehow associated with, say, living in southern Transdanubia, being a Hungarian, and being a Calvinist—all conditions to be satisfied simultaneously—is perhaps not overly edifying. A more significant lesson, however, lies in the demonstration that identical behaviour was generated in a variety of greatly differing cultural environments. In each instance, this happened in the face of official disapproval, in the absence of modern methods of contraception, and without much exposure to any form of mass media. One must conclude that common forces were at work which transcended religion or race, but were triggered into unusually early action in certain cultural settings. Unfortunately, these fundamental factors are elusive, and it is difficult, if not impossible, to isolate them statistically. In the present instance, significant evidence points to the paramount importance of economic aspirations—specifically the desire to acquire, to hold on to, and to accumulate land under the increasingly adverse combination of growing population pressures, stable or expanding latifundia, and limited availability of alternative employment opportunities. More vaguely and speculatively, a number of features in the area's historic background may be pertinent to the early decline. It should be noted in this context that much of the land was repopulated during the eighteenth century as a result of organized settlement schemes, and for a long time, segments of the repopulated land were administered as part of the Military Frontier Region. Undoubtedly the fact that the area was a meeting point of at least four major nationalities and at least three major religions, unseparated by political boundaries, is not without relevance in itself.

Finally, it should be mentioned that the detailed analysis of intra-provincial differences reconfirms to some extent the importance of at least two factors emphasized by traditional transition theory: infant mortality and literacy. Although inspection of the average values of these indices does not single out the seven provinces as likely candidates for early fertility decline, *within* each province early decline does tend to show an association with both lower infant mortality and higher literacy. This proposition remains valid even when the disturbing influence of other correlated factors (notably nationality and religion) is eliminated. Once again, the role of these factors is facilitating and permissive, rather than decisive. Interestingly, the experience of the region in question shows that infant mortality rates that are very high by modern standards even for the less-developed countries (such as two hundred or more infant deaths per thousand live births) are quite consistent with drastic and increasing limitation of marital fertility.

Massimo Livi-Bacci

Fertility and population growth in Spain in the eighteenth and nineteenth centuries

Demographers have for some time been devoting their attention to the secular (long-term) decline of fertility in the Western populations—its determinants, concomitants, and consequences. Although a completely satisfactory theory explaining the decline has yet to be formulated, it is clear that the decline is closely related to the spread of birth control during the nineteenth and twentieth centuries. The increasing acceptance of a neo-Malthusian attitude toward procreation and, also, the voluntary limitation of family size within marriage are characteristic features of the demographic development of Western populations during the last hundred years.

In recent decades, the demographers' attention has turned increasingly to the problem of the nature of fertility in pre-modern populations. Their interest lies in charting what happened before the onset of the decline. Were birth-control techniques spread by the 'diffusion' of already existing techniques practised at least among certain 'upper' sectors of the population or by genuine 'innovation', involving modification of old models of behaviour?

It has long been commonly held that populations do not experience substantial changes in the level of legitimate fertility before systematic and continuous decline in fertility. According to this assumption, modifications in the birth rate are attributable to changes in the frequency of marriage and illegitimacy or to shifts in the population's age-sex distribution. Deeper analysis, however, has shown that the levels of fertility may change because of the varying impact of sterility, pregnancy wastage, duration of breast feeding, and so forth. Thus, the birth rate may vary not only because of changes in a population's age-sex marital-status structure, but also because of the action of biological factors. If we follow Louis Henry's definition, pre-modern populations lived in a *régime* of natural fertility that was unaffected by volitional factors. Even such taboos as the abstention from sexual intercourse during lactation cannot be defined as a voluntary check on fertility.[1]

Nevertheless, it has not yet been demonstrated that biological factors account for all the differences in the levels of fertility among and within pre-modern populations. The conspicuous variations in fertility among populations, the strong rural-urban or class differentials within the same population, the notable diffusion of neo-Malthusian habits among selected (upper) sectors of the society, long-term changes in fertility within the same population (when controls are made for other factors) are elements that may support the theory that voluntary control of fertility was also at work in pre-Malthusian populations. This theory gathers further support when one examines the birth-control techniques employed before the large-scale diffusion of manufactured devices—techniques, such as *coitus interruptus*, that could be used by any sufficiently motivate couple.[2]

When more material is analysed with the tools of modern demography, the distinction between 'natural' and 'controlled' fertility will probably become less clear cut. This distinction will remain useful, but on theoretical, rather than empirical, grounds.

GENERAL CHARACTERISTICS OF THE SPANISH DEMOGRAPHIC DEVELOPMENT

Official data for Spain are unreliable until the end of the nineteenth century, but they do indicate that fertility had begun to decline there by the turn of the century, two or three decades later than it had in most Western European countries. As in other European countries, however, recurrent ravages of 'catastrophic' mortality affected population growth in Spain from the sixteenth century to the beginning of the eighteenth. As far as demographic development is concerned, the notable features of Spain's catastrophic century are the plagues of 1598–1602 and 1649–52, the expulsion of the Moriscos in 1609, the emigration to the New World, and the years of very high mortality caused by poor harvests. Various enumerations in 1591–4 put Spain's total population at 8·5 million; this figure is reduced to 7·5 million in 1717 and increased to 9·3 million in 1768, date of the first modern census. Little reliability can be claimed for the figures of 1591–4 and 1717; nevertheless, all the available indicators, together with the historical events of the

[1] Louis Henry, 'Some Data on Natural Fertility', *Eugenics Quarterly* (June 1961).
[2] See sections 2.6 and 2.7 of my article, 'Fertility and Nuptiality Changes in Spain from the Late 18th to the Early 20th Century', V, Part I, *Population Studies*, XXII, 1, 1968, pp. 98–102.

period, point towards a stabilization or reduction of the Spanish population.

The eighteenth century marks the beginning of a cycle of population growth. A period of relative prosperity follows the Peace of Utrecht in 1713. The plague disappears, and, in spite of frequent outbreaks of yellow fever and smallpox, catastrophic mortality is effectively checked. From 1768 to 1900, the population doubles in size, rising from 9·309 million to 18·608; the growth appears to be steady, without sudden depressions and accelerations (as is shown in Table 1, where the country's demographic development is traced through the census enumerations).[3]

The 1717 enumeration of households, whose reliability is still severely in question, was followed by three censuses having nearly modern characteristics: those taken by Aranda in 1768–9, by Floridablanca in 1787, and by Larruga in 1797.[4]

Table 1   Growth of the Spanish population, 1717–1910

Year	Population (000)	Average intercensal rate of increase (%)
1717	7,500·0	—
1768	9,308·9	0·42
1787	10,409·9	0·59
1797	10,541·2	0·13
1860	15,649·1	0·63
1887	17,560·1	0·43
1900	18,608·1	0·45
1910	19,944·6	0·70

Aranda based his census on the country's ecclesiastical subdivisions. As this method excludes from the count not only those villages belonging to the military orders but also those under the jurisdiction *nullius*, the census probably understates the population. Nevertheless, for the first time, at least at the national level, the census unit was the individual instead of the household subject to tribute. Unlike Aranda's tabulation, the 1787 census (considered the most complete of the three) and the 1797 one (which, like Aranda's probably understates the population) are based on a civilian subdivision of the country. The territorial data can, therefore, be com-

---

[3] For a general treatment of Spanish population development, see especially J. Nadal, *La población Española: Siglos XVI a XX* (Barcelona, 1966). See also. J. Vicens Vives, *Historia Social y Economica de España y America* (Barcelona, 1958), Books 3–4.

[4] *Censo Español Executado de Orden del Rey Communicado por el Excelentisimo Señor Conde de Floridablanca, Primer Secretario de Estado y del Despacho en el Año de 1787* (Madrid, no date). *Censo de la Población de España de el Año de 1797 Executado de Orden del Rey en el Año de 1801* (Madrid, no date).

pared with those of later enumerations.[5] Besides their use of the
individual as the unit of enumeration, the three census of the
second half of the eighteenth century have in common a sex-age
distribution combined with marital status.

A gap of sixty years separates Larruga's censuses from the first
modern census, taken in nominative form in 1857. During this interval, many unreliable counts of the population were made, either
officially or unofficially for administrative or fiscal reasons; none
of these provides sex-age details.[6] The year 1857 marks the beginning
of the modern statistical era; after 1857, censuses were taken in
1860, 1877, 1897, 1900, and every ten years thereafter. As far
as vital statistics are concerned, official data on births, deaths, and
marriages are unavailable until 1858. Between 1858 and 1870, data
were collected by parishes and published with provincial detail.
After the creation of a 'civil register' in 1878, demographic events
were systematically recorded by the civil authorities. The same
official sources warn, however, that these statistics remain largely
unreliable until the beginning of this century.[7]

The data in Table 1 show that the rate of Spain's population
growth was steady from the eighteenth century to the beginning
of the twentieth. Unlike England and Wales, the Scandinavian
countries, and other Western populations, Spain did not experience a rise in the rate of increase and a major decrease in mortality
as a result of a reduction in both 'normal' and 'catastrophic' mortality. As late as 1900, expectation of life at birth in Spain was
below thirty-five years, a level surpassed by the Scandinavian
countries one hundred and fifty years earlier.

The relatively stable rate of increase during the eighteenth and
nineteenth centuries implies a parallelism in the trends of the birth
and death rates. One must ask whether this stability was maintained through unchanged levels of fertility and mortality or
through their equal change. Owing to a marked stabilization of
living conditions—mainly the result of fewer shortages of foodstuffs—mortality must have declined during the first fifty or sixty
years of the nineteenth century. Still, the recurrent epidemics of
yellow fever, smallpox, and cholera probably reversed this trend
fairly often.

[5] For a discussion of the quality of the three censuses, see J. Nadal, La Poblacion Española:
Siglos XVI a XX, pp. 24–6; J. Vicens Vives, Historia Social y Economica de España y America,
Vol. 1, Book 4, pp. 8–9; J. Ruiz Almansa, 'El Censo de la Poblacion de España de 1797',
Revista Internacional de Sociologia (1947), n. 19; P. Vilar, 'Problèmes de Démographie
Historique de Espagne', Annales de Démographie Historique 1965 (1966), pp. 24–5.
[6] Enumerations of 1822, 1826, 1831, 1832, 1836, 1837, 1842, and 1846. See Anuario
Estadistico de España, 1859–60 (Madrid, 1860), pp. xxv–xxxviii; Anuario Estadistico de
España, 1860–61 (Madrid, 1862–63), 'Trabajos Estadisticos de España', pp. xxiv ff.
[7] Movimiento de la Poblacion de España, 1886–92 (Madrid, 1895).

STABLE TECHNIQUES OF ANALYSIS AND THE MORTALITY OF THE SPANISH POPULATION

On the basis of the pioneering work of Alfred Lotka, a complex methodology has been developed for estimating vital rates from census age distributions. Lotka has mathematically demonstrated that every population experiencing the same mortality risks and fertility rates tends to assume an unvarying or 'stable' age distribution, with constant birth, death, and growth rates. Because premodern populations often approximate conditions of stability, they can be treated as if they were stable.

Estimates of vital rates, based on stable techniques, are reached essentially by two successive stages. In the first stage, a model stable population is chosen. This selection can be made using two nonredundant parameters, such as rate of growth, level of mortality or fertility, or age distribution. In the second stage, the characteristics of the model—birth, death, growth rates, and so forth—can be assumed to represent those of the actual population. The work involved in selecting the model is greatly facilitated by the large number of pre-calculated stable populations corresponding to different levels of mortality and rates of increase.[8]

We may assume with a certain degree of confidence that the Spanish population approached stability during the eighteenth century, since the rate of growth was steady, catastrophic mortality was reduced, although by no means eliminated, and migration was negligible.

The census age distribution provides one of the two parameters needed in selecting the model; either the intercensal rate of growth or the level of mortality may be used for the other. Computation of the rate of growth is affected by the varying completeness of the eighteenth-century censuses. This type of distortion tends to be reduced, however, when the rate of growth is computed for a sufficiently wide interval. There is no direct and reliable information on the levels of mortality in Spain during the eighteenth century.

In an effort to estimate mortality, we have combined the 1768–97 rate of growth with the 1797 age distribution.[9] The 1768–97 period has been selected because the rate of increase appears to equal that of the 1717–68 period, and because the higher completeness

[8] A. J. Coale and P. Demeny, *Regional Model Life Tables and Stable Populations* (Princeton, 1966), Ch. 3.

[9] The model stable populations adopted for the various estimates are drawn from the 'South' set of the Princeton tables. As a matter of fact, the South model tables closely fit the official Spanish life tables, 1900–50. (See Coale and Demeny, *Regional Model Life Tables and Stable Populations*, Fig. 2, p. 26).

of the 1787 census would have produced a rate of growth too high for 1768–87 and too low for 1787–97. The method outlined above leads to the following estimates: rate of growth (1768–97), 4·3 per thousand; birth rate, 42·3 per thousand; and expectation of life at birth, 26·8 years. The estimated level can be assumed to represent the mortality prevailing during the eighteenth century, once we have decided whether an expectation of life slightly below twenty-seven years is consistent with the evolution of mortality in Spain during the nineteenth and early-twentieth centuries; with the social, economic, and sanitary conditions of that time; and with the mortality levels then prevalent in Western populations.

The gains in expectation of life in Spain from the eighteenth century to the 1860s and 70s are very slight, reflecting only a moderate improvement in the country's sanitary conditions. That

Table 2 Expectation of life of the Spanish population, 1797–1910

Date	Years
Prior to 1797*	26·8
1861–70**	29·1
1877–87**	28·9
1900**	34·8
1910**	40·5

* Our estimate.
** Inst. Geog. y Est.

mortality should have decreased during this period had to be expected. The plague disappeared—for causes still unknown, but probably related to the improvement of nutritional standards and the adoption of effective measures against its dissemination. Other epidemic diseases, such as yellow fever, smallpox, and cholera, appeared upon dissipation of the plague, but their consequence were less terrible than those of the plague. After the beginning of the nineteenth century, the deadly effects of smallpox were checked by the diffusion of Jenner's vaccination. Data collected by J. Nadal for the Cataluñian city of Palamos show a drastic decrease in infant mortality, beginning about 1820.[10] Living conditions and nutritional standards undergo a general improvement during the eighteenth and nineteenth centuries. Famines became more infrequent, and the improved system of communication and transportation allowed better internal redistribution of foodstuffs (particularly during the nineteenth century).[11] In 1834, Moreau de Jonnès, a Frenchman,

[10] J. Nadal, 'Sur La Population Catalane au XVIII¹, Siecle', *International Population Conference* (United Nations; New York, 1961), Vol. 1, pp. 591–600.
[11] J. Vicens Vives, *Historia Social y Economica de España y America*, Vol. 1, Book 4, pp. 160–1.

could write in his statistical work on Spain: 'Production of agriculture has doubled in quantity, exceeding all public needs, and famine does not come every third year as before to decimate the population of some province of the nation.'[12]

Although reliable national life tables are lacking (with the exception of Sweden), levels of expectation of life below thirty years seem to have been quite common in Europe during the eighteenth century. According to R. Duvillard's table, the expectation of life of the French population before the Revolution was around twenty-nine years.[13] Judging from the incidence of extraordinary mortality, sanitary conditions were probably worse in Spain than in France. In Italy, expectation of life was around twenty-six years in Bologna (1811–12); twenty-eight in Verona (1761–66); twenty-nine in Liguria (1807–12) and Naples (1826–44); and thirty in Milan (1804–5).

A level of mortality corresponding to an expectation of life at birth of around twenty-seven years is, therefore, a likely estimate for eighteenth-century Spain. This estimate is consistent with both the evolution of social and sanitary conditions in the nineteenth and early-twentieth centuries and the mortality levels of other European countries, particularly France and Italy.

THE EVOLUTION OF FERTILITY 1768–1910

With the help of the stable techniques outlined in the preceding paragraphs[14] and using the official statistics of births after 1858, we have computed the following measures of fertility from 1768 to 1910: the birth rate; the marital fertility rate (MFR), or the number of legitimate births per 1,000 married females of fecund age (15–49 years); and a measure of marital fertility (I_g) standardized

[12] A Moreau de Jonnès, *Statistique de L'Espagne* (Paris, 1834), pp. 34 ff.

[13] Louis Henry, 'The Population of France in the XVIII Century', *Population in History*, eds. Glass and Eversley (London, 1965), pp. 445–6. According to Henry, Duvillard's estimate, based on Halley's method, overestimates mortality. In fact, since the population of France increased during the eighteenth century, Duvillard's estimate of $^0e_0$ (28·8) has to be raised well over twenty-nine years.

[14] For 1768, 1787, and 1797, the estimated level of mortality has been combined with the cumulative proportion of the census population (cx) under seven, sixteen, twenty-five, forty, and sixty (only for 1797) years of age. Then for each of the six combinations of the mortality level and cx, the appropriate stable population has been selected, and the corresponding birth rates recorded. Of the six estimates of the birth rate, the median has been selected as the 'final' and 'true' value for each sex; the two medians (one derived from the male and the other from the female age distribution) have been averaged to get the final estimate for the whole population. For 1860, 1887, 1900, 1910, the birth rate has been computed on the basis of the registered births adjusted for under-registration. (See the Appendix of my article, 'Fertility and Nuptiality Changes in Spain from the Late 18th to the Early 20th Century', Part 2, in *Population Studies*, XXII, 2, 1968, pp. 232–3.)

by age (ratio of the legitimate births of the actual population to the legitimate births that the married population would have produced had it experienced the maximum 'empirical' fertility—that of the Hutterites). Because both MFR and I_g are independent of the changing marital status and (but only I_g) of the age structure of the female population of reproductive age, they are more precise measures of fertility than the birth rate.

The fertility measures are supplemented by an index of the age structure of the married female population (the ratio of the married women aged sixteen to twenty-five to the married women forty to fifty). For 1858–62, 1900–1904, and 1908–12, we have also indicated the proportion of illegitimate births over the total number of births; this proportion is unknown for earlier dates.

The estimates of the birth rates for 1768, 1787, and 1797 are based on the census age distribution, which is determined by the joint action of mortality and fertility over several decades previous to the census date. Even though the birth rate reflects a situation that antedates the census, we speak of the '1768', '1787', and '1797' birth rates for the sake of simplicity.

The data collected in Table 3 give an interesting picture of the development of Spanish fertility. The birth rate drops substantially between 1768 and 1860. This decline accelerates after 1860, and by 1910 the birth rate is less than three fourths the 1768 level.

Table 3   Measures of fertility, 1768–1910

Year	Birth rate	% Married females 16–50 over total population	% Illeg. births over total births	Married females 16–25/100 married females 40–50	MFR	I_g
1768	43·84	14·76	..	42·1	280·4‡	0·767
1787	43·16	14·71	..	48·4	277·0‡	0·745
1797	42·27	14·53	..	53·5	274·6‡	0·735
1860	39·50*	15·05†	5·6**	..	247·8	0·659†
1887	37·03*	15·16	..	54·5	232·6	0·616
1900	36·05*	14·82	4·4**	50·8	232·6	0·622
1910	32·75*	14·36	4·8**	46·4	217·2	0·582
		Index numbers, 1768=100				
1768	100·0	100·0	..	100·0	100·0	100·0
1787	98·4	99·7	..	115·0	98·3	97·1
1797	96·4	98·4	..	127·1	97·9	95·8
1860	90·1	102·0	..	..	88·4	85·9
1887	84·5	102·7	..	129·5	83·0	80·3
1900	82·2	100·4	..	120·7	83·0	81·1
1910	74·7	97·3	..	110·2	77·5	75·9

* Birth rates computed considering the average births for 1861–64, 1886–89, 1900–3, 1909–12.
† Estimated value.
** 1858–62, 1900–4, and 1909–12.
‡ Values computed discounting an illegitimacy equal to the 1858–62 value.

The decline between 1768 and 1887 becomes even more evident when we turn our attention to measures of marital fertility. By 1887, MFR and I_g are 17 to 20 per cent below the 1768 values (15 per cent for the birth rate). In the second half of the nineteenth century, therefore, both the population's marital structure and age composition were more favourable to a high number of births than they were during the eighteenth century. By 1910, marital fertility had fallen to slightly over three fourths the 1768 estimated levels.

By subdividing the country into four large regions, each having a certain social or geographic homogeneity, and analysing regional data, we uncover certain interesting features.

The East experiences the largest decline, during both the 1768–1860 and the 1860–1910 periods; the overall decline is inconspicuous in the Centre and the North; in the South, fertility falls rapidly after 1860. The Catalan-speaking area, part of the former Crown of Aragon, shows a continuous decline that is certainly associated with the increasing diffusion of neo-Malthusian attitudes. H. Puig i

Table 4   The decline in marital fertility, 1787–1910

Year	Marital fertility rate (MFR)				Index numbers, 1787 = 100			
	East*	South†	Centre**	North‡	East	South	Centre	North
1787	283	274	260	279	100	100	100	100
1860	243	261	242	247	86	95	93	89
1910	180	218	229	248	64	80	88	89

* The East: Old Crown of Aragón, Cataluña, Baleares and Valencia.
† The South: Andalusia and Murcia.
** The Centre: Castilla la Nueva, Extremadura, and León.
‡ The North: Galicia, Castilla la Vieja, Vascongadas y Navarra, Asturias.

Sais has indicated that the spread of certain contraceptive practices (primarily *coitus interruptus*) was the main factor in the fall of Catalan fertility.[15] Because Cataluña enjoyed a relatively high social level, was receptive to French influences, and entertained close cultural ties with other Catalan-speaking populations, it can be considered the ideal place for the start and diffusion of neo-Malthusianism in Spain.

The transition the Spanish population underwent between the eighteenth and nineteenth centuries would provide substantiation for a theory that marital fertility declined because of a wider use of birth control. The data on which we founded our analysis are,

[15] H. Puig i Sais, *El Problema de la Natalitat a Catalunya* (Barcelona, 1915). See also, J. A. Vandellós, *Catalunya: Poble Decadent* (Barcelona, 1935).

however, by no means perfect. It is well known that the eighteenth-century censuses are not blameless. We have assumed that age distribution was unaffected by census errors, but this assumption could prove to be wishful thinking. Moreover, the estimate of eighteenth-century mortality is little more than an elaborate guess, although one consistent with what is known about mortality in that period. Finally, we have assumed that the Spanish population, like other pre-modern populations, approached a situation of stability during this period. The precision and reliability of this approximation cannot be measured. Wars, epidemics, and extraordinary events of all sorts often prevented pre-modern populations from reaching stability, thereby distorting their age distribution and affecting the reliability of estimates based on stable techniques.

Nevertheless, little more can be done on the basis of the available data. We have aimed to test whether the fertility of the Spanish population remained stable from the end of the eighteenth century to the end of the nineteenth. Our evidence leads to the conclusion that fertility dropped, although prudential use of this finding must be recommended.

Careful consideration has to be given to another aspect of the problem. The level of marital fertility remains substantially lower in Spain than it does in other Western populations.[16] Although

Table 5   European fertility levels circa 1870 (I_g)

Prussia	0·90
Netherlands	0·85
Norway	0·76
Sweden	0·71
Switzerland	0·69
England and Wales	0·68
Italy	0·68
Ireland	0·68
Spain (1860)	0·66
Spain (1887)	0·62

the diffusion of neo-Malthusianism was already under way among certain sectors of the other Western populations (upper classes, urban areas), Spanish fertility is well at the bottom of the list. Can biological factors alone explain the 30 per cent difference between Spain and Prussia, or must the action of possible volitional factors be taken into account when determining the causes of so large a gap?

If volitional factors must be considered, and if the decline from the end of the eighteenth century to the end of the nineteenth is

[16] A. J. Coale, 'Factors Associated with the Development of Low Fertility: An Historic Summary', World Population Conference (Belgrade, 1965), n. 194.

real, we have created more problems than we have solved. Why did fertility decline in Spain, a deeply Catholic, strongly rural society with low social mobility and late, limited industrialization? Even when one accepts a 'diffusion' or 'adjustment' theory of fertility decline, the factors of the decline remain largely unexplained. According to this theory:

> Birth control, and especially contraception, need not be regarded as recent or new in human society. There may have been a 'steady state' in which birth control was practised by part of the population, or it may have been practised with higher fertility targets. The decline in fertility is then regarded as an adjustment to a new set of forces, defining a new equilibrium level of modern or 'controlled' fertility.[17]

The usual demographic explanations of fertility decline do not fit the Spanish experience. Although the secularization of life, the diffusion of education, and the process of industrialization and urbanization are probably important factors in the decline of fertility in many European countries and in Cataluña, their impact on the development of Spanish society was rather weak, at least during the first part of the nineteenth century.

Demographers should, perhaps, devote more attention to other, no less important, modifications in Spanish society. In 1787, one seventh to one eighth of all males about fifty years of age had never been married; by 1887, this proportion had fallen to one sixteenth. The reduced frequency of celibacy is, on the one hand, an effect of the decreased numerical importance of the clergy (6 per cent of the adult population by the mid-eighteenth century). On the other, it is a consequence of both the decreasing number of people claiming a noble origin (some 8 per cent of the total population in 1768) and the crisis of the institution of the *mayorazgo* (the practice of entailing land to the elder son). According to G. M. Jovellanos:

> The most notable evil (produced by *mayorazgos*)—if not the worst of all evils—falls on those same families for which the *mayorazgo* is created. Nothing is more repugnant than seeing the cadet sons of noble families, with no position and no career, condemned to poverty, celibacy, and idleness.[18]

Many class and caste preclusions to marriage were wiped out during the nineteenth century, in part because the war against France, 'intermingling men of different classes, had destroyed many social

[17] G. Carlsson, 'The Decline of Fertility: Innovation or Adjustment Process', *Population Studies*, Vol. 20, No. 2 (1966), p. 150.

[18] G. M. Jovellanos, *Informe de la Sociedad Economica de Esta Corte al Real y Supremo Consejo de Castilla en el Expediente de Ley Agraria* (Madrid, 1795), p. 73.

divisions, many imaginary differences, many local rivalries, once insuperable obstacles to the foundation of new families'.[19] It is possible that the disappearance of many preventive, or 'Malthusian' checks to the birth rate (the elimination of the obstacles to marriage), gave way to the diffusion of a 'neo-Malthusian' check, or the voluntary control of fertility within marriage.[20]

[19] A. Moreau de Jonnès, *Statistique de l'Espagne* (Paris, 1834), pp. 34 ff.
[20] A full discussion of the problems and the data presented in this paper will be found in my article 'Fertility and Nuptiality Changes in Spain from the Late 18th to the Early 19th Century', *op. cit.*

Michael Drake

Fertility controls in pre-industrial Norway

'Tell me Ole, you married when you were twenty-three years of age: don't you think now, when you reflect on the matter, that it was folly to marry so early?'

'No. I cannot say that . . . I thought it was best what I did, for when one marries so early one has one's youth in which to work for the children and can get them out in the world before old age arrives.'

'Nonsense, you didn't think in that way about it.'

'Yes I did—for it is something one often sees, people falling into complete destitution when, in old age, they find themselves with small children—one can have a lot of children even if one marries rather late. That was the case with my parents. I was the eldest and in service, but at home there were many youngsters and earnings were small so conditions were bad.'[1]

'Tell me Nils, how was it possible that such an active boy as you could go out and take such an old one for a wife? She looks to me a capable body, but she is so much older than you.

'I thought when I took such an old woman, the crowd of young ones would not be so great, for it is difficult for one who is in small circumstances to feed so many.'[2]

These two extracts from Eilert Sundt's (1817–75) major work on marriage in Norway purport to represent conversations between him and a number of cottars (*husmenn*) during the early 1850s. As a pioneer in sociology and social anthropology, Sundt spent some twenty years examining the conditions of life of the Norwegian peasantry. At that time Norway had virtually no industry, apart from that conducted in the home and no towns of any size. (Christiania, or Oslo as it is now known, was the biggest settlement and in 1855 had a population of only a little over 40,000; Bergen, the next largest, had about half this number of inhabitants.) Most of the population

[1] Eilert Sundt, *Om Giftermaal i Noege* (Christiania, 1855), p. 204.
[2] Eilert Sundt, *op. cit.*, p. 217.

worked on the land, with important subsidiary earnings from fisheries, shipping, and forestry. Farms were relatively small and were worked by the farmer's family, unmarried servants living in, and married labourers, the so-called cottars or *husmenn*. The latter were often given a small plot of land and a cottage in return for their labour. It was with these men, the cottars, that Sundt spent much of his time. The extracts cited above, from his conversations with them, give rise to several interesting reflections.

First of all, there is the assumption that marriage at twenty-three years was early for a man of the labouring class. By comparison with his peers, 'Ole' did marry early. In the mid-1850s the mean age at first marriage (bachelor-spinster) in Norway was about twenty-nine years for men and twenty-seven years for women.

Table 1   Average age at first marriage (i.e. bachelors with spinsters), in the rural and urban areas of Norway, 1856–65

	Males	Females	Age difference
Norway	29·02	26·64	2·38
Rural districts	29·12	26·63	2·49
Urban districts	27·14	26·67	0·47
Rural districts of:			
Akershus diocese	29·02	26·53	2·49
Hamar diocese	27·91	26·42	1·49
Kristiansands diocese	29·06	26·03	3·03
Bergen diocese	29·05	27·10	1·95
Trondheim diocese	29·72	27·30	2·42
Tromsø diocese	29·12	26·63	2·49

Source: Ældre Række, C. no. 1, *Tabeller vedkommende folkemængdens bevægelse* [*i Norge*] *i aarene 1856–65* (Christiania, 1868–69), p. xxxii.

In a survey he conducted throughout Southern Norway, Sundt discovered that the mean age of cottars at first marriage in 1851–52 was 27·3 years and of their brides 26·8 years. The mean age at first marriage of farmers, in the same area and period, was 29·5 years and of their brides 26·0 years. The farmers thus married, on average, a couple of years later than their cottars, though the farmers' brides were, on average, younger than those of the cottars.

The second point arising from the quotations is the rather singular one that a man might deliberately lighten his burden of dependency by marrying a relatively old woman. Again there is ample statistical evidence to suggest that many men did this, although the reason for their choice might be rather different. The fact that the mean age at marriage of cottars and their wives was virtually identical would suggest that in many cases the wife was older than the husband. For example, if we look at Western Hedmark, where in 1801 the number of cottars was large relative to farmers (1,000 : 651), we discover that in 46·4 per cent of the marriages existing at that time, in which neither partner had previously been married, the husband was older than his wife; in 47·5 per cent, however, the wife was older than her husband; and in 6.1 per cent both partners were the same age. To go behind these aggregates, we find that in almost a quarter (23·6 per cent) of the marriages the wife was *at least* five years older than her husband, and in almost a tenth (8·9 per cent) of marriages she was ten or more years older. Much greater gaps than these are found, of course, if one considers second marriages, whether between bachelors and widows or spinsters and widowers.[3]

It also appears to be the case that the earlier a man married, the greater the chance that he would marry a woman some years his senior. For instance, a study made of the ages at which men and women entered their first marriage in a part of S.E. Østfold, an area where the age at marriage was earlier than in most other parts of the country, showed that in the years 1816–85 out of 9,709 marriages 7,072 took place between men and women who were under thirty years of age. The relationship between the ages at marriage was found to be as follows (Table 2). An analysis of the data in ten-year periods (1816–25, 1826–35, and so on) showed the relationship to be constant over time. Very few men married under the age of twenty-one years (less than 5 per cent), but of those who did, two-thirds married women *over* twenty-one years of age (309 out of 459).

Table 2   Relationship between ages of husbands and wives at marriage in S.E. Østfold, 1816–85: for couples marrying under age 30

Age of bridegroom (years)	Age of bride (years)
20	22·5
21	22·8
22	22·9
23	23·1
24	23·3
25	23·5
26	23·7
27	24·0
28	24·2
29	24·4
30	24·6

Source: Data drawn from marriage registers of the parishes of Glemmen, Tune, Øst and Vest Fredrikstad, Skjeberg, Sarpsborg, Onsøy and Borge.

The third and perhaps most striking feature of the quotations at the head of this article is that they suggest age at marriage was the most important, if not the only, control on fertility. In view of the comment of the first cottar to the effect that even when people married relatively late they might have more children than they

[3] Michael Drake, *Population and Society in Norway, 1735–1865* (Cambridge, 1969), pp. 125–32.

could adequately cope with, it also seems to have been recognized as not a particularly satisfactory control. Direct evidence to refute the suggestion that marriage was the main, if not the sole method of controlling fertility is hard to find. Condoms appear to have been made from the intestines of sheep and goats. Various brews involving the use of needles from yew trees or other evergreens, of ergot, saffron, turpentine, camomile tea, aloe, and cinnamon were concocted to facilitate abortion. But how effective they were is unknown. There is also evidence of prolonged lactation being used as a means of reducing the chances of conception. Periods of one to three years were reported as quite common with instances of up to twelve years being remarked upon![4]

Indirect evidence of a statistical nature suggests that fertility controls, whatever they might have been, were sharpened during periods of crisis—for example, when there were grave food shortages. During the period 1771–76, the diocese of Akershus, which embraced some 40 per cent of the country's inhabitants, experienced a major demographic crisis. The behaviour of the birth, marriage, and death rates during this period is shown in Table 3.

Table 3   Birth, deaths, and marriages per 1,000 mean population in the diocese of Akershus, 1771–76

	1771	1772	1773	1774	1775	1776
Deaths	21	26	64	29	26	20
Marriages	7	6	6	9	10	9
Births	34	28	22	29	35	32

Source: Michael Drake, *Population and Society in Norway, 1735–1865* (Cambridge, 1969), p. 69.

One can think of several factors contributing to the low birth rate of 1773. One would be the deaths of pregnant women; another, a decline in fecundity as a result of malnutrition; still another, the age composition of the population, which was probably unfavourable to a high birth rate. This latter observation is based on the fact that cohorts which would normally contribute most to the fertility of the population were probably small due to the very high death rates of 1741–43 and 1748 (they were respectively 42·4; 67·3; 34·2, and 40·3 per 1,000 mean population). It would seem unlikely, however, that these factors, either individually or combined, could produce the very low birth rate of 1773. One is left with the possibility of birth control within marriage.

That crisis years produced a sharpening of the birth control mechanism is suggested by a calculation made by Kiær, the first director of the Norwegian Central Statistical Office. He applied the reproductive quotients of married women in the period 1871–92 to

[4] Michael Drake, *op. cit.*, p. 70.

the populations recorded at the censuses of 1835, 1845, 1855, 1865, 1875, and 1890. He found that in each case the actual number of births recorded in the years centred on the census year was within 3 per cent of those arrived at by applying the reproductive quotients to the married female population. He also did the same calculation for the year 1801, but did not publish it, merely noting that it was much below the expected figure—a fact he ascribed to a deficiency in the data at that time. He may have been correct in this, but the years 1800–1 were crisis ones, with bad harvests, in Norway as in many other parts of Europe. The Akershus diocese had a death rate of 27·7 in 1800 and 34·0 per 1,000 in 1801. It is possible, therefore, that births were deliberately limited in this period. My calculation shows the births recorded at that time were only 86 per cent of those estimated by applying the 1871–92 reproductive quotients to the married women recorded in the 1801 census.

Whatever the possibilities of birth control within marriage, the fact that both men and women married relatively so late would suggest that marriage was an important control on fertility. The proportion of the population in the fertile age group who were married remained very stable throughout that part of the pre-industrial period for which we have adequate statistical information (Table 4).

Table 4 Unmarrieds as percentage of total men and women at ages 15–49 years in 1769, 1801, and 1865

Year	Males	Females
1769	48·7	51·0
1801	49·1	47·9
1865	52·5	49·8

Source: Norwegian official statistics, Statistical Survey 1948 (Oslo, 1949), x. 178, p. 31.

What were the factors delaying entry into marriage? And why, if a man married relatively early, did he so often marry a somewhat older woman? The main reason given to Sundt in the mid-nineteenth century was that a somewhat elderly woman would bring to marriage not only a wealth of domestic experience (learned on the farm where she had worked), but probably some worldly goods as well. In view of the enormous responsibilities carried by Norwegian women, particularly of the cottar class, marriage to other than such a woman involved all too obvious hazards. Many cottars spent long periods away from home lumbering, fishing during the winter months, or working on their landlord's farm. During these periods of absence, the cottar's wife carried on the management of his holding as well as looking after the family. To encourage men to marry women who, if not long in the tooth, were hardly in the first bloom of youth, farmers might promise crofts to the men who would take them.

When Malthus toured Norway in the summer of 1799, he was struck by the obvious hindrances to marriage and believed that the vigour of the population of Norway was due to the strength of the 'preventive check' there. He remarked that farmers were reluctant to let their servants have crofts (without which they would not have the wherewithal to marry and raise a family) because this meant reducing the area of land used to produce hay for winter fodder, which in turn meant reducing their flocks and thereby under-utilizing the mountain pastures. Further, in forested areas, the farmers would have to allow their crofters to take timber for building and fuel which would reduce another important source of their income. These limitations on new settlements were so obvious to all, and the absence of towns blocked another possible source of employment, that marriages had to be delayed until crofts fell vacant. Only on the seacoast, Malthus believed, where fishing offered an opportunity of earning a living, was the preventive check less strong. *A priori* Malthus was no doubt right. It is rather ironic, however, that some fifty years later it was on an island off the west coast of Norway that Eilert Sundt found the most extreme case, in his experience, of farmers limiting access to holdings.

On the island of Vigren there were in 1855 only fifty-three farms. The same number had been recorded at each of the censuses of 1801, 1825, 1835, and 1845. The farmers not only had refused to divide their farms; they also placed strict limits on the number of cottars they would allow to settle on them. In 1856, Sundt found only five cottars with land (*husmenn med jord*) and one cottar without land (*husmann uten jord*). The farmers of Vigren needed labour over and above what their families could supply; but as there were so few cottars, the major source of labour in the eastern part of the country, they had to import them. In 1856, there were 118 male farm servants living on the farms. Of these, twenty-seven were the sons of farmers on the island; the other ninety-one were not related. Of the ninety-one, only two had been born on Vigren. When these farms' servants wanted to marry and set up their own households, they had to leave; the farmers of Vigren would not provide them with crofts. Sundt commented:

> In many districts, especially in eastern Norway, I have often heard farmers speak about how desirable it would be if one could put a stop to the formation of the working class and the increase of pauperism. But nowhere have I found this thought so carried out in practice as in Vigren.[5]

[5] Eilert Sundt, 'Harham. Et exempel fra fiskeri distrikterne', *Folkevennen* (1858), pp. 378–9.

Restrictions on entry to marriage were made more acceptable, and hence more effective, in most parts of the country by the generally lax control of pre-marital relations. In many parts of Norway, it was usual for the male and female farm servants to share the same sleeping accommodation. Often this was in lofts above the stables and byres. On Saturday nights it was usual for men to wander from farm to farm and spend the night where they fancied, without being disturbed by the farmer or his family. Among the farming class the way to marriage might well involve a lengthy period of courtship during which the prospective couple would at least share the same bed. Whether sexual intercourse took place and if so how often we cannot now say. That it did occur and that it did precipiatate marriage is suggested by some calculations of Sundt's from the 1850s. These show (Table 5) the number of premarital conceptions in the cottar and farmer class. There were, it is apparent, regional variations. The

Table 5   Number of married couples in Class I (mostly cottars) and Class II (mostly farmers) who had children before marriage, within 4 months and between 4 and 8 months of marriage per 100 of all couples married in 1855–56 in different parts of Norway

| | | Of 100 married couples the following had children | | | | | | |
| | | Class I | | | | Class II | | |
Deanery groups*	Before marriage	Within 4 months after marriage	From 4–8 months after marriage	Total	Before marriage	Within 4 months after marriage	From 4–8 months after marriage	Total
1	5	17	10	32	11	23	12	46
2	9	20	12	41	24	25	16	65
3	6	20	15	41	13	25	13	51
4	3	17	11	31	10	25	11	46
5	2	10	11	23	6	21	13	40
6	1	9	12	22	3	12	11	26
7	5	18	9	32	8	30	13	51
8	3	14	13	30	9	26	11	46
9	10	22	13	45	18	23	10	51
10	5	12	13	30	14	23	10	47
11	14	17	13	44	30	15	11	56
12	13	12	6	31	25	14	8	47
13	9	18	14	41	15	25	11	51
14	17	13	13	43	30	14	12	56
15	12	9	9	30	26	9	10	45

*Sundt grouped the deaneries as follows: (1) Nedre, Mellem, Vestre and Østre Borgesyssel, Nedre Romerike. (2) Øvre Romerike, Soløer and Odalen, Østerdalen, Hedemarken, Gudbrandsdalen. (3) Toten, Valdres, Hadeland Ringerike and Hallingdal, Kongsberg. (4) Drammen, Nordre and Søndre Jarlsberg, Larvik, Bamble, Nedre Telemark (5) Øvre Telemark Østenfjeldske and Vestenfjeldske, Østre and Vestre Nedenæs, Råbygdelaget. (6) Mandal, Lister, Dalerne. (7) Jæren, Stavanger, Karmsund, Ryfylke. (8) Hardanger and Voss, Sunnhordland, Nordhordland. (9) Ytre and Indre Sogn. (10) Sunnfjord, Nordfjord, Søndre and Nordre Sunnmøre. (11) Romsdal, Nordmøre, Fosen. (12) Søndre and Nordre Dalerne. (13) Søndre and Nordre Innherad, Namdalen. (14) Søndre and Nordre Helgeland, Søndre and Nordre Salten, Lofoten, Vesterålen. (15) Tromsø, Vest and Øst Finnmark.

Source: Eilert Sundt, *Fortsatte bidrag angaaende soedelicheds tilstanden i Norge* (Christiania 1864), p. 44.

table also makes clear that not all pre-marital conceptions led immediately to marriage. A not inconsiderable number appear to have borne illegitimate children, only marrying perhaps when the second or third child arrived.

The nuptiality and fertility pattern of Norway was not untypical of most West European societies, at least by the mid-nineteenth century. (See tables in statistical appendix.) To the extent that the theory of the demographic transition posits high and uncontrolled fertility, it is, in societies like Norway, obviously wrong. It is correct, however, in suggesting that the sustained rise in population, which began in Western Europe some two centuries ago, was due primarily to a fall in the death rate (Table 6).

As Table 6 shows, the average death rate before 1815 was in the

Table 6 Births and deaths per 1,000 mean population in Norway in the years 1736–75, 1776–1815, and 1816–55

Per 1,000 mean population	1736–75	1776–1815	1816–55
Births	30·9	29·9	31·6
Deaths	26·2	24·0	18·9

mid-20s. This average conceals, however, very marked annual fluctuations and even greater regional fluctuations. Thus the national death rate rose to 41 per 1,000 in 1741; 52 in 1742; 32 in 1748; 36 in 1763; 48 in 1773; 33 in 1785; 30 in 1789; and 36 in 1809. In many of the intervening years, however, it was as low as 20 per 1,000. Some of the most marked regional fluctuations occurred in the Akershus diocese where, as noted earlier, the death rate reached nearly 70 per 1,000 in 1742, was 64 in 1773, and 56 in 1809.[6]

This pattern of markedly fluctuating and often high (by almost any standards) death rates changed abruptly in the second decade of the nineteenth century. In the half century 1815–65, the crude death rate reached 20 per 1,000 in only 9 years: its highest point being 22·5 in 1834. On the other hand, it fell below 17 per 1,000 in only four years.

This sharp once-and-for-all fall in the death rate around 1815 caused the population to expand more rapidly than that of most other European countries (Table 7).

Why the pattern of the death rate changed in this way is not easy to explain. There was no Industrial Revolution; and in the early years of rapid population growth, demand for timber and shipping—

[6] For annual death rates, 1735–1865, in each of the Norwegian dioceses, see Drake, *Population and Society in Norway, 1735–1865.* Table 7, pp. 192–5.

Table 7   The growth of population in various European states from approximately
1815 to 1865

State	Population ca. 1815 (actual date in brackets)	Population ca. 1865 (actual date in brackets)	Annual average rate of growth ca. 1815 to ca. 1865 per cent
Norway	885,431 (1815)	1,701,756 (1865)	1·30
Sweden	2,465,066 (1815)	4,114,141 (1865)	1·03
Denmark	1,018,180 (1815)	1,600,551 (1860)	1·01
Russia	45,000,000 (1815)	61,081,801 (1863)	0·64
Prussia	10,349,031 (1816)	19,675,990 (1867)	1·27
Hanover	1,680,285 (1836)	1,937,637 (1867)	0·46
Saxony	1,558,153 (1832)	2,423,587 (1867)	1·25
Bremen	47,797 (1812)	109,572 (1867)	1·52
Bavaria	3,707,966 (1818)	4,824,421 (1867)	0·54
Austria	26,500,000 (1818)	35,500,000 (1867)	0·64
Holland	2,613,487 (1829)	3,293,577 (1859)	0·74
Belgium	3,785,814 (1831)	4,984,351 (1865)	0·81
England and Wales	10,454,529 (1811)	20,066,244 (1861)	1·31
France	30,461,875 (1821)	37,394,000 (1866)	0·46
Spain	12,286,941 (1833)	15,658,531 (1860)	0·90
Portugal	3,412,500 (1841)	3,693,363 (1861)	0·40
Switzerland	2,188,009 (1837)	2,510,494 (1860)	0·60

Source; Norges officielle statistik. Ældre Række. C. no. 1, Tabeller vedkommende folkemængdens
bevægelse i aarene, 1856–65 (Christiania, 1868–69), p. viii.

two of Norway's most important non-agricultural products—was
depressed. The rapid introduction of the potato, in the early years of
the nineteenth century, together with the spread of other innovations,
led to a marked rise in agricultural output per man, which no doubt
helped to eradicate subsistence crises.[7] The spread of vaccination
against smallpox probably also reduced the death rate.

That fertility did not decline to match the fall in mortality and so
bring down the rate of population growth to its previous modest level
would suggest either that the economy was expanding sufficiently
fast to keep up per capita incomes, or that, if it was not doing so, the
controls on fertility were not sufficiently strong or flexible to adjust to
the new situation. If the main control was delayed marriage, one can
readily understand this; for to bring down fertility to the required
level would have meant a further average delay of upwards of ten
years in the age at marriage. Coming on top of what was already a
relatively late age at marriage, such a further delay was hardly
tolerable. If there was birth control within marriage, then this too

[7] These changes have been very well documented in Fortein Valen-Sendstad, *Norske
landbruks-redskaper, 1800–1850 årene*, De Sandvigske samlinger (Lillehammer, 1964); this
book has an English summary.

would have had to be radically reorganized. It has been suggested above that in years of crisis fertility within marriage was sharply controlled. Birth control was thus an emergency procedure. For example, the birth rate was as low as 25·7 per 1,000 in 1742, 23·4 in 1773, 22·3 in 1809; all years of crisis. In the years after 1815 there were no such crisis years, and the birth rate never fell to such levels, and age specific fertility rates, as noted above, remained remarkably stable from 1835 to the 1880s.

The foregoing suggests that the population of pre-industrial Norway was subject to both the 'preventive' and the 'positive' check. The 'positive' check could on occasion be extremely savage, wiping out between a fifteenth and a twentieth of the population in a single year. Such crisis years were comparatively infrequent, however, in the eighteenth century and totally absent, after 1813, in the nineteenth; a result it seems of advances in agriculture, particularly the widespread adoption of the potato as a daily food. The threat of such crises, which if not always the result of harvest failures were widely thought to be so by contemporaries, and the desire to maintain living standards well above subsistence level caused the population to curtail fertility. In the main, this was done by not entering marriage until the late twenties. When subsistence crises occurred, however, there appears to have been some birth control within marriage. The disappearance of crises after 1815 presumably eradicated the need for this emergency-generated birth control within marriage, which probably accounts for the smaller fluctuations in and the slightly higher level (Table 6) of the birth rate after 1815 than before. That the age at marriage was not raised very much further appears to have been partly because the economy did expand to meet the needs of the increased population (apart from advances in agriculture, earnings from lumbering, the fisheries, and shipping increased from the mid-1820s) and partly because the social and psychological implications of such a shift, given the already advanced age at marriage, would have been very grave.

Without these checks on fertility in pre-industrial Norway, one can assume the country would have had a lower per capita income and a higher burden of dependency. A population that adopts such checks has, one might also assume, a less passive attitude toward its fate than one which is held in check by high mortality. Such a population is, therefore, a priori more likely to experience economic growth. That Norway did not enjoy an industrial revolution during her period of most rapid population growth (1815–65) was then more probably due to her lack of finance, raw materials, trading connections, and so forth, than to the inappropriateness of her demographic profile.

STATISTICAL APPENDIX

Table 8 Proportions married in various European countries. c. 1860

Of 1,000 males in following age groups there were:

Marital condition and age	Norway 1865	Denmark 1860	Switzerland 1860	Holland 1859	Belgium 1856	England and Wales 1861	Scotland 1861	France 1861	Italy 1860	Average of foregoing
SINGLE										
15–20	998·5	999·8	995·7	998·7	997·3	994·6	996·5	995·9	980·7	993
20–25	912	929·2	894	935	922	775	833	873	817	845
25–30	594	622·8	625	632	677	402	477	559	495	522
30–35	308	309	417	355	443	226	283	301	282	294
35–40	178	176	303	223	325	153	199	190	190	193
40–45	119	114	233	167	240	130	164	144	166	152
45–50	95	91	197	130	201	108	138	118	144	128
Total 15–50	525	522	581	560	597	473	535	487	486	497
MARRIED										
15–20	1·5	0·2	3·5	1·3	2·7	5·3	3·4	3·6	19	7
20–25	87	70·1	95	63·9	77·2	223	165	125	179·8	153
25–30	400	371·7	345	360	318	587	513	432	494	468
30–35	676	677	542	627	544	755	698	680	698	686
35–40	797	804	645	748	652	817	772	780	780	777
40–45	846	857	697	789	720	826	793	812	789	804
45–50	855	865	707	805	736	831	801	822	789	809
Total 15–50	459	464	382	421	386	508	447	492	493	482

Table 8—continued

Marital condition and age	Norway 1865	Denmark 1860	Switzerland 1860	Holland 1859	Belgium 1856	England and Wales 1961	Scotland 1861	France 1861	Italy 1860	Average of foregoing
				Of 1,000 females in following age groups there were:						
SINGLE										
15–20	989·2	985	973·8	993·7	982·7	969	978·7	946	896·6	946
20–25	802	794·7	771	853·4	825	664	741	651	539	655
25–30	498	471	500	536·0	568	369	460	374	287	375
30–35	291	249	356	311	373	232	311	240	195	244
35–40	213	162	276	214	280	173	253	177	157	182
40–45	153	121	220	169	216	142	220	148	143	154
45–50	137	105	196	143	195	122	199	129	130	137
Total 15–50	498	466	522	521	539	445	519	412	383	431
MARRIED										
15–20	10·7	12·9	23·3	6·2	17·2	30·5	21·1	53·6	101·5	53
20–25	196	203·2	210	144	173·1	331	255	343	449	338
25–30	491	518	460	452	424	613	520	607	680	603
30–35	685	727	586	661	606	729	645	724	752	716
35–40	743	796	639	734	680	765	672	764	749	750
40–45	778	811	654	742	713	761	662	761	728	747
45–50	757	783	624	717	691	744	642	738	659	713
Total 15–50	471	503	416	442	430	515	435	544	553	522

Source: Ældre Række C. no. 1, Tabeller vedkommende folkemængdens bevægelse [i Norgi] aarene, 1856–65 (Christiania 1865–68), p. xxii.

Table 9 Births per 100 women aged 20–45 years in various European countries, c. 1860

Country	Year	Women aged 20–45 years	Of which married	Live births per annum	Of which legitimate	Live births per 100 women aged 20–45 years	
						All births to all women	Legitimate births to married women
Norway	1856–65	284,449	153,698	52,055	47,840	18·30	31·13
Sweden	1861–65	725,004	(389,000)	132,540	120.358	18·28	30·94
Denmark	1850–59	273,814	154,331	48,608	43.293	17·75	28·05
Prussia	1856–61	3,224,109	(1,817,000)	680,529	626.089	21·11	34·46
Hanover	1858	328,555	(185,000)	60,567	54.151	18·43	29·27
Holland	1850–59	591,000	298,600	107,598	103.052	18·21	34·51
Belgium	1851–60	800,260	396,941	137,120	126.274	17·13	31·81
England and Wales	1851–60	3,553,786	2,154,000	647,165	604,848	18·21	28·08
France	1851–61	6,864,465	4,185,553	953,593	883,018	13·89	21·10
Spain	1858–63	2,977,000	(1,986,000)	582,567	550.000	19·57	27·69
Italy	1863–66	4,060,000	2,678,000	855,037	811,200	21·06	30·29
The above countries	ca. 1851–65	23,682,442	14,398,123	4,257,379	3,970,123	18·05	27·58

Source: Ældre Række, op. cit., p. xxxvii.

Table 10 Age at marriage in various European countries, c. 1860

Country	Under 20 years	20–25	25–30	30–35	35–40	40–45	45–50	Over 50	Total	Average age
	Among 1,000 males who entered marriage there were:									
Norway	8	200	363	222	95	48	24	40	1,000	30·8
Sweden	0·4	209	370	207	98	52	28	36	1,000	30·9
Denmark	{161	}	364	241	115	55	27	37	1,000	31·5
Belgium	27	175	328	210	116	64	37	43	1,000	31·56
England	28	472	254	101	51	36	22	36	1,000	27·94
France	28	247	325	186	94	{76	}	47	1,000	30·5
Italy	11	221	354	198	90	54	30	42	1,000	30·9
	Among 1,000 females who entered marriage there were:									
Norway	54	340	309	153	72	37	19	16	1,000	28·2
Sweden	49	317	317	164	81	41	19	12	1,000	28·4
Denmark	52	314	298	173	85	43	21	14	1,000	28·5
Belgium	111	263	287	164	86	46	25	18	1,000	28·55
England	131	496	196	76	41	27	16	17	1,000	25·39
France	188	365	222	108	54	{44	}	19	1,000	26·1
Italy	164	335	222	87	41	25	14	12	1,000	25·6

Source: Ældre Række, *op. cit.,* p. xxx.

P. C. Matthiessen

Replacement for generations of Danish females, 1840/1844–1920/1924

INTRODUCTION

One of the outstanding events of modern times has been what demographers call 'the demographic transition'.[1] By this term is meant the change from traditional societies, with high fertility and mortality, to modern societies, where fertility and mortality are low. There was by no means coincidence between the change in the two demographic components. In all societies that have experienced this transition, the mortality started to decline whereas the fall in fertility began several decades later.

In Northern and Western Europe and North America, the crude death rate began to decline around 1800 from a level of about 30 per 1,000 or more. Apart from France, where the fertility decline set in early in the nineteenth century, the crude birth rate began at first to fall from the former level of 30 to 40 per 1,000 or more in the second half of the nineteenth century. Today the value of the crude birth and death rates is in all these countries about 15 to 20 and 10 per 1,000 respectively, which produces a population growth per year of about 5 to 10 per 1,000.

Denmark fits rather well into this demographic picture.[2] Figure 1 shows the crude birth and death rate in Denmark in the period 1735–1965.

In the eighteenth century the size of both components is, on the average, about 30 per 1,000 with no clear secular trend. The crude birth rate is much more stable than the crude death rate, which fluctuates between 22 and 40 per 1,000. This fertility and mortality

[1] This study was completed during my stay at the London School of Economics and Political Science in the summer term 1968. I am especially indebted to Professor D. V. Glass, Professor G. W. Roberts, and Dr. S. Thapar for their interest in the work.
[2] As the demographic development has been entirely different in Greenland and the Faroe Islands, they are not included in the present study. After 1920 Southern Jutland has been included.

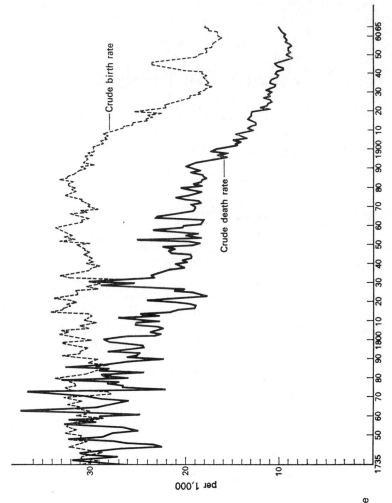

Figure 1 The crude birth and death rate in Denmark, 1735–1965

level resulted in rather slow growth of population per year—namely, about 3 per 1,000 in the period 1735–1800. The social and economic background of this demographic picture was a stationary agricultural society which, at certain intervals, was hit by hunger and epidemics.[3]

Around the year 1800 a decline in the crude death rate set in, which more or less has continued until now. The fall reduced the crude death rate to a level of about 10 per 1,000, which corresponds to an average expectation of life at birth of about seventy-two years.

As the crude birth rate remained unchanged until the end of the nineteenth century, an accelerating growth of the Danish population resulted from this development. Just before the end of the nineteenth century the *natural* population growth (excess of births over deaths) per year attained a level of nearly 15 per 1,000. The *actual* population growth was, however, somewhat lower, due to the considerable overseas emigration after 1870. From 1801 to 1901 the Danish population (Southern Jutland excluded) was increased from 1 million to 2·6 million people.

Since 1890, the decline in the crude birth rate amounted to about 50 per cent during the following forty years, which gave a crude birth rate of about 17 per 1,000 at the beginning of the thirties. After a temporary increase in the forties, the crude birth rate has today stabilized at a level of about 17 per 1,000 corresponding to a value of a gross reproduction rate of 1·2.

The present fertility and mortality level has produced a natural population growth per year of about 7 per 1,000. Today the Danish population is about 4·8 million people (Southern Jutland included).

Like other Northern and Western European countries, Denmark has experienced a huge economic and social transformation during the last 150 to 200 years. In 1801, only 20 per cent of the population lived in towns which apart from the capital (100,000 inhabitants) in no case had more than 6,000 inhabitants. In 1965, more than 63 per cent of the population lived in cities with more than 10,000 inhabitants. At the census in 1801, 67 per cent of the population were enumerated as attached to agriculture compared with only 14 per cent today. Measured in fixed prices the per capita income quadrupled between 1870–4 and 1956–9. In 1814, school education became compulsory for all children.

The demographic transition has been the focus of a large amount of demographic work. Before World War II the studies were based on transversal analysis—that is, an analysis in which all events refer to a certain period of time. In the last decades a new approach has been largely used—namely, longitudinal analysis. Here the analysis is

[3] Halvor Gille, 'The Demographic History of the Northern European Countries in the Eighteenth Century', *Population Studies*, Vol. 3, No. 1 (London, 1949).

based on the experience of a generation (a collection of individuals born in the same period of time) or a marriage cohort (that is, all marriages contracted in the same period of time). This new point of view has resulted in a considerable number of works in many countries.[4] In these studies, the fertility and the reproduction history for generations and marriage cohorts has been analysed as far back in time as possible. As a rule, it has only been possible to compute measures of fertility, mortality, and reproduction for generations or marriage cohorts after the middle of the nineteenth century.

The following remarks present some observations concerning the fertility, mortality, and reproduction for generations of Danish females born 1840/44–1920/24.[5] The results should represent a fairly high degree of reliability, because they are based on the following basic data:

1. The Danish censuses which have been held every ten years since 1840.

2. The national vital statistics which, after 1860, supply information about the distribution of births by age of mother.[6]

---

[4] See, for example, N. H. Carrier, 'An Examination of Generation Fertility in England and Wales', *Population Studies*, Vol. 9, No. 1 (London, 1955); P. Delaporte, 'Évolution de la Mortalité en Europe depuis l'Origine des Statistiques de l'Etat Civil', *Statistiques Générale de la France* (Paris, 1941); P. Depoid, 'Reproduction nette en Europe depuis l'Origine des Statistiques de l'Etat Civil', *Statistiques Générale de la France* (Paris, 1941); D. V. Glass and E. Grebenik, *The Trend and Pattern of Fertility in Great Britain. A Report on the Family Census of 1946*. Parts I–II (London, 1954); D. V. Glass, 'Fertility Trends in Europe since the Second World War', *Population Studies*, Vol. 22, No. 1 (London, 1968); T. Hjortkjær and E. og Kjeldgaard, 'Frugtbarheden i Danmark, En underøsogelse af generationerne 1865–1925', *National-økonomisk Tidsskrift*, 94 bind. 1–2 Hefte (Kobenhavn, 1956); Erland von Hofsten, 'Fertility for Birth Cohorts of Swedish Women 1870/1', *Statistisk Tidskrift* (Stockholm, 1966); G. Jahn, 'Barnetallet i Norske Ekteskap', *Census of Norway 1950*. Vol. 5 (Oslo, 1957); P. C. Matthiessen, 'The Fertility for Birth Cohorts of Danish Women', *World Views of Population Problems* (Budapest, 1968); C. E. Quensel, 'Den äktenskabeliga fruksamheten i Sveriges Städer 1911–1953 efter äktenskapens varatighet och hustrues ålder' (mimeographed; Lund, 1956); C. E. Quensel, 'Medelbarnantalet inom skilda kohorter 31/12 1960 samt ändringarna däri under senaste år', *Statistisk Tidskrift* (Stockholm, 1962); J. Vogt, 'En undersökelse over generasjonenes frugtbarhet i Norge', *Statsoekonomisk Tidsskrift* (Oslo, 1956); P. K. Whelpton, *Cohort Fertility* (Princeton, 1954); P. K. Whelpton and A. A. Campbell, *Fertility Tables for Birth Cohorts of American Women*, Part 1 (U.S. Department of Health, Education, and Welfare; Washington D.C., 1960).

[5] Some preliminary results concerning the fertility were published in 1968; see *Matthiessen*, 'The Fertility for Birth Cohorts of Danish Women'. The results presented here are some of the first results from a study going on at the Statistical Institute, University of Copenhagen. In the generation study attention will also be drawn to fertility in and out wedlock and the distribution by marital status in different areas of the country.

[6] In the first decades after 1860 we only know the distribution of the number of deliveries, not the number of live births; for all the birth cohorts, therefore, we have used the number of deliveries. As is well known, the difference between the number of deliveries and the number of live births is negligible. As our birth observations only cover the period 1860–1964, we do not possess the entire fertility history for the birth cohorts 1840/44, 1915/19, and 1920/24. For the first generation, we are missing the age-specific fertility

3. National life tables for females which have been constructed since 1840.

Figure 1 shows clearly that we are not able to give a picture of the demography of generations living before the outset of the demographic transition. The oldest of the generations were living in the phase of declining mortality. As far as fertility is concerned, the situation is different. The phase of declining fertility starts about 1890; as the fertility level among females is zero after the age of fifty and very low beyond the age of forty, the oldest of the generations ought to give a fairly acceptable impression of the fertility level and pattern before the secular fertility decline.

FERTILITY

Table 1, column 1, shows that the oldest birth cohort (1840/44) gave birth to about 4·4 children per female. The three subsequent generations (1845/49–1855/9) also gave birth to about the same

Table 1   Fertility for generations of Danish females 1840/44–1920/24

Generation	Total fertility rate (per 1,000 females) (1)	Percentage of total fertility before age 30 (2)	Mean age of mothers (3)
1840–44	4.394	39·8	32·03
1845–49	4,406	40·6	31·87
1850–54	4,436	42·3	31·64
1855–59	4,380	44·5	31·35
1860–64	4,162	45·8	31·11
1865–69	3,919	47·1	30·90
1870–74	3,771	49·6	30·58
1875–79	3,578	52·4	30·19
1880–84	3,332	54·9	29·78
1885–89	3,029	57·1	29·36
1890–94	2,709	59·7	28·98
1895–99	2,441	61·5	28·76
1900–4	2,259	60·5	28·86
1905–9	2,254	57·8	29·11
1910–14	2,304	58·4	28·93
1915–19	2,351	64·1	28·27
1920–24	2,391	69·3	27·59

rate for the age group 15–19 (number of births per 1,000 females in age group 15–19). Moreover, we have no information of the age-specific fertility rate in the age groups 45–9 and 40–9 so far as the generations 1915/19 and 1920/24 are concerned. These fertility rates are estimated, but as the fertility level in these age groups is very low, the total fertility rate (total number of births per female or per 1,000 females by age fifty assuming no mortality for the generation in question) for these three generations can be estimated with a high degree of accuracy.

number of children per female. Hence, it seems justified to argue that the four oldest generations present a fairly good picture of the generation fertility before the secular decline set in. This hypothesis is also supported by the fact that a computation of the total fertility rate based on the calendar years 1860–69 gives a value of 4,450 births per 1,000 females—about the same level as the four oldest generations.

The decline of the secular trend in fertility was very clear for the generation 1860/64 and continued until the generation 1905/9, which only gave birth to about 2·3 children per female. This is a total decline of almost 49 per cent.

For the youngest generations a slight recovery is visible. The generation 1920/4 will give birth to about 2·4 children—about 6 per cent above the level of the generation 1905/9. The preliminary fertility rates for the generation 1925/9 point to a stabilization around that level.[7]

The change of the generation fertility from about 4·4 children to the present level of 2·4 children has been followed by a considerable change in the pattern of the age-specific fertility rates. The fertility level has increased in the two youngest age groups (15–19 and 20–4 years), whereas the opposite has been the case for the other age groups with the strongest decline in the highest age groups. These movements have naturally produced a comparatively strong concentration of childbirths in the younger age groups.

In Table 1, column 2, a simple measure of this trend is indicated by calculating the percentage of children born before the age of thirty. It appears that this proportion grows from 39·8 per cent to 69·3 per cent. A more exhaustive measure of this change can be obtained by computing the mean age of mothers (Table 1, column 3).[8] The mean age of mothers declines from about 32·0 years to 27·6 years. A careful investigation of the age-specific fertility rates reveals that Denmark shows the classical European form of the transition from high to low fertility. The decline in fertility began by lopping off birth at the oldest ages of women and then proceeded down through the younger age groups. Here the fragmentary age-specific fertility rates for the generations 1815/19–1835/9 may be very helpful.[9]

---

[7] Most of this recent improvement in the fertility level is caused by a higher proportion of ever married females. This phenomenon appears together with an increase in the number of males per 1,000 females in the age groups where marriages usually take place.

[8] The mean age of mothers for a generation is based on the assumption that no mortality loss occurs before the age of fifty. When calculating this measure, only the age-specific fertility rates are applied.

[9] As our observation period starts off after 1860, we are only able to compute the age-specific fertility rates in some age groups for the generations born before 1840. For the age group 45–9, computations can be carried out for generations born after 1815. For the age group 40–4, it is only possible to make computations for generations born after 1820.

Looking at the fertility level in the age groups 40–4 and 45–9, a clear trend of decline appears for all generations born before 1840, whereas the decrease in the age group 30–9 does not begin until generations born after 1855. A change in the age group 25–9 is not visible until generations born after 1875.

This fact seems to indicate that family limitation rather than family planning (which also includes spacing) was the mechanism of fertility reduction, with family planning as such not becoming widespread until later.[10]

MORTALITY

In the following a short analysis of the mortality level and pattern for the generations of females will be given. Life tables have, therefore, been constructed for all the generations 1840/44–1920/24.[11] Special attention will be drawn to the influence of mortality on the reproductive capacity—that is, the mortality loss before the end of the reproductive period.

Obviously, it is not possible to construct life tables for the youngest of the generations as members of these are still alive. If we want to follow the generations to the age of ninety, complete life tables can at the present time only be made for the generations 1840/44–1870/74. For the next generations the lacking l_x-values have been computed on the assumption that the generations in the remaining part of their life will die according to the mortality level prevailing in the calendar years 1961–5.

The average expectation of life (e_0) is shown in Table 2, column 1. Whereas the value of e_0 for the oldest generation was only 47·4 years, the youngest generation displays a value of 68·5 years—an increase of more than twenty-one years. The speed of the increase is not equal. For the generations 1840/44–1875/9 the average gain of e_0 per five-year generation is about 0·69 years, whereas the average increase for the subsequent generations amounts to 1·89 years— three times more.

[10] It is interesting to note the generations 1900/4–1910/14 which very clearly deviate from the general trend in the fertility pattern. This is to a very high degree caused by the general increase of the fertility level during the forties, which influenced all age groups but mostly the higher age groups, perhaps because these generations postponed their births in the thirties. The generations 1900/4–1910/14 were in the upper end of the reproductive period in the forties.

[11] The life table f.inst. for the generation of females 1840/44 tells us how many of 10,000 females born 1840/44 ($l_0 = 10,000$) will still be alive at each successive age (l_x) only taking account of the mortality loss. Thus l_{40} shows the number still alive by age 40. Assuming a maximum age of f.ins t. 100 ($l_{100} = 0$) a conclusion of the life table will demand observations from a period covering around 100 years, i.e. 1840–44 to 1940–44.

Table 2   Mortality for generations of Danish females 1840/44–1920/24

Generation	Average expectation of life: e_0 (1)	Reproductive power: $a_{15,50}/35 \cdot l_0$ (2)	$p_{0,1} = l_1/l_0$ (3)	$p_{1,15} = l_{15}/l_1$ (4)	$a_{15,50}/35 \cdot l_{15}$ (5)
1840–44	47·35	0·644	0·874	0·834	0·880
1845–49	46·97	0·635	0·863	0·834	0·883
1850–54	47·38	0·640	0·877	0·825	0·884
1855–59	48·11	0·649	0·878	0·831	0·890
1860–64	48·49	0·652	0·878	0·829	0·896
1865–69	49·96	0·671	0·875	0·849	0·903
1870–74	51·54	0·689	0·880	0·859	0·911
1875–79	52·21	0·694	0·873	0·867	0·917
1880–84	53·35	0·705	0·872	0·876	0·923
1885–89	54·70	0·717	0·878	0·882	0·925
1890–94	56·58	0·737	0·875	0·906	0·931
1895–99	59·32	0·769	0·880	0·932	0·937
1900–4	61·79	0·800	0·894	0·945	0·947
1905–9	63·68	0·822	0·903	0·952	0·956
1910–14	65·43	0·844	0·916	0·957	0·963
1915–19	66·45	0·857	0·918	0·962	0·971
1920–24	68·49	0·884	0·930	0·974	0·976
Calendar years 1961–65	74·12	0·964	0·983	0·994	0·986

In order to evaluate the influence of the decline in mortality upon the ability of the generations to reproduce themselves, we will introduce the concept of the *reproductive power* of a generation. Using the life tables we will define this concept as the ratio between the *actual* number of years spent in the reproductive period ($a_{15,50}$) and the number of years spent in absence of any mortality before the age of fifty (the *potential* number of years). For $l_0 = 10,000$ the potential number of years will be $35 \cdot l_0 = 350,000$. In Table 2, column 2, the size of the reproductive power is shown.

Whereas the size of the reproductive power for the oldest generation only amounts to 0·644, it has increased to 0·884 for the generation 1920/24. The present mortality level gives a value as high as 0·964—that is, the mortality loss today is negligible.

The size of the reproductive power can be considered as the final result of a mortality loss which takes place in three different age intervals; viz. (0,1), (1,15), and (15,50). The value of the reproductive power can be expressed as the product of $p_{0,1}$ (the probability of survival from 0 till 1 year), $p_{1,15}$ (the probability of survival from 1 to 15 years), and $\dfrac{a_{15,50}}{35 \cdot l_{15}}$ (the ratio between the number of years actually spent in the reproductive period and the number of years in absence of any mortality between 15 and 50 years).[12]

Table 2, columns 3–5, indicates that the mortality loss is fluctuating from 12 to almost 17 per cent in these three age intervals for the oldest generations. The most substantial loss takes place in the age group 1–15. The improvement in the size of the reproductive power for all the generations born in the nineteenth century (0·644 to 0·769) was exclusively caused by a decline in the mortality after the first year of life and especially in the age group 1–15, as there was no appreciable decline in infant mortality, which remained at a level of more than 12 per cent. For the generations born in this century, the improvement in the reproductive power has been produced by a mortality decline in all three age groups. For the youngest generation the mortality loss in the first year of life is still considerable (7 per cent), whereas the loss in the other two age groups is small (below 3 per cent). The present mortality level (1961–5) gives a rather insignificant loss in all three age groups (below 2 per cent).

REPRODUCTION

Migration neglected. By means of the fertility and mortality rates we will now compute the usual measures of reproduction for the generations—the gross reproduction rate (GRR),[13] the net reproduction rate (NRR),[14] and the intrinsic rate of natural increase (r).[15] As all these measures are based on the fertility and the mortality level before the age of fifty they will have a very high degree of reliability for all the generations included in the present study.

---

[12] $p_{0,1}$ can simply be explained as the proportion of newborn surviving their first year of life, i.e. $\frac{l_1}{l_0}$. The proportion of newborn died during their first year of life is: $l_0 \equiv p_{0,1}$. In the same way $p_{1,15} \equiv \frac{l_{15}}{l_1}$. The correctness of the above mentioned way of expressing the reproductive power appears very easily by means of this equation: $\frac{l_1}{l_0} \cdot \frac{l_{15}}{l_1} \cdot \frac{{}^{a}15.50}{35 \cdot l_{15}} = \frac{{}^{a}15.50}{35 \cdot l_0}$. l_1 and l_{15} can be cancelled on the left side.

[13] The GRR is the total number of newborn girls per female by age fifty assuming no mortality for the generation in question. As the proportion of girls among newborn children is almost constant, the GRR will constitute a constant fraction of the total fertility rate, which includes both newborn boys as well as girls.

[14] The NRR is the total number of newborn girls per female by age fifty, taking the mortality among females into consideration.

[15] If for a very long period all generations of population were subject to the mentioned generation fertility and mortality and there were no migration, the annual rate of population increase would be identical to the intrinsic rate of natural increase for the generation in question.

Due to the fixed sex-ratio at birth, the size of the GRR will be a constant fraction of the total fertility rate. Values of the GRR below 1 indicate an insufficient fertility level in order to insure reproduction, even in absence of any mortality before the age of fifty. Table 3, column 1, indicates that none of the generations have experienced such a low fertility. Even the generation with the lowest fertility level (1905/9) displays a value of 1·098—that is, almost 10 per cent above the level which is necessary to insure reproduction.

When we take account of the effect of mortality by introducing the NRR, the situation of reproduction changes dramatically (Table 3,

Table 3   Measures of reproduction for generations of Danish females, 1840/44–1920/24

Generation	Gross reproduction rate: GRR (1)	Net reproduction rate: NRR (2)	Average age of mothers: $\bar{x}$ (3)	Intrinsic rate of natural increase: r (4)
				per 1,000
1840–44	2·140	1·387	31·68	10·3
1845–49	2·146	1·373	31·55	10·1
1850–54	2·160	1·392	31·34	10·6
1855–59	2·133	1·396	31·06	10·7
1860–64	2·027	1·335	30·85	9·4
1865–69	1·909	1·294	30·66	8·4
1870–74	1·836	1·280	30·37	8·1
1875–79	1·746	1·226	30·00	6·8
1880–84	1·623	1·161	29·60	5·0
1885–89	1·475	1·075	29·17	2·5
1890–94	1·319	0·987	28·82	—0·5
1895–99	1·189	0·927	28·63	—2·7
1900–4	1·100	0·890	28·73	—4·1
1905–9	1·098	0·910	29·01	—3·3
1910–14	1·122	0·955	28·86	—1·6
1915–19	1·144	0·989	28·21	—0·4
1920–24	1·164	1·039	27·54	1·4

column 2). Apart from the youngest generation, only the generations 1840/94–1885/9 have been able to reproduce themselves. For the birth cohorts 1890/94–1915/19, the fertility decline has been so considerable that reproduction was not possible even though the mortality level was declining quite fast. The lowest level of reproduction is experienced by the generation 1900/04, which displays a value for the NRR of only 0·890. For the subsequent generations, the combined effect of a slightly increasing fertility and a rather substantial mortality decline results in an increasing value of the NRR, which just attains a value slightly above 1 (1·039) for the youngest generation.

The average age of mothers ($\bar{x}$) resulting from the age-specific fertility and mortality pattern for the generation in question has declined rather substantially (Table 3, column 3).[16] The mothers from the generation 1840/44 had an average age of 31·7, compared with only 27·5 years for mothers from the youngest generation. This decline is primarily due to the change in the age-specific fertility pattern, described earlier, which has produced a strong concentration of births before the age of thirty. The decline in the average age is restricted—but only to a very limited degree—by the decline in the mortality level, which has caused a slightly higher proportion in the higher age groups. The weak influence from the mortality decline is, for example, shown by the fact that a combination of the age-specific fertility rates for the generation 1920/24 and of the life table of the generation 1840/44 results in an average age of 27·33 compared with a real value of 27·54 years.

The intrinsic rate of natural increase (r) for the generations (Table 3, column 4) indicates the joint effects of a change in the net reproduction rate and the average age of mothers. As mentioned earlier, it shows the annual rate of increase for a closed population.[17] which has for a very long time been subject to the generation fertility and mortality in question. For the four oldest generations the value of r is about 1 per cent, which is tantamount to a doubling period of nearly seventy years. For the subsequent birth cohorts, the value of r decreases very fast and becomes naturally negative for the generations with a value of the NRR below 1. For the youngest generation the value of r attains the very low positive value of about 1 per 1,000.

For values above zero, r is positively correlated with the value of the NRR and negatively correlated with the value of $\bar{x}$. When comparing the generations 1840/44 and 1920/24, the decrease in $\bar{x}$ has naturally counteracted the decline of r produced by the lower value of the NRR. But the influence has, in fact, been rather limited. Without any drop in the average age of mothers, the value of r would have declined from 10·3 to 1·2 per 1,000 compared with a real decline from 10·3 to 1·4 per 1,000.

The decline of mortality has naturally implied that reproduction has been possible for a much lower fertility level among the younger generations. In other words, today a value of the NRR above 1 can be produced by a much lower value of the GRR or the total fertility rate. Whereas the mortality level of the generation 1840/44 required about 3·2 children per female on average, the mortality level of the

---

[16] In contrast to the *mean* age of mothers used in the section on fertility, the *average* age of mothers takes account of the generation mortality before age fifty. Hence, this measure is based both on the age-specific fertility and mortality rates.
[17] A population which is not subject to any migration.

birth cohort 1920/24 only requires 2·3 children per female. With the present mortality level, only 2·1 children per female are necessary to insure reproduction of the generation.

Migration included: The analysis of the level of reproduction for the generations 1840/4–1920/4 in the preceding section was in fact based on a closed population—that is, a population which is not subject to any migration. As the amount of migration (primarily emigration) in certain periods of the demographic transition was rather substantial, it seems sensible to estimate the influence of that phenomenon on the level of reproduction.

Substantial emigration can be found in most European countries during the period of demographic transition, with a considerable mortality decline and a fertility level that is still high. It may be a matter of argument as to the extent to which overseas emigration was linked to the demographic transition in Europe. Although the emigration was naturally caused by many factors, strong population pressure in a certain period of the demographic transition undoubtedly played a substantial role.

As far as migration is concerned, it may be relevant to distinguish between *direct* and *indirect* effects on the level of reproduction. By direct effects, we mean a gain or loss in the number of females in the reproductive period caused by migration among females. By indirect effects, we mean an influence exerted on the proportion of ever-married females by a change in the sex ratio, which is produced by a different level of net emigration among females and males. A smaller proportion of ever-married females will, *ceteris paribus*, result in a lower fertility level and hence a reduced level of reproduction. It is evident, however, that the direct and indirect effects cannot be separated. In the present context we will only treat the direct effects.

From official statistical publications before 1933, we have no knowledge of the amount of net migration in the different age groups and, therefore, cannot compute the gain or loss caused by migrations among the generations. Consequently, when we want to calculate an estimate of the amount of net migration among the generations of females with the purpose of evaluating the influence on the level of reproduction, it is necessary to rely on indirect methods.

By means of the life tables it is possible to calculate the *expected* number of females in five-year age groups in the reproductive period for all the generations. The method simply implies a reduction of the number of live births of which the generation originally consisted. For example, for the generation 1840/44, we reduce the number of newborn females from the period 1840/44 by means of the life table for that generation. The expected number of females is equivalent to the number of females in absence of any migration. By comparing the *actual* and the *expected* number of females, it is possible to obtain an estimate of the relative net gain or net loss due to migration. Only the gain or loss in the age group between fifteen and fifty is relevant in connection with the study of reproduction. But as there is no important migration after the age of fifty, we will get a picture that includes almost all the net migration.

Table 4, column 1, shows the magnitude of the net migration and

Table 4 Influence of migration on the level of reproduction for generations of Danish females, 1840/44–1920/24

Generation	The gain (+) or loss (−) in the reproductive period in per cent (1)	NRR (migration included) (2)	NRR (migration neglected) (3)
1840–44	+3·1	1·434	1·387
1845–49	+2·1	1·408	1·373
1850–54	−0·6	1·387	1·392
1855–59	−5·8	1·320	1·396
1860–64	−3·1	1·299	1·335
1865–69	−5·0	1·232	1·294
1870–74	−4·1	1·230	1·280
1875–79	−6·5	1·146	1·226
1880–84	−5·3	1·096	1·161
1885–89	−4·4	1·025	1·075
1890–94	+0·1	0·989	0·987
1895–99	−1·2	0·918	0·927
1900–4	−2·0	0·873	0·890
1905–9	−2·8	0·887	0·910
1910–14	−1·9	0·940	0·955
1915–19	+2·3	1·015	0·989
1920–24	−5·6	0·983	1·039

reveals a somewhat fluctuating picture. From a net immigration among the two oldest generations, the situation changes to net emigration for all the subsequent generations except for the generations 1890/94 and 1915/19, of which only the last one shows a substantial net immigration. The predominant trait is, as one would expect, a loss by net emigration. For any generation this loss does not exceed 6·5 per cent.

Table 4 shows, moreover, the values of the NRR (including migration) together with the earlier values of the NRR (based on a closed population). The deviations between these two sets of values are naturally of the same size as the deviations between the actual and the expected number of females in the reproductive period. Consequently, the effect of migration on the NRR has been rather limited, compared with the influence of the change in the level of fertility and mortality. When the value of the NRR is just about 1, however, then the amount of migration may determine whether or not the generation in question will be reproduced. This point is revealed very clearly for the two youngest generations. The amount of migration increases the value of the NRR for the generation 1915/19 from 0·989 to 1·105 and lowers the NRR for the youngest generation from 1·039 to 0·983.

Jacques Henripin and Yves Péron

The demographic transition
of the province of Quebec

Even the title of this paper presents problems. It is not possible to follow exactly the same population through the last centuries, and one has to switch from one population to another, according to the information available. Broadly, if not precisely, the history that we have tried to reconstitute is the history of the French Canadians. The information we have at hand relates to French Canadians up to 1760, when New France was ceded to England. Most of this population lived along the St. Lawrence valley, but a substantial part settled in what was then known as 'Acadia'. These two settlements, like the first settlements of the English colonies of North America, date from the early seventeenth century, but their progress was much slower. In 1760, there were only around 70,000 French-speaking people in North America, of which approximately 60,000 lived in the St. Lawrence valley. They came from a quite parsimonious flow of immigrants from France: about 10,000, during a period of 150 years.

From 1760 to 1883, the data correspond to the Catholics of the Province of Quebec. Since, at the beginning of the English Regime, there were few non-French and even fewer non-French Catholics, the switch from the French to the Catholic population is smooth. The first wave of British immigrants began with the Loyalists around 1776. In any case, most of the Catholics of the Province of Quebec were French, as can be seen from Table 1. In these circumstances, it is relatively safe to assume that rates calculated for the Catholics constitute a good estimation of the behaviour of the Quebequers of French origin.

From 1884 on, populations differ according to the phenomenon considered. Births of Catholic children were registered up to 1925; then one must switch to births of French origin. From 1884 to 1925, it is possible to calculate marriage and death rates for total population only; but from 1926 to 1951, statistics are available on deaths of persons of French origin and on marriages for Catholics.

Although these data are far from ideal—and there are other difficulties than the ones relating to continuity—it is possible to

Table 1   Total, Catholic and French population of the province of Quebec, 1831
to 1961
(population in thousands)

Year	Total	Catholics	French	French/Catholics
1831	553	470*	—	—
1852	890	752*	672*	89·4%
1871	1,192	1,021	940	91·0%
1901	1,649	1,431	1,322	92·4%
1931	2,875	2,460	2,270	92·3%
1961	5,259	4,636	4,241	91·5%

Sources: Canadian censuses.
    * Corrected for unknown religion or ethnic origin.

derive from them a reliable image of the main trends in the French
Canadian population changes. That population realized a phenomenal growth. From 1760 to 1960, the world population was multiplied by 4; the European stock by 5 or 6; Canadians of French origin
by 80, despite an appreciable outflow of emigrants to the United
States. It is estimated that between 1840 and 1930 the net migration
of French Canadians was probably between 600,000 and 800,000.[1]
The ones who remained or returned to Canada produced a population of 5·54 millions in 1961, of which 77 per cent lived in the
Province of Quebec. But a substantial proportion of those who
settled in other provinces has been assimilated into the English-
speaking population so that Quebec contained 83 per cent of the
French-speaking Canadians in 1961.

A NEW LOOK AT THE ANCIENT
DEMOGRAPHIC PATTERN 1711 to 1880

SOURCES

The abundance of data that permit one to follow the evolution of the
Catholic population of the Province of Quebec, from its origin to the
end of the last century, is now well known. With few exceptions,
the parish registers kept by the clergy have been preserved; from 1666
on, numerous censuses give the population. One must add to these
classical sources, registries of notaries, administrative documents,
and the works of Champlain, Charlevoix, Ferland, Faillon, and so
forth.

We owe to Mgr. Tanguay the first systematic exploitation of the
sources. Twenty-five years of patient research in the parish registers

[1] Yolande Lavoie, *L'émigration des Canadiens aux Etats-Unis avant 1930*, M.A. dissertation
presented at the Department of Demography, University of Montreal, 1969.

permitted him to compile annual statistics of births, marriages, and deaths from 1608 to 1883, and to reconstitute the families formed during the seventeenth and eighteenth centuries.[2] Mgr. Tanguay's work is coloured by mistakes and omissions that make desirable the revision already under way. Godbout has undertaken the reconstitution of families formed in New France during the seventeenth century[3] and, at the University of Montreal, a team of researchers is presently working at building as complete a bank of demographic data as possible.[4] These efforts will undoubtedly lead to a better knowledge of the evolution of the French Canadian population. It is possible, however, to submit the already available data to new analysis in order to uncover weaknesses in our present knowledge and perhaps to indicate where corrections might be useful.[5]

EVOLUTION OF THE CATHOLIC POPULATION, 1700 TO 1881

Censuses made before 1831 do not give any breakdown of the population by religion. Until 1760 the French Canadian population, almost wholly Catholic, is obtained by subtracting the Indians. The estimate of Catholic population for the following seventy years, however, is most difficult. There were only four censuses during this period, but thirty-six between 1666 and 1760 and seven between 1831 and 1881. Moreover, the 1765 and 1790 censuses do not cover the two most important towns—Montréal and Québec—and there are good reasons to believe that the population was overestimated in the censuses of 1852 and 1861.

New and probably better estimates of the Catholic population can be derived by comparing the population enumerated at different dates to the cumulative natural increase from 1608 (Figure 1). The correspondence is good for the periods 1710–40 and 1830–60. Discrepancies before 1710 can be explained by net immigration and after 1860 by net emigration. Since emigration started around 1840 one should observe discrepancies in 1852 and 1861 also; their absence is probably due to the over-enumeration of the population in these two years.

It is generally admitted that the migration of Catholics was very low at the beginning of the English Regime, so that the deviations

---

[2] Cyprien Tanguay, *Dictionnaire généalogique des familles canadiennes*, Montréal, E. Senécal, 1871 à 1890 (7 volumes); *A travers les registres* (même éditeur).

[3] Archange Godbout, *Nos ancêtres au XVII⁰ siècle*, Rapport de l'archiviste de la province de Québec pour 1951–1952 et 1952–1953, . . .–1965.

[4] H. Charbonneau, J. Légaré, R. Durocher, G. Paquet, and J.-P. Wallot, 'La démographie historique au Canada', in *Recherches sociographiques*, Vol. 8, No. 2 (May–August 1967).

[5] See Georges Langlois, *Histoire de la population canadienne-française* (Montréal, 1934); J. Henripin, *La population canadienne au début du XVIII⁰ siècle* (Paris, 1954); and *Tendances et facteurs de la fécondité au Canada* (Ottawa, 1968), Ch. 1.

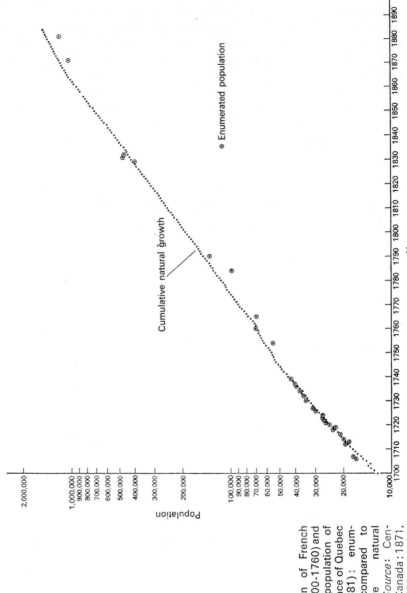

Figure 1 Population of French origin (1700-1760) and Catholic population of the province of Quebec (1760-1881): enumeration compared to cumulative natural growth. *Source:* Censuses of Canada: 1871, vol. V; 1881, vol. IV

Population

Year

⊚ Enumerated population

Cumulative natural growth

2,000,000

1,000,000
900,000
800,000
700,000
600,000
500,000

400,000

300,000

200,000

100,000
90,000
80,000
70,000
60,000
50,000

40,000

30,000

20,000

10,000

1700 1710 1720 1730 1740 1750 1760 1770 1780 1790 1800 1810 1820 1830 1840 1850 1860 1870 1880 1890

observed between the enumerated population and the cumulative natural increase must be the result of under-enumeration in the censuses of 1765, 1785, and 1790. This set of presumptions lead us to adopt, for the period 1710 to 1844, population estimates based on cumulative natural growth. From 1844 to 1861, our estimates are also based on natural growth of the Catholic population, but we have corrected this first estimate by subtracting the estimated net emigration: 25,000 from 1844 to 1852 and 55,000 from 1852 to 1861.[6] After 1861, we have relied on the populations as given in the censuses.

These estimates were used to calculate average population for decades or five-year periods. These new average populations as well as former estimates based on census data are given for decades in Table 2. Of course, the new estimates will change all the rates based

Table 2 Average French Canadian or Catholic population by decade, 1711 to 1880

Decade	Previous estimate*	New estimate
1711–20	20,800	21,400
1721–30	28,500	29,400
1731–40	39,000	39,300
1741–50	47,500	52,100
1751–60	57,000	64,200
1761–70	70,000	80,300
1771–80	87,000	104,300
1781–90	110,000	133,800
1791–1800	147,000	172,000
1801–10	197,000	223,800
1811–20	261,000	288,200
1821–30	350,000	375,500
1831–40	460,000	485,300
1841–50	600,000	620,000
1851–60	830,000	778,000
1861–70	980,000	940,000
1871–80	1,080,000	1,090,000

* Based on estimations given in Lavoie, *L'émigration des Canadiens*. Our estimate of the Catholic population is 720,000 for 1852 and 875,000 for 1861.

on population. The most striking aspect of this change is to reduce appreciably the phenomenal crude birth rates of the period 1760–1800.

CRUDE BIRTH RATE

Former calculations give crude birth rates higher than 60 per cent for the 1761–1800 period.[7] Such a level is superior to what can be estimated for the beginning of the eighteenth century. If the quality of the statistical data is not questioned, the only possible explanation

[6] Henripin, *Tendances et facteurs*, p. 5.   [7] Henripin, *Tendances et facteurs*, p. 5.

HP

is a rise of legitimate fertility, which was already quite high during the first half of the eighteenth century, since nuptiality was relatively stable.

With the new population estimates, the evolution of the birth rate is much more plausible. Table 3 lists the new crude birth rates, by

Table 3   Birth, marriage and death rates per 1,000 population, by decade, 1711 to 1860: comparison of previous and new estimates

Decade	Birth rate		Marriage rate		Death rate	
	Previous estimates*	New estimates	Previous estimates*	New estimates	Previous estimates*	New estimates
1711–20	57·5	56·8	10·2	9·9	25·1	24·4
1721–30	55·2	53·5	10·2	9·9	24·2	23·4
1731–40	56·6	56·2	9·4	9·3	25·6	25·4
1741–50	55·9	51·0	10·4	9·5	32·2	29·3
1751–60	59·6	52·9	11·3	10·0	38·2	33·9
1761–70	65·2	56·8	11·3	9·9	33·8	28·2
1771–80	64·9	54·1	10·3	8·6	34·7	28·8
1781–90	62·1	51·0	9·9	8·2	32·4	26·7
1791–1800	61·1	52·2	10·2	8·7	29·5	25·2
1801–10	58·4	51·4	9·7	8·5	30·0	26·4
1811–20	56·0	50·7	9·7	8·8	27·5	25·6
1821–30	56·0	52·2	9·3	8·6	27·1	25·3
1831–40	54·0	51·1	8·9	8·4	27·3	25·9
1841–50	53·0	51·2	8·8	8·5	23·8	23·0
1851–60	45·8	48·8	7·4	7·9	19·6	21·0

* Henripin, *Tendances et facteurs*, p. 5.

decade, as well as the ones previously calculated. The two sets of rates have been reproduced in the upper part of Figure 2. The curve representing the new rates does not leave much of the rise from the beginning to the end of the century. The general tendency is a slow decrease from around 57 per cent in 1711–20 to 51 per cent in 1781–90, followed by a remarkable stability until 1835. The first phase of the decline is probably due to the regularization of the age structure; it is accentuated in 1741–60 by the disturbances caused by the war activities; this last movement is followed by a recovery in 1761–70.

Our claim that the population was under-enumerated and that there is no long-term increasing trend in the birth rate during the eighteenth century is confirmed by the results that we have obtained in calculating the number of births per marriage.

NUMBER OF BIRTHS PER MARRIAGE

It is possible to verify in a simple way that the fertility of marriages has been relatively constant over the long run. Using the data of our previous study on the fertility of marriages celebrated in 1700–30, we

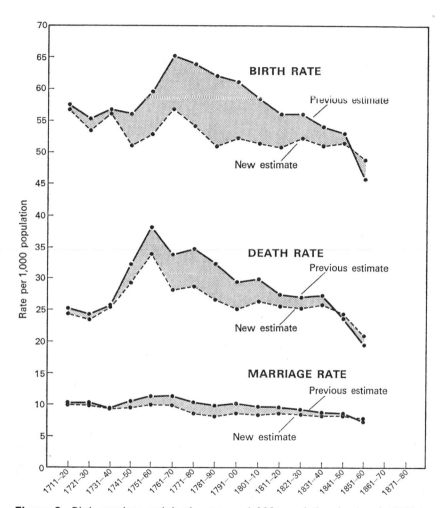

Figure 2 Birth, marriage and death rates per 1,000 population, by decade 1711 to 1860. *Source:* Table 3

have established the distribution of births by duration of marriage. Assuming that this distribution has not varied, we can derive a series of weighting coefficients that can be applied for calculating the number of marriages to which the births of every five-year period must be reported. The results appear in Table 4 and Figure 3.

Table 4   Number of births per marriage, by five-year period, 1711 to 1880

1711–15	7·2	1796–1800	7·4
1716–20	7·5	1801–5	7·5
1721–25	6·9	1806–10	7·2
1726–30	7·0	1811–15	7·1
1731–35	7·3	1816–20	7·2
1736–40	7·1	1821–25	7·4
1741–45	7·0	1826–30	7·4
1746–50	6·7	1831–35	7·5
1751–55	6·8	1836–40	6·9
1756–60	6·1	1841–45	7·4
1761–65	6·4	1846–50	7·3
1766–70	6·8	1851–55	7·0
1771–75	7·1	1856–60	7·1
1776–80	7·0	1861–65	7·4
1781–85	7·3	1866–70	6·6
1786–90	7·4	1871–75	6·7
1791–95	7·5	1876–80	6·7

Note: The number of births is slightly over-estimated due to the inclusion of illegitimate births (less than 2 per cent).

Except for the depression of 1746–70, there is a remarkable stability until 1865, when a slow and long-term decline probably started.

But the number of children per marriage is very high, with an average of 7·1 for the period 1711 to 1865. According to Mgr. Tanguay's genealogies, marriages celebrated between 1700 and 1730 and which persisted up to the end of the wife's fecundity period had 8·4 children; those which were interrupted by the death of one spouse had 4·4. By weighting these two categories, one finds an

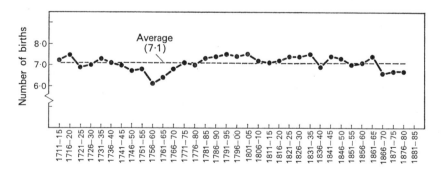

Figure 3   Number of births per marriage, by five-year period 1711 to 1880. *Source:* Table 4

average of 6·0 children. That figure is much less than what we have just found.

Such a difference is difficult to explain without questioning Mgr. Tanguay's work—his statistical computations, which we used for the number of births per marriage, or his genealogies, which we employed in our previous work to analyse the fertility of families formed in 1700–30. Using Godbout's partial revision of Tanguay's work for marriages celebrated during the seventeenth century, a provisional choice may be made between these two results. Our colleague Hubert Charbonneau has worked on Godbout's genealogies, and he was kind enough to give us information from which we could establish the number of children born per *fertile* marriage; we found 8·16 children for first marriages, 5·13 for marriages of higher order, and an average of 7·9 children. The proportion of sterile marriages can be safely estimated at 10 per cent. Thus, the number of births per marriage would be: $7·9 \times 0·9 = 7·1$. That figure is exactly what we have found. It is generally believed, however, that women married at a younger age at the end of the seventeenth century than at the beginning of the eighteenth century; on the other hand, this younger age at marriage might well have been balanced by an earlier dissolution of families by death.

Nevertheless, we would be inclined to think that the average number of children per marriage is nearer 7 than 6. A simple counting of marriage and birth certificates is undoubtedly an easier computation than the correct allocation of children to their parents. Thus Tanguay probably made fewer omissions in the first operation than in the second. Moreover, because Tanguay was not able to find all the parish registers, he could not reconstitute completely the families that migrated from a parish of which the register was found to one of which the register was lost. In the simple computation of total number of births and marriages, a missing register has equivalent effects on births and marriages and does not effect the consistency of their comparison. In these circumstances, the exploitation of Tanguay's *Dictionary of Genealogies* leads necessarily to an underevaluation of the legitimate fertility, unless the families affected by the absence of registers can be eliminated.

MORTALITY

New population estimates have the same effect on death rates as on birth rates (Table 3 and Figure 2). The most remarkable change introduced by the new estimates is the substitution of a stable level for declining rates for the period 1781–1840. This plateau is a little higher than the rates observed for the period 1711–40.

There are good reasons to believe that this similarity between the first and last part of the eighteenth century is purely accidental. The upward trend of mortality after 1740 can be partially explained by the war and epidemics of this period, but other factors such as the improvement of death registration and the stabilization of the age structure must also be taken into account.

Inspection of genealogies from the beginning of the century show a great proportion of persons whose death certificate has not been found: persons born before 1670 (Godbout), 36 per cent; persons born in 1690–99 (Godbout), 43 per cent; persons married in 1700–1730 (Tanguay), 38 per cent. The absence of death certificates has many explanations: definitive emigration; impossibility of linking the death certificate to other documents; loss of registers; absence of death registration. The proportions just mentioned must represent an upper limit of the omissions of the death statistics.

If the statistics were perfect, the cumulative natural increase would be equal to the enumerated population less net immigration. If, in reality, the cumulative natural increase is equal to the enumerated population, two interpretations are possible: either there is no net migration, or the omission of deaths is equal to net immigration. According to what we know of migrations during the first century of colonization, it can be estimated that the omission of deaths is of the order of 33 per cent. This would raise the death rate from 24 to 36 per cent around 1700–10. For the last years of the seventeenth century, H. Charbonneau gives an estimate of 30 per cent, after comparing enumerated populations, vital statistics, and migrations.[8] The level of mortality during the first half of the eighteenth century can, therefore, be estimated at 30–35 deaths per 1,000 population.

If, for instance, we assume that Tanguay has omitted a substantial proportion of deaths, the correction would lead to an estimate (by cumulative natural increase) much lower than the enumerated Catholic population in 1831 or 1832. The difference would be too great to be explained reasonably by net immigration (which is the only factor that can account for the difference).

THE DEPARTURE FROM THE TRADITIONAL DEMOGRAPHIC PATTERN

Tanguay's statistical series stop at 1883, and after that date one must rely on other sources. Nearly all information for the period 1884–

[8] Unpublished work.

1925 comes from the *Statistical Year Book of the Province of Quebec;*[9] the data relate to Catholic births, marriages, and deaths for the whole population. From 1926 to 1951, the *Vital Statistics* annual reports of the Dominion Bureau of Statistics give the number of births and deaths of French origin and the number of Catholic marriages. Rates were computed for five-year periods and have been reproduced on Figure 4, together with rates already examined from 1711 to 1883.

The time series of birth and death rates over the last two and a half centuries of French Canadian demography are not characterized by the classical pattern of demographic transition as it is described in most textbooks. It would be difficult to discern the beginning of a permanent and progressive fall of the death rate somewhere between 1750 and 1800. Nor is the birth rate constant until the last quarter of the nineteenth century. A cursory glance at Figure 4 would show that birth and death rates have been decreasing at approximately the same pace since 1770 or 1780, with a tendency for the birth rate to decline rather more rapidly after 1850. A closer look at each curve yields a more refined view:

Birth rate: from 1710 to 1775, the rate fluctuates around a quasi-stable level of 54·7 per 1,000; this is followed by a period of seventy-five years (1776 to 1850) during which natality is nearly constant, with an average rate of 51·9 per 1,000; a century of decline begins around 1850; the trend could be described as starting at 51 per 1,000 in 1841–5 and decreasing by 12 points in eighty years; this leads to a rate of 39 per 1,000 in 1921–5; then there is a sharp drop (27 per 1,000 in 1936–40) and the commonly observed revival after the Great Depression.

Marriage rate: there are three successive levels of gross nuptiality rate, covering the whole period: 9·9 per 1,000 in 1711–65; 8·5 per 1,000 in 1766–1850; and 7·4 per cent in 1886–1930.

Death rate: we have already explained why we believe that the crude death rate is largely underestimated for the first half of the eighteenth century, so that mortality must have been lower during the second half than the first half of this century. From 1785 to 1835, it seems to have remained almost constant at the level of 26 per 1,000. There is a decline of 6 points from 1835 to 1860, followed by a rise up to 1875 and then a regular decline from 24·6 per 1,000 in 1871–5 to 8·4 per cent in 1951.

[9] There is one exception: Catholic births from 1894 to 1900 are taken from R. Kuczinski, *Birth Registration and Birth Statistics in Canada* (Washington, Brookings Institution, 1930), p. 59.

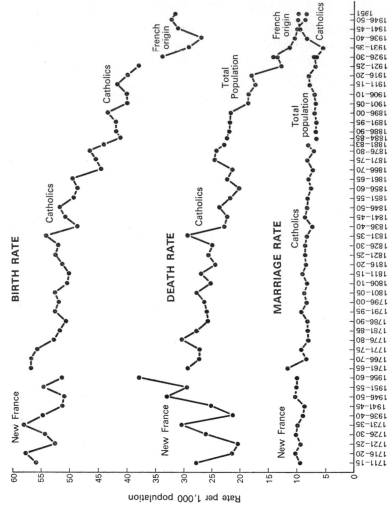

Figure 4 Birth, marriage and death rates per 1,000 population, by five-year period, for total Catholic or French population of the province of Quebec. *Source:* Tables 6 and 7

Catholic or French mortality was higher than that of the rest of the population. For the period 1926–30, the crude death rate was 13·5 per 1,000 for the total population and 14·2 per 1,000 for French Canadians.

This statement is confirmed by the high infant mortality of the French Canadians of the Province of Quebec. In 1926–30, they had a rate of 133 per 1,000 live births, compared to 89 per 1,000 for the rest of the population. In 1951, the rates were respectively 52 and 27 per 1,000. Let us recall that the estimate for the first half of the eighteenth century is 246 per 1,000.[10] No reliable information is available for the period 1750–1926.

NUPTIALITY

Nuptiality decreased from a level of 9·9 per 1,000 in 1711–65 to levels of 8·5 in 1766–1850 and 7·4 in 1851–1930. Two explanations can be put forward to account for the first shift: net immigration before 1760 might have caused the crude marriage rate to be exceptionally high; or a smaller proportion of the population might have got married after 1765. There is no information available yet to check either of these possibilities. From the first to the last level, the relative decrease is 14 per cent; this change is greater than that occurring later in the birth rate (5 per cent). Since there was no change in the number of births per marriage, there was probably a small reduction after 1765 in the proportion married. The most important factor in the reduction of nuptiality, however, was undoubtedly the cessation of net immigration.

The second downward shift, around 1850, can be safely attributed to emigration. Around 1830, the lands easily available to the French Canadian peasants were filled, and agricultural conditions were bad. The new industries of New England were a convenient outlet for the natural increase of Quebec population, and emigration was substantial. Yolande Lavoie's estimates of emigration from the Province of Quebec are:

1840–50	40,000*
1850–60	65,000*
1860–71	80,000*
1871–81	117,600
1881–91	219,200
1891–1901	218,600
1901–11	95,400
1911–21	199,500
1921–31	185,600

* These figures are very rough estimates.   [10] Henripin, *La population canadienne*, p. 106.

Probably three-quarters of these emigrants were of French origin and a little more were Catholics. A substantial proportion came back to Quebec, although specific measurements are difficult here.

It seems also that the proportions married decreased significantly from 1852 to 1871. Census informations on marital status and age distribution are difficult to deal with, but we can estimate the following proportions married for the women of the Province of Quebec by five-year age groups:[11]

Age	1852	1871	1891	1911
15–19	10·2%	7·7%	5·7%	5·4%
20–24	42·3%	33·9%	38·1%	39·0%
25–29	79·0%	63·9%	64·8%	66·6%
30–34	81·1%	78·5%	76·0%	77·2%
35–39	80·9%	79·9%	79·3%	80·4%
40–44	83·8%	82·2%	78·7%	79·7%
45–49	82·9%	80·8%	78·3%	78·8%

According to these figures, women who were 15–29 years of age in 1871 married later than those of the same ages in 1852. But the first group of women who stayed in the Province of Quebec finally reached the same proportions married at later ages. It has been estimated that this postponement of marriage after 1852 reduced the legitimate fertility by 14 per cent between 1852 and 1871. On the whole, nuptiality did not become much more favourable to legitimate fertility until the 1940s.[12]

BIRTH RATE AND FERTILITY

We have already suggested that the downward shift of the birth rates from a first level of 54·7 per 1,000 (1711–75) to the second level of 51·9 per 1,000 (1776–1850) was caused by a concomitant change in the marriage rate. Around 1850, the birth rate started to decline rather regularly. Since the number of births per marriage was stable until 1865, the early stage of this decline (1850–65) must then be related to the fall in the marriage rate. But the possible effect of a reduction in legitimate fertility, even before 1870, should not be discarded. An estimate of legitimate fertility rates by age for the total population of Quebec in 1871 gives smaller rates than the ones observed for the eighteenth century.[13] Applied to the married female population of 1871, the 1871 rates give a birth 'deficit' of 8·4 per cent compared to what would be obtained with the eighteenth-century rates. If this deficit was due entirely to the non-French population, the legitimate

[11] Henripin, *Tendances et facteurs*, p. 380.   [12] Henripin, *Tendances et facteurs*, p. 62.
[13] Henripin, *Tendances et facteurs*, p. 40.

fertility of non-French women would be about 40 per cent lower than that observed for the eighteenth century.[14] Due to the uncertainty which affects the estimated fertility rates of married women, the most reliable information is probably the number of births per marriage. According to this measure, the fertility of marriages clearly declined after 1865 (Figure 3). Compared to the constant level of 7·1 children that had been maintained since 1711, the three five-year periods that followed 1865 had respectively 6·6, 6·7, and 6·8 children.

Estimate of age specific legitimate fertility rates have also been made for the Province of Quebec for 1891, 1911, and ten-year intervals since 1921. On the whole, variations in legitimate fertility have been as follows:[15]

	Province of Quebec	*Province of Ontario*
1871–91	– 11%	– 27%
1891–1911	– 4%	– 14%
1911–21	– 1%	– 20%
1921–31	– 16%	– 17%
1931–41	– 11%	– 20%
1941–51	– 7%	+ 13%
1951–61	– 11%	+ 7%

In comparison with the Province of Ontario, the legitimate fertility decline was much slower in Quebec. The maintenance of this high level of fertility is mostly due to the French Canadians of Quebec, whose family size manifested a remarkable resistance to the fertility decline observed in all industrializing countries.

DIFFERENTIAL FERTILITY

The Canadian censuses of 1941 and 1961 included a question on the number of children ever-born to ever-married women. In 1941, the oldest age group (sixty-five years and over) corresponded to women whose year of birth was centred in 1867. Information on this age group is limited to figures by province and type of residence. Ever-married women who lived in rural areas had 7·24 children and those who lived in urban areas had 5·96.[16] But these figures are lower than those that would be obtained for the French Canadians. In fact, we

[14] It is possible that the estimate of legitimate fertility rates, for 1871, is underevaluated by up to 5 per cent. If this was the case, the deficit would be only 3·4 per cent and if it was assumed by non-French only, their legitimate fertility would then be about 17 per cent lower than the eighteenth-century level.

[15] Henripin, *Tendances et facteurs*, p. 62.

[16] D. B. S., *Census of Canada 1941*, Vol. III, Table 52 (Ottawa, Queen's Printer).

find higher figures for Quebec women whose mother tongue is French and were aged sixty-five years or over in 1961 (born around 1887). These data are given in Table 5, together with the figures for younger women.

Table 5 Number of children born per woman ever-married, by type of residence, province of Quebec, women of French mother-tongue, by age-group in 1961

Age in 1961	Total residence	Urban	Rural non-farm	Rural farm
65 and over	6·40	5·90	7·25	8·32
60–64	5·59	4·95	6·59	8·18
55–59	5·06	4·33	6·06	7·82
50–54	4·58	3·82	5·51	7·52
45–49	4·31	3·56	5·46	7·27
40–44	4·34	3·66	5·59	6·86

Source: D.B.S., *Census of Canada 1961*, Bulletin 4.1–8, Table H9.

Ever-married French Canadian women who were born around 1887 (sixty-five and over in 1961) and who lived on farms in 1961 had almost as many children (8·3) as their ancestors of the eighteenth century who were married until the age of fifty. This figure has been reduced by only one child in twenty-five years, since women born around 1913 (forty-five to forty-nine years of age in 1961) had 7·3 children. It is not possible to know when the urban-rural differential in fertility started. The oldest women (sixty-five and over) who lived in urban areas in 1961 had only 5·9 children. The fertility of urban women decreased much more rapidly than that of women still living on farms in 1961. When the trend of urban fertility is represented on a chart and projected backward, the level of 8·4 children is reached for the women born around 1855 and who had most of their children between 1875 and 1890. This is a little later than what we assume to be the starting point of the decline of the French Canadian legitimate fertility. But it is more probable that the downward trend started slowly and then began somewhat earlier than 1875.

The number of children born was 6·40 for ever-married women of all residence, aged sixty-five years or over in 1961 (born around 1887). If we assume that the long-term decline in the French Canadian legitimate fertility started with the cohorts born around 1845, there would have been a decrease of the order of 25 per cent in about forty years; a further decrease of 25 per cent took place over the following eighteen years (women born around 1905). Quebec French Canadian women who were completing their fertility period in 1961 (aged forty-five to forty-nine) had had 4·3 children. This is a high figure for an urbanized and industrialized population. Forty-eight per cent of these women lived in cities with a population of 100,000 or more; another 15 per cent in towns of 10,000 to 100,000 inhabitants, and only 12 per cent lived on farms. We have estimated that the figure of 4·3 children per ever-married woman corresponds to a net reproduction rate of approximately 1·7.

CONCLUDING COMMENTS

We will not try to explore the reasons for this high fertility. Perhaps most of the French Canadian families simply did not have the knowledge necessary to limit the size of their family sooner. Catholic obedience was probably an important instrument in this lack of knowledge and surely in the abstention from birth control methods. Perhaps nowhere in the world was the Catholic large-family ideal more efficiently put into practice. It was reinforced by outspoken nationalist propaganda in favour of the *revanche des berceaux*, and there can be no doubt about the success of these ideas. The high fertility of the French Canadians enabled them to balance the English-speaking immigrants, and the proportion of the population of French origin was maintained at a remarkably stable level of 30 per cent until 1951.

Perhaps this was necessary for the political survival of the French-speaking community in Canada. But that also had a price: Quebec French Canadian families had to support an excessive number of children. Compared to the English-speaking families, this excess runs from 100 per cent for women born around 1890 to 50 per cent for those who had just completed their families by 1961. That is a heavy load and one would be tempted to believe that certain qualitative objectives were sacrificed for quantitative ones. That is verified at least for one important aspect of the French Canadian society: education.

It seems now that this society is going to put more emphasis on quality and much less on quantity. But a crucial problem is already present in the minds of their leaders: Is the declining relative importance of French Canadians in Canada a threat to their survival as a political force?

ACKNOWLEDGEMENT

The authors are most grateful to Miss Yolande Lavoie, research assistant in the Department of Demography of the University of Montréal, for her contribution to this study.

STATISTICAL APPENDIX

Table 6 Average population and average annual birth, marriage and death rates per 1,000 population, by five-year period, French Canadian population (1711–60) and Catholic population of the province of Quebec (1761–1883)

Periods	Average population (in thousands)	Average annual number of			Average annual rate per 1,000 population		
		Births	Marriages	Deaths	Births	Marriages	Deaths
1711–15	19·8	1,107	188	551	55·9	9·5	27·8
1716–20	22·9	1,323	236	492	57·8	10·3	21·5
1721–25	27·2	1,432	257	552	52·6	9·4	20·3
1726–30	31·6	1,713	323	825	54·2	10·2	26·1
1731–35	36·2	2,104	359	1,101	58·1	9·9	30·4
1736–40	42·3	2,312	375	898	54·7	8·9	21·2
1741–45	49·1	2,513	426	1,234	51·2	8·7	25·1
1746–50	55·0	2,801	566	1,822	50·9	10·3	33·1
1751–55	61·2	3,338	617	1,804	54·5	10·1	29·5
1756–60	67·2	3,457	670	2,549	51·4	10·0	37·9
1761–65	74·4	4,224	866	2,183	56·8	11·6	29·3
1766–70	86·2	4,897	717	2,350	56·8	8·3	27·3
1771–75	98·1	5,463	903	2,667	55·7	9·2	27·2
1776–80	110·4	5,828	895	3,346	52·8	8·1	30·3
1781–85	125·7	6,487	1,023	3,482	51·6	8·1	27·7
1786–90	141·9	7,177	1,163	3,653	50·6	8·2	25·7
1791–95	160·3	8,408	1,482	4,158	52·5	9·2	25·9
1796–1800	183·7	9,543	1,521	4,519	51·9	8·3	24·6
1801–5	208·9	10,993	1,829	5,813	52·6	8·8	27·8
1806–10	238·6	12,025	1,989	6,015	50·4	8·3	25·2
1811–15	269·3	13,504	2,440	7,251	50·1	9·1	26·9
1816–20	307·0	15,717	2,606	7,508	51·2	8·5	24·5
1821–25	349·8	18,354	3,031	8,956	52·5	8·7	25·6
1826–30	401·2	20,881	3,457	10,032	52·0	8·6	25·0
1831–35	453·6	24,519	4,276	13,308	54·1	9·4	29·3
1836–40	517·0	25,117	3,898	11,790	48·6	7·5	22·8
1841–45	590·3	29,991	5,157	13,154	50·8	8·7	22·3
1846–50	650·0	33,593	5,407	15,360	51·7	8·3	23·6
1851–55	735·0	36,027	6,033	16,041	49·0	8·2	21·8
1856–60	820·0	39,922	6,238	16,572	48·7	7·6	20·2
1861–65	900·0	44,505	7,191	20,152	49·5	8·0	22·4
1866–70	980·0	43,607	7,186	21,038	44·5	7·3	21·5
1871–75	1,060·0	48,118	8,728	26,033	45·4	8·2	24·6
1876–80	1,120·0	52,148	8,006	27,180	46·6	7·1	24·3
1881–83	1,180·0	55,346	9,633	27,127	44·1	8·1	23·0

Sources: (a) Population: Based on informations published in the censuses of Canada (1871 and 1881) and on cumulative natural increase (see text).
(b) Births, marriages and deaths: Tanguay's series published in the *Census of Canada 1871*. Vol. V and *Census of Canada 1881*, Vol. IV.

Table 7 Average population and average annual birth, marriage and death rates per 1,000 population, by five-year period, for different populations of the province of Quebec, 1884 to 1951

Periods	Average population (in thousands)			Average annual number of			Average annual rate per 1,000 population		
	Total	Catholic	French	Births*	Marriages**	Deaths†	Births*	Marriages**	Deaths†
1884–85	1,408	1,215		49,886	9,320	31,415	41·1	6·6	22·3
1886–90	1,449	1,260		52,875	9,700	31,754	42·0	6·7	21·9
1891–95	1,518	1,320		55,396	10,024	33,234	41·9	6·6	21·9
1896–1900	1,599	1,380		59,708	11,151	34,739	43·3	7·0	21·6
1901–5	1,715	1,480		59,115	11,636	32,050	39·9	6·8	18·7
1906–10	1,891	1,640		65,705	13,307	34,943	40·0	7·0	18·5
1911–15	2,072	1,790		74,642	16,260	35,948	41·7	7·9	17·4
1916–20	2,248	1,935		77,267	18,092	40,495	39·9	8·1	18·0
1921–25	2,579	2,115		80,250	17,529	33,339	37·9	6·3	12·9
1926–30	2,715	—		—	18,731	36,645	—	6·9	13·5
1926–30		2,330	2,145	72,703	15,527	30,430	33·9	6·7	14·2
1931–35		2,550	2,360	68,892	13,975	26,817	29·2	5·5	11·4
1936–40		2,765	2,570	69,194	22,959	27,109	26·9	8·3	10·6
1941–45		3,025	2,780	86,667	28,548	27,779	31·2	9·4	10·0
1946–50		3,375	3,125	100,884	30,127	27,972	32·3	8·9	8·6
1951		3,564	3,327	104,725	31,243	27,897	31·5	8·3	8·4

Sources: (a) Population: 1. Total population: 1884–93: *Canada Year Book 1936*; 1894–1930: *Statistical Year Book of the Province of Quebec,* 1921, 1923 and 1934.
2. Catholic and French population: interpolated from census information.
(b) Births: 1884–93: *Statistical Year Book of the Province of Quebec,* 1921; 1894–1900: R. Kuczinski, *Birth Registration and Birth Statistics in Canada,* Washington, Brookings Institution, 1930, p. 59; 1901–5: interpolation; 1906–25: *Statistical Year Book of the Province of Quebec,* 1921 and 1928; 1926–51: D.B.S., *Vital Statistics.*
(c) Marriages and deaths: 1884–1930: *Statistical Year Book of the Province of Quebec,* 1921 and 1934; 1926–51: *Vital Statistics.*

Notes: * Catholic births up to 1925; births of French origin from 1926 to 1951.
** Total marriages up to 1930; Catholic marriages from 1926 to 1951.
† Total deaths up to 1930; deaths of French origin from 1926 to 1951.

Jean-Noël Biraben

Certain demographic characteristics of the plague epidemic in France, 1720–1722

The epidemic that began in Marseilles in 1720 was the last important epidemic of the plague in Western Europe. Details about this epidemic can be gleaned from the abundant administrative reports that were made. On 25 May 1720, the *Grand St. Antoine* arrived at Marseilles. This vessel had left Saida (the Sidon of antiquity) in Syria on 30 January, when the plague was raging in that country. It stopped at Tripoli and at Cyprus; it was refused entry at the port of Leghorn, however, because seven of its sailors had died en route, although their deaths were attributed to poor food and defective hygiene aboard ship. The health commissioners at the port of Marseilles took the precaution of impounding the ship's merchandise; they also quarantined the eight passengers and the crew for fifteen days in a lazaretto on an island in the middle of the port.

The passengers finally obtained permission to land on 14 June; one went to Paris, two others to Holland. That same day, the sailors who had also been released came into contact with the people of Marseilles, who bought several contraband lengths of cloth from them. Shortly thereafter, the street porters who had carried the wares (cotton and wool material) as well as several of the sailors fell sick. They were taken to hospitals where they died one after another. The surviving crew members and all suspect merchandise were transferred to the Isle of Jarros; the captain of the ship, Chataud, was imprisoned in the Chateau d'If.[1] After an inventory, the confiscated merchandise was burned in September. The people in the city who had bought the contraband goods, however, fell sick and died rapidly: first a woman, then on 28 June a tailor and his family, and on 1 July two more women. By the following week, all the houses in the street contained invalids. These families were very poor, and it was not until 9 July that two doctors, Peyssonnel and his son, saw a case: They were

---

[1] After a long trial his case was to be declared *nola contendere* in a judgment of 8 July 1723. The registers of the commissioners of the Health Department do not contain a faithful transcription of his declaration.

called to the bedside of a sick thirteen-year-old boy, who died before their eyes within several hours. The malignity of the disease did not escape them, and they alerted the aldermen, who had the whole family hospitalized and ordered an investigation.

On 14 July, the malady spread to another street, and a Dr. Sicard first spoke of plague. Dr. Bauzon, however, whom the aldermen had asked for an expert opinion, maintained that it was only a question of malignant fevers, possibly caused by intestinal worms. Public opinion became alarmed, but as no new cases occurred between 15 and 21 July, it went from one extreme to the other. Dr. Sicard and the aldermen were accused of having frightened everyone for nothing.

On 22 July, however, new cases were announced; fourteen people died on 23 July. The aldermen began to think of extreme measures, but because many deaths were wrongly attributed to the plague, confusion continued for several more days. On 29 July, the number of deaths increased suddenly; the municipality was overwhelmed by the urgency of the measures that had to be taken and of the help that had to be given. When, at last, a decree of the Parliament of Aix put the city of Marseilles under an interdict and the Chamber of Commerce (*Chambre des Vacations*) forbade all commerce between the city and the province, it was too late to stop the epidemic. Nearly ten thousand inhabitants had already fled.

At the same time, it was too early to close the city, for no stock of provisons existed, and food was lacking. After 6 August, strikes broke out, protesting the rising prices and lack of bread. This agitation aggravated the pestilence, which rapidly became worse. By 8 August, it was necessary to conscript beggars to bury the dead because the *corbeaux*, special bearers of plague-striken corpses, no longer sufficed for the task. On 10 August, the malady had reached all quarters of the city. Municipal services were overwhelmed by 11 August. The violence of the contagion left them completely disorganized. By the end of August, the plague had reached its maximum virulence. After 15 August, it was no longer possible to bury all the dead. Employees counted on the day before fell sick daily. It was estimated that the enlisted drivers of the death carts worked, on an average, only two days; by the third, they fell in their turn. Of 217 convicts taken to bury the dead during the month of August, only twelve remained alive by the first of September. On this date, volunteers gathered together between twelve and thirteen hundred infants who had lost their mothers and tried to nourish them with soup and goat's milk. The babies died at the rate of thirty to forty a day.

During the entire month of September the plague raged and the dead accumulated. The new commandant, Langeron, arrived on 4 September and attempted to take the situation in hand. He succeeded, but not without difficulty. The Chevalier Roze offered his help and, with a group of forty volunteer soldiers, went to remove the mounds of cadavers from the Place de la Tourette, where no living person had dared penetrate for several days. All contracted the plague; the Chevalier Roze was lucky enough to be among the five who survived the disease.

Some statistics may give an idea of the violence of the epidemic. Of about ninety thousand inhabitants, ten thousand fled before the protective cordons were established; of the eighty thousand who remained, 39,334 died. All but three of the millers died. The surviving bakers fled on 21 August when they were forbidden to abandon their ovens, and it was necessary to enlist fifty volunteers immediately to replace them. In the butcher shops, the provisioners of livestock were miraculously immune, but only three meat-cutters remained alive after 9 September. The personnel of the slaughterhouses all died, and the butchers were so decimated that it was necessary to replace them. Public services were practically nonexistent: All policemen, all captains except one, all lieutenants except two, all public servants (almost five hundred), the thirty guards recruited for the plague, and almost all of the three hundred and fifty men of the company of guards died. In the health services, of the twelve doctors who remained, six contracted the plague and four died; of thirty-five surgeons, thirty-two died. Various professions were affected differently, insofar as it is possible to estimate the number of members in each group before the epidemic and the subsequent number of deaths.

Master hatters:	50 deaths out of 100
Assistant hatters:	270 deaths out of 300
Carpenters:	84 deaths out of 134
Tailors:	78 deaths out of 138
Shoemakers:	110 deaths out of 200
Cobblers:	350 deaths out of 400
Masons:	350 deaths out of 500

Out of a total of 784 galley convicts, 543 deaths were counted. Among the 696 put at the disposal of the city of Marseilles, 486 died, twenty-eight out of thirty-four in the stores selling wheat.

Thus, the epidemic continued, slowly becoming less violent. There were only several dozen cases between 18 April 1721, and 19 August 1721, when the last case was recorded. Two severe quarantines followed immediately: the first from 20 August to 29 September, the second from 1 October to 9 November. No new case was discovered; the city was freed at last. The work of restoring order was in full swing, when, on 3 February 1722, a relapse occurred which obliged immediate reinstatement of Draconian measures. This time only 260 persons were attacked, of which 194 died. The city lived in fear, however, and took a long time to recuperate from this last blow.

During this long ordeal, what was occurring outside Marseilles?

On 1 August 1720, a blockade of the city was instituted, although inefficiently at first, with only a few posts. On 4 August, a decision was made to install protective cordons, but the necessary troops could not be assembled and put in place until 20 August. From that time on, people could not cross the barriers; merchandise was allowed to pass only at four specified points, and infinite precaution was exercised. It was, however, much too late, as many of the escaped citizens had already brought the plague to numerous localities in Provence. The cordons were extended considerably and imposed on neighbouring provinces, and precautions were extended to include all of France. These were imitated by Piedmont, Spain, Switzerland, and several other foreign countries.

Nevertheless, the plague was at Aix and at Apt on 1 August 1720. On 15 August, it reached Aubagne. It spread to Toulon on 20 August, where, after a long calm, it reappeared very violently on 7 October. On 12 October, it was at Martigues; on 4 November, at Salon; on 17 December, at Tarascon. It reached Marvéjols in Languedoc on 12 July 1721, entering Mende a little later, Avignon on 17 August, and Alès on 9 September.

It was ended at Mende at the end of September 1722, and at Avignon on 2 October. After having ravaged Provence, the Venaissin, and part of Languedoc for more than two years, it seemed that the plague had run its course. In Provence alone on 31 August 1722, there were 94,184 recorded cases; it is probable, in reality, that this figure exceeded 100,000

During the course of the epidemic, the government of Provence demanded a weekly report on the situation from all infected localities. A general report for all contaminated cities and places of Provence—giving for each the date of the plague's first appearance, the number of deaths, and the date of the last death or case—was drawn up which covered the period up to 1 June 1721.[2] A more complete register was compiled on 1 October, when the epidemic had almost disappeared in Provence. In this province alone, the number of deaths due to plague reached 89,119 by 1 October 1721.[3]

We have tried to assemble the essential information into a picture of the plague in Provence;[4] comparable figures are not available for the Venaissin and Languedoc. Table 1 lists, in chronological order

---

[2] *Archives Nationales* G⁷1730.   [3] *Archives Nationales* G⁷1733.
[4] This information comes principally from the departmental archives of Bouches du Rhône, Série C.

by first appearance, the results of the plague in the localities in Provence known to have been affected.

Table 1 The plague in Provence, Comtat, and Languedoc

Place	Approximate number of inhabitants before the plague	Date of first appearance of the plague	Number of deaths from the plague	% of deaths
Provence				
1 Marseilles and *terroir* (environs)	90,000	20 June 1720	39,334	43·7
2 Cassis	3,500	21 July	216	6·9
3 Aix	24,000	1 August	7,534	31·4
4 Apt	6,000	1 August	271	4·5
5 Vitrolles	770	2 August	210	27·3
6 Ste Tulle	810	7 August	430	53·1
7 Aubagne	7,000	15 August	2,116	30·2
8 Mayrargue	850	15 August	382	44·9
9 Les Pennes Mirabeau	540	15 August	223	41·3
10 Gignac	470	15 August	42	8·9
11 Allauch	5,000	20 August	1,017	20·3
12 Toulon	26,276	20 August	13,283	50·6
13 Lançon	1,800	22 August	816	45·3
14 Roussillon	1,100	25 August	138	12·5
15 Septèmes	940	26 August	200	21·3
16 La Penne sur Huveaume	462	26 August	165	35·7
17 Le Puy Ste Réparade	900	29 August	43	4·8
18 St. Canadet	125	29 August	34	27·2
19 St. Zacharie	1,050	30 August	254	24·2
20 Gaubert	500	4 September	29	5·8
21 Rognac	370	18 September	148	40·0
22 St. Cannat	1,500	22 September	342	22·8
23 Caseneuve	1,100	22 September	18	1·6
24 Corbières	400	22 September	131	32·8
25 Nans	500	27 September	125	25·0
26 Berre	2,000	28 September	1,080	54·0
27 St. Martin de Castillon	1,500	29 September	326	21·7
28 Cucuron	3,500	1 October	832	23·8
29 Gardane	2,000	3 October	6	0·3
30 Auriol	3,200	3 October	1,319	41·2
31 Pourrières	1,200	4 October	1	0·2
32 Bandol	187	5 October	29	15·5
33 Perthuis	4,000	6 October	364	9·1
34 Pelissanne	2,200	6 October	223	10·1
35 Villars Brancas	300	9 October	12	4·0
36 Simiane	774	15 October	257	33·2
37 Le Canet	600	18 October	198	33·0
38 St. Savournin	400	22 October	206	51·5
39 Carry	450	25 October	11	2·4
40 Martigues	6,000	1 November 1720	2,200	36·7
41 St. Rémy	3,000	1 November	1,005	33·5
42 Venelles	410	1 November	33	8·0
43 Salon	4,000	1 November	(894)	22·3
44 Rustrel	750	14 November	13	1·7
45 Arles	22,000	26 November	9,400	42·7

Table 1—*continued*

Place	Approximate number of inhabitants before the plague	Date of first appearance of the plague	Number of deaths from the plague	% of deaths
46 Vaugines	200	2 December	33	16·5
47 Tarascon	10,000	17 December	210	2·1
48 Mazaugues	441	17 December	168	38·1
49 Géménos	1,100	20 December	54	4·9
50 Orgon	1,700	29 December	105	6·2
51 Ollioules	2,600	1 January 1721	1,370	52·7
52 La Seyne	5,000	4 January	2,006	40·1
53 Maillanes	750	7 January	106	14·1
54 Sues	58	18 January	7	12·1
55 La Valette	1,660	20 February	1,068	64·3
56 Ste Marguerite	276	20 March	22	8·0
57 Forcalqueyret	230	27 May	174	75·7
58 Le Revest	650	1 June	367	64·8
59 La Garde (de Toulon)	544	3 June	300	55·1
60 Trinquetaille les Arles	1,157	11 June	80	6·9
61 Garéoult	1,200	13 June	168	14·0
62 Ste Anastasie	500	14 June	310	62·0
63 Cuers	3,000	27 June	?	?
64 Six Fours	2,226	? June	40	1·8
65 St. Nazaire (Sanary)	1,200	1 July	51	4·2
66 La Foux (le Puget)	213	3 July	98	46·0
67 Roquevaire	2,500	9 July	46	1·8
68 Frigoulet (abbaye)	60	12 July	19	31·7
69 Néoules	450	17 July	313	69·6
70 La Roquebrussane	997	14 August	201	20·1
71 Graveson	1,100	15 August	11	1·0
72 Noves	1,228	16 August	178	14·5
73 Besse et Blanquefort	1,900	24 August	374	19·7
74 Flassans	540	end of August	?	?
74 Lambesc	2,200	19 September	1	0·5
75 Le Vernégues	440	?	?	?
76 La Cadière	2,480	?	?	?
77 Le Luc (près Toulon)	2,235	?	?	?
78 Solliès	4,895	?	?	?
79 Brignolles	4,831	?	?	?
Comtat				
1 Avignon	23,041	23 September 1720 to 17 August 1721	7,224	31·3
2 Caumont/Durance	?	16 November 1720	?	?
3 Bedarrides	?	15 August 1721	?	?
4 Monteux	?	?	?	?
Languedoc				
1 Auxillac (Correjac)	109	23 November 1720	58	53·2
2 La Canourgue	1,633	8 December 1720	945	57·9
3 Banassac	?	31 May 1721	46	?
4 Marvejols	4,600	12 July	3,000	65·2
5 La Mouline	?	end of August	?	?
6 Bergonhon	?	end of August	?	?
7 Ste. Colombe de Peyre	?	end of August	?	?

Table 1—*continued*

Place	Approximate number of inhabitants before the plague	Date of first appearance of the plague	Number of deaths from the plague	% of deaths
8 Montferrand	?	end of August	?	?
9 Valladou	?	beginning of September	?	?
10 St. Léger de Peyre	?	beginning of September	?	?
11 La Chaze	?	beginning of September	?	?
12 La Capelle (Fontjulien)	?	2 September	?	?
13 St. Georges (Serres)	?	? September	?	?
14 Defret	?	? September	?	?
15 Genolhac	?	beginning of September	?	?
16 Alès	10,000	9 September	336	3·4
17 Le Chambon (abbaye)	?	beginning of September	?	?
18 Lousgratous	?	mid-September	20	?
19 Altier (et Conzes)	?	mid-September	?	?
20 La Rousse	?	mid-September	?	?
21 Chirac	?	?	?	?
22 Mende	?	?	?	?

This picture contains important gaps and uncertainties.[5] The figures in parentheses are incomplete, as they were collected before the end of the epidemic. Few communities had, like Toulon, the leisure to take a census before the plague arrived; for most, there is only a rough evaluation taken from the head-tax rolls. The date of the first appearance of the plague corresponds sometimes to the date of the first known sickness, sometimes to that of the first death; occasionally an attack at first affected only one person or one family, but several months later carried off several thousand, as at Avignon. When a daily nominative list was kept, the number of deaths is sometimes fairly precise. Unfortunately, the people who kept these lists often perished, and their notes were burned. Thus, it was necessary to reconstitute the number of deaths, and only a very approximate reconstitution was possible. The figures for the population and for the number of deaths used in calculating the percentage of deaths in relation to the pre-epidemic population are full of errors.

With all its faults, however, this picture allows us to make a certain number of observations on demographic factors in an epidemic of plague. First of all, the localities do not seem to have been touched at random. They clearly tend to follow the important routes of communication of the period. The concentration of the population also seems to have been a decisive factor. Given the uncertainty of contemporary estimates of population figures and the absence of

[5] This list gives a total of deaths from the plague in Provence of only 93,790. Documents of the period give this figure as 94,184, the difference coming from contemporary errors in addition and the gaps in our information.

figures for those places that were unaffected, we have used the Census of 1764, which, on a relative scale, can be considered reliable as far back as 1720. If one looks at the *vigueries*, typical districts of southern France before the Revolution, of Aix, Apt, Brignolles, St. Maximin, Hyeres, Tarascon, Toulon, Marseilles, and their *terres adjacentes* (environs)—all of which were heavily affected by the plague—one notes that the less populated localities were often less affected, and those that were almost all along the main arteries of communication. Regardless of place, however, all cities of ten thousand or more inhabitants were affected.

Table 2

Number of inhabitants	Total number of communities	Communities affected by plague	% of communities affected
0–99	17	2	11·8
100–499	65	9	13·8
500–699	22	7	31·8
700–999	27	9	33·3
1,000–1,999	52	19	36·5
2,000–4,999	35	17	48·6
5,000–9,999	6	4	66·7
10,000 and more	4	4	100·0
Totals	228	71	

There seems to be no correlation between the size of the city and the violence of the epidemic. The distribution of localities according to the proportion of deaths in the population, however, seems significant. Table 3 lists the relationship for the seventy-eight localities with which we are acquainted.

Table 3

Percentage of deaths	Number of localities
0·0– 9·9	24
10·0–19·9	9
20·0–29·9	11
30·0–39·9	11
40·0–49·9	9
50·0–59·9	8
60·0–69·9	5
70·0–79·9	1
80·0–89·9	—

Such a distribution suggests the existence of two divisions: On the one hand, a large number of places had few deaths, sometimes only one; on the other, a large number were severely affected by the plague, losing between 20 and 50 per cent of their population. Between these two categories, there are only three places which lost between 15 and 20 per cent.[6]

Do epidemiological reasons explain this bimodal division? Are there two different explanations for the propagation of the plague? Because the plague follows communication routes, the role played by wild rodents would seem to have been less important than is true today in the Near and Middle East. Nevertheless, are urban rats always attacked? Are other factors at work? Does, for example, the pseudo-tuberculosis bacillus of Malassex and Vignal provide immunity against the plague bacillus? The question remains to be answered, but numerous factors in the plague epidemic of southern France in 1720–22 can be found which militate in favour of an hypothesis of Ricardo Jorge.[7] He argues that human fleas played an important part in the transmission of the plague in Western Europe from the Middle Ages until the present.

New studies are necessary on this subject; perhaps they will bring us more satisfactory results. The seasonal rhythm which rules the advances and retreats of the illness shows that climatic factors are also very important.[8]

This article was translated from the French by Patricia Cumming.

[6] The London epidemic of 1665 was much less violent than that of Marseilles; only about 15 per cent of the population died, and whole quarters remained untouched.

[7] Ricardo Jorge, *Les anciennes épidémies de peste en Europe, comparées avec les épidemies modernes* (Lisbon, 1932).

[8] See also, Gaston Rambert, *Histoire du commerce de Marseille*, Vol. 4 (1660–1789; Paris, 1954); Paul Gaffarel and Marquis de Duranty, *La peste de 1720 à Marseille d'après des documents inédits* (Paris, 1911); Marc and Pierre Genton, *Contribution à l'étude historique de la peste dans la région Toulonnaise, au 18e siècle en particulier* (Paris, 1929). For the archive documents, see *Archives départementales des Bouches du Rhône*, Series C, Nos. 910, 916, 917, 918, 919, 920, 927, 944; *Archives Nationales, correspondence du Contrôle Général*, Series G⁷, Nos. for 1730, 1733, and 1736, and Series H, No. 1198. Forthcoming: J. N. Biraben, *Les hommes et la peste en France et dans les pays européens et méditerranéens*.

E. A. Wrigley

Mortality in pre-industrial England: the example of Colyton, Devon, over three centuries

In a recent article, T. McKeown and R. G. Record, analysing the Registrar-General's mortality statistics for England and Wales in the nineteenth century, express forcefully the view that the substantial falls in mortality which occurred in the second half of the nineteenth century were due primarily to improved standards of living. Until the last years of the century neither public health measures nor medical therapy is accorded a major role in reducing death rates.[1] If marked falls in mortality rates occurred in the nineteenth century after the Industrial Revolution but before medical science or public health measures had contributed much to the struggle against early death, it is clearly possible that there were comparable fluctuations in mortality in earlier centuries. It would be as unwise to assume that mortality rates in pre-industrial times were invariably high as to make the same assumption about fertility rates.[2]

Unquestionably many factors besides living standards had a bearing on pre-industrial mortality rates. In the short term, weather, harvest conditions, and epidemic infections exerted a tremendous influence. In the longer term, general economic circumstances, the degree of urbanization, the density of settlement, changes in the virulence of particular diseases and their unpredictable appearances and disappearances, and genetic characteristics—all played a part. In various combinations, the interplay of these factors might produce very different levels of mortality.

There is clear, indeed dramatic, evidence of the crushing nature of the periodic crises which overwhelmed local communities in pre-industrial Western Europe when food prices shot up after bad

[1] T. McKeown and R. G. Record, 'Reasons for the Decline of Mortality in England and Wales During the Nineteenth Century', *Population Studies*, Vol. 16, No. 2 (1962), pp. 94–122.

[2] For evidence of fluctuations in fertility, see E. A. Wrigley, 'Family Limitation in Pre-Industrial England', *Economic History Review*, Second Series, Vol. 19, No. 1 (1966), pp. 82–109.

harvests.[3] There is also much evidence of the terrible impact of the great epidemics of plague, smallpox, typhus, and influenza which might occur either independently or as part of a food crisis, attacking a weakened population with many people on the move from place to place and consequently liable to spread disease. There is, however, much less evidence about the levels of mortality which prevailed generally. Still less clear is the size of regional and local differences in mortality or the extent of change over time.

The comparative abundance of information about short-term crises and the relative lack of other studies are partly due to a technical problem in the analysis of the available sources. In England, for example, the parish registers are the only major source of information before the nineteenth century. They record by date and name the vital events of the parish—baptisms, burials, and marriages—and lend themselves readily to aggregative analysis. This permits analysis of the effects, say, of a harvest crisis because the month-by-month changes in the totals of burials, marriages, and baptisms can be correlated with data about the price of foodstuffs. Aggregative methods will not, however, yield age-specific mortality rates, and so permit the construction of life tables and the investigation of a wider range of questions, unless deaths are divided by age group and an additional source is available giving totals of population at risk by age. Until 1813, when the provisions of Rose's Act of 1812 enjoined the recording of an age for each entry in the burial register, very few English parish registers record age at death, and censuses with detailed age divisions began only in 1841. Only in recent years has this problem been circumvented for earlier centuries by the development of the technique of family reconstitution using parish register entries.[4]

The purpose of this article is to present the results of a family reconstitution study of mortality in Colyton during the period 1538–1837 and to examine some of the problems of interpretation which accompany studies of this type. The analysis which follows is neither exhaustive nor definitive. The data on the family reconstitution forms (FRFs) have all been punched onto paper tape and will be more fully analysed by computer shortly. When this has been done, and when parallel information for other parishes has become available, it will be possible to treat more fully some topics mentioned only summarily here or omitted altogether.[5]

[3] See, for example, Pierre Goubert, *Beauvais et le Beauvaisis de 1600 à 1730* (2 vols.; Paris, 1960), esp. Part I, Ch. 3.
[4] See M. Fleury and L. Henry, *Nouveau manuel de dépouillement et d'exploitation de l'état civil ancien* (Paris, 1965); and E. A. Wrigley (ed.), *An Introduction to English Historical Demography* (London, 1966), Ch. 4.
[5] Family reconstitution studies on the following parish registers are well advanced: Hartland, Devon; Banbury, Oxfordshire; Easingwold, Yorkshire; Aldenham, Hertfordshire; and a group of contiguous parishes in Bedfordshire (Campton-with-Shefford, Southill, and Clophill).

The essence of the family reconstitution method is to assemble all the information about the vital events in a given family which can be gleaned from the register of a parish or group of parishes.[6] This is done in accordance with a set of rules designed to minimize the danger that wrong linkages will be made (for example, to try to ensure that the Elizabeth Green married on 15 November 1622 was the same Elizabeth Green baptized on 6 April 1593).[7]

FAMILY RECONSTITUTION AND MORTALITY STUDIES

Each type of demographic calculation based on family reconstitution material has its own pitfalls. For example, a major problem in the study of infant and child mortality is to determine the period of time during which an individual is in observation. Clearly it is essential that the period be defined in such a way that it is independent of the event whose frequency of occurrence is to be measured. It would not do, for instance, to include the death of a four-year-old child in a count of mortality of children of that age if the only evidence of his presence in the parish were the recording of his burial, and other four-year-olds who did not die went uncounted for that reason. Failure to grasp the importance of this point in work of the reconstitution type can produce highly misleading results, as in a recent study of sixteenth-century York.[8]

In order to give a clearer picture of the problems of interpreting the Colyton data, it is perhaps useful first to describe briefly the type of information given in the burial register. The normal form of entry consists of the first name and surname of the deceased person, the date of his burial, and his relationship to the head of his family (except, of course, where the entry refers to the head himself). The

[6] Where possible, it is often best to work on a group of neighbouring parishes since this enables many individuals migrating short distances to be kept in observation. The frequency of short-distance migration is the greatest single factor tending to reduce the proportion of a parish's population whose demographic characteristics can be studied.

[7] For details of the rules to be followed, see Wrigley (ed.), *An Introduction to English Historical Demography*, Ch. 4; also Wrigley, 'Some Problems of Family Reconstitution Using English Parish Register Material', cyclostyled paper for Section 7, Third International Economic History Conference, Munich, 1965.

[8] See U. M. Cowgill, 'Life and Death in the Sixteenth Century in the City of York', *Population Studies*, Vol. 21, No. 1 (1967), pp. 53–62. In this study, the ages at death of 34 per cent of the children born in six York parishes between 1538 and 1601 were identified, and implicitly the assumption was made that the ages at death which could not be discovered were distributed in the same way as those which had been established. There is, however, a much better chance of linking a baptism entry to an early death than to later deaths and, in consequence, mortality was greatly overestimated. (Almost half the birth population is shown as dying in the first year of life. See Table 2, p. 56.)

description of the relationship to the head of the family is vital if links between baptism and burial entries are to be made with confidence. Where it is lacking (as it usually was in the Colyton register from 1709 to 1735), reconstitution, in general, and mortality studies, in particular, are always gravely handicapped and become impossible if the period of poor registration is prolonged. The relationship of a child to the head of the family continued to be recorded until he or she married. There are many entries in the form 'son of' and 'daughter of' where the son or daughter is fully adult, in his or her twenties, thirties, or even occasionally forties.[9]

In addition to this basic information, other details of the dead person are sometimes given—marital status, occupation, residence, cause of death, age, and so on. In the period 1670–79, for example, 561 burials were recorded, with details as follows: 90 'son of'; 84 'daughter of'; 87 'wife of'; 74 'widow'; 1 'bachelor'; 169 males and 56 females without indication of relationship or marital status. Of the 169 men, however, there were further details for 82: in 41 cases, place of residence; in 11, occupation; in 6, rank; 22 were distinguished as 'the older' or 'the younger', 1 was a bastard, and 1 a stranger. Of the 55 women, 17 were distinguished in a comparable fashion. At other periods, much more supplementary information was given. Between 1765 and 1779, for example, occupation was almost always recorded.

In the process of reconstitution, as many burial entries as possible are linked to a preceding baptism either directly, or indirectly by linking first to a marriage entry and then to a baptism. (In the case of married women, the middle link is, of course, essential since their surnames change at marriage.) Until the link has been made, age at death cannot be known unless it happens to be one of the supplementary items of information given in the register. Where an age at burial is recorded in the register, it is usually less accurate than an age calculated as the interval between baptism and burial, especially where death occurs at an advanced age.[10]

The necessity of conforming to independent criteria defining the period during which an individual is in observation tends to restrict mortality studies based on family reconstitution to infant and child deaths. The birth of later children in the family or the death of a parent provides in most cases evidence of the continued presence of the family in the parish up to a certain date. As long as the child at

[9] Mary, daughter of Barnard Vickary, is an extreme example of this. She was described in this way when buried in 1697, aged 46 (her father died in the following year, aged 79).

[10] In the early-nineteenth century, when baptism was frequently delayed for several weeks or months after birth, an age at death given in the register is frequently more accurate for young children than an age calculated as the interval between baptism and burial.

that date is under 10, or even under 15, there is a strong probability that he is still living with his parents. In this way, his presence in observation can be tested. The period 10–14 is more doubtful than earlier periods because of the increasing likelihood with growing years that a boy or girl will go out to service in another family, often in a different parish. This carries the attendant danger that death and burial may take place elsewhere.

Unmarried adults are at the other extreme. Their presence in the parish cannot be tested in any comparable fashion and, thus, no use can be made of information about their deaths. Married adults cause fewer problems, and estimates of adult mortality rates based on married people are possible, though the margins of error tend to be rather wide.

THE CALCULATION OF MORTALITY RATES

Rules for the calculation of mortality rates after families in a parish have been reconstituted were defined by E. Gautier and Louis Henry in their Crulai study.[11] Their exposition, with minor modifications enforced by the nature of the English parish registers, is followed here.

For the purpose of studying infant and child mortality, a family enters into observation from the date when the marriage is contracted or, in its absence, from the date of baptism of the earliest child recorded on the FRF. It passes from observation with the death of the later of the two parents to die where dates of burial for both of them are known. If the date of burial of only one parent is known, but it is also known that the other parent survived (as, for example, when a woman is described at burial as 'wife of——'), this date marks the passage from observation of the family. If the date of burial of only one parent is known, but it is not clear whether the other parent died earlier or later, and also when the date of burial of neither parent is known, the family passes from observation on the date of baptism of the youngest child in the family. The limits of observation defined in this way apply to all the children in a family. Within these limits, any individual child is in observation from the day of his birth (or baptism) until his latest birthday which occurs within the period of observation defined. Figure 1 may help to illustrate the operation of these rules with an imaginary example.

[11] E. Gautier and L. Henry, *La population de Crulai* (Paris, 1956), Ch. 8; see also L. Henry, *Manuel de démographie historique* (Paris, 1967), Ch. 6.

Figure 1   Date of entry into observation 3.9.1624 (William Bagshaw marries Elizabeth Hawkins)

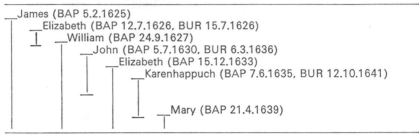

__James (BAP 5.2.1625)
 __Elizabeth (BAP 12.7.1626, BUR 15.7.1626)
  __William (BAP 24.9.1627)
   __John (BAP 5.7.1630, BUR 6.3.1636)
    __Elizabeth (BAP 15.12.1633)
     __Karenhappuch (BAP 7.6.1635, BUR 12.10.1641)

      __Mary (BAP 21.4.1639)

Date of passage from observation 9.12.1641 (Elizabeth, wife of William Bagshaw buried—William's burial not recorded)

Children to the marriage:

James—in observation to fifteenth birthday
Elizabeth (1)— dies in observation in first year of life.
William—in observation to fourteenth birthday
John—dies in observation aged five
Elizabeth (2)—in observation to seventh birthday
Karenhappuch—in observation to sixth birthday
   (death occurs outside observation and not counted in deaths of children aged six)
Mary—in observation to second birthday

When details from all FRFs have been collated, life-table death rates (1,000 q_x) can be calculated. Thus, for example (in Table 1), 182 babies died in families which are in observation from their baptism to a point in time at least one year later. The total number of babies in observation for a full year from their birth is 1,679, including those who died. The infant mortality rate, therefore, is $\frac{182}{1,679} \times 1,000 = 108$ per 1,000. The number of children in observation for the second year of life is depleted by the infant deaths and by the passage from observation of forty-one children between their first and second birthdays. This reduces the number in observation throughout their second year of life to 1,456 (1,295 children in observation until their second birthday or later, plus 161 children who died in observation aged 1 or more). Forty-nine children died at age 1, and this gives a mortality rate of 34 per 1,000 $(\frac{49}{1,456} \times 1,000)$. Values are given for the life-table death rates age 0–1, 1–4, 5–9, and 10–14.[12]

---

[12] See Henry, *Manuel de démographie historique*, pp. 125–8, for further details of methods of calculation.

Table 1 The calculation of life-table death rates (1,000 q_x) for infants and children from reconstitution data: Colyton 1538–99

A Age in years	B Deaths	C No. leaving observation	D Cumulative total of B	E Cumulative total of C	F D+E	G Death rate
0	182		343	1,336	1,679	108
1	49	41	161	1,295	1,456	34
2	29	45	112	1,250	1,362	21
3	20	39	83	1,211	1,294	15
4	15	41	63	1,170	1,233	12
5	13	40	48	1,130	1,178	11
6	5	43	35	1,087	1,122	4
7	4	36	30	1,051	1,081	4
8	7	26	26	1,025	1,051	7
9	1	30	19	995	1,014	1
10	1	30	18	965	983	1
11	2	25	17	940	957	2
12	5	22	15	918	933	5
13	7	22	10	896	906	8
14	3	18	3	878	881	3
15		878				

Life-table death rates (per 1,000)

0–1	108
1–4	80
5–9	27
10–14	21

The calculation of adult mortality rates is based on all married men and women whose age at marriage is known because a link has been made from the marriage entry to a preceding baptism entry. In analysing the Colyton FRFs, only those marrying under 35 were included in this group. They married on an average at 25 years of age (see Table 10 below) and can be treated as entering observation at this age.[13] Their numbers were steadily depleted by death. The survivors at given ages can be calculated and related to the base population, thus permitting survival ratios and mortality rates to be derived. There is, however, a serious problem in using this material. It arises from the absence of information about the date of burial of a substantial fraction of the original group, and this introduces uncertainties into the calculation of all adult mortality rates. The problem can be met in two ways—by eliminating from the group as a whole subgroups peculiarly liable to be missing from the burial register; and by manipulating the data to produce high and low estimates of mortality between which the truth must lie. Both methods were used by Gautier and Henry in their study of Crulai. After experimenting, for example, they eliminated from their female group all women

[13] See Gautier and Henry, *La population de Crulai*, p. 179, for discussion of this question.

IP

whose husbands' dates of baptism were unknown because they proved especially likely to have moved from the parish and introduced an unacceptably large uncertainty into mortality calculations. Again, in order to obtain high and low estimates of mortality, ages at death which were unknown were distributed as if all had died at the date at which their existence was last attested in the register (as at the baptism of a child, for example); and as if all had lived to age 60 and had then conformed to the age pattern of mortality observed in those whose age at death was known. When added to the known ages at death, the two alternative distributions can be made to yield high and low mortality estimates.

In analysing the Colyton data, the following conventions were observed:

1. All those whose spouse's age is unknown were excluded wherever no further information of any sort was available on the FRF. There were very few men in this situation (only 8 in 165 in the period 1538–1624), but many more women (49 in 237 in the same period). The difference probably arises because of the prevalence of the habit of marrying in the bride's parish when the husband came from a different parish, though the couple would then usually settle in the husband's parish. In such cases the partners to the marriage are in observation only at the moment of their marriage and not thereafter. To include them increases the margin between the high and low estimates without compensating advantages.

2. High and low estimates were obtained by distributing the deaths of all whose age at death is unknown as if none had lived beyond 69, and deaths in the age divisions up to that age had been distributed as in the population whose age at death is known, and as if all had reached 60 and had then been reduced by death in the same way as those whose age at death is known.

As an example of the operations involved, the treatment of the FRFs of marriages formed 1538–1624 is described. There were 345 men and women who married in this period and whose FRFs survived the test of the first convention cited above. Their average age at marriage was 25·4 years. The age at death of 227 of them is known, and Table 2 shows the distribution of these ages.

Table 2 Distribution of known ages at death of married men and women of marriages formed 1538–1624 (sexes combined)

Under 40	40–9	50–9	60–9	70–9	80 and over	Total
48	28	51	46	40	14	227

Table 3 What is known of those whose precise age at death is not known

lowest age known not to have been reached

highest age at which known still to be living		Under 40	40–9	50–9	60–9	70–9	80 and over	Total
	Under 40			2		2	88	92
	40–9			1			19	20
	50–9						4	4
	60–9						2	2
	70–9							
	80 and Over							
	Total			3		2	113	118

Table 3 shows what is known of the remaining 118. To obtain high and low estimates of the mortality experience of the group as a whole, two distributions of the deaths recorded in Table 3 must be made in conformity with the rules set out above in the second convention. Table 4 shows the results of this exercise. The horizontal totals line of Table 3 shows that three individuals did not reach 60 and two did not reach 80; they form the second line of Table 4A. The vertical totals line shows that none of the remaining 113 men and women reached a minimum age higher than the 60–69 age group.

Table 4 The redistribution of deaths in several age groups according to low and high mortality assumptions

A. *Low mortality assumptions*

	Under 40	40–9	50–9	60–9	70–9	80 and over	Total
Known ages at death	48	28	51	46	40	14	227
			3		2		5
				52	45	16	113
Total	48	28	54	98	87	30	345

B. *High mortality assumptions*

	Under 40	40–9	50–9	60–9	70–9	80 and over	Total
Known ages at death	48	28	51	46	40	14	227
	1		1				2
	25	14	26	25			90
			1				1
		5	7	7			19
			4				4
				2			2
Total	74	47	90	80	40	14	345

All, therefore, can be distributed in the same proportions as the known deaths above 60, as shown on line three of Table 4A. The totals line of this part of the table then represents the distribution of deaths on the low mortality assumptions. In Section B of the table, a parallel exercise produces the distribution of deaths by age on high mortality assumptions. In this case, the vertical totals column is the main guide since it shows the number of men and women known to have reached certain ages (those who cannot have died earlier than the age groups in which they fall in the totals column). The top line of Table 3 shows that two individuals did not reach 60, and the distrition of known ages at death suggests that they should be allotted as shown on line two of Section B. The remaining 90 individuals on the top line of Table 3 may have died at any age up to 69, and their deaths are divided accordingly on the next line of Section B. Line four of the section consists of the one man known to have reached 40, but not 60 (he appears on the second line of Table 3). Immediately beneath him on line five are the other 19 individuals from the second line of Table 3. Finally, those on the third and fourth lines of the totals column in Table 3 are to be found on lines six and seven.

Table 5 shows the rate at which the population of 345 married

Table 5 Survivors to certain ages on low and high mortality assumptions (actual numbers and related to a base population of 1,000)

Age	Low mortality	High mortality	Low	High	Medium
25	345	345	1,000	1,000	1,000
40	297	271	861	786	823
50	269	224	780	649	714
60	215	134	623	388	505
70	117	54	339	157	248
80	30	14	87	41	64

people is depleted on low and high mortality assumptions, and the same expressed in relation to a base population of 1,000, together with a medium estimate halfway between the two extremes. An average age at death can be calculated both for those whose age at death is known and for the distributions of deaths on low and high mortality assumptions. To calculate these figures, it is assumed that deaths in the six successive age groups occurred on average at 32, 45, 55, 65, 75, and 83 respectively.[14] The results are shown in Table 6.

[14] The average age of a sample of 50 married persons dying under age 40 in Colyton was 32·2 years. In all, 30 men and women died at age 80 and above at an average age of 83·2 years (the highest age at death was 91 years). For other age groups, it was assumed that deaths were spread evenly and that the midpoint age could be taken.

Table 6   Average age at death

a. Those whose age at death is known	56·2 years
b. On low mortality assumption	61·3 years
c. On high mortality assumption	54·5 years

Note: The two extremes vary from the middle point of the range by 3·4 years or 5·9 per cent.

THE MORTALITY HISTORY OF COLYTON

Having described the methods by which a picture of the mortality of certain age groups can be built up using suitable parish registers, we may consider what happened in Colyton between the sixteenth and nineteenth centuries. Figure 2 shows the fluctuations in baptisms, burials, and marriages in Colyton in the form of nine-year moving averages. It suggests four chief divisions of the three centuries as regards the relationship between births and deaths: an initial period of about a century during which population was apparently rising fast, baptisms were almost always more numerous than burials, and there was a marked inverse correlation between movements in births and deaths; a second period beginning in the 1640s and lasting until the 1730s, when the inverse relationship continued, but with burials normally more numerous than baptisms and population apparently falling; a third period of half a century when baptisms and burials were very close to each other in number and without decisive trend; and a final period beginning about 1790 when baptisms, as in the first period, soared high above burials. If annual totals are consulted, one year in particular stands out in these three centuries, partially masked in Figure 2 by the moving average. Between the beginning of November 1645, and the end of October 1646, 392 names were written into the burial register, the great majority probably being victims of a last and violent outbreak of plague in the parish. The danger of depending upon Anglican parish registers for a complete coverage of vital events in an English parish at any time (but especially as the eighteenth century wore on) are well known, and it would be foolish to place too much credence in the absolute totals shown on the graph. Nevertheless, the major changes are shown up well enough.

The fertility changes which help to explain why the relationship between the crude totals of baptisms and burials changed so drastically have been described elsewhere.[15] Marital fertility was high until the 1630s, fell sharply for two or three generations thereafter, during which family limitation appears to have been widely practised,

[15] Wrigley, 'Family Limitation in Pre-Industrial England'.

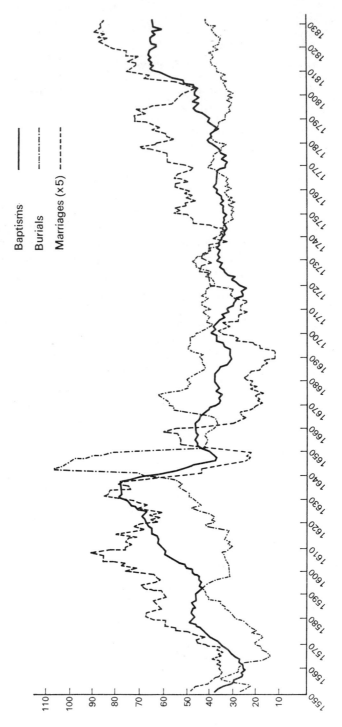

Figure 2 Baptisms, burials, and marriages in Colyton (nine-year moving averages)

recovered slowly during the middle years of the eighteenth century, and returned to Elizabethan levels by the early-nineteenth century. During the seventeenth and eighteenth centuries, there were also important changes in the average age at first marriage of women which tended to exaggerate the effect upon general fertility rates of the changes which occurred in marital fertility. Women married late in the second half of the seventeenth century, but early by the beginning of the nineteenth. Were there also changes in mortality between the sixteenth and nineteenth centuries? If so, were the periods of high fertility also periods of high mortality? Was the reverse the case? Or were the variations in fertility and mortality quite out of phase with each other.

CHILD MORTALITY

Table 7 gives the results of a series of calculations made by the method shown in Table 1. The figures in the table differ slightly from the few published previously[16] because the latter were the fruits of a preliminary calculation based only on those FRFs on which a date of marriage is recorded, whereas those in Table 7 are derived from all Colyton FRFs which meet the conditions described above, whether a date of marriage is known or not. The size of the populations at risk was of the same order of magnitude in each period. For example, Table 1 shows that the number in observation in the first year of life in 1538–99 was 1,679; the comparable figures for the four later periods are 2,077, 1,309, 985, and 2,576, a total of 8,626—or 68 per cent of the total of baptisms in Colyton 1538–1837.

Table 7 Infant and child life-table death rates ($1,000q_x$) in Colyton (sexes combined)

	1538–99	1600–49	1650–99	1700–49	1750–1837
0–1	108	81 (77)*	79	98	72
1–4	80	93 (85)	113	82	75
5–9	27	50 (32)	65	23	28
10–14	21	44 (24)	35	23	20

* Figures in parentheses for 1600–49 show the death rates which result after deducting all deaths which occurred during the plague period 1645–46.

The extremely low infant mortality rates are the most notable feature of Table 7 and call for further analysis, but they are most conveniently dealt with after examining child and adult mortality, and these are, therefore, discussed first.

Mortality in childhood varied considerably from period to period.

[16] Wrigley, 'Family limitation in Pre-industrial England', p. 101.

In order to judge what the changes imply, it is instructive to compare them with the sets of specimen life-table death rates published by the Population Branch of the United Nations Department of Social Affairs. Each set is related to a particular expectation of life at birth. The rates are set out in Table 8, while Table 9 shows how many of an initial population of 1,000 at age 1 die before reaching 15 under the several U.N. specimen tables and the comparable figures for Colyton.

Table 8 Life-table death rates ($1,000q_x$) for various expectations of life at birth taken from U.N. specimen life tables (sexes combined)

	$^0e_0$ 27·5	$^0e_0$ 30·0	$^0e_0$ 32·5	$^0e_0$ 35·0	$^0e_0$ 37·5	$^0e_0$ 40·0	$^0e_0$ 42·5	$^0e_0$ 45·0	$^0e_0$ 47·5
1–4	186	166	147	131	117	104	93	82	72
5–9	62	54	48	43	38	33	29	26	23
10–14	41	37	33	29	26	23	21	18	16

Source: United Nations, Department of Social Affairs, Population Branch, Report No. 25, *Methods for Population Projection by Sex and Age* (New York, 1956), p. 74. The death rates for the sexes combined are a simple average of the male and female figures.

It is apparent from the two tables that death rates in the age groups 1–14 for children born in the period 1538–99, whether taken separately or combined, are closely similar to those of the U.N. table which relates to an expectation of life at birth of 45 years. In the next half century, 1600–1649, even after excluding the heavy mortality of 1645–6, death rates appear to have risen somewhat and conform best to the U.N. figures for an expectation of life of 42·5 years. Death rates in the second half of the seventeenth century rose very sharply, particularly for children above the age of 5. Indeed, rates for the age groups 5–9 and 10–14 are high enough to suggest an expectation of life of less than 30, but the rate for the age group 1–4 is relatively much lower. The combined figure in Table 9 suggests an expectation

Table 9 Numbers dying before age 15 of a population of 1,000 at age 1 ($1,000_{14}q_1$) (sexes combined)

U.N. Specimen tables		Colyton	
Expectation of life	Death rate 1–14	Period	Death rate 1–14
27·5	267	1538–99	124
30·0	240	1600–49	176 (135)*
32·5	215	1650–99	200
35·0	192	1700–49	124
37·5	173	1750–1837	119
40·0	154		
42·5	138		
45·0	122		
47·5	108		

* The figure in parentheses for 1600–49 is the rate after deduction of all plague deaths 1645–6.

of life of about 34 years, a drop of ten years or so from Elizabethan times.

In the next period 1700–1749, the death rates suggest a return to the mortality conditions prevailing in the sixteenth century, but the rates for this period are minimal. There is a strong probability that the true rates would be considerably higher, for the burial register gives less detail in the early-eighteenth century than at other periods. The register at this time, and especially between 1709 and 1735, frequently mentions only the name of a deceased person without any other distinguishing characteristic. Experience in reconstitution shows that unless relationship to the head of the family is stated where appropriate, the difficulty of identification becomes very great. It is often impossible to decide between related people who bear the same name (whether, for example, the dead John Green is the uncle or the nephew, and so on). This tends to cut down the period of time a family is in observation because some dates of passage out of observation may prove impossible to determine. (It is symptomatic of this difficulty that fewer children were in observation in this period than at other times; see p. 255 above.) Even when a family technically conforms to the rules for being in observation, there remains a danger that a death may occur among the children in the family followed by an entry in the burial register which is too ambiguous to permit confident identification.

Before the middle of the eighteenth century, the register improved, and indeed in the 1760s and 1770s contains unusually full information by normal English parochial standards, though there were again short periods of poor detail at the turn of the century. From 1813, when registration of burials took place for the first time on printed sheets to conform to the requirements of Rose's Act, relationship was again not stated, but in compensation age at death was always given and ambiguities remain at a low level. By this period, the child death rates suggest an expectation of life at birth of about 45 years, as in the sixteenth century.

At all periods there was, of course, some under-registration of child deaths where these occurred during the temporary absence of the family in another parish. An arbitary method of allowing for this is described below (see p. 270).

ADULT MORTALITY

The death rates of married people in Colyton fall well into the pattern of mortality suggested by the child death rates. Table 10 shows the main features of adult mortality revealed by the method of

Table 10a Mortality of married men and women marrying under age 35 by date of marriage cohorts (sexes combined)

	1538–1624	1625–99	1700–74
Number in group	345 (157 m., 188 f.)	285 (140 m., 145 f.)	239 (128 m., 111 f.)
Number whose age at death known	227 (112 m., 115 f.)	179 (86 m., 93 f.)	142 (76 m., 66 f.)
Average age at marriage (in years)	25·4	25·3	24·8
Average age at death			
(a) where date of death known	56·2	52·2	57·7
(b) on low mortality assumptions	61·3	58·6	63·3
(c) on high mortality assumptions	54·5	50·8	54·9

Table 10b Survivors to certain ages (population at age 25 = 1,000) on three assumptions about mortality

	1538–1624			1625–99			1700–74		
Age	Low	High	Medium	Low	High	Medium	Low	High	Medium
25	1,000	1,000	1,000	1,000	1,000	1,000	1,000	1,000	1,000
40	861	786	823	839	751	795	895	803	849
50	780	649	714	695	512	603	795	615	705
60	623	388	505	554	277	415	695	418	556
70	339	157	248	270	98	184	414	184	299
80	87	41	64	67	25	46	80	33	56

analysis described earlier, while Table 11 shows some comparable material derived from the U.N. specimen life-tables. Needless to say, both because there are high percentages of men and women whose date of death is not known and because of the varying sex composition of the three groups in Table 10, any interpretation of adult

Table 11 Survivors to certain ages (population at age 25 = 1,000) derived from U.N. life-tables (sexes combined)

	$^0e_0$	$^0e_0$	$^0e_0$	$^0e_0$	$^0e_0$	$^0e_0$	$^0e_0$
Age	30·0	32·5	35·0	37·5	40·0	42·5	45·0
25	1,000	1,000	1,000	1,000	1,000	1,000	1,000
40	766	788	808	827	844	861	876
50	591	627	660	691	719	747	771
60	401	443	481	517	555	590	622
70	204	236	268	301	336	354	404
80	51	63	77	93	109	128	144

Source: United Nations, *Methods for Population Projection by Sex and Age,* p. 76. Totals of survivors for the sexes combined were taken as a simple average of the male and female figures.

mortality in Colyton is subject to wide margins of error. The difference between the low and high mortality survivorship tables is very wide, so that the low mortality figures of the middle period when death rates were high show better survivorship rates than the high mortality figures for the other two periods. Nevertheless, for all its deficiencies, Table 10 does suggest strongly that the period 1625–99 suffered from substantially higher mortality than the earlier and later periods.

The tables of medium mortality (calculated simply by taking the midpoint between the two extremes) might appear to be the best general guide to the mortality changes which took place since it is most likely either that no person whose date of death is unknown died before 60 (low mortality hypothesis) or that all had died before reaching 70 (high mortality hypothesis). There is reason, however, for inclining to the view that the low mortality hypothesis is nearer to the truth, particularly for the later ages. Imagine, for example, that a quarter of all married couples emigrated ten years after marriage. During the period one such couple is in observation, if either the husband or wife dies, the death will be recorded in the register and reflected in the distribution of known ages at death. If no death occurs, however, all that will be known is an age at which the husband and wife passed from observation. There is, therefore, a bias in the distribution of known ages at death tending to overstate the number dying young. Relatively fewer young than old deaths will be missing from the table of known ages at death. Although the low mortality hypothesis is too extreme, it is probably nearer the truth than the high mortality hypothesis for the higher ages. It is always conceivable, of course, that this effect might be counterbalanced by an association between emigration and early death, but there is no evidence as yet on this point.

Bearing these considerations in mind, it is reasonable to suppose that in the period 1538–1624 the adult death rates conform best to the U.N. life-table relating to an expectation of life at birth of 40·0 years; that in the period 1625–99, they are closest to the table giving an expectation of life of 32·5 years; and in the period 1700–1774 to the table for 42·5 years. Thus, the pattern of change in adult death rates, as with the rates for children, suggests a substantially lower expectation of life at birth in the second half of the seventeenth century than in Elizabethan times or in Georgian England. If the mortality data is broken up into short time periods, the number of individuals involved grows small, and firm conclusions necessarily become impossible. Nevertheless, it is interesting that if such sub-divisions are attempted, they suggest that mortality rates tended to increase, though very slowly at first, from the late-sixteenth century until the third quarter of the seventeenth century, only to fall back toward their earlier level during the eighteenth, so that by its end they were no higher, and even possibly a little lower, than in Elizabeth's reign. Comparison of the Colyton death rates with the U.N. figures suggests that the whole cycle of change brought expectation of life down from a high figure in the range 40 to 45 years to a low in the range 30 to 35, before returning to its earlier level.

The periods used for the study of adult mortality differ from those used for child mortality. This is largely a result of the different techniques involved. Marriage cohorts beginning after 1775 include a growing number of men and women who were still living in 1837, the closing years of the Colyton study. Child mortality, on the other hand, can be examined right down to 1837 because passage from observation is precisely defined. Again, the lack of detail in the burial register in the early part of the eighteenth century makes it necessary to treat this period as a unit in the study of child mortality, but, even though the adult deaths are also harder to identify in this period, fewer problems are created. At worst, the percentage of deaths whose date is unknown is increased. Similarly, the differences between the techniques of analysing the two bodies of data make it desirable to treat 1625–99, rather than 1650–99, as a block in the study of adult mortality because deaths from a marriage cohort are spread out over a much longer period than deaths under 15 from a birth cohort. The higher death rates of the late-seventeenth century affected cohorts marrying before 1650 as well as those marrying later. The plague year 1645–6 falls in this middle period and helps to account for the higher death rates, but its over-all impact was relatively slight in so long a period. Even if the marriages which took place before 1646 are excluded, the death rates are only slightly lowered.

The periodization problem, however, is a major difficulty in the analysis of reconstitution data; in a more extended study, it would be valuable to conduct an analysis in the form of a moving average—taking in and relegating ten-year or twenty-five-year cohorts from a moving block of data covering, say, seventy-five or one hundred years. This might also prove valuable in attempting to solve another teasing problem—the welding together of information about child and adult mortality into a single life-table. Children born in, say, 1580–89 married chiefly in the period 1600–1119, and a significant fraction of the original birth cohort was still living in 1645 when the plague struck. Thus, to produce cohort life-tables, a time lag must be allowed for. For current life-tables, on the other hand, the information about death rates at all ages must come from the same span of time. Each kind of table has its special virtues. For example, a smallpox outbreak will leave largely untouched a cohort which in childhood has already been exposed to the disease, but will devastate younger cohorts. Current life-tables which reflect this state of affairs would produce a misleadingly high cumulative mortality up to the age at which cohorts had previously been exposed to the disease, misleading because no one birth cohort would be devastated twice by smallpox, although the method of calculation from current rates subjects the population to high mortality from the disease several times over. On the other hand, a war or a run of bad harvests may produce striking effects whatever the previous history of the cohorts at risk, and here current life-tables may convey a more telling picture of the impact of the blow than the alternative method.

Where the analysis periods are long, as is inevitable in a reconstitution study of a single parish, the distinction between the two types of measurement loses much of its point. For present purposes, therefore, and particularly given the wide margin of error in the adult death rates, it is sufficient to note the parallel movement over time of the child and adult rates and their close agreement in each major period when related to specimen life-tables.

INFANT MORTALITY RECONSIDERED

Before commenting on the general import of the Colyton mortality data, infant mortality must be reconsidered. If the child mortality rates are taken to suggest that the appropriate specimen life-tables for the five periods are level 50 ($^0e_0$ 45·0), level 45 ($^0e_0$ 42·5), level 30 ($^0e_0$ 35·0), level 40 ($^0e_0$ 40·0), and level 50 ($^0e_0$ 45·0) respectively, then all the infant mortality rates calculated from the FRFs are apparently much too low, as Table 12 shows. In each period, the table suggests that infant mortality rates should be between about one-and-a-half

Table 12   Infant mortality ($1,000q_0$) in Colyton and from U.N. specimen life-tables (sexes combined)

Colyton		U.N. specimen life-tables	
Period	Infant mortality rate	$^0e_0$	Infant mortality rate
1538–99	108	45·0	159
1600–49	81	42·5	172
1650–99	79	35·0	214
1700–49	98	40·0	187
1750–1837	72	45·0	159

Source: United Nations, *Methods for Population Projection by Sex and Age*, p. 74. The infant mortality rates for the sexes combined are a simple average of the male and female rates.

and two-and-a-half times the level produced by manipulating the parish register entries.

The risk that an infant death does not give rise to an entry in the burial register is greatest for very young babies before baptism. Once a child has been baptized, it is unlikely that its subsequent death would go unregistered. It is, therefore, illuminating to study the distribution of ages at death within the first year of life. Table 13 shows the distribution of deaths within the first year of life by the apparent age of the dead child (in most cases date of burial minus date of baptism). The figures in parentheses are those which result from including those FRFs on which there were child burials without a preceding baptism entry for the child. In the overwhelming majority of cases, the child in question may be presumed to have died very young, and the timing of the other baptisms in the family shows an appropriate gap at the time of the burial. In principle, it is clearly improper in general to include such FRFs in an analysis based on strict criteria of presence in observation since the registration of the burial is the only evidence of existence. When a child died in the first days of life, however, it was usually only his death which prevented his baptism. In some cases, private baptism at home preceded the burial, but this was not always entered in the baptism register. Since almost all such burials could be given a 'manufactured' date of birth on the same day as the burial, this greatly inflates the figure of infants dying on their first day of life. (A proportion of these deaths should have been allotted to the first week rather than the first day of life, but for simplicity all were given a 'manufactured' date of birth on the same day as the burial where this was possible.) The figures for older babies rise too, but only because FRFs in this class include, of course, many other burials of young children which were preceded by a baptism in the normal way. If infant mortality rates are calculated using these FRFs as well as those in the main group, the rates for each rise are as follows (rates of Table 7 in parentheses): 119 (108), 92 (81), 95 (79), 113 (98) and 94 (72).

Absurdly low numbers of infant first-day deaths in the figures based on the main group of FRFs arise mainly because baptism did not usually take place on the same day as birth in Colyton, except in the earliest of the five periods. By the 1770s, when for the first time the baptism register contains dates of both birth and baptism, only half of all baptisms (50 per cent) took place within the first month of life (33 per cent in the third and fourth weeks). As many as a quarter of all baptisms were delayed more than three months after birth. Thus, at this time, the totals of deaths in the first month after baptism refer to the second month of life as much as the first. Some revision of the crude figures is clearly necessary. How should this be done?

Table 13 Distribution of infant deaths within the first year of life

	Days 0–	1–6	Weeks 1–4	Months 0–	1–	2–	3–5	6–8	9–11	Total
1538–99	23 (44)	26 (29)	41 (46)	90 (119)	22 (26)	20 (20)	26 (32)	12 (14)	12 (17)	182 (228)
1600–49	2 (36)	24 (29)	30 (35)	56 (100)	36 (41)	12 (19)	27 (35)	19 (22)	18 (24)	168 (241)
1650–99	3 (31)	15 (16)	21 (26)	39 (73)	15 (24)	6 (8)	19 (26)	12 (14)	12 (13)	103 (158)
1700–49	1 (18)	5 (7)	29 (32)	35 (57)	15 (17)	6 (9)	15 (20)	14 (16)	12 (12)	97 (131)
1750–1837	1 (54)	19 (22)	37 (41)	57 (117)	21 (29)	17 (22)	41 (46)	23 (28)	26 (27)	185 (269)

It is convenient to begin by considering the distribution of deaths under age one revealed by infant mortality studies of parishes where there is less reason to fear under-registration. Table 14 contains details of several such parishes. It shows that where there is little reason to doubt the completeness of registration, the percentage of all children dying under one year of age who died in the first month of life fell usually in the range of 45 to 60 per cent. Crulai had a higher figure, but Gautier and Henry stress the exceptionally high proportion of first-day deaths in the parish (30 per cent of all deaths under age one), and suggest that a substantial fraction of these deaths represents the burial of children born dead, but baptized by the midwife.[17]

P. Galliano goes so far as to eliminate all infants dying in these circumstances from his data, and this produces an over-all figure of 46 per cent for those dying one month from a very large body of information. At Sainghin-en-Mélantois, both when all such children are included and when half have been eliminated, the proportion of children dying in the first month lies between 50 and 60 per cent. The figures for the parishes of Thézels-St. Sernin reveal similar, but lower percentages.

The York register is included in this table because for a time in the late-sixteenth century the register was kept with the most scrupulous care and included ages at death down to the nearest hour in the case of very young children. The deaths of twenty-nine very young children were registered without any corresponding baptism entry, though usually with a note to the effect that baptism had been carried out at home, 'being baptised at home by the midwyf'. There seems more reason to fear that some children born dead were registered as if they had briefly lived than to expect under-registration in St. Michael le Belfrey at this period when 59 per cent of all deaths under age one were in the first month of life, a figure closely similar to those of Crulai and Sainghin-en-Mélantois. It is, incidentally, entirely possible that if the Colyton register had been kept in greater detail, the burial entries for which there were no corresponding baptisms would prove to have arisen in the same way as those in the register of St. Michael le Belfrey. (Much later, an eighteenth-century vicar of Linton in Cambridgeshire noted in his register: 'It has been usual for many years past not to register the sickly children who are named at home, till they are brought to Church to be incorporated. Consequently, all that die and are never incorporated come into the List of Burials, but not of Baptisms.')

The modified figures for Colyton in 1538–99 (the 'b' figures in Table 14) show a percentage of deaths in the first month of life little lower than that in the French parishes or at York, and indeed higher

---

[17] Gautier and Henry, *La population de Crulai*, p. 170.

Table 14 Distribution of infant deaths within the first year of life

		Days 0–	1–6	Weeks 1–4	Months 0–	1–	2–	3–5	6–11	Total
Colyton 1538–99	a.	23	26	41	90 (49%)	22	20	26	24	182
	b.	44	29	46	119 (52%)	26	20	32	31	228
Colyton 1600–49	a.	2	24	30	56 (33%)	36	12	27	37	168
	b.	36	29	35	100 (41%)	41	19	35	46	241
St. Michael le Belfrey, York 1571–86		33	28	21	82 (59%)	9	8	20	21	140
Crulai 1688–1759	c.	99	131 }	131	230 (69%)					331
		50	131 }	131	181 (64%)					282
Sainghin-en-Mélantois 1740–89	c.				163 (59%)	15	15	31	54	278
					129 (53%)	15	15	31	54	244
Thézels-St.-Sernin 1747–92		62 }		34	96 (54%)	8	11	15	49	179
	d.	34		34	68 (45%)	8	11	15	49	151
19 parishes on the southern outskirts of Paris 1774–94	e.	264	308	333	905 (46%)	176	119	284	477	1,961

a. excluding all FRFs with 'manufactured' dates of birth.
b. including all FRFs with 'manufactured' dates of birth.
c. assuming that one half of all first-day deaths were born dead. (See Henry's remarks on Sainghin-en-Mélantois. *Manuel de démographie historique*, p. 137.)
d. excluding the children baptized at home.
e. Galliano eliminated all children who died after baptism at home by the midwife from his totals at risk and dying on the ground that probably a large proportion were born dead. (Galliano, *Annales de démographie historique 1966*, p. 143.)

Note: For Crulai, see Gautier and Henry, *La population de Crulai*, pp. 169–70; for Sainghin-en-Mélantois, see Henry, *Manuel de démographie historique*, p. 143; for Thézels-St.-Sernin, see P. Valmary, *Families paysannes au XVIIIe siècle en Bas-Quercy*, (Paris, 1965), p. 147; for the nineteen parishes, see P. Galliano, 'La mortalité infantile (indigènes et nourrisons) dans la banlieue sud de Paris à la fin du XVIIIe siècle (1774–1794)', *Annales de démographie historique 1966* (Paris, 1967), p. 159·

than in the large group of parishes just south of Paris studied by Galliano. In view of this, it would be difficult to find justification for adding more than, say, twenty-five deaths to the first month total in the modified Colyton data (to make the total 57 per cent of all first year deaths). This would raise infant mortality to only 131 per 1,000. Paradoxically, comparing the early Colyton data with the French material gives almost more warrant for supposing that there was under-registration of deaths in the second half of the first year of life than in the first half. In Sainghin-en-Mélantois, Thézels-St.-Sernin, and the nineteen parishes south of Paris, about a quarter of all first-year deaths fell in this period whereas in Colyton (and in St. Michael le Belfrey) the fraction was much smaller. Further study of the differences between French and English parishes in this respect might prove rewarding.

After 1600, the unmodified totals of deaths in the first days and weeks of life shown in Table 13 are clearly much too low in Colyton. Any method of inflating these totals is bound to be arbitrary since much of the information necessary for a satisfactory system of correction is lacking. As an illustration, however, of the effect of a plausible system of correction, the following procedure might be employed. Assume that deaths in the first month of life represent between 50 and 60 per cent of all deaths in the first year, and that the number of deaths in the period 1–11 months is understated because a proportion of those apparently dying under one month were, in fact, more than one month old, but their true age was concealed by the delay between birth and baptism (which would have the effect of reducing their apparent age). Assume further that during the seventeenth century one third of all deaths apparently under one month should be transferred to the 1–11 month group, and that thereafter one half should be transferred. A new range of infant mortality rates can then be calculated. As an example, in the period 1600–1649, 56 children died under one month. One third of this number is added to the 1–11 month group to produce a new total for that group of 131, which is now taken to represent 40 to 50 per cent of all deaths under age one. The total of deaths now lies in the range 262 to 328, instead of 168; the infant mortality rate lies in the range 126 to 158 per 1,000.[18] Similar calculations may be made for other periods with the results shown in Table 15.

[18] This range of infant mortality rates and those for later periods are approximate calculations made by inflating the rates given in Table 12 in the ratio of new totals of children dying under one to the original totals. Thus, for 1600–49, the lower end of the range is calculated as $81 \times \frac{262}{168} = 128$; and so on. In a stricter calculation, the larger number of children in observation and at risk which results from the inflation of the number of deaths should be taken into account, and slightly lower infant mortality rates would result.

Table 15 Revised infant mortality rates ($1{,}000q_0$)

Period	Infant mortality rate
1538–99	120–140
1600–49	126–158
1650–99	118–147
1700–49	162–203
1750–1837	122–153

The revised figures are higher than those given previously, but they are still below, and in most cases substantially below, those to be expected from the U.N. life-tables. Are they necessarily suspect for this reason?

T. H. Hollingsworth suggests elsewhere in this volume that infant mortality rates in pre-industrial Europe below the range of 200 to 250 per 1,000 are unlikely to be accurate. Comparison of his data about the British aristocracy with the Colyton data suggests that it may be premature to generalize in this way. Table 16 shows the infant mortality rates of the British aristocracy and also their life-table death rates age 1–14 and some comparable Colyton material.

Two points about the mortality of the British aristocracy revealed in Table 16 should be noted. First, infant mortality only once

Table 16 Life-table death rates ($1{,}000q_0$ and $1{,}000{_{14}}q_1$: sexes combined)

	British aristocracy			Colyton	
	0–1	1–14		0–1	1–14
1550–74	182	99	1538–99	120–140	124
1575–99	189	93	1600–49	126–158	176
1600–24	189	128	1650–99	118–147	200
1625–49	199	162	1700–49	162–203	124
1650–74	210	200	1750–1837	122–153	119
1675–99	196	163			
1700–24	169	181			
1725–49	166	199			
1750–74	102	143			
1775–99	85	123			
1800–24	82	102			

Source: The rates for the British aristocracy were calculated from data in T. H. Hollingsworth, *The Demography of the British Peerage*, Supplement to *Population Studies*, Vol. 18, No. 2 (1964), Table 52, p. 67. Totals for the sexes combined were taken as a simple average of the male and female figures.

exceeded 200 per 1,000 between the sixteenth and nineteenth centuries. This happened during the bad years of the third quarter of the seventeenth century. It may seem reasonable to expect a lower infant mortality among the aristocracy than in a parish community, but until more is known of the childbed conditions, the exposure to infection, and the suckling habits of mothers and babies in the two groups, the issue must remain uncertain. Secondly, the remarkable lack of parallelism in the behaviour of the death rates age 0–1 and 1–14 deserves stress. Although, in the main, when one series is rising, the other tends to move in sympathy and vice versa, there were notable differences in the speed and extent of the changes involved. In the late-sixteenth century, the rate 1–14 is little more than half the infant mortality rate, whereas by the mid-eighteenth century it was considerably the higher of the two. Towards the end of the eighteenth century, infant mortality was little more than half what it had been in the late-sixteenth, yet over the same period, mortality 1–14 was a third higher. Each rate had first risen and then fallen in the interim, but in widely different proportions. There is in this table no warrant for the view that the two rates are closely related to each other. Therefore, it does not follow that where infant mortality rates are unknown or thought to be too low, they can be read off from a knowledge of death rates later in childhood. If we judge by the relationship between the two rates shown by the aristocracy data in the late-sixteenth century, the Colyton figures in Table 16 will seem improbable, but if we judge by their relationship in the early-eighteenth century, this will not be so.

There are other reasons for caution in assuming that infant mortality rates in pre-industrial communities were always high. Indeed, perhaps pre-industrial European communities will prove frequently to have differed in this respect from the developing countries today on whose data the U.N. life-tables were based. It is notable, for example, that the infant mortality rate in Crulai is below what would be expected on the basis of mortality 1–14 and comparison with U.N. life-tables. The Crulai infant mortality rate corrected for possible under-registration was put at 210 to 230 per 1,000 by Gautier and Henry.[19] This estimate includes, however, the large and doubtful group of babies baptized at home and suspected often to have been born dead. If half the children apparently dying on the first day of life fall into this class, the probable range becomes 180 to 200 per 1,000, whereas the death rate 1–14 ($1,000_{14}q_1$) at 212 suggests an expectation of life at birth of 32·5 years (see Table 9) and an infant mortality of 229 per 1,000. The over-all conclusion of Gautier and Henry, that expectation of life in Crulai was about 30 years,[20] suggests an even higher infant mortality figure of 245 per 1,000.

This is not to say, of course, that infant mortality was never high in pre-industrial England. At St. Michael le Belfrey, for example, in the

[19] Gautier and Henry, *La population de Crulai*, p. 168.
[20] Gautier and Henry, *op. cit.*, p. 192.

period 1571–86 when registration was so thorough, there were 566 baptisms, to which must be added the 29 children buried, but not baptized. This produces a total of 595 live births. In the same period, there were 140 burials of infants under age one, or an infant mortality rate of 235 per 1,000. St. Michael le Belfrey was a comparatively wealthy urban parish. In the poorer urban parishes, particularly in London, infant mortality may well have been much higher.[21] It was high in some rural parishes too. In the tiny marsh parish of Wrangle in Lincolnshire, for example, infant mortality in the period 1597–1642 was 240 per 1,000.[22]

MORTALITY AS A WHOLE IN COLYTON

There are substantial uncertainties about the level of both infant and adult mortality rates in Colyton which impose great caution in advancing suggestions about expectation of life in different periods. At an earlier point in the argument, I suggested that the child and adult mortality data are consonant with a fall from an expectation of life at birth between 40 and 45 years in the second half of the sixteenth century to a low point of 30 to 35 years a century later, followed by a rise to its earlier level by the end of the eighteenth century. This question can now be re-examined in the light of the discussion of infant mortality. Table 15 shows that although the range between the high and low estimates of infant mortality is quite wide, there was no apparent tendency for rates to rise in the seventeenth century and that the peak was probably reached early in the eighteenth. If these estimates are to be relied upon, it is evident that infant mortality rates and those of later age groups were not closely in step with each other. Because infant mortality was low in the seventeenth century, the addition of infant mortality data to other mortality information tends to damp out the differences in expectation of life between this period and earlier or later times.

Combining the infant, child, and adult mortality data, it is possible to calculate high and low estimates of expectation of life at birth. For this purpose, the period as a whole was divided into three broad sub-periods—1538–1624, 1625–99, and 1700–1774—and the following procedure was adopted.

[21] Urban poverty, very high population densities, and high infant mortality seem to have been closely associated in pre-industrial Europe.

[22] Wrigley (ed.), *An Introduction to English Historical Demography*, p. 157.

INFANT MORTALITY

1538–1624 High and low estimates were made by weighting the high and low estimates for 1538–99 and 1600–1649 in the proportion 2:1 to derive a composite figure for the period as a whole. Thus, the high estimate of infant mortality in 1538–99 is 140 per 1,000, and in 1600–1649 it is 158. The composite estimate is $\dfrac{(2 \times 140) + (1 \times 158)}{3} = 146$ per 1,000.

1625–99: The high and low estimates for 1600–1649 and 1650–99 were weighted in the proportion 1:2.

1700–1774: The high and low estimates for 1700–1749 and 1750–1837 were weighted in the proportion 2:1.

MORTALITY 1–14

1538–1624 Low estimate: the average of rates for 1538–99 and 1600–1649 (excluding the plague year) taken for each age group. High estimate: the low estimates plus 10 per cent (to cover possible under-registration due, for example, to the death of children when family temporarily absent from parish).

1625–99 Low estimate: the rates for 1650–99. High estimate: the same plus 10 per cent.

1700–1774 Low estimate: the rates of 1700–1749 plus 10 per cent (a notional allowance to offset the under-registration due to absence of detail in burial register). High estimate: the same plus a further 10 per cent.

MORTALITY 15–24

1538–1624 Low estimates: U.N. life-table death rates level 50 ($^0e_0$ 45·0 years). High estimate: level 40 ($^0e_0$ 40·0).

1625–99 Low estimate: level 30 ($^0e_0$ 35·0). High estimate: level 25 ($^0e_0$ 32·5).

1700–1774 Low estimate: level 50 ($^0e_0$ 45·0). High estimate: level 40 ($^0e_0$ 40·0).

MORTALITY 25–

1538–1624 Low estimate: U.N. life-table death rates level 45 ($^0e_0$ 42·5). High estimate: level 30 ($^0e_0$ 35·0).

1625–99 Low estimate: level 30 ($^0e_0$ 35·0). High estimate level 20 ($^0e_0$ 30·0).

1700–1774 Low estimate: level 50 ($^0e_0$ 45·0). High estimate: level 30 ($^0e_0$ 35·0).

If the high and low mortality rates for each age range are combined in a single expression, high and low estimates of expectation of life at birth can be made.[23] They are shown in Table 17. There is no

Table 17   High and low estimates of expectation of life at birth in Colyton (in years)

Period	High mortality	Low mortality	Midpoint
1538–1624	40·6	45·8	43·2
1625–99	34·9	38·9	36·9
1700–74	38·4	45·1	41·8

special magic about these estimates. All that can be said is that it is likely that the true figures of expectation of life would lie between the high and low mortality estimates. The figures cannot be said to relate in any precise sense to the periods listed for reasons which have already been discussed. They, and the material in earlier tables, show only that death rates were surprisingly low in late-Tudor Colyton; that by the Restoration period, they had risen sharply to levels broadly comparable to those in eighteenth-century Crulai (except for infant mortality which explains the higher expectation of life at birth in Colyton); and that, as the eighteenth century wore on, death rates fell back towards their Tudor levels.

Many aspects of infant, child, and adult mortality in Colyton would repay more extensive analysis than has been attempted here. No division of the material by sex has been made, for example, though there is much of interest to investigate (female rates were apparently higher than male in the adult married population in the sixteenth and seventeenth centuries). The problem of correcting the infant mortality rates has not been exhausted. The whole question of the interplay of fertility and mortality, the changes in reproduction rates over time, deserves full analysis. These are, however, deliberate omissions.[24] I have attempted to do no more than to show that suitable sources and appropriate techniques exist to enable mortality in many pre-industrial European communities to be studied in greater detail than once seemed possible. I have pursued the analysis of mortality in one parish far enough to leave little doubt that expectation of life at birth might change considerably in the course of two and a half centuries.

What can be learned from the study of one parish in Devon is necessarily limited. Colyton may have been typical of much of England, but equally it may have been exceptional. Its mortality

[23] The approximations used in calculating expectation of life at birth are those described in United Nations, *Methods for Population Projections by Sex and Age*, pp. 23–4.

[24] I hope to take some of these questions further in a comparative study of the results of family reconstitution in several parishes.

history, like its fertility history, shows only that big changes *may* be found in the past, not that big changes were common or sufficiently widespread and uniform to affect regional or national aggregates. Historical demography is in its heroic age when exciting, and sometimes puzzling, discoveries are to be expected. No mass of carefully worked material as yet exists against which new discoveries can be measured. The significance of what happened in Colyton cannot be assessed without a mass of comparable data. For some time, therefore, there will be increasing marginal returns to research effort in historical demography. Each new parish register or listing of inhabitants analysed will help to narrow the uncertainties raised by earlier studies as well as raising problems and opportunities of its own.

When more is known, for example, about the mortality of different occupational and social groups in pre-industrial populations, the degree to which poverty increased mortality will be easier to assess. (Some parish registers state the occupation of the head of the family when baptism and burial entries are made, as in the register of Banbury, Oxfordshire, after 1707.) Similarly, when it becomes possible to compare the demographic history of parishes with different types of economy, or those parishes on major traffic arteries with those comfortably remote from the danger of casual infection, or those parishes on marshland with the surrounding higher land, the interplay of demographic, economic, social, and other variables will grow less mysterious than at present when our ignorance extends so widely. Most important of all, a fuller knowledge of changes in fertility and mortality in parishes all over England at the time of the Industrial Revolution may serve to make clearer many functional relationships at present shrouded in obscurity.

The manipulation of data to provide estimates of fertility and mortality in the past is only a first step in the general study of the historical demography of a community. The knowledge, for example, that mortality in Colyton varied considerably in the course of three centuries does not in itself serve either to substantiate or disprove for Colyton in earlier years the general hypothesis of McKeown and Record for the nineteenth century—that changes in living standards played the major part in changing mortality rates. There is already reason to expect that the Colyton mortality pattern may prove to be repeated in many parishes since simple aggregative studies of baptism, burial, and marriage totals so often show either burial surpluses or much reduced baptism surpluses in the later seventeenth century.[25]

---

[25] The Cambridge Group for the History of Population and Social Structure now has aggregative returns for 400 English parishes. When the material has been fully analysed, the degree to which this pattern is apparent in different types of parish and in different regions will be much easier to specify.

In England as a whole, however, there seems no reason to suppose that living standards reached a nadir in the late-seventeenth century.[26] Indeed, there might seem more reason to find support in the Colyton data for J. D. Durand's recent thesis—that the exchange of infectious diseases between the continents following the triumphs of European navigation in the sixteenth century increased death rates all over the world in the seventeenth.[27] Only the collation of the results of detailed studies extending into many aspects of parish life can give support to some hypotheses and enable others to be put out of court.

The strictly demographic data about communities in the past are significant in their own right, but they are of prime historical importance because a community's demography was sensitive to many influences in its economic, social, and physical environment. Pierre Goubert's study of the Beauvaisis provides a classic demonstration of this point.[28] Moreover, the demographic changes of the past were not simply passive reflections of change elsewhere in the life of the community. They also helped to determine in their turn the economic fortunes and social circumstances of the times.[29] Only when the demographic changes which occurred in parishes like Colyton can be related with confidence to other changes in parish life will the full value of good fertility and mortality series be realized. Potentially, however, they provide a nexus into which other types of information can be tied so that the relationships between them can be better understood. The fact that the changes can be quantified facilitates the testing of hypotheses about the relationships involved. Few aspects of the pre-industrial past can be quantified with such precision as fertility and mortality trends where suitable records exist,[30] and, by a fortunate coincidence, what it is possible to do, it is also important to do.

[26] In a recent and authoritative review of English economic history in the seventeenth and eighteenth centuries for example, Wilson remarks: 'After a half century during which depression and maladjustment had been a chronic feature of English economic life, the Restoration was the occasion for economic as well as political renewal.' C. H. Wilson, *England's Apprenticeship* (London, 1965), p. 160. There seems good reason to regard this as a just summary of the contrast between the two halves of the century.

[27] J. D. Durand, 'The Modern Expansion of World Population', *Proceedings of the American Philosophical Society*, Vol. 111, No. 3 (1967), p. 142.

[28] Goubert, *Beauvais et le Beauvaisis*.

[29] I have recently tried to analyse one set of relationships which illustrate this point. E. A. Wrigley, 'A Simple Model of London's Importance in Changing English Society and Economy 1650–1750', *Past and Present*, No. 37 (1967), pp. 44–70.

[30] See E. A. Wrigley, *Population and History* (London, 1969), pp. 12–14 and 28–9.

D. V. Glass

Notes on the demography of London at the end of the seventeenth century

Initially, I was attracted to the demography of seventeenth-century London because of its association with the origins of demography in Britain. Both John Graunt and Gregory King—the two major pioneers—paid special attention to London. Indeed, Graunt's work is almost wholly focused on London and the Bills of Mortality, while much of the empirical basis of King's analysis also relates to that city.[1] London is also particularly attractive because it was a major metropolitan centre in the seventeenth century and has not ceased to be one today. A study of continuity and change might thus represent a valuable contribution to the understanding of urban demographic history. More practically, in accepting an invitation from the London Record Society to write an introduction to *London Inhabitants Within the Walls, 1695*,[2] I found that the basic data for London at the end of the seventeenth century are very extensive and offer possibilities for detailed analysis. What began as a small-scale trial was extended to include an analysis of nineteenth-century primary materials.[3]

As to the work itself, three main lines are being followed, two of which relate to data collected under the 1694 Act (6 & 7 Wm. & M., c. 6). The stated purpose of this Act was to help finance the war

[1] My earlier work on Gregory King is reprinted in D. V. Glass and D. E. C. Eversley (eds.), *Population in History* (London, 1965), Ch. 8, while that on John Graunt will be found in a paper on 'John Graunt and His *Natural and Political Observations*', *Proceedings of the Royal Society*, Series B, No. 974 (10 December 1963).

[2] London Record Society Publications, Vol. 2, Hon.-General ed. W. Kellaway (London, 1966).

[3] In carrying out this trial, T. R. Gourvish acted most ably and conscientiously as my research assistant. When the study was extended, he supervised the work of extraction, which was undertaken by a group of graduate assistants during the summer of 1966. He has been continuing to help me (in collaboration with Miss A. Davies) in the analysis of the material. I am greatly indebted to him. I should also like to express my particular indebtedness to Mr. P. E. Jones, Deputy Archivist to the City of London Corporation, for his unfailing help at every stage of the study.

against France by levying taxes on marriages, births, and deaths, and annual dues on bachelors above the age of twenty-five and on childless widowers. As this Act has been discussed in detail elsewhere, it will perhaps be sufficient to say that it specified two kinds of demographic data—namely, a complete enumeration of the inhabitants, with indications of marital condition and socio-economic status and a record of births, deaths, and marriages distinct from, though not completely independent of, the normal parish registration of baptisms, burials, and marriages. The Act had a national coverage, but so far the statistical returns found relate to relatively few areas. The returns for London are the most comprehensive and, as compared with other seventeenth-century official returns, seem to have been collected and compiled with unusual conscientiousness. Some of the enumerations, indeed, go beyond the requirements of the Act and list occupations. The Act was in force for ten years, and there were supposed to be annual revisions of the enumeration. Only two revised enumerations have been found for London, although revisions have been found for other areas—Southampton, Shrewsbury, and Lyme Regis, for example. For London, therefore, the basic population analysis has been confined to the data for 1695, while the analysis of vital events has been based largely on the period 1696–8. The third line of work relates to a slightly earlier set of returns—those of the 1692 Poll Tax (under the Act of 3 Wm. & M., c. 6).[4] These returns list the occupations—and they appear to be real occupations and not simply guild designations—of a large part of the employed population of London.[5] The administrative basis is that customary for seventeenth-century taxation—namely the wards—whereas the basis of the 1694 Act returns is the parish. It is possible, however, to obtain a fairly close match between the two sets of areas by using precincts within the wards. Although individuals and households are not being matched between the two 'enumerations', demographic and occupational structure can be shown for the same parishes, approximately three years apart.

The analysis of the primary materials is time-consuming. Partly for this reason—though also because a rather less detailed analysis of the 1694 Act returns for the whole group of London parishes had already been undertaken by P. E. Jones and A. V. Judges[6]—the study is being restricted to a sample of parishes within the Walls. The City of London was divided into four approximately equal geo-

---

[4] *Statutes of the Realm*, Vol. 6 (London, 1819), pp. 302–8.

[5] Some of the London returns under the 1694 Act also list occupations, and the final report on this study will contain an analysis of that material.

[6] P. E. Jones and A. V. Judges, 'London Population in the Late Seventeenth Century', *Economic History Review*, Vol. 6 (October, 1935).

graphical segments; within each segment, a 1-in-2 sample of parishes was selected from an alphabetically ordered list, yielding a total of forty parishes out of the ninety-seven within the Walls.[7] The main analysis has been undertaken for this group. Before discussing the results of that analysis, it is desirable to refer to some of the general characteristics of the City of London, as shown in the earlier, pioneer study by Jones and Judges.

That study covered both the parishes within the Walls and thirteen parishes without the Walls. On the basis of the 1694 Act enumeration, the total population was estimated to have amounted to almost seventy thousand within the Walls and almost fifty-four thousand for the thirteen parishes without, a total of 124,000. This is a much smaller population than that given by Gregory King, but his estimate of 528,000 (including an allowance for omissions) covered three additional parishes without the Walls, fifteen parishes in Middlesex and Surrey, and seven parishes in Westminster. The returns for these additional areas—save for a fragment of a parish in Westminster—have not so far been discovered, and King's own journals list the summary data (houses and total population) for only a few of them. The grand total would be for the contemporary equivalent of a conurbation, the East End of London being a large element in it—with a population of some eighty thousand, according to King's own figures.[8] Thus, the Jones and Judges data, and still more those for the parishes within the Walls, describe the core of London, an area which almost certainly declined in population by the beginning of the nineteenth century, and perhaps had even shown some fall after the middle of the seventeenth century. At the same time, London was an area with a fairly distinctive pre-industrial ecology. The proportions of upper-status households were higher in the centre, and the lower-status households showed the greatest relative frequency on the periphery and in many of the parishes without the Walls. This kind of pattern was still visible in the London of the 1830s, but it was changing by the middle of the nineteenth century. Taking the sample of forty parishes within the 'core' of London, some of the data derived from the enumeration in 1695 are summarized in Tables 1 and 2.

The first table gives an indication of some of the social characteristics of the total population. In this analysis, socio-economic status is classified on a simple twofold basis—whether the individual in question was liable to the standard rate of tax or to a surtax. The surtax itself was graduated in accordance with a person's wealth or

[7] The returns are available for eighty of the ninety-seven parishes; no trace has been found of the missing seventeen returns, and no copies have been located in other archives.

[8] For the whole area of Tower Hamlets, King gives a figure of 19,443 houses and a population of 86,882.

Table 1   City of London within the Walls, 1695. Population in a sample of forty parishes (absolute numbers)

Total population	Houses	Persons liable to surtax	Children	Servants	Apprentices	Lodgers
28,507	4,724	4,733	6,526	5,805	755	2,475

Table 2   City of London within the Walls, 1695. Demographic structure of a sample of forty parishes (absolute numbers)

	Single			Married	Widowed	Total
	Under 25	25 and over	All			
Males	7,221	1,350	8,571	4,392	273	13,236
Females	—	—	9,915	4,418	929	15,262
Total	—	—	18,486	8,810	1,202	28,498*

* Excludes 9 persons of unknown sex.

standing in the society. The lowest rate was paid by individuals with a personal estate of £600 or £50 per year, and the highest by dukes and members of their immediate families (wives, sons, and daughters). It would, however, have been cumbersome to distinguish the gradations. Even the simpler classification used shows a considerable range of variation within the city, from just under 5 per cent of the population liable to surtax in the poorest parishes (St. Mary Staining and St. Andrew by the Wardrobe) on the north-west and south-west edges of the city respectively, to almost 40 per cent in St. Matthew Friday Street, one of the central parishes in the south-west quadrant. Taking the sample as a whole, 16·6 per cent of the population came within the surtax category, counting dependents as well as heads of families.

Some of the headings in Table 1 are not entirely unambiguous. 'Children', for example, include not only individuals described explicitly in that way in the enumeration, but also others referred to as sons and daughters. The number of 'children' per house cannot be regarded as an index of relative fertility, as it might be to some extent if there were a definite and consistent age reference to the term 'child', 'servants' and 'apprentices' are also not entirely distinct categories. It is likely that the term "apprentice' was used fairly rigorously. In the parish of St. Mary le Bow, for example—a district of relatively high socio-economic status, with substantial numbers of merchants and professional people—the sixty-nine apprentices are listed clearly. In that parish, too, the internal evidence suggests that most of the servants were domestics. That is, however, not the case for all the parishes, and some of the servants may well be assistants or individuals serving in something comparable to an apprenticeship role. This perhaps partly explains the inconsistencies in the ratios of servants per house found among the different parishes. Not all the high-status parishes have the highest ratios of servants per house. If the parishes of high socio-economic status are taken as a group—covering both the four parishes in the general sample with the highest percentage of the population liable to surtax and the three highest among the remaining parishes within the Walls—the ratio of servants per house is higher than the average for the forty parishes in the general sample. The ratios of persons and children per house are also higher, as may be seen from Table 3. The picture will be clearer

Table 3   City of London within the Walls, 1695. Some social characteristics of total sample of forty parishes and seven parishes with highest proportions of population liable to surtax

		Per cent of population liable to surtax	Persons per house	Children per house	Servants per house	Servants and apprentices per house
1	Total of sample parishes	16·6	6·03	1·38	1·27	1·43
2	7 parishes with highest percentages in surtax categories*	34·4	6·68	1·46	2·18	2·37

* The total population of these seven parishes is 2,797.

when the data have been more fully analysed, for the analysis will then include a study of individual houses and households within the parishes.

Table 2 shows the composition of the population by sex and marital condition, and in Table 4 these absolute figures are expressed as percentages and are compared with similar data for the group of high-status parishes. The situation of London as a whole (that is, the geographical region covered by the census) is also shown in 1851, this point of time having been chosen because urban mortality and fertility were both high then.

The table suggests a greater difference between the higher-status parishes and the general sample in 1695 than between the general sample and the characteristics of London as a whole in 1851. The proportion of unmarried men and women, in particular, is strongly influenced by the social status of the area—this being in considerable measure a reflection of the proportion of servants and apprentices, almost all of whom were unmarried. For example, in St. Mary le Bow, a parish with 35 per cent of its population liable to surtax and

Table 4 City of London within the Walls, 1695. Demographic structure of total sample of forty parishes and of seven parishes with highest proportions of population liable to surtax (percentage distribution by marital condition)

	Males						Females				
	Single Under 25	Single 25 and over	All	Married	Widowed	Total	Single	Married	Widowed	Total	Ratio M/100 F
1 Total sample of parishes	54·6	10·2	64·8	33·2	2·1	100·1	65·0	29·0	6·1	100·1	87
2 7 parishes with highest percentages in surtax categories	55·1	15·5	70·6	27·0	2·3	99·9	70·8	25·9	3·4	100·1	97
3 London 1851 Census	50·5	10·1	60·6	36·1	3·3	100·0	58·6	32·6	8·8	100·0	88

with a ratio of just over two servants and apprentices per house, none of the apprentices and only two of the servants (both men) were married. This heavy weighting by the unmarried must, of course, be taken into account in interpreting the crude birth rates of large cities. Servants and apprentices were also likely to be relatively short-term migrants. Some of them must certainly have settled in London. It is not improbable, however, that, in general, they gave rise to a signifi-cant turnover of the population and to that extent promoted contact and communication between London's inhabitants and those in other parts of the country.

Where revised enumerations under the 1694 Act have been found, it may be possible to measure this turnover and perhaps also to obtain some indication of the kinds of people involved in it. For London, unfortunately, only two revised enumerations (for 1696) have been discovered, and one of them is for a parish (St. Peter, Paul's Wharf) for which there is no 1695 enumeration in the Guild-hall archives. As an illustration of possibilities and problems, how-ever, the other parish (St. Benet, Paul's Wharf) is of interest. Between the two enumerations, the population of the parish appeared to increase from 562 to 670 persons, a net growth of just over 19 per cent. A comparison of the individuals named in the two enumerations shows, however, that behind this net balance there was an apparent loss of seventy-five of the people listed in 1695 and a gross intake of 183 people between 1695 and 1696. The losses are equivalent to just over 13 per cent of the 1695 population and the gross gains to about 27 per cent of that population. A yearly turnover of this magnitude certainly appears extremely high. More information is available about the out-migration than the in-migration, for the 1695 enu-meration gives occupations for most of the inhabitants. Thus, of the seventy-five out-migrants, sixteen were servants, nineteen were men (and their families) in what would seem to be migratory occupations (painters, masons, a lieutenant, and a sailor), and three were widows who might, perhaps, have moved to be with relatives. In addition, the deaths of four people (two children and two adults) were traced in the parish register. Thus, in respect to forty-two of the seventy-five losses, the statistics do not seem implausible. The figures of apparent in-migration between 1695 and 1696 are much more difficult to check. Of the total of 183 newcomers, nine were traced through the 1695 list of inhabitants as being in other parishes in the city at the time of the first enumeration, while twenty-six were servants and might thus have been genuine newcomers. The 1696 assessment for St. Benet, Paul's Wharf, is a copy in the handwriting of Gregory King, and King himself lists as 'additions' the names of 106 persons—possibly these were, in his view, real additions to the

KP

population since 1695. If so, then 143 out of the 183 new names can be explained in not too unrealistic terms. It is of course, no less possible that there was more undercounting in the first enumeration of 1695 than in that of 1696. King, who appears to have undertaken —or to have sponsored—a post-enumeration check in St. Benet, Paul's Wharf in 1696, notes forty-three persons as having been omitted and six as having been counted twice. There is, however, no comparable evidence of the volume of omissions in 1695. Before we can reasonably evaluate population shifts of the kind suggested by the data for this particular parish, more work will clearly need to be done, especially on the 1694 Act assessments for cities other than London.[9]

In the introduction to *London Inhabitants*, I gave examples of two other types of analysis of the 1694 Act data, one concerning household size and structure and the other bearing upon the degree of completeness of vital registration in London. Nothing further will be said here on the first type, for the rather detailed study of household structure in a subsample of fourteen parishes is not yet complete. The attempt to estimate the completeness of birth and death registration, however, has now been extended to cover a much larger number of parishes, and it is thus possible to make a rather more confident statement about the results.

In essence—though this was not realized until after the first trials were made—the method used is that proposed in 1949 by C. Chandrasekar and W. Edwards Deming for estimating the 'true' numbers of births and deaths by means of surveys in areas lacking effective vital registration.[10] Given two independent surveys, each recording births or deaths in a given area in a specified period and listing the names of the individuals born or dying, it should be possible to compare the names of the individuals in the two surveys. Taking births as an example (if PR refers to one survey and CR to the second), a comparison or matching of individual names and specified characteristics would produce the following results: names included in both PR and CR, which we may call (PR, CR); names in PR, but not in CR; and names in CR, but not in PR. If the surveys are independent, the best estimate of the 'true' number of births would consist of

[9] P. Laslett's analysis of the population changes in Clayworth and Cogenhoe suggests a very high turnover in these two rural areas in the seventeenth century. He finds, in particular, that 62 per cent of the inhabitants of Clayworth in 1688 had not been there in 1676. See P. Laslett, *The World We Have Lost* (London, 1965), p. 147.

[10] 'On a Method of Estimating Birth and Death Rates and the Extent of Registration', *Journal of the American Statistical Association*, Vol. 44 (March 1949). A useful summary with reference to the application of this technique to current estimates in Pakistan is given by W. Parker Mauldin, 'Estimating Rates of Population Growth', *Family Planning and Population Programs*, eds. B. Berelson *et al.* (Chicago, 1966), pp. 642–7.

$(PR, CR) + PR + CR +$ an allowance for births that escaped recording in both surveys, which we shall call E. Then $E = (PR + CR)/(PR, CR)$. The technique would apply equally to recorded deaths.

While the 1694 Act was in force, two sets of vital records were available—the normal parish registration entries and the special returns compiled by the collectors appointed under the Act, which levied duties on births, burials, and marriages. Each set listed and named the individuals. Although matching is not easy, it seems generally to be possible so far as the London returns are concerned. This matching has been done for all those parishes in the general sample for which both collectors' returns and parish registers are available, namely thirty-eight parishes within the Walls. In addition, two of the parishes without the Walls (St. Bartholomew the Great and St. Bartholomew the Less) were treated in the same way.[11] Since the Act did not come into force until mid-1695 and may well have encountered initial difficulties, it seemed better to begin with the second full year of operation. Thus, the returns and parish-register entries for the three-year period—1 May 1696, to 30 April 1699—were used.[12] The main elements in, and the results of, the analysis are summarized in Table 5. The estimates of 'true' numbers of baptisms and burials are those given in the column headed 'Total'; the last two columns in the table give the ratios by which it was found

Table 5 Components used in estimating 'true' numbers of baptisms and burials in the City of London, 1696–8

A.	PR, CR	CR	PR	E	Total	Inflation ratios Total/CR	Total/PR
Baptisms (i) 38 parishes within the Walls	2,324	779	770	258	4,131	1·331	1·335
(ii) 2 outer parishes	228	34	55	8	325	1·240	1·148
B. *Burials* (i) 38 parishes within the Walls	2,253	611	1,058	287	4,209	1·470	1·271
(ii) 2 outer parishes	265	16	33	2	316	1·125	1·060

[11] For the remaining outer parishes, there are problems arising from the differences in areas covered by the collectors' returns and the parish registers.

[12] In a few cases, collectors' returns were available for only two of the three years. In such cases, the events recorded have been multiplied by 1·5. Foundlings were included, but not those individuals listed as normally resident in other parishes.

necessary to multiply the numbers recorded in the collectors' returns and in the parish registers in order to 'inflate' them to the 'true' totals.

Three conclusions seem to follow from the analysis. First, both registration systems were subject to serious omissions in the parishes within the Walls, the collectors' returns showing especially large omissions in respect to burials. Secondly, omissions seem to be much less serious in the two outer parishes, the parish registers appearing to be rather better than the collectors' returns both for burials and for baptisms. Finally, when the 'corrected' totals of baptisms and burials are used, the balance of births and deaths appears more favourable than is often assumed to have been the case for London. It is true, of course, that these estimates relate to a period subsequent to that in which John Graunt was writing and after bubonic plague had ceased to play a significant part in mortality in England. It is possible—and is at least worth investigating—that for some time after the 1660s London was far less a 'consumer of men' than is generally assumed, though the position may have worsened considerably with the development of smallpox mortality in the eighteenth century.

In considering these suggestions, it is important to acknowledge that the two systems of vital registration were unlikely to have been completely independent of each other, and that this assumption in the calculation is unrealistic. Nor was one system completely dependent on the other as is evident from the elements in Table 5. The error involved in the assumption is small in relation to the actual 'non-matching', If an allowance were made for this error, the 'inflation ratios' would have to be increased slightly. What is more important—and again this needs further study—is that parish registration may have been still less complete, both before and after the period during which the 1694 Act was in force, because the Act and its subsequent amendments provided for specific improvements in the existing parochial system, both in respect to coverage and to speed of registration. In addition, insofar as the two systems of registration were not independent, each might have benefited from the other. Even with these limitations, it is at least useful to have some definite basis for looking at the reliability of ecclesiastical registration in earlier and later periods.[13]

It is convenient to bring this 'report on progress' to an end here. The analysis is continuing, and in the final report it may be possible

---

[13] The completeness of the data in the London Bills of Mortality is also being investigated, though there are special difficulties regarding the statistics of christenings. These data, too, were not independent of the parish-registration system and, hence, may also have improved during the period in question.

to include material for communities outside London.[14] If so, there will be some hope of providing better estimates of the level of fertility and mortality for England in the late-seventeenth century than have so far been available, though to do so will not only involve tests of the completeness of registration, but will also require attempts to estimate under-enumeration in the 1694 Act assessments.[15]

[14] I have made some provisional estimates of completeness of registration in Southampton during the period, but hope to amplify them. It should also be possible later to carry out similar computations for Shrewsbury. In the work on London, I shall also be drawing upon other data to which my attention was drawn by Mr. P. E. Jones, namely the records of apprentices who acquired their freedom from the City of London. These records indicate previous place of residence and would thus prove of considerable value in studying the migration of a select group of young men.

[15] When Dr. E. A. Wrigley saw this paper in June 1967 he wondered whether the apparent differences in completeness of vital registration between the inner and outer parishes of the City of London might be a function of the relative populations of these parishes. The inner parishes have small populations; the outer, large ones. For a resident in a small parish, the possibility of recording a birth or death at a church in a nearby parish might obviously be quite high, yet the matching described in this paper had been undertaken only within the same parish.

To answer Dr. Wrigley's question, the matching process for one year was greatly extended. The entries for the sample parishes were matched against the parish registers and collectors' returns for all the London parishes for which the records were available. The detailed findings will be published later. The general result was that the inflation ratios derived from this extended matching did not differ significantly from the original ratios. It would seem, therefore, that in the City of London vital events were very largely recorded in the parish of residence.

Since this paper first appeared, further analysis has been undertaken, based on the Marriage Act data and also on the statistics of the 1692 Poll Tax. See my paper on 'Socio-Economic Status and Occupations, in the City of London at the End of the Seventeenth Century' (in *Studies in London History presented to Philip Edmund Jones*, London, 1969). Reference should also be made to the publication in full by Bristol Rural Society of the Marriage Act returns for Bristol for 1696 (E. Ralph and M. E. Williams, *The Inhabitants of Bristol in 1696*, Bristol, 1968). The editors checked the names of apprentices and servants against the entries in the Bristol Apprentice Book and found that most of the men described as servants in the Marriage Act returns (but not the women) were in fact apprentices.

Ian Sutherland

When was the Great Plague?
Mortality in London, 1563 to 1665

John Graunt's classic, his *Natural and Political Observations Made upon the Bills of Mortality*, was first published in 1662.[1] The third edition appeared in July, 1665, during the early weeks of the Great Plague. It contained some new material in an appendix, which was obviously prompted by the reappearance of plague in the capital, and which included the following statement:

> In this place I think fit to intimate, that considering the present increase of the City from *Anno* 1625 to this time, which is from eight to thirteen, that until the Burials exceed 8,400 *per week*, the Mortality will not exceed that of 1625. Which God for ever avert.

Within two months of the publication of this intimation, the weekly burials in London had twice exceeded 8,250, but never 8,400. Thus, in terms of the peak of the epidemic, the mortality in 1665 was no greater than that in at least one previous plague year in London. But the peak of an epidemic is not necessarily a good indication of its total magnitude, and any interim conclusion drawn from so limited a criterion should be checked by considering the mortality during the whole epidemic. Graunt, who had already compared the total mortality during earlier plague years in the original edition of his book, may well have returned to this point after 1665, but he published nothing further on the topic.[2]

Because Graunt's criterion relates only to the peak of the epidemic, and also leads to what may be described as an epidemiological photo-finish, it is clearly worth examining this particular point more thoroughly. What began several years ago with a casual check on my part as to whether or not the plague in 1665 surpassed Graunt's criterion gradually developed into a study of the relative mortality in

---

[1] The first edition of Graunt's book was reprinted by Willcox (1939). The fifth edition (1676), which included all the material in the earlier editions, was reprinted by Hull (1899). Recent studies of Graunt and his work were made by Glass (1963) and Sutherland (1963).

[2] There was a fourth edition a few weeks later, in September or October, 1665, but the fifth edition (1676) did not appear until after Graunt's death.

London during the major plague years and has now been extended into a more comprehensive survey of mortality in London throughout the century preceding the plague of 1665, together with a tentative series of population estimates.

No one since Graunt, so far as I am aware, has tried to compare the mortality (as distinct from the numbers of deaths) in different years in London in the sixteenth and seventeenth centuries, and it seems to be possible to get considerably further than Graunt did. Although some of the data available to Graunt have not survived, other relevant material, which he did not know of, has since come to light. In all, sufficient information has survived, either in the original weekly or annual Bills of Mortality, or as abstracts (nearly all contemporary) from these bills, to give a picture of burials and christenings in London which is continuous since 1603 and covers thirteen of the previous forty years, including the two years of highest mortality during the earlier period.[3] The basic approach to this material is closely similar to that used by Graunt, but the data, despite their imperfections, can be handled more comprehensively.

GRAUNT'S METHODS OF ASSESSING THE RELATIVE MORTALITY IN DIFFERENT PLAGUE YEARS

It is of interest first to recapitulate the sections of Graunt (1662) in which he compared the mortality in different plague years. He told us that 'There have been in *London*, within this Age, four Times of great *Mortality*, that is to say, the years 1592, and 1593, 1603, 1625, and 1636', and he listed the numbers of burials.[4] 'Now it is manifest of it self, in which of these years most died; but in which of them was the greatest *Mortality* of all Diseases in general, or of the *Plague* in particular, we discover thus.'

He then looked at the proportion of total burials which had been attributed to plague—that is, the proportionate mortality from this cause. The highest figures were in 1603 (about 80 per cent) and in 1625 (about 70 per cent). 'We must therefore conclude the Year 1603. to have been the greatest *Plague*-Year of this age.' Graunt next noted, however, that both in 1603 and 1625 the ratio of the burials from all causes to the christenings was 8 to 1, and concluded that the total mortality in the two years was equal. He reconciled these differing conclusions by asserting that in 1625 'more died of the *Plague* than were accompted for under that name', and he verified

---

[3] For sources see Appendix 1 at the end of this study.

[4] Graunt was in error in including 1592 among the years of great mortality. See Appendix 1.

this statement by comparing the numbers of burials attributed to causes other than plague in 1625 with those in the preceding and following years.[5] This led him to a corrected proportionate mortality of 80 per cent for plague in 1625, 'rendering the said year 1625 to be as great a *Plague* year as that of 1603, and no greater'. Thus, in the course of his examination of plague mortality, Graunt incidentally showed the limitations of an approach by proportionate mortality.

Finally, Graunt (1665) derived his criterion for judging the severity of the outbreak which was then developing. The highest number of weekly deaths in 1625 was 5,205, and this, when multiplied by the factor of 13 over 8, for the increase in the population of London during the forty years, gives about 8,450, which tallies with Graunt's figure of 8,400 for the critical peak number of weekly deaths in 1665. Graunt does not explain how he arrived at the ratio of 13 to 8. Using his own methods for assessing the population increase during this period, which are based on the increase in the numbers of deaths in years with little or no plague, the increase in population appears to have been at least as great, and probably greater, than this.[6] Thus Graunt's critical value may have been too low a figure, and if so it would follow that the mortality in 1665 was lower than that in 1625.

THE INFORMATION IN THE LONDON BILLS OF MORTALITY

The Bills of Mortality for London had their origin during the early years of the sixteenth century. The earliest extant bills consist of a manuscript list of the number of burials in each London parish for a period of a week, distinguishing deaths from the plague, with totals for the whole of London. Christenings were added to the bills at a fairly early date, and throughout the period of this study the basic information provided by the bills consists of three items—namely,

[5] There are contemporary references to the absence of clinical signs in those who died in 1625, which indicate that the pneumonic form of the disease was commoner than in 1603, and was often regarded as a disease other than plague. See Wilson (1963), pp. 134, 207–8.

[6] The area covered by the weekly bills for 1625 was the City, the Liberties and out-parishes; for 1665 the distant parishes were also included. Taking figures for two adjacent plague-free years, as Graunt (1662) did, the ratio of the burials in the larger area in 1663–64 to those in the smaller area in 1623–24 was 33,653/23,322, representing an increase of 44 per cent. However, as Graunt had noted, mortality from causes other than plague was particularly high in both 1623 and 1624; it follows that 44 per cent is likely to be an underestimate of the increase in population. Avoiding these years the corresponding ratio of the burials in 1661–62 to those in 1621–22 was 36,325/17,559, representing an increase of 107 per cent. However, Graunt's ratio of 13/8 corresponds to a population increase of only 62 per cent. The ratio of the population indices for 1665 and 1625, derived in Table 3 of the present study, is 16,717/8,455, representing a population increase of 98 per cent.

the total burials, the number of these attributed to plague, and the total christenings in London.

To begin with, the bills were probably compiled only in times of plague, although at some uncertain time they became a continuous weekly series. Relatively little of the information from these weekly bills before 1665 has survived to the present day. However, annual totals of the weekly figures were prepared, at first unofficially and later by the Company of Parish Clerks, and there is as a result a more extensive surviving series of annual totals.

There was naturally much more contemporary interest in the bills when plague was prevalent than at other times, and for this reason more information from the bills has survived for plague years than for the intervening periods. Thus the printed weekly and annual bills, which contain much more information than totals for the whole of London, first appeared only during and after each major plague. Throughout, the item of most general interest was the number of plague deaths, and that of least general interest was the number of christenings. Consequently, less information is available on christenings than on burials, and the deaths from plague are sometimes quoted without the corresponding figure for total burials. These considerations all help to explain the rather patchy nature of the surviving information, particularly in the second half of the sixteenth century, and the uncertainties about the origin and development of the series of weekly and annual bills.

During the period up to 1665, the area regarded as 'London', and included in the bills, was extended from time to time. The earliest bills list only the parishes in the City of London—that is, 'within the Walls', and omit certain precincts in the City which were added later. From 1603 onwards the returns for the City of London covered a total of ninety-seven parishes and precincts. A group of sixteen parishes outside the walls, lying 'part within and part without the Liberties', was included in the bills regularly before the end of the sixteenth century, the whole often being referred to as 'the City and the Liberties thereof', although the Liberties of London technically included the City, and parts of the sixteen parishes lay outside the Liberties. From 14 July 1603, a further group of nine 'out-parishes' (later divided into ten) was 'joyned with the Citie and Liberties' and from 1636 figures for the City of Westminster and six other 'distant' parishes were included in the bills.[7] In addition, during plague years

[7] The parishes included in these groups are listed in the annual bills for 1603 and 1625 reproduced by Wilson (1927; 1963). The pest-house is usually included on the bills with the group of 16 parishes (though not in Annual Bill, 1625a). In 1660 the grouping of the 10 out-parishes and the 7 distant parishes was rearranged in the bills into a grouping of 12 parishes in Middlesex and Surrey and the 5 parishes in the City and Liberties of Westminster. For this grouping see the annual bill for 1665 reproduced by Sutherland (1963).

information was often assembled from parishes not at that time included regularly in the bills.

The responsibility for the returns from each parish lay with the sexton, who from an early date had two 'searchers' to assist him. The returns were assembled, and the weekly totals prepared, by the Company of Parish Clerks of London, which was responsible for publishing both the weekly and the annual bills.

Because of the method of compilation of the bills from weekly parish returns, the bills are potentially as reliable as the parish registers as records of burials and christenings. In 1892, W. Ogle made a comparison of the numbers of burials recorded in the annual bills and in the registers for five London parishes during the ten years 1657 to 1666. Although there were numerous individual discrepancies, these tended to balance one another. There was a total of 1,879 burials according to the bills, and 1,843 according to the registers. Moreover, the totals in the plague year 1665 were 586 and 580 respectively, indicating as good an agreement when plague was prevalent as when it was not. F. P. Wilson made a similar comparison in 1927 for fourteen parishes in the plague year 1625; there were 2,517 burials according to the bills and 2,495 in the registers. No similar comparison of christenings has been made.[8]

There were few secret burials in the sixteenth and early seventeenth century and no dissenters' burial grounds, as Wilson has pointed out, but the completeness of burial recording is likely to have varied from parish to parish, and from time to time in the same parish. It is thus likely that the total burials recorded in the bills underestimate the total number of deaths. The deficiency may have been a little greater after 1642, as a consequence of the great increase in numbers of dissenters following the Civil War, but, as indicated below, this affected christenings to a very much greater extent than burials in the years between then and 1665.

Graunt noted in 1662 the growing deficiency in the numbers of christenings, compared with burials, after 1642. Until 1642, the christenings were about equal to the burials; by 1648, the christenings were about two-thirds, and by 1659 they were less than half, the burials. The two main causes, according to Graunt, 'why the Accompt of *Christnings* hath been neglected more then that of *Burials*' were 'a Religious Opinion against *Baptizing of Infants*, either as unlawfull, or unnecessary' and 'The scruples, which many Publick *Ministers* would make of the worthiness of Parents to have their Children Baptized', which forced some parents to have their

---

[8] Such a comparison would be possible only for Westminster in 1626 and from 1629 to 1659, and for the other six distant parishes from 1636 to 1659, because the christenings in individual parishes are not otherwise available from the bills of mortality.

children baptized by other ministers who could not then register the baptism. Before 1642, however, it is likely that few children went unbaptized for religious reasons. The total christenings recorded in the bills before 1642 will, however, underestimate the total number of births to a rather larger extent than the burials underestimate the deaths. In addition to incomplete recording, chrisoms—that is, children dying before they were a month old—were numerous because of the high infant mortality, and, as Wilson put it, 'a man has to be buried, but he need not be baptized'.

There is no doubt that the returns of deaths attributed to plague are very much less trustworthy than those of the total burials. Graunt, as already noted, produced good numerical evidence of this in comparing the plague mortality in 1603 and 1625, and also commented unfavourably on the ability of the 'Old-women *Searchers*' to distinguish between various causes of death.

In addition to these various defects in the information in the bills, there are certainly also gratuitous errors (which will tend to balance) arising from mistakes in addition, copying errors, and misprints. Some of these give rise to detectable discrepancies, especially in the earlier returns, but these cannot often be resolved.

The present study is based almost entirely upon the total burials (up to 1665) and the total christenings (up to 1641), as recorded in the bills of mortality. Little use is made of the total deaths attributed to plague. A full discussion of the effect of the deficiencies in the bills on the calculations which follow is given below; it is sufficient for the present to regard the recorded burials (to 1665) and the christenings (to 1641) as giving a reasonably good indication of the total numbers of deaths and births from year to year in London.

THE OCCURRENCE OF PLAGUE IN LONDON FROM 1563 TO 1665

The period covered in this study is from 1563—the first year for which the totals of burials in London are still available—to 1665, the year of the last major epidemic of plague. It is convenient to classify each year during this period into one of three groups according to the importance of plague as a cause of death. Years have been classed as 'plague-free' if the proportion of the total burials which were attributed to plague was less than 1 per cent. Those with a higher proportion of plague burials have been termed 'plague-endemic', and among them is a small number of years in which the total mortality appears (from the analyses below) to have risen to at least 50 per cent above the normal plague-free level. These, following the usage of the time, have been called 'plague years'.

During the first forty years of the period, from 1563 to 1602, annual totals of burials and plague deaths are available for thirteen years only, namely for 1563, 1578 to 1582, 1593 to 1595, and 1597 to 1600. From this and other scattered numerical information, supplemented by the general historical record, we know that 1563 was a plague year, and that London was then almost free of the disease until at least 1566. There were, however, several years between then and 1577 in which plague was endemic, although it does not appear to have reached epidemic levels in any of them. The years 1578 and 1582 were plague years separated by a period of endemicity, and it is likely that the disease then remained endemic until the plague of 1593. From 1595 to 1602, however, London appears to have been again almost free of plague.[9]

For the sixty-three years from 1603 to 1665 there is an uninterrupted series of annual totals of burials and plague deaths. Following the plague of 1603, there was a period of endemicity until 1611 (1609 being a plague year), followed by a long plague-free period until 1624. The year 1625 was a plague year, and was followed by another plague-free period until 1635, apart from the years 1630 and 1631, in which the disease was endemic. In 1636 a further epidemic of plague occurred, and the disease then remained endemic until 1648. There was another long plague-free period from 1649, culminating in the plague of 1665.

In all, among the seventy-six years for which annual totals of burials and plague deaths are available, nine come within the definition of a plague year, namely 1563, 1578, 1582, 1593, 1603, 1609, 1625, 1636, and 1665.

INDICES OF POPULATION SIZE IN THE DIFFERENT PLAGUE YEARS

Direct information on the size of London's population during the period under study is lacking (apart from one count, which will be

[9] I have come across references to plague in London in 1568, 1569, 1570, 1573, 1574, 1575, and 1577, usually in connection with the issue of plague orders, the removal of the Court to a place of 'safety', or the arrangements for the installation of the Lord Mayor. Stow (1570) reports 152 burials, including 51 from plague, in the 'Citie and oute paryshes' in the week ending 28 October 1569, and Stow (1575) reports 166 burials, including 75 from plague, in the same week in 1574. These totals, at this time of the year, are well short of what would be expected if 1569 or 1574 had been a plague year as defined in this study. Between 1583 and 1602 I have come across similar references to plague in London only in 1592, 1593, and 1594. In 1595, and from 1597–1600 the bills of mortality confirm the virtual freedom of London from plague.

referred to below). It is consequently not possible to calculate mortality rates in the customary way, in terms of deaths related to population size. In order, however, to compare the levels of mortality in different years, it is enough to have an indication of the *relative* size of the population in those years.

In his comparisons of mortality in different plague years, Graunt used the number of christenings in the year as an indicator of the size of London's population at the time of the plague. But he also showed that the number of christenings fell below its normal level in each plague year and in the following year. This suggests that it would be preferable to use an estimate of the number of christenings *expected* in the plague year, in the absence of plague, as an indicator of the size of the population. In case the numbers of christenings were affected when plague was endemic as well as when it was epidemic, it was decided to consider plague-free years only, and to use the figures for christenings in those years to indicate trends in the size of the population, and hence provide an index of population size for each plague year.[10] Because of the later deficiencies in the records, christenings may be used for this purpose only before 1642. From this date, however, burials in plague-free years may be used similarly to provide an index of population size for 1665. Although Graunt observed in 1662 that 'The *Decrease*, and *Increase* of People is to be be reckoned chiefly by *Christnings*, because few bear children in *London* but *Inhabitants*, though others die there', he also was obliged to use burials in plague-free years as the basis for his estimates of the increase in London's population up to 1659.

The use of christenings in this way implies the assumption that the birth rate (strictly, the christening rate) was constant throughout the period of study, and the corresponding use of burials implies a constant death rate (in the absence of plague). It is preferable to use christenings rather than burials before 1642 (although less geographical detail is available for christenings) because they show less variation from year to year. Many infections other than plague were common in London in the sixteenth and seventeenth centuries (though not on the same scale as plague), and the assumption of a constant death rate in plague-free years is therefore less realistic than that of a constant birth rate.

All the available information on the numbers of christenings in different parts of London in plague-free years up to 1641 is given in Table 1 and Figure 1. The christenings in the year 1580 have been

---

[10] The christenings in plague-endemic years were subsequently found to follow closely the trends derived from the plague-free years only, and this provides justification for the extension of the trend lines for the City, Liberties, and out-parishes backwards to 1603 and forwards to 1641, as shown in Figure 1.

Table 1   Recorded annual totals of christenings in London in those years during the period 1578 to 1641 in which the proportionate mortality attributed to plague was less than 1 per cent*

| Year | Christenings in | |
	City of London and the Liberties	City of London, the Liberties and out-parishes
1580	3,568	
1597	4,256	
1598	4,236	
1599	4,674	
1600	4,760	
1612		6,986
1613		6,846
1614		7,208
1615		7,682
1616		7,985
1617		7,747
1618		7,735
1619		8,127
1620	6,525	8,314
1621		8,039
1622		7,894
1623		7,945
1624	6,368	8,299
1627		8,408
1628		8,564
1629		9,901
1632		9,584
1633		9,997
1634		9,855
1635		10,034

* Except for 1580, in which the proportionate mortality attributed to plague was 4·5 per cent. For the years 1583 to 1592, 1596, 1601 and 1602, no record of the total numbers of christenings or burials is currently known.

included, although there were some deaths from plague in that year (the proportionate mortality was 4·5 per cent), because this represents the earliest available figure from the bills which may be accepted as indicating the normal level of christenings in London.

Two points are apparent from these data. First, there seems to have been a reasonably steady upward trend in the numbers of christenings during the period from 1580 to 1635, indicating a substantial increase in the population of London during the period. Moreover, the increase, as noted by Graunt and as might be expected, was greater in the out-parishes than in the City and Liberties. Secondly, there appears to have been remarkably little interruption

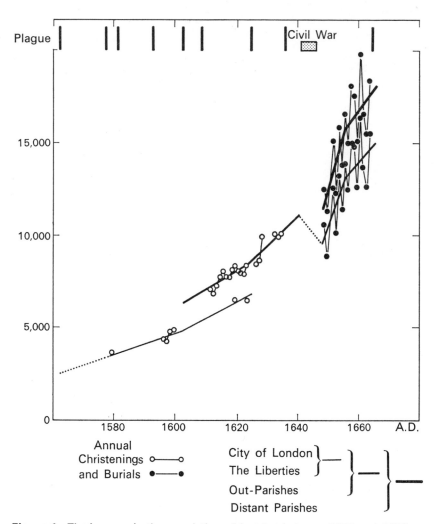

Figure 1 The increase in the population of London between 1563 and 1665, as indicated by trend-lines fitted to the recorded christenings in plague-free years before 1642, and to recorded burials in plague-free years thereafter with the nine main plague years and the period of the Civil War indicated

of the long-term trend by the plague years, even after the particularly severe plagues in 1603 and 1625. As Graunt observed, London
apparently re-peopled itself completely by the second year after each
plague. It would therefore appear that the figures for christenings in
Table 1 can be used to provide realistic estimates of the expected
number of christenings in each plague year, and that these would
represent acceptable indices of population size. Moreover, it would
even be acceptable to make an estimate *backwards* in time if no
forward estimate was possible.

The total burials in the City, the Liberties and out-parishes, and
in the City, the Liberties, out-parishes and distant parishes, in the
plague-free years during the period from 1642 to 1665, are shown in
Table 2 and in Figure 1. They indicate considerable variation

Table 2 Recorded annual totals of burials in London in those years during the
period 1642 to 1665 in which the proportionate mortality attributed to
plague was less than 1 per cent*

	Burials in	
Year	City of London, the Liberties and out-parishes	City of London, the Liberties, out-parishes and distant parishes
1649	10,566	12,373
1650	8,764	10,314
1651	10,827	12,918
1652	12,569	15,052
1653	10,087	12,242
1654	13,247	15,818
1655	11,357	13,763
1656	13,921	16,625
1657	12,434	15,046
1658	14,993	17,951
1659	14,756	17,584
1660	12,681	15,118
1661	16,265	19,771
1662	13,652	16,554
1663	12,741	15,356
1664	15,449	18,297

* Because of the rearrangement of the parishes into different groupings in 1660 (see footnote 7),
the total burials in the City of London, the Liberties, and out-parishes from 1660 to 1664 in this
table were reconstructed from the figures for individual parishes in the annual bills.

from year to year, but an upward trend in the population of London
during this period. The increase appears to have been slower towards
the end of the period.

The expected numbers of christenings in the first eight of the nine
plague years listed above were derived from four straight regression
lines: two for the City and Liberties up to and after 1603, and two for

the City, the Liberties, and out-parishes up to and after 1625.[11]
These four lines are shown in Figure 1. The expected numbers of
christenings in each plague year, derived from them, are given in
Table 3, column 4. Two further straight regression lines were
fitted to the burials in the latter part of the plague-free period
shown in Table 2—namely, from 1654 to 1664.[12] The expected
numbers of burials in 1665, derived from these lines, were reduced to
the expected numbers of christenings in 1665, shown in Table 3, by
multiplying them by 0·9998, this being the ratio of christenings to
burials during the plague-free period 1632–5. This period, which
has been taken as a base-line for mortality in this study, was not only
free of plague, but was also relatively free of other infections (apart
from an epidemic of smallpox in 1634). This reduction of the
expected burials to expected christenings implies an assumption that
the mortality in London was the same during the two plague-free
periods 1632–5 and 1654–64.

The use of this series of expected christenings as population indices
presupposes that there was a steady increase in the population from
year to year and makes no allowances for any short-term fluctuations
in population size. For some of the plague years an alternative

[11] The regression lines were as follows, Y representing the estimated christenings and x
the calendar year (measured from 1600):

City and Liberties:
(a) for years from 1563 to 1603, derived from figures from 1580 to 1600:
$Y = 4,569 + 51 \cdot 99x$
(b) for years from 1603 to 1625, derived from figures from 1597 to 1624:
$Y = 4,611 + 83 \cdot 05x$

City, Liberties and out-parishes:
(a) for years from 1603 to 1625, derived from figures from 1612 to 1624:
$Y = 5,952 \cdot 2 + 100 \cdot 12x$
(b) for years from 1627 to 1641, derived from figures from 1627 to 1635:
$Y = 3,787 \cdot 4 + 182 \cdot 73x$

[12] Separate regression lines were also fitted to the burials during the earlier part of the
plague-free period, namely from 1649 to 1654. The four regression lines were as follows,
Y representing the estimated burials and x the calendar year (measured from 1600):

City, Liberties, and out-parishes:
(a) for years from 1649 to 1654, derived from figures from the same years:
$Y = -17,118 + 546 \cdot 17x$
(b) for years from 1655 to 1666, derived from figures from 1654 to 1664:
$Y = 2,461 + 191 \cdot 72x$

City, Liberties, out-parishes, and distant parishes:
(a) for years from 1649 to 1654:
$Y = 23,877 + 718 \cdot 37x$
(b) for years from 1655 to 1666:
$Y = 3,034 + 228 \cdot 83x$

These lines were reduced to trend lines for expected christenings by multiplying them
by 0·9998. as explained in the text.

population index may be derived from the actual numbers of christenings recorded just before the outbreak of the epidemic. The total christenings in the year before the plague year, and those for the first thirteen weeks of the plague year (which always preceded the start of the epidemic) were totalled, and four-fifths of this total was taken as an alternative expected number of christenings in the plague year.[13] These expected numbers are also given, where available, in Table 3, column 5.

RELATIVE MORTALITY IN THE NINE PLAGUE YEARS

Using these figures for expected christenings as indices of the size of London's population at the time of each plague, mortality indices may be calculated, and are shown in the last two columns of Table 3. These express the ratio of the recorded burials to the expected christenings in each plague year in terms of the observed ratio of burials to christenings in the City, the Liberties, and out-parishes in the plague-free period 1632–5. Thus the mortality index represents the ratio of the mortality in the plague year to a 'normal' level of mortality, in the absence of plague, in London in the early seventeenth century.

In four of the nine plague years—namely, 1578, 1582, 1609, and 1636—the mortality, so estimated, lay between 1·7 and 2·3 times the normal level. In 1593 the mortality was more than four times the normal level, in 1665 more than five times, in 1603 and in 1625 more than six times, and in 1563 more than seven times the normal level. Taking these figures at their face value, the mortality appears to have become slightly less severe in each successive major plague.

The least reliable of these measures of relative mortality are the earliest and the latest, namely, those for 1563 and 1665. The derivation of the population index for 1563 involved a linear extrapolation backwards in time for seventeen years from the earliest available total of christenings (in 1580), a period which includes the plague year 1578. A moderate increase in the number of expected christenings, from 2,646 to just over 3,000, would suffice to reduce the relative mortality index in 1563 to the figure of 6·74 for the same

---

[13] Complete, or nearly complete, information on the weekly christenings in plague-free years is available only for 1597 to 1600, 1660 and 1664 (see Appendix 1). This information confirms that in the absence of plague the christenings were evenly distributed throughout the year, and thus justifies the use of the fraction four-fifths in this context.

Table 3 Estimated mortality in London in nine plague years from 1563 to 1665, relative to the mortality in the plague-free period 1632–35, using indices of population size derived from the recorded christenings in periods free of plague.

Area	Year	Recorded burials	Population index (expected christenings)		Relative mortality index*	
			(1) Derived from trend lines	(2) Derived from preceding 15 months	(1)	(2)
City of London and the Liberties	1563	20,372	2,646	—	7·70	—
	1578	7,830	3,425	—	2·29	—
	1582	6,930	3,633	(3,526)**	1·91	1·97
	1593	17,893	4,205	—	4·25	—
	1603	31,861	4,725	—	6·74	—
	1609	—	5,358	—	—	—
	1625	41,312	6,687	(6,530)	6·18	6·33
City of London, the Liberties and out-parishes	1603	(38,876)	6,253	—	6·22	—
	1609	11,785	6,853	6,875	1·72	1·71
	1625	54,265	8,455	8,510	6·42	6·38
	1636	23,359	10,366	10,332	2·25	2·26
	1665	80,696	14,920	15,810	5·41	5·10
City of London, the Liberties, out-parishes and distant parishes	1636	27,415	12,342	(12,420)	2·22	2·21
	1665	97,306	17,904	18,771	5·43	5·18

* Taking the mortality in the City of London, the Liberties and out-parishes in 1632–35 as 1·00.
** The figures in brackets have been derived directly from recorded totals, but for various reasons contain an element of estimation. See note to Table 3 opposite.

area in 1603.[14] The measures for 1665 all depend upon the assumption that the mortality in the plague-free period 1654–64 was the same as in the plague-free period 1632–35. If it is assumed instead that the mortality was the same in 1654–64 as it had been during the earlier plague-free period 1612–22, the relative mortality indices in the City, the Liberties, and out-parishes for 1665 would have been 5·05 and 4·76 respectively, instead of 5·41 and 5·10.

The indices derived from the alternative estimates of expected christenings are closely similar to those derived from the trend lines. The largest discrepancy is in 1665, where the estimates were of necessity based on burials, which are inherently more variable than christenings. The estimates derived from the trend lines will be used in preference later in this study, partly because they cover all the plague years, and partly because they provide population indices for the intervening years also.

[14] The only surviving information on the numbers of christenings before 1580 is that there were 52 in 'London and the suburbs' in the week ending 30 July 1563 (Hamerton, 1563); see Appendix 1. This corresponds to about 47 in the City and Liberties (by reducing 52 in the ratio 289/320, these being the recorded numbers of plague deaths in the two areas in that week). From the information on weekly christenings during 1603 a reduction of about one-sixth in the normal level of christenings might have been expected by this stage of the 1563 plague. Thus the available information suggests an expected level of about 55 christenings a week in the City and Liberties in 1563, or 2,860 in the whole year. This is rather larger than the expected total of 2,646 obtained by backwards extrapolation.

Table 3:
(a) The annual bill for 1603 gives a composite total of burials, for the City and Liberties up to 14 July, and for the City, Liberties, and out-parishes thereafter. Because of inconsistencies on the annual bill between the weekly totals and the parish totals for the latter part of the year, the figure of 31,861 burials in the City and Liberties in this table was derived from the annual bill (from 23 December 1602 to 14 July 1603) and from the separate totals for the City and for the Liberties on the weekly bills (from 14 July to 22 December). However, for the week ending 21 July, the totals for two parishes (Bartholomew the Great, and St. Trinity Minories) were transferred from the section for the out-parishes to that for the Liberties (where they were listed thereafter) and for the week ending 28 July (the bill for which contains more discrepant sub-totals than any other surviving bill) the total for the Liberties was built up from the totals for the individual parishes and for the pesthouse.
(b) The figure of 38,786 burials in the City, Liberties, and out-parishes in 1603 was derived by scaling up the burials in the City and Liberties (up to 14 July) in the ratio 34,131/27,972, these being the recorded burials in these areas from 14 July to 22 December, and adding the total so obtained to the total burials in the City, Liberties, and out-parishes for the latter part of the year.
(c) The estimate of 12,342 expected christenings in the City, Liberties, out-parishes, and distant parishes in 1636 was derived by scaling up the estimate for the City, Liberties, and out-parishes in the same year in the ratio 24,362/20,461, these being the recorded christenings in these areas in the two years 1638 and 1639.
(d) The estimate of 3,526 expected christenings for 1582 involved estimating the number of christenings in seven weeks at the end of 1581 for which records are missing (see Appendix 1). The average of the recorded numbers in the preceding and following seven weeks was used.
(e) The estimate of 6,530 expected christenings in the City and Liberties in 1625 involved estimating the number of christenings in this area in the first 13 weeks of 1625. The recorded number in the City, Liberties, and out-parishes in this period was reduced in the ratio 6,368/8,299, these being the recorded christenings in the respective areas in 1624.
(f) The estimate of 12,420 expected christenings in the City, Liberties, out-parishes, and distant parishes in 1636 involved estimating the number of christenings in this area in the first 13 weeks of 1636. The recorded number in the City, Liberties, and out-parishes in this period was increased in the ratio 11,446/9,522, these being the recorded christenings in the respective areas in the whole of 1636.

MORTALITY IN DIFFERENT PARTS OF LONDON IN EACH PLAGUE YEAR

For some of the plague years, Table 3 gives recorded burials and expected christenings for a part as well as the 'whole' of London. This suggests the possibility of using these figures, specifically, to calculate mortality indices for the out-parishes in 1603 and 1625, separately from those for the City and Liberties, and for the distant parishes in 1636 and 1665, separately from those for the City, the Liberties, and the out-parishes. Such an analysis would be inherently unreliable, however, because the calculations for the out-parishes alone and for the distant parishes alone would be based upon a relatively small difference between two estimates of expected christenings of differing precision, some of which involved extrapolation, whereas the calculations for the rest of London would be based upon a single larger estimate of expected christenings.

A more reliable, and also more comprehensive, way of examining the same point is in terms of the proportionate mortality attributed to plague in the different groups of London parishes in each plague year. Although Graunt rightly pointed out that the proportion of deaths attributed to plague could be a misleading measure in attempting to compare one plague year with another, it is less likely to be misleading as a measure of the relative plague mortality in different parts of London during the same epidemic. The available information is presented in Table 4. The differences in proportionate mortality among the groups of parishes in each epidemic are not great, and it therefore seems that in a plague year all parts of London were nearly equally involved. However, there appears to be some tendency for the plague mortality to have been more severe in the City and Liberties than in the suburbs before 1603, and more severe in the suburbs than in the City and Liberties thereafter. The latter tendency is particularly noticeable in 1665.

It would be possible also to compare the proportionate mortality from plague in individual parishes in some of the plague years. This has not been done here partly because the totals would be smaller, and partly because the figures might reflect the opinions of the local searchers more closely than the true mortality from plague.

Table 4 The proportion of the recorded burials which was attributed to plague in the different groups of London parishes, during nine plague years from 1563 to 1665.

Year	City of London (within the Walls)			The Liberties (outside the Walls)			The out-parishes			The distant parishes		
	Recorded burials	Plague no.	%	Recorded burials	Plague no.	%	Recorded burials	Plague no.	%	Recorded burials	Plague no.	%
1563	—	—	—	20,372*	17,404	85	3,288	2,732	83	—	—	—
1578	—	—	—	7,830*	3,568	46	—	—	—	—	—	—
1582	—	—	—	6,930*	3,075	44	430	239	56	—	—	—
1593	8,598	5,390	63	9,295	5,285	57	—	—	—	7,993†	4,328	54
1603	(13,059)‡	(9,955)	76	(18,802)	(15,090)	80	(7,015)	(5,583)	80	—	—	—
1609	—	—	—	—	—	—	11,785**	4,240	36	—	—	—
1625	14,340	9,197	64	26,972	17,153	64	12,953	9,067	70	8,736	5,896	67
1636	4,025	1,200	30	12,880	5,956	46	6,454	3,244	50	4,056	1,702	42
1665	15,207	9,887	65	41,351	28,888	70	24,138	17,022	71	16,610	12,788	77

* In the City and the Liberties combined.

† Derived by subtracting the totals for the City and the Liberties from the totals 'in London in all' given in the parish register for St Peter upon Cornhill; judging by the size of the difference, these figures probably relate to the out-parishes and distant parishes combined.

‡ The figures in brackets have been derived directly from recorded totals, but contain an element of estimation. In 1603 the totals of burials and plague deaths for the City and Liberties combined are those recorded, derived as explained in note to Table 3. They have been divided between the City and the Liberties in the proportion 11,465 : 16,507 (for burials) and 9,484 : 14,375 (for plague deaths), these being the recorded totals in the respective areas from 14 July to 22 December. The totals of burials and plague deaths in the out-parishes were obtained by scaling up the recorded totals from July 14 to 22 December in the ratio 31,861/27,972 (for burials) and 25,045/23,859 (for plague deaths), these being the recorded totals in the City and Liberties for the whole and the latter part of the year respectively.

** In the City, the Liberties, and out-parishes combined.

THE MORTALITY IN DIFFERENT PLAGUE YEARS, AS JUDGED BY THE REDUCTIONS IN CHRISTEN-INGS AND IN BURIALS FROM OTHER CAUSES

Graunt directed attention to the reduction in the weekly numbers of christenings in the course of the plagues of 1603 and 1625 and attributed it in varying measure to 'flying, and death, as well as miscarriages and Abortions'. He observed, however, that 'the City hath been *Re-peopled* after a great *Plague* . . . by the second year'; the number of christenings was also much reduced during the year after the plague, but in the following year the christenings were back to their previous level. This suggests that the extent of the reduction in the christenings, below their expected level, might also provide a measure of the severity of the epidemic. Because this measure would be based upon the reduction in christenings and not upon the increase in burials, it would be independent of the relative mortality index.

Similarly, the reduction in the number of burials below their previous level, after the end of the epidemic, might also provide an alternative measure of its severity. Moreover, both approaches might lead to direct estimates of the proportion of the population that did not survive the epidemic.

Some experimental analyses on both these lines have been made on the available weekly figures, but so far without a great deal of success. The numbers of burials following the epidemic will have been affected by the proportion of the resident population which fled, by the proportion which returned, and how rapidly they did so, and by the rapidity with which new residents migrated into London. The numbers of christenings during and following the epidemic will have been affected by the same influences. In addition, the effect of the deaths of pregnant women during the epidemic on the level of christenings is not immediate, but is spread over the next nine months; this period extends into the early summer of the following year, when fear of a repetition of the epidemic appears sometimes to have led to a further exodus of the population. Christenings also seem to have been delayed, either until a family, which had fled from London, had returned, or perhaps until a parish priest, who had fled or died, had been replaced. Moreover, the proportion of the population which fled almost certainly varied in different plague years and was not necessarily closely related to the severity of the epidemic.

A further obstacle is the usual absence of a 'clean' end to the epidemic, and the lack of complete weekly information for the following year. It is particularly unfortunate that no information at all is available from the weekly bills for 1626, following a major plague which appears to have ended more abruptly and completely than any other on record.

For these various reasons, these two alternative approaches have not been considered further in the present report.

RELATIVE MORTALITY IN LONDON IN PLAGUE-FREE AND PLAGUE-ENDEMIC PERIODS FROM 1580 TO 1664

The trend lines for expected christenings, which provided indices of population size for the nine plague years in Table 3, may also be used to provide population indices for the periods between the major plagues.[15] Excluding only the year after each of the nine plague years, in view of the uncertain size and certain mobility of the population in those years, the relevant information is summarized in Table 5. Mortality indices for the various periods are calculated on the same basis as before and appear in the final column.

There was clearly some fluctuation in the 'normal' level of mortality in the periods between the major plague years, even in the absence of plague. Thus, in the plague-free periods 1597–1600, 1612–22, and 1627–9, the mortality indices were 0·95, 1·08, and 0·91 respectively. Moreover, in 1623–4, two plague-free years which have been listed separately in Table 5 because of the very large numbers of deaths recorded in those years, the index was 1·40. The whole period from 1612 to 1624, although plague-free, was marked by a number of other outbreaks of infectious disease. The bills contain no regular information on causes of death other than plague before 1629, but Wilson refers to the severe agues which raged throughout the country in the autumn of 1612 and the summer and autumn of 1616, to an epidemic of smallpox at the end of 1621, and to outbreaks of smallpox and 'a contagious, spotted or purple fever' in 1623, and of a 'spotted ague' in 1624.

When plague was endemic, the mortality indices were usually above unity. Thus, in the plague-endemic periods 1580–81, 1605–8, 1630–31, and 1638–48, the mortality indices were 1·05, 1·19, 1·03, and 1·10 respectively.

The general level of the mortality indices in the plague-free periods provides valuable confirmation of the 'normality' of the level of the

[15] The trend lines for christenings given in footnotes 11 and 12 cover the whole period apart from the plague-endemic years 1642 to 1648 inclusive, which include the Civil War (1642–46). It has been arbitrarily assumed that the population indices for the City, the Liberties and out-parishes during these troubled years followed the straight line joining the estimates for 1641 and 1649. This is shown as a dotted line on Figure 1.

Table 5 Estimated mortality in London in plague-endemic and plague-free periods from 1580 to 1664, relative to the mortality in the plague-free period 1632–5, using indices of population size derived from trends in recorded christenings in periods free of plague.

Area	Period or year*	Prevalence of plague	Number of years	Recorded burials (annual average)	Population index (annual average expected christenings from trend lines)	Relative mortality index†
City of London and the Liberties	1580–81	Endemic	2	(3,722)**	3,555	1·05
	1595	Free	1	3,507	4,309	0·82
	1597–1600	Free	4	4,234	4,492	0·95
	1605–08	Endemic	4	7,838	6,603	1·19
	1611	Endemic	1	7,343	7,054	1·05
	1612–22	Free	11	8,235	7,654	1·08
	1623–24	Free	2	11,661	8,305	1·40
City of London, the Liberties and out-parishes	1627–29	Free	3	8,076	8,904	0·91
	1630–31	Endemic	2	9,558	9,365	1·03
	1632–35	Free	4	9,870	9,909	1·00
	1638–48	Endemic	11	12,712	11,528	1·10
	1649–59	Free	11	12,138	12,089	1·00
City of London, the Liberties, out-parishes and distant parishes	1660–64	Free	5	17,019	17,218	0·99

* Omitting the nine plague years, which are shown in Table 3, and the year following each plague year.
† Taking the mortality in the City of London, the Liberties, and out-parishes in 1632–35 as 1·00.
** This figure has been derived directly from recorded totals, but contains an element of estimation. The total of 3,722 burials in 1580–81 involved estimating the number of burials in seven weeks at the end of 1581 for which records are missing (see Appendix 1). The total burials in the preceding and following three weeks, multiplied by 7/6, was used.

mortality in the period 1632–5 and justifies its adoption as a base-line for the mortality index during the whole period of study. More importantly, the general agreement between the pattern of the indices and the known prevalence of plague and of other diseases in different years, indicates that the assumption of a constant birth rate during the period of study was not unreasonable and, consequently, that the expected christenings represent a valid index of the size of London's population throughout the whole period from 1578–1665.

It follows that if the size of the population was known, or could be estimated reliably, at any point between 1578 and 1665, it would be possible to derive a series of estimates of London's population through this period of nearly ninety years.

THE POPULATION COUNT OF 1631

Graunt (1665) gives particulars of a count of the population of the City and the Liberties which was made by special command of the Privy Council in August, 1631. The recorded total of men, women, and children was 130,178. Graunt indicated that those parts of the group of sixteen parishes which lay outside the Liberties were excluded from this count, whereas, as stated above, the burials and christenings in those parts are included in the bills. According to him, 'The Liberties of the City of *London* consist of the 97 Parishes within the Walls, and of 2/3 of the 16 Parishes next without them, which estimate of mine, nevertheless, I leave to examination'. There is no means of checking the accuracy of the fraction 2/3, as applied to the population of the sixteen parishes, and it has been accepted as it stands (the exact value is not crucial).

This count has been used to estimate the population of the City, the Liberties, and out-parishes in the middle of the plague-free period 1632–5. The recorded total was scaled up to a population total for the larger area in August, 1631, in accordance with the figures for burials in different parts of London (and with the aid of the fraction 2/3). This total was then scaled up again, in accordance with the trend line for expected christenings for the larger area, to allow for the increase in population between August, 1631, and the mid-point of the period 1632–5.[16] The resultant population estimate was 234,000.

[16] During the years 1632–35, there were total burials of 10,761, 18,301 and 10,416 in the City, the Liberties, and the out-parishes respectively. The population figure of 130,178 was therefore scaled up in the ratio $(10,761 + 18,301 + 10,416)/(10,761 + 18,301 \times 2/3) = 39,478/22,962$, to give a population figure of 223,812 for the City, Liberties and out-parishes in August, 1631. This figure was then scaled up in the ratio 9,908·8/9,474·8, these being the expected annual numbers of christenings in this area, according to the fourth trend line given in footnote 12, for x = 33·5 and 31·125 respectively, to give an estimated population of 234,064 in the middle of the period 1632–5.

The recorded burials and christenings in 1632–5 were then expressed in terms of this population figure, giving estimates of the annual burial rate and the annual christening rate during this period which are each equal to 42·2 per 1,000 population.

It is likely, however, that 234,000 represents an under-estimate of the population of London at the end of 1633. First, there was probably a substantial under-enumeration in the count of 1631. Secondly, it is likely that in August, 1631, following the small outbreak of plague in the previous year, a proportion of London residents had removed temporarily to the country, for fear of a recurrence of the disease, and thereby also escaped enumeration. Moreover, it is probable that the deficiencies in the recorded population total were proportionately greater than the deficiencies in the recorded totals of burials and christenings as measures of the deaths and births. This would imply that the 'normal' burial rate and the christening rate in London were both less than 42 per 1,000 population.

The same conclusion may be reached from a more general consideration. In communities practising no limitation of births, live birth rates as high as 45 per 1,000 are exceptional, and a christening rate of 42 per 1,000 would imply a birth rate well in excess of 45 per 1,000, after making allowance for chrisoms and children not baptized.

Thus, although the population count of 1631 does not provide a reliable estimate of the size of the population of London at the time, it indicates maximum levels for the christening rate and for the 'normal' level of the burial rate.

TENTATIVE ESTIMATES OF THE SIZE OF LONDON'S POPULATION FROM 1565 TO 1665

An alternative method of obtaining a series of estimates of London's population during the period of study would be to start from a closer estimate of the christening rate than the maximum value given above. This figure could then be applied to the series of expected christenings to give population estimates at intervals during the whole period. An estimate of the burial rate at a particular time could be used similarly, and this approach is perhaps the most promising. If, for example, an estimate could be made of the proportion of the population of the City, the Liberties, and out-parishes that died in the plague of 1625, and divided by the mortality index for that year (6·42), this would give an estimate of the burial rate in 1632–35 (which was the same as the christening rate). The series of population estimates could then be derived from this estimate of the christening rate.

In the absence of a closer direct estimate of the christening rate, it is necessary to take an arbitrary figure which is rather less than the above value of 42 per 1,000. Those who have previously studied London's population during this period (Graunt, 1662; Creighton, 1891b; Wilson, 1927) have had to adopt the same approach. For the present report, three levels have been taken for the annual christening rate, namely, 30, 32·5, and 35 per 1,000 population. The corresponding annual birth rates will be higher than this because of chrisoms and unbaptized children. The advantage of using several values for the christening rate is that they indicate a likely *range* for the size of the population at different times; a single figure might suggest a spurious precision in the estimate.

Graunt makes an unsupported statement that 'in *London*, it seems manifest, that about one in 32 dies, over and above what dies of the *Plague*'. This represents a 'normal' burial rate of 31·2 per 1,000. He also found, 'by telling the number of Families in some Parishes within the walls, that 3 out of 11 families *per an.* have died'. With his allowance of 8 persons per family, this implies a burial rate of 3 in 88, which is 34·1 per 1,000. Both these figures are within the above range for the christening rate.

Table 6 shows, at five-year intervals from 1565 to 1665, the population indices for London, taken from the regression lines shown in Figure 1, together with the population sizes, in thousands, corresponding to the above three levels of christening rate. The population figures in this table for the plague years 1625 and 1665 represent estimates of the size of the population before the start of the epidemic.

DISCUSSION

This examination of the vital statistics for London, as shown in the bills of mortality up to 1665, is, to put it mildly, long overdue. The analysis follows classical demographic lines for a situation where there is no information on the size of the population, and, because of the nature of the basic data, which refer to events and not to individuals, the newer methods of demographic inquiry, illustrated in other contributions to this volume, cannot be applied.

The analysis is based upon one source of information only—the bills of mortality—and an attempt has been made to use these data comprehensively. But much of the original information has not survived to the present day, and even though all three known copies of the original annual bill for 1603, and nearly all the known weekly bills for 1603 and 1604, only came to light within the last decade, one cannot expect major additions in the future. However, the close

Table 6   Indices of population size for various areas in London at five-year intervals from 1565 to 1665, with population estimates derived from them for three levels of christening-rate.

Area	Year	Population index (expected christenings)	Estimated population (in thousands) if christenings per 1,000 population equalled		
			30	32·5	35
	1565	2,750	92	85	79
	1570	3,009	100	93	86
	1575	3,269	109	101	93
	1580	3,529	118	109	101
	1585	3,789	126	117	108
City of London	1590	4,049	135	125	116
and the	1595	4,309	144	133	123
Liberties	1600	4,569	152	141	131
	1605	5,026	168	155	144
	1610	5,441	181	167	155
	1615	5,857	195	180	167
	1620	6,272	209	193	179
	1625	6,687	223	206	191
	1605	6,453	215	199	184
	1610	6,953	232	214	199
	1615	7,454	248	229	213
	1620	7,955	265	245	227
	1625	8,455	282	260	242
City of London,	1630	9,269	309	285	265
the Liberties	1635	10,183	340	313	291
and out-parishes	1640	11,097	370	341	317
	1645	11,802	393	363	337
	1650	10,170	339	313	291
	1655	13,003	433	400	372
	1660	13,961	465	430	399
	1665	14,920	497	459	426
City of London,	1650	12,040	401	370	344
the Liberties,	1655	15,616	521	480	446
out-parishes and	1660	16,730	558	515	478
distant parishes	1665	17,904	597	551	512

similarity between the totals in the bills of mortality and those derived from parish registers indicates a valuable means of supplementing the surviving data from the bills of mortality. Data from parish registers might help to bridge some of the gaps in the series of annual totals before 1603 and give more information on the fluctuations in the weekly totals in relation to the prevalence of plague (Sutherland, 1970). But family reconstitution studies on the London parish registers do not appear to be a practical proposition.

It seems likely that during the period under review all the burials came to the notice of the parish authorities, and that deficiencies, perhaps of the order of 10 per cent, will have occurred by omissions either from parish registers or from the bills of mortality, as Wilson has pointed out. The deficiencies in christenings before the Civil War will certainly have been greater than those in burials, for reasons already stated; the later gross deficiencies do not affect the analysis because the recorded figures have not been used.

The mortality indices presented in this study are based essentially upon ratios of burials to a smoothed value of christenings. Moderate deficiencies in the recorded totals, even if the deficiency is greater for christenings than burials, will not have affected these indices if these deficiencies bore a similar relation to one another throughout the period of study. Indeed, the mortality indices themselves provide indirect evidence that this was so. In plague-free periods the indices were similar, lying close to unity, both early and late during the period; in plague-endemic periods the indices took larger values, again both early and late during the period. These findings also confirm that the assumption of a constant birth rate throughout the period was probably not too far from the truth. However, the explanation of the relatively high mortality index in the plague-free period 1612–22, for example, could be that there was a limitation of births during these years and not an increase in burials.

It is impossible to tell whether a larger proportion of burials was omitted from the records during plague years than in other years. The way in which the returns were compiled—namely, from sub-totals of burials each week in each parish—will have provided some safeguard against gross deficiencies, even at the height of the epidemic. Moreover, public interest and official concern may even have encouraged more complete records during plague years than in less dramatic circumstances. If, however, the deficiencies in burials were greater during plague years than at other times, the mortality indices calculated above will under-estimate the mortality during those years.

The picture presented by the mortality indices, both in plague years and in the intervening periods, may therefore be accepted as a reasonable approximation to relative mortality levels in London during the century before the plague of 1665. No categoric answer, however, can be given to the question posed in the title. In the four most severe plagues of the century, in 1563, 1603, 1625, and in 1665, the mortality rose to at least five times its normal level; although the mortality appears to have been greater in 1603 and 1625 than in 1665, and perhaps higher still in 1563, the many uncertainties make it unwise to single out any one of these plagues as clearly greater than the others. If the 'normal' burial rate was at the intermediate level of 32·5 per 1,000 adopted in Table 6, then between one sixth and one quarter of the population of London died in each of these plague years. The mortality would presumably have been greater still if a proportion of the population had not managed to escape infection by fleeing from London. It is of interest to note that J. C. Russell, from analyses of inquests upon property, estimated the general mortality in country districts during the first four epidemics of plague in England—namely, in 1348–50, 1360–61, 1369, and 1375, to have been 23·6 per cent, 18·7 per cent, 13·0 per cent, and 11·6 per cent respectively. These figures are of the same order of magnitude as those for London in the sixteenth and seventeenth centuries.

The severity of many of the outbreaks of plague before 1665 is common knowledge among historians. Trevelyan provides an excellent summary:

> The famous 'plague of London' was merely the last, and not perhaps the worst, of a series of outbreaks covering three centuries. Between the campaigns of Crecy and Poitiers, the Black Death had first swept over Europe from some unknown source in the Far East, with the ubiquity and violence usual to the incoming of a new disease. The obscurest hamlet had little chance of escape. It is thought probable that a third, and possibly that one half of the fellow countrymen of Boccaccio, of Froissart and of Chaucer, perished within three years. The Black Death remained in the soil of England, and became known as 'The Plague'. It never again swept the whole country at one time, but it perpetually broke out in different localities, particularly in the towns and the ports and the river-sides, where the ship-borne, flea-bearing rat multiplied. In London under the Lancastrian and Tudor Kings the plague was for long periods together endemic and nearly continual; under the Stuarts it came in rare but violent outbursts. The rejoicing in London for the accession of James I had been cut short by an outbreak of the Plague that carried off 30,000 persons; the accession of Charles I was the signal for another, no less destructive. In 1636, a slighter attack occurred. Then followed thirty years of comparative immunity for London, during which other events took place calculated to make men forget in their talk the plague horrors that their fathers and grandfathers had endured. So when the last outbreak came in 1665, although it did not destroy a much larger proportion of the Londoners than some of its predecessors had done, it struck the imagination more, for it came in an age of greater civilization, comfort and security, when such calamities were less remembered and less expected, and it was followed close, as though at the Divine command, by another catastrophe to which there was no parallel in the most ancient records of London.

The present study has done little more than add a modicum of arithmetical precision, and some change of emphasis, to this admirable statement.

It remains to explain why, to most of us, 1665 is so emphatically the year of 'The Great Plague'. Trevelyan gives part of the explanation. Defoe's dramatic publicity for 1665 in *A Journal of the Plague Year* provides another. But the main reason is perhaps simply that it was the last major visitation of plague in these islands. It is not generally realized that there has always been a natural tendency to refer to the most recent large plague as the 'great plague'. Thus, the anonymous compiler of the annual totals of burials and christenings in 1582 lists 'the number that died in the time of the great Plague', referring to 1563. And 'The Printer to the Reader' of *London's Dreadful Visitation* (1665) states that 'In the year 1625, the stroke of the Lord's hand was heavy upon this City and Suburbs, which year was ever since called The Great Plague.' Thus, from 1348 until 1665 there was a succession of great plagues in London; for each man The Great Plague was the one that he had lived through, or his parents had lived through. Perhaps, after all, the question in the title should only be answered at this individual level, and not in statistical terms.

ACKNOWLEDGMENTS

The author wishes to record his thanks to the librarians of the Guildhall Library, the Bodleian Library, the British Museum, the Harvard College Library, and the Henry E. Huntington Library for access to so much scarce basic material and for their assistance in various ways. He is particularly grateful to Miss K. F. Pantzer of the Houghton Library, who provided him with detailed up-to-date information on extant bills of mortality, and to Mr. D. G. Neill of the Bodleian Library. Figure 1 was drawn by Mr. V. K. Asta, Department of Medical Illustration, University College Hospital Medical School, London.

APPENDIX

I ORIGINAL SOURCES

The sources of the surviving annual and weekly information on burials (B), plague deaths (P) and christenings (C) in the London bills of mortality up to 1665 are listed below. Where there is a choice of sources, original bills have been used in preference to abstracts from them, and earlier abstracts in preference to later ones. Small discrepancies between figures from alternative sources have been treated in accordance with the above rule; large discrepancies are mentioned below. Sources marked with an asterisk are additional to those referred to by Wilson (1927, with some additions in the preface to the reprint of 1963). The principal collections of original

LP

bills and other source material are at the Guildhall Library, London (GL), the Bodleian Library, Oxford (O), the British Museum, London (BM), and the Houghton Library, Harvard University. The location of the documents consulted is given; those in America were consulted in photocopies. A dagger indicates an original document consulted only in transcription.

An annotated abstract of the annual totals of burials, plague deaths and christenings in the City, the Liberties, the out-parishes, and the distant parishes, as recorded in these sources, has been deposited for reference with each of the above libraries. Copies of this abstract may also be obtained from the author.

Annual totals

1563   Stow (1565)* Fol. 244: B and P only.

1578–81   Salisbury MS† (Hatfield House), transcribed by Creighton (1891a), *1*, 341, with some inconsistencies between the weekly and annual totals. The totals of the transcribed weekly figures have been used here. The totals for 1581 require adjustment for 7 missing weeks. See footnotes to Tables 3 and 5.

1582   Anon. (1582) (GL): This is an unofficial printed 'annual bill'. Salisbury MS† (Hatfield House) also covers 1582 but is not quite complete.

1592   Weekly Bills (1603b): P 'in and about London' given as '2000'.
            Graunt (1662), p. 34: C, apparently (from its similarity to the total for 1593) for the City and Liberties. His totals for B and P (pp. 33–4), however, refer to the larger area 'in and about London' in 1593 (q.v.).

1593   (a) In the City and Liberties.
            Parish Register, St. Peter upon Cornhill (1593)* (GL) (Harleian Society transcripts, *1*, 143): B and P only.
            Stow (1598)*, p. 438: same figures for B and P.
            Graunt (1662), p. 33: C, with slightly different B and P from Stow.
            (b) 'In London in all' (see footnotes to Table 4).
            Parish Register, St. Peter upon Cornhill (1593)* (GL) (Harleian Society transcripts, *1*, 143): B and P only.
            Weekly Bills (1603b): same figures, for B and P, 'in and about London'.
            Broadside (1636b): C, with the same B as the last, but P = 11,503 instead of the more plausible earlier figure of 15,003.
            Broadside (1637) gives the same B, P and C, and

Graunt (1662, p. 33) the same B and P, as Broadside (1636b) but both attribute them incorrectly to 1592.

1594–5   Graunt (1662), p. 53. B and P only. In the context 1593 is an evident misprint for 1594.

1597–1600 Ashmole MS (O), transcribed by Hull (1899), *1*, 433.

1603   Annual bill (BM; Houghton Library, Harvard University; H. E. Huntington Library, California). This annual bill, printed by John Windet, was later reprinted by William Stansby in two different versions, one not dated but presumably after Stansby was licensed to print the bills in September, 1611 (GL), and one in 1625 (O). The Houghton Library copy is reproduced by Wilson (1963) and the Bodleian Library copy of the 1625 version by Wilson (1927). The totals given cannot be used as they stand, because they cover the City and Liberties until 14 July, and (with inconsistencies) the City, Liberties and out-parishes thereafter. See footnotes to Table 3.

1604–5   Graunt (1662), p. 75. Bell (1665) agrees for 1604.

1606   Annual bill† (whereabouts unknown), transcribed by Walford (1878)*, with errors which can be corrected by reference to Graunt (1662). Bell (1665) agrees.

1607–9   Graunt (1662), p. 75. Bell (1665) agrees.

1610   Bell (1665). Graunt (1662) gives the same P and C, but a different B. Bell has been preferred because his total B checks with the total of his weekly figures.

1611–19   Graunt (1662), p. 75.

1620   'Annual bill'* (H. E. Huntington Library, California). This document consists of a printed form for a weekly bill, dated 1621, on part of which totals of B, P, and C for the period 23 December 1619 to 17 December 1620 have been entered in manuscript. (The rest of the brief has been used for a manuscript index to the copy of Stow (1618) into which it was pasted, presumably in 1621 or soon after.) The figures for the City, Liberties and out-parishes (B=8,415, P=10, C=8,314) are substantially different from those given by Graunt (1662) (B=9,712, P=21, C=7,845), but are to be preferred, although the document is not an official annual bill, because it represents an earlier abstract; it also contains other totals (notably C in the City and Liberties) not given by Graunt.

1621–3   Graunt (1662), p. 75. In his main table Graunt gives B – P for the City, the Liberties and the out-parishes separately and together, with a single total of P and C for the whole area. The first three of these figures sometimes do not tally with the fourth, either as a result of mistakes in subtraction or misprints. For 1622 the total B derived from the three areas separately (9,436) has been preferred to the alternative total (8,959) because none of the separate figures looks 'wrong' in relation to those in the preceding or succeeding year.

1624 Graunt (1662), p.5*. This is a transcript of the annual bill.

1625 (a) In the City, Liberties, and out-parishes. Annual bill. There are two printed versions of this bill, one (1625a) including weekly totals of B, P, and C, and printed on the same sheet as the 1625 reprint of the 1603 bill (O), the other (1625b) without any weekly figures (GL). The Guildhall Library copy of 1625b is reproduced by Wilson (1927; 1963).
(b) For six of the distant parishes. A separate printed bill (1625c) (GL; O) contains totals of B and P only for the parishes of Westminster, Islington, Lambeth, Stepney, Newington, and Hackney.

1626–8 Graunt (1662), p. 75.

1629–36 Annual bills (GL).

1637–40 Graunt (1662), p. 76. Bell (1665) agrees for 1637 and for 1640.

1641 Annual bill (GL). Graunt (1662) gives substantially different figures from these, whereas Bell (1665) almost agrees with the annual bill.

1642 Bell (1665). Graunt (1662) gives substantially different figures from these, but Peacham (1669)* almost agrees with Bell on B and P.

1643–5 Graunt (1662), p. 76. Bell (1665) agrees, for all three years, with one minor discrepancy.

1646 Bell (1665). Graunt (1662) gives substantially different figures from these, but Peacham (1669)* agrees with Bell on B and P.

1647–8 Graunt (1662), p. 76. Bell (1665) agrees for 1647.

1649–56 Annual bills (* for 1649–51 and 1654–6) (GL).

1657 Annual bill* (O).

1658–65 Annual bills (BM; GL, except for 1662).
A copy of the annual bill for 1665 is reproduced by Sutherland (1963).

Weekly totals

This list includes all those weekly series which are complete or nearly complete for a large part of a year. For other sporadic and isolated weekly information see Wilson (1927).

1563–66   Stow MS† (Lambeth Palace Library), transcribed by
           Gairdner (1880). P only, for the City and the Liberties,
           from 5 June 1563 to 26 July 1566. Hamerton (1563)†
           gives B, P, and C in 'London and the suburbs' in the
           week ending 30 July 1563, P being rather higher (320)
           than Stow's figure (289).
1569   Stow (1570)*: B and P for 'the Citie and oute paryshes'
           for the week ending 28 October.
1574   Stow (1575)*, p. 564: B and P, presumably for the City
           and Liberties for the week ending 28 October. Holinshed
           (1577) ii, 1870 quotes the same figures.
1578–82   Salisbury MS† (Hatfield House), transcribed by Creigh-
           ton (1891a), *1*, 341. Information for the seven weeks from
           9 November–28 December 1581 and for the week ending
           20 December 1582 (C also for the previous week) is
           missing. The series continues until 31 January 1583.
1593   Broadside (1636b). B and P only, from 10 March to
           22 December. Broadside (1637) gives the same weekly
           figures, but attributes them to 1592.
1597–1600 Ashmole MS (O), transcribed, with a few minor errors,
           by Hull (1899), *1*, 433.
1603   (a) In the City and Liberties, up to 14 July: Annual
           bill (1603). Also on the two reprints of this bill, with
           C = 69 for week ending (? beginning) 23 December
           1602 instead of 96.
           (b) In the City, Liberties and out-parishes, from 14
           July to 22 December:
           Weekly bills (Houghton Library, Harvard University;
           BM, lacking weeks ending 11 August, 22 September and
           27 October; Photocopies of complete series at GL, O
           and BM). Figures for these weeks also appear on the
           annual bills, with C = 138 for week ending 28 July,
           instead of 158. There are two versions of the printed
           weekly bills from 14 July. One version (1603a) contains
           figures only for the current week, and this was apparently
           replaced in September by the other version (1603b),
           which also includes totals of B and P only, for earlier
           weeks in 1603. For the two weeks 22 September–
           6 October both versions of the bill are known (1603a:
           Houghton Library, Harvard University; 1603b: BM,
           for the first week only in a fragment). In addition a
           printed bill (1603c) gives summary totals for the eight-
           week period from 14 July to 8 September (Houghton
           Library, Harvard University; photocopy at GL, O, BM).

Broadside (1636a) (GL), quotes the weekly totals from 10 March to 2 December 1603. Broadsides (1636b—GL, O; 1636c—GL, BM; 1637—O, BM) quote B and P only for the same period.

1604   29 December 1603 to 12 April, and 24 May to 21 June 1604:
Weekly bills (Houghton Library, Harvard University, lacking week ending 19 January; BM, five weeks only, 29 December 1603 to 19 January, and 2 to 16 February 1604; photocopies of complete series at GL, O, BM). These printed weekly bills are similar in style to the series (1603a), and contain figures only for the current week.

1606–10   Bell (1665).

1625   Annual bill (1625a) (O). Weekly bills are known only for the weeks ending 21 July (O), 11 August (BM), 27 October (O) and 15 December (O), and their totals of B, P, and C tally with those on the annual bill (1625a). Bell (1665) gives slightly different totals in some instances. Broadsides (1636a; 1636b; 1636c; 1637) quote weekly totals of B and P (and 1636a includes C) from 10 March to 22 December 1625.

1630   Bell (1665).

1636   (a) In the City, Liberties and out-parishes. Bell (1665). Broadsides (1636a; 1636b; 1636c; 1637) quote weekly totals of B and P (and 1636a includes C) from 10 March, but only Broadsides (1637) and one copy of (1636a) are complete to the end of the year (the latter in manuscript —see below).
Printed weekly bills are extant for 20 of the 26 weeks between 28 April and 27 October 1636 (O).
(b) In the seven distant parishes. Broadside (1636a). One of the two copies in the Guildhall Library (Gr. 5. 2. 3(21)) quotes weekly totals of B and P for the seven distant parishes separately from 14 April to 22 December 1636; these are printed up to 23 June and in manuscript thereafter. The incomplete series of printed weekly bills referred to above also contains figures for the distant parishes.

1637   Bell (1665). One copy of Broadside (1637) (O) quotes weekly totals of B and P up to 11 May 1637.

1640–47   Bell (1665).

1660   Weekly bills (O). The bill for the week ending 11 December 1660 is missing.

1664   Weekly bills (GL).
1665   Weekly bills (GL, BM). The complete series of weekly
            bills for 1665 was also issued with a title page and
            preface as London's Dreadful Visitation (Anon. 1665).
1666   Weekly bills (BM). After the week ending 28 August
            1666 the returns were disrupted by the Fire.

2 BIBLIOGRAPHY

Anon. (1582), 'The number of all those that hath dyed in . . .
    London . . . 1582' (London).
Anon. (1665), *London's Dreadful Visitation* (London).
Bell, J. (1665), *London's Remembrancer* (London).
Broadside (1636a), 'Lord have mercy upon us. Preservatives and
    Medicines' (London).
Broadside (1636b), 'Lord have mercy upon us. This is the humble
    petition of England' (London).
Broadside (1636c), 'Lord have mercy upon us. A speciall remedy
    for the plague' (London).
Broadside (1637), 'London's Lord have mercy upon us' (London).
Creighton, C. (1891a; reprinted 1965), *A History of Epidemics in
    Britain* (Cambridge University Press).
Creighton, C. (1891b), 'The Population of Old London' *Blackwoods
    Magazine*, April 1891 (Edinburgh).
Defoe, D. (1722) (Ed.), *A Journal of the Plague Year* (London).
Gairdner, J. (Ed.) (1880) 'Three fifteenth-century Chronicles,
    with historical memoranda by J. Stowe', Camden Society, NS
    28 (London).
Glass, D. V. (1963), 'John Graunt and his Natural and Political
    Observations', *Proc. Roy. Soc.* B, *159*, 1–32.
Graunt, J. (1662), *Natural and Political Observations mentioned in a
    following index, and made upon the Bills of Mortality* (London).
Graunt, J. (1665), *Natural and Political Observations . . . upon the Bills
    of Mortality*, 3rd edition (London).
Hamerton, W. (1563), MS. enclosure with a letter of 3 August to
    the Earl of Shrewsbury (Hatfield House). Transcribed in Hist.
    MSS. Commission (1877), Report *6*, 455a.
Holinshed, R. (1577), *The Chronicles of England, Scotlande, and Irelande*
    (London).
Hull, C. H. (Ed.) (1899; reprinted 1963), *The Economic Writings of
    Sir William Petty together with the Observations on the bills of mortality
    more probably by Captain John Graunt* (including a reprint of the
    fifth edition of the *Observations*, 1676) (Cambridge University
    Press).

Ogle, W. (1892), 'An Inquiry into the Trustworthiness of the Old Bills of Mortality', *Jl. Roy. statist. Soc.*, *55*, 437.

Peacham, H. (1669), *The Worth of a Penny*, with a catalogue of the bills of mortality from 1642 to 1669 (London).

Russell, J. C. (1948), *British Medieval Population* (Albuquerque).

Stow, J. (1565), *A Summarie of Englyshe Chronicles* (London).

Stow, J. (1570), *A Summarie of Englyshe Chronicles* (London).

Stow, J. (1575), *A Summarie of Englyshe Chronicles* (London).

Stow, J. (1598), *A Summarie of the Chronicles of England* (London).

Stow, J. (1618), *The Survay of London* (London).

Sutherland, Ian (1963), 'John Graunt: A Tercentenary Tribute', *Jl. Roy. statist. Soc. A*, *126*, 537–56.

Sutherland, Ian (1970), 'Parish Registers and the London Bills of Mortality', *Jl. Soc. Archivists*, *4*, 65.

Trevelyan, G. M. (1943), *English Social History* (London).

Walford, C. (1878), 'Early Bills of Mortality', *Trans. Roy. hist. Soc.*, *7*, 212.

Willcox, W. F. (Ed.) (1939), *Natural and Political Observations made upon the bills of mortality by John Graunt.* (A reprint of the first edition of the *Observations*, 1662.) Baltimore: Johns Hopkins Press.

Wilson, F. P. (1927, is reprinted with slight changes 1963), *The Plague in Shakespeare's London* (Oxford University Press).

Pierre Goubert

Legitimate fertility and infant mortality in France during the eighteenth century: a comparison

This article proposes to study the birth and child death rates in France during the eighteenth century in order to discover whether they were uniform throughout. Since 1962, research has been conducted on Brittany, a populous province which had more than two million inhabitants by 1700. Brittany is a unique province, with its own language (Celtic in the western half), a long history of independence (until the sixteenth century), special legislation (the common law of Brittany until the Revolution), a semi-autonomous spirit, a powerful nobility and gentry, and a curious economy which was both agrarian and maritime. The historian, and the demographic historian in particular, will be interested in the province's high fertility and Catholic fervour, supported and commanded by the numerous priests, who were popular as well as imperious. The clergy, strongly controlled by the episcopal administration, exercised the greatest strictness and seriousness in drawing up the parochial registers after the sixteenth century. Fortunate circumstances, like Brittany's remoteness from war zones, have insured the excellent preservation of these basic documents. The registers of baptisms, marriages, and burials are entirely preserved in numerous localities from 1600 until 1792, and sometimes even from a date prior to 1500. Moreover, the influence of Protestanism was weak, limited, and well defined in Brittany; thus, for almost every period, the Catholic parochial registers concern the total population. Since the seventeenth century at least, the deaths of children of low age were also registered, which was not the case in all of France, especially the south.

With the numerous and excellent sources, the method of family reconstitution can be applied, according to the principles established by Michel Fleury and Louis Henry.[1] This method consists of reconstituting the complete demographic history of a married couple from the birth of either of the two spouses until the dissolution

---

[1] Michel Fleury and Louis Henry, *Nouveau manuel de dépouillement et d'exploitation de l'etat civil ancien* (Paris, 1965).

of the household; it includes the birth and death of their children. If the parochial registers are complete, and if the family remained in one location, the results obtained by this method are accurate and will satisfy most of the demographer's curiosity.

I have encouraged three students at Rennes to study localities in the interior of the Haute-Bretagne (upper Brittany), according to the method of Henry. Jacqueline Caro worked on La Guerche for the period 1733 to 1792 (which represents approximately four thousand inhabitants); Jean Besnard, on Saint-Méen Le Grand for the period 1720 to 1792 (approximately 1,800 inhabitants); and Michel Renouard, on Saint-Aubin d'Aubigné for the period 1740 to 1789 (approximately 1,000 inhabitants). These three large parishes, which now belong to the *département* of Ille-et-Vilaine, are within thirty or forty kilometres of Rennes—the first to the south, the second to the west, and the third to the north of the city. Caro, Besnard, and Renouard have drawn up more than 30,000 individual case histories and have succeeded in reconstituting more than 14,000 peasant families of the eighteenth century.

The first characteristic of fertility in Brittany is not surprising to the historical demographer who is familiar with old France: Nearly 99 per cent of the births are legitimate. Of 14,947 registered baptisms, only 201 concern illegitimate children. This rate illustrates the pressures exerted by both Catholicism and society and is not exceptional for the heart of the provinces, where the situation of the unmarried mother was exceptional and difficult. The rates of illegitimacy were much higher in the cities and the ports. Never, however, do they reach the high figures one finds in England during the seventeenth and eighteenth centuries. In this period, virtue is French, even in the lower classes.

The second characteristic is more surprising: Women start to have children very late, seldom before their twenty-sixth or twenty-seventh year. In other words, the age at marriage is high. In the whole century and in all three localities, the average age at first marriage for women is always higher than twenty-five years; at Saint-Aubin d'Aubigné, it is twenty-seven years. Men are usually two to four years older than their spouses. This phenomenon, rather common in the old peasant France, has never been fully explained. It might be related to the age at which a person reached his majority—twenty-five years in most of the provinces, although there is no general rule for the entire country. Young men or women did not fully enjoy their civil rights until they reached age twenty-five, when they could inherit property, acquire goods, and appear in court, and paternal power remained strong for a long time. In Brittany, a marriage could not take place without paternal authorization; even after age twenty-five, one had to ask for it, if only out of politeness. Before age twenty-five, young people could only exist within the security of the family.

Women started to have children late, and they also stopped early. The cause of this cessation was physiological. At the time of their last delivery, women were usually between forty-one and forty-three years of age. After age forty, fertility is weak; after forty-five, it is practically non-existent.

What is the rhythm of births during this rather short period between a woman's twenty-sixth and forty-second year?

About 6 per cent of married couples are sterile for reasons that are unknown, but can be assumed to be physiological. In rural France during the eighteenth century, about half of the young women gave birth for the first time less than a year after their marriage; about 75 to 80 per cent, within less than eighteen months.

The study of other intervals gives the following results:

Interval (between births)	La Guerche	St.-Aubin	St.-Méen	St.-Méen, women with a 'rapid rhythm' (the third part)
1–2	18·6 months	18·2 months	20·2 months	15·3 months
2–3	19·5	19·9	21·6	15·1
3–4	21·2	21·4	22·6	17·1
4–5	21·0	25·0	25·0	19·4
Before the last:	27·5	26·5	25·8	19·8

These intervals are by far the shortest of those that have been observed in eighteenth-century France.

Using a technical method to correlate observations based on 1,047 families, we can show the legitimate fertility by age groups. No other part of France shows so high a rate as Brittany. In the eighteenth century, only the results from Canada and Sainghin-en-Mélantois, a village in the north of France, are comparable, although they do not reach the same levels.[2] By isolating that third

Women aged	20–24	25–29	30–34	35–39
St.-Aubin	0·582	0·520	0·489	0·358
La Guerche	0·507	0·487	0·458	0·270
St.-Méen	0·582	0·548	0·476	0·385

[2] Jacques Henripin, *La population canadienne au début du XVIIIe siècle* (Travaux et documents, I.N.E.D., No. 22; Paris, 1954). Raymond Deniel and Louis Henry, 'La population d'un village du Nord de la France. Sainghin-en Mélentois, de 1665 à 1851', *Population* (1965), pp. 564–602.

of the women at Saint-Méen le Grand whose childbearing was most rapid—those aged twenty to thirty-four—one arrives at a rate between 0·775 and 0·669, or three to four children in five years.

The fertility of these women does not diminish in the course of the eighteenth century. When one isolates those women at Saint-Méen le Grand who married between 1720 and 1755 from those who married between 1756 and 1792, one discovers with surprise that the latter are the most fertile (at twenty to twenty-four years, 0·632, as against 0·560; at thirty to thirty-four years, 0·502 as against 0·464).

Other methodologies exist by which one can present this fertility, which is both exceptional for France and rising. One can, for example, multiply by 5 the sum of the fecundity rate for women twenty to forty-nine years of age, as Henry did for Sainghin-en-Mélantois.[3] One obtains 11·1 for Saint-Méen for the first half of the eighteenth century and 12 for the second half. Not a single calculation given by Louis Henry exceeds 10·8. These figures sensitively express the average number of children per family for women who married at age twenty and lived in the marriage state until age fifty.

The following are the real numbers of children in those families that were studied at Saint-Méen: 52 per cent of the families had less than five children; 36 per cent had between five and nine children; and 12 per cent had ten to twenty-one children.

If one reverses the methodology, taking the children as the starting point, one obtains the following results: 21 per cent of the children born at Saint-Méen came from families with less than five children; 50 per cent from families that had five to nine children; and 29 per cent from families with ten or more children.

The legitimate fertility in the three Breton villages is exceptionally high and does not diminish, but, on the contrary, rises during the second half of the century. There does not seem to have been the slightest trace of birth control in that province. These three Breton villages do not, however, exemplify all of eighteenth-century France; a comparison is necessary for the wider picture.

For this comparison, I shall take two examples, most unlike those in Brittany, from the south-west of France—the one is from a study by Pierre Valmary, published by the I.N.E.D. (Institut National d'Etudes Démographiques) on Thézels and Saint-Sernin in Bas Quercy[4] and the other is from a thesis, published in 1969 in

[3] Louis Henry, 'La Nuptialité à la fin de l'Ancien Régime', *Population* (July–September 1953), p. 593.
[4] Pierre Valmary, *Familles paysannes en Bas-Quercy* (Travaux et documents, I.N.E.D., No. 45; Paris, 1965).

Paris by Anne Zink, on Azereix near Tarbes at the foot of the Pyrenees. I shall also use the famous monograph by E. Gautier and Louis Henry on Crulai, a Norman village.[5] To simplify the account, I shall use only the intervals between births (the number of births within five years of marriage) and births classified according to the age of the women, both of which are likely to be good indicators of marital fertility.

In terms of months, the following are the intervals between births:

	Thézels	Azereix	La Guerche (Brittany)
Interval 1–2	25 months	29 months	19 months
Interval 2–3	30	31	20
Interval 3–4	32	33	21
Interval 4–5	32	32	21
Before the last	31	37	28

In Brittany, the intervals between successive births are close to twenty months; in the south-west, they are close to thirty months. Such a marked difference cannot be the result of chance.

The number of births (given in five-year intervals), when correlated to the age of the women, yields observations of the same kind:

Age of women	20–24 years	25–29 years	30–34 years	35–39 years
St.-Méen, 1756–92	3·16	2·95	2·51	2·00
Crulai, 1674–1742	2·33	2·19	1·68	1·49
Thézels, 18th century	1·89	1·82	1·51	1·13

The contrast between the parish in Brittany (St.-Méen) and the parish in Quercy (Thezels) is obvious. The rates for Crulai (Normandy) are intermediate, but still closer to the distant Quercy than to the bordering Brittany.

This comparison underlines the great differences between the exceptional fertility of the Breton women and the rather weak fecundity of women in the south-west. Other monographs are necessary, but if the given examples prove to be truly representative, one must ask what caused such a wide disparity.

Two hypotheses, and two only, seem to me to be possible. We are either confronted with two types of women, with two types of couples, whose biological characters differ profoundly, or with two types of behaviour, two types of society or civilization. In

[5] Etienne Gautier and Louis Henry, *La Population de Crulai, paroisse normande* (Travaux et documents, I.N.E.D., No. 33; Paris, 1958).

Brittany, couples accept all the children 'that God sends them'; in the south-west, they do not. In Brittany, the Catholic priests exercised strict control on private life, especially through confession; in the south-west, this control was weak. In Brittany, birth control was probably not practised until the end of the eighteenth century; in the south-west, a sporadic and intermittent limitation (*coitus interruptus?*) was practised in order to delay the succession of births.

It is usually held that rural districts in France passed from a state of uncontrolled births to one of controlled births during the eighteenth century. Thus far, this affirmation has been proved for only four villages, and one little town, Meulan, all of which are north of Paris—Sainghin and the three villages in the Ile-de-France studied by M. Ganiage.[6] Results for Brittany and the south-west do not confirm such a rapid transition. In these provinces, there seems to have been no change in birth-control practices from one end of the eighteenth century to the other. In Saint-Méen le Grand, fertility increased, rather than decreased.

In a France that was divided by differences in language and law, the diversity and regional contrast prevailed, maintained in part by a poor transportation system. The real eighteenth century, as far as rural and provincial populations are concerned, remains to be discovered. We must descend from gossipy generalities to humble realities.

Does the study of infant mortality in Brittany and the south-west confirm these observations? (It is difficult to know the mortality of adults because of their mobility.)

The ecclesiastics that kept the parochial registers in Brittany were particularly attentive in inscribing the deaths of very young children, even those that died immediately after birth and the stillborn. The reasons for this attention were based in religious conviction. In contrast, the ecclesiastics of the south were much less careful. Frequently they did not even inscribe in their registers the deaths of children under ten years of age. Since these children had not taken communion, they were considered to be 'incomplete' Christians. Moreover, the south was much less devout than the north. M. Valmary himself could not use the parochial registers of Thézels and Saint-Sernin before 1746 in his study of infant mortality there.

The Breton figures, therefore, are much more reliable than the figures of the south-west; the Breton rates are certain and have

---

[6] Jean Ganiage, *Trots villages d'Ile-de-France au XVIIIe siècle* (Travaux et documents, I.N.E.D., No. 40) Paris, 1963). Marcel Lachiver, *La Population de Meulan du XVIIe an XIXe siècle*, Paris, S.E.V.P.E.N., 1969.

been calculated from five to ten times as many cases as the others that have been published for France thus far.

The following are the results for Brittany's infant mortality (the proportion of children that died during their first year):

La Guerche (1720–92)	285 out of 1,000
Saint-Méen (1720–92)	237 out of 1,000
Saint-Aubin (1749–89)	243 out of 1,000

Roughly one child in four died during his first year. This rate is higher than what I calculated a short time ago for Beauvais between 1665 and 1735.[7] Certain historians found this rate exaggerated, but did not provide acceptable arguments for their criticism.

The rates for the south-west and Crulai were:

Thézels (1747–82)	191 out of 1,000
Azereix (18th century)	156 out of 1,000
Crulai (1674–1742)	172 out of 1,000

Roughly one child out of every six or seven died during his first year. One discovers this rather low rate in some villages in the region of Paris, in Normandy, and in the south.

Thus, the notion of 'infant mortality' is far from satisfying. The grave dangers to young children do not cease one year after they are born. The difficulties of weaning are added to others. Of much more utility are the rates of child mortality from zero to four years, or from zero to nine years. I shall content myself with giving the rate at which children survive until age ten. Beyond ten years, the children have often moved and cannot be easily traced. Furthermore, after age ten a child is less threatened.

Children surviving to age ten in three Breton localities

Saint-Aubin (1748–89)	580 out of 1,000
La Guerche (1720–90)	510 out of 1,000
Saint-Méen (1720–92)	463 out of 1,000

Roughly half of the children do not reach their tenth year. The situation does not improve in the course of the eighteenth century. At the beginning of the second half of the century, the rate of survival at Saint-Méen declines from 475 to 451. This decline corresponds to a slight increase in fertility.

Children surviving to age ten in the south-west and Normandy

Thézels	645 out of 1,000
Azereix	639 out of 1,000
Crulai	672 out of 1,000

[7] Pierre Goubert, *Beauvais et le Beauvaisis* (Paris, 1960), pp. 39–40.

Nearly two thirds of the children reach their tenth year in these areas. The two groups, thus, vary in their rate of infant mortality as well as their rate of marital fertility.

The phenomenon of mortality is perhaps more complex than the phenomenon of fertility, as more factors are involved. The demographic explanation of the demographic phenomenon of mortality is not satisfactory. It is only one point of view, one aspect, one element of the total picture; it is not sufficient by itself.

A comparison between the interior of Brittany and the interior of Aquitaine may prove useful. The natural conditions are not the same. Upper Brittany has neither cold winters nor sunny summers, and the climate there is very humid. A lot of water becomes stagnant, and the months of August and September are stormy, dull, and wretched. Thus, the majority of children die in summer: The poor quality of water, the swarms of parasitic insects, and the lack of hygiene probably played their role in the high death tolls during the summer. The south-west seems to offer a more healthful climate, one that is more sunny. Did these climatic differences count for much in the eighteenth century?

After the end of the seventeenth century, the two regions under consideration were spared the great famines which struck other French provinces. In both cases, a diversified agriculture sheltered them from poverty and famine. From this point of view, the superiority of the regions of Aquitaine is striking. Since the seventeenth century, the cultivation of corn assured the population of enough food. The numerous secondary cultivations—grapes, fruit, trees, poultry, and vegetables—enabled the population to maintain a level of subsistence through trade with other regions. Inner Brittany fed itself solely on buckwheat pancakes, salty butter which was often rancid, salty lard, and black bread. People drank bad cider, and too much hard cider, which they sometimes gave (and still give) to children. The filth of the Breton farms, although proverbial, is not apocryphal: the well next to dung, dung in front of the door, animals in the house. Moreover, the quacks, the matrons (midwives without any qualifications), and the sorcerers of the villages aggravated the situation in Brittany. The south-west seems to have been less dirty and less superstitious.

The economic and social conditions also acted in the opposite direction in the two regions. The rights of the feudal lords and aristocrats always weighed heavily on the peasants of Brittany. Moreover, the rural development was limited, dispersed, and insufficient. The south of France was less subject to seignorial and 'feudal' dues, but the extent of peasant cultivation is not known.

These are only possible explanations for the contrast between the very high infant mortality in Brittany and the more moderate mortality in the south-west. The exact causes are still unknown.

What do these observations concerning two French provinces during the eighteenth century teach us?

It is certain that the Bretons were ignorant of all birth control during the entire eighteenth century. It is likely that the married couples in the south-west practised some birth control throughout the century, although not systematically. In neither case can a significant change be observed, nor is there any evidence of systematic contraception aimed at limiting the total number of children, rather than the interval between births. There are considerably more differences between regions than between periods.

This observation holds true for infant mortality: It is high in Brittany and does not diminish in the course of the eighteenth century; although much weaker in the south-west, it maintains a constant level throughout the century.

Neither Brittany nor the south-west represents all of France. The area around Paris constitutes a quite different case, as it was shaken by great demographic crises during the seventeenth and part of the eighteenth centuries. (These became attenuated about 1750.) Such phenomena are the exception in Brittany and the south-west. The area around Paris is characterized by a rather high fertility, one clearly much stronger than that of the south-west, but perceptibly weaker than that of Brittany. Around Paris, one can observe a slight decrease in mortality during the eighteenth century and the beginning of systematic contraception after 1780 or 1750.

Are there, then, several 'demographic regimes' in the interior of the kingdom of France, several types of behaviour, or even several types of civilization that demographic analysis can help to reveal? Analysis of the demographic, economic, and social phenomena of ancient France can be undertaken only for regions. Nothing has as yet been determined with any degree of certainty, and historians must stop teaching unfounded ideas about comprehensive demographic development, which has not thus far been sufficiently explored.

One can object that although our comparison dealt with two disparate elements, they produced the same results. Indeed, the Breton families had a lot of children, but lost a lot of them. The families in the south-west had fewer children, but did not lose so many. Do these conditions not produce the same results? If they do, it is a disturbing situation.

A little reflection is in order. One hundred Breton families in the three localities considered here produced 460 children; of these, about 230 reached adulthood. One hundred and twenty of the 230 were women. To maintain the total population, it was necesssary for one hundred of these women to marry, given the same demographic conditions. The rate of celibacy for women wavers between 10 and 15 per cent, and the rate of sterility for married women is close to 6 per cent. These summary, and partly hypothetical, calculations lead to the conclusion that the Breton population could not grow during the eighteenth century. On the other hand, it is known that between 1770 and 1787 the number of deaths exceeded the number of baptisms by more than one hundred thousand.[8] The demographic documentation is not so precise for the south-west. Nevertheless, historians often support the thesis that the southern population increased after 1740, although as far this has not been established.[9] It is fortunate that Louis Henry could prove that the rural population in the area around Paris underwent a strong growth after 1750, because proof for the other regions is missing or not very convincing.[10]

Is it necessary to doubt the theory that French population increased during the eighteenth century? I do not think so. It is merely necessary to examine the phenomenon very closely—for the course of the century, from one province to another—in order to demonstrate without doubt that the subject is more complicated, more diverse, and more varied than it was thought to be for a long time. As a Danish prince said: 'There are more things in heaven and earth, Horatio, than are dreamt of in your philosophy.' Much work remains for the historical demographer.

This article was translated from the French by Marlis Fette.

[8] Numerical data published by Edmond Esmonin, *Etudes et Chroniques de Démographie Historique 1964* (Paris, Société de Démographie Historique), p. 123.

[9] Jacques Godechot and Suzanne Moncassin, 'Démographie et subsistances en Languedoc du XVIIIe siècle au debut du XIXe', *Bulletin d'Histoire économique et sociale de la Révolution française* (Paris, 1965). Critical review by Pierre Goubert, *Annales de Démographie Historique 1965*, pp. 231–5.

[10] Louis Henry and Mlle. Claude Levy, 'Quelques donnees sur la region autour de Paris au VIIIe siècle', *Population* (1962), pp. 297–326.

Bernard H. Slicher van Bath

Historical demography and the social and economic development of the Netherlands

Studies in economic and social history have advanced rapidly since 1950; not only have they used new methods and techniques, but they have dealt with problems that have changed radically. During the first stage in the development of studies in economic history, each sector of economic life was treated separately, thus producing histories of agriculture, commerce, industry, banking, and so forth. In the second stage, the separate histories were joined on a national scale, but still not integrated. The internal development of each of the segments remained divorced from the other parts of economic life, resulting in the segmentation characteristic of the well-known textbooks of economic history—the economies of the United States, England, the Netherlands, and so on. Since 1950, however, the various economic activities have come to be considered part of an economic and social totality. We know that a change in one of the segments causes repercussions in many other parts of the economy and the social structure. The ideal equilibrium of the old economic theories is constantly disturbed. From a historical point of view, the disturbing factors are particularly interesting.

Before 1800, the greatest changes occurred mostly in the population figures and the relations among prices. Increase or decrease of population affected both production and consumption. Growth of population is not always correlated with an increase of productive forces because the age distribution and the occupational structure can change. Moreover, different dietary and spending habits within the social stratification can influence consumption. Before 1800, many people spent most of their income on food.

In integral economic history, based on a holistic viewpoint, the most important problems of the pre-industrial period have become demographic changes and the price relations of goods and wages. Problems are now studied which remained unexplored in the older segmental national economic histories. Quantification, especially of population and prices, is the backbone of new researches in the history of economic and social development.

The researches on the Netherlands being done by the Department of Rural History at Wageningen University focus on the period between 1500 and 1800; the statistical data, therefore, are often lacking or incomplete. Each investigation relates to a definite territorial and administrative unit—a province or a major part of a province. Prior to 1800 each province had its own administration because the Republic of the United Provinces was a federation. Thus, diverse source materials are available for the various provinces. A regional treatment is also justified because a great variety of patterns existed in the various areas between 1500 and 1800.

The regions investigated so far are widely distributed over the country: Friesland, studied by J. A. Faber; Holland, by A. M. van der Woude; the Veluwe by H. K. Roessingh; the bailiwick of Bois-le-Duc by H. J. van Xanten; and Overijssel, by myself. The investigations cover 56 to 66 per cent of the total population living between 1500 and 1800 on the present territorial area of the Netherlands.

The investigations are focused on long-term developments, so that considerable attention is paid to reconstructing the evolution of the absolute number of inhabitants. Other aspects of the demographic past are also taken into account—birth rate, death rate, migration, age distribution, fertility, age at marriage, nuptiality, family size, family structure, the distribution of the population among the various religious denominations, demographic differences among the religious groups, and so forth. In regard to some of the latter aspects, the work has sometimes met with great difficulties owing to the extensive migration and religious diversity within the Dutch population.

Demographic investigations form only a subsidiary part of the study, which embraces the entire economic and social life of the area concerned. Attention is paid to such different phenomena as the occupational pattern, the distribution of wealth, the social stratification, agriculture, rural industries, navigation, fishing and peat-digging, the incidence of taxation, drainage duties, ground rent, and the prices of land and produce.

THE SOURCES

Sources used for demographic analyses were general and local population censuses, reports of the number of communicants, lists of men capable of bearing arms, reports of the numbers of hearths, homes, or families, tribute registers, poll-tax registers, revenues of taxes on such necessities as corn and meat, and, finally, parish registers. All of these sources present peculiar difficulties in interpretation. The first true national census dates from 1795–6; previously, incidental censuses had been taken in the various provinces, mostly for purposes of taxation. The results of these censuses are often imperfectly preserved, and only fragments are available.

In order to infer the total number of inhabitants from the number of communicants, men capable of bearing arms, and hearths, homes, or families, it is necessary to have conversion coefficients. These are related to such factors as age structure, ratio of males to females, and average size of the household or family. In interpreting the tax registers, the evasion factor must obviously be taken into consideration.

The perusal of parish registers is beset with other kinds of pit-falls. Because the registers of deaths and burials are scarce, this important aspect of the demographic development generally falls outside our scope. Few registers of baptisms and marriages ante-date 1650. Such registers as exist relate mainly to the congregations of the Reformed Church. It is questionable if they represent the trend in the total number of inhabitants. Unfortunately, the baptism registers of the Roman Catholics usually begin after 1700 and the registers of births of the Mennonites in the second half of the eighteenth century. Moreover, the Roman Catholic missionary stations and the Mennonite congregations usually cover a wider area than do the Reformed Church congregations, the latter being limited chiefly to a single town or village. There exists a possibility of double registration of the Roman Catholics, for their baptisms and marriages should have been entered in the Protestant registers, although Catholics backed out of this obligation when possible.

Even when the available baptism statistics are representative of the birth rate of the entire population, it is still an open question as to what extent the trend in the number of births is an index of the trend of that population. Strictly speaking, this would only be the case if the birth rate remained stationary. Obviously there are annual fluctuations in this figure. Owing to changes in the marriage rate, the marriage age, natural fertility, female mortality, and intentional interference with marital fertility, differences may also occur over a longer period.

G. J. Mentink and A. M. van der Woude have used parish registers in their study of the demographic development of Rotterdam during the seventeenth and eighteenth centuries. The Amsterdam registers of bridegrooms and brides will be a rich source for investigation. Researches into these registers have only been made for migration and the marriage age of brides, but the registers also contain interesting information, such as data on occupations and literacy.

Family reconstitution, a method being used by Louis Henry for France and the Cambridge Group for England, is complicated in the Netherlands because many people among the lower classes had no family names before the introduction of civil registration in 1811. They were called by their Christian name combined with the genitive of their father's Christian name. Sometimes the Christian name was linked with the name of a trade or a farm.

For the economic and social history, use is made of a host of new records, many of which have not been previously studied. Although differing in value according to the investigation concerned, important sources are assessment lists and related materials from which data have been deduced about wealth, occupation, acreage of land under cultivation, balance between crop farming and cattle breeding, size of the livestock population, number and size of farms, balance between leased and owned property, extent of poverty, industry, and tax revenues; also used are weigh-house records, rent accounts, administration of dike contributions, data on land reclamations and utilization, peat-digging, cattle plague, dispensation of taxes, village accounts, and deeds in notarial files. Publications in the field of price history are also most pertinent.

THE DEMOGRAPHIC DEVELOPMENT

It is possible, using the 1795–6 national census and the knowledge of the development in the five areas studied (Friesland,[1] the Veluwe,[2] Overijssel,[3] the bailiwick of Bois-le-Duc,[4] and Holland[5]), to calculate the hypothetical number of inhabitants of the present territorial area of the Netherlands from 1500 to the present day (see Figure 1).

[1] In Friesland, the increase before 1689 occurred in the towns, the centre and south-west of the province, and in the sandy regions to the east; the decline after 1650 hit the towns and the livestock-farming area in the west of the province. The renewed growth was less pronounced in the clay pasture area and the towns.

[2] In the Veluwe area, there was a steady, continuous increase in population which was free from any drastic changes. During the sixteenth century and the first half of the seventeenth, the growth was modest, although the rate of growth gradually increased. Between 1650 and 1750, the increase occurred mainly in the rural areas. The urban population showed little increase during this period, the only marked growth being in the small towns of Nijkerk and Wageningen where tobacco cultivation and trading rose to prosperous heights. After 1750, the stagnation in urban growth came to an end, and the rate of growth in the rural area remained at practically the same level.

[3] Overijssel suffered considerably as a result of the Eighty Years' War, during which there was fierce fighting, particularly in the eastern part of the province. The country districts were plundered and laid under ransom. A good many persons emigrated from these districts to Amsterdam and other towns in Holland during this period. When peace was restored, a surprisingly rapid increase of the population set in, mainly between 1675 and 1748, especially in the eastern part. The growth occurred chiefly in the rural areas and hamlets during the first period from 1675 to 1723. Between 1723 and 1748, the increase was most striking in the parish-villages and the towns. The rapid increase in population between 1675 and 1748 was due to the excess of births over deaths, as appears from the

large number of children. The increase in the eastern part is paralleled by that in the adjoining German districts, the bishoprics of Münster and Osnabrück. In the western part of the province, the increase was far less spectacular, much more regular. This area is very similar to the Veluwe on the other side of the river IJssel.

In some towns and villages on the Zuiderzee coast, the population even declined, just as it did in areas of Holland and Friesland, which were situated along the Zuiderzee.

The pattern underwent a complete change during the second half of the eighteenth century: In many parts of Overijssel, the population remained stationary or even declined.

4 In the bailiwick of Bois-le-Duc, the population increased very rapidly during the first half of the sixteenth century. The growth was particularly marked in the pasture districts and the centres of the textile industry—Tilburg, Helmond, Eindhoven, and their surrounding districts. The growth was less marked in the high lands with sandy soil.

An industrial crisis in the cloth industry, religious struggles, the loss of trade routes, and finally the Eighty Years' War contributed to a rapid decline in population of the town of Bois-le-Duc—falling from 23,000 in 1526 to 9,000 in 1665. In the rural districts, the war had less disastrous results. Characteristically, the number of inhabitants in the countryside was as high and probably even somewhat higher in 1665 than it was in 1526. The western part gained 15 to 20 per cent, but the pasture district lost a few per cent.

After the war, the town of Bois-le-Duc saw a considerable growth in population, reaching almost 14,000 in 1747. After that date, the number of inhabitants continued at the same level for the remainder of the century. From 1665 to 1766, there was a slight growth in the rural population. During these hundred years, the bailiwick underwent a period of rise between 1665 and 1700, of decline between 1700 and 1750, followed by some revival after 1750.

5 In Holland, a period of continued growth began with the early-sixteenth century and lasted for one hundred and fifty years. In the first stage, between 1514 and 1569, the growth was focused particularly in the countryside and the smaller towns. The expansion of Amsterdam, Leyden, Haarlem, Delft, Rotterdam, and other towns did not start in earnest until after 1580. Towards the end of the sixteenth century, the countryside of Holland was becoming so overpopulated that many countrypeople could no longer make a living there and had to go to the cities; moreover, the stream of immigrants, mainly from the southern Low Countries and Germany, was directed to the larger cities. The growth of the towns at the end of the sixteenth and the beginning of the seventeenth century far exceeded that of the countryside. In 1514, more than 46 per cent of the population of Holland lived in towns; this percentage was 54 in 1622.

After 1650, the population in the area north of Amsterdam began to decrease—slowly at first, but catastrophically after 1700. In this area, the numbers of inhabitants decreased from more than 200,000 in 1650 to about 130,000 in 1750. In large parts of North Holland, the decrease even came to 50 per cent.

In the area of Holland south of Amsterdam, which was the largest part and where most of the inhabitants lived, the demographic development was not uniform. There was a stagnation or even a slight decrease in the countryside. With exception of Amsterdam, Rotterdam, the Hague, and Schiedam, the towns saw their population decrease, often considerably. Their demographic development can be divided into three phases: from 1622 to about 1680, there was continued growth; between 1680 and 1750, a rapid decrease; and between 1750 and 1795, a slow decrease. The total decrease between 1650 and 1750 for the whole province of Holland may be estimated at about 120,000 persons.

The causes of the decrease are not yet clear. Many possibilities exist—such as a higher mortality, a lower average number of children per marriage, a higher age at marriage, and an increase of celibacy. In Amsterdam, the age of brides at first marriage was higher in the eighteenth century than in the seventeenth. In 1626-7, 51·5 per cent of the brides were twenty to twenty-four years of age; in the eighteenth century, this figure was 30·6 to 32·4 per cent. Many brides were thirty to thirty-four years old: 18 per cent in the eighteenth century, against 7·3 per cent in the seventeenth. During the eighteenth century, there was a very remakable stagnation in the Protestant denominations, while the Roman Catholics increased, or did not decrease to such an extent. Statistics for Rotterdam, Delft, and some other towns indicate that Protestants had fewer children per marriage. At Rotterdam, Protestants had, on an average, one child less per marriage than did the Roman Catholics during the eighteenth century.

Figure 1

I. HOLLAND
  Ia. North Holland
  Ib. South Holland
    1. Amsterdam
    2. Haarlem
    3. Leyden
    4. The Hague
    5. Delft
    6. Schiedam
    7. Rotterdam
    8. Gouda
    9. Den Briel
    10. Dordrecht
    11. Schoonhoven
    12. Gorkum

II. FRIESLAND
  IIa. clay pasture
       district

IIb. peat pasture
     district
IIc. 'Wouden'
IId. clay arable district
    1. Leeuwarden
    2. Harlingen
    3. Sneek
    4. Hindeloopen
    5. Staveren
    6. Sloten

III. OVERIJSSEL
  IIIa. Salland
    a¹. arable farming
        area
    a². livestock farm-
        ing area
  IIIb. Twente

IIIc. Vollenhove
    1. Zwolle
    2. Deventer
    3. Kampen

IV. VELUWE
    1. Arnhem
    2. Wageningen
    3. Nijkerk
    4. Hattem

V. TOWN and BAILIWICK
   of BOIS-LE-DUC
  Va. Maasland
  Vb. Peelland
  Vc. Kempenland
  Vd. Oisterwijk
    1. Bois-le-Duc
       with its freedom

Although the figures relating to periods prior to 1795 are hypothetical and provisional, their calculation is not entirely a matter of guesswork. Only 35 to 40 per cent of the calculations were made

Table 1 Population of the Netherlands, 1500–1950

Year	Population	Year	Population
1500	900,000 to 1,000,000	1750	1,900,000 to 1,950,000
1550	1,200,000 to 1,300,000	1795	2,078,000
1600	1,400,000 to 1,600,000	1850	3,057,000
1650	1,850,000 to 1,900,000	1900	5,104,000
1700	1,850,000 to 1,950,000	1950	10,200,000

solely by means of geographical interpolation, the remaining 60 to 65 per cent being based on sufficiently reliable factual material.

There is great regional and chronological variety in the demographic development of the five areas studied, as is shown in the following table of the absolute numbers of inhabitants and the indices and percentages.

Table 2 Total number of inhabitants of the five areas

Area	c. 1500	c. 1650	1795
Friesland	75,000	145,000	162,000
Veluwe	36,000	41,000	66,000
Overijssel	53,000	71,000	135,000
Bailiwick B.	96,000	82,000	117,000
Holland	275,000	903,000	783,000
Total	535,000	1,242,000	1,263,000

Table 3 Indices of the demographic development of the five areas

Area	c. 1500	1795	c. 1500	c. 1650	c. 1650	1795
Friesland	100	216	100	193	100	112
Veluwe	100	186	100	114	100	163
Overijssel	100	255	100	134	100	190
Bailiwick B.	100	122	100	85	100	143
Holland	100	285	100	328	100	87
Netherlands	100	219	100	197	100	111

	Indices 1650–1795				Percentages 1500–1795		
Area	c. 1650	c. 1700	c. 1750	1795	c. 1500	a. 1650	1795
Friesland	100	90	93	112	7·9	7·7	7·8
Veluwe	100	121	132	163	3·8	2·2	3·2
Overijssel	100	117	172	190	5·6	3·8	6·5
Bailiwick B.	100	134	138	143	10·1	4·4	5·6
Holland	100	98	87	87	28·9	48·2	37·7
Other provinces	—	—	—	—	43·7	33·7	39·2
Netherlands	—	—	—	—	100·0	100·0	100·0

A turning point occurred about 1650. Between 1500 and 1650, demographic growth predominated, especially in Holland and, in a lesser degree, in Friesland. The growth was not so spectacular in Overijssel and the Veluwe. In the second half of the sixteenth and the first half of the seventeenth century, a decline set in in the bailiwick of Bois-le-Duc, owing to the Eighty Years' War (1568–1648). The eastern parts of Overijssel also suffered badly during this war.

The period from 1650 to 1795 shows considerable growth in Overijssel and the Veluwe, moderate growth in the bailiwick of Bois-le-Duc, but stagnation in Friesland and decline in Holland. The growth in the bailiwick took place between 1650 and 1700, a recovery after the Eighty Years' War. In Overijssel, much of the growth occurred during the first half of the eighteenth century, and in the Veluwe during the second half of the same century. In Friesland, a decline between 1650 and 1700 was followed by a recovery during the second half of the eighteenth century. Stagnation characterized the second half of the seventeenth century in Holland; the decline appeared in the first half of the eighteenth century. There is a decline in population after 1650, especially along the coasts of the Zuiderzee—in North Holland and the coastal areas of Friesland and Overijssel.

THE ECONOMIC AND SOCIAL CONDITIONS

It is difficult to explain the many changes in population numbers. To what extent was the growth of population a consequence of a natural increase, of immigration? Was the decline in population caused by higher mortality, by emigration, or by a lower marriage rate? Extensive migration took place inside the country. People from the countryside came to the parish-villages and the neighbouring towns. Amsterdam attracted people from the whole country, and great numbers came from the villages and towns in North Holland. The republic was an asylum for persecuted people from other countries: Calvinists, Huguenots, Lutherans, Mennonites, and Jews. The prosperity of the Netherlands lured some who sought a change in fortune; still others came as soldiers. Numerous persons also emigrated to the East and West Indies, South Africa, Brazil, the New Netherlands, Scandinavia, Germany, and Eastern Europe; we do not know the extent to which emigration counterbalanced immigration.

There are no signs that mortality was higher after 1650 due to the spread of contagious diseases. We know of ten plagues and three other epidemics between 1500 and 1650; during the period from 1650 to 1800, there were four plague attacks and six epidemics. The last attack of the plague was in 1668–70. The plague had, therefore, already disappeared when the population in Holland and the Zuiderzee area started to decline.

The country suffered from many wars, but its heaviest losses were incurred during the Eighty Years' War. The southern and eastern parts of the Republic endured particularly severe hardships in this struggle. Despite such heavy costs, the country reached the culminating point of its Golden Age during the last phases of this war. In most parts of Holland, the population continued to increase; in Overijssel and the bailiwick of Bois-le-Duc, population growth began again. The succeeding wars did not result in heavy losses of human lives.

Between 1650 and 1800, inundations became more frequent. There were nine inundations between 1500 and 1650 but nineteen after 1650. Agricultural prices were low during this period, and the costs of maintaining the dikes and polders were high. There were many complaints against high dike taxes, which weighed heavily on the rural population. The inundations were most probably the result of the dikes being inadequately maintained. During this period, the piles at the foot of the sea-dikes were destroyed by the teredo plague, and large sums were required to replace these wooden defences with stone ones, chiefly imported from Norway.

An increase in population always coincides with new economic possibilities in agriculture, industry, shipping, and peat-digging, whereas a decline in population is attended by recession in trade, agriculture, and industry. It is impossible to solve the problem of causality: A growing population means expansion of production and consumption, and new economic possibilities vreate opportunities for population growth. A decreasing population results in the restriction of production and consumption, and a decline in economic possibilities leads to a decrease in the marriage rate, a higher age at marriage, and more celibacy. Once the process has started, there is always a reinforcing secondary effect. The process of population growth can be observed in the province of Overijssel after the Eighty Years' War. Agricultural potentialities were exploited by resettling abandoned farms and fields. Further land clearance was restricted because wastelands were a source of heather sods and humus for the arable lands (turf-manuring). When the price of cereals dropped, the textile industry relieved the burden of imminent overpopulation. At first, the cottage weavers lived among the farmers. Eventually they broke away from this environment and became professional weavers, settling mostly in certain villages and towns. The various wars fought between 1688 and 1748 were exceptionally favourable to the sale of textile products.

The Veluwe is an area with a continued modest growth in population. Before 1650, during the period of relatively high and rising cereal prices, the reclamation of wastelands kept pace with population growth. Buckwheat cultivation was expanded on the higher lands, thereby enabling a greater number of persons to subsist on the same acreage. During the depression in arable farming between 1650 and 1750, the expanded activity of the tobacco, paper-making, and textile industries led to a substantial increase in employment. The economic situation for the industries and the tobacco growers became less favourable after 1750, but the appearance of the potato corrected it by opening up new prospects for smallholders.

A classic Malthusian pattern is enacted in the neighbouring eastern part of Overijssel. A rise in population was founded on the small base of the textile industry. After nearly a hundred years of population growth, the general state of health, diet, housing, education, and medical and spiritual care had deteriorated to a low level. After 1750, the keen foreign competition led to a structural crisis in the textile industry. Universal poverty resulted, and the growth in population came to an end.

The dependence on one industry may be at the root of the small resistance this region had against economic misfortune. Still, no region was hit harder by the economic depression and decline in population than North Holland with its shipping centres, fisheries, livestock farms, and diverse industries along the river Zaan and elsewhere. A many-sided economic development, thus, does not guarantee the uninterrupted continuation of prosperity. The whole economic life of North Holland was closely connected with shipping and foreign trade, mainly with the Dutch shipping in the Sound. The Baltic trade flourished from 1550 to 1650, owing to the increasing demand for cereals in Western and Southern Europe. After 1650, the situation changed. The general stagnation in population growth had a negative effect on the demand for cereals. Moreover, Southern and Western Europe were beginning to produce more because of the increase in acreage devoted to rice, maize, and buckwheat. The steep decline in the demand for Baltic cereals adversely affected Dutch shipping in the Sound, a change fatal to the situation in North Holland.

In general, a region that had more economic opportunities was also more dependent on the market and economic fluctuations. The economic diversity in the Netherlands perhaps postponed, but certainly did not prevent, the penetration of the general European depression in the seventeenth century.

Various possibilities for economic expansion were available to the Netherlands. Agriculture could have been developed in all five districts; peat-digging combined with shipping and industry, in Friesland and Overijssel; shipping, in Friesland and Holland; sea fishery, in Holland; industries connected with trade, shipping, and export, in Holland; textile industries, in Overijssel, the bailiwick of Bois-le-Duc and the Veluwe; and papermaking, in the Veluwe and Holland.

Between 1500 and 1800, periods of economic rise and depression alternated. There was a rise from 1500 to 1650, a depression from 1650 to 1750, and then another rise after 1750. During periods of economic expansion, the ratio between the price of grain and the prices of other commodities and wages was favourable to high grain prices. The ratio was unfavourable during the depression period.

Many new polders were made in Holland between 1500 and 1650, and thousands of people worked to drain the land. There were also reclamations in Friesland, the Veluwe, and the bailiwick of Bois-le-Duc. Reclamations started again on a more modest scale after 1750.

The high prices of wheat and rye stimulated the cultivation of other crops: buckwheat in Overijssel and the Veluwe in the sixteenth and seventeenth centuries, and the potato in Friesland, the Veluwe, Overijssel, and the bailiwick after 1750. Because buckwheat required no direct manuring, it could be grown as an unmanured last crop in the rotation after one or two rye harvests. Such a crop was important in view of the continual lack of manure. Buckwheat cultivation had a further advantage because it countered the great weed infestation resulting from the cultivation of rye as a single crop. Checking the weed infestation served to increase the rye yield. Thus, the expansion of buckwheat cultivation had a multiple effect: the same amount of manure was put to better use, there was more intensive land use, and the rye harvest was improved. All these factors meant that a greater number of persons were able to subsist on the same acreage, thereby creating conditions conducive to an increase in population.

During the depression period (1650–1750), farmers were interested not in growing grain, but in cultivating cash crops. Tobacco was grown in the Veluwe; flax, coleseed, and hops in Friesland and the bailiwick of Bois-le-Duc. The rural industries prospered during this period: The textile industry developed in Overijssel, the Veluwe, and the bailiwick of Bois-le-Duc, and papermaking flourished in the Veluwe. In all of these regions, the rural industries met with difficulties after 1750, when the economic situation began to improve.

As far as can be seen, peat-digging was not subject to economic

alternations. In Friesland, low transport costs made peat comparatively cheap, thereby favouring the establishment and development
of industries in which fuel was a relatively important cost factor—
for example, brickworks, tile-works, salt-works, lime kilns, breweries,
and distilleries.

In north-west Overijssel, peat excavation represented an important means of employment. Peat transport led to a great expansion
of shipping and, in turn, to the development of many other
branches of industry, such as shipbuilding, sail-making, rope and
shoe manufacturing, and baking. Peat-digging, however, like gold-
digging, brings only temporary prosperity. Once the peat has been
removed, all that remains are lakes and ponds. When this district
provided no further livelihood from peat, it was abandoned and
the population sought fresh possibilities in the peat reserves of
Friesland and Drenthe.

Although the depression was part of a general European phenomenon, in the Netherlands it was aggravated by domestic problems.
The government contracted large loans to finance the many wars
in the second half of the seventeenth and beginning of the eighteenth
centuries. The tax burden was increased to meet the interest on and
discharge of these loans. The economic situation, however, demanded
a decrease in taxation. The fiscal system also worked in the wrong
direction, as can be seen in Overijssel. During the period of low
grain prices, high taxes were imposed on agriculture. After 1755,
when grain prices began to rise, the highest tax incidence shifted from
agriculture to the principal foodstuffs. This measure further
aggravated the condition of the textile workers, who were already
suffering from underemployment due to crises in the textile industry.

A MALTHUSIAN EXAMPLE

Exact figures are only available for one province of the Netherlands.
These data refer to the increase in population of the province
of Overijssel. Between 1675 and 1764, the population nearly
doubled: The index was 100 in 1675, but 186·9 in 1764. All the
social and economic phenomena observable at that time point to a
relative overpopulation—the occupational structure, social stratification, housing conditions, medical and spiritual care, education, and
financial and agricultural development.

In 1795, less than half of the occupational population worked in
agriculture (45·6 per cent). The importance of industry is a striking
feature of the occupational structure; 35·5 per cent of all workers

were employed in industry and nearly half of them were in the textile trades. Commerce (11·6 per cent) and social services (5·1 per cent) were of less importance.

By classifying the population on the basis of property we can discern the numbers of persons belonging to various groups and the total value of properties owned by each group. Between 1675 and 1758, the importance of the nobility declined, and the number of citizens with fortunes of more than 10,000 guilders dwindled. The supremacy of the nobility and city patricians, who had ruled the province for many centuries, was broken. The upper-middle classes, composed of people with fortunes between 500 and 10,000 guilders, grew. This new group included lawyers and doctors, as well as linen manufacturers in Twente. They acted as money-lenders to the nobility, giving mortgages on castles and sometimes even becoming the new inhabitants of castles formerly belonging to the nobility. The lower-middle classes, made up of people with yearly incomes of less than 500 guilders and of paupers who could not pay the low poll taxes, rose enormously. The increasing pauperization was alarming. In 1675, a quarter of the total population was in the pauper class; by 1758, this percentage had risen to 35·7. All cottage weavers in Twente were paupers.

Conditions for the cottagers and weavers were aggravated by poor housing. In towns and rural areas, people lived in turf huts, sheds, bakehouses, and pigsties. Many new 'houses' had a surface area of 150 square feet, the height being under six feet. Between 1682 and 1749, the number of new houses built did not keep pace with the increase in population. The net number of houses rose by 3,235, but the number of families rose by 11,000. This lag meant that houses were available for only 30 per cent of the new families.

Poor housing conditions were most probably a factor in the increase in the number of diseases resulting in a high mortality after 1750. Medical care was on an insignificant scale. In 1795, the province had only thirty-four doctors, fifty-four surgeons (barbers), and seventeen midwives, or one doctor per 4,000 and one midwife per 8,000 inhabitants. The situation was worse in the rural areas than it was in the urban centres because the doctors and midwives were concentrated in the towns. The same inadequacy characterized spiritual care and education: one Protestant clergyman per 1,600, one Roman Catholic priest per 4,300, and one teacher per 900 inhabitants.

The financial development, as far as we can conclude from the increase in the total amount of property declared for the purpose of property taxes, remained far below the increase in population between 1675 and 1758. The index of the population in 1764 was

186·9, that of 1675 was 100; the index of the total amount of property was only 113·7 in 1758, when that of 1675 was also 100. The increase in the number of paupers unable to pay the poll tax was far greater than the population increase. In some places in Twente in 1764, paupers accounted for 50 to 60 per cent of the total population.

Taxation did not greatly increase in severity, but it was still higher than the increase in property. The index of the tax yield in 1760 was 134·1; in 1680, it was 100. It is understandable, therefore, that the government shifted the burden of taxation from property to excises on foodstuffs. The property taxes were paid only by landowners, the excise taxes by the whole population. This measure created great difficulties for the weavers, the peat diggers, and paupers. A high consumption of brandy was an accompanying feature of the universal poverty. The yield from excises levied on strong alcoholic drink was one of the province's chief sources of revenue, representing 16 per cent of the total tax yield between 1770 and 1790.

The agricultural population did not increase so rapidly as the total population: Index for the agricultural population in 1795 was 162·6 (1602, 100) and for the total population, 189·7 (1675, 100). There was an even greater lag in the growth of the acreage of arable land and pasture: In 1749, the respective indices were 106·4 and 104·2 (1602, 100). As a result, the farms became smaller and the cotter holdings more numerous. The number of horses used as draught animals on the farms remained practically unchanged between 1602 and 1812. This fact indicates that there were not more medium-sized farms in 1812 than there had been in 1602. The increase in arable acreage took place in the small cotter holdings. Pig-keeping is characteristic of cotter farming, and the number of pigs increased greatly between 1602 and 1812. There was also a decline in the number of sheep between 1602 and 1844, due mainly to the decrease of wasteland during the first half of the nineteenth century.

Before 1800, there were few possibilities for land clearance because the wastelands were used for grazing livestock and as a source of humus. In the first half of the nineteenth century, the acreage of cultivated land increased more rapidly than the population. The cultivation of turnips and fodder plants ended the dependence on earth manuring with heather sods and sand. The cattle population increased, and more pigs were kept. Potato cultivation also brought great change, by increasing the yield per acre.

During the period of its population increase, Overijssel depended on the import of cereals from other areas to supply the towns, villages, and rural districts with food, because it was unable to sustain its population on its domestic yield. Nor was the increase in livestock proportional to the growth of the human population. As a result, sufficient grain and animal proteins were unavailable to the population, which must have had an adverse affect on their health. A medical report of 1781 relates that the cottage weavers of Almelo were weak and lethargic.

The divergence between the growth of the agricultural population and the increase in the acreage of arable land and pasture produced great changes in the social stratification of the rural population. In 1602, the farmers still formed the largest group in the agricultural population (61·4 per cent), but by 1795 they were less than half (46·9 per cent); the cotters maintained their relative numbers (about 35 per cent). Owing to the steep rise in population, no additional living space was available for large numbers of country dwellers, even as cotters. A large group of day labourers developed, amounting to 18·3 per cent of the entire agricultural population by 1795. An almost landless proletariat sprang up, its sole resources being physical strength and the capacity for work. An increasing differentiation in the social stratification is observable among the rural population. The social scale tended to a large downward spreading.

All these phenomena confirm the picture of a society under the heavy stress of a too rapid increase in population. After 1764, the population growth came to a standstill, due in part to higher mortality. The age of marriage may have risen, and more people may have remained unmarried. In the nineteenth century, many three-generation households are found in the province of Overijssel; there are few indications of such households in the Census of 1748, taken during the period of growth.

In some parts of the province, hereditary laws were in force which stipulated that only one of the children in a family could inherit the farm. This law was applied to the farms of the villeins from the Middle Ages until 1795. It may be that after 1750 the custom was expanded to other farms in some villages. With the exception of the heritable child, children often remained unmarried. Researches into these problems, however, are still to be done.

H. K. Roessingh has published many exact data for the Veluwe, especially for the situation in mid-eighteenth century. We hope to get a better understanding of the interaction between changes in the population and in the social and economic conditions for the other parts of the Netherlands, but this work is still in progress.

MP

BIBLIOGRAPHICAL NOTE

J. A. Faber, H. K. Roessingh, B. H. Slicher van Bath, A. M. van der Woude, and H. J. van Xanten, 'Population Changes and Economic Developments in the Netherlands: A Historical Survey', *A. A. G. Bijdragen*, Vol. 12 (1965), pp. 47–113.

H. K. Roessingh, 'Beroep en bedrijf op de Veluwe in het midden van de achttiende eeuw', *A. A. G. Bijdragen*, Vol. 13 (1965), pp. 181–274

G. J. Mentink and A. M. van der Woude, *De demografische ontwikkeling te Rotterdam en Cool in de 17e en 18e eeuw* (Rotterdam, 1965).

J. A. Faber, 'The Decline of the Baltic Grain Trade in the Second Half of the 17th Century', *Acta historiae Neerlandica*, Vol. 1 (1966), pp. 108–31.

B. H. Slicher van Bath, *Een samenleving onder spanning. Geschiedenis van het platteland in Overijssel* (Assen, 1957).

B. H. Slicher van Bath, *The Agrarian History of Western Europe A. D. 500–1850* (London, 1963).

C. J. Erickson

Who were the English and Scots emigrants to the United States in the late nineteenth century?

I

The great migration of European peoples in the nineteenth century has been interpreted as a movement in which economic influences dominated both underlying causes and timing. Through overseas migration and intra-continental movements, people were redistributed from regions of lower to regions of higher labour productivity, from the countryside and rural occupations to urban areas and industrial occupations. Except in the case of the disaster of the Irish famine, emigration was more a means of escaping from relative rural poverty in regions touched by economic growth and structural change than a flight from pure Malthusian crisis. As one writer put it, emigrants came from areas 'first in contact with urban and commercial influences'. The inhabitants of the poorest and most isolated rural areas in Europe either did not participate in mass emigration at all or joined it late as that isolation was infringed.[1]

If mass emigration usually accompanied a reorganization of agriculture with the beginnings of industrialization, the maturing of an industrial economy tended in the long run to stem the overseas flow. This is the standard explanation of the decline of emigration from some of the older regions of emigration in North-western Europe in the early twentieth century. The gross rate of emigration from Germany, for example, declined from 49 per 10,000 of popula-

---

[1] United Nations Department of Social Studies, Population Division, Population Studies, No. 17, *The Determinants and Consequences of Population Trends* (New York, 1953), p. 111. See also Dudley Kirk, *Europe's Population in the Interwar Years*, League of Nations, II, Economic and Financial Series, 1946, II, A. 8. Princeton Office of Population Research, p. 81. 'Emigration began to achieve importance just at the point at which industrialization was making real strides in the Swedish economy.' (Dorothy Swain Thomas, *Economic Aspects of Swedish Population Movements, 1750–1933* [New York, 1941], p. 166.) Ingrid Gaustad Semmingsen, 'Norwegian Emigration in the Nineteenth Century', *Scandinavian Economic History Review*, Vol. 8, No. 2 (1960), pp. 152–3. Theodore Saloutos, *The Greeks in the United States* (Cambridge, Mass., 1964), pp. 2–3, 24.

tion in 1881 to a mere 3·9 per 10,000 in 1901.[2] Even in the short run, strong cyclical upswings in the industrial sector at home could discourage emigration, despite the stronger impact of conditions overseas upon the timing of the migration movement.[3] Moreover, the inhabitants of a few European countries which gained relatively high per capita incomes—like Belgium, France, and the Netherlands—participated as little in the great nineteenth-century migrations as did people from the most backward parts of the Continent.

Overseas emigration from England and Scotland does not seem to have conformed to the pattern of these generalizations. Per capita incomes were almost certainly higher in Great Britain (that is, excluding Ireland) than they were on the Continent of Europe. By this criterion England and Scotland should have been as unimportant as sources of overseas emigrants as were France and Belgium. Yet average rates of gross emigration from Great Britain during the entire period from 1861 to 1910 exceeded those of Sweden, Germany, Switzerland, and Austria-Hungary as well as Belgium, France, and the Netherlands. According to Gustav Sundbärg's estimates of gross annual rates of emigration from various European countries, only Sweden, Norway, and Ireland experienced higher rates of emigration during the 1880s than did England and Scotland. Emigration from England itself never reached the high annual rates attained in certain decades by regions of truly mass emigration, such as Ireland, Norway, Baden, Württemburg, and Alsace, though Scotland's loss of population in the eighties approached the Scandinavian rates.[4]

Indeed, the assumption that maturing industrialization ought to stem the flow of population overseas was so strong among some early students of British emigration that they stated flatly that the peak of emigration from England, relative to population size, had been reached by the mid-nineteenth century after which the expansion of industrial employment and the growth of towns at home absorbed migration from the countryside.[5] Implied in such a statement is the

[2] W. D. Forsyth, *The Myth of the Open Spaces* (Melbourne, 1942), p. 68. For a more complete set of estimates of comparative rates of gross emigration from European countries, see Gustav Sundbärg, *Aperçus Statistiques Internationaux*, 11e Année (Stockholm, 1908), pp. 103, 105. Semmingsen, 'Norwegian Migration', pp. 155–6.

[3] '. . . Prosperity in America was highly important as a stimulus to emigration from Sweden, but . . . cyclical upswings in Sweden were a far more powerful counter-stimulant than is generally recognised.' (Thomas, *Swedish Population Movements*, p. 169.)

[4] Richard Easterlin, 'Influence in European Overseas Emigration Before World War I', *Economic Development and Cultural Change*, Vol. 9, No. 3 (April, 1961), p. 335. Sundbärg, *Aperçus Statistiques Internationaux*, p. 105.

[5] 'After the first half of the century, however, industrial developments in Great Britain had a depressing effect on emigration.' (E.C. Snow writing in Imre Ferenczi and Walter Willcox, *Internal Migrations*, National Bureau of Economic Research [1932], Vol. 2, pp. 251–2. This statement formed the basis for similar remarks in M. R. Davie, *World Migration* (New York, 1949), pp. 58–9; United Nations, *Determinants and Consequences*, p. 99;

counter-factual proposition, which cannot be tested, that emigration from England would have been higher than it was in the last part of the nineteenth century had that country not become the workshop of the world. The statement that emigration declined is patently false. Emigration was more important in the last half of the century than it had been in the first half. Gross rates of emigration from England and Scotland were higher in the prosperous fifties than they had been in the early forties. The next bulge in emigration in the late sixties and early seventies produced a greater absolute volume of emigrants from England and Scotland than ever before, though the incidence in the population was probably slightly less than in the fifties. The rates of emigration during the eighties, however, when 67 per cent of passengers going overseas from the United Kingdom still gave the U.S.A. as their destination, were higher than those of the fifties. Again in the decade after 1900, by which time only 44 per cent of the emigrants from the United Kingdom were bound for the United States, the relative rates of emigration were again nearly as high as they had been in the eighties. The evidence suggests that some Englishmen and Scotsmen responded to the American business cycle as well as to the 'Kuznets' cycles during the last third of the nineteenth century.

Table 1 Absolute levels of outward passenger movement from Great Britain to overseas places in peak years of emigration

Year	England and Wales	Scotland
1832	50,700*	11,112*
1842	74,683*	13,108*
1854	90,966	25,872
1873	123,343	21,310
1883	183,236	31,139
1888	170,822	35,873
1907	265,229	66,355
1912	314,622	72,626

* Figures for 1832 and 1842 refer to passengers leaving from English, Welsh and Scottish ports in vessels covered by the Passenger Acts. The figures for 1854 and afterwards refer to passengers of English, Welsh, or Scottish nationality.
Sources: N. H. Carrier and J. R. Jeffery, *External Migration, a Study of the available Statistics, 1815–1950*, General Register Office, Studies on Medical and Population Subjects, No. 6 (London, H.M.S.O., 1953), pp. 93–4. Figures for 1832 and 1842 calculated from *British Parliamentary Papers*, 1831–32, XXXII, (724), p. 209; 1842, XXXI (231), p. 33.

Kirk, *Europe's Population in the Interwar Years*, p. 81. Kirk made the entirely false statement that, in relation to population size, the peak of emigration in England had been passed before the middle of the nineteenth century. See also Stanley C. Johnston, *Emigration from the United Kingdom to North America, 1763–1912*, (1913; new impression, London, 1966), p. 39.

An obvious reason for some of the confusion about emigration from industrial Britain is the relatively poor quality of its migration statistics. Before the Passenger Act of 1852 the emigration statistics of the United Kingdom related only to the total number of passengers sailing from her ports in certain types of vessels.[6] Not until 1853 were the various nationalities within the British Isles distinguished in the port records. From that date onwards, the official statistics separated English, Welsh, Scottish, and Irish passengers according to destination, age, and sex. No distinction was made between prospective settlers and transient visitors. In 1863 cabin passengers were for the first time included in the published records, but no count was taken of the return of people from overseas places (by nationality) until 1895.

With all their limitations, these published statistics attest to the strength of the emigration movement from England and Scotland in the late nineteenth century and form the basis for hypotheses as to its responsiveness to economic conditions in receiving countries.[7] The only other means of estimating the magnitude of the emigration movement from England and Scotland, a method which provides no guide to annual fluctuations, is to estimate the net outward movement from one census to the next by projecting the probable increase in population from birth and death records and then comparing this figure with the actual population recorded in the census. (See Table 2.) Under-registration of births may explain, in part, the wide gap between estimates of net and gross emigration from England in the 1850s, but it is doubtful that the explanation applies to the even wider gap shown in the 1880s. While there is good reason to believe that some of the gross emigration of the eighties was offset by the return of former emigrants and of visitors from abroad, the disparity between the two estimates suggests that nearly twice as many English people returned as remained overseas, a conclusion which is barely credible.[8] Thus while we can be certain that the permanent outward movement from England and Scotland

[6] The most convenient summary of statistics of emigration from the United Kingdom is to be found in Carrier and Jeffery, *External Migration*. See also Ferenczi and Willcox, *International Migrations*, Vol. 1, 619–58.

[7] Brinley Thomas, *Migration and Economic Growth*, National Institute of Economic and Social Research (Cambridge University Press, 1954), pp. 83–122. Harry Jerome, *Migration and the Business Cycle*, National Bureau of Economic Research (New York, 1926), pp. 156–8. Allen C. Kelley, 'International Migration and Economic Growth: Australia, 1865–1935', *Journal of Economic History*, Vol. 25, no. 3 (September 1965), pp. 333–54.

[8] Though the English and Scots cannot be disaggregated in these figures, the United Kingdom authorities reported 708,586 passengers as returning from the U.S.A., Australia, and British North America between 1881 and 1890 as compared with 2,388,619 leaving for those places. (Carrier and Jeffery, *External Migration* pp. 95–7).

was higher in many years after 1850 than it had ever been before, the precise absolute levels are not known.[9]

Table 2   Estimates of gross and net annual rates of emigration per 10,000 population from Great Britain in certain years

| Year | Gross rate/10,000 | | Year | Net rate/10,000 | |
	England and Wales	Scotland		England	Scotland
1841	−14	n.a.	1841–50	−5*	n.a.
1853–60	−32	−50	1851–60	−16	−101
1061–70	−28	−46	1861–70	7	44
1871–80	−40	−47	1871–80	−5	−28
1881–90	−59	−71	1881–90	−23	−58
1891–1900	−36	−44	1891–1900	−2	−13
1901–10	−55	−99	1901–10	−19	−57

* Refers to England and Wales.

Sources: See footnote 9.

Apart from providing information on annual fluctuations in emigration and the age and sex of migrants, British emigration statistics reveal little about emigrants from England and Scotland in the last half of the nineteenth century. Occupations of outward-bound passengers were recorded after 1854 by destination rather than by place of origin. The only possibility of separating the British from the Irish, by occupation, is to use the separate series on the occupations of Irish emigrants provided after 1877, and to subtract.[10]

[9] Estimates of gross and net emigration from England and Scotland may be found in Sundbärg, *Aperçus Statistiques*, pp. 105, 339. The figures of net emigration given in table 2 were taken from estimates by Carrier and Jeffery in *External Migration*, p. 14 and by Brinley Thomas in *Wales and the Atlantic Economy* (Cardiff, 1962), p. 7. The estimates of gross emigration from England and Wales for 1853–1910 are based upon the passenger statistics of the U.K. as summarized in Carrier and Jeffery, *External Migration*, pp. 92–3. The estimate for 1841 has been made by using figures of emigration from individual counties in England and Wales as recorded in the U.K. Census, 1841, *Abstracts of the Answers and Returns, England and Wales* (London, 1843), pp. 399, 458. An estimate of the share of the year's emigrants who departed during the first five months of the year (included in the census of emigrants) was calculated from *British Parliamentary Papers* 1841, 2 sess., III (61), pp. 4–7, and used to gain an estimate of the total emigration of English and Welsh people for the entire year, 1841. This method gave an estimate of 20,484 English emigrants and 22,487 English and Welsh emigrants for the year 1841. If one assumes that the proportion of English and Welsh people in the total emigration from English and Welsh ports in 1841 was the same as that recorded in 1853, one gets a lower figure for total emigration—that is, 15,867 English and Welsh emigrants in 1841. Almost certainly more Irish were emigrating by way of English ports in 1853 than in 1841. The years 1841 and 1842 marked the peak of departures from English and Welsh ports before 1846, and thus the 1841 estimate of gross emigration rate gives the highest annual rate before 1846.

[10] Separate series of statistics of emigration from Ireland were begun in 1851 by the Census Commissioners. They included information about sex, age, occupation, county of origin in Ireland, destination abroad, and intended length of residence abroad. Thus they constitute a much more satisfactory guide to Irish emigration than exists for the English or Scots. For further details see Carrier and Jeffery, *External Migration*, p. 145.

Instead, scholars have turned to the records of immigrant-receiving countries for data on occupations of immigrants from various parts of the British Isles. The most important of these, the United States, did not make a satisfactory effort to disaggregate the British immigrants according to occupation until 1875.[11] These much-used American statistics form the basis of the common generalization that skilled workers constituted a higher proportion of the immigrants America received from England and Scotland than of any other immigrant group in the last quarter of the nineteenth century. They also reveal a pronounced shift in the composition of the English and Scottish immigrants by occupation between the peak inflow of the 1880s and the next great secular upswing after 1900. As America slumped dramatically as a destination for British emigrants in the latter period, those who did enter the United States included an even higher proportion of skilled workers than formerly.[12]

If our knowledge of the occupations of British emigrants is thus seriously limited, we have no comprehensive information at all about certain other characteristics of the emigrants from England and Scotland. We know little about the particular counties or the size of communities from which emigrants departed for places overseas after 1851. Professor Arthur Redford's account of the geographical origins of English overseas emigrants in the 1830s and 1840s was based upon comments by census enumerators and the emigration census of 1841.[13] After 1851, as the public debate about emigration dwindled, the census authorities stopped publishing comments on the subject. For the last part of the century, the only analyses of the composition of emigrant populations are those by Philip Taylor of the Mormons and by Ross Duncan of a group of emigrants assisted to go to New South Wales.[14] Clearly these groups may not have been typical of the much larger voluntary, unassisted emigration.

Not all writers have ignored the increasing emigration after 1850. Because of the want of contemporary statistical data, however, those who have sought to explain the continued emigration have relied upon literacy evidence and supposition as to which groups

[11] These were the figures used by Brinley Thomas. The American census also gave information on jobs held by English and Scots-born inhabitants of the U.S.A. from 1870 to 1910. For discussion, see E. P. Hutchinson, *Immigrants and Their Children, 1850–1950* (New York, 1956).

[12] Thomas, *Migration and Economic Growth*, pp. 60–5. Carrier and Jeffery, *External Migration*, p. 115.

[13] Arthur Redford, *Labour Migration in England, 1750–1850*, 1926, 2nd edition (Manchester University Press, 1964), pp. 124, 173–6.

[14] Philip Taylor, *Expectations Westward* (Edinburgh, 1965), pp. 147–51. Ross Duncan, 'Case Studies in Emigration: Cornwall, Gloucestershire and New South Wales, 1877–1886', *Economic History Review*, 2nd Series, Vol. 16, No. 2 (December 1963), pp. 272–89.

might have been induced by hardship to leave the country. Maldwyn
Jones assumed that since there was distress in certain branches of
English agriculture at the time of the Great Depression, 'tens of
thousands of farmers and agricultural labourers were driven to
emigrate'.[15] Convinced that rising real wages in the towns in the
eighties deprived townworkers of an incentive to emigrate, Professor A. K. Cairncross also thought that the 'combined force of depression in British agriculture and expansion abroad resulted in a
tremendous rural exodus, not so much to the towns as to America
and the colonies'.[16] Other writers, on equally slender evidence,
tended to emphasize the difficulties of specific groups of industrial
workers during the so-called Great Depression in explaining the
relatively large emigration of the eighties.[17] In fact, we are still
very much in the dark about the main characteristics of emigrants
from England and Scotland as well as about any changes in the composition of the movement as it swelled in certain years in the latter
half of the century.

The historical data available on these questions is so sparse that
a hypothesis might be entertained that English emigration was
entirely an individualistic movement, drawing off persons from all
occupations and regions of the country at times when opportunities
abroad looked promising. Since it is clear that parts of the countryside were losing population, however, what one would most like to
know is the relationship between the rural exodus and overseas
emigration. Were the rural labourers and handicraftsmen going
overseas, as suggested by Jones and Cairncross, or were they attracted
in the first instance by the possibility of employment in English
towns? Norway was another country in which emigration continued
after industrialization was well begun. In her study of Norwegian
port records, Ingrid Semmingsen found that, as industrial development matured, more and more rural migrants went first to Norwegian
towns for a period of time before emigrating and that towns became
more common as the last place of residence before emigration.

[15] Maldwyn Jones, *American Immigration* (Chicago, 1960) p. 194. Dr. William Farr in the
39th Report of the Register General, 1877, 'took the case of an agricultural labourer as
being synonymous with that of the emigrant'. (Johnston, *Emigration from the United
Kingdom*, p. 306.) These writers at least examined the course of emigration. A contrary
view was expressed by those who followed the *Interpretations* of the N.B.E.R. M. R. Davie,
in *World Migration*, p. 58, stated that farmers and labourers went to towns rather than
abroad after the mid-century. See also Kirk, *Europe's Population in the Interwar Years*, p. 82;
Ferenczi and Willcox, *International Migrations*, Vol. 2, p. 250.

[16] A. K. Cairncross, *Home and Foreign Investment, 1870–1913* (Cambridge University
Press, 1953), p. 211.

[17] W. A. Carrothers, *Emigration from the British Isles* (London, 1929), pp. 216, 218, 227–8.
H. Leak and T. Priday, 'Migration from and to the United Kingdom', *Journal of the
Royal Statistical Society*, Vol. 46 (1933), Part 2, pp. 188–9. Jones, *American Immigration*,
p. 195.

She also discovered that skilled workers came to constitute a higher share of emigrants towards the end of the nineteenth century, but that these skilled workers were more likely to be handicraft than factory workers.[18] It is plausible that in England and Scotland as well, the movement overseas reflected the so-called rural exodus only indirectly, and that towns and industries at home became the favoured destination of the emigrant from agricultural areas in the last part of the nineteenth century.

II

A certain amount of information about some of these mysterious English and Scots emigrants of the late nineteenth century does survive on the microfilms of ship lists in the National Archives in Washington. Most of these lists give a bare minimum of information. Occasionally the captains of ships carrying immigrants to New York took the trouble to fill out carefully the official forms for describing their passengers. Some ship lists contain not only the name of the passenger, his age, and that of other members of his family who accompanied him, but also his occupation, his country of birth, and his place of last residence. A few captains even provided information about the destinations of their passengers in the U.S.A. or Canada, and whether or not they intended to settle permanently in the New World. For the mid-century period of heavy immigration from 1846–54, twenty-seven ships arriving at New York from Liverpool, Bristol, London, and Glasgow provided satisfactory details about the English and Scottish passengers they carried. Roughly 850 adult men from England and Scotland were on these ships, about 9 per cent of the total number of English and Scottish males reported as entering the United States during these years.[19] Dipping into the ship lists in the next immigration peak in the early seventies produced no 'good' ship lists. After the Federal Government took over the regulation of immigration in the eighties, a new effort was made to get full details about passengers arriving in American ports. From 1885 through 1888, most captains conscientiously filled in the new form in the early part of each year, until the seasonal flood of migrants seemingly overwhelmed them some time in April or May. For the first few months of these four years it was possible to analyse the returns of English and Scottish immigrants from London, Liverpool, and Glasgow on 129 ships. The

[18] Semmingsen, 'Norwegian Emigration in the Nineteenth Century', pp. 156–7.
[19] The United States records clearly under-estimated the numbers of immigrants from England and Scotland during this period because the largest category of immigrants from the British Isles were returned as 'Great Britain, not stated' until the 1870s. See Appendix A for ships analysed.

10,000-odd adult males on these ships who had been born in England or Scotland constituted about 5 per cent of the total males reported in the American immigration records as coming from England or Scotland during these years.[20]

The contrast between the 'good' lists and the usual passenger list submitted adds to any suspicions one might already have as to the reliability of published immigration statistics. The lazier or more harassed captain was likely to fill in the blank for occupation at the top of the form with the word 'labourer' or 'mechanic' and use ditto marks for the rest of the page. This liberal use of ditto marks accounts for the large numbers of immigrants to the United States recorded as coming from 'Great Britain, not stated' until the mid-seventies. Because published records were based upon such carelessly compiled lists, the documents that were completed carefully become the more interesting. Yet, as sources, they have drawbacks that make it unwise to treat them formally as random samples of the entire emigration from England and Scotland. They yield information about migrants who went to North America, but not about the rest of the overseas movement. They are biased towards certain years and the migration of the first few months of those years. One's confidence is perhaps enhanced by the fact that both small vessels and large ships carrying hundreds of steerage passengers are included. Nevertheless, I have not ventured to assign tests of significance to the data because the criteria for randomness could not be applied.

In this article the 'good' ship lists have been exploited for three types of information: the occupations of male immigrants arriving in New York from England and Scotland; the counties from which they emigrated; and the size of the communities which they reported as their 'place of last residence'.[21] The view-point of the analysis is that of the sending rather than the receiving country. Instead of comparing the structure of the emigrant population with that of the receiving country or of other immigrant groups, as writers concerned with the impact of British immigrants upon the American economy have done, I have compared the emigrant groups with the English and Scottish populations as recorded in the nearest census. The question to be answered was whether this evidence suggested that certain occupations and regions were losing an excessive share of

[20] See Appendix A for ships analysed. It is quite possible that satisfactory ship lists exist for some of the years of low immigration. Limitations of time enabled me to search for clues as to the migrants of peak years of emigration only. Not until 1891 were federal immigration officials required to check the manifests provided by the ship captains by interviewing immigrants to ascertain whether or not details were correct. It is quite clear that even after this date harassed officials were unable to carry out the requirements of the law in peak months and years of immigration.

[21] On some lists this column was headed 'Starting point' or 'Hailing from.'

their population through emigration to the United States. In an attempt to find an answer, experiments were carried out comparing the characteristics of adult male emigrants with those of all adult males in the census of England and Scotland in 1851 and 1881.

The samples from ship lists seemed too small to presume to say anything from them about emigration from particular counties. Instead, the English counties were grouped into four classes, according to the share of the labour force in agriculture and the level of nominal weekly wages in agriculture reported in Bowley. If more than a third of the male labour force was employed in agriculture, the county was ranked as an agricultural county; and if the weekly wages in agriculture in 1851 were lower than 10 shillings, the county was ranked as a low-wage county. For 1881 the cut-off point for a low-wage county was raised to 15 shillings. The Scottish labour force was divided into two classes, one in counties in the Highlands and Lowlands in which agriculture was the principal employment, and the other in those Lowland counties in which agriculture employed less than a third of the labour force.[22] Comparing the emigrants with the census afforded one means of testing the hypothesis that emigrants came mainly from the least industrialized and poorest counties in England and Scotland.

In order to discover whether the men on these particular ships were coming from the countryside in excessive numbers, an effort was made to find all the towns of 20,000 or more inhabitants in the 1851 and 1881 census. These communities were designated as urban. The question was whether the male emigrants from England and Scotland were more or less urbanized than the entire population at the time they went overseas.[23]

The most complex comparison with the census related to occupations. I rejected, perhaps somewhat perversely, the occupational classifications suggested by the census authorities themselves and those employed by the American immigration authorities,[24] because the conventional distinction between skilled and unskilled manual workers, which has formed the basis of so many summaries of migrant occupations, reveals less about the skilled men who emigrated than one would like to know. The fact that men were skilled was of significance to the American economy; but in attempting to explain why people emigrated, one would like to know whether

[22] The counties in each class in 1851 and 1881 are listed in Appendix B.

[23] These towns are not all included in the table in Phyllis Deane and B. R. Mitchell, *Abstract of British Historical Statistics* (Cambridge University Press, 1962), pp. 24–7.

[24] In an unpublished paper on the census occupational classification, William Armstrong has urged all researchers to employ the census classes of 1951 for social classification and Booth's scheme for industrial classification in working on nineteenth century census materials.

the factory workers in the forefront of the Industrial Revolution emigrated in excessive numbers, or whether the emigration of skilled men was primarily a movement from the countryside of handi-craftsmen whose skills were undermined as much from declining local populations as from the competition of factory production. The census occupations and the emigrant occupations were grouped into six classes:[25]

1. *Agricultural workers.*

2. *Labourers.* This group includes all non-agricultural labourers listed in the census under whatever industrial classification. If this class was returned in small numbers because respondents did not like to describe themselves simply as labourers to census enumerators, the same considerations might be assumed to arise when such people were asked their occupation by a ship's captain or mate.

3. *Pre-industrial tertiary workers.* This class was made up very largely of servants, one of the subdivisions used in the American immigration statistics. Since those statistics did not always distinguish between males and females by occupation, they provide no indication of the numbers of male servants among English and Scottish emigrants. This class also includes such occupations as messengers, road and barge workers, grooms and coachmen.

4. *Pre-industrial skilled workers.* Here an attempt has been made to single out occupations and industries that did not undergo significant technological change before 1880. The group contains building-trades workers; miners; clothing workers, such as tailors and shoemakers; food processors, such as millers, butchers, and grocers; metalworkers, such as blacksmiths; woodworkers, such as cabinet-makers, coopers, and wheelwrights. These were occupations in which the job description was probably not very different in 1880 from what it had been in 1800. Thus these workers did not experience a sharp leap forward in productivity in the course of the nineteenth century though some increase was possible. In emigrating to less developed regions overseas, they might expect to follow their traditional occupations with only minor modifications. These occupations were fairly widely dispersed in England and Scotland in both cities and villages, agricultural and industrial regions. These people probably did not face direct technological unemployment by the substitution of machinery for their labour in the community in which they worked, though some of their activities might be indirectly displaced

[25] For a more detailed listing of occupations in each group, see Appendix C.

by concentrated manufacturing activities elsewhere. If they emigrated because of lack of opportunity, that factor might be connected
with declining population in the area where they practised their
trades. This, then, is an attempt to distinguish handicraft workers
whose jobs changed little, and many of whom, like building-trades
workers and miners, found expanding opportunities to practise
old trades with the advance of industrialization. These were people
more likely to suffer cyclical than technological unemployment.
Their opportunities might change with internal population movements, for most of them (apart from miners) served primarily
local markets. The one common feature was the limited advance
in productivity that established some kind of ceiling on earnings and
might make higher wages paid in more labour-scarce regions seem
the only means to substantially higher earnings for roughly the same
work.

5. *Industrial skilled workers.* This group contains workers in new and
changing industries in which job classifications were changed
markedly some time during the nineteenth century and the productivity of many jobs raised through the introduction of improved
technology. The workers placed in this category were all skilled
workers engaged in these changing industries—both those displaced
by new machinery and those gaining from it. Into this industrial
class went all workers attached to the great nineteenth-century
industries of textiles, iron and steel, engineering, and most of the
secondary branches of metal manufacture. Thus, because of the
difficulties of interpreting census classifications, this group includes
both the workers in new occupations specifically created by industrialization as well as those suffering at some point from technological unemployment, such as handloom-weavers and framework-
knitters. In the 1850s the class clearly contains both workers in
collapsing occupations and those in more modern sectors of industry.
By the 1880s, the class can be taken to represent primarily the skilled
workers in the industrialized sectors of the economy.

6. *Modern tertiary workers.* This class contains service workers in
the distinctly nineteenth-century railway industry as well as workers
in commercial, clerical, and professional occupations which can
be distinguished from producers in the census. Where a class
was returned as 'maker and dealer', the occupation was placed in
a skilled industrial group.

Obviously this classification is in part a compromise forced upon
one by the categories of workers singled out by the census authorities.
It does, however, form some basis for estimating whether the workers
on these ships came primarily from more traditional industries

and occupations or from new and changing industries produced by nineteenth-century technology.

III

The passenger lists give some information about emigrants during two periods of peak emigration. After declining between 1842 and 1843, emigration from British ports began a long upward movement not significantly interrupted until 1855. In spite of the growing confidence and prosperity in the British economy, this mid-century emigration generated rates of gross emigration higher than those of the thirties and forties. The published statistics, however, afford no possibility of estimating the exact numbers of English and Scottish people who emigrated between 1846 and 1854. This was probably the largest emigration from England and Scotland during the whole nineteenth century, with the exception of the decade of the 1880s, which stands out as the most important, whether one looks at estimates of gross or net emigration. The year 1885, the first for which we have good ship lists, was the second of two years of falling emigration after the huge upswing which had begun in 1879. Emigration to America then rose in 1886 and 1887, to decline very slightly in 1888. Approximately 130,000 English, Welsh, and Scottish passengers left for the United States in 1887 and in 1888, which were the peak years for movement into America for the entire century.

These 'samples' of emigrants based upon port lists relate to passengers entering the U.S.A. in years of heaviest emigration there from England and Scotland. The characteristics of the migrant population in those years may have been quite different from the migrant stream in troughs of emigration. Moreover, the structure of the migrant population may have changed from one emigration peak to another. Thus the data to be examined here cannot be generalized for years other than those specifically treated, and cannot be interpreted as a cross section of English and Scottish emigration, even to the U.S.A., throughout the last half of the nineteenth century. Only a tentative comparison can be made between the emigrants of the two peak periods. That in itself is some advance in knowledge, since we presently know practically nothing.

The ship lists cast doubt upon the idea that the emigration from England and Scotland to the United States in the eighties could be characterized by the term 'rural exodus'. Almost four out of five men who came to New York on these ships in the late eighties gave a principal town as his place of last residence. Since not quite half the population of England and Scotland was concentrated in towns of 20,000 or more inhabitants in 1881 (53 per cent in 1891), town-dwellers were over-represented among emigrants. This over-representation was greater during the three years of rising immigration from 1885–7 and waned in 1888 as the crest of the migration wave was reached. It was also slightly more pronounced among the Scottish emigrants than it was among the English. (Table 3.)

Table 3   Percentage of adult male emigrants from England and Scotland giving principal towns as places of last residence, by date of emigration to the U.S.A.

	Date of ship lists	
	1846–54	1885–88
1. Total number in group	848	10,074
2. % from principal towns	26·8	78·0
3. % living in towns at nearest census	35·0	49·4
4. Index of representation: 2/3 × 100	77	158

Sources: Principal towns with populations of 20,000 or more for 1851 taken from *Census of Great Britain,* 1851, Vol. 1, *Summary Tables,* pp. ccvi, ccxviii, cxxvi. In most instances the boundaries used were those of municipal boroughs. The following towns were also included, with boundaries as designated.
  Birkenhead, Burnley, Stalybridge (Local registrar's districts).
  Brighton (Parish).
  Dudley, Cheltenham (Parliamentary borough and Parish).
  Huddersfield (Parliamentary borough and Township).
  Leicester, Stockport (Municipal and Parliamentary borough).
  Stoke-on-Trent (Township).
  Bury, Chatham, Rochdale (Parliamentary borough).
Principal towns with populations of 20,000 or more for 1881 were taken from the *Census of England and Wales,* 1891, *Preliminary Report,* p. 18; Vol. 2, p. vi; and *Ninth Census of Scotland,* 1891, Vol. 1, Report and Tables, *B.P.P.,* 1892, XCIV, 1, p. 123. Definition of towns was in all cases Urban Sanitary Districts.

According to the ship lists, town-dwellers had not been over-represented among the emigrants of the mid-century emigration. At that time, relatively more men were leaving for America directly from agricultural villages and small towns, and the inhabitants of larger towns were under-represented among emigrants. The switch in origins between the two periods was much greater than could be accounted for simply by rising urbanization in England and Scotland during the intervening years. As urban growth advanced in the United States (by 40 per cent in the decade of the eighties), urban rather than rural workers, were attracted there from England and Scotland. Many of these emigrants may previously have come into British towns from the countryside, later to set off for the United States, but our data do not enable us to see these previous migrations. It is also quite possible that the English and Scots emigrants to Canada and Australia at this time were proceeding more frequently directly from rural communities. In the late eighties, it appears that the United States was attracting, selectively, urban workers from Britain and that the character of English and

Scottish emigration was very different in this respect from what it had been in the middle of the century.

Table 4   English and Scottish adult male immigrants on New York ship lists by size of place of last residence

	1885	1886	1887	1888	Census 1881	Census 1891
England						
from towns	1,113	2,024	1,704	1,154		
total male immigrants	1,478	2,591	2,098	1,492		
% from towns	75·3	78·1	81·2	77·3	50·9	55·3
Scotland						
from towns	361	697	413	398		
total male immigrants	461	857	500	610		
% from towns	78·3	81·3	82·6	65·2	39·7	43·5

Analysis of the types of counties from which emigrants were proceeding to the United States also reveals a marked change in the composition of emigration between the fifties and the eighties. In the mid-century, agricultural counties were still fairly well represented as places of last residence of emigrants to America. Yet the migrants of these years were not going overseas mainly from the least industrialized counties with the lowest agricultural wages. The most pronounced movement to America was coming from low-wage industrial counties—Cornwall and the Midlands (Worcestershire, Leicestershire, Staffordshire, Warwickshire, and Gloucestershire). The poorer agricultural counties produced as many emigrants for these ships, nearly a quarter of the total, but they contained almost a third of the adult male labour force of the country (see Table 5).

The ship lists of the eighties cast doubt on the idea of considering the depression in agriculture as a direct explanation for the swelling overseas emigration of the decade. Only 4 per cent of the migrants studied came from agricultural counties, while 14 per cent of England's male labour force still lived in them in 1881. At this time, the older and richer industrial counties were supplying proportionately more emigrants to the States; indeed, 77 per cent of those studied came from the counties classified as high-wage industrial counties. Since opportunities to emigrate had by this time been enhanced, as compared with the fifties, both with respect to the information available to prospective emigrants and to the predictable cost of the journey and loss of earnings, the shift in the origins of migrants towards the industrial counties suggests that most young men who were leaving rural communities in England were seeking opportunities first of all in English industrial areas. The over-representation of Lowland industrial counties in the Scottish movement overseas in the late-eighties was not so pronounced, but one highland city, Aberdeen, was sending quite extraordinary numbers of building-trades workers to New York in 1887 and 1888, though its county has been ranked as agricultural.[26]

Table 5   Adult male emigrants from England and Scotland found on New York ship lists, according to type of county in which they last resided before emigration, by date of emigration

	Ship lists		Census		Index	
	1846–54	1885–88	1851	1881	1846–54	1885–88
	(1)	(2)	(3)	(4)	1/3	2/4
	%	%	%	%	×100	×100
Counties						
England:						
I Agricultural low wage	24·3	4·6	32·2	14·0	75	33
II Agricultural high wage	8·6	—	9·5	—	91	—
III Industrial low wage	23·8	20·9	16·3	29·3	146	71
IV Industrial high wage	43·3	74·5	42·0	56·7	103	131
Totals	100·0	100·0	100·0	100·0		
Absolute numbers	608	7,238	4,788,000	7,231,000		
Scotland:						
I Agricultural	41·1	20·1	40·4	24·8	102	81
II Industrial	58·9	79·9	59·6	75·2	99	106
Totals	100·0	100·0	100·0	100·0		
Absolute numbers	68	2,421	873,000	1,109,000		
Unknowns*	172	415				

Yorkshire had to be omitted entirely from the 1846–54 analysis because too many migrants were returned without identification as to which part of Yorkshire they came from, and the different Ridings of Yorkshire fell into different classes of counties.

*Most of the unknowns were migrants for whom the place of residence could not be identified, or the village name was given without a county and villages of the same name appeared in more than one county.

Sources: Census of Great Britain, 1851, Vol. II, sections V, IX. *Census cf England and Wales*, 1881, Vol. III, secton VI, p. 24; section IV, p. 7. *Census of Scotland*, 1881, *British Parliamentary Papers*, 1881, LXXXI, 1, section VI, pp. 24–5; section IV, p. 7. Sir Arthur Lyon Bowley, *Wages in the United Kingdom in the 19th century* (London, 1900), Table at back of book. Ship lists.

This evidence that emigrants of the late-eighties were departing not so much from the countryside and agricultural regions, as from the principal towns and the leading industrial counties of Britain might seem to suggest that the bulge in emigration was related, after all, to industrial unemployment in Britain's major industries

[26] 'After a particularly dull winter in the Scottish trade, nearly every stonemason who could scrape together the passage money emigrated to recoup his fortunes. Two thousand landed in New York during six weeks of the spring of 1887. . . .' R. T. Berthoff, *British Immigrants in Industrial America* (Cambridge, Mass., 1954), p. 82, citing *Scottish American*, 25 May, 1887.

despite rising real wages in the towns. A look at the occupations
of the emigrants dispels this impression. (See Table 6.)

Table 6 Occupations of adult male emigrants from England and Scotland on certain ships arriving in the port of New York

	Ship lists		Census		Index	
	1846–54 (1) %	1885–8 (2) %	1851 (3) %	1881 (4) %	1846–54 1/3 x100	1885–8 2/4 x100
I A. Farmers	14·2	8·4	6·5	4·1	219	204
B. Farm labourers	0·5	1·1	20·4	11·4	2	10
Total agriculture	14·7	9·5	27·3*	15·6	54	61
II Labourers	22·6	29·5	6·9	8·2	328	360
III Servants, etc.	3·1	3·2	9·3	12·8	33	25
IV Building trades	10·1	18·1	7·4	9·1	136	199
Mining	5·2	8·0	5·2	6·4	100	125
Food	5·9	2·1	4·2	4·2	140	50
Metal	4·4	1·7	2·8	2·6	157	65
Clothing	6·7	1·5	6·4	4·4	105	34
Woodworking	2·1	0·5	2·2	2·0	95	25
Miscellaneous	1·8	0·9	2·0	1·2	90	75
Mechanics	0·6	1·5	—	0·4	—	375
Total pre-industrial	36·7	34·3	30·2	30·3	122	113
V Textiles	7·4	2·0	8·9	5·4	83	37
Steel and Engineering	7·3	4·0	4·8	7·9	152	51
Miscellaneous	2·6	1·8	2·0	3·8	130	47
Total industrial	17·3	7·8	15·7	17·0	110	46
VI Railways	—	0·1	0·3	2·1	—	5
Clerical	1·2	5·6	2·1	3·7	57	151
Commercial	3·9	8·0	5·9	7·1	66	113
Professional	0·5	1·9	2·5	3·3	20	58
Total tertiary†	5·6	15·7	10·7	16·1	52	98
Total percentages	100·0	100·0	100·1	100·0		
Absolute numbers	848	8,698	6,625,000	8,892,985		
Omissions†	—	753	26,593	626		
Unknowns†	—	632				

* A few miscellaneous agricultural workers included in total for agriculture not classified under farmers or agricultural labourers.
† The only class of male migrants omitted from this occupation table was gentlemen, of whom 753 were found on the 129 ship lists. Unknowns included illegible occupations and men listed with 'none' in the occupation column.

Source: Census of Great Britain, 1851, Population Tables II, Vol. I, Table 54, pp. cxxviii–cxl; Table XXIV, pp. ccxviii–ccxxi. *Census of England and Wales,* 1881, III, Table 5, pp. x–xvii. *Ninth Census of Scotland,* Vol. II, *British Parliamentary Papers,* 1883, LXXXI, 1, Table XV, pp. 406–13.

Skilled industrial workers were fairly well represented in the mid-century emigration from England and Scotland according to the ship lists. Apart from building-trades workers, who will be discussed shortly, two groups of industrial workers were somewhat over represented in the migration of this period: first, workers associated with preparing and distributing food, such as millers, grocers, and butchers and second, metalworkers and engineers of all kinds. The analysis does not suggest that the men classified as pre-industrial metalworkers showed a greater tendency to emigrate at this time than did workers in the more modern branches of the iron and machinery industries. Members of the two most numerous occupations, blacksmiths and engineers, appeared in approximately equal numbers in the ship lists. Very few practised trades that were particularly depressed in the fifties: two nailers, one caster, and one stamper and a shuttle-maker were identified. But six coachmakers, eight moulders as well as a pattern-maker, an engine-smith, a boiler-maker, two steel rollers were also there. Textile workers were not well represented, neither the prosperous cotton workers nor the depressed handloom-weavers of the woollen industry. The impression that emigration was not at this time serving as a safety-valve against technological unemployment to any significant degree is further enhanced by noting that these skilled workers were leaving mostly from principal towns, not small communities. (See Table 7.)

Table 7   Share of English and Scottish male immigrants on ships arriving in New York between 1828 and 1854 who gave principal towns as places of last residence

Occupation	Number from towns	Total on ships	% from towns
Labourers	29	198	14·6
Building trades	39	111	35·1
Miners	2	42	4·8
Other handicrafts	85	128	66·4
Textile workers	30	94	31·9
Ironworkers/engineers	36	63	57·1
Other industrial workers	11	28	39·2
All males on ships	316	1,163	27·2
Census, 1851			35·0

The attraction that the American economy exercised upon Britain's skilled workers seems to have been much diminished by the late-eighties. With the exception of building-trades workers and miners, men following handicraft occupations were far less well represented in the emigrant labour force than they had been in the fifties. When they did emigrate, they were as likely to go to the Empire as to the United States. (See Table 8.) Similarly workers in the industrialized sector of the economy formed a smaller share of the emigrant labour force than they had in the fifties. The textile workers who did emigrate at this time went almost exclusively to the United States, but their under-representation in the emigrant labour force suggests that they were not choosing emigration as a means of adapting to the difficulties of that decade in a manner suggestive of a social movement.[27] Workers in heavy industry—such as iron and steel workers, engineers, shipbuilders, and boiler-makers—did not show a similar preference for the United States as a destination, and they, too, were under-represented among emigrants to New York. Clearly, in the great migration of these years, many skilled industrial workers did emigrate, both to the U.S.A. and to other parts of the world, but they did not leave in such large numbers that one can explain the heavy emigration in terms of skilled workers who sought this means of escape from uncertain employment.[28] Even in 1886, and 1887 when trade unions in Britain reported relatively high rates of unemployment and the upward movement in real wages abated, skilled industrial workers were not flocking to America.

Two groups of skilled workers in Britain did demonstrate a responsiveness to the American boom of the eighties, however: miners and building-trades workers. These occupations were fairly well represented among the emigrants of the mid-century, but both groups were over-represented in the emigration of the late-eighties. Miners formed 8 per cent and building-trades workers no less than 18 per cent of the passengers analysed in the eighties. The striking mobility of these workers, who might hope to practise their trades with little modification in many parts of the world, is indicated in Table 8. While the United States was undergoing rapid industrial advance combined with a building boom in the eighties, both groups clearly preferred America as a destination. No other occupational groups among those studied changed the direction of their migration so sharply during the nineties when American building slumped and new mines were being opened in Australia and South Africa.

[27] A contemporary, Thomas Ellison, referred to the large numbers of impoverished textile workers emigrating to the U.S.A. in the 1880s. (*The Cotton Trade of Great Britain* [1886], p. 103, cited in J. Parry Lewis, *Building Cycles and Britain's Growth* [London 1965], p. 124.)

[28] 'In most American industries—iron and steel by 1870, coal and iron mining by 1880, most textile processes by 1900, and even upstarts like tinplating by 1905—the original English, Welsh and Scottish skilled hands lost their place to peasant greenhorns, Irish or French Canadians before 1880, southern and eastern Europeans thereafter. Many were able to move up into managerial jobs or even ownership, but, for their countrymen who might have followed them to America, opportunities were drying up.' (Berthoff, *British Immigrants in Industrial America*, p. 87.) The evidence of port records suggests that Berthoff antedated the decline of opportunities in coal mining and postdated that for textile workers.

Table 8   Percentage of adult male passengers, by occupation, leaving U.K. ports for the U.S.A. in two periods*

	1885–8	1895–8
Per cent of all occupied males giving U.S.A. as destination	68·5	56·1
Occupations with a high preference for U.S.A. during eighties:		
Farm labourers	66·9	93·4
Labourers	77·8	75·0
Building trades workers	70·7	44·1
Miners	72·9	22·4
Mechanics not otherwise designated	83·8	88·1
Textile workers	86·6	96·4
Occupations with relatively low preference for U.S.A. during eighties:		
Farmers	60·3	51·8
Handicraftsmen	52·7	61·1
Iron, Steel, Engineering	55·0	37·0
Clerks	55·7	51·7
Commercial occupations	52·9	48·3
Professional occupations†	43·9	21·5
Servants, etc.	59·4	63·8

* Since these figures are based upon official U.K. emigration statistics, the Irish are included with the British.

† Includes merchants, students, and gentlemen who cannot be separated in the original data.

Sources: Statistical Tables Relating to Emigration from and into the United Kingdom in the Year 1885, British Parliamentary Papers, 1886, LXXI (3), pp. 14–15; *in 1886, B.P.P.,* 1887, LXXXIX (32), pp. 16–17; *in 1887, B.P.P.,* 1888, CVII (2), pp. 16–17; *in 1888, B.P.P.,* 1889, LXXXIV (10), pp. 16–17; *in 1895, B.P.P.,* 1896, XCIII (130), pp. 22–3; *in 1896, B.P.P.,* 1897, XCIX (165), pp. 22–3; *in 1897, B.P.P.,* 1898, CIII (154), pp. 22–3; *in 1897, B.P.P.,* CVII (154), pp. 22–3; *in 1898, B.P.P.,* 1899, CVII (188), pp. 24–5.

This remarkable prominence of building-trades workers among emigrants of the late eighties (they formed 36 per cent of the male emigrants from Scotland alone) coincided with a period of low building activity in most English and Scottish towns.[29] Four out of five of these building craftsmen found on ships arriving in New York came from principal towns, a slightly higher percentage than that for all male immigrants studied.[30] Writers who have elucidated fluctuations in building activity in Britain, which (depending upon which index one uses) reached a peak sometime about 1878 and a trough in the late eighties, have also called attention to connections

[29] Lewis, *Building Cycles,* pp. 316–17. Cairncross, *Home and Foreign Investment,* pp. 16–17 213. Thomas, *Migration and Economic Growth,* p. 297.

[30] Percentage of building-trades workers on New York ship lists coming from principal towns:

1885	—82·1
1886	—84·8
1887	—83·2
1888	—70·2
1885–88	—80·7

between British overseas emigration and capital movements and domestic building activity.[31] Professor Cairncross has noted the emigration of building-trades workers to Canada after 1907 when domestic building activity was again at a low ebb. The port records indicate that these workers were behaving as though the Atlantic formed a single economy for building activity in the eighties as well. A very large number of these English and Scottish emigrants went back and forth across the Atlantic each season during the eighties, to work during the peak of activity in the States and spend the winter in England or Scotland.[32] Cairncross and Lewis have provided persuasive evidence that the decline in building activity in most English and Scottish towns in the eighties was itself a consequence of the huge emigration that began its upswing in 1879. The emigration of young people—those people who, as Lewis suggests, might shortly have been marrying and demanding housing had they remained in Britain—was one factor in the weak market for housing in the eighties.[33] The published occupational statistics of the U.K. and the U.S.A. indicate that this emigration of building trades workers was relatively weaker in the early-eighties, as a share of total emigrants, and reached its peak during the latter half of the decade.[34] (See Table 9 and Appendix D, Tables 12 and 13.) The building-trades workers did not initiate the migration movement of the eighties, but they found migration, permanent or seasonal, a means of adapting to one of its consequences—the decline in house-building.

The origins of the great emigration of the eighties itself are found in the sharp rise in the numbers of unskilled labourers going overseas, especially from England, after 1879. The responsiveness of unskilled labourers to conditions in the American economy is indicated by the seven-and-a-half-fold increase in the numbers reported by the American authorities as arriving from England between the trough of 1879 and the peak of 1882. The number of skilled workers arriving in the States from England rose only four times during those years. Both the American and the British statistics imply that unskilled labourers formed a higher share of total emigrants from England to the U.S.A. in the early eighties than they did in the latter half of the decade. Yet the analysis of the ship lists for 1885–8 reported 33 per cent of the English and 20 per cent

---

[31] Lewis, *Building Cycles*, pp. 164–85. Cairncross, *Home and Foreign Investment*, pp. 209–21. Thomas, *Migration and Economic Growth*, pp. 175–89.

[32] Berthoff, *British Immigrants*, p. 82. Charlotte Erickson, *American Industry and the European Immigrant* (Cambridge, Mass., 1957), pp. 49–50. Roger Simon, 'Birds of Passage', M.A. Thesis, University of Wisconsin, 1966, pp. 3–4.

[33] Lewis, *Building Cycles*, pp. 179–80.

[34] The share of building-trades workers recorded in the ship lists rose from 10 per cent of the immigrants of 1885 to 20 per cent in 1888.

of the Scotsmen arriving in New York as general labourers.[35]

Labour had also been the most over-represented occupation among the emigrants of the mid-century. In that period, the labourers had been going out directly from the countryside and smaller towns. (See Table 7. Only 14 per cent of the labourers came from principal towns.) The unskilled labourers who emigrated in the late eighties had been, like the entire emigration, highly urbanized.[36] The share of labourers from the countryside was highest, at 30 per cent in 1885, the year of lowest emigration in the four years analysed in the eighties. As prosperity seemed to be returning to the towns in 1887 and 1888 the share of emigrant labourers coming from principal towns rose.[37]

The chief feature, then, of the large emigration of the late-nineteenth century was the exodus of some of the least qualified members of the urban labour force in England and Scotland, of the disadvantaged for whom the continued high rate of population increase and entries to the labour force narrowed the range of opportunities, particularly in a decade when building activity was low. The port records suggest that farm labourers and pre-industrial tertiary workers were the least well represented among the emigrants to the U.S.A. at this time. Farmers themselves were still emigrating in larger numbers than their share in the labour force might warrant, as they had been in the fifties. The poorer people from the countryside were being drawn first of all to English towns, though some of them may have proceeded overseas from those towns in the eighties. Contemporary accounts of the emigration of farm labourers in the seventies and eighties mentioned emigration to the towns with greater frequency than they did overseas migration. Only one of the Assistant Commissioners for the Richmond Commission mentioned the U.S.A.

[35] These percentages are slightly lower than those recorded in the published American immigration statistics for these years which recorded peaks of 48 per cent of English immigrants in 1885 and 29 per cent of Scots in 1887 as labourers. (Thomas, *Migration and Economic Growth*, pp. 269, 271.) The ship lists may bias the share of labourers downwards by their concentration in the early months of the year. A breakdown of occupations of immigrants by months of immigration for the four years shows the proportion of labourers to have been higher in April than in the earlier months.

[36] Percentage of labourers from principal towns:

1885	—71·2
1886	—80·3
1887	—87·9
1888	—80·3
1885–88	—80·3

[37] On the beginning of a slight improvement in the home economy' in 1887 and recovery in 1888, see Lewis, *Building Cycles*, p. 202; H. L. Beales, 'The Great Depression in Industry and Trade', *Economic History Review*, Vol. 5 (1934), reprinted in E. M. Carus-Wilson (ed.), *Essays in Economic History* (London, 1954), Vol. 1, p. 413. Unemployment reported by trade unions peaked in 1886 and was falling in 1887 and 1888. (Deane and Mitchell, *British Historical Statistics*, p. 64.)

as a destination for young men leaving the countryside. Mr. Little, in the report on Devonshire, quoted a landowner and M.P. who reported that 'hundreds of labourers have gone . . . [to the Welsh coalfields.] Many too have emigrated to America, and no parish is without its representative in Canada and the United States.[38] More characteristic were reports of young men going to the towns to become porters, policemen, or postmen, or seeking employment in mines or on the railways.[39] Thus, this evidence does not support Brinley Thomas's suggestion that during periods, such as the seventies, of low emigration, high internal mobility, and building investment in England, the ambitious young people from the countryside left for British towns. but that in the succeeding decade such people chose to go overseas.[40] The towns continued to attract the better-educated, ambitious young men from the countryside in the eighties.

In contrast to farmers, industrial workers and labourers, people in service occupations had been weakly represented on the ship lists of the mid-century. While the traditional tertiary occupations, such as domestic service, continued to trail far behind as a source of male emigrants to the United States in the eighties, Class VI, consisting principally of white-collar workers and professional and commercial people, tended to be somewhat better represented in the eighties. Yet the ship lists do not suggest any over-representation of them in the flow to America. These classes were not so responsive as building-trades workers and labourers to economic conditions in the States. Railway workers were not significant in the emigration of either the fifties or the eighties. As Table 7 indicates, none of these groups showed a high preference for the United States as a field emigration during the eighties.

Professor Frank Musgrove has suggested that the brain drain from

[38] Royal Commission on Agriculture, *Reports of the Assistant Commissioners, British Parliamentary Papers*, 1882, XV (C. 3375–I), p. 21.

[39] *Ibid.* (C. 3375–II) p. 42. Little's summary for the ten counties he investigated, including Devon, Cornwall, and Somerset, mentioned young men drifting away into the towns or railway service. *Ibid.* (C. 3375–I), p. 54. Mr. Druce made roughly the same remark about Bedfordshire and reported from Essex that the best and youngest workmen left villages to seek employment in London, on the railways, or in the manufacturing districts. *Ibid* (C. 3375–II), pp. 9, 30. For similar reports from Lincolnshire, Norfolk, Suffolk, Lancashire, Yorkshire, Buckinghamshire, and Hertfordshire, see *ibid*, pp. 56, 67, 94; (C. 3375–V), p. 43. *Digest and Appendix to Part I of Evidence, B.P.P.*, 1881, XVI (C. 2778–II), pp. 141, 364, 368. For similar reports from Forfar, Clackmannan and Fife, see Mr. Walker's report, *ibid.*, pp. 544, 547, 549. Frederick Ernest Green remarked that by the late seventies emigration had gone out of fashion amongst the men of Norfolk. 'It began to be considered derogatory to be an exile.' The young men went to navvying, or into the police force, or on to the railways lines, the mines, or the contractor's yard. (*A History of the English Agricultural Labourers* [London, 1920], pp. 89, 150.) See also Arthur Clayden, *The Revolt of the Field* (1874), p. 160.

[40] Brinley Thomas (ed.), *Wales and the Atlantic Economy* (Cardiff, 1962), p. 6.

Britain abroad, and particularly to America, began in the 1860s and has become more pronounced ever since.[41] In support of this view, he used the percentages of U.K. passengers, by occupation, worked out by N. H. Carrier and J. R. Jeffery.[42] In comparing a period of high emigration in the late-sixties with a period of low emigration in the nineties, Musgrove misinterpreted a cyclical fluctuation as a trend. As can be seen in Table 9, for example, in

Table 9   Estimates of shares of male emigrants leaving the U.K. for all places (with Irish subtracted) by occupation at selected dates

Occupation	1878	1882	1888	1897
Farmers	9·6	2·4	7·5	5·9
Farm Labourers	20·9	7·0	28·1	10·5
Labourers	2·9	50·2	13·0	8·6
Servants, etc.	0·3	0·3	1·0	2·1
Building trades	6·0	4·4	6·0	5·4
Miners	3·6	4·1	5·9	8·6
Mechanics n.o.d.	10·6	7·6	12·5	8·7
Other handicrafts	1·5	1·4	2·8	3·2
Textile workers	—	0·3	0·7	1·5
Other industrial	1·3	0·7	2·0	3·1
Railway workers	0·3	0·2	0·5	1·2
Clerical	3·3	1·2	3·4	6·9
Commercial	1·3	1·3	1·5	3·8
Other tertiary*	38·4	18·9	15·1	30·4
Total	100·0	100·0	100·0	99·9
Total males stating occupation	28,931	73,276	79,720	43,026

*This is the broad class included in the original emigration data as comprised of gentlemen, professional men, merchants and students.

Sources: *Statistical Tables Relating to Emigration and Immigration from and into the U.K. in 1878,* British Parliamentary Papers, 1878–9, LXXV (32), pp. 12–13; *Ireland* (C. 2221), pp. 10–11; *in 1882, B.P.P.,* 1883, LXXVI (89), pp. 16–17; *Ireland* (C. 3489), pp. 10–11; *in 1888, B.P.P.,* 1889, LXXXIV (10), pp. 16–17; *Ireland* (C. 5647), pp. 10–11; *in 1897, B.P.P.,* 1898, CIII (154), pp. 22–3, *Ireland* (C. 8748), pp. 10–11.

years of relatively low emigration, members of trades which might be called relatively insensitive to the short-term forces governing migration, such as farmers, skilled industrial workers, and the class designated by Carrier and Jeffery as 'commerce, finance, insurance, professions,' formed a higher share of the reduced number of emigrants. Another source of confusion is that the class entitled 'commerce, finance, insurance and professions' included gentlemen in the original published data on which Carrier and Jeffery's percentages are based. The inclusion of more and more gentlemen travellers in the original data distorted the picture to give the illusion of an increasing exodus of trained people. The ship lists of the eighties recorded the arrival of 753 gentlemen in New York from England

[41] Frank Musgrove, *The Migratory Elite* (London, 1963), pp. 18–19.
[42] Carrier and Jeffery, *External Migration*, p. 102.

and Scotland, or 8 per cent of the adult males reported. Omitting from the analysis these gentlemen, who may not have had the specialized training involved in the term 'brain drain', gives a better indication of the migrant stream, as is evident in Table 6. The ship lists indicate only a slight increase in the proportion of professional people among the immigrants of the eighties as compared with the fifties; professional people were still markedly under-represented among the people emigrating to America. The increase in Class VI was accounted for mainly by clerical workers. It would seem that the American economy and society were no more attractive to specialized and trained tertiary workers in Britain in the eighties than they were to skilled secondary workers.

The appearance of so many commercial men and gentlemen in the data of the eighties is related to another feature of the emigration of that period. A higher proportion of the Britons who embarked for the United States in this decade were transient visitors who sailed with no intention of remaining abroad. These data are not so complete, since some ship captains who gave other useful information failed to ask this question of their passengers. But of 503 passengers clearly marked as temporary visitors, 70 per cent came from Class VI, commercial men and gentlemen accounting for most of them. Another 7 per cent of the transients were building-trades workers, and an equal number represented the modern sectors of industry, especially iron, steel, and engineering.

One other feature of the migration of the eighties highlights the changed character of emigration from England and Scotland in the eighties as compared with the fifties. Most of the migrants of the later decade went out as young men who were either un-married or had left their families behind. On any single ship there was a complement of English and Scots wives and children, but they were not legally attached to the men on the same ships. They were probably going out to join husbands and fathers already in America, just as dependents of West Indian immigrants to Britain in recent years here followed their fathers and husbands. The sex ratios in published migration data which suggest that one English woman emigrated to America for every two men in the eighties are mis-leading in that they greatly underestimate the extent to which this was a movement of young unattached males rather than a family migration. On ships arriving in New York before 1854 single men outnumbered men travelling with families and dependents by less than 2:1. In the eighties the ratio was 8:1.

In conclusion, three points may be made. First of all, the similarity between the data from ship lists about English and Scots migrants of the eighties and Mrs. Semmingsen's conclusions about the character of Norwegian emigration in the last decades of the nineteenth century are striking. In this period, she wrote, 'those who wanted to find open land and conformed to the old pattern of emigration turned North, to the prairie provinces of Canada; the rest, to a much larger extent than before, found work in various industries and trades in the towns—a particularly large number in the building trades.[43] Among Norwegian migrants on the eve of World War I, 'there was a growing proportion of men to women, of young people to older people and of single persons to married persons'. By World War I 'there was little left of the family character of Norwegian emigration.'[44] Our data on the eighties suggest that most of these remarks might have been made of English and Scottish emigrants. In only one respect do the findings differ. No significant trend towards younger males was found in the eighties.[45]

As Professor Richard Easterlin has pointed out, Norway and Britain were two regions of emigration in which the rate of population growth remained high, by European standards, as industrialization progressed. In the conventional accounts of American immigration, both of these groups ranked as 'older immigration', and their character was contrasted with that of the newer immigrants from southern and eastern Europe from the nineties onwards. The tentative conclusion to be drawn from this analysis of ship lists and from Mrs. Semmingsen's study of the superior Norwegian records is that the character of the migration from England, Scotland, and Norway also changed as America became more industrialized and opportunities in agriculture waned. One can speak of an 'old migration' from England and Scotland before 1854 of farmers and skilled industrial workers, many of whom hoped to establish themselves

---

[43] Semmingsen, 'Norwegian Emigration', pp. 157–8.   [44] *Ibid.*, p. 158.

[45] Unfortunately I do not have the microfilms of the ship lists of 1846–54 with me in London to make possible a breakdown of all male emigrants from England and Scotland by age group, in order to be able to compare my findings with Mrs. Semmingsen's. She found 30·6 per cent of male emigrants in 1866–70 in the age group 15–30 years and 78 per cent in 1911–15. Since in my abstracts from the microfilms in Washington, I took details only of males over the age of 15, I can only conclude that there was no trend towards the younger age group as compared with the older. The inclusion of children might change the ratios:

Percentage adult male passengers on New York ship lists

	15–30 years of age %	above 30 years of age %
1846–9	65	35
1850–54	78	22
1885	65	35
1886	67	33
1887	67	33
1888	71	29

on the land or in towns in developing regions.[46] Many of the migrants
of the eighties were 'new immigrants' like the migrants who were
soon to start going to the U.S.A. in large numbers from Italy,
Hungary, and elsewhere: young unattached males, without industrial skills.

In one respect the labourers from England and Scotland of the
eighties differed from the new immigrants from southern and eastern
Europe: they came from the towns of Britain, not the countryside.
One cannot judge from the data available whether or not these town
labourers who left England and Scotland in the eighties had themselves recently come into towns from the British countryside.[47] The
available evidence indicates that by the eighties general labourers
from agricultural regions in Britain tended to go first to British
towns, not to American towns, unlike the Italians a couple of decades
later. The slump in building in many British towns from the late
seventies onwards may have been one of the factors dislodging
marginal urban workers and causing them to be the most responsive
group to the return of prosperity in America after 1879. They were
departing from towns in England and did not remain in the eighties
to see whether or not they could find employment or opportunities
which might enable them to marry and possibly even to demand
houseroom. Thus their migration, beginning in the early eighties,
may partly explain the quite extraordinary flow, both seasonal
and permanent, of building trades workers from England and Scotland to the U.S.A., in the late eighties.

ACKNOWLEDGMENTS

The author wishes to thank Gwenda Moseley for valuable assistance in research and her
colleague Dudley Baines for reading and commenting on this paper.

[46] Charlotte Erickson, 'The Agrarian Myths of English Immigrants', in O. F. Ander
(ed.), *In the Trek of the Immigrants* (Rock Island, Ill., 1964), pp. 59–80.

[47] The U.K. emigration records recorded a higher percentage of agricultural labourers
among emigrants, even when the Irish are subtracted, than did the American statistics
or the ship lists. (See Table 14, Appendix D.)

APPENDIX A

Table 10 Ships arriving in New York port whose English and Scottish-born adult male passengers were analysed in this study. National Archives Microfilm series 237.

Reel Number	Ship Number	Date	No. English and Scottish males
61	321	1846	54
71	328	1848	45
72	397	1848	37
77	63, 178, 156	1848	54
78	250, 237, 403	1849	87
79	560, 636	1849	66
81	878	1849	115
82	1066	1849	28
83	1264, 1304, 1302	1849	79
86	52	1850	33
88	349	1850	41
101	854	1851	74
109	127	1852	11
135	24	1854	10
137	347	1854	19
144	1032	1854	7
145	1275	1854	64
146	1365	1854	14
			848
483	42, 50, 65, 66, 72, 78, 88, 89, 97, 110, 111, 120, 127, 133, 166, 169, 178, 180, 187, 200, 209, 221, 234, 236, 237, 247, 273, 282.	1885	1,253
484	296, 319, 327, 336, 339, 369, 370, 374, 383, 396, 405.	1885	767
493	269, 273, 286, 290, 304, 306, 324, 322, 330, 337, 343, 349, 364, 360, 374, 378, 379, 396, 397, 413, 415.	1886	1,760
494	426, 434, 455, 456, 460, 477, 485, 487, 491, 502, 507, 526, 530, 542, 543.	1886	1,570
503	10, 13, 23, 38, 42, 48, 60, 62, 66, 75, 89, 94, 102, 108, 113, 130, 139, 150, 153a, 153, 166, 170, 177, 179a, 193, 197, 204.	1887	1,359
504	214, 217, 237, 243, 244, 265, 285, 319, 325.	1887	1,344
516	196, 214, 230, 239, 242, 257, 258, 279, 288, 292, 302, 312, 319, 334, 350, 354, 357.	1888	2,021
			10,074

APPENDIX B

Table 11 English and Scottish counties by share of labour force in agriculture, and average weekly earnings in agriculture

1851	% Male labour force in agriculture	Weekly wages in agriculture
I. *Low wage—agricultural counties*		
Buckinghamshire	50	8/6
Bedfordshire	52	9/0
Cambridgeshire	53	7/6
Devonshire	39	8/6
Dorset	44	7/6
Berkshire	47	7/6
Essex	50	8/0
Herefordshire	55	8/5
Hertfordshire	49	7/6
Hampshire	34	9/0
Huntingdonshire	56	8/6
Norfolk	45	8/6
Northamptonshire	44	9/0
Oxfordshire	48	9/0
Rutland	52	not returned
Shropshire	43	7/3
Somerset	38	8/7
Surrey (ex metropolitan)	41	9/6
Wiltshire	50	7/3
Suffolk	52	7/0
II. *High wage—agricultural counties*		
Kent	37	11/6
Cumberland	34	13/0
Lincolnshire	52	10/0
Sussex	43	10/6
Westmorland	46	not returned
(N.R. Yorks. omitted)	48	11/0
III. *Low wage—industrial counties*		
Cornwall	31	8/8
Gloucestershire	28	7/0
Leicestershire	30	9/6
Warwickshire	19	8/6
Worcestershire	26	7/8
IV. *High wage—industrial counties*		
Cheshire	25	12/0
Derbyshire	23	11/0
Durham	13	11/0
Lancashire	10	13/6
London	2	13/6
Middlesex (ex metropolitan)	29	11/0
Northumberland	22	11/0
Nottinghamshire	27	10/0
East Riding, Yorks. (omitted)	32	12/0
West Riding, Yorks. (omitted)	14	14/0

Table 11—*continued*

1881	% Labour force in agriculture	Average weekly wages in agriculture
I. *Agricultural—low wage counties*		
Bedfordshire	40	12/6
Berkshire	33	12/3
Buckinghamshire	36	12/9
Cambridgeshire	47	13/6
Dorsetshire	35	10/9
Herefordshire	45	11/9
Huntingdonshire	51	12/6
Hertfordshire	35	13/6
Lincolnshire	40	13/6–15/0
Norfolk	38	12/6
Oxfordshire	39	12/9
Rutland	48	not returned
Shropshire	33	13/3
Suffolk	42	12/6
Westmorland	36	18/0
Wiltshire	38	11/9
III. *Industrial—low wage counties*		
Cheshire	15	12/6
Cornwall	29	13/9
Devon	27	13/0
Essex	28	12/6
Gloucester	19	13/3
Hampshire	21	12/0
Leicestershire	18	13/0
Nottinghamshire	15	14/0
Northamptonshire	28	13/6
Staffordshire	8	14/6
Somerset	29	12/6
Sussex	28	13/6
Warwick	11	14/3
Worcester	18	13/0
IV. *Industrial—high wage counties*		
Cumberland	22	18/0
Derby	13	16/6
Durham	5	17/9
Lancashire	11	17/6
Kent	24	15/9
London	1	—
Northumberland	11	17/0
Middlesex	9	15/6
Surrey	17	15/6
Yorkshire East Riding	20	15/0
Yorkshire North Riding	25	16/6
Yorkshire West Riding	8	16/6

Table 11—*continued*

Scotland

1851 Agricultural counties	% Male labour force in agriculture	1851 Industrial counties	% Male labour force in agriculture
Dumfriesshire	41	Ayrshire	24
Kirkcudbrightshire	48	Renfrewshire	11
Wigtownshire	55	Dunbartonshire	20
Bute	36	Lanarkshire	7
Peeblesshire	53	Stirlingshire	22
Roxburghshire	38	Linlithgow	25
Berwickshire	51	Edinburgh	10
Haddington	44	Selkirkshire	29
Kinross-shire	35	Fifeshire	20
Perthshire	36	Clackmannanshire	12
Kincardine	53	Forfar	18
Aberdeenshire	45		
Elgin	42		
Banffshire	53		
Nairnshire	49		
Inverness-shire	56		
Argyllshire	48		
Ross and Cromarty	55		
Sutherland	50		
Orkney and Shetland	41		
Caithness	45		

1881 Agricultural counties		1881 Industrial counties	
Kirkcudbrightshire	37	Dumfriesshire	31
Wigtownshire	44	Bute	26
Berwickshire	43	Peeblesshire	31
Haddington	36	Roxburghshire	30
Kinross-shire	35	Perthshire	29
Kincardine	44	Ayrshire	13
Aberdeenshire	33	Renfrewshire	5
Elgin	35	Dunbartonshire	8
Banffshire	42	Lanarkshire	3
Nairnshire	36	Stirlingshire	11
Inverness-shire	39	Linlithgow	12
Argyllshire	35	Edinburgh	4
Ross and Cromarty	41	Selkirkshire	12
Sutherland	43	Fifeshire	15
Orkney and Shetland	56	Clackmannanshire	7
Caithness	36	Forfar	12

Sources: See Table 5.

Np

APPENDIX C

Classification of occupations

Male labour force only included. Major occupations included in each class:

I *Agriculture*
A. Farmers, graziers, bailiffs, and working relatives of farmers
B. Agricultural labourers, shepherds, woodsmen, gardeners

II *Labourers*
All labourers, except farm

III *Tertiary, pre-industrial*
Domestic servants; soldiers and seamen; messengers; police; workers on roads and waterways; gamekeepers, grooms, fishermen and others
Chimney sweeps, crossing sweepers, scavengers

IV *Pre-industrial and unchanging skills*
1 Building trades: bricklayers, carpenters, masons, painter, thatcher, plasterer, plumber, slater, brickmaker
2 Mining: all kinds of miners and quarrymen
3 Food trades: baker, grocer, butcher, confectioner, miller, brewer, maltster
4 Metal trades: blacksmiths, whitesmiths, lead, copper, brass, zinc manufacturers; tinsmiths, goldsmiths
5 Clothing trades: glover; hatter; milliner; tailor; shoemaker, etc.
6 Wood-working trades: cabinet maker, cooper, sawyer, wheelwright, wood carver
7 Miscellaneous: currier, saddler, tanner, soap maker, tallow chandler, willow, cane, rush makers, carver, brush maker
9 Mechanics not otherwise designated

V *Industrial, new, and changing skills*
8 Textiles: woollen, silk, cotton, linen, hemp and jute clothmakers and finishers; hosiery manufacturers
10a Iron and steel industries: toolmaking, engineering; coach and railway carriagemakers; shipbuilders; gun and ordnance makers; cutlers, tin manufacturers, watch instrument makers
10b Miscellaneous: printers; chemical workers; cement manufacturers; earthenware and glass manufacturers; gas workers; paper manufacture; machinists and machine workers; toy and game makers; oil and colourmen; bookbinders and publishers; printers

VI *Tertiary, industrial*
10c Railway workers: railway driver, pointsmen, plate layers, guard and engine drivers and stokers
1 Clerical: civil servants; telegraph and telephone service; railway officials and servants; warehousemen, commercial clerks
2 Commercial: all dealers distinguished only as such; contractors; keepers of inns, lodging houses and coffee houses
3 Professional: accountants, army and navy officers, veterinary surgeons in addition to the learned professions distinguished as such
4 Gentlemen, not otherwise distinguished

APPENDIX D

Table 12 Occupations of British and Irish male passengers leaving the U.K. for the United States of America at selected dates. Percentage distribution

	1878	1882	1888	1897
I *Agriculture*				
1 Farmers	9·7	4·7	5·6	5·4
2 Farm Labourers	0·5	0·4	20·1	14·6
II *Labourers*	43·3	68·8	39·6	35·7
III *Servants, etc.*	0·8	0·3	0·8	2·0
IV *Pre-industrial skilled*				
1 Building trades	4·6	2·7	5·3	3·1
2 Mining	3·7	3·4	4·0	3·0
3 Other crafts	2·0	1·3	2·4	2·2
4 Mechanics n.o.d.	9·3	5·4	10·4	11·5
Total pre-industrial	19·6	12·8	22·1	19·8
V *Industrial skilled*				
1 Textile	0·0	0·4	0·6	2·0
2 Iron, steel, engineering				
other	0·9	0·4	1·3	1·4
Total industrial	0·9	0·8	1·9	3·4
VI *Tertiary*	25·2	12·2	9·9	19·0
Total	100·0	100·0	100·0	99·9
Total stating occupation	20,669	75,736	81,470	29,072

Sources: See Table 9.

Table 13 Occupations of English and Scottish passengers arriving in the U.S.A. at selected dates (includes women). Percentage distribution

	1878	1882	1888	1897
I *Agriculture*				
1 Farmers	12·6	7·9	5·9	5·9
2 Farm Labourers	2·7	0·6	0·8	1·7
Total agricultural	15·3	8·5	6·6	7·6
II *Labourers*	26·7	47·1	35·1	14·0
III *Servants, etc.**	9·3	7·1	11·0	19·2
IV *Pre-industrial skilled*				
1 Building trades	5·9	5·2	10·2	6·1
2 Mining	7·6	7·8	7·8	10·2
3 Food trades	2·2	1·8	2·0	4·8
4 Metal trades	1·4	1·1	2·0	1·7
5 Clothing trades	2·9	1·5	2·2	5·1
6 Wood trades	0·3	0·3	0·6	0·6
7 Miscellaneous	0·4	0·3	0·5	0·4
8 Mechanics	1·7	4·3	4·1	1·5
Total pre-industrial	22·6	22·4	29·2	30·3
V *Industrial skilled*				
1 Textiles	2·6	2·5	2·7	9·5
2 Iron, steel, engineering	5·4	3·2	4·7	6·0
3 Miscellaneous	1·0	0·7	1·0	1·0
Total industrial	8·9	6·3	8·4	16·6
VI *Tertiary*				
1 Railway workers	0·1	0·1	0·4	—
2 Clerical	4·7	2·5	3·1	5·8
3 Commercial	9·1	4·3	3·8	3·4
4 Professional	2·9	1·6	2·3	3·0
5 Gentlemen	0·2	0·2	—	—
Total tertiary	17·1	8·8	9·7	12·2
Total	99·9	100·2	100·0	99·9
Total stating occupation	10,117	47,851	54,269	5,977
Errors	—	—	10	6

* 85 per cent of the English and Scots women returned with occupations in the ship lists, 1885–88, were servants. This explains the very much higher share of pre-industrial tertiary workers in the published statistics which did not distinguish females from males by occupation during these years.

Sources: U.S. Treasury Department, Statistics Bureau, *Annual Report on Foreign Commerce and Navigation*, 1878, pp. 752–91; 1882, pp. 698–725; 1888, pp. 744–95; 1897, pp. 25–31.

Table 14 Occupational distribution of British male immigrants to the U.S.A. according to U.K., U.S.A. official records and selected ship lists, 1885–88

Occupational groups	U.K. records Irish included %	U.S.A. records English and Scots women included %	Ship lists English and Scots %
I. *Agriculture*			
1 Farmers	5·9	6·2	8·4
2 Farm labourers	16·3	0·6	1·1
Total agricultural	22·2	6·8	9·5
II. *Labourers*	42·6	38·9	29·5
III. *Servants*	0·8	11·1	3·2
IV. *Pre-industrial skills*			
1 Building trades	5·1	8·2	18·1
2 Mining	4·9	6·8	8·0
3 Food trades		1·9	2·1
4 Metal trades		1·4	1·7
5 Clothing trades		2·1	1·5
6 Wood trades		0·5	0·5
7 Miscellaneous	2·1	0·3	0·9
8 Mechanics, n.o.d.	9·1	3·4	1·5
Total pre-industrial	21·2	24·8	34·3
V. *Industrial skills*			
1 Textile	0·6	2·9	2·0
2 Iron, steel, engineering	1·6	4·2	4·0
3 Miscellaneous	—	1·0	1·8
Total industrial	2·2	8·1	7·8
VI. *Tertiary*			
1 Railway workers	—	0·3	0·1
2 Clerical	2·5	3·7	5·6
3 Commercial	1·2	4·3	8·0
4 Professional	7·2*	2·1	1·9
Total tertiary	10·9	10·3	15·7
Total	99·9	100·0	100·0
Total stating occupation	281,514	163,098	8,698
Omissions, unknown, errors		17	1,385

* Includes gentlemen.

Sources: U.S. Treasury Department, Statistics Bureau, *Annual Report on Foreign Commerce and Navigation,* 1885, pp. 726–49; 1886, pp. 720–41; 1887, pp. 735–55; 1888, pp. 744–97. See also Table 8.

H. E. Lewis,[1] *D. F. Roberts, and A. W. F. Edwards*

Biological problems, and opportunities, of isolation among the islanders of Tristan da Cunha

THE ISLANDERS OF TRISTAN DA CUNHA

Tristan da Cunha is a tiny volcanic island in the South Atlantic on the fortieth parallel. It is 1,700 miles from Cape Town, 1,900 miles from South America. The nearest land is the island of St. Helena, 1,500 miles north-east.

In 1961 the volcano erupted, and the inhabitants, 270 in all, were taken safely off and brought to Cape Town by a boat that happened to be in the nearby waters.[2] From Cape Town they all sailed to England where they were warmly received. For generations they had enjoyed fame as the stalwarts who lived happily on the loneliest island in the world. They were to be relied on in the days of sail for their brave and generous help to ships in trouble in the 'roaring forties'; they were god-fearing and, among other things, had a splendid reputation for good health, especially dental health.[3]

The story of the people and their island goes back over a century and a half to Napoleon's exile to St. Helena. There was a fear that an effort would be made to bring about his release and, for any adventure of this sort, it seemed strategically prudent to guard the southern approach by stationing a garrison on Tristan da Cunha. The detachment came from the British Colony at the Cape of Good Hope.

Towards the end of his life Napoleon was infirm and no longer a 'menace'. In 1817 the garrison returned to the South African Colony, but three men, of whom one, Corporal William Glass, was accompanied by his wife and two children, asked to remain on the

---

[1] Dr. H. E. Lewis died at a tragically early age on 21 June 1971. Without his vision and intense personal effort as co-ordinator of the Tristan investigation, very few of the studies mentioned in this article would have been undertaken and would not have achieved the degree of interrlatedness that makes the Tristan work unique.—D. F. R.

[2] P. J. Wheeler, 'Death of an Island', *National Geographic*, Vol. 121 (1962), pp. 678–97.

[3] T. Whiteside, 'Annals of Migration', *The New Yorker* (9 November, 1963), pp. 154–207.

island. The request was granted. This little group was joined over the next few decades by others—English and American sàilors, St. Helena women, and a shipwrecked Dutchman. Another St. Helena woman arrived in 1863; in 1892, two shipwrecked Italians decided to remain on the island; and in 1908 two Irish sisters migrated to Tristan to stay permanently. Although dozens of people came to the island, very few found it sufficiently attractive to remain. The few that did established a tough and resilient little population, and all the present Tristanians count descent from these fifteen ancestors. In fact, the 270 islanders are disposed into seventy family groups, but have only seven surnames. This shorthand description of their numbers emphasizes the degree of inter-marriage. It appears all the more intensive when one knows that, of the women who came from St. Helena in 1827, two were sisters and a third was the daughter of one of them.

The island itself is bleak. It rises spectacularly over 6,000 feet as a steep volcanic mountain from its roughly circular base, which is about 30 square miles in area. It is so steep that there is little flat ground, barely 3 square miles. To land on the island is difficult because, except for a small bay, almost all the periphery consists of steep cliffs. Initially the settlement was successfuly based on fishing and sealing and producing fresh vegetables and meat, the latter being especially in demand by passing ships stopping for supplies of fresh water. But after the middle of the nineteenth century, when steam replaced sail, ships bypassed Tristan da Cunha, and the Islanders were almost completely isolated and came near to starvation. They refused offers by the British Government to take them off the island and became objects of charity.

Their life until World War II has been well recorded in a series of books by missionaries and teachers,[4] and particularly by the reports of a Norwegian Expedition in 1937, which concluded:

> Infectious disease is very rare, and the same is true of all kinds of diseases of children. Further, diseases of the heart, kidney, liver and other internal organs seem to occur seldom. On the whole, the Tristanites seem to have a fair chance of getting old unless they are drowned or fall down from the mountain.[5]

World War II made an impact on their lives. The island once again was thought to have strategic value, and a Royal Navy contingent was posted there with a South African Air Force unit

[4] R. A. Rogers, *The Lonely Island* (London, 1926); K. M. Barrow, *Three Years in Tristan da Cunha* (London, 1910).
[5] E. Christopherson, *Results of the Norwegian Scientific Expedition to Tristan da Cunha, 1937–1938* (Oslo: Norske Videnskaps-Akademie, 1946).

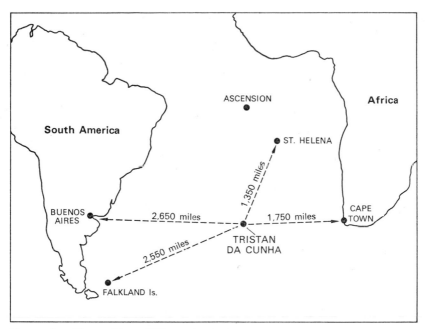

Figure 1a   The position of Tristan da Cunha

responsible for meteorological work. The islanders were employed by the station and for the first time they used money. With their wages they were able to buy imported food from the serviceman's store, for example, refined flour, sweets and biscuits.

After the war, it was realized that the South Atlantic waters around Tristan abounded with fish, especially the spiny lobster (*Jasus lalandii*). Thanks to the initiative of the Reverend Lawrence, previously a padre to the islanders, a fish canning factory was set up, which ensured employment. The islanders now enjoyed a modest prosperity. There had, since 1884, been a Tristan Charity Fund, and at the beginning of 1961 it was decided to wind this up.

But in October of that year the volcano erupted, destroying the fish factory, and the islanders were brought to England, heavily dependent again on charity. Soon they were housed in comfortable cottages in an empty R.A.F. camp at Calshot, Southampton, and jobs were found nearby. Their coming aroused great public interest and sympathy. It also awakened scientific interest. For people to survive as the Tristanites had they must be hardy. Their reputation for fitness and good health had preceded them. Comparatively little is known about the natural history of health, in contrast with the enormous knowledge of disease, and today any community with particularly high standards of health provides a challenge to

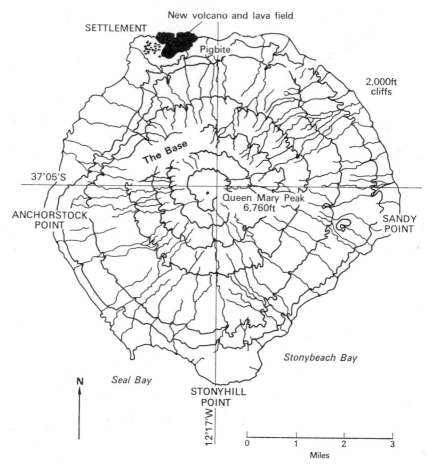

Figure 1b Relief diagram of Tristan da Cunha

medical scientists. Was there perhaps something specially advan-
tageous about the environment of Tristan? Did the islanders have a
particularly beneficial genetic endowment? It was because of their
reputation for good health that the Medical Research Council
survey was originally conceived.[6] Its initial object was to measure
the levels of health of this unique population. But it became apparent
that the islanders were not paragons of good health.[7] There was a
peculiar chronic asthmatic state that affected almost half the people,
a low resistance to respiratory infection, a high incidence of round-
worm infestation, and other conditions that might be found typically

[6] H. E. Lewis, 'The Tristan Islanders: A Medical Study of Isolation', *New Scientist*, Vol.
20 (1963), pp. 720–22.
[7] H. E. Lewis, *op. cit.*, also A. Sakula, 'Tuberculosis in the Tristan da Cunha Community', *Tubercle*, Vol. 44 (1963), pp. 225–29.

in an underdeveloped country; there was, moreover, serious dental deterioration, and the suggestion of widespread congenital anomalies.[8]

The research emphasis shifted, and a working party was set up that included experts in epidemiology, virology, public health, dentistry, genetics, and tropical medicine. Tristan da Cunha is not in the tropics, but disease is not affected by lines of latitude and longitude so much as by the poverty and ignorance that occur frequently in the tropics.

The first job was a thorough clinical examination of all the islanders. The widespread ill health and congenital abnormality were confirmed, and unsuspected morbidity revealed. Some islanders were in need of relatively minor surgery or gynaecological treatment; and there were two children whose urogenital anatomy was only partly developed; one of them, a boy, had been mistakenly brought up as a girl and after plastic surgery needed some psychotherapy.[9]

The congenital abnormalities included malformations of the skull, external ear, and fingers. Alone, they were not serious, but in some islanders there was associated deafness and mental dullness. The most serious inherited disease was retinitis pigmentosa in four people. This manifests itself in adults of early middle age and leads to blindness. The first symptoms are night blindness, and by then the sufferer is usually married with children to whom the gene responsible for the recessive disease is passed. It is probable that the responsible gene is fairly widespread in the community, but the number of carriers is not known—there may be eight among the immediate younger generation alone.[10]

The first phase of our work was a crash programme with all the satisfaction of diagnosis, treatment, and cure. But we were left with a large number of problems for example, asthma,[11] deafness,

[8] 'Dental Caries Among the Inhabitants of Tristan da Cunha', *Royal Society of Health Proceedings*, Vol. 3 (1962), pp. 134–9; also 'Symposium on Medical Problems Presented by the Tristan da Cunha Community', *Transactions of the Royal Society of Tropical Medicine and Hygiene*, Vol. 57 (1963), pp. 8–26.

[9] J. A. Black, C. K. M. Thacker, H. E. Lewis, and A. K. Thould, 'Tristan da Cunha: General Medical Investigations', *British Medical Journal Supplement*, Vol. 2 (26 October, 1963), pp. 1018–24; 'Tristan da Cunha: Some Medical Aspects. Editorial', *British Medical Journal* (26 October, 1963); J. L. Hamerton, Angela I. Taylor, Roslyn Angell, and V. Mary McGuire, 'Chromosome Investigations of a Small Isolated Human Population: Chromosome Abnormalities and Distribution of Chromosome Counts According to Age and Sex Among the Population of Tristan da Cunha', *Nature*, Vol. 206, No. 4990 (1965), pp. 1232–4.

[10] 'Symposium on Medical Problems Presented by the Tristan da Cunha Community', *Transactions of the Royal Society*.

[11] K. M. Citron and J. Pepys, 'An Investigation of Asthma Among the Tristan da Cunha Islanders', *British Journal of Diseases of the Chest*, Vol. 58 (1964), pp. 119–23.

dental deterioration,[12] retinitis pigmentosa, for which there were no immediate answers. Since we were committed to a thorough study of the islanders' health we embarked on a series of long-term clinical investigations to get to the bottom of these problems. The main object of the Medical Research Council project was to improve the health lot of the Tristan islanders, and it would have been a very patchy job indeed if we had stopped at the point when the few obvious conditions were treated. Curing disease is not the same as creating health and happiness, and to achieve this part of our assignment we needed to know a great deal more about the islanders.

When we started the work, our role was that of 'Doctor', a stereo-type figure easy for the islanders to understand, someone dispensing medicines and giving treatment for painful conditions. For the long-term studies, our role had to change somewhat; we were becoming clinical investigators or detectives. The islanders were not familiar with this form of doctoring, and we had to be specially meticulous not to generate conflict. It was not easy to explain to relatively simple people the long-term reasons for seemingly irrelevant tests and investigations—a difficult problem among far more sophisticated laymen. In the event, successful rapport was created, particularly with the influential older people who were quite alert to the scourges of night-blindness and asthma. Opposition tended to come from well-meaning outsiders who felt that we should not be doing so many tests on the poor islanders. These people rather fancied themselves as guardians of the islanders' welfare, although they were in fact acting most unethically because time is not on the side of the Tristan-ians, as we will discuss presently. There was a revealing conversation with one of the 'guardians' when he was asked: 'If an island child were your son, how would you feel about the problem of his health?' He replied: 'Oh, that would be different. I'd see that he got every possible bit of help from medical research and education.'

How were we to approach a long-term study to find out the obscure underlying factors causing disease or denying health? We were led immediately to examine some of the basic aspects of the islanders' human biology, particularly their complicated genetic structure. This involved a study of the available markers: such as blood groups,

---

[12] P. T. Heffer and B. B. J. Lovius, 'An Orthodontic Survey of the Islanders of Tristan da Cunha', *The Dental Practitioner*, Vol. 14 (1963), pp. 129–38; P. J. Holloway, P. M. C. James, and G. L. Slack, 'Dental Disease in the Inhabitants of Tristan da Cunha in 1962', *Proceedings of the 9th ORCA Congress* (1963), pp. 337, 340; P. J. Holloway, P. M. C. James, and G. L. Slack, 'Dental Disease in Tristan da Cunha', *British Dentistry Journal*, Vol. 115 (1963), pp. 19–25.

haptoglob.

cholinesterase & Tristan

—the quantitative aspects of ...ve aspects like facial features,[15]

To answer this question, dietary ...ere undertaken[18]; growth and ...ere studied.[19] Had their dietary ...ssible immunity from cardio- ...leterioration)?[20]

...environment; we observed their ...he relationship of the individual ...re a basis for zoonotic disease,

...interdisciplinary research into ...cluding, of course, the islanders' ...nization[21] and education.[22] In

[13] H. Harris, D. A. Hopkinson, Elizabeth B. Robson, and Mary Whittaker, 'Genetical ... on a New Variant of Serum Cholinest...ase Detected by Electrophoresis', *Annals of ...man Genetics*, Vol. 2... (1963), pp. ...; H. Harris and E. B. Robson, 'Haptoglobins in Tristan da Cunha', *Vox Sang*, Vol. 8 (1963), p. 226-30.

[14] Hamerton, *et al.*, 'Chromosome Investigations. . . .'

[15] D. R. Brothwell and R. G. Harvey, 'Facial Variation: Some Problems of Recording ...hapes and Determining the Affinities of Human Populations by Means of Facial Differ...ces, with Special Reference to the People of Tristan da Cunha', *Eugenics Review*, Vol. 57 (1965), pp. 167-81.

[16] Angela I. Taylor, 'Eye Colour in the Tristan da Cunha Population', *Human Biology*, Vol. 39, No. 3 (1967), pp. 316-18.

[17] E. Sunderland, 'Hair Colour of the Population of Tristan da Cunha', *Nature*, Vol. 208, No. 5008 (1965), p. 412.

[18] Elaine C. Taylor, Dorothy F. Hollingsworth, and Margaret A. Chambers, 'The Diet of the Tristan da Cunha Islanders', *British Journal of Nutrition*, Vol. 20 (1966), pp. 393–411; Margaret A. Chambers and D. A. T. Southgate, 'Nutritional Study of the Islanders on Tristan da Cunha, 1966', *British Journal of Nutrition*, Vol. 23 (1969), pp. 227–47; Annotation, 'Diets of the People on Tristan da Cunha', *Nutrition Review*, Vol. 25, No. 4 (1967), pp. 104–8.

[19] S. M. Lewis, 'Nutritional Anaemia in an Isolated Community', *Israel Journal of Medical Science*, Vol. 2 (1966), pp. 507–9; A. W. Woodruff and L. E. Pettitt, 'Plasma Proteins in Tristan da Cunha Islanders', *Transactions of the Royal Society of Tropical Medicine and Hygiene*, Vol. 59 (1965), pp. 356–7.

[20] F. J. Fisher, 'A Field Survey of Dental Caries, Peridontal Disease and Enamel Defects in Tristan da Cunha', *British Dentistry Journal*, Vol. 125 (1968), pp. 398–401, 447–53; P. J. Holloway, R. L. Speirs, and G. L. Slack, 'Fluoride Content of Extracted Teeth from Some Islanders of Tristan da Cunha', *British Dentistry Journal*, Vol. 118 (1965), pp. 283–5.

[21] D. G. Fleck, 'Toxoplasmosis and Tristan da Cunha *Journal of Hygiene*, Vol. 63 (1965), pp. 389–93; J. B. Loudon, 'Social Aspects of Ideas about Treatment', *Transcultural Psychiatry*, eds. A. V. S. de Reuck and Ruth Porter (Ciba Foundation Symposium: London, 1965), pp. 137–61; Peter A. Munch, 'Culture and Superculture in a Displaced Community: Tristan da Cunha', *Ethnology*, Vol. 3 (1964), pp. 369–76; Peter A. Munch, 'Tristan Islanders Find Freedom', *The Times* (16 November 1965), p. 13.

[22] Gertrude Keir, 'The Psychological Assessment of the Children from the Island of Tristan da Cunha', *Studies in Psychology*, eds. Charlotte Banks and P. L. Broadhurst (1965), pp. 129–72.

fact, over eighty lines of study have developed, each coming on to the stage as a natural open-ended process and returning when needed, perhaps in company of different groups of disciplines. This effort has been achieved largely because of the central position the Medical Research Council occupies in Britain, and because of the active help by dozens of experts who have willingly given a little or a lot of their time when presented with a piece of the human jigsaw puzzle.

It became apparent quite early in the project that the sheet anchor of our work must be a thorough knowledge of the genealogical background of the Tristan islanders. The presence of the congenital abnormalities would have been sufficient mandate, but there was another long-term reason.

In medicine there has always been debate on the relative importance of genetic predisposition—the soil—and the disease process (for example, an infecting organism)—the seed. Both roles are acknowledged, but while a great deal of information has been generated about, say, the virulence of bacteria, knowledge about the human soil is less complete, if only because past generations were born and died before their biological characteristics could be systematically recorded. In the case of the unique population of Tristan da Cunha, there had fortunately been some extremely good note taking.

We were fortunate, indeed, in assembling the genealogy. Over the years, long before the islanders arrived in Britain in 1961, there had been studies of their family tree. It was a favourite interest of the padres, accustomed to parish registers in Britain; the Tristan genealogy was, to say the least, of some complexity. In 1937 the Norwegian Scientific Expedition attempted genealogies to show the inheritance of deformed ears and asthma.[23]

During World War II, the late Dr. E. J. S. Woolley was posted to Tristan as Surgeon Commander, Royal Navy, and though he was also required to double as Governor of the island, he still had time to practise as an amateur genealogist. In the few years of his posting, he drank innumerable cups of tea ('very strong with condensed milk') in the Tristan homes and, by perceptive questioning, he was able to elicit from the oldest people much information about the founders and their first Tristan generation. He prepared a card for practically every known islander since the settlement and noted the degree of intelligence, the presence of night blindness, asthma, and other conditions. When our survey started, Dr. Woolley, then a consultant physician in Derby, generously offered us the cards he had prepared

[23] Christopherson, *Results of the Norwegian Scientific Expedition to Tristan da Cunha.*

twenty years earlier. They formed the basis of our genealogical studies.

There were for a time certain gaps, particularly before 1882, but here we were helped by the inscriptions in family Bibles and other Tristan documents in the British Museum. After 1882, the current official register of Tristan births, marriages, and deaths was started; the earliest register had been taken to South Africa in 1857.

Bringing the population records up to date was a task undertaken mainly by Dr. J. Loudon, as part of his own work on the social anthropology of the islanders. A further check was given by Professor Peter A. Munch, now of the Department of Sociology, University of Southern Illinois. He had been a member of the Norwegian Expedition and in 1962 travelled to Britain to renew contact with the islanders.

These data were collated at the Galton Laboratory, University College, London, by Professor L. S. Penrose and his assistant Helen Lang-Brown. An attempt was made to recreate the genealogy from the beginning, using peg board and coloured thread; if the earlier missionaries found it complex, by the 1960s it had become almost impossibly so. But this attempt was particularly useful for small sections of the family tree. A different representation, however, was necessary for genetic studies of blood groups and biochemical markers examined in the present population. The simple solution chosen by Dr. Betty Robson and her colleagues for the work on haptoglobins and cholinesterases at the Galton Laboratory took as a base the individual islanders then being tested, and worked backwards to give a pedigree showing their ancestry and relationship.[24]

Both of these were subsequently developed in the Newcastle Human Genetics Laboratory to answer dynamic problems of population genetics. Complete tracing down of the population from its founders was undertaken to show the contributions of individual ancestors to the present gene pool and thus to demonstrate the effects of population size reductions on the genetic constitution of the population[25] as well as to trace the effects of differential fertility and migration on gene frequency change.[26] Tracing backwards was completed to show which of the present population derived what proportion of their genes from which ancestors, and for the examination of inbreeding.[27] Both of these in combination gave,

[24] Harris and Robson, 'Haptoglobins in Tristan da Cunha'.

[25] D. F. Roberts, 'Genetic Effects of Population Size Reduction', *Nature*, Vol. 220 (1968), pp. 1087–8.

[26] D. F. Roberts, 'Differential Fertility and the Genetic Constitution of an Isolated Population', *Proceedings of the 8th International Congress of Anthropological Sciences* (Tokyo), Vol. 1 (1968), pp. 350–56

[27] D. F. Roberts, 'The Development of Inbreeding in an Island Population', *Proceedings of the International Symposium on Genetics, Piracicaba: In Ciencia e Cul'ura*, Vol. 19 (1967), pp. 78–84; reprinted in the *Yearbook of Physical Anthropology*, Vol. 15 (1967), pp. 150–160.

for example, an answer to the question of how many retinitis pigmentosa genes there are likely to be in the present population—
eighteen in all.

But it soon became quite clear that traditional methods of pedigree
depiction were not adequate for the present population and were
likely to be still less so as new generations accrue. Attention was
therefore turned to computer methods of data storage and retrieval.
So far all the data on genetic markers in the population have been
put on punch cards, as has the material relating to demography,
movement of individuals to and from the island, and so forth.
Undoubtedly the task of record-keeping is made much easier,
and the straightforward statistical presentation of information
facilitated, by computer storage.

COMPUTER TECHNIQUES IN GENE FLOW STUDIES

The genealogy of this closed community, accurate for six generations,
provides a rare opportunity for the use of the most advanced
computer methods. The tasks of record-keeping, when there is
continuous accretion of new material, the retrieval of individual
entries, and statistical presentation of summarized information are
well suited to computer handling. But the real advantage comes in
computer analysis of such stored data and, from the nature of this
community, particularly in the investigation of the genetical
situation.

Accurate knowledge of the structure of a population is of the
greatest interest to the geneticist, for it enables him to predict the
genetic properties both of the population and of the individuals that
comprise it. Genes may be thought of as 'flowing through' a population structure, defined by the mutual relationships of its members,
in the same way as electrons flow through an electrical network.
The precise manner in which the electrons flow is determined
by the units, such as capacities and resistances, in the network and
the way they are joined together. Similarly, the genetic properties
of a population structure are determined by the way in which the
individuals are 'joined together' in families, in sibships, by ancestry
and by marriage.

Consider first the individuals. At each locus on his autosomes, an
individual inherits one gene from his mother and one gene from his
father chosen, according to Mendel's law, at random from the pair
of maternal genes and the pair of paternal genes respectively. If the
mother and father are related, through having at least one common

ancestor, then there is a possibility that the gene inherited from the mother is derived from exactly the same ancestral gene as the one inherited from the father. When this possibility is realized, we speak of the two genes being *identical by descent*. On an evolutionary time-scale it is, of course, remotely possible that *all* the genes of a particular kind may owe their existence to a single mutation, so that every homozygote may claim that, ultimately, its two genes are identical by descent. But over the period of a few generations for which, in man, we are likely to have genealogical information it is conceptually profitable to regard every gene, even though alike in state, as being formally identical only to its precursors and its direct descendants. Two genes of the same generation can, therefore, only be identical by descent if they share an ancestral precursor.

This powerful concept is due to Cotterman,[28] and it enables us to measure genetic relationship in terms of the *probability of gene-identity by descent*, otherwise termed the inbreeding coefficient. Thus the inbreeding coefficient of an individual may be concisely defined as the probability that the maternal and paternal genes at a locus are identical by descent, an event that can only happen if the parents are related through a common ancestor. When we speak of 'probability' in this connection, we are not forgetting that the structure of a particular population is unique, but are referring to the frequency of the event among all the loci, which are presumed independent. Another assumption is that in the limited time for which we have records mutation may safely be neglected.

The inbreeding coefficient is a most important parameter. It enables us to make probability statements about the genotype of an individual, given the population gene frequency, and it provides an index of the extent of inbreeding against which we can compare the incidences or means of other traits.

Whereas the inbreeding coefficient conveys the extent to which the maternal and paternal 'halves' of an indivudual are related, similar coefficients measure the genetic relationship of distinct individuals. Suppose we label the two genes of an individual at a particular locus A and B, and those of a relative C and D. If by $P(X = Y)$ we mean 'the probability that X and Y are identical by descent', then $P(A = B)$ and $P(C = D)$ are the inbreeding coefficients of the two individuals. But, further, we may also evaluate $P(A = C)$, $P(A = D)$, $P(B = C)$, and $P(B = D)$. Now the genetic correlation of two related individuals turns out to be equal to half the sum of these last four probabilities, and other informative coefficients of relationship can be defined in terms of similar, but more complex, proba-

[28] C. Cotterman, 'A Calculus for Statistical Genetics', Ph.D. Dissertation, Ohio State University, 1940.

bilities (such as P [A = C *and* B = D]).[29] Given these measures of relationship, not only are we equipped to make probability statements about the genotypes of pairs of individuals (such as those of relatives intending to marry), but we can also examine observed similarities between relatives to see whether the traits concerned behave as would be expected if they were in part inherited.

But how are these coefficients to be calculated in a particular case? Even quite simple genealogies lead to rather difficult computations, but the computer can help us in a novel way. Instead of instructing it in the precise rules for calculating the probabilities, which turns out to be a formidable task, [30]we can take advantage of the rapidity with which it can *simulate* the flow of genes through the population structure. We actually invoke the concept on which our ideas are based! All that is necessary is to list the individuals in the genealogy so that each is preceded (though not usually immediately) by his parents in the new list. Those who are founder-members (that is, those about whose parents nothing is known) head the list, and they are each allocated two numbered genes, 2N in all if there are N founders. Straightforward Mendelian gene flow is then repeatedly simulated, and gene-correspondences are counted in order to derive estimates of the probabilities of gene-identity by descent. Thus if, in 10,000 runs, the two genes of an individual have the same reference number on 312 occasions, the inbreeding coefficient is estimated to be 0·0312.

Armed with this technique, we may also attack the other problem —that of the genetic properties of the population as a whole. By computer simulation, we can follow the fate of particular genes and examine the genetic contribution of any particular individual to the gene pool at any time. Given the genotypes of some individuals, we can predict the genotypes of others, perhaps even of remote ancestors, and we can study random genetic drift, the spread of mutants, and selection. With little difficulty, we can extend the investigation to linked loci and polygenic variation. The computer technique provides us, in essence, with an analogue of the true population, which we may interrogate at will.

The above investigations require a knowledge of the population structure, but not, for the most part, of the genotypes of the individuals. Where these are also known, however, the work is easily extended to an examination of whether the genotypes accord satisfactorily with Mendelian expectations or whether selective forces must be invoked.

[29] O. Kempthorne, *An Introduction to Genetic Statistics* (New York, 1957).

[30] R. MacCluer, R. Griffith, C. F. Sing, and W. J. Schull, 'Use of Computers in Human Genetics', *American Journal of Human Genetics* (Supplement), Vol. 19 (1967), pp. 189–221.

Sometimes, indeed, genetic information may be available without the corresponding genealogical information. Here the computer can, in principle, come to our aid by offering us the possibility of re-constructing the genealogy from the genotypes. If sufficient genetic information is available, the computer should be able to sift through the individuals and detect the pattern of relationships that best corresponds to the genetic similarities. It is, as yet, too early to predict the ultimate success of such a method, but trial runs based on simu-lated data have proved quite encouraging.

The application of these methods to the Tristan population (or any other, for that matter) is still in its infancy. Thus far, the inbreed-ing coefficients, ancestral contributions to the gene pool, and so forth have been computed by electronic desk calculators, but the basic pedigree material is now prepared on cards ready for computer use, and programmes are in operation which, for example, enable computation of the pair-wise coefficient of relationship for any two individuals in the genealogy. The application of the new methods to the Tristan data may be expected to reveal facts about the genetic properties of the population structure that cannot be elucidated in any other way, for example, in the analysis of polygenic characters, quite apart from the simpler tasks of probability calculations to be made in individual circumstances or even checking the acceptability of laboratory findings for particular individuals!

THE PERVASION OF ISOLATION

I   GENETIC

The founder fathers set about their creation in a business-like way. The product of its period, it was conceived as a utopian community based on the principles of equality, communal ownership, and free-dom from Government control. These could only be achieved in relative isolation from the economic bustle of the world. In their remarkable founding charter, in the British Museum, they agreed that 'all stock and stores of every description should be considered as belonging equally to each, all profits should be equally divided; and that in order to ensure the harmony of the Firm, no member should assume any superiority whatever, but all to be considered as equal in every respect.'

This conception attracted others—sailors tired of the sea, adven-turers and within five years it was necessary to modify the charter, allocating specific areas of responsibility. But the harsh environment, the remoteness from the outside world, the loss of contact with 'ordinary' activities, the inability on this little isolated speck of land to get away from some other member of the community with whom there was temporary friction, were all too much for some individuals. Most of the late-comers did not stay long, and only a few lived out their lives on the island, as indeed did only one of the original founder men. But within a generation, this collective enterprise had evolved into an aggregate of independent households where each man was his own master and nobody's servant, an acephalous society where the spirit of independence and equality prevailed to become a living force and a dominant element of the community's system of values that has lasted to the present day. It has coloured their attitudes throughout their history. The islanders time and time again risked their lives to rescue survivors from the shipwrecks that occurred and to shelter the survivors in their own small houses until they could be taken off. Many throughout their history have tried to persuade them to leave the island, to take up an easier and more affluent way of life, but though segments of the community have emigrated, the majority consistently have refused to leave the island. The founding fathers, and those they accepted as permanent companions, were no undisciplined rabble of adventurers, but serious-minded, disciplined men who endeavoured to retain in their remoteness the values of their society.

The tiny community built up gradually, as is to be expected in a situation where numbers are dependent on the fertility of a small parental generation. The earliest members were indeed highly fertile and natural increase was high. But the numbers were greatly reduced by a large emigration in 1855–57 and by a boat disaster in 1885, when the drowning of fifteen active men turned Tristan into an island of widows, with only four adult men left to support the remaining population. During the six years that followed there was further large-scale emigration that reduced the population to less than sixty inhabitants.

Right from the foundation of the settlement individuals had a very restricted choice of mates. In the earliest years the founder's wife was often the only adult woman on the island. When it became clear that several other men intended to remain as permanent settlers, wives were obtained for them from St. Helena, the nearest inhabited island— five adult women for the then five unmarried men. With the passage of time, as new generations were born, it became very difficult for a man who wanted to marry to find a spouse of the right age; what is also important, there were soon only relatives from whom to choose. When potential husbands sought to wed in 1871 and 1876, there were no other available women on the island other than the ones they chose. For the last few decades, any marriages between islanders have been marriages between relatives. They have tried to avoid marriage with close relatives, by carefully observing the prohibited degrees of marriage, and it is only in extremely few instances that these have been transgressed in irregular matings. But the combination of small population size and marriage with relatives brought about by their isolation has made the population more and more inbred.[31]

The degree of inbreeding in a population can be measured in terms of the probability that both the genes an individual possesses at a given autosomal locus are identical. This probability is known as the coefficient of inbreeding. It has been calculated for each member of the population, past and present, and there is a clear steady increase over the years, For instance, islanders born between 1850 and 1860 had a mean inbreeding coefficient of 0·014; those born between 1950 and 1960, a hundred years later, had a mean inbreeding coefficient of 0·05, over three times as high. Now this may sound a large rise, but in fact the island population as a whole today is still not highly inbred. The mean inbreeding coefficient of the total population when our study started in 1961 was 0·04. This value is only two-thirds that of the offspring of a first-cousin marriage. Indeed, it is less than in other small populations where it has been calculated over a comparable number of generations, like the Samaritans of Israel and Jordan. But it must be emphasized that this is the mean figure, and there are indeed individuals within the population who have high inbreeding coefficients just as there are others who are not inbred. And it is in the more highly inbred individuals that we detect signs of the deleterious effects that may accompany inbreeding—the occurrence of recessive diseases, diminution of mental vigour[32], diminished survival.[33] This is what makes the study of the population at the present time so valuable, for we can observe a whole range of inbreeding coefficients in different individuals, compare with them the observed biological characters, and thereby calculate the genetic load and discover which features attributable to inbreeding are the price the islanders are paying for their heritage.

Although the average level of inbreeding in the population is not at all high and is only today surpassing the value expected had random mating occurred, the effects have already begun to show. What is equally important is that the inbreeding that has so far

[31] Roberts, 'The Development of Inbreeding in an Island Population'.

[32] D. F. Roberts, 'Incest, Inbreeding, and Mental Abilities', *British Medical Journal*, Vol. 4 (1967), pp. 336–7.

[33] D. F. Roberts, 'Consanguineous Marriages and Calculation of the Genetic Load', *Annals of Human Genetics*, Vol. 32 (1969), pp. 407–10; D. F. Roberts, 'Demography of Tristan da Cunha', *Population Studies*, November 1971, pp. 465–79.

occurred is only high in respect to half the founding ancestors; in respect to four major ancestors there has been no inbreeding— that is, the replicated genes have not yet had an opportunity of coming together in any descendant, and we simply do not know yet what deleterious genes these four ancestors endowed the population with. If the inbreeding continues, these genes too will show their effects, and again the implications may be serious. The only way that further inbreeding can be prevented from developing is to have a steady flow of new genes from outside in each new generation. But even to keep inbreeding at its present mean level, 10 per cent of all matings should take place with outsiders, given the population size, structure, breeding pattern and so forth of the Tristanites. This would keep the load of genetic defects at its present level. But as things are, this possibility seems unlikely.

2   DEMOGRAPHIC

It is not only the quality of the future population of the island that is important, but also whether the population can continue to exist in its isolation as a viable demographic entity. Projection of the population trends is not just an academic exercise, but is of practical importance as the following case-study demonstrates.

In 1969 we received a letter from a senior administrator in the Commonwealth Office.

[He asked] 'whether the [Medical Research] Council would be able to undertake a study of population trends in Tristan with a view to forecasting likely developments in years to come? As far as I am aware this has not yet been done. The sorts of questions which I would like to have answered are: Is there an overall natural increase or decrease of population taking place? Has the number of children of school age increased? Or is the balance of the population shifting towards the older groups? What are the prospects for maintaining or increasing the able-bodied male labour force?

I realize that it may well be difficult to answer these questions in view of the interruption of life on the island by the removal of the community to Britain after the eruption and their subsequent return, which has probably dislocated the course of events on which demographers have to base their conclusions. However, I feel that it is necessary for the Commonwealth Office to have some projection of future trends and I should be very glad to know whether your experts consider that it would be possible to produce some information on these lines.'

This request was certainly a perceptive one. We tried to answer it, fully aware of the complications arising from the islanders' upheaval It was therefore not sufficient merely to look at the rate of population growth over the decades and extrapolate from that. Instead, the several factors that affect human fertility and survival had to be dissected and estimates made of how each is likely to tend in the future.

The population of Tristan da Cunha is particularly subject to features making any such projection unwise—a very small population size, its remoteness, the change in its relationship to the outside world, the change in the awareness of its population—all of which make any detailed computation of future trends unrealistic. Yet from studies so far of the biological demography of the island population, there emerge data from which some estimate of future developments can be made.[34]

3   IS AN OVERALL NATURAL INCREASE OR DECREASE TAKING PLACE?

The population has increased from the time of its establishment as a viable entity with an adequate sex ratio in 1827, when the numbers were twenty-three, until October, 1961, when the population size was 267. This is an overall increase at the rate of 0·0183 (that is, 1·83 per cent) per annum. But this overall population increase has been far from regular. Figure 2 shows that there have been three periods of steady increase, at rates which the slopes of the graph suggest were fairly similar, but which in fact were not (0·054, 0·040, and 0·022 respectively). These three periods were separated by two brief phases of drastic population reduction. The overall rate of increase over the population history, therefore, is not particularly meaningful. Moreover, for projection of trends, it is more fruitful to examine the variations in the underlying biological factors of population increase and then to employ a measure more closely related to these rather than to use their observed resultant alone.

Table 1 sets out maternal and paternal ages at the birth of first offspring, according to the year of birth of the parents. The entry for the last cohort, 1940–49, is undoubtedly an underestimate for both sexes, since several individuals have not yet commenced reproduction: the same bias, though to a lesser extent, may also apply to the 1930–39 cohort. The cohorts are of different durations on account of the small number of individuals in some decadal groups. There has obviously been little change in maternal age at birth of first child with the passage of time, but by contrast there was a steady

[34] D. F. Roberts, 'Demography of Tristan da Cunha'.

Figure 2   The size of the population of Tristan da Cunha on 31 December of each year from 1816 to 1960. Reproduced by permission of *Nature*

reduction in mean paternal age until the turn of the century, and there has since occurred a slight tendency to increase. In other words, women have started producing their families at generally the same age throughout the whole of the island's history, whereas men commenced fatherhood at fairly late ages at first, then at younger ages until the present century, during which there has been a tendency to postpone reproduction. Data for parental ages at birth of the final child are only complete to 1920 for women and 1910 for men, for it is by no means certain that reproduction has

Table 1   Parental age at birth of first child

| | Mother | | | Father | |
Mother born	Mean	S.D.	Father born	Mean	S.D.
−1839	21·7	5·06	−1839	30·7	8·01
1840–69	21·2	4·26	1840–69	28·1	5·16
1870–89	22·4	6·29	1870–89	26·3	5·81
1890–99	23·2	4·32	1890–99	24·3	5·85
1900–9	24·1	3·53	1900–9	25·1	4·12
1910–19	20·5	2·25	1910–19	26·2	4·54
1920–29	23·3	4·99	1920–29	26·8	4·85
1930–39	23·2	2·73	1930–39	27·4	4·06
1940–49	(22·1	2·17)	1940–49	(22·9	2·55)

ceased for cohorts born after these dates. In both sexes the trend is clear; there has been a steady decline in the age of cessation of repro-

Table 2   Parental age at birth of last child

Mother born	Mother Mean	S.D.	Father born	Father Mean	S.D.
−1829	42·7	4·63	−1829	53·6	8·00
1830–69	40·3	2·69	1830–69	47·1	6·33
1870–89	40·8	3·46	1870–89	42·6	8·03
1890–99	37·3	3·50	1890–99	40·7	8·73
1900–9	37·3	4·71	1900–9	37·6	6·76
1910–19	(32·3	8·33)	1910–19	(37·5	7·12)

duction both in women and in men, as Table 2 shows. Thus there has been a steady reduction in the duration of the reproductive span in the Tristan population. There has moreover occurred an increase in the mean interval between births from a mean of 1·9 years in the earliest cohorts born before 1830 (women) to 4·3 for women born between 1930 and 1939. Thus, overall, there has been a steady decline in the number of births per parent throughout the history of the population. Not all adults were parents and in Table 3 are shown for each cohort the mean numbers of total births per

Table 3 Mean fertility of individuals remaining on the island

Cohort	Female	Male
−1830	8·82	7·43
−1870	4·26	4·41
−1890	5·00	4·00
−1900	4·70	5·22
−1910	4·36	3·60
−1920	3·69	3·69

individual remaining on the island until any time during adulthood. These trends in fertility factors can be summarized diagrammatically. Dividing the population into three main cohorts—those born before 1840, those born 1840–79, and those born 1880–1919—Figure 3 represents the age specific fecundity schedule for an islander according to date of birth. This shows the number of children he or she could expect to produce in a given five-year age interval. In the diagram for men, the steady decrease in the area of the three triangles shows the diminution in total fertility, and the shift to the left of the three triangles shows the earlier fertility; for women, the shift to the left is less pronounced, but again the diminishing area of the three polygons shows the trend to decreasing fertility.

While these calculations show the general trends in Tristanian

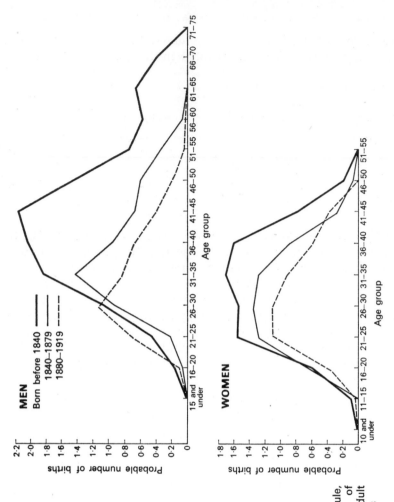

Figure 3 Age-specific fecundity schedule, showing the probable number of births per five years for the adult islanders born at different periods

reproduction, they do not show whether the reproduction was sufficient to maintain the population. A first indication of this is given
by the net reproduction rate, which is the rate of multiplication in
one generation; it is expressed as the ratio of female births to female
parents and male births to male parents in two successive generations.
It is, in other words, the sum of the product at each age of the probability of survival to that age and the probable fecundity at that age.
An approximation to the net reproduction rates for each cohort is
set out in Table 4. (It is an approximation since total births were

Table 4   Net reproduction rate for each cohort

Cohort	Women	Men
−1815	7·63	6·14
1815–30	3·5	2·00
1830–40	1·5	1·93
1840–60	0·81	0·44
1860–70	1·33	1·29
1870–80	0·9	0·95
1880–90	1·36	0·57
1890–1900	1·96	2·61
1900–10	2·18	1·72
1910–20	1·72	1·60
Subtotals		
−1840	2·94	2·64
1840–80	0·87	0·70
1880–1920	1·74	1·50
Total		
1800–1920	1·58	1·31

assumed to comprise equal numbers of each sex.) The table shows
that twice in the population's history reproduction was not sufficient
to balance wastage, the first occasion affecting the cohorts born
1840–60, and the second occasion women born 1870–80 and men
born 1870–90.

All these variables can be summarized by the constant r, the
intrinsic rate of increase of the population. This is defined as the
rate of growth per head under specified physical conditions in an
unlimited environment where the effects of increasing density do
not need to be considered, conditions which apply to the Tristan
population. Table 5 sets out for each cohort the intrinsic rate of
natural increase for each sex. The figures are different for the two
sexes, since these reproduce at different ages. From this table it
appears that the cohorts drastically affected by the heavy emigrations were in fact so heavily affected that the rate was negative.
Thus, the periods of massive emigration despoiled the population

Table 5 The intrinsic rate of natural increase in the island population

Cohort	Women	Men
−1815	0·076	0·044
1815–30	0·045	0·021
1830–40	0·013	0·023
1840–60	−0·006	−0·007
1860–70	0·011	0·003
1870–80	−0·004	−0·002
1880–90	0·010	−0·017
1890–1900	0·022	0·031
1900–10	0·026	0·016
1910–20	0·019	0·015
Subtotals		
−1840	0·036	0·032
1840–80	−0·005	−0·001
1880–1920	0·019	0·014
Total		
1800–1920	0·016	0·014

of much of its reproductive potential. In two cohorts of women and three of men, the rate was negative; in all other cohorts, the rate of increase has remained positive. A tendency to population increase has therefore been general throughout the population's history. While any general trend is difficult to identify because of the variations caused by the emigrations, the highest values occurred in the earliest cohorts. There seems to have been a general secular diminution in the rate of increase until after the turn of the present century when the rate settled down to a medium level, with fertility characterized by smaller families completed at an earlier age than in the cohorts of the previous century. The rate of increase as determined by the pattern of reproduction, mortality, and emigration of individuals born in the first two decades of the twentieth century is approximately 0·022 in women and 0·016 in men. A similarity to the overall value throughout the history of the population (0·015) is coincidental, for the latter is an intermediate value, determined by the high rates of the earliest cohorts and the low rates of those experiencing severe emigration.

As regards the future, if the reproductive pattern of the population continues to resemble that in the earlier cohorts of the twentieth century, and if the emigration and mortality patterns remain similar, then the capacity for increase will continue at approximately the same rate, 0·018. This figure should, however, be regarded as a maximum. With increasing awareness of the outside world and the greater contacts maintained through outside staff of the various services on the island, emigration is likely to increase above that characteristic of the 1900–20 cohorts. This will reduce the rate of increase, particularly since the younger members of the population will be affected. Moreover, the reproductive pattern shows a clear trend to lower fertility; this tendency seems likely to continue and again, though offset to some extent by the earlier completion of fertility, will result in a reduction in the capacity for increase. There is some room for earlier age at male marriage to offset this, but age at marriage has remained stable in women, and there is no sign that any change is taking place. The most likely figure on a purely subjective assessment for the rate of increase over the next few decades seems to be of the order of 0·012 to 0·015.

Table 6 gives the expected size of the population over the next

Table 6   Expected size of Tristan population for various rates of increase

Year	0·022	0·020	0·018	0·015	0·012
1980	322	315	307	297	286
1990	400	383	367	344	322
2000	498	467	439	399	363
2010	619	570	525	464	409

forty years for various values of the rate of increase. These predicted sizes assume that population size and density will not themselves inhibit growth. There is no evidence as yet from which the maximum population size can be calculated.

4   HAS THE NUMBER OF CHILDREN OF SCHOOL-AGE INCREASED

There occurred a steady increase in the number of children in the age groups five to fifteen from 1890 until 1950 (Figure 4). There was thereafter some decline due to a drop in fertility. The effects of the temporary migration to Britain obscure subsequent developments. In 1968 there was a slight increase in the number of children under 5 (Figure 5), which suggests that the number of children in the school-age group may be about to recommence its increase. From the present structure of the population, the expected number of children of school-age will be sixty-three in 1980.

For further prediction, in view of the disturbance of the Tristan population in the past few years, it is perhaps more useful to calculate the number of children of school-age to be expected when the anticipated population growth rate becomes established. If this becomes established at the rate of 0·015, then the percentage of the

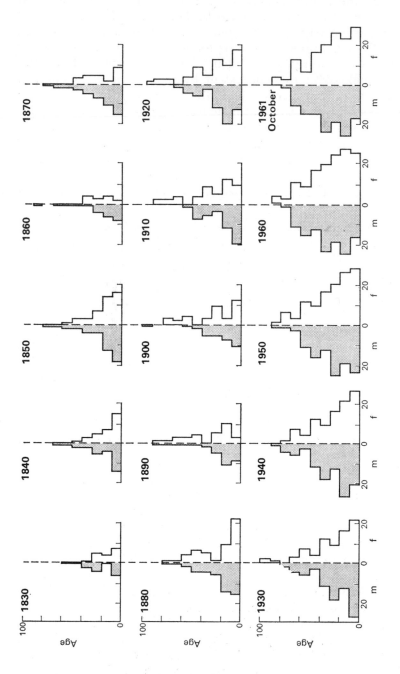

Figure 4 Population pyramids at the end of each tenth year from 1830 onwards

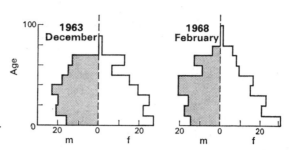

Figure 5 Recent popu-
lation pyramids

population between the ages of five and fifteen will be approximately
18 per cent. This proportion suggests that the school-age population
may be as high as seventy-three in the year 2000.

5 IS THE BALANCE OF THE POPULATION SHIFTING TOWARDS THE OLDER GROUPS?

Comparison of the population pyramids from 1900 onwards
(Figure 4) shows that in the first few decades births were sufficiently
numerous to promise an increase in the older age groups in due
course. By 1960, however, there had been some reduction in the
number of infants, which suggested that by 1990 there would be a
reduction in the thirty-year-old segment of the population. This
suggestion was reinforced by the structure of the population that
returned to the island in 1963, where again there was a suggestion
of a deficit of children and young adults, but by 1968 the situation
was beginning to be redressed (Figure 5).

From the present structure of the population, the number of
adults in the twenty-year-old and thirty-year-old groups expected
in 1980 is thirty-nine and forty-three respectively; in 1990, forty-
nine and thirty-nine respectively. For further prediction, the numbers
in the older age groups expected when the population settles down
to its new rate of increase can be calculated. The number of adults
in the twenty-year-old age groups expected in 2000 may be as high
as sixty-three, assuming a rate of increase of 0·015. There is no reason
to believe that there will be an excessive burden of the older age
groups when the population settles down to its new rate of increase.

6 WHAT ARE THE PROSPECTS FOR MAINTAINING THE ABLE-BODIED MALE LABOUR FORCE?

Information on this point derives from the sex ratio in children. In
February, 1968, there were nineteen boys under fifteen as compared

with forty-two girls (Figure 5). For this difference between the sexes, random fluctuation in the sex ratio at birth is largely responsible. The immediate prospects, therefore, are that there will be a slight decline in the male labour force and that its effects will be most noticeable in about twenty years time. On the other hand, the population has survived in the past with a much more marked depletion of males, and there seems no real reason for concern on this score as regards the island's economy, although it may give rise to matrimony difficulties and probably to some female emigration and some male immigration.

7 GENERAL COMMENTS

There is no doubt about the demographic trends observed in the past population. But it is extremely hazardous to extrapolate these into the future; there is no real reason to assume that present patterns of fertility and mortality will be maintained. There is nothing on which to base estimates of future emigration and immigration. Most serious, there is no evidence from which the upper azymptote of the growth curve can be calculated, so that all the calculations envisage numerical expansion unchecked by a limited environment. The estimates of future developments must, therefore, be considered tentative at best.

The conspicuous feature of forecasts of even large populations is that they are rarely realized, and the population of Tristan is particularly subject to features, stemming from its isolation, that make numerical projections unwise. But it would have been wrong not to attempt some estimate, however tentative, when we had such complete biological information. This line of reasoning led us to attempt a partial answer to a subsequent request from the Government Actuary's Department in London for information to enable consideration of the financial and actuarial aspects of a pension scheme for the island. We were asked for the expected numbers of each sex by age groups over the next thirty years or so and for a sub-division of the expected numbers of women and men by marital status. The previous calculations provided the necessary information on the expected age distributions of the total population, but we did not feel able, because of small numbers, to make any useful attempt at prediction of sex ratio by age group. It was interesting to see that the present age distribution is not much different from the predicted, and so the Actuary was able to judge whether or not the proposed system of finance for the pension scheme would be adequate in the long term.

MIGRATIONS AFTER THE VOLCANO

Biological predictions such as these are often upset by events of history. In the case of Tristan, who would have predicted the volcanic eruption in 1961? And at that date how many would have predicted that two years later the Tristanians would return to their island? It is worthwhile considering the circumstances prior to this return.

After the novelty of Britain wore off, they had to face the realities and complexities of life. They found themselves in the south of England, a prosperous, affluent, and socially competitive region. One of the biggest employers, the Esso Oil refinery, pays extremely good wages for skilled men. Unfortunately, the islanders were sub-literate and unskilled in the sense that the mechanical revolution had passed them by. Their average earning capacity was at the lowest level.

Fortunately, their rent was very low, but although the cottages in the old Royal Air Force camp near Southampton were attractive and had been furnished from the Tristan Fund, the islanders did not really appreciate this benefit. On Tristan they were property owners: in Britain, they saw their precious shillings disappear each week as rent. For their jobs, perhaps several miles away, they were dependent on buses: they found it irksome to have to be punctual; time had never been much of a factor in their lives.

Daily living was complex. In the welfare state, which they took or granted, there were many authorities to deal with: the labour exchange, the police, welfare office, post office, and so forth, each with its own set of bewildering forms. The presence of a sympathetic sociologist from the survey helped to reassure them to some extent.

There were also difficulties facing the children of these sub-literate parents. In 1962, there were about sixty Tristan children who had to be integrated into the British educational system. Normally it is difficult to get to the upper streams. How much more so for a youngster whose background was completely unlike that of a child born in Britain? This problem confronts the children of migrants to Britain from other Commonwealth countries like India, Pakistan, and the West Indies.

At the time, it was widely expected in Britain that the Tristanians would remain and many felt it most desirable to help the Tristan children to integrate easily, reach the various landmarks in their schooling, and have happy young lives with a minimum of frustration— and, just as important, get reasonable jobs afterwards. These pious

Op

hopes are fairly easy to express, but difficult to achieve; therefore, as a first effort, a study was made of the fundamentals of their educational psychology.

Normally, education is a matter outside the scope of the Medical Research Council, but a research project was supported since it concerned the total health of the community. It was undertaken by a group from the psychology department of University College London under the direction of Dr. Gertrude Keir. It turned out to be larger than originally conceived because the psychologists realized that for their study to be valid they would also have to measure the attainments of the English boys and girls who were providing the new environment of the Tristan children.

The children were studied as soon as they joined the schools in order to find out what effects their Tristan upbringing might have had in the development of their intelligence, their educational attainments, and their social and personal interactions. We wanted to follow up their adaptation to the very different educational and environmental conditions in which they found themselves in Britain. They were given intelligence tests, tests of basic educational attainment, and some personality tests. The children's behaviour was observed closely, their own teachers helping to rate some characteristics of it. In addition, there was a test of intellectual maturation for the schoolchildren between $2\frac{1}{2}$ and 5 years. Ratings of intelligence were obtained from a number of independent judges who knew them on the island. While the means of assessment were certainly not ideal, they did at least ensure that some conclusions could be drawn about the personality characteristics of the children at the beginning of their school life in Britain and also about changes that took place over the period of the followup.

Life within the Tristan community, it turned out, results in some lack of personal initiative, very limited competitiveness, and self-acceptance. The children were free of anxiety, had a strong sense of belonging together distinct from 'the outsiders', and a certain fatalism or passivity. They are not a talkative people so it is not surprising that the children had diminished linguistic skills, limited imagination, lack of curiosity, and a certain immaturity of thought. Although some were of normal intelligence, there were many among the older children especially who appeared to be of limited intellectual capacity. They were all slow in the basic school subjects.

After eighteen months, there were very few changes in their general personality characteristics. A few children were perhaps showing rather more interest in their new environment, while passivity decreased and aggression increased. This period is too short to allow definite conclusions about adaptation to a new environment. The essence really is whether an individual wants to adapt. In the case of the Tristanians, the motivation seemed to be slim.[35]

The research by the educational psychologists has been presented at some length because not only was it aimed primarily at the welfare of the Tristan children, but also because it is widely pertinent to situations in the world today. It illustrates the closely interlocking nature of the studies made on this community; it has laid the basis for a genetic study of the intelligence of the community, particularly in relation to the effect of inbreeding. A preliminary analysis, based on Dr. Woolley's clinical notes, shows significant associations between the extent of inbreeding and lowered intelligence. It suggests that some of the worse mental conditions in the population are due to the inbreeding that has so far occurred, with intelligence under polygenic control with directional dominance.[36] To correlate the findings from different fields of investigation and to follow them up in long-term studies are but two of the many possibilities for scientific inquiry that an isolated community such as Tristan presents.

Had the islanders remained in Britain, it would have been only fair to give them additional help with their education, and this we planned to do. Britain is intellectually competitive and much in future life depends on school attainment. But in 1963 events overtook these plans. The islanders went back to Tristan.

To the reasons already mentioned for their dissatisfaction, others must be added. It was their justifiable complaint that the weather was always bad. They were upset to read continually about violence, especially assaults on babies which made headline news. One of the older islanders was, in fact, set upon by hooligans and robbed. The Tristanians are not aggressive, and their non-competitiveness left them rather bewildered. Their conditioning to the concept that no man could be of greater position than the next did not serve them well in the industrialized south of England. Because the Industrial Revolution had largely passed them by and left them in the nineteenth century, they were, in a manner of speaking, temporal British foreigners. Over a century and a half they had come into a fine equilibrium with their environment on Tristan, but this experience did not help them to face life in Britain. So they returned to their island 'We must go back', an elderly Tristanian said. 'We know all about the volcano, and we know all about the blindness—but leastways, on Tristan, you don't get killed crossing the road'.

[35] A. G. Davey, 'The Tristan da Cunha Children's Concepts of Equivalence', *British Journal of Educational Psychology*, Vol. 38 (1968), pp. 162–70; also Keir, 'The Psychological Assessment of the Children from the Island of Tristan da Cunha', and Keir, 'The Merrill-Palmer Test in Use with the Children from the Island of Tristan da Cunha', *Journal of Child Psychology and Psychiatry*, Vol. 7 (1966), pp. 133–42.
[36] Roberts, 'Incest, Inbreeding, and Mental Abilities'.

It might perhaps have been more realistic to settle the Tristanians on one of the islands off the coast of Scotland—for example, the Shetlands or the Hebrides. Or, since the weather was an important factor in their lives, they might have gone to the Pacific or to the Caribbean, where they would have been only a few hours from a neighbouring island. But the Tristanians had almost an obsessional vision of returning to their Promised Land.

The Medical Research Council was not asked to help in making the decision whether or when they should go. It would have been a thankless decision, even though, ironically, as a result of the survey we already knew more about the Tristanians than about the average man in the United Kingdom!

In 1962, two islanders went back with a Royal Society expedition of geophysicists and biologists.[37] Then twelve men went as an advance party to repair damage on the island in anticipation of the first batch of fifty-two islanders who left England in May, 1963. The volcano had done very little damage to their houses; in fact, only one was destroyed when sparks set the roof alight. But the fish canning factory had been completely engulfed and destroyed by the volcano. Towards the end of the year, 198 more islanders made the journey, leaving only fourteen in England.

The community settled down, but the new Administrator, who travelled from London with the early party for a year's tour of duty, was oppressed by the stark isolation of the place. He felt that there could be no future for the people on Tristan and considered it his moral duty to encourage them to leave. If they returned to England, he said, houses and jobs would be easy to come by. Forty islanders responded to these inducements, but, back in England, they found that reality was different.

When they had arrived in 1961, their reputation had preceded them; they were lionized by well-wishers and subsidized accommodation was found for them. Now, their novelty worn off, they had to fend for themselves and, in fact, compete in a high-priced market for accommodation.

Some of them became farm labourers, the main attraction being a house; but they were the loneliest and most miserable of the islanders because they felt so utterly separated from other Tristan families, whom they could only visit by a five-mile journey on an inconvenient bus service, an expensive and major expedition for them. In 1967 nine of them returned once again to Tristan, followed by six more

[37] D. E. Baird, J. H. Dickson, M. W. Holgate, M. N. Wace, 'Biological Report of the Royal Society Expedition to Tristan da Cunha, 1962', *Philosophical Transactions of the Royal Society*, Vol. 249 (1965), pp. 257–434.

in August, 1968. Plans have been made for a dozen more to leave England.

For the time being the exiles yearn for home, and those on the island are content to remain.

THE FUTURE

I   THE IMPORTANT ROLE OF EDUCATION

At present it seems that the island children are caught in a vicious circle. The island itself is bleak, and *prime facie* evidence suggests that there is little to stimulate young minds. The pre-volcano picture appears to confirm this. Our educational research has pointed to the relatively low level of attainment. Inquiries are afoot to discover how much of this is due to inbreeding and how much to the lack of mental stimulation.

But for immediate purposes it seems useful to ask the more practical question: 'What sort of education is best suited to the *realistic needs* of the Tristan islanders?'

The men can now obtain employment from the administration or from the fishing company. They work an eight-hour day. The best jobs include fairly skilled carpentry and electrical maintenance; this is a measure of the rapidity with which the intelligent islanders learn useful trades. The majority are ordinary labourers. When the weather allows the islanders to go fishing, less than a hundred days per year, most of the able-bodied men between twenty and forty years of age take part. They leave other jobs if it suits them to do so that day, and they work long hours. In the evenings the older men and young boys process the crawfish catch. The most capable girls obtain employment either as maids, pupil teachers, or in the hospital. Married women do not usually take jobs outside the house.

Since the establishment of the fish-freezing factory and the emphasis on cash economy, island tasks now take second place; cultivation of their potato patches and animal husbandry are left for evenings and weekends, though the women work at the patches during the week.[38] Our nutritional research has confirmed the low efficiency with which the islanders conduct their agronomy.

All these points confirm the urgent need for a specially imaginative type of education, especially devised for their isolated circumstances. It should be based on rural studies, or the modern concept 'ecological studies'. The foundation should be a showpiece school farm, where gradually, over a few years, the benefits of rational practice would

[38] Chambers and Southgate, 'Nutritional Study of the Islanders of Tristan da Cunha'.

become obvious. The children would clearly see from it the possibilities of their island environment and, it is to be hoped, would not become frustrated teenagers. The exemplar approach is important when the older generation is set in its ways. In developing communities it has often been found that disproportionate effort and expense have to be devoted to an obstinate older generation; in fact, the result may be antagonism rather than cooperation. It is usually prudent in the long run to invest in the children—that is, of course, if the country can afford to wait a decade.

2 NATURAL RESOURCES ON TRISTAN

How many people can be supported on an island whose flat ground is a mere three square miles? The answer hinges on the intelligent mobilization of resources and the population growth.

The main economy depends on the fishing industry. At present this is thriving; the islanders have become largely dependent on it for their cash income. They would suffer badly if lobster tails ceased to be a delicacy in the United States market; or if the fishing company decided to concentrate its activities on factory ships and withdraw its industry from the island (it amounts to only 20 per cent of its fishing activities); or, a third unhappy possibility, if the waters became fished out. There is, in fact, some evidence that smaller and younger fish are appearing in the catch in increasing numbers.

With the present emphasis, the acreage of land for cultivation, though an important consideration, is not the most vital. Nor is the secondary importance assigned to food crop cultivation by the men, nor the slight attention given to livestock utilization of the mountain slopes where there is considerable scope for improvement. But for stability it is desirable for the islanders to strike a balance between the cash and subsistence economies. It would be quite possible to adjust the economy so that an individual could choose, without sacrifice, to earn wages or grow food. At present, the latter is badly neglected, and the islanders buy from the store many imported foods which they could grow for themselves. If there were an economic recession, food production could at least continue.

From the ecological point of view there are many opportunities to study the balance between animals, food production, land usage, and marine resources. In this ecologic system, the best documented section is the human population, as a result of the Medical Research Council endeavours. Zoologists and botanists have conducted excellent research in the last decade,[39] and there is the possibility

[39] Baird, et al., 'Biological Report of the Royal Society Expedition to Tristan da Cunha'; J. H. Flint, Oryx, Vol. 9, No. 1 (1967).

of setting up a biological research station. An important development would be a study of the effect of man on this natural system. In the opposite direction, the Tristanians are almost certainly affected by zoonoses.

For a study of the total ecology of an island Tristan is a unique opportunity. The Tristan da Cunha 'laboratory' could well be exploited by the International Biological Programme. Its interdisciplinary philosophy (productivity, conservation, marine and terrestrial resources, and so forth) could be put to the test on this small island; Tristan might prove scientifically more valuable than some venues where perhaps only one discipline can be applied in an almost totally unknown environment.

AN ANALOGUE UNDERDEVELOPED COUNTRY?

In this paper, we have referred from time to time to the islanders' medical problems, their subliteracy, poor agronomy, negligible technology, waste, cussedness, turning away from subsistence in favour of cash crops, and a dependence on cash crops that makes the Tristanians hostages to fortune. These problems are seen in many underdeveloped countries. Aid to these countries amounts annually to billions of dollars from the United States, France, Britain, the Soviet Union, and other technologically advanced countries, but it is not always evident that the money is spent in order to obtain the greatest amount of good for the greatest number of people. There may often be shrewd political reasons for not embracing Benthamism; but more often it is because the problem is inherently complex and perhaps because economists, in whose hands is the disposition of the funds, do not use the experimental method, but rely almost solely on intuition.

Those in the biological and physical sciences also rely on intuition, yet put their theories to rigid experimental test. Such scientists work also by analogy, and some of the most exciting advances, for example, in medicine, have often come from an application of knowledge gained from the physiology of some very distant organism, say, a lowly animal like an amoeba or a squid.

We suggest that Tristan da Cunha could be an analogy to the larger world. It would satisfy many criteria: it is a tiny island, utterly isolated and therefore in no danger of being 'contaminated' We could know everything that comes in and goes out. We know a great deal about its people, their health, nutrition, education, agronomy, and pattern of activities.

It would not be too difficult to initiate a series of micro-economic studies: assessing the cost effectiveness of ridding the island of rodents, or putting an extra acre under cultivation, or culling the cattle, or starting a small cooperative dairy.

We are the first to admit that Tristan is very different from countries in South America, Asia, or Africa. Nevertheless, there is a long list of ingredients of misery common to all these countries. Because of the splendid documentation already available as a foundation, such micro-economic studies may reveal certain principles that could be of use when applied to the larger world in need of aid. It is in this context that an unexpected benefit might come from the most isolated population in the world.[40]

CONCLUSIONS

Isolation has left its mark on the Tristan islanders. The concepts on which the community was founded could only have been successful in remoteness, and they have permeated the islanders' attitudes right up to the present day. In the past, isolation has created biological and social problems—in demography, in economic and social life, in genetics, in health. In the recent past and today these problems have intensified along with the increased contact with the outside world, and other problems—particularly those related to welfare and social progress—have arisen from the temporal dysphasia of the culture.

But isolation has also brought the opportunities to investigate these problems. Intensive interdisciplinary research, sponsored by the British Medical Research Council, has involved almost eighty groups of scientists, covering the islanders' history, education, social anthropology, genetics, nutrition, dental health, and many

[40] For other sources on Tristan da Cunha, see H. L. Bailit, S. T. Damon, and A. Damon, 'Consanguinity on Tristan da Cunha in 1938', *Eugenics Quarterly*, Vol. 13, No. 1 (1966), pp. 30–33; H. E. Lewis, 'Tristan da Cunha, The Human Biology of Isolation', *The Listener*, Vol. 81 (1969), pp. 65–8; J. B. Loudon, 'Private Stress and Public Ritual', *Journal of Psychosomatic Res.*, Vol. 10 (1966), pp. 101–8; D. F. Roberts, 'Genetic Fitness in a Colonizing Human Population', *Human Biology*, Vol. 40 (1968), p. 4; A. Sakula, 'Tuberculosis in Tristan da Cunha', *Chest and Heart Bulletin*, Vol. 26 (1963), pp. 180–82; N. Samuels, 'Experiences of a Medical Officer on Tristan da Cunha, June–October 1961', *British Medical Journal* (26 October, 1963), Vol. 2, pp. 1013–17; M. Shibli, 'Heat as the Cause of Dental Decay', *Lancet* (1967), pp. 992–3; D. A. J. Tyrrell, 'Serological Studies of Infections by Respiratory Viruses on the Inhabitants of Tristan da Cunha', *Journal of Hygiene*, Vol. 65 (1967), pp. 327–41. M. A. Chambers and H. E. Lewis, 'The Energy Expenditure and Food Intake of Tristan Islanders', *British Journal of Nutrition*, Vol. 23 (1969), pp. 237–47. M. A. Chambers and D. A. T. Southgate, 'The Foods Eaten by Tristan Islanders, their methods of preparation and composition', *British Journal of Nutrition*, Vol. 23 (1969), pp. 227–35. W. A. Marshall, J. M. Tanner, H. E. Lewis and M. A. Richardson 'Anthropometric Measurements of the Tristan da Cunha Islanders 1962–1968', *Human Biology*, Vol. 43 (1971), pp. 112–39.

fields of clinical and laboratory medicine. In practically every one of these aspects the pervasive influence of their isolation is found. Some of the opportunities such research yields are indeed unique— for example, that of applying modern computer techniques in gene flow studies making use of the accurate genealogy and other documentation that is available, or examining the applicability of models of the spread of virus diseases. An unexpected dividend may accrue as a result of the detailed documentation of this isolated island. It would be possible to institute micro-economic studies pursuing the theme that Tristan is an analogue to an underdeveloped country. A study of this nature would be pertinent to unravelling some of the problems that beset aid to developing countries.

Ajit Das Gupta

Study of the historical demography of India

INTRODUCTION

The study of the historical demography of India is of international importance in the sense that India through the ages has comprised one of the largest population entities. The history of India has received the attention of eminent scholars, both Indian and foreign, as has the demography of India; but, in contrast, study of its historical demography has been surprisingly meagre.

Though China is credited with the earliest population enumeration anywhere, about 2000 B.C. during the Hsia dynasty,[1] registration of population was apparently well established in India[2] by the beginning of the Christian era. And all evidence tends to show that India from ancient times carried teeming millions of population.[3]

Indians in the past were not mindful of maintaining any continuity of objective historical facts. Moreover, the quick deterioration caused by the humid hot climate was supplemented by the wanton destruction by invaders and conquerors. The instances of indiscriminate destruction through the ages, particularly in medieval times, are too numerous to recount.[4]

Coins, monuments, rock inscriptions, and edicts, along with travel accounts of visiting foreigners preserved in their own countries, provide the most fruitful sources of ancient and early medieval Indian history.[5] Coins and inscriptions, by their very nature, do not mention the number and composition of people or the changes in them, which form the core of demography. When the ancients,

[1] Tai Shih Kuang, *1953 Population Census of China* (mimeographed; Calcutta, 1956). Ping-ti Ho, *Studies in the Population of China* (Cambridge, Mass., 1959).

[2] R. Shamasastry, *Kautilya's Arthasāstra* (Mysore, 1961).

[3] For Japan's early enumeration, see Irene B. Taeuber, *The Population of Japan* (Princeton, 1958).

[4] One example is the wanton destruction of the great University of Nalanda and its library and wholesale slaughter of the learned men of the University in 1197 by Qutbud Din's generals. Akbar's great collection of manuscript library has similarly been lost. K. M. Panikkar, *A Survey of Indian History* (Bombay, 1962).

[5] Damodar Kosambi, *Indian History* (Bombay, 1956).

whether Indian or foreign, provided estimates of the army or other population segments, they were prone to use figures more in the figurative than in the substantive sense. Inflation of numbers invested grandeur and drama; the greater the adversary's armies that were vanquished the greater the victory of one's own side. Figures quoted in old narratives often have to be taken with some reservation.

Ancient and medieval travellers generally referred to India as a very populous country in their accounts; they also noted changes in the fortunes of particular regions. It is to be expected that natural or man-made catastrophes fell on parts of India at different times: populations of certain principalities flourished and multiplied, and then suddenly declined or nearly disappeared. There is an ancient Indian theory of cycles of population overweight and large-scale annihilation. Given the climatic conditions of India, a crop failure once in five years is not an unlikely event. In the moderate growth situation likely to characterize societies prior to the advance of modern science, a catastrophe eliminating a quarter of the population every generation would maintain a population ceiling. The decline of numerous principalities, once prosperous and populous, demonstrates these turns of history, although the role of catastrophe in shaping the past populations in India can only be guessed.

The first all-India modern census was taken in 1871,[6] and regular decennial censuses have been taken since then. We have, therefore, limited this study to the period prior to 1871. The Births, Deaths and Marriages Registration Act of 1886 provided for voluntary registration of vital events, and registration was made compulsory in succeeding decades; but registration statistics remain grossly defective, and we have not been able to use registration data in this study.

The major emphasis of the present study is on the nineteenth century, extending somewhat speculatively into the eighteenth and seventeenth centuries, and dealing even more tentatively with earlier medieval and ancient times with the object of providing a framework for the more recent estimates rather than establishing any firm population quantities for these earlier times. We have tried to relate our study and estimates to the areas of the Indian sub-continent that comprise present-day India; this has meant omitting the Vangas, and Sindhu, Yaudheya, Madra and Gandhara principalities of ancient India;[7] and Sindh and West Punjab and territories west of them, and East Bengal of subsequent times.

[6] *Census of India 1872*, Vol. I, Part 1.

[7] The boundaries of the ancient principalities going under these names are only roughly known; a map is given in R. C. Majumdar, H. C. Raychaudhuri, Kalinkinkar Datta, *An Advanced History of India*. Any adjustments for ancient and early medieval times have to be very approximate.

TECHNIQUES OF ESTIMATION

It is appropriate at this stage to discuss the alternative techniques used for estimation of population numbers and growth rates which form the core of inquiry in historical demography when, as is usual, these facts are not available. The techniques used could be placed in three broad classes, according to the emphasis of approach.

1. *Historical-Static*, under which the contemporary socio-economic conditions are examined and analysed for their probable impact on population, and an informed judgment is made about the population size and the growth rate. Works done by Moreland (1920)[8] and Datta (1960)[9] on the populations of the Indian sub-continent in the seventeenth century employ this approach.

2. *Historical-Mathematical*, under which some kind of growth curve model, say the logistic, is fitted to the recent known series of populations (in the case of India, the post-1871 decennial census series), and then the earlier populations read off from the backward projection of the curve. Works done by Swaroop (1938),[10] Davis (1951)[11] and Durand (1965)[12] on nineteenth- to seventeenth-century populations of the Indian sub-continent can be properly classified under this approach (though Durand used different growth rates for different epochs on consideration of historical evidence).

3. *Historical-Component*, under which the historical material, as available, is first examined for the component segments of the country, shifted, and evaluated against collateral evidence and circumstances following the methods of history; then the component data, spread over space and time, are joined to provide the overall trends and quantities for the country as a whole, on area and other adjustments, following the methods of demography. This approach appears to be most appropriate for the study of historical demography in recent epochs. While the historical-static technique could be applied to any period, the historical-mathematical and particularly the historical-component techniques could be applied only to more recent times.

[8] W. H. Moreland, *India at the Death of Akbar* (London, 1920).

[9] Jatindra Mohan Datta, 'A Re-examination of Moreland's Estimate of the Population of India at the Death of Akbar', *Indian Population Bulletin*, Vol. I, No. 1 (Delhi, 1960).

[10] Satya Swaroop and R. B. Lal, 'Logistic Laws of Growth and Structure of Indian Population', *Population*, Vol. 2 (London, 1938).

[11] Kingsley Davis, *The Population of India and Pakistan* (Princeton, 1951).

[12] John D. Durand, *World Population Estimates 1750–2000*, World Population Conference, Belgrade, 1965 (New York, 1967).

In an attempt to estimate the populations of nineteenth-century India, the author has recently employed the historical-component approach in collaboration with colleagues drawn from the discipline of demography and history. Time and resources at our disposal have been limited; to suit the convenience of demographic periodization, we have taken a simplified non-rigorous view of history, and even rounded out dates. Though we were able to pay fair attention to the historical-demographic source materials of the nineteenth century, we were not able to analyse those of the seventeenth or eighteenth century (for example, the *Khānāpuri* village revenue, the *Jāziya* poll tax records, some of the excellent genealogical trees maintained by Indians, or church and temple records). These records will throw interesting sidelights on demographic composition and characteristics of sections of contemporary populations. We have not been able to go beyond numbers into either the vital rates or the demographic characteristics. This tentative report is released in the hope that it will stimulate interest and draw more resources to this neglected field.

ANCIENT INDIA: UP TO A.D. 1000

Study of the historical demography of India should properly begin with the epics, Rāmāyana and Mahābhārata, though the dating of these epics is somewhat uncertain. Various epochs added to these ballads about adventure and victory, and when they first assumed the form of connected epic narrative is not known. There is no reference to Pātaliputra in the epics, and their times therefore must have preceded the Mauryas (fourth century B.C.) by a few centuries.[13]

Rāmāyana depicts a countryside relatively unpopulated, almost undeveloped. The India of the Mahābhārata, on the other hand, gives the impression of a populous country. Many flourishing principalities are locked in a devastating war, both sides deploying huge armies in the battlefield of Kurukshetra. Some scholars place Rāmāyana in a later period;[14] if Rāmāyana does represent a later period, the population and habitations of India must have been reduced drastically in the meantime, whether from the great war of Kurukshetra and the pestilences and disorganization that followed it, or from other catastrophes.

Herodotus (490 B.C.) referred to India as the most populous of the countries of the world.[15] Dhana Nanda (Agrammes of the Greek

[13] Majumdar, Raychaudhuri, Datta, *An Advanced History of India.*
[14] Radha Kumud Mookerji, *Hindu Civilization* (Bombay, 1957).
[15] R. C. Majumdar, *The Classical Accounts of India* (Calcutta, 1960).

classical writers), the last of the Nandas whom Chandragupta Maurya probably deposed, is credited in the Purānas and Buddhist chronicles as possessing a colossal army.[16] According to Pliny, the army of Chandragupta Maurya (320 B.C.) included 600,000 foot soldiers, 30,000 cavalry, and 9,000 elephants. Diodorus Siculus (60 B.C.) referred to the armed strength of the king of Eastern India (Prasii and Gangaridae) as 200,000 foot soldiers, 20,000 cavalry (some Greek sources raise it to 80,000), 4,000 elephants, and 2,000 chariots.[17] Only colossal populations can support such armies, in segments not exceeding a fifth of India.

But Kautilya's Arthasāstra,[18] placed between 300 B.C. and A.D. 300, conveys the impression that the countryside was not well populated; acquiring population was considered an important means of adding strength to the state. The population of the country might have experienced another slump, between the time of the later Nandas and the later Mauryas.

Arthasāstra records a sophisticated system of population registration not delegated to the local headman or restricted to counts of 'doors' and 'mouths' alone as in ancient China, but entrusted to paid accountants and extended to cover occupations, old and young listed separately with their means of sustenance and characteristics, and sometimes even reports on suspicious diseases.[19] A chain of flourishing towns about the time of Buddha (sixth century B.C.) are mentioned in Buddhist chronicles, and the Republic of Sakiyas is reputed to have counted 80,000 families. The Republic of Lichhavis according to Tibetan tradition had three districts, with a population of 42,000, while their capital contained 'twice 84,000' according to Mahavastu chronicles.[20] From these records it appears that the counting of families and persons was in vogue in ancient India much before the Arthasāstra. None of the records of actual local counts or aggregate reports based on them, however, have been discovered from the Arthasāstra times. In India, in contrast to China and Japan, the system of population registration fell into disuse early in the Christian era. Fa Hein, who visited the country about A.D. 400 during the reign of Chandra Gupta II Vikramāditya, noticed that people did not have to register their households.[21] For several centuries before the rise of the imperial Guptas, Saka, Parithan, and Kushan inroads and conquests had unsettled conditions in India.

But India reached another peak under the imperial Guptas, and Fa Hein (A.D. 400), referring to the middle kingdom (Madhya Desa), observed that the people were numerous and happy.[22] On the decline

---

[16] See note 14.   [17] See note 15.   [18] See note 2.
[19] Arthasāstra, Ch. 35, Art. 142, and Ch. 36, Art. 144.   [20] See note 14.
[21] B. G. Gokhle, *Ancient India* (Bombay, 1952).   [22] See note 21.

of the Guptas, the Huns made incursions into India for about a century. The next high point was during the reign of Harsha, who assumed full regal title in A.D. 612. Bāna, the historian of Harsha, records that the army was increased to 100,000 cavalry and 60,000 elephants during his time: this is consistent with the references in Chinese chronicles of serious disturbances in India during A.D. 612–A.D. 627, with Harsha punishing the kings of four parts of India.[23] Harsha's empire extended over northern and perhaps near-eastern India.

Hiuen Tsang, the Chinese pilgrim who visited India during this period, noticed that vast stretches of the eastern part of the middle kingdom (which Fa Hien had found flourishing two centuries before) appeared desolate. The seat of learning which Fa Hien found at Pataliputra had shifted to Nalanda where, according to Hiuen Tsang, thousands of brethren, all highly esteemed men of great ability and learning, deliberated on 'possible and impossible' things. About A.D. 640, Hiuen Tsang witnessed a great gathering at Prayāga, the arena of charitable offerings and discourses, to which over 500,000 people mustered from all corners of the five Indies.[24]

Through succeeding centuries until late medieval times, India remained divided and subject to invasions and wars. Kalhāna in Rajtarangini, *History of Kashmir*, placed the strength of the army of the famous Kashmiri prince Lalitāditya (A.D. 750) at over 100,000.[25]

Thus, we have occasional glimpses of the population facts of ancient India, apparently during her prosperous periods and at intervals of a couple of centuries or more. In this situation, no quantitative speculation can be hazarded except to observe that during the stable periods India attained vast populations with colossal armies; the principalities went subject to the ups and downs of fortune, with their populations briskly pressing ahead for centuries and then slumping.

Pran Nath (1929), after calculations based on the reported number of *grāma* estates and contemporary socio-economic conditions, estimated the population of the Indian sub-continent at 100 to 140 millions[26] around 300 B.C. or during the time of Chandragupta Maurya. Going by the minimum estimate which allows for exclusion of areas now in Pakistan, this figure is of the same order as the estimated population of India around A.D. 1600, about the end of

[23] See note 13.   [24] See note 13.
[25] P. N. K. Bamzai, *A History of Kashmir* (Delhi, 1962).
[26] Pran Nath, *A Study in Economic Conditions of Ancient India*, Royal Asiatic Society (London, 1929).

Akbar's reign.[27] It is possible that populations of the order of 100 millions were attained by India during the peaks of the country's ancient and medieval periods under Chandragupta Maurya (300 B.C.), Asoka, Chandra Gupta II Vikramāditya (A.D. 400), Harsha (A.D. 650), Akbar (A.D. 1600) and his immediate successors, with populations dwindling during the intervening unsettled periods.

MEDIEVAL INDIA: A.D. 1000–1800

Medieval India, as to be expected, is fairly rich in population records scattered over the state and national archives and other institutions, but it has not been possible for us to analyse and use even a small fraction of them. According to historian Ferishta, in 1190, Prithwiraj opposed the invading armies of Muhammad Ghor with 200,000 cavalry and 3,000 elephants,[28] while historian Zia-uddin Barni relates that Muhammad bin Tughluk (1325) enrolled 3,700,000 men to prepare for his dreams of great conquests.[29] Muhammad bin Tughluk transferred his capital from Delhi to Devagiri, seven hundred miles away, and then returned to Delhi when the new site did not work. Some years later, in 1334, the African traveller Ibn Batuta found Delhi deserted in some places and bearing marks of ruin.[30] Firuz Shah (1350), according to his official historian Shams-i-Siraj Afif, marshalled 90,000 cavalry and 4,000 boats, in addition to infantry and elephants, against the Jams of Sind who had 20,000 cavalry and 400,000 infantry. While Ala-ud-din had 50,000 slaves, the number rose to 200,000 under Firuz;[31] most of the slaves, however, could be counted among the soldiery.

India continued to be divided into a number of warring principalities during the period and lacked either internal or external stability. When Amir Timur invaded India in 1398, Delhi was in chaos. Opposed by Sultan Mahmud and Mallu Igbal with 10,000 cavalry and 40,000 infantry, Timur captured and massacred over 100,000 male captives, besides butchering many of the inhabitants of Delhi. Famine and pestilence descended in the wake of his destruction.

Although also involved in wars, South India perhaps remained more organized and suffered less devastation. In 1420, Nicolo de Conti, the Italian traveller, described the city of Vijaynagar as being sixty miles in circumference, with 90,000 men fit to bear arms within its walls.[32] In 1442, Abdul Razzak, the Persian traveller,

---

[27] See note 8.
[28] R. H. Major, *India in the 15th Century* (London, 1857). P. Saran, *Studies in Medieval Indian History* (Delhi, 1952).
[29] See note 28.   [30] See note 13.   [31] See note 13.   [32] See note 28.

found the country of Vijaynagar so well populated that it was impossible in a reasonable space to convey an idea of it.[33] Althanasius Nikitin, the Russian traveller (1470), observed that Bedar was overstocked with people;[34] while the few nobles were opulent, the commoners were miserable. According to him, the personal arm of Sultan of Bedar exceeded 300,000. Eduardo Barbosa visiting India in 1516 described a highly populous Vijaynagar.[35] The end of Vijaynagar's prosperity came with defeat in the battle of Talikota in 1565.

In 1527, Rana Sanga is reported to have given battle to Babar, the Mughal invader, with 80,000 horses and 500 war elephants.[36] Sher Shah (1542) had 150,000 cavalry, 25,000 infantry, and 300 elephants under his command.[37] Until 1556, the time of Akbar, the contest of supremacy among the Mughals and the Afghans dragged on. Akbar was himself engaged in extending frontiers and consolidating his conquests at the end of his reign in early 1600, but even then the far south remained outside his sway.

Confidence was restored and foundations of good administration laid in the late sixteenth century during Akbar's time. Ralph Fitch, the English traveller, writing in 1585 observed that Agra and Fatehpur were two very great cities, each of them more populous than London; the 12-mile stretch of road between Agra and Fatehpur was as full of people as though one were still in town, with as many men as in a market. Other cities of eastern and western India were described in similarly glowing terms.[38]

Nizamud Din Ahmed, the first historian of Akbar, wrote in his sketch of 'Conclusions' that in 1595 (A.H. 1002) Hindustan contained 3,200 towns, of which 120 were large cities, and upon each town depended 200 to 1,000 villages; he promised to draw up a detailed list of towns in alphabetical order, but could not accomplish the work.[39] If Nazamud Din's *minimum* town-to-village dependency factor is taken and an average village is assumed to contain a population of 150 (roughly 30 households), the rural population of the Indian sub-continent would have been about 100 million.

Terrible famines are also on record during this period: in 1556–57 around Agra, in 1573–74 and again in 1594–98 in Gujarat, and later on in 1630–32 in Gujarat and Deccan.[40]

Though there were palace intrigues, coups, and battles of succession as well as battles on the frontiers, particularly the south, the stability and prosperity of the latter part of Akbar's reign were

[33] See note 28.   [34] See note 28.   [35] See note 13.
[36] See note 13.   [37] See note 13.   [38] See note 13.
[39] Nizamud Din Ahmed, *Tabakat-i Akbar-shahi*, trans. H. Elliot (Calcutta, 1871).
[40] See note 13.

maintained during the next fifty years in the reigns of Jehangir and Shah Jehan. Aurangzib's battles of succession were more bitter and dislocating, although at first he tried to alleviate the distress of the people caused by the administrative disorder of the battles of succession. Aurangzib also organized the revenue system and agriculture of the Southern province. The actual armed strength of the empire in 1647 was 200,000 troopers; 40,000 foot musketeers, gunners, rocket-men; 185,000 additional troopers of the subsidiary princes, apart from officers and ancillaries.[41] But, as the reign of Aurangzib progressed, he involved the country in more and more wars. In 1679 Aurangzib re-imposed the *jāziyā* poll tax on Hindus (non-believers). There were first the rebellions of the Jāts, then the Bundelas, the Sikhs, the Rājputs of Jodhpur, Marāthās, and finally with his army of 70,000 men Prince Akbar rebelled in 1681. Bijapur was annexed after a siege in 1686, but the city was deserted and ruined in the process; and famine followed.[42] Aurangzib moved his headquarters south, and the north and the centre of the administration were neglected. The Marāthās affair eventually developed into a people's war, and Mughal administration in the south dissolved towards the close of Aurangzib's reign and the beginning of the eighteenth century. According to Manucci (Storia do Mogor 1653–1708),[43] about 100,000 men died in Aurangzib's army annually during his late southern campaigns, and plague visited the Deccan province.

The *jāziyā* poll tax, reimposed in 1679, varied from Rs3 to Rs13 (12 to 48 dirhams) a year from the poor to the rich; women, children below 14, slaves, and invalids or monks were untaxed.[44] The tax yielded Rs 500,000 a year from Gujarat;[45] this would apply realization from a total Hindu population of about 500,000 only, assuming Rs 4 as the average rate of *jāziyā* poll tax per person assessable (exempting 50 per cent women, 20 per cent male children below age 14, and 5 per cent others). Although there must have been widespread evasions, connivance, and non-realization of the tax, the detailed *jāziyā* tax records deserve close scrutiny for the potential demographic information they might reveal.

The death of Aurangzib in 1707 was the signal for disintegration of the central authority and fresh battles of succession and intrigues. Administration and economic as well as social organization were hastening to utter ruin. Warlordism and worse characterized Indian history during this period. Apart from wars between organized powers, the plunder and devastation of the countryside were also perpetrated by the Marāthās, the Sikhs, the Jāts, the

[41] J. N. Sarkar, *A Short History of Aurangzib* (Calcutta, 1954).   [42] See note 41.
[43] See note 41.   [44] See note 41.   [45] See note 41.

Firangee pirates, and invading bands. Nadir Shah invaded northern India in 1739, and the whole province of Punjab fell into great disorder. Nadir Shah massacred the citizens of Delhi, plundered marketplaces and the surrounding countryside, and sealed granaries. Ahmad Shah Abdali led several expeditions into India from 1748 to 1767. The final showdown between Abdali with an army 60,000 strong and the Mārāthās, who mustered 45,000, came at Panipat in 1761, in which the Mārāthās suffered a bad defeat.

In the meantime, the British had become a power in India during the 1750s. Bengal was then disturbed by political instability, and Carnatic was distracted by wars on its soil. The first Anglo-Mysore war was fought in 1767–69. Mārāthās, though weakened by dissensions and internal fights, emerged in force again by 1770, and the first Anglo-Maratha war was fought at different places in 1775–82. The second, third, and fourth Anglo-Mysore wars were fought in 1780–84, 1790–92, and 1799.

India of the eighteenth century was the site of war, plunder, massacre, lawlessness, and the breakdown of normal life. There were several famines; one of the worst, in Bengal in 1770–72, wiped out a third of the population of Bengal—about 8 to 10 million people.[46] Great economic waste and drain were common following the end of Aurangzib's reign. Due to such dire conditions, one can assume that the population of India did not grow during the century and a quarter from 1675 to 1800. The limits of this sterile period are placed arbitrarily, and the hypothesis itself will have to be supported by substantive evidence of population growth or decline in various tracts of India during the period (which we hope is available in contemporary records not yet studied with an eye for the population component).

It appears that in outlying parts of India, like Assam and Kashmir, there was some type of population enumeration during the late medieval period. The Assam Buranjis, chronicles written in the local language and in some cases dating from the sixth century A.D., refer to censuses in the modern sense in Assam at the time of Pratap Singh in the seventeenth century and later in the eighteenth century; the objects of these censuses were reported to be both political and economic.[47] Saif Khan is reputed to have conducted a rough census around 1670 and found 1,243,033 persons in Kashmir.[48] Incidentally, Kashmir is supposed to have been well populated in ancient times, but the population dwindled with the Afghan occupation.[49]

It is relevant to observe here that institutions like *sati* (self-

[46] See note 9.
[47] E. A. Gait, B. K. Barua, H. V. S. Murthy, *A History of Assam* (Calcutta, 1933).
[48] See note 25.   [49] See note 25.

immolation of the widow on her husband's funeral pyre) and taboo on the remarriage of a widow are of ancient origin in India, though restricted mostly to upper classes of Hindus. Similarly, infanticide (particularly of the female child) was widespread in medieval Indian culture,[50] as it was in the other ancient Asian cultures of China and Japan. Methods not only of abortion but of contraception[51] were known in ancient and medieval Indian culture. There were, thus, a number of cultural curbs on the free growth of population in the Indian society.

A carefully considered estimate of the population of the Indian sub-continent was made by Moreland (1920)[52] at 100 million at the death of Akbar (1600). Moreland estimated the population of the northern part of the Indian sub-continent to have been 70 million on the basis of area cultivated, the labour needed for cultivation of unit area, and the ratio of dependents to agricultural labour. He thus omitted about 25 per cent of the population dependent on means of subsistence other than agriculture. He also omitted the populations of the outlying states of Bengal, Assam, and Gujarat, which might have comprised 20 per cent of the population of the northern part of the sub-continent. Moreland's estimates of the northern part of the sub-continent could thus be raised to 105 million, with adjustment for the omissions.

Moreland estimated the population of South India from the sizes of the armies that fought at Talikota in 1565. He borrowed the soldier-to-civilian ratio from France and Germany of 1914, and assumed a total of 30 people in aggregate to each fighting man. He thus arrived at an estimated population for south India of 30 million. Travellers in the late Mughal empire (1660), like François Bernier, observed the incredible number of troops in India.[53] According to him, the cavalry in Deccan amounted to 25,000 and it was even greater in Bengal. Nikitin, the Russian traveller, had observed the similarly large retinue and armies of the Sultans of the relatively small principality of Bedar, running to over 300,000 of his own and about the same number of his vassals.[54]

The proportion of fighting men could have been higher in medieval India than in France or Germany in 1914 as the rulers were mostly alien and had to depend on the strength of the army; moreover, by 1914 mechanization enabled substantial reduction in human numbers. But all the troops of South India did not participate

[50] Kanti Pakrasi, 'Female Infanticide in India—A Century Ago', *Bulletin of the Socio-Economic Research Institute*, Vol. 2, No. 2 (Calcutta, 1968).

[51] Norman E. Himes, *Medical History of Contraception* (New York, 1963).

[52] See note 8.

[53] F. Bernier, *The Travels in the Moghul Empire* (Delhi, 1968).

[54] See note 28.

in the battle of Talikota, and therefore we decided not to increase Moreland's estimate for South India. We accordingly revised Moreland's estimate for the Indian sub-continent to 105 plus 30 millions.[55]

Datta (1960)[56] pointed to the deficiencies of Moreland's estimate, but his own estimate of the population of the Indian subcontinent at the beginning of the seventeenth century was 110 million. According to Datta, the population was increasing in the seventeenth century, though at a slow rate, as evidenced by the spread of cultivation, land reclamation, and increased salt consumption. His assumption also involved a high degree of arbitrariness. Other authors[57] thought that the population of contemporary India was higher. Going by Moreland's estimate as revised to 135 million for the Indian sub-continent, and taking out a sixth for the populations of the sub-continent outside the Indian dominion, we estimate the population of the present boundaries of India in 1600 at 115 million.

MODERN INDIA: AFTER 1800

Though the first modern all-India census was taken in 1871, administrative enumerations started in tracts of India much earlier. For example, before the nineteenth century enumerations were made in the ceded districts of Madras; later, around the middle of the century or earlier, enumeration of larger segments, whole Presidencies (areas comprising one or more of the present states) started. We shifted these available segmental materials, evaluated them against other collateral evidence, tied them on to the post-1871 census series of progression of population for these segments, and arrived at pre-1871 growth rates for these component segments: we then estimated the populations of the whole of India from these components by forward and backward projections.

Before presenting our own and other standard recent estimates of the populations of India for the earlier part of the nineteenth century, we first cite some of the contemporary late-eighteenth and early-nineteenth-century local estimates which came to our notice and which demonstrate the ingenuity exercised and the urge to get a measure of the population.

[55] Davis (1951) and Durand (1965) estimated the population of the Indian sub-continent in 1600 at 125 million and 140 million respectively.
[56] See note 9.   [57] See note 55.

SOME NINETEENTH-CENTURY CONTEMPORARY ESTIMATES

In 1789, Duncan estimated the population of Varanshi (Benaras) city from consumption of grain.

In 1789, Redfern estimated the population of Nadia district from a house count, assuming 7 persons on an average in each house.

In 1789, Heatly estimated the population of Purnea district by making actual enumeration in 3 villages and multiplying the average by the total number of villages in the district. Later, Willes and Smyth introduced greater refinement and assumed varying averages for different *mahals* to estimate the population of Sylhet district.[58]

In 1814, Bailey estimated the population of Burdwan district by allowing 5·5 persons per house.[59]

In 1807–14 and again in 1828–35, Buchanan[60] multiplied the number of ploughs by 5 to estimate the total population dependent on agriculture; and then from the most 'intelligible' person of the locality got the proportion of population in agriculture. In this manner, in the course of his long drawn-out surveys, he estimated the population of a quarter of Bengal Presidency.

In 1822, an estimate of the population of the lower provinces was made and embodied in the Report of the Police Superintendent (H. Shakespeare).[61]

In 1829, Phukon in his Assam Buranji[62] mentioned the estimate from the population enumeration of Assam in 1826–27.

In 1838, Martin[63] estimated the population of Bengal Presidency in 1822 at 39,957,561 by assuming 5 persons per house and making some adjustments; past estimators had used a higher number of persons per house, and subsequent census enumerations showed that Martin's assumption about the number of persons per house was much too low.

There were many other contemporary estimates of population,

---

[58] Earlier estimates are mentioned in: Henry Thomas Colebrook, *Remarks on the Present State of the Husbandry and Commerce of Bengal* (Calcutta, 1795); Walter Hamilton, *The East India Gazetteer* (London, 1828); Great Britain, House of Commons, *First Appendix to the Third Report of Select Committee* (London, 1832); R. M. Martin, *History, Antiquities, Topography and Statistics of Eastern India* (London, 1838).

[59] See note 59.

[60] F. Buchanan, *An Account of the District of Purnea 1809–10* (Patna, 1928); *An Account of the District of Patna 1811–12* (Patna, 1935).

[61] House of Commons, *First Appendix to the Third Report of Select Committee*.

[62] H. D. Phukon, *Assam Buranji* (Shillong, 1829).

[63] Martin, *History . . . of Eastern India*.

but they involved a similar or even higher degree of guesswork and tended to underestimate the population.[64]

The Historical-Component Estimate. For our estimates, we adopted the contemporary Madras, Bengal, and Bombay Presidencies and the North West Province as the four segments, excluding and adjusting for areas now in Pakistan.[65] The aggregate area of the four selected segments covered a little more than 50 per cent of the area of India and represented about 70 per cent of the total population of India. The growth rates referred to below are all linear exponential rates considered appropriate for the times, before either the birth rates or death rates would experience any accelerated decline.

The Madras Presidency, comprising the present states of Madras and Andhra, had the earliest series of enumerations of the ceded districts in the beginning of the nineteenth century, but our attempts to link these with the subsequent enumerations of 1821 and then the quinquennial series 1851, 1856, 1861, and 1866, were not successful despite careful adjustments of area to make the enumerations comparable.[66] It was claimed in a recent Census of India report[67] that the method of census taking in Madras had been perfected shortly after 1851; but our experience has been that the Madras enumerations represent a series of progressively improving quality of work which imparts a spurious inflation to the growth rate. The reported populations, adjusted for areal changes, increased by about 20 per cent in the six years between the 1866 enumeration and the first regular census of 1871–72; in the absence of a brisk in-migration, such a high rate of population growth is clearly untenable.

Census of India 1911 report, however, mentioned that the estimates of population totals of Madras Presidency obtained through the agency of the revenue staff in 1822 and some subsequent years were not sufficiently reliable to be worth quoting; census 1911 report also mentioned that the first regular census of 1871, like all first assays in a work of such magnitude, lacked completeness, and many persons escaped enumeration.[68] Census of India 1881 report referred

---

[64] Thornton (1854) gave an interesting description as to how some of the estimates were arrived at. Edward Thornton, *A Gazetteer of the Territories under the Government of the East India Company and the Native States on the Continent of India* (London, 1854). The Census of India recently established a Pre-Census Project, which has done valuable work in digging out old references to the eighteenth- and nineteenth-century population of India.

[65] Suranjan Sen Gupta, Murari Ghosh, Alok Kumar Datta, Ajit Das Gupta, 'Estimates of the 19th Century Population of India', *Bulletin of the Socio-Economic Research Institute*, Vol. 3, No. 1 (Calcutta, 1969).

[66] References to earlier enumerations in Madras found in House of Commons, *First Appendix to the Third Report of the Select Committee, Transactions of the Bombay Geographical Society*, Vol. 4 (1840), and *Census of India 1951*, Vol. IX, Part I-A (i).

[67] *Census of India 1961*, Vol. IX, Part I-A (i).

[68] *Census of India 1911*, Vol. I, Part 1.

to the concealment or omission of females from the earlier enumerations in the Presidency.[69]

We accordingly accepted the view of census 1911 report, which was much nearer the times: the census report mentioned 0·6 per cent per year as the prevailing growth rate in the area in the middle of the nineteenth century[70] and the incidence of recurring famines and scarcities. The growth rate of the segment during the census period 1871–1921 was 0·7 per cent per year; and, given other considerations, this growth rate was accepted by us as the prevailing one for the pre-1871 period in the Madras Presidency segment.[71]

The Bengal Presidency, comprising the present states of West Bengal, Bihar, and Orissa (excluding areas now forming part of East Pakistan), had an enumeration of houses in 1822, when a total number of 7,781,240 houses was reported.[72] Taking the average number of persons per house as 5·8 (the average for the Presidency in 1871–72 census), the population of the Presidency in 1822 is estimated at 45 million. Taken with the census series of 1872–1921, the 45 million estimate of 1822 implied a growth rate of about 0·6 per cent per year.

The 1872–1921 censal growth rate for the Indian part of Bengal Presidency was only about 0·5 per cent per year. Considering the political and economic dislocation of the times[73] as well as allowing for the spurious inflation in recorded growth rate from progressively improving enumerations, a growth rate of 0·5 per cent was accepted for the pre-1871 period for Bengal Presidency.

The Bombay Presidency comprises the present states of Maharastra and Gujarat, excluding the tracts now forming part of West Pakistan. The earliest enumeration was held in the Presidency in 1846; both the 1846 enumeration and the first regular census of 1872 suffered from the defect of under-enumeration of females.[74] Indeed, census 1911 report stated that the first regular census of 1871–72 was taken without any pretensions to accuracy.[75] Females reported in enumeration 1846 and census 1872 were accordingly adjusted up to make them comparable and render the same sex ratio as the subsequent censuses.

The growth rate implied by the adjusted enumeration of 1846, taken with the census series of 1872–1921, was a little higher than 0·4 per cent a year. The pre-1871 growth rate for the segment during the nineteenth century was accepted as 0·4 per cent a year on these considerations.[76]

---

[69] *Census of India 1881*, Vol. I, Part 1.   [70] See note 68.   [71] See note 65.

[72] This house count was apparently done through the agency of the Police, and the Bengal Government thought the calculations not far wide of the truth. See note 61.

[73] See note 65.   [74] See note 6.   [75] See note 68.   [76] See note 65.

The North West Province comprises the present state of Uttar Pradesh of India. The first population survey of the province in 1841–42 turned out, from contemporary evidence, to be a gross undercount. The next enumeration of 1853 was contemporarily adjudged an overcount;[77] but census 1881 report[78] was of the view that the enumeration of 1853 could have given a better approximation of the true population (the usual errors of omission being compensated by counting of absentees) than the subsequent enumeration of 1865.[79]

Under-enumeration of females was perhaps at its worst in this province. Census 1872 report[80] stated that the apparent increase in population found at the census was often to be attributed to more accurate registration, especially of females. Census 1881 report[81] particularly refers to Varanshi (Benaras) Division, where concealment of females was most conspicuous even at census 1872, which gave a male-to-female sex-ratio as 112·5 per cent. Only male populations were considered for estimation of growth rate, in view of such gross defect.

The 1853 enumeration, taken with the census series of 1872–1921, implied a growth rate of 0·2 per cent per year.[82] Contemporary administration reports[83] described the conditions of the province as very 'parlous' around 1840, owing to repeated Sikh invasions, and constant internal feuds, which made cultivation unsure and reduced the population greatly. The 0·2 per cent per year growth rate was accordingly accepted for the pre-1871 period for this segment.

All-India Estimates. The four selected segments on the four corners of India, comprising in aggregate about 70 per cent of the population of India, grew at rates varying from 0·2 per cent to 0·7 per cent per year during the pre-1871 period. On the assumption that a uniform proportion of the country around the component segments grew in step with the segments, an overall growth rate of 0·42 per cent per year for the whole of India was rendered.

It should be remembered that there were about eight wars or widespread revolts and ten major famines (as distinguished from distress or scarcity) during this pre-1871 period.[84] Estimates of deaths from famines are not available in most cases, but the famine of the upper *doāb* of 1860–61 is credited with 2 million deaths.[85]

---

[77] *Report of the Census of the North West Province 1865* thought that the decrease in population found in enumeration of 1865 in comparison to the enumeration of 1853 arose from errors in the earlier enumeration, and thus came to the conclusion that the 1853 enumeration overestimated the population.

[78] See note 69.   [79] See note 77.   [80] See note 6.   [81] See note 69.

[82] See note 65.   [83] See note 68.   [84] See note 65.

[85] Charles Blair, *Indian Famines* (London, 1874); *Famine Commission Report 1880;* B. M. Bhatia, *Famines in India (1860–1945)* (Bombay, 1963).

Estimates of nineteenth-century populations of India on the basis of the composite pre-1871 growth rate established by us were: 154 million in 1800, 189 million in 1850, and 237 million in 1900.[86]

As compared to our estimates of 154 million for the population of India in 1800, Swaroop (1938),[87] Davis (1951),[88] Datta (1960),[89] and Durand (1965)[90] estimated the populations of India and Pakistan at 139 million, 225 million, 162–76 million, and 150–210 million respectively; if the population of Pakistan were taken to have comprised only a sixth of the population of the sub-continent, their estimates of the population of India work out to 116 million, 188 million, 135–47 million, and 125–75 million respectively.

SUMMARY

This essay embodies a tentative report on the study of the historical demography of India undertaken by the author in collaboration with both historians and demographers. For lack of resources and time, analysis of the rich source materials of the late-medieval period remains to be done.

Regular decennial all-India censuses started in 1871. Population estimates are therefore available from the Census of India reports, which also adjusted the first few census counts for deficiencies of coverage.

The essay quotes:

1. Pran Nath's figure of 100 million[91] (1929) for ancient India (300 B.C., and later till A.D. 600) as the rounded ceiling of population attained by India during peaks of stability and prosperity, centuries apart.

2. Moreland's estimate of 115 million (1920) for mid-medieval India (A.D. 1600),[92] as adjusted by Datta (1960)[93] and the author.

3. The author's own[94,95] estimate of 154 million in 1800 and 189 million in 1850 for nineteenth-century India, built up by the historical-component technique from varying growth rates of major component segments.

As a Consultant, the author has been engaged by different organizations at different times; the views are the author's own in his personal capacity. The author is grateful for the assistance received from Alok Kumar Datta, Murari Ghosh, David V. Glass, Suranjan Sen Gupta, Ranjan K. Som, and W. F. Wertheim.

[86] Ajit Das Gupta, Suranjan Sen Gupta, Alok Kumar Datta, Murari Ghosh, *1800 A.D. to 1968 A.D. Population of Asia—A Reconstruct*, International Population Conference (London, 1969).
[87] See note 10.   [88] See note 11.   [89] See note 9.   [90] See note 12.
[91] See note 26.   [92] See note 8.   [93] See note 9.   [94] See note 65.   [95] See note 86.

Susan B. Hanley

Population trends and economic development in Tokugawa Japan: the case of Bizen province in Okayama

Despite the existence of national population statistics dating as far back as 1721 and evidence of striking changes in population trends during the pre-modern period, until recently little interest has been shown in Japan's demographic history. Sources for the study of the pre-modern population in Japan are far better than those for most other countries, but many of these have either been ignored or used inefficiently. The traditional view of population trends in this period has been based on unadjusted Tokugawa government figures; until the last three or four years, the potentially rich village sources remained virtually untapped.

During the Tokugawa period (1600–1868), Japan's population almost doubled, going from an estimated eighteen million to around thirty-five million. Rapid urbanization accompanied this marked increase in population. Edo (now Tokyo), the administrative capital of Japan, was a village in the early-seventeenth century, but by the eighteenth and nineteenth centuries, it was probably the largest city in the world, containing between 500,000 and one million inhabitants. The population of the urban area surrounding the commercial centre of Osaka was nearly as large. These two cities did not, however, constitute isolated phenomena; large administrative and market centres grew up around the castle town of each Japanese domain.

The usual image of the Tokugawa population has been one of rapid growth in the first half of the period with a subsequent levelling off of the population at around thirty million.[1] The rapid

---

[1] The official figure is twenty-six or twenty-seven million, but some adjustment must be made because the warrior class, usually estimated at about 10 per cent of the entire population, and other smaller groups were not included in population surveys.

growth in the first century has been attributed to the economic development that took place in a Japan at peace and unified after years of civil war. When the Tokugawa house gained hegemony over the contending *daimyō* and set up its administration in Edo in the early-seventeenth century, it initiated a number of policies which were to have far-reaching effects. Foreign trade and intercourse ceased except in amounts too small to have much economic effect, and Christianity was prohibited. The supply of reclaimable land dwindled during the 200 years in which Japan was isolated, both politically and economically. These two factors have been used to explain the levelling off in the population growth rate. In essence, Malthusian theory has been applied to Tokugawa Japan.

According to the stereotype of Tokugawa population, the Malthusian limitations at work in a closed economy kept the population constant after its period of growth and subsequent levelling off. An increasing interest in modernization and the preconditions for modern economic growth have, however, led to new research on the population of Tokugawa Japan.

Excellent sources exist for the study of Tokugawa population. The Japanese showed an earlier and greater interest in the quantification of economic resources and the significance of population numbers than did Europeans. A strong government coupled with a large bureaucracy made fairly accurate surveys possible. In 1721, the shogunate ordered an enumeration of the population of the domains comprising Japan; these surveys were then made at regular intervals until the mid-nineteenth century. Surveys, dating from the late-seventeenth century, were also taken of various domains with differing degrees of depth and accuracy.

The domain (*han*) statistics were compiled basically from village records. In certain areas, registers enumerating the households, persons, and draft animals in a village were drawn up as a kind of census. More prevalent are the *shūmon = aratame = chō*, the religious investigation records. These surveys were first undertaken in the seventeenth century as a means of preventing the practice and dissemination of Christianity. The documents purport to record the name, age, relationship to head of household, and temple affiliation of every person in a village. Since they are fairly thorough, their reliability can be evaluated by examining the internal consistencies. Their reliability is greater for the earlier years, however, because Christianity soon disappeared for the most part, thus obviating the original religious purpose of the surveys. The function of the surveys gradually shifted to an assessment of population. The first national survey of population, conducted in 1721, was based on existing surveys; the order for the census stated specifically that no new survey was necessary.

For those villages for which a continuous time series exists, the records can be analysed by the method of family reconstitution, without the painstaking work of assembling families from scattered baptismal, marriage, and burial registers.[2] Unfortunately, not enough records exist to permit an entire area to analysed in this way, but relatively unbroken records do exist for a significant number of villages.

Traditional views of Tokugawa population trends are being revised and modified, according to information gleaned from applying new techniques of analysis to both local records and aggregate statistics. New research particularly calls into question the theory of the stabilization of the population during the second half of the Tokugawa period. If the conclusions of studies on the Meiji period (1868–1912) are pushed back into the Tokugawa period, it becomes obvious that the growth during the latter half of the Tokugawa period must have been sufficient to bring the population of the mid-nineteenth century to the level of the early Meiji period. The survey of 1872, certainly more accurate than those at the end of the Tokugawa period, showed a population of thirty-five million persons, a difference of five million. The political unrest and the lack of any indication of a rapid rise in population in any contemporary records make a rapid growth in the early Meiji period unlikely, if not impossible. Thus, the population growth rate was probably higher at the end of the Tokugawa period than the government records indicate. The growth of urban areas increased social mobility, a supposition borne out by the incomplete recording of city populations.

Aggregate figures for the population of Tokugawa Japan by no means give the entire picture of demographic development and often cloak significant trends. While the national population statistics suggest that the population became stable during the eighteenth century, various regions show vastly different trends. Decreases in population in three regions in central and northern Japan were great enough to counterbalance the large increases that occurred in the outlying regions, particularly in the west. Only the northeast (Tōhoku region), which suffered from unusually inclement weather in the eighteenth century, and the regions with the largest urban populations (the Edo and Osaka areas) showed

<hr/>

[2] The work of family reconstitution has been pioneered in Japan by Professor Akira Hayami of the Department of Economics, Keio University, Tokyo. The findings of Professor Hayami have been published in English in the *Keio Economic Studies* and in excerpts in the *Mita Gakkai Zasshi*.

decreases in population according to the official shogunal statistics[3]

In order to obtain a clear picture of Tokugawa population trends, it is necessary to focus on a smaller unit than the nation and to supplement available statistics with analyses of existing village documents. The domain of Okayama has proved to be excellent for a regional study, because more sources are available for Okayama than for most areas.[4] Not only do good documents exist for a number of villages, but there are breakdowns of the domain population by district for at least seven different years in the Tokugawa period. For at least one year, there is an analysis of the composition of the population by occupation, including the samurai or warrior class, which is one of the hardest groups to pinpoint in terms of numbers during the Tokugawa period. Although Okayama may not be completely representative because of the great differences among Japan's two hundred and fifty-odd domains, it cannot be considered atypical. In the sense that aggregate population statistics tend to hide the important developments taking place, the demographic history of this one domain reflects the national trend. Because of the geographical similarities between Okayama and its neighbouring domains located along the Inland Sea, many of the trends and developments in Okayama were typical of the neighbouring domains in Southern Honshū.

This report on population trends within Okayama and their implications is only a preliminary one. The statistics used here are those of the domain, primarily the aggregate figures for the various districts. At least four or five villages can be analysed in depth by the family-reconstitution method. The results of such an analysis will add much information to the existing knowledge, but they will not be available for probably another year. The findings herein

[3] The urban population of Tokugawa Japan constitutes one of the great demographic mysteries in Japanese history. It is difficult even to calculate what the approximate populations of these areas were, and the figures quoted earlier of one million are extraordinarily rough estimates. There is much conflicting evidence, though the enormous size of these cities has never been disputed. Part of the problem in estimating the size of Edo (Tokyo) and Osaka is due to the composition of the population. The warrior class and their immediate attendants were not required to register. If they did, they registered not in the city, but in the home domain. As time passed and social mobility increased, there was an increase in the number of unregistered persons living in the cities, or persons who had registered in their own villages in rural areas. During one famine, the government asked persons in desperate need of food to register for relief, and 1·3 million persons registered in the Edo area alone. This figure seems entirely out of proportion, but does indicate the existence of extremely large urban populations in pre-modern Japan. Why they seemed to have decreased in population during the late-eighteenth and nineteenth centuries is unknown. In the case of Osaka, the decrease seems to have been related to a change in the commercial structure in the direction of a decentralization of markets.

[4] For maps of this area during the Tokugawa period, see Richard Beardsley, John W. Hall, and Robert E. Ward (eds.), *Village Japan* (Chicago, 1959), especially p. 38.

may well have to be revised in the future, but the trends are clear enough to warrant the present discussion.

The modern prefecture of Okayama is located about one hundred miles west of Osaka, along the northern shore of the Inland Sea. This prefecture takes its name from the domain of Okayama, located in one of the three major areas from which the modern prefecture was formed. The domain of Okayama was composed of a number of scattered areas, but its basic component was the province of Bizen. Since the other areas in the domain were scattered- and their size and population fluctuated over time, discussion of the domain's population will be based on Bizen, which included the basic eight districts and the administrative capital of Okayama.

The population of Okayama domain went from an estimated 300,000 in the latter half of the seventeenth century, to a peak of over 360,000 in the early-eighteenth century, but then declined to 340,000 in the early-nineteenth century. The figures for the province of Bizen plus the castle town show a similar trend. The figures for the years 1721, 1798, and 1834 listed in Table 1 include persons age two and above. No correction has been made, because there is no evidence that figures for the other years include infants under age two. (Usually, children were not recorded until they reached at least age two.) Moreover, such corrections cannot be made until the results of some village studies on Bizen become available.

Table 1   The population of Bizen and the castle town of Okayama

Year	Bizen Figures	Index	Castle town Figures	Index	Total Figures	Index
1679	244,180	100·0	30,033*	100·0	274,213	100·0
1707	284,503	116·5	30,635	102·0	315,138	114·9
1721	338,513	138·6	30,296	100·9	368,809	134·5
1738	304,135	124·6	26,349	87·7	330,484	120·5
1798	320,795	131·4	21,218	70·6	342,013	124·7
1834	318,207	130·3	20,173†	67·2	338,380	123·4

Notes: * The castle town figure is for 1680.
   † The figure is for 1838, the only year in this period for which there is a figure.
Sources: The Bizen figures for 1679 and 1834 listed in Tables 1 and 2 are from the *Gogungun Mononaridaka narabi ni Ninzū sono Ta* and the *Ninzū Chō*, respectively, and are quoted in Taniguchi Sumio, *Okayama Hansei Shi no Kenkyū* (A Study of the History of the Domain of Okayama; Tokyo, 1964), pp. 460–61. The remaining Bizen figures were compiled from documents from Okayama in the collection of Professor John W. Hall. The 1707 figure is from the *Arinin Aratame Chō*, that for 1721 from the *Ryochi Tahata Chōbu Ninzū Chō*, and those for 1738 and 1798 from the *Ninzū Aratame Chō*. The castle town figures were obtained respectively from the *Uenin Sodate Mokuroku, Arinin Aratame Chō, Okayama Shi Shi, Biyōki, Tome Chō,* and *Okayama Shi Shi,* as quoted in Taniguchi, *Okayama Hansei Shi no Kenkyū,* pp. 465–6.

The warrior class is known to have been omitted from these data. Statistics for Okayama on this class exist only for the year 1707, when 10,027 persons were recorded as belonging to it. This

PP

figure constitutes about 3 per cent of the domain's population, an extremely low proportion since the estimated average for Japan is 10 per cent. Because the proportion of *sumarai* to the rest of the population in a domain was unlikely to have increased after the end of the seventeenth century, the omission of this group from the statistics does not affect basic trends, except in the castle town where most of this class lived.

A breakdown of the population of Bizen into its eight constituent districts (see Table 2) gives a very different picture of population trends than do aggregate figures. The total population of the domain followed the same trend as the national population, but trends within Bizen differed considerably. The three districts of Mino, Kamimichi, and Kojima showed a substantial rise in population during the entire period, a remarkable increase for an area which had been well populated for over a thousand years and had a traditional economy. None of the other five districts showed substantial decreases, nor did they increase in any significant way considering the length of the period and the reliability of the statistics.

During the century and a half from 1679 to 1834, the population of Kojima increased by 75 per cent, that of Kamimichi by 47 per cent, but that of Mino by nearly 130 per cent. The figures for Mino are probably seriously in error, since an increase from 21,558 in 1707 to 51,817 in 1721 would have been virtually impossible without some sort of mass migration, and there is no record of any social phenomenon of this magnitude. Nevertheless, population undeniably tended to increase in these three districts.[5]

What accounted for the radical variation in population trends within an area united politically and economically? The two groups

[5] An index has been added to the figures for comparative purposes. Growth rates were also computed for the district population, but they must be used cautiously. They are less revealing than the index, partly because of the levelling off the growth in the inner districts, and partly because of the long time periods between years for which statistics exist. Inaccuracies such as the one in the Mino statistics create distorted growth rates. For the period from 1679–1834, Mino appears to have grown by an average of 0·6 per cent per year, Kojima by 0·3 per cent, Kamimichi by 0·2 per cent; the remaining districts showed almost no annual growth. The average for Bizen as a whole was 0·2 per cent per year.

Growth rates become more significant when the 155-year period is divided into two parts. In the first half of the period. Kamimichi and Tsutaka grew by 0·7 per cent per year. Kojima and Akasaka by 0·5 per cent, and Oku, Wake, and Iwanashi by 0·4 per cent. The distorted Mino rates are at a high 2·3 per cent. The average for Bizen is 0·5 per cent. The second half of the period witnessed very different growth rates. These were, in fact, zero or negative for all of the districts except Kojima, which had a 0·2 per cent annual average rate of increase, and Kamimichi, which had 0·1 per cent. The average for the province was a decrease of 0·2 per year. On the whole, there was very little growth in Oku, Wake, and Tsutaka, while there seems to have been a slight decrease in numbers in Iwanashi and Akasaka during the 155-year period. These are all compounded rates. As they have been calculated from unadjusted figures, they are useful only for comparative purposes.

Table 2 The population of the eight districts of Bizen

District Year	Mino* Figure	Index	Kamimichi Figure	Index	Oku Figure	Index	Wake Figure	Index	Iwanashi Figure	Index
1679	17,579	100·0	35,021	100·0	42,886	100·0	30,287	100·0	17,815	100·0
1707	21,558	121·9	38,094	108·8	46,107	107·5	34,040	112·4	20,780	116·6
1721	51,317	293·1	46,293	132·2	50,561	117·9	35,697	117·9	21,231	119·2
1726	51,163	289·4	47,456	135·6	51,989	121·2	36,562	120·7	21,536	120·9
1738	23,444	132·6	39,021	111·4	48,469	113·0	35,432	117·0	21,795	122·3
1798	40,933	231·5	50,782	145·0	44,599	104·0	32,755	108·1	17,930	100·6
1834	40,630	229·8	51,354	146·6	44,578	103·9	32,187	106·3	16,223	91·1

District Year	Akasaka Figure	Index	Tsutaka Figure	Index	Kojima Figure	Index	Total Figure	Index
1679	27,224	100·0	31,825	100·0	41,443	100·0	244,180	100·0
1707	32,478	119·3	39,707	124·8	51,738	124·9	284,503	116·5
1721	34,156	125·5	42,816	134·5	55,942	135·0	338,513	138·6
1726	34,688	127·4	43,295	136·0	58,379	140·9	345,068	141·3
1738	33,651	123·6	42,820	134·5	59,503	143·6	304,135	124·6
1798	27,839	102·3	37,342	117·3	68,615	165·6	320,795	131·4
1834	26,073	95·8	34,652	108·9	72,510	175·0	318,207	130·3

* The Mino figures are obviously inaccurate for some years, but they have been left unadjusted because it s not yet known just which years are inaccurate or how inaccurate they really are.

of districts differ significantly in geographical location. The three districts which sustained large population increases were in the southern half of Bizen on the Okayama Plain, one of the few broad flat areas in this part of Japan; all three were located on the sea or Kojima Bay and had excellent access to transportation and water facilities. The further north the location within Bizen, the more mountainous it is. (North of the Okayama Plain lie the Kibi Plateau and then the Chūgoku Mountains.) Tsutaka, Akasaka, and Iwanashi were located in this inner part of Bizen and had no access to the sea. These areas were composed largely of low mountains and valleys, where there was little room for the creation of new fields through land reclamation. In contrast to this, land reclamation was fairly extensive throughout much of the Tokugawa period in Kojima, Mino, Kamimichi, and Oku. Kojima was an island until the thirteenth century, but through reclamation in Kojima Bay it was gradually attached to the mainland. The large amount of land reclaimed from the sea differentiates Okayama from other domains, although land reclamation was carried out during the Tokugawa period throughout Japan.

In Okayama, small-scale private reclamation began in the last quarter of the sixteenth century; large-scale reclamation was initiated in the mid-seventeenth century under the direction of the domain government. Land fronting on the sea was reclaimed in the lower reaches of the three rivers which flowed through Bizen to Kojima Bay. By the time three large-scale projects, one in Oku and two in Kamimichi, had been completed at the end of the seventeenth century, land with a productivity totalling more than five hundred thousand bushels of grain had been added to Okayama

Table 3 Percentage of cultivated land and population of each district in total Bizen figures

Year District	Population† 1679	1726	1834	Cultivated land 1702	(1702 in chō*)
Mino	7·2	14·8	12·8	12·9	2,803
Kamimichi	14·3	13·8	16·1	18·0	3,893
Oku	17·6	15·1	14·0	12·9	2,790
Wake	12·4	10·6	10·1	9·3	2,007
Iwanashi	7·3	6·2	5·1	7·4	1,605
Akasaka	11·1	10·1	8·2	12·8	2,770
Tsutaka	13·0	12·5	10·9	15·7	3,392
Kojima	17·0	16·9	22·8	11·1	2,393
Total	99·9	100·0	100·0	100·1	21,653

* One chō equals 2·45 acres.
† Percentages of population were calculated from the figures in Table 2. The land figures are those quoted by Taniguchi Sumio, *Okayama Hansei Shi no Kenkyū*, p. 330. Since the major reclamation projects were carried out in the seventeenth century, the comparison between population and land is more valid than it would otherwise be when data on land are available for only one year.

domain. From this time on, reclamation lagged, probably because there was no more land that could be easily reclaimed from the sea.

Reclamation projects not only added land to the existing area, but often improved the original land. Irrigation and drainage channels were constructed as part of the seventeenth-century efforts in reclamation. The 17-kilometre-long Kurayasu River, completed in 1679, provided water for the reclaimed land in Kamimichi as well as for a large area outside the project. Another drainage channel was built in the seventeenth century across the same district to prevent flooding of the castle town. Both projects were of immense importance to Kamimichi as a whole and undoubtedly contributed to its productivity.

The economic development of the districts was also closely correlated to population trends. Although it is impossible at this stage in the research to draw causal relationships, the correlation is too close to be coincidental. The economy of Okayama changed radically during the Tokugawa period. Over 80 per cent of the population was engaged in agriculture in 1707; even at the end of the Tokugawa period, Bizen was overwhelmingly rural. But by the nineteenth century, striking developments had taken place in the domain's economy with the development of commerce, pre-modern manufacture, and commercial agriculture on a large scale.

The villages witnessed the intensification of rural trade, increasing progress toward a rural money economy, and the commercialization of agriculture. Cotton, the basis of the area's commercial agriculture, was increasingly cultivated in Kojima, Kamimichi, and Oku,[6] primarily in the newly reclaimed fields. The development of cotton culture began in the mid-Tokugawa period; by 1846, 44·8 per cent of the cultivated land belonging to the five villages in one of the reclamation projects in Kojima was planted in cotton. Rice cultivation did not suffer since cotton could be planted as a winter crop.

The development of cotton cultivation and the commercialization of agriculture fostered the emergence of a cotton textile industry, largely carried on as a handicraft enterprise in the home. Many of these developments took place in Kojima and the areas bordering the newly reclaimed land. This new economic activity would explain Kojima's ability to maintain an increasing population with progressively less land per person.

---

[6] Oku seems to remain the exception to many of the trends in Bizen. Among the districts in which extensive land reclamation was carried on, only Oku failed to show an increase in population in the second half of the Tokugawa period. Other factors not yet known must account for the difference between Oku and the seemingly similar districts which sustained population increases.

There are other reasons for increases in population in Kojima. The fishing industry was well developed by the early part of the Tokugawa period. Indeed, in terms of earning power a fishing boat was considered as valuable as owning paddy land. The trading industry expanded, and Kojima became a port centre for the coastal trade. The development of trade and fishing as well as commercial agriculture and manufacture stimulated the economy of this region, enabling it to support a larger and growing population on far less acreage per person than the other districts. Even as far back as 1702, Kojima had twice as many people in relation to its production of grain as most of the other districts.

Mino and Kamimichi also benefited from the commercialization of agriculture and the development of trade. During the early Tokugawa period, the castle town, the largest market in the domain, was located in this area and controlled virtually all important trade and commerce. Rural commerce was centred in thirteen rural towns maintained by traders based in the castle town. The castle town of Okayama had a registered population of more than thirty thousand in the eighteenth century; it was probably far larger than this, however, because most of the warrior class and their attendants lived there.

By the end of the seventeenth century, traders began to appear even in small rural villages. They were usually men who had farmed on a scale that was not economically viable. With the commercialization of large segments of agriculture and the spread of manufacture and trade to the villages, merchants of the castle town lost their monopoly on commerce, a possible explanation for the decline in the registered population of that city. (By the 1830s, its population was only twenty thousand, or two thirds of what it had been in the early-eighteenth century.) Although this subject needs further study, the centre of trade clearly shifted from the castle town to the rural areas, and Mino and Kamimichi were among the first to benefit from this.

The innermost districts of Bizen were not so capable of developing economically or benefiting from land reclamation and the new type of agriculture which it fostered. They created the fewest new fields, showed the least amount of economic change, and sustained the smallest increases in population during the period.

There is little evidence of extensive famine and crop failure, though poor crop years were not unusual. Contemporary records do not mention any widespread epidemics. There were severe famines in Western Japan during the 1730s due to insect pests, but these ended with the discovery that whale oil would kill the pests without harming the crop. These crop failures probably contributed to the drop in population during the 1730s. There were national crop failures in the 1780s and the 1830s, and their effect on the population of Bizen must not be ignored. Nevertheless, the population in the most densely populated areas continued to increase even in these periods.

Population control is one of the most debated subjects in Tokugawa demography. Infanticide and abortion were carried out to such an extent that both the shogunal and domain governments felt it necessary to pass edicts concerning these practices. The domain government does not seem to have resorted to this expedient in Okayama, where its concern centred more on the practice of abandoning fields and villages in order to work in the cities and towns. There is, unfortunately, little information on the extent of migration in Bizen. In the village of Fujito in Kojima, a large number of workers were hired from the surrounding villages for work in Fujito, but a large number of persons from that village also worked in other places.

It is often difficult for the historical demographer to uncover the relationship between population trends and general social and economic patterns. This is true to some extent in the case of Japan. It is extremely clear, however, that the relationship between economic development and population changes in the Okayama domain are too consistent to be coincidental. This correlation between economic development and population trends is not restricted to Okayama. The population of the entire country grew only 3·23 per cent between 1721 and 1846, but the population of the four domains considered the most influential areas in the carrying out of the Meiji Restoration increased by 30·25 per cent during this same period.[7] This would seem to imply that the areas strong enough to challenge the Tokugawa government were also those capable of supporting the largest increases in population, an indication of strong economies.

To people who are not immersed in Japanese history, the conclusions which can be drawn from the statistics on Bizen and Okayama domain will not seem particularly striking. No definitive statement can be made with regard to many of the most important aspects of population growth and composition. To those steeped in the traditional studies on Tokugawa Japan, however, the difference in growth trends within the province of Bizen is most startling. That aggregate figures hide regional and local differences

[7] This figure was calculated by aggregating the figures of the provinces of Suo, Nagato, Osumi, Satsuma, Tosa, and Hizen, and thus is weighted by the size of the population in each province. Figures are from Sekiyama Naotarō, *Kinsei Nihon no Jinkō Kōzo*. (The Population Structure of Tokugawa Japan; Tokyo, 1958), pp. 137–9.

in growth is a truism, but one too often forgotten in studying a pre-modern period in which documents are difficult to find and even more difficult to interpret. There is a tendency for trends in one area or in the country as a whole to be taken as representative of each area in the country individually. Yet trends differed widely according to region during the Tokugawa period. Okayama exemplifies the diversification of both demographic and economic developments within a fairly small and supposedly integrated area.

Furthermore, these developments have been discerned from a kind of statistic which traditional demographers have largely ignored, and demographers using the most recent techniques of analysis have increasingly scorned. There are certainly many inaccuracies and omissions in the regional statistics. Moreover, because there is no breakdown further than that by sex, it is impossible to determine their accuracy by testing internal consistencies. Nevertheless, these statistics were compiled from the basic village registers and can be presumed to be nearly as accurate as the registers; they certainly reflect the same basic population trends.

These statistics have the advantage of being aggregates of local areas. The documents, lying between the national aggregates and the individual village statistics, can prove to be extremely valuable in filling in gaps in knowledge. Nevertheless, just as aggregates hide differences in trends in areas smaller than the one aggregated, so is there danger in using statistics on a village with a population of four hundred and assuming that the results are representative of the surrounding area. There seem to have been substantial differences in population trends in certain villages in Kojima for example.

Although demographic research on Bizen and the domain of Okayama has only just begun, a correlation between economic development and population trends is apparent. Further research, including analysis of the four or five villages whose records lend themselves to family reconstitution, should provide much additional knowledge on this subject. Even with the present level of knowledge, however, it is evident that significant changes occurred behind the façade of population stagnation during the latter half of the Tokugawa period. Neither the economy nor the population remained constant. Fundamental economic development took place with the growth of trade and the commercialization of agriculture; the resulting increases in economic production enabled certain areas to support growing populations. The outstanding example is Kojima.

In fact, the domain of Okayama seems to have acquired the preconditions to industrialization: the growth of a money economy, improved communications, the commercialization of agriculture, the penetration of commerce and trade into the rural areas, and the development of pre-modern manufacture. Both the level of living and the population size rose in areas where these developments took place. The role played by population in the economic developments prior to industrialization is still a matter for conjecture. Further study of Japan may help to isolate the exact nature of the relationship between economic and demographic phenomena. It may point out what in population trends is significant in terms of industrialization and its preconditions.

BIBLIOGRAPHICAL NOTE

While this book was in press, the analysis of the *shūmon-aratame-chō* for the village of Fujito in Kojima was completed and will appear in 'Toward an Analysis of Demographic and Economic Change in Tokugawa Japan: A Village Study', to be published in the *Journal of Asian Studies*, Vol. XXXI, No. 3 (May 1972). The results of the analysis support the hypothesis advanced in this essay.

ACKNOWLEDGMENTS

The author wishes to express her indebtedness to Professor John W. Hall of Yale University and Professor Sumio Taniguchi of Okayama University, who made their sources available. Their research and guidance form the background from which this study was drawn.

Susan B. Hanley and Kozo Yamamura

Population trends and economic growth in pre-industrial Japan

Recent demographic studies on England have indicated that its population prior to the Industrial Revolution increased at an extremely low rate, averaging perhaps one quarter of 1 per cent per year between 1500 and 1700 and about five twelfths of 1 per cent per year between 1700 and 1750. Similar low rates prevailed in other European countries. and are in sharp contrast to the annual growth rates of 2 per cent and above with which the developing nations of the mid-twentieth century must contend.[1] If these findings on Europe's population can be accepted, one may be permitted to conclude that for England, at the very least, such low average rates of population growth for nearly three centuries, while total output was known to have been growing at a faster pace, were an essential ingredient of her successful industrialization.[2]

Though numerous studies have been made comparing the process of industrialization in Japan and in the West, the relationship of the pre-industrial period in Japan to her industrialization and the similarities or dissimilarities with the comparable period in Western Europe have largely been ignored. Because of the increasing knowledge of the importance of the pre-industrial period for industrialization, we ask the following questions with regard to Japan: What were the relative growth rates of population and output through the Tokugawa period (1600–1868) to the early Meiji years (1868–73)? What inferences or conclusions can be drawn from these observations in further explaining Japan's successful industrialization after the Meiji Restoration of 1868? And, finally, how do the demographic trends and patterns compare with those for Europe during the pre-industrial period?

Data on population exist for the Tokugawa period, both on a nation-wide basis and on a regional and village basis. These data

---

[1] Joseph J. Spengler, 'Demographic Factors and Early Modern Economic Development' (pp. 87–98, the present volume).

[2] Phyllis Deane and W. A. Cole, *British Economic Growth, 1688–1959* (Cambridge, 1967), Second Edition, pp. 96–7.

are, however, incomplete for various reasons and remain largely unanalysed beyond impressionistic generalizations and occasional case studies using only a fraction of the existing data. This lack of attention to Japanese historical demography, coupled with the difficulty in obtaining evidence on output and agricultural productivity—thus on the living standard—has led to facile speculations arising from the uncritical reiteration of observations based on the limited use of qualitative information on population and the unqualified use of the available data on the rice output. Thus, two contradictory hypotheses on preindustrial Japan's demographic changes and economic development have been developed.

The most widely accepted views on the Tokugawa population have emphasized the economic distress of the Bakufu, the samurai or warrior class, and the peasantry, which led them to practise abortion and infanticide.[3] According to the proponents of this view, after a major population increase during the seventeenth century,[4]

[3] Honjō Eijirō's 'The Population of Japan in the "Tokugawa" Era', *Tokugawa Bakufu no beika chōsetsu* (Tokyo, 1924) probably provides the best summary in English of this view. See also Irene B. Taeuber, *The Population of Japan* (Princeton, 1958), Chapter 2, for a summary of the views of the major Japanese scholars on this subject. (In this article all Japanese names are listed with the surname first, following the Japanese custom. All sources are listed in the language in which they were published; only quotations from the text have been translated. See Appendix A for a glossary of Japanese terms.)

[4] We will confine this paper to a discussion of the population of the eighteenth and nineteenth centuries because there exist no reliable data or information to use in estimating the nationwide population of the seventeenth century. The most widely quoted estimate for the beginning of the seventeenth century is Yoshida Tōgō's 18·5 million persons. There is no statistical basis for this population figure, however. Since there was a handy correlation of *kokudaka* (rice output) and population figures in 1721, both estimated at about 26 million, and since the traditional estimate of how much rice it took to feed one person one year was one *koku*, Yoshida extrapolated backwards and hypothesized that the estimated 18·5 million *koku* of rice in 1600 would have supported a population of 18·5 million persons. Even should this rice output estimate be reliable, it scarcely forms the basis for estimating the population. This estimate would mean a population increase of approximately 40 per cent from 1600 to 1721, the first date for which we have nation-wide population figures. Such an increase infers an annual average growth rate of around 0·3 per cent. Other data quoted for the seventeenth century are the estimates made in 1721 by the ten *daimyō* holding the largest domains in Japan. See Honjō Eijirō, 'The Population of Japan in the "Tokugawa" Era', pp. 32–3, and *Jinkō oyobi jinkō mondai* (Tokyo, 1930), pp. 43–6; and Taeuber, *The Population of Japan*, p. 21. These figures were, however, 'guesstimates' on the part of the *daimyō* who had been ordered to estimate the population in their domains seventy to eighty years previously.

Hayami Akira attempted to re-estimate the national population in 1600 on the basis of local case studies and arrived at a rate of natural increase of 1 per cent, resulting in a population ranging from 6·2–9·8 million in 1600. See Hayami Akira, 'The Population at the Beginning of the Tokugawa Period', *Keio Economic Studies*, Vol. 4 (1966–67), especially pp. 22–3. Hayami admits that his estimate is inconclusive, and his data are inevitably biased in that they come from villages with known rapid increases in population. Because no other data exist, except for scattered figures or short time series from the late seventeenth century, we have omitted this subject from our discussion, but it must be noted that all sources do indicate a rising population in the seventeenth century, the magnitude of which is yet unknown.

following the peace brought about by the Tokugawa hegemony, nearly absolute population limits were reached by the first quarter of the eighteenth century. Thereafter the population remained more or less stationary with the help of at least three major famines and a great many local disasters, along with a negligible increase in agricultural productivity. A major check in restraining population growth was the limitation on births through the practice of abortion and infanticide by all classes of Japanese society.

The picture so often depicted by Japanese scholars of a distressed population living to the limits of its resources during most of the Tokugawa period, is incongruent with the rapid increases in population and rising agricultural output that occurred during the early Meiji period prior to the diffusion of Western technology and modern agricultural techniques. This view of economic and demographic stagnation during these centuries has therefore come under critical review during the last decade. Thomas C. Smith, Sydney Crawcour, John W. Hall,[5] and an increasing number of the postwar generation of Japanese scholars have come to emphasize the economic developments occurring during this period, but so far there has been little attempt to reconcile this view of the economy with what is known about demographic trends.

We propose here a synthesis of the demographic and economic data of the Tokugawa period. We have studied all the obtainable demographic data available for meaningful time-series analyses and the nation-wide rice output figures sufficiently reliable for our use. To provide evidence for our synthesis, we will first summarize the findings of the major scholars on the Tokugawa population, and then analyse the nation-wide data for all of the *kuni* (provinces) in Japan and for the accumulated samples of thirty-seven regions and villages. We will then examine rice output and other evidence on economic development in relation to demographic growth. Finally, we will discuss other factors affecting the rate of population growth, notably population control and the effect of famines and

[5] For example, see Thomas C. Smith, 'The Land Tax in the Tokugawa Period', in John W. Hall and Marius B. Jansen (eds.), *Studies in the Institutional story of Early Modern Japan* (Princeton, 1968), pp. 288–99; E. Sydney Crawcour, 'The Tokugawa Heritage', in William W. Lockwood (ed.), *The State and Economic Enterprise in Japan* (Princeton, 1965), pp. 17–44; and John Whitney Hall, 'Aspects of Japanese Economic Development', in John W. Hall and Richard K. Beardsley, *Twelve Doors to Japan* (New York, 1965), pp. 546–9. George Sansom is an example of a Western writer who changed his mind on the question of economic development and the standard of living in the Tokugawa period, as can be seen from his references to decreases in the farming population, distressing conditions of the peasants, and so forth—problems which he considered largely due to the rise of a money economy. See his *A Short Cultural History* (New York, 1943), pp. 466–9, 514–18. But in his later work, Sansom emphasized increases in the output of rice, rising living standards, and the rapid growth of a commercial economy. See his *A History of Japan, 1615–1867* (Stanford, 1963), pp. 107–23, 185–7.

other disasters. We conclude by comparing the demographic and economic trends that took place in Japan with those in pre-industrial Europe and by contrasting these findings with what the under-developed nations of the world face today.

CONTRIBUTIONS TO THE STUDY OF JAPANESE HISTORICAL DEMOGRAPHY

The contributions of Japanese and Western scholars to the study of Japan's pre-modern population can be summarized briefly since so little interest has been shown on this subject until very recently. The classic studies—and just about the only studies— were made by Honjō Eijirō, Sekiyama Naotarō, and Takahashi Bonsen.[6] Honjō was interested only in the national aggregate data and explained the stationary population, as seen in the total figures, purely by positive population checks in the form of abortion, infanticide, and famines. Sekiyama based his studies primarily on the *kuni* or provincial data collected by the Bakufu at regular intervals from 1721 to the end of the Tokugawa period. Sekiyama's major contribution has been to show that while the population was stationary when taken in the aggregate, a breakdown of the data into ten regions indicates that the decreases in three of the regions— Kinki, Kantō, and Tōhoku—were balanced by growth in the seven remaining regions.[7] Thus, he suggested, the aggregate population figures show a very distorted picture of demographic trends during the Tokugawa period, although he adhered to the position that the total picture was one of stagnation and, in doing so, failed to examine inter-regional differentials in demographic patterns against possible variations in economic changes among regions during the period.[8]

Takahashi Bonsen's major interest has been confined to a description of abortion and infanticide in Tokugawa Japan and the documentation of contemporary literature concerning these practices. He does supply numerous demographic data on regions ranging from *han* (a domain) to a section of a village, but he has attempted

[6] See Honjō Eijirō, 'The Population of Japan in the "Tokugawa" Era'; 'Population Problems in the Tokugawa Era', *Kyoto University Economic Review*, Vol. 2, No. 2 (1927); *The Social and Economic History of Japan* (Kyoto, 1935); *Jinkō oyobi jinkō mondai* (Tokyo, 1930); *Nihon jinkōshi* (Tokyo, 1941); Sekiyama Naotarō. *Kinsei Nihon jinkō no kenkyū* (Tokyo, 1948); *Kinsei Nihon no jinkō kōzō* (Tokyo, 1958); *Nihon no jinkō* (Tokyo, 1962); and Takahashi Bonsen, *Nihon jinkōshi no kenkyū*, Vol. 1 (Tokyo, 1941), Vol. 2 (Tokyo. 1955), and Vol. 3 (Tokyo, 1962); and *Datai-mabiki no kenkyū* (Tokyo, 1936).

[7] Sekiyama, *Kinsei Nihon no jinkō kōzō* pp. 140–41. See Map 1 for the location of these three regions.

[8] Sekiyama, *op. cit.*, p. 143.

little or no analysis of what he so assiduously collected. In reading his three-volume series the predominant impression conveyed to the reader is the importance of the 'immoral' (*fudōtoku*) practices of abortion and infanticide as the primary cause for the general stationary trend of Tokugawa population.[9]

Even though none of these scholars attempted to analyse the data in any systematic way, the superficial view of the Tokugawa population they presented became the stereotyped staple of economic historical literature on Tokugawa Japan. Then in the early 1950s, Nomura Kanetarō of Keiō University became interested in Japanese historical demography and began to ask a number of questions about the cultural and economic relationships between demographic trends and economic developments.[10] He also subjected to a new and more thorough kind of analysis the basic source of population data, the *shūmon-aratame-chō* or religious investigation registers, which recorded the Japanese population over the entire country at the village level from the late-seventeenth century.[11] With an excellent command of Japan's economic history, Nomura, despite his lack of demographic evidence, seriously questioned whether the traditional view of Tokugawa Japan's demographic changes was accurate. He hypothesized that due to the underestimation of the population and economic growth the effects of abortion and infanticide had been over-emphasized.

Unfortunately, this promising start was cut short by Nomura's death while he and a group of students were analysing the first village data, using the registers of Kōmi village in Mino province.[12] In the mid-1960s, however, Nomura's student, Hayami Akira, began a thorough analysis of the Tokugawa population using the religious investigation registers. Hayami, stimulated by the work of French and English demographers on parish registers, adapted the method of family reconstruction to fit the Japanese demographic

[9] Takahashi noted that 'the corrupted morality in cities caused numerous unwanted pregnancies, and this was one of the major reasons for infanticides and abortion.' Takahashi, *Nihon jinkoshi no kenkyū*, Vol. 1, p. 361. Though he made frequent comments on the poverty of the peasants and the immortality of the urban population, he did not find it contradictory to mention also a 1754 document which stated: 'Until fifty or sixty years ago, peasants raised five or six, at times even seven to eight children, but this is not done any more. . . . Is it because people have begun to enjoy better living to the point of wanting only a few children?' Takahashi, *Nihon jinkoshi no kenkyū*, Vol. 2, p. 32.

[10] See Nomura Kanetarō, 'On Cultural Conditions Affecting Population Trends in Japan', The Science Council of Japan, Economic Series No. 2, Tokyo, 1953.

[11] Tsuchiya Takao originally suggested using religious investigation registers as a source for the study of Japanese social and economic history in his 'Shūmon-aratame-chō no shakai keizai kōsatsu', *Shakai Keizai Shigaku*, Vol. 3, No. 8 (1933).

[12] Nomura Kenkyūkai, Kōmi Mura Kyōdō Kenkyū Han, 'Ogaki Hanryō Mino no kuni Motosu no kōri Kōmi mura no kokō tōkei', *Mita Gakkai Zasshi*, Vols. 10–11 (1960), pp. 166–208.

sources.[13] To date, two villages[14] have been analysed using the family reconstitution method and more are currently being studied. While the scale of this research is still obviously extremely small, it does provide revealing insights into fertility, mortality, nuptiality, family size, population composition, life expectancy, birth intervals, migration, and the family structure, all of which are directly comparable with the studies on population now coming out of England, France, and other European countries.

We know of only two attempts to draw together these scattered sources of data and to analyse them in comparison with quantitative data and qualitative evidence on economic developments and changes in output during the same period. The first is in Irene Taeuber's *The Population of Japan* published in 1958. Though without the benefit of the most recent studies, she provided a comprehensive summary of much of the work then available in Japanese. Despite her expressed misgivings that the Japanese view on abortion and infanticide was overly impressionistic, Mrs Taeuber was in the end influenced by these views and the consensus of Japanese scholars. While she stated that she did not think that poverty and the problem of subsistence alone were sufficient to explain the practice of abortion and infanticide, she concluded with the rather vague statement that the balance of the forces of change throughout the economy and society were such that population emerged as a major problem during the eighteenth and early nineteenth centuries in Japan.[15]

The second attempt at synthesis appeared in 1965 in an article by Umemura Mataji and others in *Keizai Kenkyū*, a Japanese economics periodical.[16] This study, again, was an excellent attempt to summarize economic and demographic changes, although its authors accepted without much caution Sekiyama's data and his regionalization and merely restated what earlier Japanese authors had observed about the relationship between these changes.

In short, despite the recent interest in Japanese demography, the studies on Tokugawa population leave this important subject still relatively unanalysed. In this study, we have attempted to combine both the *kuni* and local (village, district, and *han*) levels of data so that each category of data can supplement as well as provide a check on the other. The *kuni* data used here are from Sekiyama's work which provides the Bakufu population figures

---

[13] Hayami Akira and Yasumoto Minoru, 'Jinkōshi kenkyū ni okeru Family Reconstitution', *Shakai Keizai Shigaku*, Vol. 34, No. 2 (1968), pp. 123–56.

[14] Yokouchi village and Kando-*shinden*. See Appendix C.

[15] Taeuber, *The Population of Japan*, pp. 29–34.

[16] Umemura Mataji *et al*, 'Tokugawa jidai no jinkō sūsei to sono kisei yōin', *Keizai Kenkyū*, Vol. 16, No. 2 (1965), pp. 135–54.

for 1721, 1750, 1756, 1786, 1798, 1804, 1822, 1828, 1834, and 1846; and the Meiji government's census data by *kuni* for 1872.[17] The Tokugawa figures were compiled by the Bakufu on the basis of information received from the several *han* or domains.

To supplement the *kuni* data, thirty-six time-series data have been collected and analysed. These include twenty-five villages and eleven larger units. These are enumerated in Appendix C along with the location, dates of coverage, and the size of the population at the beginning of the time series to give the magnitude of each sample.[18]

While data of this scope, some providing excellent time series, are extremely rare for a pre-modern country, the data presented here can be criticized on a number of grounds. The first source of data, the *kuni* figures, has been called unreliable because: 1. the method of survey and the information included varied by *kuni*; 2. it excluded various elements of the population, most notably the samurai or warrior class and almost certainly others, such as the Japanese outcasts[19] and the servants of the samurai and their families; and 3. it is available only for ten interspersed time periods during the latter half of the Tokugawa period. We consider these data extremely important, however, because they provide the only source of general population figures on a nation-wide level, even if these are to be taken only as a general or rough indicator of demographic developments. Moreover, this source provides some clue as to how applicable trends in villages and other local areas are to a province or even the country as a whole.

But there are indications that these data underestimate the population even more than it has been thought up to now. We have supplemental data providing *kuni* totals for at least two *kuni* in Japan. The first data are for the province of Bizen, which was most of Okayama *han*. The *kuni* totals listed in Sekiyama are approximately the same for three dates as the aggregate population figures for the eight districts of Bizen if the population of the castle town of Okayama is excluded.[20] The second example is that of Kōchi *han*, which was geographically identical to Tosa province.[21] The Sekiyama figures for Tosa are smaller by forty to fifty thousand, or nearly one tenth, than the Kōchi *han* annual data. These two bits of information are

[17] Sekiyama, *Kinsei Nihon no jinkō kōzō*, pp. 137-9.

[18] For economy of space, only a small part of the results of our analysis of these thirty-seven areas is presented in this paper. Those interested in further details may write to the authors.

[19] The Japanese outcasts are known as *eta* or *hinin*.

[20] Compare the figures for Okayama in Susan B. Hanley, 'Population Trends and Economic Development in Tokugawa Japan; The Case of Bizen Province in Okayama', see pp. 437-449 of the present volume, with Sekiyama, *Kinsei Nihon no jinkō kōzō*, p. 139.

[21] Compare the figures for Kōchi *han* in Takahashi Bonsen, *Nihon jinkōshi*, Vol. 2, pp. 229-35, with Sekiyama, *Kinsei Nihon no jinkō kōzō*, p. 139.

inconclusive in themselves, but they do strongly suggest that the population totals of the *kuni* were underestimated by possibly as much as 10 per cent, and that in many or most cases the population of the castle town was not included in the *kuni* figures. This would mean that the *kuni* figures refer not only to just the commoner population, but primarily to the rural commoner population.

One other important note must be made with regard to the use of the statistics: The 1872 data are not strictly comparable with the other observations because the survey for that year was undertaken by the new Meiji government and included many elements of the population omitted from the earlier surveys. Hence, growth rates from 1846–72 are overstated considerably as they originate from the underestimated portion of the 1846 population. We have no further indicators of the reliability of the Sekiyama data at this time, but it must be kept in mind that however valuable these data are as sources, they can provide only a rough indication of demographic trends.

While village and local studies have been widely criticized for being on too small a scale to give any true indication of nationwide trends, these studies not only provide a counterbalance to the nation-wide data since their reliability can be more easily checked, but they supplement the national data with information on sex ratios, the number of households, and, at the village level, with information usually to be obtained only from a modern census.

Too much can be made of the differences in the local and national data. In general, all of the statistics were derived from the same sources. These were the *shūmon-aratame-chō* or religious registration registers, originally compiled in the mid-seventeenth century in order to prevent the dissemination of Christianity throughout Japan. After making the decision to prohibit this foreign religion, the Bakufu ordered all Japanese to become members of a recognized Buddhist sect and to register every year with the temples with which they were affiliated. This registration resulted, from our point of view, in a demographic survey of Japan. Since most families belonged to the same temple, most of the registers record families under the head of household, giving name, age, and relationship to the head of the household of all persons living within the household, including servants, and any changes in the status of family members or their whereabouts, including births and deaths, in many cases. This registration was nation wide in scope after 1671, but the basic unit of registration was the village.[22]

Earlier surveys, and ones undertaken explicitly for the purpose of

[22] For further discussion on the *shūmon-aratame-chō* and their value and drawbacks as demographic sources, see Sekiyama, *Kinsei Nihon no jinkō kōzō*, Chapter 1; Sekiyama, *Nihon no jinkō*, Chapter 2; and Honjō, 'The Population of Japan in the "Tokugawa" Era'.

enumerating the population and domestic animals in one area, do exist. These were generally called *ninbetsu-aratame-chō*, one of the most famous of which was undertaken by Kokura *han* in the provinces of Buzen and Bungo in the early seventeenth century.[23] The *shūmon-aratame* system was undoubtedly patterned after earlier local population surveys as a convenient and well-established method of survey. In any case, in 1721 when the Shōgun Yoshimune wished to find out how many Japanese there were, he ordered each *han* to report their population using existing surveys, and the *shūmon-aratame-chō* provided this basic record of population.

Despite the common base of the *kuni* figures, a problem in comparing the *kuni* statistics arises because not all of the *shūmon-aratame-chō* included the same information, and most, in fact, omitted the counting of large groups of persons. The most obvious omissions were children, especially infants. If the purpose of the population surveys in the Tokugawa period was to obtain some estimate of the productive population, young children were relatively unimportant, particularly as they had a high mortality rate. Thus in Wakayama *han* children under the age of eight were not reported.[24] Children were usually first recorded in their second year of life, which meant they were about age one in the Western method of counting, as babies were considered one year old at birth in Japan and gained another year at their first New Year's. Okayama is apparently rather unusual as children were reported from birth, with the month and day recorded, but even there it was not uncommon for a child to first appear in the records at age two or three.[25] This means that there was a consistent underestimation of the population of Japan in the national statistics, and one borne out by the sharp jump in the population between the last Tokugawa survey in 1846 and the first Meiji survey in 1872.

A number of other problems arise with regard to the reliability of the data on population. First, there was undoubtedly an under-reporting of the city population that grew greater over time with the increased mobility of the Japanese and the flow of persons from the rural areas into the cities.[26] Persons were supposed to change their

[23] For an analysis of this data, see Hayami, 'The population at the beginning of the Tokugawa Period', and 'Kokura han ninbetsu-aratame-chō no bunseki to kinsei shoki zenkoku jinkō suikei no kokoromi', *Mita Gakkai Zasshi*, Vol. 59, No. 3 (1966), pp. 221–56.

[24] Sekiyama Naotarō, 'Wakayama han no jinkō chōsa to jinkō jōtai', *Keizai Riron*, Vols. 15–18 (1953), p. 189.

[25] See the *shūmon-aratame-chō* of Fujito and Fukiage villages in the possession of the Okayama University Library, Okayama.

[26] We do not discuss the population trends and their relationship to economic activities in those provinces including the major cities of Edo and Osaka. As all Japanese authors confess, any detailed discussion of these provinces is extremely difficult for various reasons. To begin with, the population of these cities did not follow national patterns. The popula-

place of registration officially when they moved, but many moved without official permission and hence could not change their records. In any case, it was difficult, if not impossible, for a city to trace and account for all of its transients, particularly in a metropolis such as Edo (present-day Tokyo) where the population numbered over a million in the early eighteenth century. It is probable also that many *hōkōnin* or servants and workers in the rural districts were counted twice, being registered both in their own villages and in the ones where they were temporarily working. But we do not know what proportion of the population went uncounted and what proportion was counted twice in the population surveys. Further village case studies will provide an indication of the latter, but we shall probably never know the former.

There exist, then, numerous pieces of pertinent information which infer varying degrees of a lack of reliability or underestimation of the population in all levels of the data for the Tokugawa period. Because of the diverse nature of the data obtainable for this study, we have relied on one simple test for the general reliability of the demographic data presented here. That is the sex ratio. In general, more male infants are born than female, but they tend to have a higher infant mortality. Any infant bias would in general be lacking in our data because most persons were not reported until the age of two or above. There were no wars or other phenomena that we know of which would tend to raise the mortality of one sex above that of the other. Thus, we can conclude that a sex ratio close to one would signify a fairly high reliability of demographic information.

---

tion of Osaka rose until 1760, but because of the development of rural trade which began to reduce Osaka's importance as the major commercial entrepôt of Japan, its population declined after that year. The population pattern of Edo was opposite that of Osaka. From about 1720, the time for which we have the first usable data, the population declined from a peak of about one million and reached its eighteenth-century minimum during the Temmei famine which severely affected the Kantō region. But the population increased steadily after this famine to the point of necessitating the Bakufu policy to reduce the population by means of 'back to the village' measures and the dispersion of the samurai quarters to the outskirts of Edo. During the early nineteenth century, the major problem facing Edo was rising price levels which were caused by relatively large demands for all types of goods supplied by inadequate distribution facilities and by the continued debasements of coins.

These large cities are known, however, to have had a large number of transients (*mushuku-mono* and *rōnin*) who were not all accounted for in the city records. Because of our general lack of precise knowledge of the magnitude of the total economic activities in these cities and of more reliable population data which account for migration into and out of the cities and for the effects of epidemics and changing demographic trends, particularly in the birth and death rates of the urban population, we must, at this stage of our research on historical demography, leave these provinces as questions in need of further examination. For useful literature on this subject see Honjō, *Nihon jinkōshi*, pp. 91–4, 98–103; Umemura *et al*, 'Tokugawa jidai no jinkō susei to sono kisei yōin', pp. 141–2; and Sekiyama, *Kinsei Nihon no jinkō kōzō*, Chapter 5, pp. 211–42. The last is perhaps the best.

This hypothesis is partially substantiated because the sex ratios of the various villages for which detailed analyses exist are very good—that is, the ratios are close to one for the entire period for which there are data. Kando-shinden, Yokouchi, and Kōmi villages have reasonable sex ratios, always ranging around one, but with a somewhat cyclical trend. For example, in Kando-shinden during the eighteenth century the sex ratio was first slightly over one and then slightly below. From 1788–1800 it ranged from 1·01 to 1·08, but from 1816–43 it was at no time above one. Then from 1843–71 it was again consistently slightly above one. Other villages for which we have less supporting information than the above three showed a variety of trends in the sex ratio with no general pattern emerging at the village level. A few showed a slight upward trend over time, while others indicated a gradual but definite negative trend. All village trends could be termed natural. Any deviations were not significant enough to invalidate the population figures, particularly since these figures are only being considered here as a rough indicator of population trends.

A very different picture emerges when the sex ratios of larger areas are examined. Yonezawa *han* had a sex ratio of 1·5 for the late seventeenth century. There was a statistically significant downward trend, however, bringing this ratio to 1·06 by the mid-1830s.[27] Morioka *han*, also in the Tōhoku region, can also be taken as an example of an area in which considerable under-reporting of females must have taken place. There was an average of ninety-four observations for each of ten districts with the domain. At no time in any of the districts did the sex ratio fall below one, though there was a general negative trend.[28] Though Takahashi failed to make the point when he included these data in his three volume series, it seems conclusive to us that females were definitely under-reported, and by as much as 20 per cent. This bias in the figures tended to correct itself over time, but the sex ratio was still above one at the end of the observed period for every district, and we judged the statistics for the Morioka area too unreliable for use in further analysis.[29]

[27] The slope was −0·003; t-test = −11·28; n = 144.

[28] A typical sample would be the seventh district in which the sex ratio started from a base of 1·24 and had a negative slope of 0·0015; t-test = −9·33; n = 94.

[29] We judged the Morioka data unreliable not just on the basis of unnatural sex ratios, but also because of frequently observed discrepancies in the annual data—for example, increases or decreases in population of a magnitude and in a manner which cannot be explained by any known factors. We do not believe the imbalance in the sex ratio could have been caused by female infanticide. First, the earliest ratios are too unbalanced to reflect a normal population, and should the sex ratio have in fact been so unbalanced, subsequent ratios would be expected to be extremely abnormal. Second, infanticide would have been more prevalent in famine years, but the ratio steadily improves with no noticeable fluctuations even though some of the worst famines occurred towards the end of the Tokugawa period.

The other areas for which the sex ratio could be analysed over time all show ratios over one with statistically insignificant trends. In general, however, it can be concluded that smaller local and village units tend to have more reliable or believable sex ratios. The Tōhoku region in Northern Honshū shows by far the most inaccurate reporting as seen by sex ratios, but these tend to have a negative trend and approach one by the end of the Tokugawa period. If the national or regional statistics were compiled from the local, why does there exist such a difference in their reliability as seen by sex ratio? One answer might be that the villages for which data exist come from different regions than do the larger areas examined. Another answer might be that the mere fact that certain village records are extant gives them a bias towards being more accurate than would be an average of all the village statistics in Japan, were it possible to obtain them. This might result because a village headman and his descendants interested enough in village records to preserve the copies of the documents sent to the *han* administration over a number of generations, would also be the kind of headman interested in obtaining accurate records.

Despite the various ways in which data at all levels are under-stated or biased, we have made no attempt to correct these deficiencies or to adjust any of the figures to obtain a more accurate picture of the Tokugawa population. We have considered most of the data extremely rough in nature, and indicative only of general trends. Our present knowledge of the extent of underestimation for each set of figures is too limited to permit any adjustment of the figures.

ANALYSIS OF THE DATA AND FINDINGS

I RE-EXAMINATION OF THE SEKIYAMA DATA ON KUNI

Keeping the shortcomings of the Sekiyama data in mind, we calculated linear trend lines for each *kuni* (see Appendix B, Table 6, and footnote[30]) and annual average growth rates between the

[30] The linear trend lines in this article were calculated using the standard least squares method. The equation $Y = a + bX$ is the standard form in which Y is the dependant variable, a is the intercept, b is the regression coefficient or slope, and X is the independent variable. In the trend lines, t in year units replaces X as the independent variable. When $t = 0$, Y is obviously equal to a. Thus a is the calculated amount of Y at the base year. Throughout this article, Y is population, replaced here by the symbols TP which stand for total population. Therefore, b, the slope, indicates the calculated amount of change in population per year. The calculated and the actual population for both the slope and intercept are not necessarily identical unless R^2 (coefficient of determination) happens to be 1 or -1. R^2 can range between -1 to 1 and indicates 'the goodness of the fit' of the calculated trend line to the actual data. The standard error given to the coefficient (and written directly beneath it) indicates the degree of reliability of the regression coefficient.

years for which data are available (see Appendix B, Table 7). Of the 69 *kuni* for the period 1721–1872, the regression coefficients (slopes) of 53 *kuni* were significant at least at the 0·01 level; and of these 53, regression coefficients were significant at the 0·01 level for as many as 40 *kuni*. All but eight of the 53 significant slopes were positive, and there were only three negative slopes significant at the 0·01 level.[31] Map 1 shows the regional distribution of the signs of the slopes.

Examining the results presented in Appendix B, Tables 6 and 7, and Map 1, we have reached the following broad conclusions: Between 1721 and 1872, the population of Japan *as a whole* showed a distinct upward trend. The average annual growth rate for the entire period was ·16 per cent. Even if the periods affected by nation-wide famines and the 1846–72 years are deleted, the average annual growth rate is still slightly under ·20 per cent. This 0·16 per cent

Statistically, the magnitude of the t-test referred to in the article is obtained by dividing the regression coefficient by its standard error. The level of significance refers to the degree of statistical reliability. For example, a 0·01 level of significance simply means that the 'confidence coefficient' is 99 per cent—that is, chance of obtaining such high values for the t-test and R^2 had the original data been entirely random is only one out of a hundred. The above are very free descriptions of statistical terms. Those seeking fuller discussion of the statistical terms should see Taro Yamane, *Statistics: An Introductory Analysis* (New York, 1964), Chapter 12 on 'Time Series—Trend Line', pp. 330–49 or any other standard statistics text.

[31] These are the results for the trend lines calculated for the eleven observations from 1721–1872, in which the 1872 data were compiled by a different method of survey and included groups in the population excluded from the Tokugawa surveys. Table 1 includes the results of trend lines calculated both for the eleven observations and for the ten observations from 1721–1846. The coefficient of determination tends to improve by dropping the 1872 Meiji observation because of discontinuities in the data. For both positive and negative slopes, the absolute value of the slope is smaller without the eleventh observation because there was a significant increase in population in nearly all *kuni* after the Tempō famine and because of the inclusion in the Meiji data of previously non-enumerated population, such as samurai, *rōnin*, and unregistered commoners. Satsuma (no. 66 on Table 1), for example, had a slope almost twice as steep for the 1721–1872 data as for the 1721–1846 data, partly because of the large proportion of samurai in the population who went unenumerated until 1872, and possibly because of under reporting during the Tokugawa period. The slope of both trend lines, however, is positive and sig-nificant at the ·01 level.

For comparative purposes, the 1721–1872 data have been used in this article. First, these data are most comparable to the rice output data discussed later in the article, for which the final observation is also early Meiji. Second, it is not known how much of the increase between the 1846 and 1872 figures is due to an increase in the population and how much to the inclusion of groups formerly omitted from the surveys. Except for the qualifications made above, however, the differences observed in calculated trend lines are such that they do not materially affect our conclusions. It should be noted that eleven of the slopes changed signs, all from positive to negative, when the eleventh observation was dropped. Six of the results were statistically insignificant in both trend lines, four went from statistically insignificant to significant at the 0·05 level, and one became statistically significant at the 0·10 level when the eleventh observation was omitted. Since the slope for all these *kuni* are statistically insignificant when the 1872 data are included, no entry was made for them on Map 1.

growth rate was, however, the net result of the averaging of various regional differences in the pattern of growth. Excluding Ezo (Hokkaidō), which experienced steady in-migration, the annual average rate of growth for the entire period varied between -0.18 per cent and $+0.86$ per cent.

Table 1   Frequency of annual average *kuni* growth rates 1721–1872

Rate of growth (per cent)	Negative	0·00–0·10	0·11–0·20	0·21–0·30	0·31–0·40	Over 0·40
Frequency (no. of *kuni*)	10	12	18	15	7	7

The growth rates showed distinct regional patterns in that Western Japan (Kyūshū, Shikoku, and Western Honshū) and the Chūbu region gained steadily while the Tōhoku, Kantō, and Kinki regions either remained nearly constant or declined over time at uneven rates. The growth rates for the nation as a whole varied over the period, as is shown below in Table 2.

Table 2   Average annual growth rates for Japan by sub-period

Year	1721–50	1750–56	1756–86	1786–98	1798–1804	1804–22	1822–28	1828–36	1836–46	1846–72
Total growth rate	−0·02	0·10	−0·13	0·13	0·10	0·21	0·37	−0·03	−0·05	0·08

Another noteworthy finding is the pattern seen in a frequency table of *kuni* growth rates. The high number of negative growth rates for nearly every period shows that famine was affecting a fairly large section of the country during nearly every sub-period from 1721 to 1872, but a look at Appendix B, Table 7, will demonstrate that famine was affecting different parts of the country at different times. If one compares Table 3 with Table 2, one might conclude

Table 3   Frequencies of *kuni* growth rates (per cent) by rate-class and by sub-period

Period	Negative	0·00–0·10	0·11–0·20	0·21–0·30	0·31–0·40	0·41–0·50	Over 0·50
1721–50	36	6	10	8	3	0	6
1750–56	22	9	9	5	7	3	14
1756–86	38	13	8	2	1	3	4
1786–98	23	8	10	8	6	5	9
1798–1804	26	11	10	9	6	2	5
1804–22	8	7	12	14	13	2	13
1822–28	11	9	6	10	7	10	16
1828–34	26	9	7	7	7	7	6
1834–46	42	11	5	5	1	1	4
1846–72	3	1	2	9	5	6	43

that the Tempō famine was slightly more widespread over the country than was the Temmei famine, as evidenced by a larger number of negative and smaller growth rates in the 1834–46 period than in the 1756–98 period. The country as a whole, however, experienced its largest negative growth rate, – 0·13 per cent, during the 1756–86 period, when regional famines were common. The effects of the Kyōhō famine, which took place during the 1721–50 period, were also widespread. Since the final period is skewed by the inclusion of a greater proportion of the population in the survey in 1872 than in 1846, the only obvious period of steady population growth took place between 1804 and 1828, after the eighteenth century famines and just prior to the Tempō famine.

Despite a distinct but broad regional pattern and the dominant upward trend for the nation as a whole, the magnitudes of the growth rates clearly differed rather significanly by *kuni* and by sub-period during the century and a half covered by the data. And it is evident from the *kuni* data that the incidence of famine was high.

2 ANALYSIS OF THE REGIONAL DATA

We have also intensively examined the available regional and local data described earlier. Because of a lack of uniformity in the coverage, duration, and level of aggregation (ranging from a section of a large village called an *ōaza* to a *han*), we shall present only a broad outline of our findings in this paper.

Of the total of thirty-six areas for which we were able to gather time-series data for the total population, all but seven regions yielded statistically significant positive trend lines. Four of these seven were villages or sections of a village, two were *kōri* (districts, a section of a *kuni*), and one was Aizu *han*. When these seven areas were analysed more closely, it was seen that they were mostly enclaves of declining population within a growing region (the Ario section of Kamitado village, two districts in Tsushima, and two out of fourteen villages in the growing Owashi area of Kii province). Only Kamiizumi village in Shimotsuke province and Aizu *han* in Mutsu province were in the Kantō-Tōhoku regions (Eastern and Northeastern Honshū) in which population trends were negative during the Tokugawa period.

The values of the regression coefficients and the coefficients of determination for these areas generally followed the pattern of the province in which these areas were located, and we can, therefore, consider that these regional findings support the validity of the population trends observed for the *kuni* data.

The kuni (provinces) of Japan

1 Yamashiro
2 Yamato
3 Kawachi
4 Izumi
5 Settsu
6 Iga
7 Ise
8 Shima
9 Owari
10 Mikawa
11 Tōtomi
12 Suruga
13 Izu
14 Kai
15 Sagami
16 Musashi
17 Awa (1)
18 Kazusa
19 Shimo-osa
20 Hitachi
21 Omi
22 Mino
23 Hida
24 Shinano
25 Kōzuke
26 Shimotsuke
27 Tōhoku (kuni of Iwaki, Iwashiro, Rikuzen, Rikuchū, and Mutsu)
28 Uzen-Ugo
29 Wakasa
30 Echizen
31 Kaga
32 Noto
33 Etchū

34 Echigo
35 Sado
36 Tamba
37 Tango
38 Tajima
39 Inaba
40 Hōki
41 Izumo
42 Iwami
43 Oki
44 Harima
45 Mimasaka
46 Bizen
47 Bitchū
48 Bingo
49 Aki
50 Suō
51 Nagato
52 Kii
53 Awaji
54 Awa (2)
55 Sanuki
56 Iyo
57 Tosa
58 Chikuzen
59 Chikugo
60 Buzen
61 Bungo
62 Hizen
63 Higo
64 Hyūga

65 Osumi
66 Satsuma
67 Iki
68 Tsushima

The regions of Japan

Kinki — 1-5, 21, 36-38, 44, 52, 53
Tōkai — 6-15
Kantō — 15-20, 25, 26
Tōhoku — 27, 28
Tōsan — 14, 22-24
Hokuriku — 29-35
San'in — 39-43
San'yō — 45-51
Shikoku — 54-57
Kyūshū — 58-68

Note: Due to the lack of statistical reliability of the data on Ezo (Hokkaidō), this region was not included on the map

⊕ = Positive regression coefficient significant at the 0·01 level
+ = Positive   at the 0·05 level
⊖ = Negative   at the 0·01 level
– = Negative   at the 0·05 level

Map 1 Significant population trends by kuni, 1721–1872

A closer look at regional changes in terms of the rate of increase in the total population, however, shows that it is not possible to generalize the pattern of change over time. For example, for the eleven villages out of the fourteen examined in Kii, we were able to fit linear trend lines for four sub-periods because of the existence of nearly continuous data for almost a century (1775–1871). The results are shown in Table 4. The sub-period with the best fit was 1775–1837. All eleven villages and the total of the fourteen villages had positive slopes, all of which were significant at least at the 0·10 level. All of the slopes were also positive for the sub-period 1794–1871, and all but one were significant at the 5 per cent (one) or 1 per cent level (ten). These subdivisions were made in our attempt to discern significant differences in trends before and after known major famines, those of Temmei (1780s) and Tempō (1830s). Interestingly enough, the only negative slope seen in the total for this region was for the 1855–71 period, during which seven of the twelve trend lines calculated had negative slopes, though only three of these were significant at even the 0·05 level.

For the other villages in our sample where sufficiently long time-series data were available, we fitted second order polynomial trend equations.[32] If the often-generated Tokugawa population trend—that of a steady rise tapering off and stagnating in the 1720s—were to be observed, the signs of the coefficient should be $TP = a + bt - ct^2$.[33] But here the signs varied to yield all possible combinations except a $TP = a - bt + ct^2$ of any significance. A few of the better fitting examples are shown below:

1. Higashifunabori village (Musashi province)

$$TP = 630.85 + 7.12t - 0.057t \qquad R^2 = 0.814 \qquad n = 53$$
$$(0.973) \quad (0.014)$$

2. Gōmura (Rural area of Tsushima)

$$TP = 14778.33 + 1.664t + 1.876t^2 \qquad R^2 = 0.960 \qquad n = 35$$
$$(11.379) \quad (0.293)$$

3. Fuchū (Principal town of Tsushima)

$$TP = 13216.88 + 308.38t - 9.377t^2 \qquad R^2 = 0.762 \qquad n = 35$$
$$(40.804) \quad (1.046)$$

[32] We calculated other forms of equations, but these second-order polynomials best fitted the largest number of the samples.

[33] This form is known as a second-order polynomial; a non-linear form of the trend line discussed in Footnote 30. If the total population change rises at a decreasing rate to reach some set maximum asymptotically before some value of t, then the coefficient of t must be positive in sign and that of t^2 must be negative.

Table 4 Trend lines for Kii villages 1775–1871 and sub-periods

Village Trend		R²	n	Village Trend		R²	n
1 Haidaura				**2 Kukiura**			
I 259·84	−0·20t	(0·026)	84	I 499·66	1·17t	0·527**	78
II 215·82	1·56t	0·669**	57	II 466·39	2·45t	0·909**	53
III 274·52	−0·669t	0·410**	27	III 704·38	−1·5t	0·302**	25
IV 271·1	0·36t	0·114*	39	IV 496·63	1·78t	0·791**	35
V 230·50	−0·19t	(0·009)	14	V 748·79	−2·06t	(0·241)	13
3 Osoneura				**4 Mukaimura**			
I 145·88	0·003t	(0·000)	88	I 179·30	1·56t	0·912**	82
II 124·93	0·80t	0·797**	62	II 177·43	1·56t	0·819**	55
III 162·88	−0·35t	0·158*	26	III 238·85	0·79t	0·350**	27
IV 128·73	0·70t	0·719**	44	IV 139·28	2·40t	0·957**	37
V 145·49	0·92t	(0·098)	13	V 339·16	−0·35t	(0·020)	13
5 Yanohamamura				**6 Hayashiura**			
I 433·19	1·12t	0·506**	80	I 742·77	9·32t	0·186**	84
II 435·09	1·23t	0·580**	53	II 670·14	3·95t	0·918**	55
III 122·26	4·83t	0·880**	27	III 699·73	1·01t	0·144*	29
IV 394·82	2·09t	0·729**	35	IV 613·78	5·21t	0·962**	37
V 247·08	3·47t	0·646**	14	V 264·39	5·78t	0·519**	15
7 Minamiura				**8 Nôjimura**			
I 754·46	0·49t	(0·029)	86	I 370·61	2·18t	0·604**	79
II 651·59	4·54t	0·884**	56	II 314·79	4·56t	0·920**	54
III 960·21	−2·66t	0·256**	30	III 231·44	3·44t	0·762**	25
IV 612·59	5·38t	0·817**	38	IV 299·44	4·93t	0·882**	36
V 1,052·36	−3·87t	(0·228)	13	V 705·63	−1·79t	0·427*	31
9 Horikitaura				**10 Tenmaura**			
I 543·34	0·25t	(0·012)	86	I 136·25	0·26t	0·241**	82
II 465·93	3·56t	0·923**	55	II 124·03	0·76t	0·619**	56
III 322·56	2·45t	0·524**	31	III 141·76	0·12t	(0·021)	26
IV 435·96	4·25t	0·971**	37	IV 148·91	0·20t	(0·081)	38
V 795·12	−2·74t	0·681**	14	V 327·66	−1·95t	0·903**	14
11 Sugariura				**Total of 14 Villages**			
I 353·43	0·82t	0·491**	93	I 5,980·57	9·37t	0·274**	66
II 350·49	0·91t	0·593**	63	II 5,444·06	33·85t	0·979**	44
III 408·77	1·35t	(0·002)	30	III 5,867·91	6·76t	0·258*	22
IV 333·71	1·29t	0·619**	45	IV 5,362·90	35·75t	0·959**	26
V 193·97	2·52t	(0·056)	15	V 8,336·39	−2·07t	0·505**	11

For Yukunoura, Nakaiura, and Suijiura, trend lines were not calculated because of gaps in the data, but the total includes these villages also.

Note:
I refers to the years 1775–1871, the entire period for which we have data.
II refers to the years 1775–1837.
III refers to the period 1838–71. A break was made in 1837–38 to try to see if population behaved in discernibly different trends before and after the Tempō famine.
IV runs from 1794–1871.
V from 1855–71.

* The levels of significance for R² for the respective *n*'s are: ** for 0·01 and for 0·05.
For an explanation of terms relating to linear regression, see footnote 30.

We found, however that for some of the areas to which we fitted second order polynomial equations a linear regression had a better fit. These areas include Kōchi *han* (Tosa province), which had a positive slope of 697·4; t-test = 15·50; n = 123; Kando-shinden of Owari province, which had a positive slope of 3·16; t-test = 79·20; n = 89; and Yonezawa *han* of Uzen province, which showed a significant negative slope of − 136·65; t-test = − 10·17; n = 144.

Because of the diversity in time coverage and gaps in the data, it is difficult to give annual average growth rates for these areas in any concise fashion. From the annual average growth rates calculated when the data were fairly complete, we can generally say that the rate of population growth followed the national pattern over time with wider amplitude, but that the annual rate of growth was well under a ceiling of 1 per cent when areas were on an upward trend. While on a downward trend, barring famine years during which losses of approximately 10 per cent were frequently sustained, the rate was at a maximum of minus 1 per cent per annum.[34]

Another general observation that can be made for the regional samples because of the availability of data for a sufficient number of villages is that the number of persons per household declined during the period covered by our data. With the two exceptions of Kando-*shinden* in Owari province and Funabori village in Musashi province, the calculated ratios of total population over the total number of households showed the pattern represented in the following examples:

1. Yokoya, of Kamitado village (Mino province)

   $TP/H = 7\cdot33 - 0\cdot023t$ $R^2 = 0\cdot418$ $n = 27$ (1697–1813)

2. Fukiage village (Bizen province)

   $TP/H = 5.94 - 0\cdot016t$ $R^2 = 0\cdot871$ $n = 24$ (1693–1854)

The actual observations of TP/H ranged from 9·0 in Yokoya (Example 1 above) in 1704 to around 3·8 in Kōmi village of Mino province in the late-eighteenth century and during the 1840s.

Data on the birth rate (B/TP) and on the death rate (D/TP) is extremely limited. From the data available we calculated rates of birth and death which we have summarized in the following tables. There was no significant trend in either the pattern of births or deaths, and thus we have given this information in the form of frequency tables. (See Table 5.) There is a significant difference

[34] These observations exclude those cases in which the population growth rates were obviously influenced by known in-migration—the case of Sado Island— or instances of declines in population during famine years.

Table 5 Frequency of birth and death rates for four villages (per mille)

Range in per mille	Birth No. of years in which the rate was within the range	Death No. of years in which the rate was within the range
(a) Imafuku village (Kai province) 1816–75 (n = 40)		
0–10°/$_{oo}$	1	3
11–20	5	11
21–30	13	14
31–40	16	7
41–50	4	3
51–60	1	1
Over 60	0	2
(b) The three areas of Tsushima 1701–12 (n = 36)		
0–10	4	0
11–20	14	5
21–30	18	17
31–40	0	11
41–50	0	3
(c) Kōmi village (Mino province) 1674–1819 (n = 67D, 68B)		
0–10	7	9
11–20	34	26
21–30	20	23
31–40	4	3
41–50	2	3
51–60	1	0
Over 60	0	3
(d) Yokouchi village (Shinano province) 1671–1867 (n = 140D, 141B)		
0–10	6	10
11–20	32	60
21–30	46	45
31–40	28	15
41–50	23	9
51–60	4	1

in the mode of birth and death rates. The mode for both rates was the same for Tsushima taken as a whole, where differences in the birth and death rates for the decreasing and increasing areas would be balanced out, and for Kōmi village of Mino province for which the population showed no definite trend. The mode for birth rates was higher than that for death rates in Yokouchi village of Shinano province, and it was slightly higher for Imafuku village of Kai province. It can be seen that the pattern of birth and deaths in general followed the same pattern seen in Europe in the pre-industrial period, one of both high fertility and high mortality.

POPULATION AND ECONOMIC GROWTH

What was the relationship between the patterns of change in population and economic growth during the Tokugawa period? We believe that total output was growing at a faster rate than that of population and, thus, that the average standard of living was rising during the Tokugawa period. Moreover the growth of population in a region seems to have been highly correlated with the growth of the economy of that region. Thus, we argue, *a fortiori*, that the low rate of population increase during the Tokugawa period, especially after the beginning of the eighteenth century, was not the result of the Japanese economy being trapped in a low-level equilibrium, but occurred because, as in England, the pre-industrial natural growth rate of population was low.

Many Japanese economic historians begin their examination of the Tokugawa economy by citing the 18·5 million *koku* estimate of the total grain output (in rice equivalent) for the early seventeenth century. This figure, however, is based on untested assumptions and subjective estimates and is no more useful than the numerous 'guesstimates' for total national grain output (in rice equivalent) advanced by some Japanese economic historians on the basis of their limited regional case studies.[35] For our purposes, the data which we deemed sufficiently reliable for analysis are the existing results of three national surveys out of the six conducted by the Bakufu. These three were for the years 1645, 1697, and 1829.[36] To be sure, the surveys were products of counter-pressures between the peasants' efforts to under-report and the official attempts to increase the tax base. But these surveys were known to have been conducted in such a way as to take account of increases in arable land and in productivity as well as to correct previous under-reporting of various kinds and adjust for changes in the standard measures of land.[37]

[35] Kikuchi Toshio, *Shinden kaihatsu* (Tokyo, 1964), pp. 2–3. See also Takayanagi Mitsutoshi, *Toyotomi Hideyoshi no kenchi*, Iwanami Kōza Nihon Rekishi XVII, No. 6 (Tokyo, 1934), and Miyakawa Mitsuru, *Taikō kenchi ron* (Tokyo, 1957). The Taikō Kenchi (Hideyoshi's cadastral survey), conducted between 1582 and 1598, measured the amount of arable land; however, we do not know much about the productivity of the land; no known records of total output exist.

[36] Kikuchi Toshio, *Shinden kaihatsu* (Tokyo, 1958), Vol. 1 of 2 vols., p. 137.

[37] Though Bakufu officials compiled the rice output figures, the village headmen made the necessary adjustments in the area of land under cultivation and reported the figures to the *han* and Bakufu officials when changes were made in the standard measures of land in the Jōkyō era (1684–88). The defined area of the *tan* was 10·25 per cent greater in the 1645 survey than in the 1697 survey, but adjustments were made so that the rice output surveys are comparable. See Kikuchi Toshio, *Shinden kaihatsu*, Vol. 1, pp. 208–9 for detailed information on adjustments made and James I. Nakamura, *Agricultural Production and the Economic Development of Japan, 1873–1922* (Princeton, 1966), p. 75, for changes in the land measure.

Changes in yield per *tan* were adjusted by re-classifying paddy and upland fields based on locally adjusted schedules of yields.[38] Appendix B, Table 8 provides the results of these three surveys[39] and the 1873 survey made by the Meiji government[40] along with growth rates computed for each of the periods between surveys and for the entire period, 1645–1873. Certainly, a great deal of caution must be taken in using these figures as estimates, because it is, for example, unthinkable that the rice output for Satsuma remained precisely the same between 1697 and 1829. If anything, the official figures are understated.

The major reason for the increases in the total output of rice and other grains seen in Table 8 of Appendix B was probably the increase in land under cultivation during the Tokugawa period. Reliable aggregate data cannot be obtained from the large body of literature on this subject, but there is sufficient evidence to show that the period can be characterized by continuous land reclamation, irrigation projects, and the conversion of marsh and forest land into arable. Approximately seventy articles examining the creation of *shinden* literally, 'new fields' give detailed descriptions of the changes brought about to the Tokugawa village economy by *shinden*.[41]

Though the all-important information on the size of each *shinden* is lacking, we have fairly reliable data on the number of *shinden* created during the sub-periods of the Tokugawa rule. Compared to twenty-eight *shinden* known to have been created from 1551–1600, the number of *shinden* created during the first fifty years of the Tokugawa regime (1600–1650) jumped to 243, a number made possible because Japan was completely at peace for the first time in several hundred years. The creation of *shinden*, encouraged by the Bakufu, reached a peak during the 1651–1700 period when the number totalled 434. The amount of reclamation carried on during the eighteenth century fell sharply, probably because all of the land readily and economically reclaimable under existing technology had been reclaimed. The first half of the century recorded 182 *shinden* and the last half 142. But during the last sixty-eight years of the Tokugawa period (1801–68), the number of *shinden* created rose

---

[38] For a detailed discussion on these points, see Kikuchi, *Shinden kaihatsu* (1964), p. 125–48.

[39] The Tokugawa survey data was obtained from Kikuchi, *Shinden kaihatsu*, Vol. 1, p. 137.

[40] The Meiji data was obtained from Meiji Zaiseishi Hensankai, *Meiji zaiseishi* (Tokyo, 1905), Vol. 5, pp. 361–78.

[41] In addition to what is cited in the Kikuchi volumes, the major works are: Furushima Toshio, *Nihon nōgyō gijitsushi* (Tokyo, 1949); Matsuyoshi Sadao, *Shinden no kenkyū* (Tokyo, (1926); Kimura Motoi *Kinsei no shinden mura* (Tokyo, 1964); and Nōrinshō Nōmukyoku, *Kyūhan jidai no kōchi kakuchō kairyo jigyō ni kansuru chōsa* (Tokyo, 1927). The articles written on this subject are widely contributed by historians, geographers, and economists.

to 788 because of technological development and the Bakufu's near desperate efforts to increase its tax base.[42]

The types and sizes of *shinden* varied widely by period and by region. The *shinden* created during the nineteenth century were undoubtedly smaller in size and less productive than the earlier ones, Also, the *shinden* in the Kyūshu, Chūgoku, and Shikoku areas were more numerous and tended to be larger in size than those found in the Tōhoku or Kantō regions.[43]

The following comparison may be useful for gaining some impression of the total magnitude of the arable area added by *shinden*, provided that we are aware of the weaknesses contained in the estimations. The 1873 survey put the total arable land at 4,126,771 *chō* of paddy and upland fields. If we compare this figure with the oft-cited estimate of about 2·06 million *chō* for the beginning of the Tokugawa period, we can conclude that the amount of land reclaimed during the Tokugawa period doubled the size of the total arable area.[44] As reclamations increased, the productivity of the new fields tended to be lower. The increase in acreage under cultivation does indicate, however, an increased economic base on which an increase in population could have been supported.

It is even more difficult to obtain reliable measures of increases in agricultural productivity than of gains in the cultivated area. (Witness the controversy on the Meiji period!) Since it is not possible to estimate with any degree of confidence the rate of increase in productivity on an aggregate level, let us describe a few categories of evidence to show that agricultural productivity was definitely rising during the Tokugawa period. A fuller discussion of this topic can easily fill a lengthy volume; thus, what is here described is to be taken only as a capsule version of the evidence available.

First, many recent case studies contain direct reports of increases in agricultural productivity. Studies on the village level are most numerous, followed by household studies, and then by studies on the *kori* or district level. This work, most frequently done by historians, does not satisfy the needs of the economist, but the conclusion to be drawn is unmistakably that of a rising agricultural productivity. A few examples may be useful. Naitō Jirō, after a detailed study on the basis of families in Numa village in Bizen province, noted that the productivity of the peasants there rose remarkably from 1780 to the beginning of the nineteenth century. In addition, this village

---

[42] Kimura, *Kinsei no shinden mura*, pp. 5–6, and the sources cited in footnote 41.

[43] For details, see Vol. 2 of Doboku Gakkai (ed.), *Meiji izen Nihon dobokushi* (Tokyo, 1936). Numerous works on the subject referred to earlier in the text are also useful. See footnote 41.

[44] Kimura, *Kinsei no shinden mura*, p. 6, and the sources cited in footnote 41.

QP

had an increasing amount of income from subsidiary crops as well.[45]

Takeyasu found in his intensive study of the records of a peasant family in Kawachi province that the output per male labour increased by 27 per cent in the period between 1822–3 and 1865–7.[46] We should also recall in this connection Thomas C. Smith's findings based on Kaga *han* and eleven villages scattered around Japan. He concluded that 'the productivity of land was generally rising', and he has careful analysis that supports this statement.[47]

Second, one can gather an impressive amount of more recent evidence on the increasing use of fertilizers of various kinds, on the evolution of agricultural tools and the regional dissemination of them, and on the increasing use of better seed rice over the period.[48]

Confining ourselves here to the output of rice and other grains, the most important element in the Japanese diet of the period, let us compare the rate of growth in the grain output and that of population. Table 8, Appendix B presents average annual growth rates in the grain output between 1645 and 1873 by sub-periods and for the entire period. When we compare Table 8 with Table 7 (both in Appendix B) on population, we obtain the results seen on Map 2. When the annual average growth rate of rice for a *kuni* for the 1645–1873 period exceeded that of population by at least 0·1 per cent, that *kuni* is marked ⊕ on the map, and if by less than 0·1 per cent by +. The signs ⊖ and — conversely indicate those cases in which the rate of population growth exceeded that of rice. In several cases, when the growth rates of rice and population were identical or virtually so (the difference either way being less than 0·5 per cent), the *kuni* was marked ⊙.

What this map reveals is significant. The regions of Kantō, northern Tōhoku, and the environs of Osaka, Kyoto, and Nagoya, which showed population trends ranging from statistically insignificant and positive to statistically significant and negative on Map 1, are the very regions showing positive signs on Map 2. The reverse holds true in that those regions in Western Japan, and the region sandwiched between Nagoya and Edo show negative signs, indicating that the rate of increase in the rice yield was falling behind that of population growth.

These results are puzzling at first glance, especially to those familiar with Japanese literature which reiterates the relative poverty of the northern Kantō regions and the relative prosperity of Western Japan.

---

[45] Naitō Jirō *Honbyakushō no kenkyū* (Tokyo, 1968), p. 167.

[46] Takeyasu Shigeji, *Kinsei Kinai nōgyō no kōzo* (Tokyo 1969), p. 197–203.

[47] Smith, 'The Land Tax in the Tokugawa Period', p. 293.

[48] The most comprehensive studies were made by Furushima Toshio in his *Kinsei Nihon nōgyō no kōzō* (Tokyo, 1967), 3d ed., pp. 205–77, and in his book cited in footnote 36.

The kuni (provinces) of Japan

1 Yamashiro	34 Echigo	65 Osumi
2 Yamato	35 Sado	66 Satsuma
3 Kawachi	36 Tamba	67 Iki
4 Izumi	37 Tango	68 Tsushima
5 Settsu	38 Tajima	
6 Iga	39 Inaba	*The regions of Japan*
7 Ise	40 Hōki	Kinki – 1-5, 21, 36-38, 44,
8 Shima	41 Izumo	52, 53
9 Owari	42 Iwami	Tōkai – 6-15
10 Mikawa	43 Oki	Kantō – 15-20, 25, 26
11 Tōtomi	44 Harima	Tōhoku – 27, 28
12 Suruga	45 Mimasaka	Tōsan – 14, 22-24
13 Izu	46 Bizen	Hokuriku – 29-35
14 Kai	47 Bitchū	San' in – 39-43
15 Sagami	48 Bingo	San'yō – 45-51
16 Musashi	49 Aki	Chikoku – 54-57
17 Awa (1)	50 Suō	Kyūshū – 58-68
18 Kazusa	51 Nagato	
19 Shimo-osa	52 Kii	
20 Hitachi	53 Awaji	
21 Omi	54 Awa (2)	
22 Mino	55 Sanuki	
23 Hida	56 Iyo	
24 Shinano	57 Tosa	
25 Kōzuke	58 Chikuzen	
26 Shimotsuke	59 Chikugo	
27 Tōhoku (*kuni* of Iwaki,	60 Buzen	
Iwashiro, Rikuzen,	61 Bungo	
Rikuchū, and Mutsu)	62 Hizen	
28 Uzen-Ugo	63 Higo	
29 Wakasa	64 Hyūga	
30 Echizen		
31 Kaga		
32 Noto		
33 Etchū		

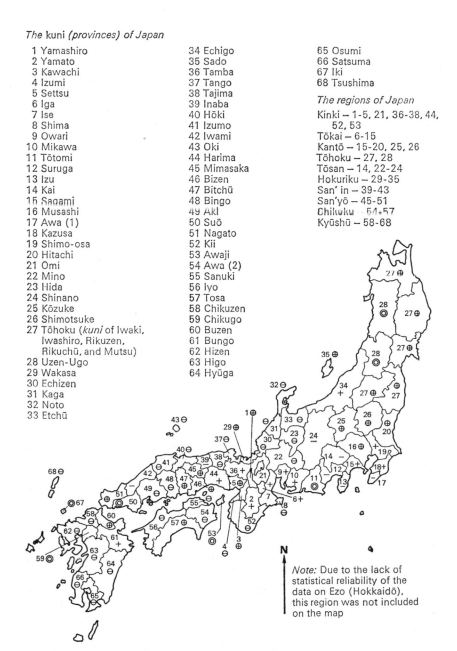

N

Note: Due to the lack of statistical reliability of the data on Ezo (Hokkaidō), this region was not included on the map

⊕ = Growth rates of rice output exceed those for population by at least 0·1%
+ = Growth rates of rice output exceed those for population by 0·05–0·1%
◎ = Virtually identical rates, differing less than 0·05%
⊖ = Growth rates of population exceed those for rice output by at least 0·1%
– = Growth rates of population exceed those for rice output by 0·05–0·1%

Map 2 A comparison of signs and relative magnitudes of annual average growth rates of rice output (1645–1873) and population (1721–1872)

We believe that the following diagrams will explain the puzzling contrast in the patterns of the growth rates of rice and population between Western Japan and North-eastern Japan.[49]

We hypothesize that what happened in Tōhoku and its adjacent *kuni* was schematically as shown in Figure 1, and what happened in Western Japan, in Figure 2. In North-eastern Japan, the growth

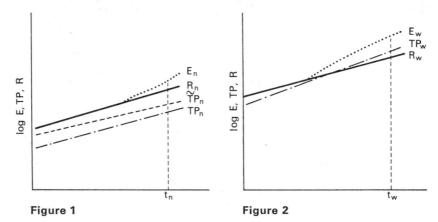

Figure 1   **Figure 2**

rates of grain output (r_n) were larger than the population growth rates (p_n). But as we have seen from the Morioka and Yonezawa examples of sex ratios, the population in North-eastern Japan was considerably understated. Allowing for this we have added $\widetilde{TP}_n$ for the adjusted population growth rate, $\tilde{p}_n$. However, $p_n < r_n$, as is shown in Appendix B, Tables 7 and 8, and the difference between p_n and $\tilde{p}_n$ tends to diminish over time as indicated by the significant negative regression coefficients for the trend lines fitted to the Morioka and Yonezawa sex ratios. E_n indicates the economic activity—that is, manufacturing and commercial activities which increased the total income and, thus, per-capita income of the region, and this is added to the total output of rice, R_n. As is well established, E_n increased from the mid-Tokugawa period.[50]

On the other hand, in Figure 2, $r_w < p_w$, as is shown in Appendix B, Tables 7 and 8 and as can be seen most vividly on Map 2. Due to the relative reliability of the village and other regional data

[49] For a discussion of city population, see footnote 26.

[50] For evidence on the increasing commercial, manufacturing, and market-oriented agricultural activities during the Tokugawa period, see the following sources which were used as our bases in evaluating the significance of E and the patterns of economic growth in the North and West: Toyota Takeshi and Kodama Kōta (eds.), *Ryūtsū-shi* (Tokyo, 1969); Hayashi Reiko, *Edo tonya nakama no kenkyū* (Tokyo, 1967); Honjō Eijirō (ed.), *Kinsei no Osaka* (Osaka, 1959); and several other recent books in Japanese and numerous articles which are readily available. In English, E. Sydney Crawcour's 'Changes in Japanese Commerce in the Tokugawa Period', in Hall and Jansen (eds.), *Studies in the Institutional History of Early Modern Japan*, pp. 189–202 is useful.

examined from Western Japan, we feel that it is not necessary to adjust p_w upward for the comparison at hand. However, note that the slope of E_w is steeper than that of E_n and rises earlier in time.

A comparison of the diagrams as drawn show that, as on Map 2, $r_w < p_w$ but that $r_n > \tilde{p}_n$, but because of the differences in the rates of increase and the levels of the contributions made by E_w and E_n the per-capita income of the north east (E_n divided by $\widetilde{TP}_n$ at t_n) is smaller than E_w divided by TP_w at t_w. The distance between TP_n and $\widetilde{TP}_n$ may vary by location in the north east, but the diagram is drawn to show that the per-capita income in the north east was always lower than in the west.

The preceding hypothesis implies that in neither of these two regions of Japan were population limits reached, and that the poverty of North-eastern Japan was only relative to the prosperity of Western Japan. Moreover, in Western Japan, E_w grew more quickly than TP_w to assure a rise in per-capita income in spite of $r_w < p_w$. We need not argue that the living standard in Tōhoku and adjacent *kuni* necessarily rose, but only that it was most likely that the per-capita output of rice remained relatively constant or slightly larger while E_n increased over time.

The importance of E can perhaps be seen in the fact that Spears man's rank correlation coefficients calculated between growth-rate of rice and population were not high. The coefficients were 0·208 for rice (1697–1829) and population (1721–1828) and 0·226 for rice (1829–73) and population (1828–72). When we calculated the coefficient for the entire period, for rice (1697–1873) and for population (1721–1872), we obtained a higher coefficient, 0·408, which one would expect in an agricultural economy in the long run. The magnitude of the coefficient is sufficiently low, however, to indicate the relative importance of other crops and other economic activities.

To buttress the above hypotheses, including the argument that Japan was not in a low-level equilibrium in the Tokugawa period, it is essential to show that economic activities besides rice culture were increasing over time and increasing more in Western Japan than in the Tōhoku region. There is plenty of evidence to show that a 'surplus' was generated in the Tokugawa economy by the increasing agricultural productivity, and especially by the increasing commercial and manufacturing activities, and that Western Japan enjoyed a more rapid rate of increase in such activities than North-eastern Japan. We need cite here only some of the more important evidence since an impressive amount has been made available by the post-war efforts of Japanese economic historians. This includes the following points:

1. All commercial activities developed at an accelerated pace from the Genroku period (1688–1704). Osaka was at the centre of these activities until the mid-eighteenth century when commercial activity became more widely distributed over the country with the rise of the *zaikata* (rural) merchants. Much of this activity was concerned with the flow of goods and foodstuffs from all parts of the nation into Edo, the administrative capital, and a metropolis with a population in the neighbourhood of a million.[51]

2. The output from the manufacturing of rapeseed oil, *sake*, pottery, cotton cloth, silk, fertilizer (fish cakes), the mining of various kinds of minerals, and the production of various other goods rose steadily. The regional distribution of these activities increasingly favoured the west.[52]

3. In the agricultural sector, too, winter crops expanded in wheat, cotton, and marketable vegetables. New crops were cultivated on a large scale, one of the most notable of which is the sweet potato famous in Kyūshū. It was impossible to carry out winter cropping in Eastern and Northern Japan because of the climate.[53]

4. The costly reclamation of land into *shinden* carried out by merchant capital (rather than by government funds, as had been more prevalent in the seventeenth century) increased after the beginning of the eighteenth century and was concentrated in the West. Most *shinden* were tax exempt, at least for a considerable length of time after they had been developed, with the consequence of raising the income of merchants and peasants.[54]

5. Complaints of people migrating to the cities, a labour shortage in villages, and accounts of uncultivated land combined with a rise in city consumption indicate a 'slack' in the economy. From various well-documented evidence we know that a labour shortage developed in the agricultural areas, especially in Western Japan. The marginal productivity of agricultural labour was not only positive, but this evidence indicated also that income which could be earned outside agriculture was higher.[55]

6. There was an increasing amount of regional specialization in the economy, with a much greater concentration of commercial crops and area specialities emerging in the west. Sugar, pottery, tallow wax, flint, and straw matting were widely produced in Kyūshū, paper, salt, lumber, and cotton in Shikoku, while paper, indigo,

[51] See in addition to the works cited in footnote 50, Kodama Kōta (ed.), *Sangyōshi* (Tokyo, 1967), Vol. 2.
[52] Many works support this point; the best and most comprehensive is Furushima Toshio, *Kindai Nihon nōgyō no tenkai* (Tokyo, 1968), especially pp. 153–442.
[53] Furushima Toshio, *op. cit.*   [54] See footnote 41.
[55] Though there are numerous Japanese sources which can be referred to, T. C. Smith's article cited in footnote 5 makes this point well. See especially pp. 289–90.

carrots, silver, and iron were among the major products marketed in Western Honshū. Kansai was famous for mandarin oranges, cotton and leather products, umbrellas, fish fertilizers and oil, and masonry products. Special goods were far fewer in the Tōhoku region where rice was listed as the major item produced there, though Kōfu grew grapes and Toyama was noted for its medicine. Yonezawa *han* in the North suffered an economic recession when some of the *kuni* in the Chūgoku region in Western Honshū developed in the eighteenth century a kind of wax superior to that formerly produced on a wide scale in Yonezawa.[56]

7. The average number of persons per household was steadily falling throughout most of Japan, as has been observed. The ability to set up branch families and permit younger brothers to marry or to send younger sons away from home to earn their living in economic activities outside agriculture indicates an increase in both accumulated capital and in economic opportunities.

8. There is strong evidence for the argument that the over-all standard of living of the Japanese was rising in the Tokugawa period, despite the increasing relative impoverishment of the samurai who lived on a relatively fixed real income throughout the Tokugawa period. First, it is highly likely that the larger share of increases in productivity were accrued to the peasant cultivators, certainly according to the studies of T. C. Smith on Kaga *han* and on scattered villages throughout central Japan.[57] This would, in turn, account for the failure of the tax base to rise sufficiently to meet the needs of the Bakufu and the *daimyō*, though it is unknown why authorities allowed this phenomenon to occur.

There is also concrete evidence to prove that the demand for an increasing number of products was rising not only in the cities, but in many rural areas as well. By the nineteenth century, numerous items were *sold* in the rural villages of Okayama—for example, for the everyday household use of the peasants—that were not on the market a hundred years earlier.[58] Ogyū Sorai (1666–1728) commented on the rise in the rural standard of living, saying that the peasants in the eighteenth century now used straw matting on the floor, mosquito nets, and paper room dividers, drank good *sake*, and bought clothes.[59]

9. The steady development of bank-like institutions, led by the 'Big Ten' money-exchangers (*jūnin ryōgaeya*) of Osaka, and of several

[56] See Kodama, *Sangyōshi, passim.*, and Kodama and Toyoda, (eds.), *Ryūtsūshi*, pp. 123–76.
[57] See Smith's article cited in footnote 5.
[58] E. Sydney Crawcour, 'The Tokugawa Heritage', p. 41. (See footnote 5.)
[59] J. R. McEwan, *The Political Writings of Ogyū Sorai.* (Cambridge, 1962), p. 44.

credit instruments during the Tokugawa period testifies to continuous increases in commercial and manufacturing activities. Were it not for the rapidly increasing volume of the Edo–Osaka trade and for the expanded transactions between local producers and merchants in cities and towns, especially after the mid-eighteenth century, there would have been little need for these surprisingly advanced methods of exchange bills, speculations in fluctuating gold-silver bills, and elaborate mechanisms for credit creations practised among city merchants.[60] Or, to put it differently, these were signs of an expanding economy which enjoyed a level of existence considerably above that which one associates with the subsistence existence.

The preceding evidence was presented to illustrate the contrasting patterns of change in population and economic activities in Western Japan vis-à-vis North-eastern Japan and the advanced level of economic activity reached by the country as a whole by the last century of the Tokugawa period. One might well ask then why Japan's population did not increase any faster than it did. First, Japan's rates of natural increase are comparable to those for Europe and other nations, before the present century, where the general pattern was one of high birth and death rates which tended to cancel each other out, leaving only a small margin of increase. Second, Japan did seem to be practising various forms of population control. Unfortunately we cannot now ascertain exactly what effect the practice of abortion and infanticide, so widely quoted in Japanese literature,[61] had on the rate of increase. These practices form a convenient handle for explaining the superficially stable population of the late Tokugawa period. When examples of the prohibition of these practices and other forms of documentation are analysed, however, one sees that the examples come primarily from the Tōhoku region and the larger cities, particularly Edo and Osaka, and that they are clustered in time around the years of the Temmei and Tempō famines.[62] It must also be remembered that the entire second half of the eighteenth century was characterized by widespread natural disasters. It is not difficult to understand why persons tried to prevent the birth of additional children in the years and the places that famines struck.

To what extent these methods of population control were practised in normal times and in areas other than Tōhoku and the larger metropolises is open to some conjecture. While it was widely reported that families tried to limit the number of children born to them to

[60] A reliable standard description of the institutional development of the Tokugawa monetary system can be found in Sakudō Yōtarō *Nihon kahei kinyūshi no kenkyū* (Tokyo, 1961).

[61] See footnote 6 for a few of these works.

[62] See the Takahashi and Honjō works cited in footnote 6. It is well known that Takahashi's interest in these problems began with his study of Tōhoku.

three, either in an effort to increase their standard of living or out of social shame,[63] these reports are not easily substantiated. Mean family size was around five, but there was much greater variation in family size during the Tokugawa period than exists in modern Japan. Also, decreases in family size frequently meant a decrease in non-nuclear family members rather than in the number of children.[64]

If we examine the statistics of the villages which have been analysed to date, we find wide variation in the average number of children born to each woman. In Kando-*shinden* the average number of children born to females who lived with their first husband from marriage until at least age forty-five was above six, and more women in this classification had between six and eight children than any other number. Since the average birth interval was approximately three years, no matter what the area studied and regardless of the order of the birth, six to eight reported births does not indicate much practice of infanticide or abortion.[65]

In Yokouchi village of Shinano province, however, the fertility pattern changed over time. During the seventeenth and most of the eighteenth centuries, the pattern followed that described above, and variations were largely due to differences in age at marriage. But the birth rate dropped after 1776, and from then on women averaged between 3·3 and 3·6 births whenever they married. Hayami attributes this change to the use of birth control measures,[66] but the most apparent birth control measure in Yokouchi was the long-term absence of many of the men who left to work elsewhere in the late Tokugawa period.

How typical the pattern of Yokouchi was is not known. Kando-*shinden* showed a rise in fertility during the Tokugawa period.[67] On the other hand, in Fujito village of Bizen province, the average number of children born to each woman remained nearly constant over the ninety-year period 1775–1863. Fujito women averaged 3·5 children during this period, with almost no variation between cohort groups. The women of Fujito tended to have children during a limited period, with very few births occurring before age twenty and most childbearing completed by age thirty-seven or thirty-eight.[68]

[63] Tsuge Takeshi, "Nōson mondai no ichi to shite no mabiki ni tsuite,' *Keizaishi Kenkyū*, Vol. 2, No. 50, p. 20.

[64] See Hayami's articles, especially 'Shūmon-aratame-chō o tsūjite mita Shinshū Yokouchi mura no chōki jinkō tōkei', Management Labour Studies Series No. 202, Keiō University, p. 98. The shūmon-aratame-chō of Okayama also confirm this point.

[65] Hayami Akira, 'The Demographic Analysis of a Village in Tokugawa Japan: Kando-shinden of Owari Province, 1778–1871', *Keiō Economic Studies*, Vol. 5 (1968), p. 73.

[66] See Hayami's article cited in footnote 64, pp. 102–3.

[67] Hayami, 'Demographic Analysis', p. 78.

[68] These findings are based on data gathered from the *shūmon-aratame-chō* of Fujito village in Okayama located in the Okayama University Library, Okayama.

We can tentatively conclude from the birth rates presented earlier and from the limited amount of data resulting from family reconstitution studies that while some measures of birth control were being used, these measures cannot be considered the only reason or even the most important reason for the low rate of natural increase in population during the latter half of the Tokugawa period. And the number of villages analysed to date is so small that we cannot yet generalize as to childbearing patterns in Tokugawa Japan.

Other checks to population growth hitherto unmentioned in most Japanese writings might best be included in a category labelled social controls. Social control can be defined as the behaviour of a society as a whole which acts to limit population growth. Included in this category are limiting the number of nuclear families per household to one, limiting the number of households within the village, and sending younger sons out to work instead of permitting them to marry and set up a junior branch of the family. These measures effectively limited the number of persons who married and bore children in Tokugawa Japan.

Also included in forms of social control practised in Tokugawa Japan were the postponing of the average age of females at first marriage to reduce the number of years during which they would be exposed to the risk of childbearing and the limiting of opportunities for the remarriage of widows. Women in Tokugawa Japan did not marry in their early or mid-teens as they did in many traditional societies, such as Rome or even modern India. The average age of marriage for females in Kando-*shinden* was twenty-two.[69] Even though marriages were often or usually not registered until the wife became pregnant, the average age of marriage is still well above twenty. The age of marriage rose in Yokouchi village from seventeen in 1701–25, to nineteen in 1751–75, and then to twenty-two from 1851–71.[70] Marriages of women in their late-twenties were not uncommon in Fujito village in Bizen province in the late-eighteenth and early nineteenth centuries, and, in fact, were far more common than the marriage of teenage girls.[71] Women who were widowed or divorced in the Tokugawa period most frequently did not remarry.[72] These phenomena all worked to create a lower rate of natural increase in population.

From the results of the few village studies made to date and from the qualitative evidence, it can be safely concluded that famines were

[69] Hayami, 'Demographic Analysis', p. 74.
[70] See page 96 of the Hayami article cited in Footnote 64.
[71] See the *shūmon-aratame-chō* of Fujito village.
[72] Hayami, 'Demographic Analysis', p. 77.

probably the most important factor in restricting population growth and, in fact, may have been the primary cause of most of the abortion and infanticide that took place. The three famines of a nation-wide scale were the Kyōhō famine of the 1720s through the mid-1730s (though large areas of the country remained unaffected), the Temmei famine from 1783–7, and the Tempō famine in the 1830s. The period under study here coincidentally follows this century of famine, and it must be emphasized that in this century the Japanese suffered from wide-scale and extreme climatic disturbances, ranging from drought, flooding, and volcanic eruptions, to cold summers (disastrous for Tōhoku) and continued rain in usually dry months.[73]

The Meiji government compiled reports on the Tempō famine. One area for which there exists detailed information is Okayama *han* for 1836.[74] Rain was continuous from January, the usual dry season in Japan. The wheat yield in Kojima was 6 per cent of normal. May was unseasonably cold; the peasants had to wear heavy padded winter clothing to keep warm while transplanting the rice seedlings. Floods, storms, and intense cold continued through June, and the autumn mushrooms appeared. Both rice and wheat developed quickly and then rotted in the field. Yields were 10 to 20 per cent of normal.

Bad harvests had been the pattern since 1833, but 1836 was the first year in which mass deaths occurred in Okayama. The peasants took to the mountains and dug up roots; they ate anything edible. The bodies of the starving swelled up, acute diarrhoea was common. The *han* government forbade the selling or transportation of foodstuffs outside the *han*, and it began to dole out small portions of rice gruel to the starving at night so that those not accustomed to charity could hide their shame in the dark.

Okayama recovered from this famine within ten years, but other areas and other peoples in previous famines suffered far more and far longer. Reports of cannibalism in the Tōhoku region during the Temmei famine of the 1780s are unsubstantiated, but too numerous in contemporary documents to be ignored. Mothers killed their infants because they were not able to nurse them. Following on

---

[73] Arakawa Hidetoshi, *Kikin no rekishi* (Tokyo, 1967). See especially pp. 37–41. Arakawa concluded on the basis of data for 1902–40 that a lowering of the mean July and August temperature for the Tōhoku region by 4° C. would reduce the per *tan* yield by 0·8 *koku*, meaning about a 50 per cent reduction in yield. Evidence presented in Arakawa's *Kinsei kishō saigaishi* (Tokyo, 1963) indicates that the mean temperature of these months in both the Temmei and Tempō famines was reduced by even more than 4° C.

[74] This description was taken from the *Tempō nendo kikin jōkyō torishirabesho*, compiled by the Okayama District Administration in 1888. A copy of this document is now in the Kurashiki Municipal Library, Kurashiki, Okayama.

famines were epidemics of typhoid, dysentery, influenza, measles, and other epidemic and debilitating diseases.[75]

Japan's famines were intensified by the lack of an efficient system of transportation other than the major sea routes leading to Edo and Osaka and by the strong regionalization of the country and near autonomy of the *han*. Often one *han* suffering a severe famine would be adjacent to a domain which experienced few hardships, but out of the fear of depleting its own resources and for political considerations, the neighbour would refuse to send any food to the famine area.[76]

It has been noted that the figures show a faster rate of recovery from famine in provinces economically resilient, and recovery also tended to be faster in areas where the climate and agricultural conditions were the most favourable. Obviously recovery would occur faster in regions which usually grew winter crops than in northern mountainous areas where much of the farming was fairly marginal. This has been part of the argument of those who advanced the pessimistic view of the Tokugawa population and economy, and while we will not dispute the fact that some of the farming was being carried out on land better left to woods or mountain pasture, the statistics of growth for the Meiji period are strong evidence that any absolute limits to the amount of population were certainly not reached during Tokugawa period. From 1872 to the turn of the century, the population as a whole grew at just under 1 per cent, and the region which grew the fastest was Tōhoku. The population in the northernmost part of Honshū increased 40 per cent from 1872–85, and the region just south of Tōhoku increased by 19·0 per cent, second in growth in the nation.[77] These increases took place during the earliest stage of Japan's industrialization, but long before any major effects of such could be expected to penetrate the rural areas. In other words, though more advanced agricultural techniques and seed strains were being disseminated more widely during the early Meiji years, the agricultural output which was supporting this population growth was indigenous; foodstuffs were not imported on any significant scale until the turn of the twentieth century.[78]

[75] See Sansom, *A History of Japan, 1615–1867*, pp. 184–5; Taeuber, *The Population of Japan*, pp. 24–5; and Honjo, 'The Population of Japan in the "Tokugawa" Era', pp. 40–42, for accounts of the famines in English. For a description of the famines in Japanese see the Arakawa works cited in footnote 73; Nishimura Makoto and Yoshikawa Ichiro, (eds.), *Nihon kyōkō shikō* (Tokyo, 1936); Ono Takeo, *Nihon kinsei kikinshi* (Tokyo, 1935); and Nōmukyoku (ed.), *Dainihon nōsei ruihen* (Tokyo, 1893), reprinted in 1932 as *Dainihon nōseishi* (Tokyo).

[76] Arakawa, *Kikin no rekishi*, p. 23.   [77] Taeuber, *The Population of Japan*, p. 46.

[78] Japan was a net exporter of rice until 1892. She began importing rice about the turn of the century, but in 1902 rice imports amounted to only about 11 million yen as against total imports amounting to 271·7 million yen. Kajinishi Mitsuhaya *et al.*, *Nihon shihonshugi no hatten* (Tokyo, 1957), Vol. 1, p. 67.

CONCLUSION

The most important conclusion to be drawn from our study, though we remind the reader of the less than satisfactory aggregate data and the limited samples which we were able to analyse, is that Tokugawa Japan as a whole was clearly not trapped in a low-level economic equilibrium with a high rate of population growth ready to sap whatever surplus the economy was able to generate. The annual average rate of growth of the population for the entire period was under one-fifth of 1 per cent, due to a significant extent to intervening famines and their consequences. Perhaps the nation-wide growth rate, *sans* natural calamities, might have been closer to the famine-free period of 1822–8, which had an annual growth rate of 0·37 per cent. In any event, we are relatively certain from our examinations of those areas and sub-periods which were least affected by famines that the natural rate of population increase rarely exceeded 1 per cent per annum for any significant period.

Second, our analysis of national and village data revealed diverse patterns of population change within the nation at the *kuni* level, within *kuni* on a local level, and even from village to neighbouring village. Thus, it is apparent that the Tokugawa population must be analysed on as small a regional basis as possible if we are to find the diverse demographic characteristics of a region *vis-à-vis* the region's social, economic, and geographic characteristics. For this reason, we examined population patterns by *kuni* and by local areas rather than by the traditional ten regions used by most other scholars.

The intra-regional and intra-temporal differences in demographic patterns were indeed significant. Even the impacts of the seemingly national famines were far from even, and incidences of infanticide and abortion undoubtedly varied by region and by period. The only useful analytical distinction we feel can be made on the basis of present knowledge of the demographic and economic changes of the two centuries under discussion will deprive us of facile generalizations. From the establishment of the East India Company to the onset of the Industrial Revolution, England saw over a century and a half of social and economic changes, so did Tokugawa Japan during a comparable period.

Third, we became fully aware that there exist a set of questions which need further intensive study. Yet to be closely analysed are the extent of famines, the rapid increases in mobility, and the consequences of urbanization on Tokugawa demographic trends. We need also to examine for their effect on demographic trends the marital patterns, the widespread practice of adopting heirs, and the delayed and even prevented marriages for younger sons in a society in which only one son could inherit. Careful and more empirically oriented examinations into the motives and frequency of abortion and infanticide are clearly called for before we can better understand the changes in Tokugawa demography. To argue that the non-Christian Japanese outlook on abortion as a natural method of birth control, as attested by practices in the mid-twentieth century, affected demographic patterns in the Tokugawa period is only to beg the question. Before we are able to advance more definite views on the approximate importance and general magnitude of these practices, we must await the results of many more regional and detailed studies currently progressing in Japan and the United States.

Finally, the greatest significance of the pattern of Tokugawa population growth undoubtedly lies in its relationship to the post-1868 industrialization of Japan. We believe that Japan had living standards and a rate of population growth which made possible a surplus in the economy, and that there is substantial evidence to show that such a surplus existed. Thus, with the coming of industrialization the economy was able to support entirely from indigenous capital, most of which was contributed by the land tax, both industrialization and a population that began to grow at a faster pace. In short, the pre-industrial population and economic development of Japan can be compared most readily with that of England. Japan, like England, experienced a rate of population increase well under one half of 1 per cent per annum, while output increased steadily at a higher rate. When these growth rates are compared to the rates of estimated increases of population in the developing economies of today, Japan's industrialization can be said to have been the product of the fortuitous combination of famines, a growing economy, and a multitude of social customs, all of which were, of course, interrelated. But Japan's greatest advantage lay, perhaps, in the fact that though she was a latecomer to industrialization, she was early enough to take the first steps before world technology, medicine, and D.D.T. fundamentally changed the delicate pre-industrial balance of fertility and mortality.

BIBLIOGRAPHICAL NOTE

Since this essay was written, the following articles have been pub-
lished which further support the views expressed herein: Susan
B. Hanley and Kozo Yamamura, 'A Quiet Transformation in
Tokugawa Economic History', *Journal of Asian Studies*, Vol. XXX,
No. 2 (February 1971); Kozo Yamamura 'The Increasing Poverty
of the Samurai in Tokugawa Japan, 1600–1868' *Journal of Economic
History*, Vol. XXXI, No. 2 (June 1971); and E. S. Crawcour and
K. Yamamura, 'The Tokugawa Monetary System: 1787–1868',
Economic Development and Cultural Change, Vol. XVIII, No. 3 (July
1970).

ACKNOWLEDGMENTS

The authors are grateful to Professor Akira Hayami of Keiō University, Tokyo, for the
generous assistance rendered to them in sharing the results of his research and his knowledge of sources and for his detailed comments on this article. They would also like to
express their appreciation to Professors D. V. Glass, Harry A. Miskimin, James I. Nakamura, Hugh T. Patrick, and Henry Rosovsky for their extremely helpful comments and
criticisms. Susan Hanley wishes to thank the Foreign Area Fellowship Programme which
made her research trip to Japan possible, and Kozo Yamamura wishes to thank the
National Science Foundation for the grant which supported his research on Japanese
historical and economic demography.

APPENDIX A

GLOSSARY OF JAPANESE TERMS

Bakufu   the Tokugawa Shogunate or government

chō   a measure of land, equivalent to 2·45 acres

daimyō   feudal lords; those samurai possessing domains assessed to yield at least 10,000 *koku*

datai   abortion

eta   outcasts

han   a domain of fief; a political and economic unit ruled by a *daimyō* under the hegemony of the Tokugawa Shogunate

hinin   outcasts

hōkōnin   servant, hired worker, or apprentice. By the late-eighteenth century, it was often common for young men and women, especially, to contract to work for a specified period, usually by calendar year, and if the contracts were to be renewed, work would be taken up again after the New Year holidays. This is a very broad term specifying persons who go to work for employers other than their own families.

jūnin ryōgaeya   the 'Big Ten' money exchangers who performed various functions of modern bankers

koku   the traditional measure for rice in Japan; equivalent to 4·96 bushels

kokudaka   literally, 'amount in rice'; used *vis-à-vis* yield or stipend

kōri   a district, the administrative unit of a *han* one step down from the *han* government

kuni   province(s); geographical and administrative units originating in the prehistorical era which were maintained until the Meiji Restoration. In the Tokugawa period *kuni* boundaries often coincided with *han* or domain boundaries, but they could comprise only part of a *han* or contain a number of *han* and other political units within their boundaries

machi   a town and/or administrative part of a city (for example, Edo, Osaka, and the castle towns of the domains were made up of *machi*)

mabiki   infanticide; literally, 'thinning', a term usually applied to the thinning out of young rice plants

Meiji period   1868–1912

mura   a village, usually averaging about 500 inhabitants and governed nearly autonomously under a headman appointed by villagers

mushukumono   vagrants, homeless persons

ōaza   a section of a village (*mura*) often as large as the usual village; a subdivision created in large villages to make the governing area conform to the usual size village

rōnin   masterless samurai

samurai   'warriors'. Positions in the Bakufu and *han* governments were limited to persons belonging to this hereditary class

shinden   new field or fields, usually referring to land newly reclaimed for cultivation during the Tokugawa period. The term was often used instead of 'village' for villages settled on this land

shūmon-aratame-chō   religious investigation registers. First undertaken in the seventeenth century to control and eliminate the practice of Christianity, these surveys later became sources of data on the population

tan   a measure of land equivalent to 0·245 acres. Ten *tan* equal one *chō*.

Tokugawa period   1600–1868

zaikata   rural districts or countryside

APPENDIX B

Table 6 Trend lines for total population and for each *kuni*, 1721–1872[a] and 1721–1846[b]. (For an explanation of terms relating to linear regression, see footnote 30)

Kuni	Constant	Regression coefficient	R^2
Total	23,717,840·00[a]	30,637·98	0·402*
	25,301,328·00[b]	9,518·50	0·296*
1 Yamashiro	570,358·62	−764·68	0·850**
	566,593·69	−714·47	0·796**
2 Yamato	371,238·56	−58·22	(0·009)
	393,167·44	−350·69	0·414*
3 Kawachi	222,472·81	25·24	(0·007)
	226,644·50	−30·39	(0·009)
4 Izumi	215,657·56	−88·45	(0·169)
	219,010·25	−133·17	0·283+
5 Settsu	841,732·25	−460·38	0·528**
	829,019·50	−290·83	0·361*
6 Iga	87,976·69	2·78	(0·0004)
	91,320·88	−41·82	(0·110)
7 Ise	505,655·75	31·94	(0·002)
	534,396·25	−351·39	0·433*
8 Shima	31,774·62	58·80	0·681**
	30,065·95	81·59	0·965**
9 Owari	509,683·50	1,062·87	0·905**
	523,101·62	883·91	0·951**
10 Mikawa	400,073·25	318·72	0·590**
	410,841·31	175·11	0·624**
11 Tōtomi	314,813·12	420·08	0·591**
	325,512·62	277·38	0·463*
12 Suruga	232,288·87	416·87	0·242+
	257,064·56	86·43	(0·022)
13 Izu	88,177·86	323·03	0·681**
	90,485·56	292·25	0·576*
14 Kai	285,353·37	327·86	0·238+
	292,388·50	234·06	(0·112)
15 Sagami	290,190·87	75·86	(0·020)
	310,697·87	−197·65	0·273+
16 Musashi	1,753,755·00	−43·78	(0·0004)
	1,829,405·00	1,057·77	0·289+
17 Awa 1.	125,352·50	132·06	0·241+
	127,892·81	98·19	(0·120)
18 Kazusa	430,429·81	−387·88	0·274+
	452,034·06	−676·04	0·667**
19 Shimo-osa	525,999·37	−155·95	(0·010)
	582,012·37	−903·03	0·436*
20 Hitachi	664,718·87	−1,065·93	0·296+
	728,967·06	−1,922·84	0·801**
21 Omi	591,754·06	−328·68	0·316*
	607,631·06	−540·45	0·663**
22 Mino	504,452·44	733·45	0·799**
	516,085·19	578·31	0·742**

Table 6—*continued*

Kuni	Constant	Regression coefficient	R²
23 Hida	62,113·77	205·72	0·913**
	62,451·82	201·21	0·882**
24 Shinano	626,519·56	1,349·21	0·838**
	649,765·50	1,039·17	0·902**
25 Kōzuke	603,121·31	−954·62	0·670**
	622,354·81	−1,304·45	0·919**
26 Shimotsuke	563,623·31	−1,171·76	0·464*
	616,026·94	−1,870·58	0·918**
27 Iwaki, Iwashiro, Rikuzen,	1,727,413·00	253·73	(0·003)
Rikuchū, Mutsu	1,928,595·00	−2,429·53	0·593*
28 Uzen-Ugo	746,740·69	1,589·75	0·485**
	812,350·44	714·69	0·400*
29 Wakasa	79,882·87	13·30	(0·028)
	81,156·00	−3·69	(0·002)
30 Echizen	320,475·19	473·01	0·368*
	343,209·50	169·81	(0·140)
31 Kaga	130,063·19	929·29	0·448*
	173,634·25	348·16	0·413*
32 Noto	134,972·31	489·00	0·413*
	151,641·37	266·68	(0·205)
33 Etchū	219,794·19	1,559·48	0·644**
	268,811·50	905·72	0·788**
34 Echigo	823,495·50	2,731·38	0·850**
	852,349·56	2,346·54	0·816**
35 Sado	87,174·69	95·24	0·552**
	86,998·63	97·59	0·488*
36 Tamba	276,799·00	84·83	0·394*
	278,322·75	64·52	(0·235)
37 Tango	121,598·56	250·25	0·946**
	120,173·87	269·25	0·954**
38 Tajima	141,689·00	267·64	0·873**
	141,444·25	270·90	0·839**
39 Inaba	112,496·00	187·27	0·554**
	119,460·12	94·39	0·599*
40 Hōki	121,525·56	450·38	0·926**
	119,669·44	475·14	0·920**
41 Izumo	189,922·00	869·21	0·952**
	190,158·31	866·06	0·935**
42 Iwami	215,199·62	287·60	0·497**
	213,257·75	313·50	0·469*
43 Oki	15,407·77	73·03	0·953**
	15,623·40	70·16	0·938**
44 Harima	601,557·81	58·93	(0·013)
	610,811·69	−64·49	(0·014)
45 Mimasaka	169,419·44	9·27	(0·001)
	186,542·37	−219·09	0·550*
46 Bizen	330,412·50	−79·04	0·227+
	336,196·56	−156·18	0·794**
47 Bitchū	302,970·62	349·65	0·519**
	315,938·87	176·70	0·433*
48 Bingo	265,228·00	743·69	0·591**
	289,544·31	419·38	0·590*
49 Aki	302,634·19	1,969·12	0·963**

Table 6—*continued*

Kuni	Constant	Regression coefficient	R²
	312,769·75	1,833·95	0·963**
50 Suō	211,759·06	1,576·50	0·967**
	215,649·25	1,509·82	0·957**
51 Nagato	192,994·56	573·80	0·746**
	207,900·44	374·99	0·976**
52 Kii	480,252·06	329·58	(0·165)
	509,816·81	−64·73	(0·026)
53 Awaji	87,389·50	300·21	0·608**
	95,340·81	167·49	0·691**
54 Awa 2.	272,059·19	1,444·78	0·818**
	297,207·62	1,109·37	0·858**
55 Sanuki	289,574·56	1,167·90	0·793**
	316,172·31	837·16	0·988**
56 Iyo	419,721·56	1,407·00	0·655**
	463,596·81	821·82	0·842**
57 Tosa	310,416·87	1,082·74	0·931**
	321,116·94	940·04	0·955**
58 Chikuzen	262,678·12	654·56	0·556**
	287,990·75	316·96	0·746**
59 Chikugo	225,342·25	632·80	0·601**
	247,366·81	339·05	0·765**
60 Buzen	229,644·06	188·91	(0·193)
	245,941·31	−28·45	(0·032)
61 Bungo	501,957·69	−94·27	(0·017)
	531,365·69	−486·51	0·698**
62 Hizen	510,672·75	1,964·91	0·506**
	597,396·75	808·24	0·886**
63 Higo	513,748·62	1,876·97	0·758**
	558,469·06	1,280·52	0·899**
64 Hyūga	176,570·37	685·19	0·487**
	208,101·19	264·65	0·930**
65 Osumi	94,060·00	330·94	(0·114)
	134,704·06	−211·14	0·526*
66 Satsuma	87,201·18	1,650·50	0·532**
	155,694·95	736·97	0·842**
67 Iki	18,602·62	69·01	0·877**
	19,577·39	56·00	0·920**
68 Tsushima	10,199·82	60·24	0·338**
	13,702·78	13·53	(0·113)
69 Ezo	−14,598·62	633·54	0·834**
	−4,421·00	497·80	0·864**

Note: The levels of significance for the coefficients of determination at n = 11 and n = 10 are indicated as follows: ** for 0·01, * for 0·05, and + for 0·10. Those in parentheses are not significant.

(a) The first set of numbers for the total and for each *Kuni* is for the 11 observations from 1721–1872.

(b) The second set of numbers is for the 10 observations from 1721–1846, with the Meiji data for 1872 eliminated.

Table 7 The population of Japan by *kuni* and average annual growth rates (per cent)

No.	Kuni	Population			Annual average growth rates										
		1721	1846	1872	1721– 50	1750– 56	1756– 86	1786– 98	1798– 1804	1804– 22	1822– 28	1828– 34	1834– 46	1846– 72	1721– 1872
	Total	26,065,425	26,907,625	33,110,825	−0·02	0·10	−0·13	0·13	0·10	0·21	0·37	−0·08	−0·05	0·80	0·16
1	Yamashiro	564,994	452,140	429,030	−0·27	0·15	−0·13	−0·45	−0·40	0·11	0·67	−0·32	−0·65	−0·20	−0·18
2	Yamato	413,331	361,157	418,326	−0·34	−0·28	−0·30	−0·19	−0·16	0·09	0·49	0·16	0·03	0·57	0·01
3	Kawachi	243,820	224,055	237,678	−0·18	−1·88	−0·02	0·49	−0·24	0·72	−1·50	0·08	−0·03	0·23	−0·02
4	Izumi	218,405	197,656	209,174	−0·17	1·42	−0·57	0·36	0·27	0·09	0·27	−0·13	−0·39	0·22	−0·03
5	Settsu	809,242	763,729	729,443	−0·02	0·78	−0·17	0·06	−0·35	0·01	0·45	−0·32	−0·35	−0·18	−0·07
6	Iga	95,978	91,774	97,164	−0·17	−0·53	−0·24	−0·17	−0·09	0·36	0·44	0·24	0·23	0·22	0·01
7	Ise	543,737	499,874	585,988	−0·13	−0·12	−0·27	−0·02	−0·05	0·21	0·12	0·06	−0·00	0·61	0·05
8	Shima	31,856	40,693	37,439	0·23	0·09	0·27	0·32	−0·32	0·36	0·21	0·39	−0·24	−0·32	0·11
9	Owari	554,561	653,678	727,437	−0·01	0·68	0·11	0·14	0·02	0·23	0·38	−0·07	0·12	0·41	0·18
10	Mikawa	416,204	431,800	482,931	0·03	0·25	−0·05	0·09	−0·13	0·21	0·10	0·02	−0·16	0·43	0·10
11	Tōtomi	342,663	363,959	414,928	−0·09	0·39	−0·10	0·49	−0·46	0·67	−1·13	−0·02	0·07	0·50	0·13
12	Suruga	245,834	286,290	368,505	0·84	−3·75	−0·11	0·20	0·26	0·76	−1·08	−1·08	1·00	0·97	0·27
13	Izu	96,650	115,197	149,749	0·29	0·02	0·45	−1·35	3·37	0·39	−0·49	1·67	−1·89	1·01	0·29
14	Kai	291,168	310,273	360,068	0·23	0·33	−0·12	0·10	−0·64	−0·12	4·91	−3·44	−0·22	0·57	0·14
15	Sagami	312,638	303,271	356,638	−0·02	−0·28	−0·30	−0·07	0·05	−0·17	1·17	0·26	0·26	0·62	0·09
16	Musashi	1,903,316	1,777,371	1,943,211	−0·25	−0·03	−0·29	0·20	−0·12	0·13	0·23	−0·03	0·30	0·34	0·01
17	Awa 1.	115,579	143,500	154,683	1·09	−2·35	−0·32	0·55	−0·07	0·27	0·14	0·44	−0·06	0·29	0·19
18	Kazusa	407,552	360,761	419,969	0·37	−0·55	−0·41	−0·43	−0·19	0·12	−0·45	0·08	−0·08	0·58	0·02
19	Shimo-osa	542,661	525,041	645,029	0·15	−0·06	−0·52	0·02	−0·20	−0·74	2·87	−3·56	2·22	0·79	0·11
20	Hitachi	712,387	521,777	648,674	−0·29	−0·36	−0·74	−0·36	−0·24	0·11	0·01	−1·35	1·10	0·84	−0·06
21	Omi	602,367	541,732	576,564	−0·16	−0·04	0·06	−0·68	−0·17	0·25	−0·29	−1·13	0·47	0·24	−0·03
22	Mino	545,919	583,137	660,896	−0·08	0·32	0·08	0·11	0·07	0·31	0·30	−0·06	−0·34	0·48	0·13
23	Hida	67,032	86,338	98,378	0·26	0·59	0·13	0·15	0·49	0·52	0·29	0·43	−0·69	0·50	0·25
24	Shinano	693,947	794,698	919,115	−0·04	0·49	−0·08	0·22	0·12	0·22	0·40	0·23	−0·14	0·56	0·19

Table 7—continued

No.	Kuni	Population 1721	1846	1872	1721–50	1750–56	1756–86	1786–98	1798–1804	1804–22	1822–28	1828–34	1834–46	1846–72	1721–1872
									Annual average growth rates						
25	Kōzuke	569,550	428,092	507,235	0·04	0·11	−0·35	−0·14	−0·56	−0·47	0·26	−0·45	−0·45	0·65	−0·08
26	Shimotsuke	560,020	378,665	498,520	−0·04	−0·63	−0·68	−0·42	−0·36	−0·13	−0·83	−1·57	0·84	1·06	−0·08
27	Iwaki, Iwashiro, Rikuzen, Rikuchū, Mutsu	1,962,839	1,607,881	2,294,915	−0·23	−0·27	−0·48	0·13	0·14	0·16	0·29	0·10	−0·42	0·37	0·10
28	Uzen-Ugo	877,650	912,452	1,191,020	−0·13	−0·15	−0·14	0·48	0·33	0·24	0·66	−0·09	−0·26	1·02	0·20
29	Wakasa	86,598	77,183	85,487	−0·36	−0·07	0·07	−0·10	0·08	0·30	0·32	−0·06	−0·74	0·39	−0·01
30	Echizen	367,652	353,674	461,032	−0·19	−0·16	−0·13	0·46	0·15	0·33	−0·34	−1·30	−0·98	1·02	0·15
31	Kaga	206,933	238,291	403,357	−0·08	−3·84	0·67	−0·17	0·34	0·62	0·02	0·75	0·28	2·02	0·44
32	Noto	152,113	186,970	262,486	0·13	4·93	−1·45	1·53	0·24	0·80	0·39	−0·03	−0·47	1·30	0·36
33	Etchū	314,158	403,121	615,663	−0·01	0·01	0·04	0·51	0·40	0·58	1·28	−0·47	0·01	1·63	0·45
34	Echigo	932,461	1,172,973	1,368,428	0·14	0·73	−0·20	0·82	0·30	0·41	0·54	0·46	−0·36	0·59	0·25
35	Sado	95,748	102,265	103,098	−0·20	0·01	0·02	0·03	0·18	0·54	0·23	−0·02	−0·07	0·03	0·05
36	Tamba	284,893	280,947	295,359	−0·11	0·34	−0·01	−0·00	0·07	0·15	0·09	0·05	−0·34	0·19	0·02
37	Tango	125,276	154,308	160,932	0·24	0·11	0·14	0·32	0·07	0·27	0·28	0·19	−0·26	0·16	0·17
38	Tajima	149,732	173,573	187,086	0·15	−0·17	0·07	0·33	0·28	0·38	0·15	0·30	−0·50	0·29	0·15
39	Inaba	122,030	127,797	162,842	0·09	−0·00	−0·04	0·20	0·25	0·17	0·41	0·03	−0·53	0·93	0·19
40	Hōki	132,981	177,420	194,158	0·20	0·45	0·24	0·58	0·31	0·35	0·55	0·38	−0·62	0·35	0·25
41	Izumo	222,330	309,606	340,042	0·19	1·08	0·54	0·40	0·45	0·39	0·47	0·37	−0·15	0·36	0·28
42	Iwami	207,965	239,963	259,611	0·19	2·77	−0·41	0·66	−0·19	0·27	−0·01	0·49	−0·83	0·30	0·15
43	Oki	18,133	26,208	28,531	0·15	0·53	0·19	0·49	−0·23	0·67	0·53	0·31	0·16	0·33	0·30
44	Harima	633,725	594,560	635,791	−0·48	2·17	−0·11	0·02	−0·26	0·09	0·12	−0·35	−0·09	0·26	0·00
45	Mimasaka	194,226	165,468	215,602	−0·36	−0·26	−0·30	−0·04	−0·39	0·20	0·09	0·43	0·07	1·02	0·07
46	Bizen	338,523	310,576	331,878	−0·16	0·13	−0·04	−0·01	−0·15	−0·00	0·03	−0·01	−0·21	0·26	−0·01

Table 7—*continued*

No.	Kuni	Population			Annual average growth rates										
		1721	1846	1872	1721–50	1750–56	1756–86	1786–98	1798–1804	1804–22	1822–28	1828–34	1834–46	1846–72	1721–1872
47	Bitchū	333,731	346,927	396,880	−0·15	0·32	−0·09	0·26	0·07	0·15	0·32	0·17	−0·01	0·52	0·11
48	Bingo	321,008	360,832	456,461	−0·16	0·23	−0·08	0·31	0·17	0·40	0·45	0·42	0·00	0·90	0·23
49	Aki	361,431	553,708	667,717	0·32	0·71	0·31	0·66	0·26	0·51	0·51	0·42	−0·37	0·72	0·41
50	Suō	262,927	435,188	497,034	0·33	0·11	0·56	0·30	0·06	0·57	1·27	0·26	−0·21	0·60	0·42
51	Nagato	212,124	261,100	330,502	0·23	0·46	0·11	0·14	0·13	0·07	0·50	0·10	−0·06	0·91	0·29
52	Kii	519,022	499,826	613,925	−0·07	0·15	−0·08	−0·46	0·13	0·35	0·27	0·14	−0·34	0·79	0·11
53	Awaji	105,226	122,773	164,939	0·06	0·00	−0·03	−0·15	1·26	0·33	0·61	−0·03	−0·05	1·14	0·30
54	Awa 2.	342,386	448,287	586,046	−0·06	1·26	0·05	0·14	2·08	0·27	0·29	0·19	−0·20	1·03	0·36
55	Sanuki	334,153	433,880	559,712	0·23	0·26	0·20	0·24	−0·01	0·19	0·51	0·40	0·02	0·98	0·34
56	Iyo	504,045	599,948	775,974	−0·03	0·29	0·04	0·26	−0·05	0·34	0·33	0·31	0·20	0·99	0·29
57	Tosa	351,547	461,031	524,511	0·16	0·21	0·17	0·15	0·40	0·44	0·07	0·36	0·10	0·50	0·26
58	Chikuzen	302,160	346,942	441,175	0·06	−0·07	0·02	0·01	0·27	0·15	0·41	0·30	0·27	0·92	0·25
59	Chikugo	266,426	299,041	391,535	−0·07	0·15	0·09	0·06	0·32	0·13	0·51	0·79	−0·22	1·04	0·25
60	Buzen	248,187	249,274	304,574	−0·08	0·77	−0·23	−0·11	0·11	0·08	0·32	0·22	0·07	0·77	0·14
61	Bungo	524,394	470,875	562,318	−0·08	0·32	−0·35	−0·09	0·05	0·09	0·02	0·05	−0·09	0·68	0·05
62	Hizen	609,926	713,593	1,074,460	0·13	0·39	0·07	0·15	0·92	−0·23	0·43	−0·06	0·17	1·57	0·37
63	Higo	614,007	755,781	953,037	0·03	0·03	0·13	0·21	0·20	0·39	0·41	0·12	0·14	0·89	0·29
64	Hyūga	211,614	247,621	376,527	0·22	0·02	0·06	−0·02	0·08	0·25	0·14	0·14	0·07	1·61	0·38
65	Osumi	112,616	99,212	256,816	0·54	0·15	−0·17	−0·68	−0·29	−0·33	−0·53	−0·18	−0·32	3·66	0·55
66	Satsuma	149,039	241,797	549,440	0·91	0·92	0·49	−0·08	0·20	0·28	0·05	−0·22	−0·22	3·16	0·86
67	Iki	19,993	27,005	33,010	0·51	0·15	−0·00	0·54	0·26	0·25	0·67	−0·25	−0·06	0·77	0·33
68	Tsushima	16,467	16,904	29,684	−0·37	−3·53	0·55	−0·21	0·09	1·03	−2·37	2·39	0·09	2·17	0·39
69	Ezo	15,615	70,887	120,873	1·15	0·62	0·50	0·73	7·64	1·72	0·81	0·71	0·36	2·05	1·36

Table 8   Rice output *(koku)* and annual average growth rates (per cent)

	1645	1645–97	1697	1697–1829	1829	1839–73	1873	1645–1873
Total	24,553,757	0·10	25,876,392	0·13	30,558,917	0·11	32,008,292	0·12
1 Yamashiro	215,982	0·07	224,257	0·02	230,131	−0·08	222,265	0·01
2 Yamato	459,380	0·16	500,497	0·00	501,361	−0·02	497,404	0·03
3 Kawachi	264,952	0·08	276,329	0·05	293,786	−0·00	293,708	0·05
4 Izumi	159,326	0·03	161,692	0·05	172,847	−0·02	171,295	0·03
5 Settsu	375,478	0·09	392,707	0·05	417,391	−0·00	416,521	0·05
6 Iga	100,540	0·00	100,540	0·07	110,090	0·02	110,917	0·04
7 Ise	585,065	0·11	621,027	0·11	716,451	−0·01	714,376	0·09
8 Shima	20,061	0·00	20,061	0·05	21,470	−0·24	19,279	−0·02
9 Owari	483,432	0·15	521,480	0·03	545,875	0·77	764,976	0·20
10 Mikawa	350,888	0·17	383,413	0·15	466,080	0·03	472,373	0·13
11 Tōtomi	280,696	0·30	328,651	0·09	369,952	0·02	372,878	0·12
12 Suruga	191,315	0·49	247,437	0·01	250,530	0·01	251,865	0·12
13 Izu	79,653	0·10	83,991	0·00	84,171	−0·04	82,690	0·02
14 Kai	245,298	0·06	235,023	0·16	312,159	−0·00	311,502	0·10
15 Sagami	220,617	0·30	258,216	0·08	286,719	0·03	290,469	0·12
16 Musashi	982,327	0·33	1,168,613	0·07	1,281,431	0·00	1,282,000	0·12
17 Awa 1.	92,641	0·03	93,886	0·01	95,736	−0·00	95,641	0·01
18 Kazusa		n.a.	391,113	0·06	425,080	0·01	427,313	n.a.
19 Shimo-osa	444,829	0·47	568,331	0·14	681,062	0·01	685,027	0·19
20 Hitachi	840,048	0·14	903,778	0·08	1,005,707	−0·20	921,629	0·04
21 Omi	832,122	0·01	836,829	0·01	853,095	0·01	857,757	0·01
22 Mino	609,718	0·11	645,010	0·06	699,764	0·10	729,831	0·08
23 Hida	38,764	0·26	44,469	0·18	56,602	0·03	57,243	0·17
24 Shinano	548,600	0·22	615,818	0·17	767,788	0·03	779,462	0·15
25 Kōzuke	515,215	0·27	591,834	0·06	637,331	−0·01	635,766	0·09
26 Shimotsuke	568,733	0·35	681,702	0·09	769,905	−0·02	761,523	0·13
27 Iwaki, Iwashiro, Rikuzen, Rikuchū, Mutsu	1,431,060	0·76	2,124,941	0·23	2,874,236	0·10	2,999,417	0·32
28 Uzen-Ugo	965,674	0·30	1,126,247	0·11	1,295,322	0·35	1,514,186	0·20
29 Wakasa	85,099	0·07	88,281	0·02	91,018	0·02	91,767	0·03
30 Echizen	682,182	0·01	684,271	0·01	689,304	0·00	609,243	0·01
31 Kaga	422,957	0·07	438,281	0·07	483,665	0·11	508,609	0·08
32 Noto	225,006	0·12	239,208	0·11	275,369	0·24	305,482	0·13
33 Etchū	592,415	0·06	611,001	0·21	808,008	0·19	877,760	0·17
34 Echigo	611,960	0·56	816,775	0·25	1,142,555	0·01	1,149,017	0·28
35 Sado	24,812	3·19	130,373	0·01	132,565	0·04	135,095	0·74
36 Tamba	289,829	0·02	293,445	0·08	324,136	0·04	329,465	0·06
37 Tango	123,175	0·30	143,624	0·02	147,614	0·01	148,002	0·08
38 Tajima	129,069	0·02	130,673	0·08	144,313	0·06	148,147	0·06
39 Inaba	149,539	0·25	170,728	0·03	177,844	0·22	195,632	0·12
40 Hōki	170,254	0·26	194,416	0·09	217,990	0·32	251,067	0·17
41 Izumo	253,597	0·21	282,489	0·05	302,627	0·13	320,709	0·10
42 Iwami	139,401	0·04	142,499	0·14	172,209	0·13	182,136	0·12
43 Oki	11,601	0·09	12,165	0·02	12,559	0·00	12,562	0·03
44 Harima	562,291	0·02	568,517	0·10	651,964	0·03	660,557	0·07

Table 8—*continued*

		1645	1645–97	1697	1697–1829	1829	1829–73	1873	1645–1873
45	Mimasaka	186,500	0·63	259,353	−0·02	252,099	0·09	262,333	0·15
46	Bizen	280,200	0·06	289,224	0·28	416,581	0·01	418,960	0·18
47	Bitchū	236,691	0·61	324,455	0·09	363,915	0·05	371,441	0·20
48	Bingo	248,606	0·30	289,878	0·06	312,054	0·03	315,511	0·10
49	Aki	265,071	0·08	276,678	0·09	310,648	0·02	313,164	0·07
50	Suō	202,787	0·00	202,787	0·67	489,428	0·27	552,160	0·44
51	Nagato	166,623	0·50	216,623	0·47	404,853	0·28	458,143	0·44
52	Kii	378,393	−0·00	397,668	0·08	440,839	0·02	444,162	0·05
53	Awaji	70,186	0·01	70,428	0·24	97,164	0·77	136,637	0·29
54	Awa 2.	186,753	0·07	193,862	0·25	268,894	0·31	307,732	0·22
55	Sanuki	173,554	0·14	186,394	0·34	291,320	0·15	311,064	0·26
56	Iyo	400,271	0·13	429,163	0·05	460,997	−0·10	442,079	0·04
57	Tosa	202,626	0·54	268,486	0·16	330,026	0·99	510,572	0·41
58	Chikuzen	522,512	0·12	556,981	0·12	651,782	−0·06	633,434	0·08
59	Chikugo	302,089	0·18	331,497	0·09	375,588	0·81	536,841	0·25
60	Buzen	231,680	0·32	273,801	0·23	368,913	−0·01	366,948	0·20
61	Bungo	378,592	−0·05	369,540	0·09	417,514	0·22	459,184	0·08
62	Hizen	561,437	0·04	572,284	0·16	706,470	−0·05	691,444	0·09
63	Higo	572,980	−0·03	563,787	0·06	611,920	0·75	851,237	0·17
64	Hyūga	288,589	0·14	309,954	0·07	340,128	0·47	418,142	0·16
65	Osumi	170,828	0·00	170,843	−0·00	170,833	0·97	261,793	0·19
66	Satsuma	315,251	−0·00	315,005	0·00	315,005	0·06	323,483	0·01
67	Iki	15,982	0·24	18,072	0·45	32,742	0·15	35,042	0·34
68	Tsushima	123,711	−0·00	123,611	0·13	146,023	n.a.		n.a.

APPENDIX C

Table 9   Local data sources and coverage

Location	Period of coverage no. of observations	Population in base year and variable examined*	Source of data
Villages			
1a Kamiizumi village Shimotsuke province	1716–1819 (30)	354 TP, M, F, H	Takahashi Bonsen, *Nihon jinkō-shi no kenkyū*, Vol. I, Tokyo, 1941, pp. 199–202
1b Kamiizumi village Shimotsuke province	1834–70 (23)	275 TP, M, F	Takahashi, *op. cit.*, Vol. I, pp. 202–4
2 Funabori village Musashi province	1793–1854 (53)	685 TP, M, F, H	Takahashi, *op. cit.*, Vol. I, *ibid.*, pp. 192–7
3 Imafuku village Kai province	1816–75 (43)	344 TP, M, F, H, B, D	Takahashi, *op. cit.*, Vol. I, *ibid.*, pp. 187–90
4 Yokouchi village Shinano province	1671–1871 (144)	189 TP, M, F, H, B, D	Hayami Akira, 'Shūmon-aratame-chō o tsūjite mita Shinshū Yokouchi mura no chōki jinkō tōkei', Management and Labor Studies, Series No. 202, Keio Univ, 1967–68, Charts 2 and 3
5 Kōmi village Mino province	1674–1870 (73)	440 TP, M, F, H, B, D, b, d	Nomura Kenkyūkai, 'Ogaki *han*, Mino no Kuni Motosu no kōri Kōmi mura no kokō tōkei', *Mita Gakkai Zasshi*, Vol. 53, 1960, pp. 186–92, 202–3
6 Ario section Kamitado village Mino province	1691–1867 (62)	144 TP, M, F, H	Takahashi, *op. cit.*, Vol. I, pp. 162–7
7 Uda section Kamitado village Mino province	1685–1871 (68)	119 TP, M, F, H	Takahashi, *op. cit.*, Vol. I, pp. 168–73
8 Yokoya section Kamitado village Mino province	1694–1863 (27)	278 TP, M, F, H, B, D	Takahashi, *op. cit.*, Vol. I, pp. 174–8
9 Kando-*shinden* Owari province	1778–1871 (89)	312 TP, M, F, H	Hayami Akira, 'The Demographic Analysis of a Village in Tokugawa Japan', *Keio Economic Studies*, Vol. 5, 1968, pp. 57–61
10 Fujito village Bizen province	1708–1859 (46)	493 TP, H	*Shūmon-aratame-chō* of Fujito village

Table 9—*continued*

Location	Period of coverage no. of observations	Population in base year and variable examined	Source of data
11 Fukiage village Bizen province	1693–1860 (24)	411 TP, H	*Shūmon-aratame-chō* of Fukiage village
12 Tsubuura village Bizen province	1753–1869 (98)	415 TP, M, F, H	Nagayama Usaburo, *Kurashiki shishi*, Vol. 15, Kurashiki, 1963, pp. 397–404
13 Atochi village Iwami province	1716–1870 (36)	1,392 TP, M, F, H	Takahashi, *op. cit.*, Vol. I, pp. 125–8
14 Ikeda section Ikeno village Chikuzen province	1746–1818 (72)	701 TP, M, F, B	Takahashi, *op. cit.*, Vol. I, pp. 133–9
II *Districts and Han*			
15 Aizu *han* Iwaki-Iwashiro provinces	1648–1804 (112)	156,706 TP, M, F	Takahashi, *op. cit.*, Vol. I, pp. 208–17
16 Yonezawa *han* Uzen province	1692–1860 (144)	133,259 TP, M, F	Yoshida Yoshinobu, *Chishi minshū seikatsushi*, Yamagata, 1958, pp. 113–17
17 Sado province	1741–1815 (17)	93,394 TP, M, F, H	Takahashi, *op. cit.*, Vol. I, pp. 159–61
18 Komoro *han* Shinano province	1830–63 (34)	27,624 TP	Takahashi, *op. cit.*, Vol. II, pp. 449–51
19 Ii-ishi district Izumo province	1738–1858 (15)	9,168 TP, M, F	Takahashi, *op. cit.*, Vol. I, pp. 117–18
20 Kōchi *han* Tosa province	1681–1855 (123)	327,971 TP	Takahashi, *op. cit.*, Vol. II, pp. 229–35
21 Fuchū district Tsushima province	1677–1712 (35)	13,737 TP, B, D, b, d	Takahashi, *op. cit.*, Vol. I, pp. 149–53
22 Gōmura district Tsushima province	1677–1712 (35)	14,593 TP, B, D, b, d	Takahashi, *op. cit.*, Vol. I, pp. 149–53
23 Ginzan district Tsushima province	1677–1712 (35)	1,349 TP, B. D. b, d	Takahashi, *op. cit.*, Vol. I, pp. 149–53
III *Additional Data*			
24 14 villages in Owashi region, Kii province	1775–1871 (90+)	See Table 5	Hayami Akira, 'Kishū Owashigumi no jinkō sūsei', *Tokugawa Rinseishi Kenkyū Kiyō*, No. 3, 1969
25 Morioka *han*	1681–1840 (94)	Data unreliable See text	Takahashi, *op. cit.*, Vol. III, pp. 209–31

* TP stands for total population, M and F for male and female, H for the number of households, B and D for births and deaths and b and d for birth and death rates.

Notes on Contributors

BANKS, J. A.
Professor of Sociology, University of Leicester.
Publications: Prosperity and Parenthood, London, 1954; *Industrial Participation*, Liverpool, 1963; (with Olive Banks), *Feminism and Family Planning*, Liverpool, 1964; *Marxist Sociology in Action: A Sociological Critique of the Marxist Approach to Industrial Relations*, London, 1970.

BIRABEN, J.–N.
Research worker, Institut National d'Études Démographiques, Paris. Publications: Papers in *Population*, *Les Annales* and other Journals.

DAS GUPTA, A.
Consultant. Formerly Head of the National Sample Survey, Indian Statistical Institute; Regional Demographic Adviser, Economic Commisson on the Far East; Consultant to Economic Commission on Africa and to the Government of Trinidad.
Publications: *Couple Fertility*, National Sample Survey, Calcutta 1955; contributions to various journals, and to proceedings of international statistical and population conferences.

DEMENY, P.
Director of the East-West Population Institute, East-West Centre, and Professor of Economics, University of Hawaii:
Publications: Co-author of: *Regional Model Life Tables and Stable Populations*, Princeton, 1965; *Methods of Estimating Basic Demographic Measures from Incomplete Data*, New York, 1967; *The Demography of Tropical Africa*, Princeton, 1967.

502   NOTES ON CONTRIBUTORS

DRAKE, M.
Dean of the Faculty of Social Sciences, The Open University, Bletchworth, England.
Publications: *Population and Society in Norway 1735–1865*, Cambridge, 1969; Papers in *Economic History Review* and T. W. Moody, ed., *Historical Studies*, VI, 1968.

ERICKSON, CHARLOTTE
Senior lecturer in economic history, London School of Economics (University of London).
Publications: *American Industry and the European Immigrant 1860–85*, Cambridge, Mass., 1957; *British Industrialists; Steel and History, 1850–1950*, Cambridge, 1959.

GLASS, D. V.
Martin White Professor of Sociology, London School of Economics (University of London).
Publications: *Population Policies and Movements in Europe*, Oxford, 1940; (with E. Grebenik), *The Trend and Pattern of Fertility in Britain*, London, 1955; editor and contributor, *Social Mobility in Britain*, London, 1954; editor and contributor, *Introduction to Malthus*, London, 1954; co-editor and contributor, *Population in History*, London, 1965.

GOUBERT, P.
Professor of Modern History, University of Paris-Sorbonne.
Publications: *Beauvais et le Beauvaisis de 1600 à 1730*, Paris, 1960; *1789, les Français ont la parole*, Paris, 1964; *Louis XIV et vingt millions de Français*, Paris, 1966, London and New York, 1970; *L'ancien régime*, Paris, 1969.

HANLEY, SUSAN B.
Research Associate, East-West Population Institute, East-West Centre, Honolulu.
Publications: Papers in *Daedalus*, and *Journal of Asian Studies*: Contributor to *The Dimensions of the Past: Materials, Problems and Opportunities for Quantitative Work in History*, New Haven, 1971.

HEER, D. M.
Associate Professor of Demography, School of Public Health, Harvard University.
Publications: *After nuclear attack: a demographic inquiry*, New York, 1965; *Society and Population*, Englewood Cliffs, N.J., 1968; editor, *Readings on Population*, Englewood Cliffs, N.J., 1968; editor, *Social Statistics and the City*, Cambridge, Mass., 1968.

HENRIPIN, J.
Professor and head of the Department of Demography, University of Montreal.
Publications *La population canadienne au début de XVIIIe siècle*, Paris, 1954; *Tendance et facteurs de la fécondité au Canada*, Ottawa, 1967; *Evolution démographique du Québec et de ses régions, 1966–1986*, Quebec, 1969 And papers in various journals.

HENRY, L.
Director of Research, Institut National d'Études Démographiques, Paris.
Publications: *Fécondité des mariages—nouvelle méthode de mesure*, Paris, 1953; *Anciennes familles genevoises*, Paris, 1956; (with M. Fleury), *Des registres parossiaux à l'histoire de la population*, Paris, 1956; (with E. Gautier), *La population de Crulai, paroisse Normande*, Paris, 1958; (with A. Girard and R. Nistri), *Facteurs sociaux et culturels de la mortalité infantile*, Paris, 1960; *Leçons d'analyse démographique*, Paris, 1960 and 1964; (with M. Fleury), *Nouveau manuel de dépouillement et d'exploitation de l'état civil ancien*, Paris, 1965; *Manuel de démographaphie historique*, Paris—Geneva, 1967.

HOLLINGSWORTH, T. H.
Lecturer in Social Statistics, University of Glasgow.
Publications: *The Demography of the British Peerage* (Supplement to *Population Studies*, November, 1964); *Historical Demography*, London, 1969; *Migration: a Study based on Scottish Experience*, Edinburgh, 1969.

LANDES, D.
Professor of History, Harvard University.
Publications: *Bankers and Pashas: International Finance and Economic Imperialism*, London, 1958; *The Unbound*

Prometheus: Technological Change and Industrial Development in Western Europe since 1750, Cambridge, 1969; editor, *The Rise of Capitalism*, New York, 1968; co-editor, *History as Social Science*, Englewood Cliffs, N.J., 1971.

LEWIS, H.

Dr. Lewis unfortunately died on 21 June 1971. He had been a member of the Division of Human Physiology, National Institute for Medical Research, London, with a special responsibility for co-ordinating the inter-disciplinary research on the islanders of Tristan da Cunha.

Publications: Contributor to P. B. Beeson and W. McDermott, eds. *Textbook of Medicine*, Philadelphia, 1971; co-author of papers in *The Lancet* and *The Journal of Hygiene* (Cambridge).

LIVI-BACCI, M.

Director of the Department of Mathematical Statistics, University of Florence.

Publications: *L'immigrazione e l'assimilazione degli Italiani in America*, Milan, 1961; *I Fattori demografici dello sviluppo economico Italiano*, Rome, 1965; *A Century of Portuguese Fertility*, Princeton, 1971.

MATTHIESSEN, P. C.

Professor of Demography, Univerity of Copenhagen.

Publications: *Fertiletsforskelle i Danmark*, Copenhagen 1965; *Infant Mortality in Denmark, 1931–60*, Copenhagen 1965; *Some Aspects of the Demographic Transition in Denmark*, Copenhagen 1970.

NOONAN, J. T.

Professor of Law and Chairman of the Programme in Religious Studies, University of California, Berkeley.

Publications: *The Scholastic Analysis of Usury*, Cambridge, Mass., 1957; *Contraception*, Cambridge, Mass., 1965; *The Morality of Abortion*, Cambridge, Mass., 1970.

PÉRON, Y.

Assistant Professor, University of Montreal (Department of Demography).

Publications: Papers in *Information sociales* and in *Population*.

REVELLE, R.

Richard Saltonstall Professor of Population Policy and Director of the Centre for Population Studies, Harvard University. Deputy Foreign Secretary, National Academy of Sciences.

SLICHER VAN BATH, B. H.

Professor of Agrarian History, Wageningen University.

Publications: *The Agrarian History of Western Europe, A.D. 500–1850*, London, 1963; *Yield Ratios 810–1920*, Wageningen, 1963.

SPENGLER, J. J.

James B. Duke Professor of Economics, Duke University.

Publications: *France Faces Depopulation*, Durham, N.C., 1938; *French Predecessors to Malthus*, Durham, N.C., 1942; *Indian Economic Thought*, Durham, N.C., 1971; *Declining Population Growth Revisited*, Chapel Hill, N.C., 1971; co-editor, *Tradition, Values, and Socio-Economic Development*, Durham, N.C., 1961; co-editor, *Administration and Economic Development in India*, Durham, N.C., 1963; co-editor, *Population Theory and Policy*, Glencoe, Ill., 1956; co-editor, *Demographic Analysis*, Glencoe, Ill., 1956.

SUTHERLAND, I.

Director of the Medical Research Council Statistical and Services Unit, London.

Publications: *Stillbirths; their Epidemiology and Social Significance*, London, 1949; and papers in the *Journal of the Royal Statistical Society*, the *British Medical Journal*, and other journals.

VAN DE WALLE, E.

Research Demographer, the Office of Population Research, Princeton University.

Publications: Co-author, *The Demography of Tropical Africa*, Princeton, 1968; papers in various journals, including *Population Studies*.

WRIGLEY, E. A.

Fellow and Bursar, Peterhouse College, Cambridge University.

Publications: *Industrial Growth and Population Change*, Cambridge, 1961; *Population and History*, London, 1969; editor, *An Introduction to English Historial Demography*, London, 1966.

YAMAMURA, K.

Professor of Asian Studies and Economics, University of Washington, Seattle.

Publications: *Economic Policy in Postwar Japan*, Berkeley, 1967. Papers on the economic growth and economic history of Japan in various journals.

RP

Index

Bold figures indicate main entries